Employment Law in Scotland

Employment Law in Scotland

Sam Middlemiss
Reader in Law, Robert Gordon University

Margaret Downie
Lecturer in Law, Robert Gordon University

Bloomsbury Professional

Bloomsbury Professional Limited, Maxwelton House, 41–43 Boltro Road, Haywards Heath, West Sussex, RH16 1BJ

© Bloomsbury Professional Limited 2012

Bloomsbury Professional, an imprint of Bloomsbury Publishing Plc

A CIP Catalogue record for this book is available from the British Library.

ISBN: 978 184766 558 4

Typeset by Phoenix Photosetting, Chatham, Kent
Printed and bound in EU by GZ Digital Media

Contents

Preface

This book will appeal to everybody who needs to understand employment law in a practical sense, such as practitioners and students, but will appeal most to those that will benefit from a Scottish perspective on the topic.

This is a comprehensive text which covers all the traditional areas of employment law from a practitioner's perspective but we have added some additional areas which we thought would prove useful.

For example, increasing the resolution of disputes without going to an employment tribunal was an aim of the previous Government and is an aim of the current Government as well so we have included a chapter on Alternative Dispute Resolution (ADR). Also for employers, abiding by immigration rules in the UK in the employment of non-EU citizens has been and continues to be a problem, and we thought it would be useful to include the relevant details.

In terms of the content of the book, we have had to contend with the introduction of the Equality Act 2010 which has not been helped by the Government backtracking on introducing various measures under the Act. We have also had to recognise and deal with in the text, the Government's plans to make changes to employment law rules, which when implemented will reduce employment rights for employees and workers.

We couldn't have written the book without the help of friends who are practitioners in Scotland looking over and commenting on various chapters. We also want to thank the publishers Bloomsbury Professional who have stuck by us throughout and proven to be professional and efficient in the production of the book. We would like to thank in particular Paula O'Connell who has done a masterly job of managing the project in a patient and supportive manner.

We have tried to state the law as of December 2011 and we of course accept responsibility for any inaccuracies.

Sam Middlemiss and Margaret Downie
Aberdeen 2012

Note
The European Court of Justice (ECJ) is now the Court of Justice of the European Union (CJEU), however we have used ECJ throughout the book as for the most part it relates to case law where the citation is ECJ.

Acknowledgements

We would like to thank David Christie and Lilli Hunter, solicitors in Aberdeen who gave up their valuable time to review some of the chapters.

Thanks also go the Robert Gordon University for giving me some time off to work on the book, my family and friends in particular my daughter Rebecca and Graham who from time to time have encouraged me to carry on.

Sam Middlemiss

Thanks to Adam, Callum and Sarah Downie and to Mary and Robert Meechan for their patience, encouragement and support.

Margaret Downie

Abbreviations

Statutes

DDA 1995	Disability Discrimination Act 1995
DDA 2005	Disability Discrimination Act 2005
EA 2002	Employment Act 2002
EA 2010	Employment Act 2010
EPA 1970	Equal Pay Act 1970
ERA 1996	Employment Rights Act 1996
HASAW 1974	Health and Safety at Work Act 1974
HRA 1998	Human Rights Act 1998
NMWA 1998	National Minimum Wage Act 1998
PIDA 1998	Public Interest Disclosure Act 1998
RRA 1976	Race Relations Act 1976
SDA 1975	Sex Discrimination Act 1975
TULR(C)A 1992	Trade Union and Labour Relations (Consolidation) Act 1992
TURERA 1993	Trade Union Reform and Employment Rights Act 1993

Institutions

ACAS	Advisory, Conciliation and Arbitration Service
CA	Court of Appeal
CAC	Central Arbitration Committee
CBI	Confederation of British Industry
DTI	Department of Trade and Industry
EAT	Employment Appeal Tribunal
EC	European Communities
EHRC	Equality and Human Rights Commission
ECtHR	European Court of Human Rights
HC	High Court of Justice
HL	House of Lords
HSC	Health and Safety Commission
HSE	Health and Safety Executive
IH	Inner House of the Court of Session
ILO	International Labour Organisation
LAUTRO	Life Assurance and Unit Trust Regulating Organisation

NUJ	National Union of Journalists
OH	Outer House of the Court of Session
SLCC	Scottish Legal Complaints Commission
TUC	Trades Union Congress
UKCC	United Kingdom Central Council
UKEATS	United Kingdom Employment Appeals Tribunal

Law Reports and Journals

AC	Appeal Cases
All ER	All England Reports
CMLR	Common Market Law Reports
Ch	Chancery Cases
ECR	European Court of Justice Reports
EHRR	European Human Rights Reports
EWCA Crim	England and Wales Court of Appeal (Criminal Division)
EWHC	England and Wales High Court
GWD	Green's Weekly Digest
ICR	Industrial Cases Reports
ILJ	Industrial Law Journal
IRLR	Industrial Relations Law Reports
ITR	Industrial Tribunals Reports
KB	Law Reports, King's Bench Division (England)
MLR	Modern Law Review
Mor	Morison's Dictionary of Decisions (Court of Session)
PIQR	Personal Injury and Quantum Report
QB	Law Reports, Queen's Bench Division (England)
SC	Session Cases
SCCR	Scottish Criminal Case Reports
SCLR	Scottish Civil Law Reports
SJ	Scottish Jurist
SLT	Scots Law Times
UKHL	House of Lords
WLR	Weekly Law Reports

Other Abbreviations

ABWOR	Assistance by Way of Representation
CMD	Case Management Discussion
ECHR	European Convention on Human Rights
ETO	Economic, Technical or Organisational

EWC	Expected Week of Childbirth
GOQ	Genuine Occupational Qualification
JES	Job Evaluation Scheme
MA	Maternity Allowance
NMW	National Minimum Wage
PCP	Provision Criterion or Practice
PHR	Pre-hearing Review
PRP	Performance Related Pay
SMP	Statutory Maternity Pay
SPP	Statutory Paternity Pay
SSP	Statutory Sick Pay

Table of Statutes

[References are to paragraph number]

Table of Statutory Instruments

[References are to paragraph number]

Table of Cases

Table of Cases

N

Table of EC Materials, International Conventions etc

[References are to paragraph number]

Table of Other Material

[References are to paragraph number]

Chapter 1

Development of Employment Law

INTRODUCTION

1.1 Employment law particularly, over the last forty years, has developed into one of the most important and influential areas of law for the parties involved and also their representatives.

It can have an impact on an employers' financial position and their reputation, internally and externally, where they are successfully legally challenged by their employees or third parties in courts, and/or, at employment tribunals. The practitioner will often be called upon to minimise the impact of the legal rules on the parties to the employment relationship involved in a legal dispute, and increasingly invited in to organisations by employers to take practical steps to avoid legal claims by employees and workers. This book is concerned with covering in an interesting and accessible way all the major area of importance for employment law practitioners advising clients on employment law matters in Scotland.

In order to fully understand the subject of employment law in Scotland it is necessary to be provided with an overview of its development. Such an overview will necessarily involve analysing the sources of, and influences on, the law.

SLAVERY

1.2 While it is well known that Scottish merchants were heavily involved in the slave trade in the 18th and 19th century, it is perhaps less well known that the employment relationship that existed two hundred years ago, or more, in Scotland was most commonly that of master and slave. Exceptions to this were Artisans, who were highly skilled in their profession and formed themselves into Guilds. They had a more equal relationship with their employer, and were able to negotiate good terms and conditions for their profession. There were other exceptions, for example the pioneer employer Robert Owen, who built New Lanark, in Scotland, for his workers in 1799 was determined to improve the working conditions and housing of his employees. His new employment model lasted for around thirty years.

Under the master and slave relationship, the master not only benefitted from the fruits of the slave's labour without any substantial cost to himself, but he effectively owned the slave and could deal with the slave in any way he chose. This was illustrated by early workers in the coal and salt mines, who were transferable as chattels with the sale of a mine and, until 1799, could be criminally prosecuted if they tried to leave their job.[1]

Accordingly, the master not only had a right to the fruits of the labour of his slave, but he became the legal owner, body and soul, of a human being whom the law counted as a chattel.[2]

In an early Scottish case dealing with the legal nature of workers, the judge pronounced that the state of slavery was not recognised by the law of Scotland, and was inconsistent with its principles, but what was required for slavery to exist, was perpetual service of a worker without the payment of wages.[3] This decision was confusing, to say the least but, reflected the judiciaries' uneasiness with the relationship. This legal position of workers applied until it was replaced, in the Victorian era, with the law of master and servant.[4] This legal arrangement applied prior to the current legal position, which is referred to here as the modern law of employment, starting in the early 1960's.[5]

Law of Master and Servant

1.3 The period during which the law of master and servant applied lasted for around a hundred years, from the 1850's until the modern period that started in 1960. The contract of service was classed under the contract of *locatio conductio* and, under this heading, consisted of a combination of *locatio operis*, defined as the hiring of a person to do particular work,

---

1 Philip, J R Early Labour Law in Scotland (1934) Juridical Review Vol 46 pp 121–132.
2 Miller, I P *Industrial Law in Scotland* (1970) W Green.
3 *Knight v Wedderburn* M 14545 (1778).
4 Fraser, P Treatise on Master and Servant According to the Law of Scotland 3rd ed. (1881) T&T Clark.
5 Some commentators would argue the modern period started much earlier.

and *locatio operum*, which was the hiring of a person's services to act in a particular capacity, without relation to any specific business. Since the Industrial Revolution took hold, in the early part of the 19th century, most people left their rural lives to live in cities and work in factories. As the number of these employees rose, and working conditions worsened, it became clear over a long period of time that Governments needed to protect the rights of the workers. Unfortunately, under the law of master and servant employment law, throughout the UK, was characterised by a combination of the Poor Laws,[6] the gradual development of legal rights for trade unions,[7] Factories Acts which provided limited protection of health and safety,[8] and limited rights under the law of contract. Despite these developments, fundamental legal rights for employees were missing, and not forthcoming until well into the twentieth century. So, less than half a century ago, there was little or no protection for employees and, accordingly, employers were able to treat their employees however they wanted, often paying them low wages while also making them work for long hours. The working environment in which they worked was often poor and dirty, full of hazardous emissions, and generally unsafe. This traditional arrangement of master and servant was not, as the name suggests, one of slavery or servility, but rather one where an employer offered work, and the person to whom it was offered, the servant, was largely obliged to accept it.[9] The terms on which they were employed could be determined by the employer, or through custom and practice or, to a lesser extent, by statutory rules. The relationship was governed by the law of contract, and the rights and duties of the parties were largely express or implied. Relationships based on slavery had been abolished, and workmen were nominally free and with the same legal status as their masters. However, the master and servant relationship was significantly different to modern contractual arrangements in several important ways:

---

6 In Scotland in 1692 Magistrates were ordered to build Correction Houses or workhouses so that beggars could be made to work. See also Poor Law (Scotland) Act 1845.

7 Trade Union Act 1871, Trade Disputes Act 1906.

8 Factories Acts 1833, 1844, 1937, 1961, see Factory and Workshop Act 1878 in Scotland.

9 Breach of contract by a workman was a criminal offence until the passing of the Master and Servant Act, 1867.

the absence of mutual agreement over contractual terms, attributable in part to the significant differential in bargaining power between the parties, lack of job security for employees and an absence of full representation by collective bodies, such as trade unions.

The pressure for legislative change in the UK to provide statutory minimum rights came from international bodies, such as the International Labour Organisation (ILO), pressure groups such as women rights organisations, the Trades Union Congress (TUC) and the Confederation of British Industry (CBI) and, most significantly, the European Union. The public began to challenge a system which, up to the early 1960's, meant workers were dependent on trade unions and collective bargaining for any protection. The trade unions were not present in all industries and occupations and, even where they were, they did not represent all sectors of employment. Women were particularly unrepresented by trade unions, which were, at the time, driven by male workers' interests.[10]

MODERN EMPLOYMENT LAW

1.4 Employment law began to change in the 1960's with the introduction of minimum working rights for employees (sometimes referred to as a 'floor of rights') that were provided by statute.

Although much of modern employment law is contained in statutes and statutory instruments, the legal basis of the employment relationship was, and continues to be, the contract of employment between the employer and the employee. The contract of employment can be important in itself, providing the right to make a common law claim for its enforcement, and to obtain damages for its breach. However, it is also has an impact in areas of statutory employment law where working under a contract of employment is a prerequisite for underpinning statutory remedies such as constructive dismissal, which will be considered later. The other interaction with statutory rights arises because access to the statutory rights are mainly restricted to 'employees' and this status is defined by reference to the contractual relationship at common law. From the early

---

10 In 1951 only 27% of women in work in the UK were trade union members compared with 56% of men.

1960's onwards however, UK and European legislation has been the major influence in the creation of employment rights and obligations.

The first real statutory intervention came in 1963 with the Contract of Employment Act, which required an employer to give his employees a minimum period of notice, and to provide to their employees with a document known as the 'written statement of terms and conditions'. This latter right was established to provide employees with a summary of the main contractual provisions.[11]

Since then, a vast number of statutory rights have been added for employees and workers. These have not replaced the contractual provisions which still apply, but have supplemented them with universal rights enforceable before employment tribunals. Any employment law claims can now involve: common law actions (mainly contractual and delictual); statutory claims under UK statutes or under a combination of UK and European legislation; and, more recently, actions involving human rights, as defined in the Human Rights Act 1998.

This book covers the nature and characteristics of the modern employment relationship. It covers the rules that have been developed to distinguish an employee from other workers and independent contractors. It includes the legal rules dealing with the formation of the contract of employment, terms of a contract of employment and the consequences of breach of the contract of employment, and the remedies available for such breach. It also involves coverage of the rules dealing with termination of employment including claims for: wrongful dismissal, unfair dismissal, transfers of undertakings and statutory redundancy. Also explained, are the statutory rights of employees providing protection from different forms of discrimination such as sex, race, religion, disability, sexual orientation, age, and the provision of family-friendly rights. Other areas where legal intervention has occurred recently to provide rights to workers, involve matters such as the regulation of: the national minimum wage, maximum working hours and, for employees, unauthorised deductions from wages.

Health and safety law, and the law of trade unions, are also considered, as are the legal mechanisms for Alternative Dispute Resolution, and immigration rules affecting employment. Employment law is heavily

---

11 The form of this statement is now prescribed by s 1 of the Employment Rights Act 1996, s 1 (ERA 1996).

influenced by the EU and UK social policy and human rights, particularly those under the European Convention of Human Rights, and their impact on the growth of this dynamic area of law are also considered. It is now generally accepted that both the nature of employment, the employment market, and employment law has radically changed over the last 20 years or so. We will also look at alternative dispute resolution in employment law and the options for settling disputes without going to an employment tribunal and look at the immigration rules that impact on employers particularly when they choose to employ someone from outside the European Union.

Over this period these changes have been made partly in response to the increasingly globalised nature of modern working life. Other factors are the decreasing importance of trade unions and collective bargaining; and employers' increasingly wanting to employ people on less formal or permanent basis than previously. More recently, less favourable economic conditions, domestically and abroad, have also had an impact on the employment relationship. One change, is that increasingly workers, sometimes through choice but often because of changes introduced by employers (to offset these changes outlined), have to adapt themselves and be more flexible in terms of the contractual status of their employment, and their working hours, and get accustomed to working in a more flexible workplace. With the advent of flexible working practices, such as flexi-time, there has been a move by employers towards taking on a more flexible workforce. This takes the form of increased utilisation by employers of agency workers, casual or seasonal workers, and workers on fixed-term contracts. The result is that many workforces now consist of a mixture of permanent employees, temporary workers, casual and agency workers etc. We will look at the different forms of contractual arrangements employees and workers are employed under, that are different from the traditional permanent and open ended contract of employment. The extent to which those workers who are not permanent employees, known as atypical workers, have the benefit of statutory protection, is the subject of case law and statutory changes, which is also considered in the book.

Chapter 2

Institutions of Employment Law

2.1 This chapter explains the role of tribunals and the court system in employment law disputes in Scotland. It also gives a brief introduction to the other institutions of employment law.

What follows is a diagram which shows the various appeal stages an employment claim can go through starting at the employment tribunal stage and ending up in the Supreme Court. There is also the possibility the case will be referred to one of the two relevant European Courts for their opinion.

THE EMPLOYMENT TRIBUNAL SYSTEM

2.2

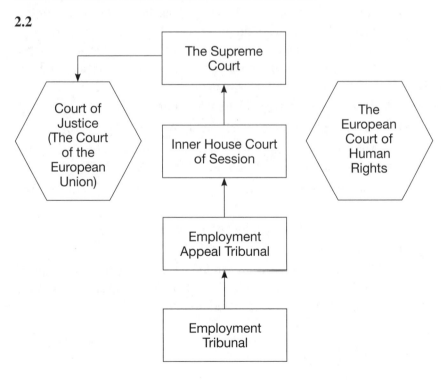

EMPLOYMENT TRIBUNALS

Jurisdiction

2.3 Jurisdiction is the authority which the court or tribunal has to hear a case. In the case of employment tribunals this authority derives from statute and unless statute has conferred jurisdiction on the tribunal then it has no authority to hear a claim.[1] There are two other types of limitations on jurisdiction, namely subject matter and territorial limitations.

The employment tribunal has jurisdiction over a wide range of subject matter in employment law, including:

(1)   Claims relating to statutory rights including employment particulars, protection of wages, guarantee payments, protection from suffering detriment in employment, time off work, suspension from work, maternity and parental leave, termination of employment, unfair dismissal, interim relief, redundancy payments, insolvency of employer.

(2)   Many union matters, including discipline by trade union, unlawful deduction of union dues, wrongful deduction or refusal to deduct union dues, refusal of employment because a member of a trade union or refusal to become one, detriment suffered because of trade union activities.

(3)   Provisions relating to the transfer of undertakings.

(4)   Equality claims under the Equality Act 2010 (EA 2010).

(5)   Appeals against improvement or prohibition notices under the Health and Safety at Work Act 1974 (HASAW 1974).

(6)   Claims under the National Minimum Wage Act 1998 (NMWA 1998).

(7)   Working Time Regulations 1998 (WTR 1998).

(8)   Public Interest Disclosure Act 1998 (PIDA 1998).

(9)   Flexible Working (Procedural Requirements) Regulations 2002/3207 and the Part-time Workers (Prevention of Less Favourable Treatment) Regulations 2000/1551.

---

1   *Aparau v Iceland Frozen Foods plc* 2000 ICR 341.

(10)   Claims for breach of contract.[2] It is important to note that breach of contract claims are only subject to the jurisdiction of the Employment tribunal if they are not for personal injuries and the claim arises, or is outstanding, on termination of the contract of employment. The maximum limit which can be claimed for breach of contract is £25,000.

A full list of the jurisdiction of the employment tribunal is available on the Employment Tribunal in Scotland website.[3]

In most of these areas, jurisdiction is exclusive and, as such, claims cannot be heard by the courts. A notable exception is breach of contract claims. The civil courts (Sheriff Court and the Court of Session) have jurisdiction in such cases and their jurisdiction is wider than that of the employment tribunal. In court there is no upper limit on the amount that can be claimed, the claim need not be outstanding on termination of the contract, and time limits within which a claim must be aired are much longer.

The territorial jurisdiction of the employment tribunal is a complicated issue. Jurisdiction generally extends to all those who are working in the United Kingdom. The tribunal may have jurisdiction over those working outside the UK in limited circumstances which are outlined below. It will often depend on the statute under which the particular claim is raised.

As far as unfair dismissal claims are concerned under s 94(1) of the Employment Rights Act 1996 the repeal of s 196 of that Act in 1999 left a vacuum in respect of jurisdiction which is required to be filled by the courts. Section 196 had excluded employees who ordinarily work outside the UK from various employment rights. This section was not replaced and it was left to the courts to decide this issue. The leading case was *Lawson v Serco*[4] which set out the principles which must be applied in establishing jurisdiction. In *Lawson v Serco*, three cases were heard together. Mr Lawson was engaged by a UK-based company, Serco, to work as a security supervisor on Ascension Island, a dependency of the British Overseas Territory of St Helena. In *Botham v Ministry of Defence,*

---

2   Industrial Tribunals Extension of Jurisdiction (Scotland) Order 1994/1624.
3   http://www.employmenttribunals.gov.uk/
4   [2006] IRLR 289.

Mr Botham was employed by the Ministry of Defence as a 'UK-based youth worker' with the British Forces Germany Youth Service. He was part of the 'civil component' of the British Forces in Germany and treated as resident in the UK rather than Germany for various purposes including taxation. In *Crofts v Veta Ltd*, the employer was a company based in Hong Kong and was a wholly-owned subsidiary of Cathay Pacific Airways Ltd (another company based in Hong Kong). Veta supplied aircrew for aircraft owned and run by Cathay Pacific. Cathay operated a 'permanent basings policy' by which some aircrew could be assigned a permanent 'home base' outside Hong Kong. Mr Crofts was based at Heathrow, which enabled him to live in the United Kingdom. The House of Lords divided claimants into three categories: claimants working in the UK, peripatetic employees (employees who travel from place to place) and expatriate employees. They held that, if an employee is working in the UK he should be entitled to protection and, therefore, the UK tribunal should have jurisdiction. If an employee is peripatetic[5] then the tribunal will only have jurisdiction if the employee is based in the UK.[6] Finally, in the case of expatriate workers, Lord Hoffman was of the opinion that it would be very unlikely that an expatriate worker would be within the scope of s 94(1) Employment Rights Act 1996 unless he was working for an employer based in Great Britain but that would not be enough on its own. The fact that the employee also happened to be British, or even that he was recruited in Britain, so that the relationship was 'rooted and forged' in this country, should not in itself be sufficient to take the case out of the general rule that the place of employment is decisive. Lord Hoffman concluded that 'something more is necessary' and, although he did not specify what was necessary, he gave the examples of employees who would come under the jurisdiction of the UK tribunal including an employee who had been posted abroad by a British employer for the purposes of a business carried on in Britain, or an

---

5   Peripatetic employees are employees who in the course of their employment move around from place to place often across different countries such as airline pilots, international management consultants and salesmen.

6   In *Anderson v Stena Drilling* UKEATS/0023/06/RN it was held by the Scottish EAT that an oil worker domiciled in Aberdeen working on a rig in far eastern waters for a company which was a subsidiary of a Swedish company was not based in the UK. Accordingly the employment tribunal did not have jurisdiction to hear a case of unfair dismissal but the question as to whether an oil rig could be a work base was left open.

expatriate employee of a British employer who was operating within what amounted for practical purposes to an extra territorial British political or social enclave in a foreign country. Given that the second example applied in two of the appeals (namely those involving Lawson and Botham) the appeal in these cases were allowed, and they were able to claim unfair dismissal. The appeal in the other case *Crofts v Veta Ltd* was dismissed.

The Scottish courts considered the issue of jurisdiction in *Ravat v Halliburton Manufacturing & Services Ltd.*[7] In this case the appellant did a small amount of work at home in Preston, Lancashire, but apart from that he worked solely in Libya, in accordance with the respondents' 'international commuter assignment policy', applied to those working outside the UK on a form of rotational working pattern which he followed. The Inner House of the Court of Session applied *Lawson v Serco* and held that for s 94(1) to apply there must be a 'strong connection' between the employee and the UK. They were satisfied there was so the appellant won the appeal.

The *Lawson v Serco* principles will apply to all claims involving domestic statutory rights, however, if the claim involves enforcement of a right which is conferred by an EU directive which has direct effect, the jurisdiction of the employment tribunal is much wider. It will have jurisdiction even over foreign nationals who work abroad but for UK based employers. In *Bleuse v MTB Transport Limited*[8] the Employment Appeals Tribunal stated that *Lawson* did not apply in such situations and such provisions had to be construed so as to give effect to EU rights.[9] This wider jurisdiction will therefore apply to any claims derived from directly effective European Directives, for example claims under the Working Time Directive and discrimination claims, whether or not the claim is against a public sector employer.[10]

---

7   [2010] CSIH 52.
8   [2008] ICR 488.
9   *Marshall v Southampton and South West Hampshire AHA* (152/84) [1986] QB 401 and *Marleasing SA v La Comercial Internacional de Alimentacion SA* (C-106/89) [1990] ECR I-4135.
10   *Mangold v Helm* [2006] All ER (EC) 383.

COMPOSITION

2.4 The purpose of the employment tribunal is to resolve disputes between employers and employees and in some cases between trade unions and employers and/or employees. Employment tribunals are the lowest tier of the legal system.[11] Appeals against decisions of employment tribunals are heard by the EAT which sits in Edinburgh. The appellate system for appeals from employment tribunals in Scotland are outlined on the first page of this chapter.

The operation of the employment tribunal system in Scotland is supervised by the President of the employment tribunals (appointed by the Lord President).[12]

A hearing before a tribunal will be before an employment judge who must either be an advocate or solicitor of not less than seven years standing, and two lay members, one drawn from either side of industry. There are certain circumstances where an employment judge may sit alone. The function of the employment judge is to preside over the proceedings; advise the lay members on the relevant law and its application to the facts of the case; and give the reasons for the tribunal's decision. When sitting with lay members, the legally qualified employment judge is not in a privileged position. The members of the tribunal are equal and the judge can be outvoted, and where his happens the judge's opinion in these cases will form the minority opinion of the tribunal.

REPRESENTATION

2.5 A party may be represented by a lay representative (paid or unpaid). It was an important objective when establishing the employment tribunals for the first time, under the Industrial Training Act 1964, that employment tribunals compared with the ordinary courts were relatively cheap, quick and informal. Unfortunately the law administered by the tribunals has become increasingly complex and subject to constant

---

11   There are Employment Tribunals based in Aberdeen, Edinburgh, Dundee, Inverness and Glasgow.

12   The Judicial Appointments Commission appoints the President of Employment Tribunals. In Scotland the President is Ms Shona Simon.

change.[13] Cases have become more protracted (and sometimes more complicated) and, because they are judicial bodies, there has still been a high degree of formality in the procedure. For these reasons there has been an increased use of legal representation over the years which has resulted in increased expense for most claimants in pursuing their case against an employer.

LEGAL AID

2.6 In England and Wales there is no legal aid available to cover the costs of representation at the employment tribunal. It is different in Scotland, where Scottish Ministers acceded to arguments that the non-availability of legal aid in employment tribunals amounted to non-compliance with Art 6(1) of the European Convention on Human Rights (the right to a fair trial). This led to the limited extension of legal aid in Scotland to cover the legal costs in some cases in employment tribunals with effect from 15 January 2001. The Scottish Legal Aid Board ensures that only the most complex employment cases are eligible for funding. Legal Aid in the form of advice and assistance may be made available to solicitors to advise a claimant on the necessary steps to apply to a tribunal, and to negotiate with the employer, but does not cover the work required to lodge a claim, or provide representation at a tribunal. In order to be paid for providing such services, it is necessary to apply for Assistance by way of Representation (ABWOR). ABWOR must be applied for in advance and will be granted if the Scottish Legal Aid Board is satisfied that the case is arguable; it is reasonable in the particular circumstances of the case that assistance by way of representation be made available; and the case is too complex to allow the applicant to present it to a minimum standard of effectiveness in person.[14] Factors which the board must take into account in deciding whether the case is too complex are whether determining the issue may involve procedural difficulty, or consideration of a substantial question of law, or of evidence of a complex or difficult nature, and the applicant may be unable to understand the proceedings or to state their

---

13 Most notably through changes in EU Law requiring UK compliance.
14 Legal Aid (Scotland Act 1986 s 6(1) and Advice and Assistance by Way of Representation (Scotland) Regulations 2003, Regulations 3 and 13.

own case because of their age, inadequate knowledge of English, mental illness, other mental or physical disability, or otherwise. Guidance and forms are available from The Scottish Legal Aid Board website.[15]

PROCEDURE

2.7 Employment tribunals are constituted and operate according to statutory rules issued by the Secretary of State.[16] The relevant rules are the Employment Tribunals Rules of Procedure, which set out the Tribunals' main objectives, procedures and other matters such as time limits for making a claim. The current rules are set out in Schedule 1 of the Employment Tribunals (Constitution and Rules of Procedure) Regulations 2004[17] which came into force on 1 October 2004. The main amendments to these regulations were made on 1 October 2004,[18] 5 April 2005,[19] and 1 October 2005.[20] The Employment Tribunals (Constitution and Rules of Procedure) (Amendment) Regulations 2008[21] made changes to take account of the ACAS Code on Discipline and Grievance Procedures.[22] These were introduced by ACAS to provide a minimum standard of behaviour for employers and employees in respect of discipline and grievances procedures in the workplace which, although not legally binding, is regarded by employment tribunals as a legal minimum in unfair dismissal cases. The nature and constitution of the Advisory, Conciliation and Arbitration Service (ACAS) and its role will be considered later in the chapter.

---

15   http://www.slab.org.uk/profession/index.html
16   Employment Rights (Dispute Resolution) Act 1998, s 1(1).
17   2004 SI 2004/1861.
18   Employment Tribunals (Constitution and Rules of Procedure) (Amendment) Regulations 2004 SI 2004/2351 which inserted rules on Equal Pay cases.
19   Employment Tribunals (Constitution and Rules of Procedure) (Amendment) Regulations 2005 SI2005/435.
20   Employment Tribunals (Constitution and Rules of Procedure) (Amendment) (No 2) Regulations 2005 SI 2005/1865.
21   SI 2008/3240.
22   Introduced in 2008 but updated in 2009.

It should be noted that in some types of case there are special rules of procedure.[23] These special rules are for use in cases involving health & safety improvement and prohibition notices, appeals against non-discrimination notices and National Security Levy Appeals.

Although the rules apply throughout the UK, there are some minor differences of procedure in Scotland from the rest of the UK. Many Practice Directions have been issued in England and Wales under the 2004 Regulations, whereas in Scotland, the President of Employment Tribunals has issued only three Practice Directions to date under Regulation 13 of the 2004 Regulations, namely: Practice Direction (Scotland) No1: Intimation of List of Documents 14 days before a Hearing, Practice Direction (Scotland) No 2: Sist for Mediation; and Practice Direction (Scotland) No 3: Counter Claims. The rules and practice directions are available on the Employment Tribunal for Scotland website.[24]

According to Regulation 3 of the 2004 Regulations, in exercising its powers the tribunal's overriding objective must be to deal with the case justly. This includes, so far as practicable:

(a)   ensuring that the parties are on an equal footing;

(b)   dealing with the case in ways which are proportionate to the complexity or importance of the issues;

(c)   ensuring that the case is dealt with expeditiously and fairly; and

(d)   saving expense.

Commencing the claim

2.8 The claim is commenced by the claimant completing and submitting the ET1 claim form. It is crucial that the claim form is completed accurately and submitted on time. In Scotland the Glasgow office of the Employment Tribunal Service is where all claims are first received and processed.[25] It is therefore best initially that claimants and respondents

---

23   Schedule 2–6 of the Employment Tribunals (Constitution and Rules of Procedure) Regulations 2004 SI 2004/1861 as amended by the Employment Tribunals (Constitution and Rules of Procedure) (Amendment) Regulations 2004 SI 2004/2351.

24   http://www.employmenttribunals.gov.uk/

25   The address for which is: Employment Tribunal Office, Eagle Building, 215 Bothwell Street, Glasgow, G27TS.

send their correspondence about the claim to that office. Although once the claim has been processed it will usually be sent from there to the tribunal office in the area where the claimant works, worked or applied for work.

Once the claim is received by the employment tribunal it will be reviewed and then either accepted or not accepted. If the claim is accepted, the claimant will be sent a letter from the employment tribunal to confirm this. However, a claim will not be accepted if it is out of time,[26] not in its correct form, or if the claimant has not provided all the information needed.[27] If this happens the form will be sent back to the claimant with a letter explaining the problem and how to remedy it, if possible.[28]

Time limits

2.9 The time limit for making a claim depends on the type of claim being made and the relevant statute should always be consulted. The following quote from the official Government source summarises the position thus:

> 'Most employment law claims must be made within very strict time limits. In most cases the tribunal must receive your claim within 3 months. In dismissal case the three months period begins from the date your employment ended. In discrimination cases or complaints relating to non-payment of wages or holiday pay the three month period begins when the matter you are complaining about happened. There are special rules for equal pay and redundancy payment claims.'[29]

The time limit for most claims is 3 months from the date of action complained of or on the date of the final part of a continuing act. For guidance as to what will be considered a continuing act see the Court of Appeal's decision in *Owusu v London Fire & Civil Defence Authority*,[30] where it was held that:

---

26   www.employmenttribunals.gov.uk/FormsGuidance/makingAClaim.htm
27   Ibid see unacceptable claims.
28   www.direct.gov.uk/en/employment/index.htm
29   Ibid.
30   [1995] IRLR 574.

'The position is that an act does not extend over a period simply because the doing of the act has continuing consequences. A specific decision not to upgrade may be a specific act with continuing consequences. The continuing consequences do not make it a continuing act. On the other hand, an act does extend over a period of time if it takes the form of some policy, rule or practice, in accordance with which decisions are taken from time to time. What is continuing is alleged in this case to be a practice which results in consistent decisions discriminatory of Mr. Owusu.'[31]

Further clarification was given by the Court of Appeal in their decision in the case of *Cast v Croydon College*.[32] They held that a decision by an employer may be an act of discrimination, whether or not it is made on the same facts as a previous decision, where it results from further consideration of a matter and not merely a reference back to an earlier decision. Where the matter is reconsidered in response to a further request, time begins to run again for the purpose of the time limit. So the last and most recent refusal is the relevant one for this purpose. This is clearly a broad interpretation of what amounts to a continuing act of discrimination.

In addition see s 48(3)(a) of the ERA 1996 which provides for time limits in cases involving a detriment under various sections of the Employment Rights Act[33] to run from the end of a series of acts. In *Arthur v London and Eastern Railways Limited*,[34] the Court of Appeal decided unanimously that in a claim under s 48(3) of ERA 1996, a tribunal had erred in ruling that a number of alleged acts of detriment did not form part of 'a series of similar acts' and that the claimant was out of time in respect of all but the last such act.

The exceptions to the three month time limit include equal pay claims under Chapter 3 of the Equality Act 2010 (Equality of Terms) and claims for a Redundancy payment under s 164 of the Employment Rights Act where the claimant has 6 months to make a claim.[35]

---

31 P 576.
32 [1998] ICR 500, CA.
33 As specified in section 48(1) of the ERA 1996.
34 [2006] EWCA Civ 1358.
35 *Abdulla v Birmingham City Council* it was held by the High Court that equal pay case that were out of time under the Equal Pay Act could bring claims to the High Court in England.

Whether or not the date of the action complained of, or date of dismissal, is included in the calculation as day 1 of any time limit depends on the exact wording of the relevant statutory provision. If the wording used is 'beginning with' then that date will be included,[36] therefore three months beginning with 1 May means on, or before, 31 July. If the wording is 'from' or 'after' a specified date then that date is not included,[37] hence three months from, or after, 1 May means 1 August. A month usually means a calendar month. There is a presumption that if a letter is sent to the tribunal by first class post it will be received two days after it was posted.[38] However, it has been held that in the case of tribunals (but not courts) Saturdays, Sundays and public holidays should be excluded from the computation.[39] The deadline for submission is midnight on the last day of the two-day period. Most claims are now made electronically but, as can be seen from the case law discussed below, this leads to problems of its own.

A claimant should not allow a time limit to expire simply because he is awaiting completion of an employer's internal procedure.[40]

The tribunal may extend the time limit in certain cases. In order to ascertain the test which the tribunal will apply in considering whether or not to extend the time limit for making a claim, it is once more necessary to examine the statutory provision under which the right was conferred. Generally, for claims made under the Employment Rights Act 1996, the tribunal will extend the time limit if it is satisfied that it was not reasonably practicable for the application to have been made in time.[41] If the claim was made under the Equality Act 2010, the tribunal is directed to allow an extension if it is satisfied that it is just and equitable to do so.[42] This latter test also applies to claims for redundancy payments.[43]

---

36 *Dorber v London Brick Co Ltd* 1974 ICT 270.
37 *Goldsmith's Co v West Metropolitan Railway Co* [1904] 1KB 1.
38 *Consignia Ltd v Sealy* [2002] EWCA Civ 878, [2002] ICR 1193.
39 *Coldridge v HM Prison Service* EAT 20/04/05.
40 *Hamm v GMB Union* EAT 15/11/2000.
41 Employment Rights Act 1996 sections 111 and 48 and Rules of Procedure 2004 rule 10.
42 Section 123 of the Equality Act.
43 Employment Rights Act 1996, s 164(2).

The reasonably practicable test under the Employment Rights Act 1996 is a two part test. First the claimant must show that it was not reasonably practicable to submit the claim on time. Then he must show that it was submitted within a reasonable time after the deadline expired.[44] The test is objective rather than subjective.[45]

In *Palmer & Saunders v Southend-on-Sea Borough Council*,[46] Lord Justice May held that the word 'practicable' was the equivalent of 'feasible'. Factors which should be taken into consideration include the likelihood of prejudice to either party by granting or refusing the extension[47] and the merits of the case.[48] The test will not usually be satisfied merely because the fault of a representative of the claimant resulted in the late submission. In *Beasley v National Grid*,[49] the claimant had received conflicting legal advice about the time limits and had submitted his own claim form electronically. The application was received 88 seconds late. The Court of Appeal stated that it is clear that what is reasonably practicable is preeminently a question of fact for the tribunal in each case, and it is seldom that an appeal from such a decision will be upheld unless the legal test has been incorrectly applied, or the decision was perverse.[50] It is clear that tribunals have little sympathy for claimants who leave it until the last minute to make a claim and then encounter a technical difficulty.[51] Perhaps one of the most harsh examples of a refusal to extend the time limit was *Miller v Community Links Trust*,[52] where an application was submitted by the claimant's paid representative, electronically at one second to midnight on the last day, but not received by the tribunal until eight seconds past

---

44   *Lezo v OCS Group UK Ltd* [2010] All ER (D) 33 (Sep), EAT.
45   *Birmingham Optical Group plc v Johnson* [1995] ICR 459.
46   [1984] ICR 372 at 375–375.
47   *Unison v Sodexho Healthcare* EAT 21/5/2001; *Kwik Save Stores v Swain* 1997 ICR 49.
48   *Aziz v Bethnal City Green Challenge Co Ltd* [2000] IRLR 111.
49   [2008] EWCA Civ 742,
50   *Walls Meat Co v Khan* [1979] ICR 52; *Marks and Spencer plc v Williams-Ryan* [2005] ICR1293; *Chief Constable of Lincolnshire Police v Caston* [2010] IRLR 327; *Mehta v Mayor and Burgesses of London Borough of Hackney* EAT 19 Jan 2010.
51   Such as a printer breaking down *Fishley v Working Men's College* [2005] All ER (D) 46 (Jan), EAT.
52   [2007] EAT Case 0486/07.

midnight. However, in *Jurkowska v Hilmad Limited*,[53] the court used its discretion and accepted a claim that was 33 minutes late.

The tribunal is not often sympathetic to cases where the failure is the fault of the party's solicitor. In *Agrico v Amanda Ireland*,[54] a tribunal decided to allow an extension of time where a solicitor went on holiday, leaving his secretary to put the claim form in the mail, and she became sick and did not send it. The Scottish EAT allowed the employer's appeal on the basis that the tribunal's decision was perverse. The EAT were of the opinion that the solicitor should have had a better system in place. Similarly, in *Northamptonshire County Council v Entwhistle*,[55] the English EAT refused to allow an extension despite the fact that the solicitor had misadvised the claimant as to the time limit.

Where a claimant has lost the chance to bring a claim because of the bad advice of a solicitor regarding time limits, they could sue the solicitor in court for negligence or professional misconduct. Alternatively they could bring a complaint before the appropriate professional body.[56] The Scottish Legal Complaints Commission (SLCC) will deal with the complaint in the first instance. If they regard it as a complaint about service they will investigate the complaint and mediate between the client and his solicitor. If mediation is unsuccessful and the claim well founded they can order any (or all) of the following:

    (a)   Decide what fees and outlays are due to the solicitor – where fees and outlays have already been paid to (or deducted by) the solicitor this may mean a reduction in the fees and repayment by the solicitor.

---

53   [2008] EWCA Civ 231, [2008] IRLR 430.
54   EAT (SCOT) 10 August 2005.
55   [2010] IRLR 740.
56   In England and Wales the Legal Complaints Service (LCS) is an organisation that was set up in 2007. It took over responsibility for complaints about solicitors from the Law Society. Initially, it will try to negotiate a settlement but, if unsuccessful, it will investigate a complaint and has the power to order the solicitor to reduce a bill, rectify any mistakes and make good any financial loss (up to a maximum of £15,000). It also has the power to order the solicitor to pay compensation for distress and inconvenience, again to a maximum of £15,000. If the loss is greater than the maximum the client will have to take his solicitor to court.

(b)   Direct that the solicitor, at the solicitor's expense, take action to put right any error, omission or other deficiency.

(c)   Where someone has been directly affected by the inadequate services, order the solicitor to pay compensation to that person up to a maximum of £20,000.

(d)   Direct that the solicitor take such other action as they specify.

Where they consider the complaint is so serious that it amounts to a conduct issue the SLCC will refer it instead to the Law Society of Scotland who will if they consider there is a case to answer refer it to the Scottish Solicitors Discipline Tribunal. If the case is founded they may:

(a)   Censure of the solicitor concerned.

(b)   Impose a fine.

(c)   Place a restriction on the practising certificate of the solicitor concerned.

(d)   Suspend the practising certificate of the solicitor concerned for a period of time.

(e)   Order the striking of the solicitor from the roll of solicitors kept by the Law Society.

(f)   Order the solicitor to make payment of the costs of the hearing, including the costs of the Law Society in conducting the complaint against him.

Where the representative at fault is not legally qualified there may be more chance that a tribunal will allow an extension, for example where the failure was due to the actions of a Citizen's Advice Bureau[57] or civil servant,[58] or where the claimant represented himself.[59]

An example of a situation where an extension may be allowed is where information becomes available after the expiry of the time limit which makes a claimant realise he may have a claim when he originally believed

---

57   *Marks and Spencer plc v Williams-Ryan* [2005] EWCA Civ 470, [2005] ICR 1293.
58   *London International College v Sen; Sorelle(Jean) Ltd v Rybak* [1991] ICR 127; *Alexander Holdings Ltd v Metheven* EAT 782/93.
59   *Zinda v Governing Body of Barn Hill Community High and ors* EAT 29/7/2010.

did not.[60] Whilst a mistaken belief as to the facts,[61] or ignorance of a fact which becomes available later, might therefore be a ground for allowing an extension,[62] ignorance of the law will probably not suffice.[63] The fact that the claimant is still making use of the employer's internal appeal processes will not mean that it was not reasonably practicable to comply with the deadline.[64]

The just and equitable test under the equality legislation is much easier to satisfy, although the case law is contradictory. In *British Coal Corporation v Keeble*,[65] the application was submitted years after the time limit because the claimant misunderstood the true effect of European law. It was not until a decision of the European Court of Justice clarified the position that the claimant's trade union realised the claimant might have a valid claim. The Court of Appeal held that the just and equitable test in discrimination cases was much wider than the reasonably practicable test. The court could take all the circumstances into account including a mistake as to the law or incorrect legal advice.[66] However, in *Perth and Kinross Council v Townsley*,[67] the Scottish EAT held that the need to consider whether a claimant was reasonably ignorant, was equally applicable when considering the grant of an extension of time under the 'just and equitable' test in race discrimination claims, or the 'not reasonably practicable' test in relation to an unfair dismissal claim. It will still be the exceptional case where an error of law will be sufficient reason to allow an extension of time, even in discrimination cases.[68]

Where the claim is lodged late because of the negligence of the legal representative there is more chance of successfully applying for an

60   *Cambridge and Peterborough Foundations Trust v Crouchman* [2009] ICR 1306, EAT; *Teva UK v Heslip* EAT 9/7/2009.

61   *Defer-Wyatt v Williams* EAT 27/4/2003.

62   *Machine Tool Industry Research Association v Simpson* 1988 ICR 558.

63   *Barber v Staffordshire County* [1996] ICR 379.

64   *Robinson v Post Office* [2000] IRLR 804; *Palmer and Saunders v Southend on Sea* BC 1984 ICR 372.

65   [1997] IRLR 336.

66   Compare the decision in this case to the decision in *Biggs v Somerset* CC [1996] IRLR 203.

67   EAT Scot 17 August 2010.

68   *University of Westminster v Bailey* EAT 22 September 2009.

extension under the just and equitable test, than under the reasonably practicable' test in an unfair dismissal claim.[69] In *Chohan v Derby Law Centre*,[70] a victimisation claim against his employer was lodged by a trainee solicitor 18 days late. The EAT held that inadequate advice given to the trainee by another solicitor, and the fact that a decision on termination of her traineeship contract was still to be made by the Office for Supervision of Solicitors, were relevant factors to be taken into account. There was a suggestion that the factors listed in the checklist in the Limitation Act 1980 (which does not apply to Scotland) should be considered,[71] however this suggestion was later disapproved in *McCarthy v HM Prison*.[72]

Orders

2.10 Under rule 10 (1) of Schedule 1 of the Employment Tribunals (Constitution and Rules of Procedure) Regulations 2004, the Employment Judge may at any time, either on the application of a party or on his own initiative, make an order in relation to any matter which appears to him to be appropriate. Such orders may be any of those listed in rule 10 (2), or such other orders as he thinks fit. Subject to the following rules, orders may be issued as a result of an Employment Judge considering the papers before him in the absence of the parties, or at a hearing. Under rule 10 (2) examples of orders which may be made under paragraph (1) are inter alia orders: '(a) as to the manner in which the proceedings are to be conducted, including any time limit to be observed; (b) that a party provide additional information; (c) requiring the attendance of any person in Great Britain either to give evidence or to produce documents or information; (d) requiring any person in Great Britain to disclose documents or information to a party or to allow a party to inspect such material as might be ordered by a sheriff (or a Country Court in England).'

The party may have been ordered by the Tribunal to disclose documents to the other party as per rule 10. However, even if he has not, the party

---

69 *Virdi v Commissioner of Metropolitan Police* [2007] IRLR 24.
70 [2004] IRLR 685.
71 This approach was also applied in *Anderson v George S Hall Ltd* UKEAT/0631/05/DA.
72 EAT 7 February 2005.

relying on and introducing documentary evidence into the proceedings must make sure that the other party has reasonable notice, (at least seven days), of these documents. Both parties can bring witnesses to the hearing to give relevant evidence. Even if the tribunal has not told the parties to let them know before the hearing how many witnesses each plans to bring, it will be helpful to them to be informed. The employment tribunal may have ordered one or both of the parties to produce a written statement of his own evidence, but even if the party has not been ordered he may wish to consider doing so. However, in Scotland the parties should not do so unless ordered by the tribunal.

Amendment of the claim

2.11 It is extremely important to include in the claim form details of any claim which the claimant wishes the tribunal to consider. The tribunal has discretion to allow amendment of the claim.[73] The likelihood of success of a claim to amend the form depends on whether the amendment seeks to rely on facts other than those already stated in the original claim form and what stage of the procedure the case has reached. It is relatively easy to persuade the tribunal to allow the correction of a clerical error or the relabeling or tidying up of a claim for which facts have already been included in the pleadings.[74] An application to amend in order to add a claim which requires new facts is more difficult, particularly if the application to amend is made outwith the time limit. In such cases the tribunal is required to consider the hardship which would be caused to each party if the amendment were to be allowed or refused. The stage at which the application for amendment is made is a relevant factor and the earlier the application is made in the process the better. An attempt to add a claim after the hearing has commenced is generally too late,[75] but not impossible if the facts are already included in the claim and the tribunal is satisfied that it is fair to allow it. In *Selkent Bus Co Ltd v Moor*,[76] the

---

73   Rule 10 (2) (q) of the 2004 rules.
74   *Jocic v LB of Hammersmith & Fulham and ors* [2007] All ER (D) 443 (Oct) EAT; *Lewis v Corus Group Ltd* [2003] All ER (D) 23 (Jun) EAT.
75   *Bradford Hospitals NHS Trust v Al Shabib* EAT 2003 IRLR 4.
76   [1996] ICR 836.

claimant was not allowed to add a ground of claim because the addition came too late and outwith the time limit to his existing claim for unfair dismissal the basis of which was his dismissal for a trade union reason. The EAT held that in exercising its discretion, a tribunal should take into account all the circumstances, including the nature of the amendment, the applicability of time limits and the timing and manner of the application, before balancing the hardship and injustice of allowing the amendment against the injustice and hardship of refusing it. An attempt may be made to add a new cause of action on different facts from those already included in the pleadings. In this type of amendment, the question of limitation must be considered and the tribunal should not allow an amendment unless the reasonably practicable test for out of time applications (discussed in detail above) is met.[77]

The response

2.12 Claims are usually administered and heard in the employment tribunal office closest to the place where the claimant normally works or applied for work.

Once the claim is accepted, the employment tribunal usually sends a copy of it to the respondent (the person the claimant is claiming against) along with a form to fill in with their response and, once the respondent's response is received, to ACAS (the Advisory, Conciliation and Arbitration Service). The respondent must send in a response within 28 days of the date that the claim is sent to them. The respondent may obtain an extension if granted by the employment tribunal. If they don't, response must be received within the time period, or if the response does not supply the information that has been asked for, the response will not be accepted. In these cases, the Employment Judge can issue what is called a 'default judgment.' This means that the employment tribunal will make a decision about the claim without proceeding to a hearing, based on the information available to it.

In the event that a response is accepted, an Employment Judge will consider how best to proceed usually by requesting further information directly from the parties where appropriate and then when satisfied setting a date for the hearing.

---

77   *Harvey v Port of Tilbury (London) Ltd* [1999] ICR 1030.

EMPLOYMENT TRIBUNAL PRE-HEARING DISCUSSIONS AND REVIEWS

2.13 The employment tribunal, or an employment judge, can carry out a preliminary hearing which will involve case management discussions or preliminary reviews. This allows the tribunal to determine any obstacle to any party bringing or contesting proceedings, to which the original claim applies. It is held before the substantive case is heard. Either of the parties can apply for such a hearing or it may be convened at the instigation of the tribunal.

Case management discussions[78]

2.14 Case management discussions (CMD's) are held in private before an employment judge sitting alone and aim to identify the issues to be determined in the case, and to consider procedural aspects such as whether a pre-hearing review or particular evidence is required, eg medical evidence in a disability discrimination case. The discussions do not extend to considering the particular merits of the case or the likelihood of a successful outcome at the hearing. The CMDs may be conducted face-to-face or if both the parties are legally represented by telephone conference, between the judge and the parties' representatives. No evidence is led by the parties or their witnesses. Following these discussions the employment judge may make orders on a wide range of matters including: that one or both of the parties provide additional information or that a hearing be postponed, adjourned or the proceedings are stayed. Where there is a failure by the employer to comply with the order their response may be struck out and they may be ordered to pay all or some of the claimant's costs.

Pre-hearing reviews[79]

2.15 Pre-hearing reviews (PHRs) are undertaken by employment tribunals to decide on preliminary issues in the case. These reviews are usually

---

78 Rule17, Employment Tribunals (Constitution and Rules of Procedure) Regulations 2004/1861.
79 Ibid, Rule 18.

heard by an employment judge sitting alone, but a full tribunal will usually be involved if one or more issues of substantive fact are likely to be determined. In a pre-hearing review both parties must explain the basis of their case, eg which witnesses (if any) they will need and the evidence they will need to provide.

Examples of issues which can be decided in this way are whether: a claimant is disabled for the purposes of a disability discrimination claim under the Equality Act 2010 (see chapter on Equality Law); whether the employment status of the claimant is that of an employee or some other category of worker; whether the claim of a claimant that is submitted outwith the time limit can proceed, or the claimant has sufficient continuous service with his employer to make a claim, eg unfair dismissal. However, a PHR may also decide whether a case should go ahead and a claim which appears to have no reasonable chance of success will usually not be allowed to proceed to hearing. Where the claim of a party has little prospect of success he may be ordered to pay a deposit of up to £500 in order to be allowed to proceed with the claim.[80] If the complaint is not settled or withdrawn at this stage it will proceed to a full hearing by an employment tribunal.

HEARING

2.16 Prior to the hearing, an ACAS conciliator will contact and maintain a dialogue with the parties to try and resolve the problem without needing to go to a hearing. In fact, ACAS is remarkably successful in this. In the year ending March 2010, 44% of all the unfair dismissal claims ended in a conciliated settlement.[81] If a case proceeds to a hearing, the employment judge is under a duty to ensure that the hearing is conducted fairly, taking into account both sides' submissions on the law and the facts. At the hearing, tribunals try to keep the proceedings as simple and informal as possible. Many claimants and respondents may put their own case to the tribunal although some choose to have a representative who may be a

---

80   Rule 20.
81   Employment Tribunals Service (2009) Employment tribunal and EAT statistics (GB) 1 April 2009 to 31 March 2010. Available online at: http://www.employmenttribunals. gov.uk/

lawyer, trade union official, support agency such as CAB, representative of an employers' organisation or simply a friend or colleague. Generally for both sides witnesses are called to give oral evidence. In England and Wales written witness statements are approved in advance, but there is no such practice or requirement in Scotland.

Where a witness is involved he will have to give his evidence on oath or affirmation. If a witness lies or omits information after swearing an oath or affirmation, he could be convicted of perjury.[82] Each witness will give his evidence in chief orally. Then he can be cross-examined by the other party, or their representative if they have one. If called upon to do so the witness may then give further evidence through re-examination to clarify matters which came up. Finally, the Employment Judge and lay members may ask some questions of the witness. This process is repeated for all the witnesses to the case. Once all the evidence has been heard, both sides will sum up before the tribunal retires to consider their judgment. Unless the tribunal reserves its judgment the Employment Judge will announce the judgment verbally to the parties at the end of the hearing. If the judgment is reserved, the parties will receive it in writing at a later date. This will usually happen in complicated cases or if there is not enough time on the day of the hearing to announce the judgment following consideration by the tribunal.

Employment tribunal hearings are often completed in one day. Decisions may be by majority vote but in fact are nearly always are unanimous decisions. The tribunal usually announces its decision and the reasons for it immediately. A written decision is also sent to the parties, generally within three to six weeks.

Expenses or costs

2.17 The general rule is that no expenses or costs are recoverable in employment tribunal proceedings. The Rules of Procedure make several exceptions to this rule. Where a claimant has requested to be reengaged or reinstated and has intimated that request to the respondent more than 7 days before the hearing, then if the hearing has to be adjourned or

---

82   In England and Wales the witness may give evidence by reading out a pre-prepared written statement.

postponed because the employer does not lead evidence regarding the availability of the claimant's job or suitable alternative employment, then the tribunal must make a costs order[83] or preparation time order[84] against the respondent.

The tribunal may make a costs order or preparation order where a hearing has to be postponed or adjourned and the party ordered to make payment has in bringing the proceedings, or in conducting them, acted vexatiously, abusively, disruptively or unreasonably, or the bringing or conducting of proceedings was misconceived. The tribunal may make a costs order or preparation time order against a party who has failed to comply with an order or practice direction.

If a party has been ordered to pay a deposit under Rule 20 and the case continues but the tribunal finds against him on the point in respect of which the order to pay the deposit was made, then the tribunal may make a costs order or preparation time order if it considers that he continued unreasonably. His deposit shall be used in part payment.

A party may make an application for costs at any time during the proceedings up until 28 days after the judgement has been issued.

Whether or not the tribunal makes a costs order or a preparation time order depends on whether the party receiving payment is legally represented or not. If they are legally represented the appropriate order is a costs order, if not then it is a preparation time order. The amount of a costs order is such sum as the tribunal shall specify not exceeding £10,000 *or* such sum as the parties agree *or* such sum as is taxed on the scale of fees applicable to sheriff court actions Therefore, the sum awarded may well exceed £10,000.

In order to calculate the amount of preparation of time the tribunal [or Employment Judge] shall make an assessment the number of hours spent on preparation time on information provided and what it feels is proportionate and reasonable. They then apply an hourly rate of £31[85] to that figure subject to a limit of £10,000.

---

83   Rule 39.
84   Rule 43.
85   The hourly rate increases by £1.00 every year on 1 April.

In deciding the amount of the costs order or preparation time order one factor which the tribunal may take into account is the paying party's ability to pay.

Under rule 48 the tribunal may hold a party's representative liable for wasted costs as a result of the representative's (a representative is anyone who is acting in pursuit of profit including under a conditional fee arrangement) improper, unreasonable or negligent act or omission. It may disallow expenses or order the representative to make a payment to any party, including his own client, and to repay to the Secretary of State any allowance paid to anyone in who has had to attend the tribunal because of his conduct. Before making a wasted costs order the tribunal must allow the representative an opportunity to make written or oral representations and it must issue written reasons for its decision within 14 days of making the order. The ordinary standard of negligence applies to such cases. In *Ridehalgh v Horsefield and Another*[86] a case concerning personal liability for court costs, the House of Lords acknowledged it was a jurisdiction which falls to be exercised with care and discretion and only in clear cases can a solicitor against whom a claim is made must have a full opportunity of rebutting the complaint, but recognises that he may be hampered in doing so by his duty of confidentiality to the client. They commented on the extreme undesirability of claims for wasted costs orders being used as a means of browbeating, bludgeoning or threatening the other side during the progress of the case as such a practice, could gravely undermine the ability of a solicitor to do so with the required objectivity and independence. The EAT has endorsed this approach to employment tribunal wasted cost orders in several cases most recently that of Godfrey *Morgan Solicitors Ltd v Cobalt Systems Ltd.*[87]

Appeals

2.18 In the event of an appeal against the employment tribunal decision on a point of law the case is referred to the Employment Appeal Tribunal (the panel comprising of one judge from the Court of Session and two or four lay members). Further appeal, if leave is granted, is to the Inner

---

86   [1994] Ch 205.
87   [2011] 6 Costs LR 1006.

House of the Court of Session (or the Court of Appeal in England & Wales and Northern Ireland) and from there to the Supreme Court (see diagram on first page).

Appeals are on a point of law or on the ground of perversity only. A decision as to whether a person is an employee or not is usually a question of fact and the EAT will rarely interfere with the tribunal's decision in such cases. A decision is perverse if no tribunal with a reasonable appreciation of the evidence before it would have reached that decision.[88] This is a very high threshold and there are few examples of successful appeals on this ground.[89] One example of perversity is the situation where a tribunal's decision failed to outline the evidence given, or to indicate the tribunal's factual findings, and contain a statement of the reasons leading to the tribunal's conclusion resulting in the appellate court being unable to determine from the decision whether a question of law arose.[90]

The party appealing (appellant) must send a fully-completed notice of appeal form to the EAT within 42 days[91] from the date of the tribunal's decision. If he does not use this form he must provide the same information in some other way and should also send the following documents: the judgment, decision, direction or order against which he is appealing, written reasons if his appeal is against a judgment, claim (ET1) which the claimant sent to the employment tribunal response, (ET3) which the respondent sent to the employment tribunal, and an application for review.[92] The Practice Direction (Employment Appeal – Procedure) 2008 sets out the detailed rules concerning the appeal procedure.[93] The principles which apply to the extension of time limits were discussed earlier in this chapter. Appeals from the EAT to the Inner House of the Court of Session are also on point of law or perversity.

88   *Crofton v Yeboah* [2002] EWCA Civ 794; [2002] IRLR 634; *Mowlem Technical Services (Scotland) Ltd v King* [2005] CSIH 46.
89   *Honey v City and County of Swansea* EAT 16 April 2010.
90   *Meek v Birmingham* DC [1987] IRLR 250.
91   See *Hine Marketing Partnership v Talbot* EAT 27/6/2011 for factors taken into account when allowing an appeal to be lodged late.
92   Section 2 of the Practice Direction (Employment Appeal – Procedure) 2008.
93   www.employmentappeals.gov.uk/FormsGuidance/practiceDirection.htm

COURTS

2.19 As the contract of employment is a contract like any other, it is important to consider the role which the civil courts have to play, because claims for breach of contract can be brought before them directly.[94] There is also the likelihood of appeals from the Employment Appeal Tribunal being heard by the Inner House of the Court of Session, and appeals from the Inner House to the Supreme Court.

The Civil Courts[95]

2.20

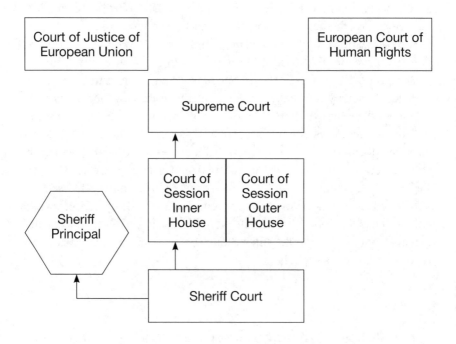

---

94   Eg common law claim for breach of contract, delictual claims and actions for interdicts
     There are aspects of the criminal law that are relevant to employment law for example
     health and safety law and trade union law.
95   http://www.scotcourts.gov.uk

The Scottish Courts Service was established as an independent statutory body by the Judiciary and Courts (Scotland) Act 2008. The same statute appointed the Lord President as head of the Scottish Judiciary. He is supported by the Judicial Office for Scotland and is responsible for the running of the efficient disposal of business in the courts, the training of the justiciary and dealing with complaints.

Jurisdiction

2.21 The civil jurisdiction of the courts in employment matters is generally restricted to appeals from the EAT, which are made to the Inner House of the Court of Session (and thereafter the Supreme Court), and claims for breach of contract or delictual claims. There are many advantages of pursuing a claim for breach of contract in the courts rather than tribunal. For example it is not possible to claim damages for personal injury at an employment tribunal. The claim is not subject to the £25000 limit which applies to claims of breach of contract before an employment tribunal. A court action for breach of contract may be pursued at any time during the subsistence of the contract of employment or after its end subject, to the 5 year prescriptive period discussed below. Full Legal Aid may be available for court actions unlike the more limited 'Advice by Way of Representation' (ABWOR) which may be available for tribunal claims. Remedies available for breach of contract claims in the civil courts, which are not available at tribunal, include specific implement and interdict.

In the civil courts, expenses will normally be ordered to be paid by the unsuccessful party to the successful party. The representative of the successful party will prepare a judicial account of his expenses when an action is settled during the course of litigation or when a court makes an award of expenses. The judicial account of expenses is prepared on the basis of a statutory fixed Table of Fees,[96] which regulates the expenses the successful party can claim. The tables of fees allow the successful party to recover their expenses, either on the basis of fixed 'block fees' for particular types of work, or by charging for the time spent on the case, by reference to fixed rates. The former basis for calculation for fees is the one most commonly used. There are different tables of fees used for

---

96   These are updated annually by statute.

expenses incurred in the Court of Session and the Sheriff Court, although the principles are the same.

Except in small claims (see below), the party must usually be represented by a solicitor or advocate, although it is always competent to represent oneself.[97]

Time limits

2.22 The time limit for bringing a claim in the civil court is much longer than that for bringing a claim to a tribunal. The Prescription and Limitation (Scotland) Act 1973 sets down the time limits for bringing claims for breach of contract and delictual claims in the civil courts. Section 6 of that statute provides that such claims will prescribe if the liability has subsisted for 5 years without a relevant claim being made, or there having been a relevant acknowledgement of the obligation. A relevant claim[98] may be made by commencement of an action in the civil courts, or presentation of a petition for sequestration. A civil claim in Scotland is brought on the day the warranted writ is successfully served on the Defender. A relevant acknowledgement[99] is either part performance of the obligation, eg the making of a payment to account, or an unequivocal acknowledgment that the obligation still exists.

Civil injury claims

2.23 Although these are not employment law claims, they can relate to delictual wrongs in the workplace, and we thought it might be useful to the reader to be given an overview of the relevant rules.

An obligation to make reparation becomes enforceable on the date the loss injury or damage occurs[100] or, in the case of a continuing act, on the date when the act neglect or default ceased.[101] In addition, ss 17 and 18 of the Prescription and Limitation (Scotland) 1973 Act prevents the

---

97   Raising and Defending Ordinary Actions in the Court of Session A Guide for Party
      Litigants August 2010 www.scotcourts.gov.uk
98   Section 8.
99   Section 10.
100 Section 11(1).
101 Section 11(2).

bringing of a claim for personal injuries, unless it is commenced within 3 years of the date of the date on which the injuries were sustained. In the situation where the act or omission to which the injuries were attributable was a continuing one, the action must be commenced within 3 years of the date on which the act or omission ceased.[102] If the injury resulted in death the action must be commenced within 3 years of the death of the injured party.[103] An action may also be brought if it is commenced within 3 years of the date on which the pursuer in the action became, or on which, in the opinion of the court, it would have been reasonably practicable for him in all the circumstances to become, aware of all the following facts:

(i)   that the injuries in question were sufficiently serious to justify his bringing an action of damages, on the assumption that the person against whom the action was brought did not dispute liability and was able to satisfy a decree;

(ii)   that the injuries were attributable in whole or in part to an act or omission; and

(iii) that the defender was a person to whose act or omission the injuries were attributable, in whole or in part, or the employer or principal of such a person.[104]

Any time during which the person who sustained the injuries was under legal disability, by reason of unsoundness of mind or was under the age of 18, is disregarded in computation of the time limit.[105]

The three year time limit also applies to claims for defamation,[106] and claims under the Protection from Harassment Act 1997.[107]

The action may be allowed to proceed, notwithstanding the fact that the limitation period has expired, if the Court is of the opinion that it is just and equitable to allow it to do so.[108]

---

102 Section 17.
103 Section 18.
104 Section 18.
105 Section 17(3).
106 Section 18(A).
107 Section 18(B).
108 Section 19A(1).

THE SHERIFF COURT AND SHERIFF PRINCIPAL

2.24 Scotland is divided into 6 sheriffdoms. There is a Sheriff Principal in charge of each sheriffdom and he is responsible for the running of courts within his sheriffdom, and also hears appeals raised against decisions made by sheriffs within his sheriffdom. Within each sheriffdom are a number of sheriff courts which hear civil claims and criminal prosecutions. There are 49 sheriff courts in total. Cases are normally heard before one sheriff. There are two types of civil action which can be pursued in the sheriff court, namely summary causes and ordinary actions.

Summary causes are further divided into two types of action. The small claims action deals with claims up to £3000.[109] This is an informal type of action designed for litigants appearing without a solicitor, although many litigants in the small claims court are in fact legally represented. The summary cause action deals with claims from £3000 to £5000.[110] The ordinary action is for claims exceeding the value of £5000.[111] There is no upper limit to ordinary actions.

THE COURT OF SESSION

2.25 The Court of Session[112] is based in Edinburgh. It deals only with civil cases. It is divided into the Outer House and Inner House. The Outer House hears cases at first instance and it may be advantageous to bring a breach of contract claim here rather than the sheriff court, particularly if a large some of money or complicated point of law is involved. An action in the Court of Session can be extremely costly, although Legal Aid may be available depending on the pursuer's financial situation. The parties will require to instruct either a solicitor and at least one advocate, or a solicitor advocate, as solicitors do not have rights of audience in the Court of Session. The Court of Session is headed by the Lord President and below him the Lord Justice Clerk. The Outer House consists of 24 Lords

---

109 Act of Sederunt (Small Claim Rules) 2002 No 133 (as amended).
110 Act of Sederunt (Summary Cause Rules) 2002 No 132.
111 Act of Sederunt (Sheriff Court Ordinary Cause Rules) 1993 No 1956.
112 Rules of the Court of Session 1994.

Ordinary. Cases are usually heard before one Lord Ordinary sitting alone although some cases will be heard by a Lord Ordinary with a civil jury.

The Inner House of the Court of Session hears appeals on a point of Law from the Sheriff Court, the Sheriff Principal and the Court of Session Outer House. Relevant employment law issues that the Inner House of the Court of Session is concerned with include hearing appeals from the Employment Appeal Tribunal on points of law and grounds of perversity; and actions for judicial review of administrative decisions. There are two Divisions of equal stature and occasionally a third division sits. The First Division is headed by the Lord President, the Second by the Lord Justice Clerk, and each division has up to 5 Lords Ordinary, although there is a quorum of 3.

THE SUPREME COURT

2.26 The Supreme Court of the United Kingdom was established by the Constitutional Reform Act 2005 which took effect from 1 October 2009. The Supreme Court took over the judicial function previously carried out by the judicial arm of the House of Lords,[113]which included final appellate jurisdiction in civil cases throughout the UK. In respect of Scotland it hears appeals from the Inner House of the Court of Session. In respect of European Union Law, the Supreme Court is subject to the decisions of the European Court of Justice. Since there can be no appeal from the Supreme Court, there is an interlocutory procedure by which the Supreme Court may refer questions about European law arising in cases before it to the European Court. The Supreme Court can then obtain a definitive ruling from the European Court before giving its final judgment. Appeals are normally heard by 5 Justices (formerly Lords of Appeal in Ordinary, or Law Lords), but there can be as many as 9. Like the House of Lords before it, the new Supreme Court includes a minority of Scottish judges, only two out of twelve of the permanent members. However, as a matter of practice, they take a prominent role in all cases before the court that raise distinct questions of Scottish law.

---

113 Law Lords sitting in the Appellate Committee.

COURT OF JUSTICE OF THE EUROPEAN UNION

2.27 The Court of Justice deals with questions of interpretation and application of the treaties promulgated by the European Union. Its function within domestic law is not that of an Appeal Court; rather it sits outwith the domestic court structure. Recourse may be had to the Court of Justice, if necessary, to answer a relevant question on a particular treaty, but that answer does not dispose of the case. The answer is then applied by the initiating domestic court, who will then continue to dispose of the case. Questions can be referred to the Court of Justice by any national court, or by the EAT. An example was the question of whether an employee may retain his pension rights when an undertaking is transferred. This has led to much speculation and controversy and resulted in more than one referral to the European Court of Justice. A decision was given in *Beckmann v Dynamco Whicheloe Macfarlane Ltd*.[114] Under Regulation 7(1) of the Transfer of Undertakings (Protection of Employment) Regulations 1982 (TUPE),[115] occupational pension schemes were excluded from Regulations 5 and 6 of TUPE, which meant that an employer's liability for pension rights, unlike other employment rights, did not pass to the purchaser. In 1993 the government added sub-para (2) to regulation 7 to reflect article 3(3) of the Acquired Rights Directive (Council Directive 77/187/EEC). This stated that the exclusion applies only to rights to old-age, invalidity, or survivors' benefits, but does not apply to other benefits under an occupational pension scheme. The *Beckman* case shows that the exclusion is far narrower than had previously been thought. Mrs Beckmann had been employed by the NHS and her employment was transferred to DWM under TUPE. When DWM dismissed her for redundancy it refused to pay her the early retirement pension, lump sum, and other benefits to which she would have been entitled under the NHS scheme, on the grounds that those benefits were excluded from TUPE. The ECJ held that: 'Early retirement benefits and benefits intended to enhance the conditions of such retirement, paid in the event of dismissal to employees who have reached a certain age, such as

---

114 Case C-164/00.
115 Replaced by the Transfer of Undertakings (Protection of Employment) Regulations 2006 No 246.

the benefits at issue in the main proceedings, are not old-age, invalidity or survivors' benefits ... within the meaning of Article 3(3) of Council Directive 77/187/EEC ...' So these rights could transfer. Although the *Beckmann* case was concerned with redundancy pensions, the wording of the decision was so wide that it seemed to include any early retirement arrangement, including the right to retire early voluntarily.[116]

THE EUROPEAN COURT OF HUMAN RIGHTS

2.28 The European Court of Human Rights concerns itself with the interpretation and application of the European Convention on Human Rights and Fundamental Freedoms. Unlike the Court of Justice, all domestic remedies must have been exhausted before an application is made. Thus, in civil cases, the claimant must have appealed his case as far as the Supreme Court before he can apply to the European Court of Human Rights. If there is no domestic remedy available, the claimant can move straight to the Court of Human Rights. This is much less likely since the European Convention of Human Rights has been introduced into UK law by the Human Rights Act 1998 and the UK courts have jurisdiction to deal with cases brought under the Convention. The role of the ECHR is discussed in more detail in Chapter 3.

OTHER INSTITUTIONS

2.29 Alongside the traditional court structure, there are a number of organisations which make an important contribution to employment law matters.

Advisory Conciliation and Arbitration Service

2.30 The Advisory Conciliation and Arbitration Service (ACAS)[117] is a non governmental body run by an independent council[118] although they

---

116 *Martin and others v South Bank University* Case C-4/01, reported at (2003) All ER (D) 85.
117 http://www.acas.org.uk/index.aspx?articleid=1342
118 Whose independence is guaranteed by the Trade Union and Labour Relations (Consolidation) Act 1992 (TULR(C)A), s 247(3).

are funded by the Department for Business Innovation and Skills (BIS).
The Chair of the Council is appointed by the Secretary of State and it has
11 additional members, of whom three represent employers and three
represent trade unions.[119]

Acas's duty is to promote improvement in industrial relations and it
does this in several ways.[120]

Codes of Practice

2.31 An important power and function of ACAS is the production of
Codes of Practice in certain areas of employment law.[121] The terms of
these Codes are not legally binding as such, but referred to by tribunals
and courts as evidence of what constitutes good practice in certain
situations. Any deviation from a Code of Practice by an employer will
generally require to be justified. A failure to comply with the ACAS Code
of Practice on Disciplinary and Grievance Procedures by an employer
may result, not only in a finding of unfair dismissal against him, but also
in an uplift of any award of compensation by up to 25%. Similarly where
an employee fails to meet the expectations of him set out in the Code, eg
does not attend an internal disciplinary hearing, then his compensation
could be reduced by up to 25%.

Advice

2.32 ACAS also assists with employment relations by providing
information, training, advice and support to employers and employee.
Their website is an invaluable source of information and guidance on
employment matters. Advice can be provided over the telephone in
individual cases, and ACAS produces guidance notes and handbooks for
employers and employees.

---

119 TULR(C)A, ss 247–253.
120 TULR(C)A, s 209.
121 TULR(C)A, s 199.

Conciliation and mediation

2.33 According to ACAS:

> 'Mediation is a completely voluntary and confidential form of alternative dispute resolution. It involves an independent, impartial person helping two or more individuals or groups reach a solution that's acceptable to everyone. The mediator can talk to both sides separately or together. Mediators do not make judgments or determine outcomes – they ask questions that help to uncover underlying problems, assist the parties to understand the issues and help them to clarify the options for resolving their difference or dispute'.

ACAS provide an important role within the Employment Tribunal System. ACAS is notified once a tribunal claim has been lodged and its officers will attempt conciliation by liaising with the parties to try to resolve matters and achieve a settlement. More information is available in their Guide on Conciliation.[122]

> 'Although similar to mediation, the term conciliation is used when an employee is making, or could make, a specific complaint against their employer to an employment tribunal. It's unlike arbitration because the conciliator has no authority to seek evidence or call witnesses, or make decisions or awards. The process involves an independent ACAS conciliator discussing the issues with both parties in order to help them reach a better understanding of each other's position and underlying interest. The impartial conciliator tries to encourage the parties in dispute to come to an agreement between themselves, and so avoid the stress and expense of contesting the issue in Tribunal.'[123]

ACAS can (for a fee) provide an independent mediator to help resolve disputes in the workplace.

---

122 Available at http://www.acas.org.uk/CHttpHandler.ashx?id=1046
123 www.acas.gov.uk

Arbitration

2.34 ACAS describe arbitration as involving an impartial outsider being asked to make a decision on a dispute. The arbitrator makes a firm decision on a case based on the evidence presented by the parties. Arbitration is voluntary, so both sides must agree to go to arbitration; they should also agree in advance that they will abide by the arbitrator's decision. It can be seen as an alternative to a court of law, with its rules for procedures such as disclosure of documents, evidence and so on, but arbitration is private rather than public. Arbitration can be used in collective employment related disputes or to settle individual disputes.

ACAS can provide arbitration in any employment-related dispute but there is an ACAS Arbitration Scheme for unfair dismissal, and in England and Wales for flexible working which can be used as an alternative to making a claim at employment tribunal. Guides to these schemes can be found on the ACAS website but they have not been widely used. According to the ACAS Arbitration Scheme: An Evaluation of Parties' Views 03/04 Report,[124] the two main reasons for this were first, the scheme's restriction to unfair dismissal cases, and second, the continuing low awareness of the scheme amongst employers, employees and representatives. The ACAS individual arbitration scheme attracted only three requests in the year 2006/2007 compared to six in 2005/2006.[125]

Certification Officer

2.35 The role of the Certification Officer was first established under statute, namely the Employment Protection Act in 1975. The post is independent of Government or any other organisation. He or she is responsible for maintaining a list of trade unions and employers' associations; ensuring compliance with statutory requirements; keeping available for public inspection annual returns from trade unions and employers' associations; determining complaints concerning trade union elections; certain other ballots and certain breaches of trade union rules; ensuring observance of statutory requirements governing mergers between trade unions and

---

124 http://www.acas.org.uk/CHttpHandler.ashx?id=328&p=0
125 ACAS Annual Report 2006/2007.

employers' associations; overseeing the political funds and the finances of trade unions and employers associations; and certifying the independence of trade unions. Further information is available from the Certification Officer website,[126] which also is a useful source of case law on these matters.

Central Arbitration Committee

2.36 The Central Arbitration Committee is a permanent, independent body with statutory powers. The Central Arbitration Committee[127] consists of a Chairman, 10 Deputy Chairmen, and 50 members, of whom 27 members are experienced as representatives of employers, and 23 are experienced as representatives of workers. It is an independent body whose main function is to adjudicate on applications relating to the statutory recognition and derecognition of trade unions for collective bargaining purposes, where such recognition or derecognition cannot be agreed voluntarily. It also has a role in determining disputes between trade unions and employers over the disclosure of information for collective bargaining purposes, and in dealing with applications and resolving complaints under various statutes.[128] In 2002,[129] the CAC dealt with a recognition dispute between National Union of Journalists (NUJ) and Emap Healthcare and Emap Public Sector Management, where there was a question raised by the employers over the validity of a voluntary recognition agreement made between the employers and the trade union. The voluntary agreement reached had been signed by all the parties and declared that the Union was to be recognised as entitled to conduct collective bargaining on behalf of full-time, part-time or temporary journalists engaged under a contract of employment with both employers. The Panel determined that the Agreement defined the bargaining unit, identified the parties to the Agreement and specified the matters in respect of which the Union was

126 http://www.certoffice.org/pages/index.cfm?pageID=home
127 http://www.cac.gov.uk/index.aspx?articleid=2213
128 The Information and Consultation of Employees Regulations 2004, The European Public Limited-Liability Company Regulations 2004, The Transnational Information and Consultation of Employees Regulations 1999, The European Cooperative Society Regulations 2006, The Companies (Cross-Border Mergers) Regulations 2007.
129 Case Number: TUR2/1/(2002).

recognised and entitled to conduct negotiations under the Agreement. Therefore the Panel declared that the voluntary agreement signed by the parties was an agreement for recognition as defined by the statute between the NUJ and Emap Healthcare, and between the NUJ and Emap Public Sector Management.

Equality and Human Rights Commission

2.37 The Commission is a statutory body set up to protect, enforce and promote equality across 7 areas: age, disability, gender, race, religion and belief, sexual orientation and gender reassignment.[130] It is also charged with protecting human rights and promoting good relations in society. They are a non-departmental public body funded by the Government. It also has a presence in Scotland. The Equality and Human Rights Commission in Scotland is there to ensure that the aims, vision and strategy of the Commission consider the specific needs of Scotland. The team is based in Glasgow and Edinburgh and is headed up by a Scottish Commissioner. The Commission works closely with the Scottish Parliament, the Scottish Commission for Human Rights and other organisations in Scotland.

The Commission was launched on 1 October 2007 and its role is to: ensure people are aware of their rights and how to use them; work with employers, service providers and organisations to help them develop best practice, work with policymakers, lawyers and the Government to make sure that social policy and the law promotes equality and utilises powers to enforce the laws that are already in place. As a single Commission, it acts as single source of information, provides advice and tackles discrimination on various levels. It combines the work of the three previous Equality Commissions[131] and also has responsibilities for newer forms of inequality protected by the law, namely, age, religion and belief, and sexual orientation. It also has the power to enforce the human rights legislation that guarantees basic rights and freedoms for everyone.[132] The EHRC has extensive powers to enforce equality law and to provide

---

130 Equality Act 2006 Part I.
131 Equal Opportunities Commission, Commission for Racial Equality and the Disability Rights Commission.
132 Human Rights Act 1998.

advice and information. It may raise legal cases on behalf of individuals, as well as legal action to prevent breaches of the Human Rights Act. However, it can only take on a limited number of cases each year, so it concentrates on the cases which test the law.[133] In addition, the EHRC provides funding to organisations that provide legal advice to members of the public and make sure that public authorities carry out their legal duties to tackle discrimination and promote equality. It has the power to launch official inquiries and formal investigations.[134] Over the first two years of its existence three formal inquiries were undertaken into race in the construction industry, the meat and poultry processing sector, and sex discrimination in the finance sector. An enquiry may be directed at a named person if there is evidence that the person has committed an unlawful act.[135] In this case the Commission can issue that person with an Unlawful Act Notice,[136] and can require the person to put in place an action plan, eg an equal pay action plan following an audit which shows areas of inequality of pay in an organisation.[137] If the Commission thinks a public authority has failed to comply with a public sector duty, it may enter into a binding agreement with the public authority under which the Commission undertakes not to issue a compliance notice, and the public authority undertakes to comply with the duty and to take, or refrain from taking, other specified action (which may include the preparation of a plan for the purpose of complying with the duty).[138] Under s 23 the EHRC can enter into a binding agreement with any employer. If the Commission thinks that a party to an agreement under s 23 has failed to comply, or is likely not to comply, with an undertaking under the Agreement, the Commission can apply to a sheriff for an order requiring the public authority to comply with its undertaking and take such other action as a sheriff may specify.[139]

---

133 More than eighty discrimination cases were provided with legal assistance over the first two years of the EHRC's operation. (October 2007 to October 2009).
134 Section 16 of the Equality Act 2006.
135 If the named person is suspected of committing an offence the inquiry will be dealt with under s 20 of the Equality Act 2006.
136 Equality Act 2006 s 21.
137 www.equalityhumanrights.com
138 Sections 23(1) and 23(5) of the Equality Act 2010.
139 Section 24(2) and (3).

The International Labour Organisation[140]

2.38 The International Labour Organisation (ILO)[141] was founded in the aftermath of World War 1 in 1919. It believes that universal lasting peace is founded on decent treatment of working people and it therefore seeks to promote good working conditions in every country. It became an agency of the UN in 1946 and brings together governments, employers and workers. The ILO has drawn up and enforces international Labour Standards. Various conventions have been produced to which the UK has signed up and declarations have been made. Adopted in 1998, the ILO Declaration on Fundamental Principles and Rights at Work is an expression of commitment by Governments (including the UK) employers' and workers' organizations to uphold basic human values. In 2008, the ILO adopted a Declaration on Social Justice for a Fair Globalization. The website of the ILO contains these documents and also statistics and other resources.[142]

The ILO has produced around 190 conventions and the UK Government has ratified some of these. The difficulty has always been the lack of an effective procedure for enforcing the conventions. It has usually been by way of supervision and declaration, rather than enforcement in individual cases. However, in 2008, the British Airline Pilots' Association (BALPA) successfully took a case against the UK Government to the ILO, because the Government has done nothing to clarify the law on strike action following a controversial decision of the European Court.[143] BALPA took the case to the ILO for breach by the UK Government of ILO Convention 87, which covers the freedom of association and right for unions to organise workers. The Committee of Experts found in favour of the union, and requested the UK Government to review the operation of the Trade Union and Labour Relation Act 1992, consider appropriate measures for the protection of workers and their organisations that engage in industrial action, and to indicate the steps taken in this regard.[144]

---

140 www.ilo.org
141 http://www.ilo.org/global/lang--en/index.htm
142 http://www.ilo.org/public/english/support/lib/resource/ilodatabases.htm
143 Joined cases of Viking (Case C-438/05) and Laval (Case C-341/05).
144 International Labour Conference, 99th Session, 2010.

FURTHER READING

Journal articles

Brearley, 'Territorial jurisdiction' (2011) CSR 34(26), 203.
Mandeep, 'The long arm of the employment tribunal' (2011) Emp LJ 118, 22–24.

Websites

http://www.scotcourts.gov.uk/
http://www.justice.gov.uk/guidance/courts-and-tribunals/tribunals/employment/rules-and-legislation.htm#scotland
http://www.justice.gov.uk/guidance/courts-and-tribunals/tribunals/employment-appeals/index.htm
http://www.eurofound.europa.eu/areas/industrialrelations/dictionary/definitions/EUROPEANCOURTOFJUSTICE.htm
http://www.echr.coe.int/ECHR/homepage_en
www.acas.org.uk
http://www.certoffice.org
http://www.cac.gov.uk
www.equalityhumanrights.com
www.ilo.org

Chapter 3

Human Rights in Employment Law

THE EUROPEAN CONVENTION OF HUMAN RIGHTS & THE HUMAN RIGHTS ACT 1998

Sources of human rights

3.1 The original source of human rights in the UK was the Bill of Rights 1689. This offered undoubted rights and liberties such as the supremacy of law, equality before the law, the prohibition of inhuman treatment and trial by jury. Within Europe, the next notable development was the French Declaration of the Rights of Man in 1789 which provided individual rights, including freedom from arrest, presumption of innocence, freedom of opinion, religion, expression and the right of property. In 1864, the Geneva Convention dealt with humanitarian issues in war such as the immunity of military hospitals, obligation to care for the sick of the enemy and protection of civilians.

Undoubtedly one of the most important landmarks in modern European human rights law is the United Nation's Universal Declaration of Human Rights in 1948, which is the basis for human rights on an international scale and of a generic nature. It also provides specific rights (eg protection against degrading treatment) and makes provision for particular sectors of humanity (eg children). In September 1953, the European Convention of Human Rights 1950 (ECHR 1950) gave specific legal content to the rights contained in the Universal Declaration.

The ECHR 1950 established the European Commission of Human Rights (ECommHR)[1] which filters applications from individuals with a

---

1   From 1954 to the entry into force of Protocol 11 of the European Convention on Human Rights in 1998 individuals did not have direct access to the European Court of Human Rights; they had to apply to the Commission, which if it found the case to be well-founded would submit a case to the Court on the individual's behalf. In 1998 the Commission was abolished and at the same time the Court's jurisdiction was enlarged and allowed individuals to take cases directly to it.

grievance against their National State under the European Convention on Human Rights. For the first time, citizens of the signatory states whose rights were infringed by the state, or whose rights were not protected by domestic law, could challenge their treatment at international level by raising an action against their state before the European Court of Human Rights (ECtHR). Pursuing such a claim was however a lengthy and costly business (see chapter on Institutions of Employment law for more on their role of the ECtHR).

The Scotland Act 1998 makes specific reference to the European Convention on Human Rights, which has important consequences for the Scottish Executive and Parliament, and for the enforcement of human rights in Scotland. Section 29 of the Act provides that an Act of the Scottish Parliament may not include provisions which are incompatible with the Convention rights, as defined in the Human Rights Act 1998 (HRA 1998). Also s 57(2) provides that a member of the Scottish Executive has no power to make any subordinate legislation, or to do any other act, which would be incompatible with Convention rights. As employment law is a reserved matter under the Scotland Act; the Act so far has had very little impact in this area.

The Human Rights Act 1998 came into force in the UK on the 3 of October 2000 and this Act incorporated the European Convention on Human Rights into UK Law. Only 17 out of 587 cases brought under HRA 1998 in the first year of it being passed were successful. The UK courts have tended to adopt a restrictive approach and there is a general feeling amongst commentators that the human rights dimension of employment law is slim.

Under the HRA 1998, there are four main methods of implementation of convention rights in the UK. The main sections which are relevant are:

Section 2 – in making a decision which involves a Convention Right, any domestic court or tribunal must take into account the judgments, decisions, declarations or advisory opinions of the European Court of Human Rights, and certain decisions of the ECommHR. They are not however bound by the jurisprudence of the ECtHR.

Section 3 – legislation (primary and delegated) must be read by the judiciary in a way that is compatible with convention rights, in so far as it is possible to do so.

Section 4 – if the court is satisfied that a provision of primary legislation is incompatible with a Convention right it may make a declaration of incompatibility. In such circumstances, a Minister of the Crown may make an order to amend the legislation to remove the incompatibility (s 10). It is important to recognise that this is a power of the court and not a duty. In Scotland the courts which have this power are the Court of Session, the High Court of Justiciary, the Supreme Court and the Privy Council.

Section 19 – a Minister of Crown in charge of a Bill in the Houses of Parliament must make a declaration of compatibility before the second reading of that Bill. However, in Scotland s 29(2)(d) of the Scotland Act provides that an Act of the Scottish Parliament must not be incompatible with any of the Convention rights of individuals. Also, prior to the introduction of an Executive Bill in the Scottish Parliament, or upon its introduction, the Scotland Act requires the Scottish Executive to provide a statement that the Bill is within the Parliament's legislative competence, including confirmation of its compatibility with the Convention. In respect of all Bills introduced into Parliament, the Presiding Officer of the Parliament must consider whether a Bill is within the Parliament's legislative competence and provide a statement setting out his decision.

Section 6 – it is unlawful for a public authority (including a court or tribunal) to act in a way which is incompatible with a Convention right.

Section 7 – an individual who claims that a public authority has acted in breach of the convention may bring judicial review proceedings against that Authority. In Scotland this would be done in the Court of Session. If an individual is a victim of breach of the Convention he can rely on the convention rights in any subsequent court proceedings.

Public Authorities

3.2 The duty to comply with the HRA 1998 is restricted to public authorities and the meaning of a 'public authority' is set out in s 6 of that Act. The HRA 1998 does not provide a list of public authorities to which the Act is applicable. Instead, it states in s 6(3)(b) that a 'public authority' includes 'any certain person of whose functions are functions of a public nature'.

Public authorities include government departments, the NHS, the police and private organisations that carry out public functions will be subject to obligations in the Act where they perform a public function.[2] Whilst it was previously thought that it was the institution or body that had to be public, it is now the view of the courts that it is the function which the body is performing is public, then they will be regarded as a public authority for the purpose of carrying it out.[3] 'It will be relevant first of all to examine with some care the nature of the function in question. It is the nature of the function – public or private – which is decisive under the section.'[4]

Compatibility of UK Law with ECHR

3.3 Under s 2(b) and (c) of the Act, UK Courts will not have the power to strike down primary legislation incompatible with the Convention. However, as has been seen, higher courts have the power to issue declarations of incompatibility (s 4) and, in such cases, fast track procedures can be used by the Government to legislate to change legislation contravening the Convention. With regards to secondary legislation, the article provides that 'if a court agrees with a person bringing the case that their rights have been breached under secondary legislation (of member states), the courts do have power to set the legislation aside if there is nothing in the primary legislation preventing them from doing so.'

Where there is an Act of Parliament that makes it impossible to comply with the Convention rights, the courts are not entitled to override Parliament but can make a declaration that the law is incompatible with the Convention, so enabling the Government to amend the incompatible law. Only the Court of Session or the High Court of Justiciary in Scotland (High Court and the Court of Appeal in England and Wales) or the Supreme Court can make a 'declaration of incompatibility'. In furtherance of legislating to change legislation contravening the Convention, government ministers

---

2   Section 6.

3   *Aston Cantlow and Wilmcote with Billesley Parochial Church Council v Wallbank* [2003] UKHL 37, [2004] 1 AC 546; *Hampshire County Council on the application of Beer t/a Hammer Trout Farm v Hampshire Farmers Market* [2004] 1 WLR 233.

4   *YL (by her litigation friend the Official Solicitor) (FC) (Appellant) v Birmingham City Council and others* (2007) UKHL 27 Lord Bingham of Cornhill Para. 6.

have the power to take immediate remedial action to remove the offending part of the legislation. If the incompatible law is not amended, changed or repealed, in Parliament then the matter can be taken by the court (where the matter is raised) to the European Court of Human Rights,[5] which can act through the Committee of Ministers to pressurise the Government into changing its legislation.

Applicable Convention Rights

3.4 Although the rights in the Convention and the Human Rights Act are couched in negative terms there is a positive obligation on States to legislate to prevent breach of these rights and the Convention. What follows is a list of the most important human rights from the perspective of employment law, although some are more significant (Article 8) than others (Article 3), in this context.

Article 3 – Right not to be subjected to torture or inhumane or degrading treatment or punishment.

Article 4 – Right not to be held in slavery or to be required to perform forced labour.

Article 6 – Right to a fair hearing.

Article 8 – Right to respect for private and family law, home and correspondence.

Article 9 – Right to freedom of thought, conscience and religion.

Article 10 – Right to freedom of expression.

Article 11 – Right to freedom of assembly and association.

Article 14 – Right not to be subjected to discrimination in the enjoyment of other Convention rights.

Article 3 provides the right not to be subjected to torture or inhumane, or degrading, treatment or punishment. This could apply if the employer's behaviour affects a person's physical or mental wellbeing and has particular application to harassment and bullying. The treatment of an individual

---

5   Their judgement is declaratory of the law and monitoring the action of a State following a finding of the court that there has been a violation of the Convention is undertaken by Committee of Ministers.

will be deemed to be degrading if it arouses in the victim feelings of fear, anguish and inferiority capable of humiliating and debasing them. It is questionable whether the applicant in *Porcelli v Strathclyde Regional Council*,[6] the leading case on sexual harassment in the UK brought under the Sex Discrimination Act 1975 (SDA 1975), would have a case under Article 3 of the Act. Mrs Porcelli was subjected to campaign of sexual harassment by her male colleagues, including verbal comments and physical gestures of a sexual nature made to her, and sexual images put up on her locker, in the workplace in an effort to get her to leave her job.

While she was successful in her case for sex discrimination, under the Sex Discrimination Act 1975, a case was not brought under the Convention (ECHR) and, if it had been, it seems unlikely that this would be sufficiently harmful behaviour to be degrading in the context of Article 3. However, in another sexual harassment case brought under the SDA 1975 in the UK, *Bracebridge Engineering Ltd v Darby*,[7] (also not a human rights action), the employee who was the victim, was physically sexually assaulted by her supervisor and a colleague. This would, undoubtedly, breach Article 3. It seems likely that only the most extreme cases of bullying and harassment would be covered by Article 3 and complainants may face the argument that harassment and bullying are adequately protected under domestic law.[8] Suffering or humiliation must go beyond the inevitable element of suffering connected with a given form of treatment or punishment.[9] 'The threshold question – whether the specific treatment complained of meets a minimum level of severity – needs to be considered with some care and inevitably involves a degree of subjective judgement.'[10]

Under **Article 4**, the right not to be held in slavery, or to be required to perform forced labour, is protected. In order to demonstrate a breach of Article 4 it must be shown that work was exacted under the menace of any penalty, and also performed against the will of the person concerned.

---

6   (1986) ICR 564.

7   (1990) IRLR 3, EAT.

8   The issue of whether an effective domestic remedy is provided will be considered and whether that remedy has been exhausted as per Article 35.

9   In *Raninen v Finland* (2097/92) 1997 – V111, handcuffing a prisoner on his way to a barracks was not sufficiently severe to breach Article 3.

10 Reed, R Murdoch, J *A Guide to Human Rights in Scotland* 2nd ed. (2008) Bloomsbury Professional p 275.

Article 4, therefore, applies only to work for which the person has not offered himself voluntarily, often referred to as forced labour. Illegal immigrants in the UK could be forced into this type of work arrangement where their illegal passage to this country is paid for through forced or compulsory labour. In *Siliadin v France*,[11] a fifteen year old girl was taken to France by a French national who, in return for arranging her education and regularising her immigration status, made her carry out unpaid household work for nine months. Thereafter, she was lent to a French couple who made her work 15 hours per day for four years until criminal proceedings were taken against them. They were acquitted on appeal and only an order for payment of damages was made against them. In proceedings before the European Court of Human Rights (ECtHR), it was argued by the applicant that she had not been afforded sufficient protection under French law. It was also contended by the victim that the circumstances of her working as a minor against her will, with the constant fear of being arrested, was forced labour. It was regarded as forced labour by the court and therefore contrary to Article 4. The court also confirmed that it is necessary that a signatory State has criminal provisions under its domestic law to deal with this type behaviour.[12] Article 4 does not prohibit obligations imposed on applicants to provide unpaid work as part of their professional responsibilities.[13] There are also certain exclusions from forced or compulsory labour under Article 4(3) namely: work required to be carried out as part of detention; military service; work that is part of civic obligations and services in a time of emergency (when the life or well being of the community is threatened).

Article 6 covers the right to a fair trial or hearing. Article 6(1) of the Convention provides that: 'In the determination of his civil rights and obligations…everyone is entitled to a fair and public hearing within a reasonable time by an independent and impartial tribunal established by law'.

---

11 2005 – V11, 43 EHRR 16.

12 In Scotland inter alia: section 22 of the Criminal Justice (Scotland) Act 2003 and sections 9–12 of the Protection of Children and Prevention of Sexual Abuse (Scotland) Act 2005 would provide such protection.

13 In Belguim pupil advocates who were unpaid were not covered by Article 4 see *Van Der Mussele v Belgium* (1983) A 70.

There have not been many employment law cases brought under this article.[14] A notable development was the extension of legal aid to cover tribunal hearings, which was introduced into the law of Scotland by the Scottish Parliament under the Advice and Assistance (Assistance by way of Representation) Scotland Regulations, to ensure compliance with Article 6.[15] This legislation was introduced in 2001 to provide, for the first time in Scotland, legal aid for claimants in employment law cases to cover the costs of representation at an employment tribunal, in anticipation of a possible challenge under Article 6. However, no corresponding measure has been introduced in England and Wales. An Article 6 claim was brought in *Liddjard v the Post Office,*[16] when the Court of Appeal refused to accept that unfair dismissal legislation in the UK was incompatible with the HRA 1998. There was an attempt by the claimant to rely upon Article 6 of the Human Rights Act, and to attack s 98 of the Employment Rights Act 1996. The Court of Appeal indicated that they did not believe that there was anything in the Human Rights Act that required s 98 to be construed, and applied any way differently, from previous unfair dismissal cases in the UK. In *Smith v Secretary of State for Trade and Industry,*[17] the issue was raised about the impartiality of employment tribunals, in particular the Secretary of State's power to appoint lay members of tribunals. Employment tribunal wing or lay members were appointed by the Secretary of State for Trade and Industry, their allowances were paid by him, the Rules of Procedure for Tribunals were made by the Secretary of State and the Department of Trade and Industry funded the Employment Tribunal Service. The question was, are employment tribunals therefore 'an independent and impartial Tribunal' within the meaning of Article 6(1) of the Convention. The EAT decided this challenge was unsuccessful.[18]

---

14 Most challenges relate to criminal law and the administration of justice.

15 SI 2001/2 Legal aid will be available in Scotland, where (a) the applicant is unable to fund or find alternative representation elsewhere (b) the case is an arguable one, and (c) the case is too complex to allow the applicant to present it to a minimum standard of effectiveness.

16 [2001] EWCA Civ 940, [2001] All ER (D) 46 (Jun).

17 (2000) IRLR 6.

18 In *McMichael v United Kingdom* (1995) A-307B, a breach of Article 6 was established in the appointment process for members of the children's hearing system in Scotland.

In the case of *Stansbury v Datapulse plc and another*,[19] an employee was found by the EAT not to have been given a fair trial when one of the lay members of an employment tribunal appeared to have been drunk and fell asleep during the hearing.

The applicability of Article 6 to internal disputes procedures arose in *Darnell v UK*,[20] where it was stated by the ECtHR that where the disputes procedure involved a claim or dispute that is genuine, of a serious nature and involves the determination of civil rights and obligations then Article 6 would apply to it. So it would not normally apply to internal disputes, but it could apply to professional misconduct hearings,[21] or court martials. It has been held ECtHR that the decision by a disciplinary tribunal to suspend or to disqualify a professional person is a determination of his civil rights and obligations within the meaning of Article 6(1).[22] However, the decision of a disciplinary tribunal to admonish a professional person is not such a determination, and it has been suggested by the Commission in *X v United Kingdom* that Article 6 does not apply to the tribunal's proceedings, even if the tribunal has power to suspend or disqualify a person.[23] In a similar case *Tehrani v UKCC*,[24] Lord Mackay of Drumadoon in the Court of Session said:

'what remains in dispute, however, is whether the disciplinary proceedings initiated against the petitioner could lead to a "determination of her civil rights and obligations" within the meaning of Article 6(1) ... In my opinion, if the petitioner can establish that the disciplinary proceedings could result in a finding that would constitute a determination of her civil rights and obligations, the decision to initiate those disciplinary proceedings is open to challenge as being incompatible with the petitioner's Convention rights.'[25]

---

19 (2003) ICR 358.
20 (1994) 18 EHRR 205.
21 *The European Court of Human Rights in Konig v Germany* (1979) 2 EHRR 170 found that Article 6 was directly applicable to an internal disciplinary hearing of the tribunal for the medical profession in Germany which had considered a doctor's ability to practise.
22 As decided in *Albert and le Compte v Belgium* (1983) 5 EHRR 533.
23 (1983) 6 EHRR 583 (a decision of the Commission).
24 [2001] IRLR 208.
25 This approach was approved by the *Court of Appeal in R (on the application of Wayne Thompson) v the Law Society* [2004] EWCA Civ 167, [2004] 2 All ER 113.

Employment tribunal and court procedures should therefore be free from delay,[26] and impartial and free from bias.[27] The same requirements apply to internal disciplinary procedures, where the employer is a public authority: if the outcome of an internal disciplinary procedure is likely to result in the employee's right to practice his profession, then Article 6 will apply to the proceedings.[28] In *R v Governors of 'X' School*,[29] the Court of Appeal held that a teaching assistant who was subjected to disciplinary proceedings should have been allowed legal representation at those proceedings, since they would have an effect on the decision of the Secretary of State for Children, Schools and Families,[30] whether or not he would be placed on the list of persons barred from working with children. The employer is not obliged to pay for such legal representation.[31]

Even when a disciplinary body does not act in compliance with Article 6 in terms of its rules or procedure, if there is an appeal from its decision to a Court of law, then it will be allowed to continue to operate. This was the decision in *Tehrani v UK Council for Nursing*,[32] when Ms Tehrani, who was a nurse, was subject to disciplinary proceedings by the United Kingdom Central Council (UKCC). She brought a claim under Article 6, claiming the UKCC breached the requirements of Article 6. In order to practise within the United Kingdom, all nurses have to be registered with the UKCC who have the power to discipline nurses for misconduct. She complained that the UKCC had breached Article 6 by convening a hearing before one of its Professional Conduct Committees. She said the Committee could not be regarded as an independent and impartial tribunal, as the UKCC was responsible for setting policy regarding nurses' conduct, investigating complaints, as well as prosecuting and adjudicating upon allegations of misconduct. The UKCC was, in effect, the policy-maker,

---

26 *Porter v Magill* [2001] UKHL 67, [2002] 2 AC 357.
27 *Whitbread t/a Whitbread Medway Inns v Hall* [2001] ICR 699 The Employment Tribunals (Constitution and Rules of Procedure) Regulations 2004 no 1861 Regulation 3(2)(c).
28 *R (on application of G) v Governors of 'X' School* [2010] EWCA Civ 1, [2010] 1 WLR 2218.
29 [2010] EWCA Civ 1.
30 Who had the power to make a direction under s 142 of the Education Act 2002 to prohibit a person from working with children in educational establishments.
31 *Botham v Ministry of Defence* [2010] EWHC 646 (QB).
32 [2001] IRLR 208.

investigator, prosecutor, judge and jury. The court found that the UKCC Committee was an administrative decision-making body, rather than a judicial tribunal and that, under Convention jurisprudence, administrative decision-makers do not themselves have to comply with Article 6, provided there exists a right of appeal to a Court with full jurisdiction, which fully complies with Article 6.[33]

Article 8 protects the right to respect for private and family life,[34] home and correspondence. The protection of this Article also extends to privacy in employment, covered by s 6 of the Human Rights Act 1998.[35] If there is an interference with an employee's privacy, in the context of employment, this does not necessary breach Article 8 rights, as such interferences are permitted if they are justified under Article 8(2). Article 8(2) states that there may be no interference with Article 8 rights by a public authority, as defined in s 6 of the HRA 1998, except as is in accordance with the law and is necessary in a democratic society, in the interests of national security, public safety, the economic wellbeing of the country, for the prevention of disorder or crime, for the protection of health or morals or for the protection of the rights and freedoms of others. An example of a situation where an exception would apply, is the investigation of crime believed by the (public authority) employer thought to have been committed by the employee. The exception relating to the interest and freedom of others is often most relevant in the employment field, as the courts and tribunals strive to achieve a balance between the employee's Article 8 rights and the employer's interests. Any interference must be justified and also a proportionate means of achieving a legitimate aim.[36]

The interception of correspondence, telephone tapping, and searches in the workplace are affected by Article 8.

---

33 In this case, nurses had a full right of appeal to the Court of Session on all questions of fact and law and therefore there was no breach of Article 6.

34 In *Niemitz v Germany* [1992] EHRR, 97 it was decided that private life has a collective dimension which extends to relationships at work.

35 Right to private life extends to employment *De Keyser v Wilson* (2001) IRLR 234.

36 *Pay v UK* [2009] IRLR 139.

'Assuming that, at its limit, the Neimitz[37] conception views working life as engaging in an important and central aspect of private life, it follows that Article 8(2) will require close scrutiny of why particular forms of workplace surveillance are necessary and for what ends; a simple balancing of employer and workers interests is not sufficient.'[38]

In *Halford v UK*,[39] the privacy of an employee (in the workplace) who had raised an action against her employer for sex discrimination was the issue. It was shown that her employer had tapped a phone, allocated to an employee, to make personal calls regarding a sex discrimination case she was bringing against her employer. This was held to be a breach of her rights under Article 8.[40]

The Telecommunications (Lawful Business Practice) (Interception of Communications) Regulations 2000,[41] provide that confidentiality of electronic communications should be respected, except for certain derogations, including interceptions for business purposes.[42] The Data Protection Act 1998, requires that personal data must be processed fairly, and lawfully, and provides another means by which domestic law can give effect to a right of privacy for workers.[43]

In the case of *Copland v UK*,[44] the ECtHR held that the monitoring of an employee's telephone, internet and email usage by her employer, Carmarthenshire College, was a breach of Article 8. Similarly, the use of intrusive CCTV footage, or vehicle tracking devices, subjecting to searches, or to drug or alcohol testing, may interfere with an employee's

---

37 Supra 34 which states that relationships in the workplace can be part of someone's private life.
38 Ford M, Two Conceptions of Worker Privacy, Industrial Law Journal, ILJ (2002), Vol. 31(2), 135–155.
39 (1997) IRLR 471.
40 The Regulation of Investigatory Powers Act 2000 as amended justifies employers operating surveillance and monitoring of employees in certain circumstances.
41 SI 2000/2699.
42 However, the employer must inform his employees of such excepted arrangements.
43 www.ico.gov.uk/for_organisations/data_protection.aspx and www.businesslink.gov.uk
44 (2007) 45 EHRR 37.

right to respect for private life, unless it can be justified under Article 8(2).[45] Employers will need to put forward strong reasons for electronic (or other kinds of) scrutiny or monitoring of employees. In *McGowan v Scottish Water*,[46] the Scottish EAT recognised that, whilst, at first sight, the covert surveillance of an employee at his own home using private detectives was an invasion of his right to a private life, this was proportionate and accordingly lawful. This was because his employer, Scottish Water, was investigating criminal activities, namely the falsification of timesheets, and, since his employee's home was a tied house, it was decided by the EAT that it was part of the workplace. The surveillance complained about was undertaken by the detectives from outside the employee's home. Also the surveillance was not carried out for whimsical or external reasons, but went to the heart of the investigation, which the employer was required to carry out in order to protect its assets and, in fact, the investigation and subsequent disciplinary proceedings resulted in the dismissal of the employee for dishonesty.

Other breaches of Article 8 include unreasonably allowing access to information about a person's identity;[47] the right to have and express an identity and sexuality;[48] and the right to protection of a person's reputation.[49] Article 8 duties may also arise in common law cases dealing with issues such as breach of confidence and breach of the implied term of trust and confidence in employment contracts, and in delictual claims for breach of confidence.[50] In hearing claims of unfair dismissal a tribunal should no doubt apply the test of reasonableness required by s 98 of the ERA 1996 in the light of Article 8.[51]

---

45 In the Copland case, supra 43 it was stated that telephone calls from business premises are prima facie covered by the notions of 'private life' and 'correspondence' for the purposes of article 8 and the Court's were of the opinion that it logically followed that emails sent from work should be similarly protected under article 8 as should information derived from the monitoring of personal internet usage.
46 (2005) IRLR 167.
47 In *Coeriel and Aurik v The Netherlands* (Communication No. 453/1991, Views of 31 October 1994), the Human Rights Committee established that a person's name, including the power to change it, falls within the realm of privacy.
48 *Gaskin v United Kingdom* (1979) 2 EHRR 245.
49 *Polanco Torres and Movilla Planco v Spain* Case No 34147/06.
50 *Campbell v MGN Ltd* [2004] UKHL 22.
51 *Pay v UK* [2009] IRLR 139.

With regard to discrimination on the ground of sexual orientation, it was decided by the ECtHR in *Smith and Grady v United Kingdom*,[52] that aggressive investigation of a soldier by military police into allegations that he was a homosexual was contrary to his Article 8 rights, as was dismissal of a homosexual on the ground of sexual orientation (which was accepted practice in the armed forces at the time).[53] However, in *McDonald v Ministry of Defence*,[54] Mr Macdonald was dismissed from the Royal Air Force because he was a homosexual. He claimed that this treatment comprised direct sex discrimination, as defined in s 1(1) (a) of the Sex Discrimination Act 1975.[55] This was unsuccessful. (The domestic law has since been changed to include sexual orientation as a protected characteristic).[56] He also claimed that the employer's behaviour was contrary to Article 8 of the European Convention on Human Rights. It was established in this case that the dismissal and other treatment accorded to Mr Macdonald infringed his rights.[57] However, his unfavourable treatment had occurred in 1996 and 1997, some time before the Human Rights Act 1998 was enacted or came into force. Mr McDonald's claim was therefore unsuccessful, and was thrown out on appeal to the House of Lords, which held that the wording of the Sex Discrimination Act 1975 could not be construed to include this type of discrimination.[58] Similarly, in *Pearce v Governing Body of Mayfield Secondary School*,[59] a lesbian teacher who was the victim of homophobic abuse by her pupils, was not covered by the SDA 1975 or Article 8. It could not be said that she had received less

---

52 [1999] IRLR 734.
53 (2001) IRLR 431 Middlemiss, S Back to Square One, *The Secretary of State for Defence v McDonald* [2001] IRLR 431 and the legal protection against discrimination in employment based on sexual orientation Scottish Law Practice Quarterly October 2001.
54 [2001] IRLR 431.
55 Equality Act 2010 Section 13.
56 Employment Equality (Religion or Belief) Regulations 2003 Equality Act 2010 section 9.
57 The Advocate-General for Scotland accepted that this treatment had violated Mr Macdonald's rights under article 8 (respect for private life) in conjunction with article 14 (discrimination).
58 *Macdonald (AP) (Appellant) v Advocate General for Scotland (Respondent)* (Scotland) *Pearce (Appellant) v Governing Body of Mayfield School* [2003] UKHL 34, [2004] 1 All ER 339.
59 [2000] IRLR 548.

favourable treatment than a hypothetical homosexual male teacher, as there was no evidence such a teacher would have been treated differently. It also failed because it was the case that, in the context of s 1 of the Sex Discrimination Act, 'sex' meant gender and did not include sexual orientation. Since that Act was not aimed at sexual orientation, there was no justification for interpreting the expression 'on the ground of her sex' in s 1 broadly, to include cases which are cases of discrimination on the ground of sexual orientation.

Article 9 provides an individual with the right to hold religious beliefs and to manifest those beliefs in worship, teaching practice and observance (religious freedom). The right to freedom of belief,[60] under Article 9, may be relevant to several employment law areas, including steps taken by employers to accommodate the beliefs and worship of their employees, and imposing uniform requirements that may be contrary to their employee's convictions. Article 9 is a qualified right, ie enjoyment of the right may be subject to restriction, so long as such restriction is: prescribed by law; for a legitimate purpose; necessary in a democratic society; and is proportionate to the purpose or the aim being pursued. Accordingly, the right to manifest one's beliefs is subject to: the interests of public safety; the protection of public order; health or morals; and the protection of the rights and freedoms of others.

The ECtHR tends to apply a restrictive interpretation of this Article, so that rights can be limited by pre-existing contractual arrangements, such as in *Ahmad v UK*,[61] where an employee was refused the right by his employer to worship at his mosque on a Friday afternoon which was during his working hours. The ECtHR found that the employer's refusal to grant time off was not a breach of Article 9, as the terms of the employment contract requiring him to work on Friday afternoons was known to him at the commencement of the employment relationship. Similarly, in *Stedman v UK*,[62] an employee refused to work on a Sunday because of his religious beliefs. It was held that he was dismissed because he refused to observe his

---

60 In *McFeely v UK*: (1981) 3 EHRR 161 it was held that belief means more than just mere opinions or deeply held feelings there must be a holding of a spiritual or philosophical conviction which has an identifiable formal content.

61 (1982) 4 EHRR 126.

62 (1997) 23 EHRR CD 168.

working hours and not because of his religious conviction.[63] It is important to note that atheism and agnosticism are protected as well as other beliefs.

A rule prohibiting a Christian employee from wearing a cross,[64] or a refusal to allow a Muslim employee time off for prayer, may interfere with the right of those employees to manifest their religious belief, but these restrictions will not be unlawful if they are justified and proportionate. There is now specific legislation prohibiting discrimination on the grounds of religion and beliefs in employment in the UK.[65] However, it would be possible for an employee to add weight to their discrimination claim, by reference to a possible breach of their Article 9 rights.

An employer can include an express clause in a contract setting out a dress code that employees have to observe. However, even if there is no explicit reference to clothing in the contract, employees are still under an implied duty to obey their employer's reasonable and lawful instructions regarding expected standards, and that includes their clothing and appearance. The issue of dress codes and religious belief has been a controversial one in the UK (and other countries) in recent years, with some employers insisting that religious symbols be removed by all their workers, and that the wearing of a veil that completely covers the face by Muslim women is incompatible with the social interaction needed in service jobs, such as teaching. These and similar issues are likely to continue to remain controversial.

The Court of Appeal, in the case of *Eweida v British Airways Plc,*[66] have recently upheld the decision of an employment tribunal that a Christian employee who was sent home because she persisted in wearing a cross around her neck in full view, against the employer's company dress code, did not suffer indirect discrimination on the grounds of her religion. The Court also found that, in relation to the footing on which the claim had been advanced, namely disadvantage to a single individual arising

---

63 In *Copsey v WWB Devon Clays Ltd, CA (Mummery, Rix and Neuberger LLJ)* [2005] EWCA Civ 932 [2005] IRLR 811, the dismissal of a Christian worker for refusal to work on Sundays was not unfair under the Employment Rights Act 1996 and did not interfere with his right to religious freedom under Article 9.

64 *Eweida v British Airways Plc* [2010] EWCA Civ 80, [2010] IRLR 322.

65 Employment Equality (Religion or Belief) Regulations 2003 now see s 12 of the Equality Act 2010.

66 [2010] EWCA Civ 80, [2010] IRLR 322.

out of her wish to manifest her faith in a particular way, the employment tribunal's findings of fact had shown that BA's staff dress code, and the ban on a visible neck adornment, was a proportionate means of achieving a legitimate aim.

The Court of Appeal also held that Miss Eweida was not assisted in her claims by Article 9 of the European Convention on Human Rights (Freedom of thought, conscience, and religion), as the European Court of Human Rights has ruled that Article 9 does not protect every act motivated by religion or belief. Employees may also try to bring claims under the Human Rights Act.

Under **Article 10**, employees are entitled to a freedom of expression which could encompass a variety of things, most notably: a choice of clothing to wear at school or at work; participating in meetings or political activities;[67] attendance at picket lines; and assertion of opinions.[68] The right to freedom of expression provided by Article 10 is, like Article 9, not absolute. Interferences with the right to freedom of expression may be permitted if they are: prescribed by law; pursue a legitimate aim; and are necessary in a democratic society. The legitimate purposes for which the right to freedom of expression may be limited are: national security; territorial integrity; or public safety; the protection of health or morals; the protection of the reputation or rights of others; and the prevention of the disclosure of information received in confidence.[69]

In *Camelot Group plc v Centaur Publications Ltd*,[70] drafts of a company's accounts had been released to the press to embarrass the company. The documents involved were stolen and a return of them to the employer would enable them to identify of the source of the disclosure *namely* the identity of the employee who had leaked the confidential information. The Court had to decide whether or not to issue an order to a journalist to return the documents. The question was could Article 10 protect the source? A balancing exercise was required, one which would differ from case to case. Here it weighed in favour of disclosure.

---

67 *Ahmed v United Kingdom* (1999) IRLR 188 ECHR.
68 *Kara v UK* (1999) EHRLR 232.
69 *Wilson and Palmer v United Kingdom* (2002) IRLR 128 see Ewing, K The implications of Wilson and Palmer Industrial Law Journal, Vol 31, No 1 March 2003 p 1.
70 (1998) IRLR 80 CA.

In this case there remained a threat of further damage from a disloyal senior employee. It was held that the public interest in finding the disloyal employee was greater than the public interest of the person escaping detection.

Although Article 10 guarantees freedom of expression, this right is severely limited in practice because of the competing interests between a worker's freedom of expression, and the employer's right to manage the workplace and to protect reputation, confidentiality and trade secrets. In *Pay v UK*,[71] a probation officer who was involved in the treatment of sex offenders was dismissed, when his employers discovered that he had an interest in a business which sold bondage equipment. The employers felt that this activity was incompatible with his role as a probation officer, and likely to bring the probation service into disrepute. He had appeared in an advertisement for the business on the internet. He claimed that the dismissal amounted to a breach of Article 8 and Article 10. The ECtHR held that his activities did not form part of his private life, since he had appeared in public on the internet therefore Article 8 was not engaged. His right of freedom of expression, under Article 10, was limited by the interests and freedoms of others, namely his employer's interest in protecting the credibility and reputation of the probation service. It is clear from this case that in domestic law of unfair dismissal any consideration of reasonableness must include consideration as to whether the decision to dismiss is a proportionate response, bearing in mind the Article 10 rights of the employee.

It is also clear that, under the HRA 1998, freedom of expression may be restricted by a contract of employment. To this extent, the rights to expression can be bargained away by the worker upon agreeing to his contractual terms.

Article 11 provides for freedom of association. While Article 11(1) includes trade union freedom as a specific aspect of freedom of association, this provision does not secure any specific treatment of trade union members by the State. There is no exclusion of a right to strike, or an obligation on employers to engage in collective bargaining. At most, Article 11(1) may be regarded as the safeguarding of trade unions

---

71 [2009] IRLR 139.

to protect the occupational interest of their members. While the right to strike represents one of the most important means by which trade unions can fulfil this function, there are others.[72] 'In Wilson and Palmer the court has gone a long way to restore confidence in Article 11 of the Convention ... it provides protection for the right to peaceful assembly, as well as the right to freedom of association with others, including the right to form and join trade unions for the protection of one's interests.'[73] Article 11 rights are dealt with more fully in Chapter 15.

Article 14 deals with discrimination, but it is not a free-standing protection against discrimination. It provides protection against discrimination in the enjoyment of the rights and freedoms set out in the European Convention on Human Rights, however, for a breach of Article 14, the issue in relation to which a person is discriminated against has to come within the scope of one of the other Convention Articles.[74] If the discrimination does not refer to one of the rights guaranteed under the Convention, Article 14 does not assist the applicant.[75]

The discriminatory behaviour does not have to amount to a breach of the other Article. What needs to be established, is that an employee has been treated differently to another employee in a similar situation, on the basis of a characteristic they have, and the behaviour complained of falls within the scope of a Convention right.[76] The House of Lords held in *R (S and Marper) v Chief Constable of Yorkshire*,[77] that the difference in treatment must be based on a personal characteristic.

Even where it can be shown that an employee has been discriminated against, and that the area in which he has been discriminated against comes within the scope of another Article, it is still possible for the Government or a public authority to argue that the discrimination is justified. They must show that there is an objective and justifiable reason for treating the person differently, and that the difference in treatment is proportionate to that reason, in other words no more than was necessary.

---

72 *Unison v United Kingdom* 2002 IRLR 128.
73 Supra 38 p 5.
74 *Nerva and others v UK* (2002) IRLR 815.
75 In *Chima v Westinghouse Signals Ltd* EAT/1106/00 articles 6 and 14 were referred to.
76 This includes all the areas covered by the equality legislation in the UK.
77 (2004) 1 WLR 2196.

Equality and Human Rights Commission

3.5 The Equality and Human Rights Commission has responsibility for race, sex, disability, religious, sexual orientation and age discrimination issues, but it also fulfils the role of a human rights commission in the UK. In Scotland the Scottish Human Rights Commission is also dedicated to helping everyone understand their rights and the shared responsibilities they have to each other and the community. The Commission is independent of the UK and Scottish Parliaments and Governments.

FURTHER READING

Books

Arnheim, M. (2004) *The Handbook of Human Rights Law: An Accessible Approach to the Issues and Principles*. Kogan Page.

Hoffman, D. and Rowe, J. (2003) 'The Convention and the United Kingdom', *Human Rights in the UK: A General Introduction to the Human Rights Act 1998*. Pearson Longman.

Journal articles

Aikin, O. (2004) 'The Limits of Liberty'. People Management. Vol 10, No 6, p19

Legal Services Commission. Community Legal Service Direct Information Leaflet 7 (2005) *The Human Rights Act: What it means for you.*

Human Rights Act and Employment Law Update. (2005) IDS Employment Law Brief. No 779, p11.

Mundlak (2007) The Right to Work: Linking Human Rights and Employment Policy. International Labour Review. Vol 146, No 3–4, p189.

Websites

United Nations Charter (online). Available at http://www.un.org/aboutun/charter/preamble.htm

Woolf, Lord H. (2005) *Review of the Working Methods of the European Court of Human Rights*. www.echr.coe.int

Chapter 4

Contracts of Employment

4.1 There are three facets to any contract of employment. Firstly it is a contract governed by the usual rules of contract, secondly it is the legal expression of a personal relationship (based on trust and confidence) that exists between employer and employee and thirdly there is a statutory framework which is superimposed on the first two facets, and which is considered in later chapters.

A contract of employment or a contract of service, as it is known, is an example of a general contract and accordingly the law of contract will apply to it. It is crucial that the employment lawyer possesses a good working knowledge of contract law.

ESSENTIAL ELEMENTS OF THE CONTRACT

4.2 There are certain fundamental elements of contracts, including a contract of service, which should not be overlooked by the practitioner, as a defect in the fundamentals or formation of the contract can be fatal.

In order for a contract to exist, there must be at least three essential elements. Firstly, there must be two parties and the parties must possess legal capacity to enter into the contract. Secondly, there must be *consensus in idem*. In other words, the parties must be in agreement about the main points of the contract. Finally, there must also be an intention to create legal obligations.

If one of the three essential elements of the contract is missing then the contract will be void.

(1) Legal capacity

4.3 The most common factors which may affect the parties' legal capacity to enter into a contract include age, insanity, intoxication and vires.

Age

4.4 There are of course many statutory provisions which apply to protect young workers and these are discussed in chapters 8 dealing with age discrimination and chapter 12 covering working time rules. The age of legal capacity in Scotland is 16[1] and children under the age of 16 may not enter into contracts,[2] except in so far as they are of a kind commonly entered into by persons of his age and circumstances, and are on terms which are not unreasonable.[3] This means that a child under 16 is permitted to enter into a contract of employment such as a paper round. A person of twelve or over has testamentary capacity and accordingly has the ability to make a will. Where someone under sixteen purports to enter a transaction not covered by any of the exceptions, the transaction is void.

Most contracts entered into by a young person aged 16 or 17 may be set aside on application to the court on grounds that they have resulted in substantial prejudice, but this provision does not apply to a transaction in the course of the claimant's trade, business or profession.[4] It is not clear whether the words 'trade business or profession' include contracts of employment as well as situations where the young person is self employed. Ordinarily this would not be a problem for employers since under the common law a contract of employment can be brought to an end simply by giving notice. However, where the notice is lengthy, or there is some contractual obligation which subsists beyond the termination of the employment relationship, the issue may become important, eg where a 17 year old employee has entered into a contract containing a restrictive covenant which he is then able to have the court set aside. The Court of Session or the Sheriff Court may set aside a prejudicial transaction by a person in the above category.

The application to court must be made before the person reaches twenty one and the application of reduction must be raised by the young person, not the other contracting party. Businessmen might be reluctant to

---

1   The Age of Legal Capacity (Scotland) Act 1991.
2   Age of Legal Capacity (Scotland) Act 1991 s 1(a).
3   Age of Legal Capacity (Scotland) Act 1991 s 2(1).
4   Age of Legal Capacity (Scotland) Act 1991 s 3(3)(f).

transact with sixteen or seventeen year olds owing to the possibility of the young person later challenging the contract as prejudicial.

The Act therefore provides that the person between sixteen and eighteen and the other party may jointly apply to the Sheriff to have the proposed transaction ratified, thus rendering it unchallengeable at a later date.

Intoxication

4.5 The fact that one of the parties was intoxicated at the time the contract was entered into is unlikely to affect the validity of the contract, although it is possible to have a contract set aside on this ground.[5] The mere fact that the contracting party is intoxicated does not result in a contract being void or voidable. If the drunkenness has reached a stage where the person is incapable of knowing what he is doing, and therefore cannot consent, the contract is voidable and can be set aside but only if the intoxicated person repudiates his actions as soon as he recovers his senses.

Insanity

4.6 An insane person cannot enter into a contract. It should be noted that legal insanity may differ slightly from a medical definition of sanity. Legal insanity is regarded as an inability to understand the consequences of one's actions and consent to entering into contractual relations. The sanity of a party will be judged at the time the contract was entered into. A person who has supplied 'necessaries' to an insane person is entitled to do so for a reasonable price. A guardian may be appointed by the court to contract on behalf of an insane person.

Vires

4.7 The contract must be within the power (vires) of the parties to enter into, and this is only an issue affecting the validity of the contract, where one of the parties to the contract is a company and the constitutional documents of the company do not permit it to enter into such contracts.

---

5   *Taylor v Provan* (1864) 2 M 1226; *Pollock v Burns* (1875)2 R 497.

Since the coming into force of the Companies Act 2006 this should rarely be a problem.

(2) *Consensus in idem*

4.8 The second requirement for a valid contract is that there must be *consensus in idem*.[6] A contract will only be formed where there is mutual agreement between the parties about the essential terms and conditions in the contract. In many instances involving a contract of service, the terms and conditions are set by the employer and presented to the prospective employee for him to accept or reject. When he is only left with this choice it will be because the employer will not be prepared to enter into negotiation over the terms of the contract. There are exceptions to this where negotiations do take place before the contract of employment is finalised, but these tend to be restricted to employment in highly skilled occupations or occupations where there is a high demand for the skills involved. Defects in the formation of the contract are discussed below and these affect *consensus in idem*.

(3) Intention to create legal obligations

4.9 In order to be a valid contract there must also be an intention to create legal obligations. A social arrangement is not a contract and neither is an agreement to do something which is immoral or illegal. Common examples of contracts of employment which turn out to be void on this ground are prostitution, contracts where the employee does not have a valid work permit,[7] and contracts where the employee is working cash in hand, or in the knowledge that the employer is not paying tax and making National Insurance Contributions.[8] If the rules of contract law are applied strictly then the contract will be completely void[9] and the parties would have no rights at all, but often the tribunals and the courts have taken the view that although the contract is void the employee may sometimes still

---

6   *Mathieson Gee (Ayrshire) Ltd v Quigley* 1952 SC (HL) 38.
7   *Vakante v Governors of Addey and Stanhope School* 2005 ICR 231.
8   *Wheeler v Quality Deep Ltd (trading as Thai Royale Restaurant)* 2005 ICR 265.
9   *Newlands v Simons and Willer (Hairdressers) Ltd* [1981] IRLR 359.

be able to take advantage of statutory rights such as unfair dismissal[10] and protection against discrimination.[11] It is more likely that the employee will be able to enforce such rights where the illegality is to do with performance of the contract rather than the substance of the contract itself.[12] This is particularly true where the employee was not aware of the illegality,[13] where the employee did not benefit significantly from the illegal act,[14] or where the illegality was relatively minor[15]. Nevertheless, the possibility of illegality should be considered in situations where there has been a failure to pay tax and National Insurance, or a scheme to avoid such payments by payments being made to service companies rather than directly to employees and the employee subsequently wishes to claim unfair dismissal,[16] discrimination or indeed to enforce contractual rights. Recently the courts have attempted to sever the parts of the contract which were illegal and enforce the other clauses. In *Blue Chip Trading Ltd v Helbawi*,[17] the claimant was a foreign student studying in the UK, who had worked in breach of the conditions imposed as a term of his student visa. He worked longer hours than was permitted during term time. He alleged that his employers were in breach of the minimum wage. The employers contended as a preliminary point that the contract was illegal. The employment tribunal rejected that contention. However, the EAT upheld the employer's appeal in part, holding that part of the contract was lawful and could be severed from the unlawful part. The claimant could recover with respect to the periods out of term and at other times when there were no restrictions on his hours, but he could not recover with respect to the periods during term time when he was knowingly infringing the hours requirement.

---

10   *Hewcastle Catering Ltd v Ahmed and Elkamah* [1992] ICR 626.
11   *Hall v Woolston Hall Leisure Ltd* [2001] ICR 99.
12   *Enfield Technical Services Ltd v Payne* [2008] IRLR 500.
13   *Hall v Woolston Hall Leisure Ltd* [2001] ICR 99.
14   *Hewcastle Catering Ltd v Ahmed and Elkamah* [1992] ICR 626.
15   *Shelley v Paddock* [1980] QB 348.
16   *Bakersfield Entertainment Ltd v Church and Stuart* UKEAT/0523/05/ZT; see also *Beauvale Furnishings Ltd v Chapmand* [2000] UKEAT 79_00_2911 and *Hunt v Power Resources Ltd* UKEAT/0545/04/ILB.
17   [2009] IRLR 128.

FORMATION OF CONTRACT

4.10 In order to be valid the contract must be formed correctly. If there is a serious defect in formation then the contract will be void.

Void and voidable

4.11 The difference between a contract which is void and a contract which is voidable is extremely important. A contract which is void is treated as if it never existed. The parties cannot enforce it and a third party cannot acquire rights under it. A voidable contract is one which is perfectly valid until the court sets it aside on the application of one of the parties. Therefore it can be enforced by a party if it has not been set aside and a third party acting in good faith can acquire rights in consequence of the contract. There are three situations in which the court will not be able to set aside a voidable contract. Firstly, if a third part acting in good faith has acquired rights. Secondly, if *restitutio in integrum* is not possible (in other words the parties cannot be put back in the position they were in before the contract was entered into) The third situation is if personal bar applies and the party seeking to have the contract set aside has allowed the other party to act in reliance on it or has acted as if the contract is not defective.

Whether a contract is void or voidable does depend on what has caused the defect and also the extent of the defect.

Formation Rules

4.12 The normal rules of formation of contract apply with the result that, despite the fact that the contract is an open ended contract of service that can last for an employee's lifetime, it does require no more formality in its construction than a contract to buy a good or service, or to travel on a bus or train. In all contracts a valid offer and acceptance is required before the contract can be finalised. In the usual employment situation: (1) the offer will be made when the recruitment and selection process is complete and a person is chosen for employment; and (2) the acceptance takes place when the person chosen accepts the post on the terms offered. This process could be undertaken by letter, by e-mail or verbally.

No matter which process is followed, there must be *consensus in idem* and this must usually result from an offer and an unconditional acceptance in order to form a contract. The offer must come before the acceptance. This will usually be an offer of employment although there may be an offer to work by the employee. The offer may be express or implied. If express, it may be verbal or in writing or a mixture of both. Unless it contains a time limit for acceptance, the offer may be withdrawn at any time until it is accepted by communicating withdrawal to the offeree.[18] If it does not contain a time limit, the offer will lapse after a reasonable time.[19] If it does contain a time limit then the offer must remain open for acceptance until the time limit and cannot be withdrawn. It will automatically lapse if the time limit is reached without acceptance.

In order to form a contract the acceptance must be unconditional, ie it must match the terms of the offer and must not contain conflicting or additional conditions. A conditional acceptance will kill off the original offer which cannot then be accepted. The conditional offer will act as a counter offer which will require an unconditional acceptance to form a contract.[20]

The process of formation of contract is important because, even if a valid contract has been entered into, the terms of the contract will be contained in the offer and unconditional acceptance. It should be borne in mind that, unlike general contract law where the advertisement will not usually form part of the contract,[21] the advert in a contract of employment may be persuasive in helping determine the terms of the contract and, indeed, following the decision in the case of *Ministry of Defence v Kettles*,[22] may in fact form part of the contract. The issue in this case was whether a specialist orthodontist consultant was an employee or not. She responded to a job advertisement for salaried part-time employment in a clinic, but on starting the job she was asked to sign contractual documentation which was applicable for an independent contractor with his own organisation

---

18   *McMillan v Caldwell* 1991 SLT 325.
19   *Flaws v International Oil Pollution Compensation Fund* 2001 SLT 897; *Wylie & Lochhead v McElroy & Sons* (1873) 1 R 41.
20   *Wolf and Wolf v Forfar Potato Co* 1984 SLT 100; *Ruttorford v Allied Brewerie Ltd* 1990 SLT 244; *Tenbey v Stolt Comex Seaway Ltd* 2002 SLT 418.
21   Boots Pharmaceutical.
22   UKEAT/0308/06/LA.

using sub-contractors. The question was whether tribunal restricted to contractual documentation or entitled to take account of job advertisement and subsequent conduct of the parties.[23] It was decided the latter applied:

'Once granted that the Tribunal Chairman was entitled to look outside the ... contract documentation ... his conclusion that Dr Kettle was an employee of the MOD is not in my judgment perverse. It is a striking feature of the case that the MOD had advertised for an employee, interviewed Dr Kettle for the advertised post, and told her that she was successful before producing contract documentation which is difficult to reconcile with the job which had been advertised and which it was intended she would do.'[24]

Defects in contract

4.13 The validity of a contract of service (and its continued existence) can also be affected by factors such as error, misrepresentation, force and fear, facility and circumvention and undue influence. Such factors will either make the contract void or voidable.

Error

4.14 If the defect in the contract concerns an essential error, in other words goes to the root of the contract, it will be void. If the defect does not relate to something which is essential to the contract then the contract will be voidable.

A common error is where the parties have made the same mistake. As *consensus in idem* is not affected, this type of error will not usually affect validity.

An error of opinion will not affect validity, and an error as to the law will not affect validity. An error of expression, where the agreement of the parties is not accurately reflected when it is reduced to writing, does not

---

23 Middlemiss, S Discriminating Material? Legal Liability of Employers for Job Advertisements International Journal of Discrimination and Law 2007 Vol. 9 p 95.
24 Honour Judge Richardson at Paragraph 65.

affect validity.[25] In this case the written contract can be amended to reflect the true agreement between the parties.[26]

A mutual error is where one party is under a misapprehension or the parties have misunderstood each other. This will affect *consensus in idem* and the contract will be void if the error is essential and voidable if it is non essential.

An essential error is something which strikes at the root of the contract. In a contract of employment aspects which are regarded as essential include the nature of the contract ie employment or contract for services (see *Ministry of Defence v Kettles* earlier), the type of job and the rate of pay. Non essential matters would include the method of payment, the specific job description and the hours of work (as opposed to the number of hours worked which is likely to be essential).

Since a contract of employment is a contract *delectus personae* an error as to the identity of the parties is likely to be essential, whereas in a contract for services it is likely to be non essential.

Misrepresentation is an error which has been induced by the words or actions of another party to the contract. The innocent party must have relied on the misrepresentation when entering into the contract. A misrepresentation may be innocent, negligent or fraudulent. Damages are not available as a remedy if the misrepresentation is innocent, but are available in the case of negligent[27] or fraudulent misrepresentation. The extent of damage is discussed below. The effect on validity of contract does not depend on whether the misrepresentation was innocent, fraudulent or negligent but rather on the seriousness of the error it induces, ie essential or non essential.

Where force or fear, involving violence or the threat of violence, is used to persuade someone to enter into a contract of service that would also make the contract void.[28]

Facility and circumvention is a situation where a party to the contract was suffering from a weakness of mind which was not so severe as to amount to insanity and another party took advantage of the situation. Undue

---

25 *Krupp v John Menzies* 1907SC 903.
26 Law Reform (Miscellaneous Provisions) (Scotland Act) 1989.
27 *Hedley Byrne & Co Ltd v Heller & Partners Ltd* [1964] 465.
28 *Earl of Orkney v Vinfra* 1606 Mor 16481.

influence occurs when a person in a position of trust induces the other party to enter into a contract. If established, facility and circumvention or undue influence can result in the contract being void.[29]

THE CONTRACT OF SERVICE AND THE CONTRACT FOR SERVICES

4.15 There are a growing number of working arrangements being used by employers in the workplace which are difficult to define from a legal point of view, commonly referred to as atypical employment (considered fully in chapter 5).

As has already been seen, the contract of employment or contract of service is regarded by the law as being of a personal nature between the employer and employees, and employees are chosen for their particular skills and attributes (*delectus personae*). This latter element will prove vital in determining what kind of contract applies in any given situation.

The term 'contract of service' is a legal term meaning contract of employment and a 'contract for services' is a contract between an employer and an independent contractor (self-employed person). There are different rights and obligations attached to each type of relationship. Persons working under a contract of service are entitled to contractual rights and a vast number of statutory employment rights, whereas those persons working under a contract for services are not entitled to most of these rights although they do tend to benefit from flexibility in any arrangement with the employer (eg no restriction on identity of persons undertaking work), and certain financial benefits, (eg lower rate of tax than employees).

Distinction between a Contract of Service and a Contract for Services

4.16 It is important to determine which applies because the workers status affects his rights in three main areas:

---

29   *Cairns v Marianski* (1850) 12 D 919; *Gray v Binnie* (1879) 7 R 332.

(1) Statutory rights

4.17 A person working under a contract of service will be entitled to rights under the Employment Rights Act 1996 such as redundancy payment, protection against unfair dismissal, maternity and paternity and adoption rights, various rights to time off work and the right to request flexible working. Regarding tax and national insurance an employer must deduct tax and national insurance from his employee's wages before he pays them.[30] A worker working under a contract of services will not benefit from these statutory rights, although protection against discrimination and many statutory rights are available to a wider category of workers.[31] Also, someone working under a contract for services is responsible for paying his own tax and making his own National Insurance contributions.

(2) Health and Safety

4.18 Section 2 of the Health and Safety at Work Act 1974 imposes a duty on employers to take care of the safety of their employees so far is as is reasonably practicable.[32] No such duty is owed to those working under a contract for services. In addition the employer owes a duty to take reasonable care for the safety of an employee under the law of delict and contract. Again no such delictual or contractual duty is owed by the employer in respect of an independent contractor. See chapter 13 for a detailed discussion of Health and Safety law and the implied duty to take reasonable care for the safety of employees.

(3) Vicarious Liability

4.19 An employer is vicariously liable for the actions of an employee whilst working within the scope of his employment.[33] The end user of the services of an independent contractor is not usually vicariously liable

---

30   Social Security Contributions and Benefits Act 1992.
31   See for example the National Minimum Wage Act 1998, the Part Time Workers (Prevention of Less Favourable Treatment Regulations, the Working Time Regulations and the Transfer of Undertakings Regulations.
32   Section 2(2) provides more specific duties to be fulfilled by an employer.
33   For an example see *Toms and another v Royal Mail Group plc* [2002] CSOH 32.

for the contractor's actions unless he has control over the actions of the contractor, or he negligently selects an incompetent contractor. See chapter 13 for a detailed discussion of vicarious liability.

It is not always clear whether a worker is engaged under a contract of service or a contract for services. Under statute an employee is defined under s 230(1) of the Employment Rights Act 1996 as '... an individual who has entered into or works under (or where the employment has ceased, worked under) a contract of employment and a contract of employment means a contract of service or apprenticeship whether express or implied (and if express) whether oral or in writing.'[34] These definitions are clear but could be more helpful in characterising what an employee and a contract of employment are. It has been left to the courts and employment tribunals to identify the essential elements of a contract of service and to distinguish it from a contract for services.

The tribunals and courts will decide the question according to the substance of the contract, not according to the label given to it by the parties. A case in point is *Ferguson v John Dawson & Partners*,[35] where the Plaintiff was employed under a system called the 'lump', which was common in the construction industry at the time, where the worker was regarded as self employed and paid a lump sum for their work. The plaintiff was injured when he fell off the roof at the defendant's construction site. Contrary to regulations, there was no guard rail on the roof. If he had been an independent contractor he would have been responsible for his own safety and couldn't sue the company he worked for. However, he was employed as an unskilled labourer, was clearly subject to the control of the site agent, where tools were required the company provided them, and he was paid an hourly wage. The Court of Appeal held that despite the label apparently given by the parties to the relationship, in substance it was a contract of employment.

For well over a hundred years,[36] the courts have developed various tests which it was hoped could be utilised uniformly to distinguish between these contracts although each of them had their limitations as will be seen. The first of these was the control test which simply asked the question

---

34   Section 230(2).
35   (1976) 1 WLR 1213 Court of Appeal.
36   *Stephen v Thurso Police Commissioners* (1876) 3 R 535.

'who was in control of who, and in what circumstances the work was done?' If it was the employer that determined this then the person carrying out the work would be an employee, and if it was the worker himself then it would be a contract for services. In an early case *Yewens v Noakes*,[37] it was stated that 'a servant is a person subject to the command of his master as to the manner in which he shall do his work'. It was also stated that 'he who could and should have exercised ultimate control should bear responsibility.' The control test was found to be unreliable as a single factor test to determine this issue, because it was apparent in a large number of jobs workers had a high degree of control over their jobs but were still employees, eg doctors, teachers, information technologists etc.

The next test to be developed was the organisational test which asked the question how important or integral is the task the worker is undertaking to the organisation? The more important the task the more likely the person undertaking it is an employee. So, in the case of *Cassidy v Ministry of Health*,[38] a doctor who was working in a hospital had been negligent in his treatment of a patient and it had to be determined for the purpose of determining the liability of the hospital if a he was an employee. The court applied the organisational test and found that his work was integral to the organisation so he was an employee and the employer was vicariously liable for his actions. Similarly, in *Whittaker v Minister of Pensions*,[39] a trapeze artist who was injured at work and claiming compensation as an employee was deemed to be an integral part of a circus. However, this test has also proved unreliable because increasingly integral tasks of an organisation are being contracted out of the organisation to other contractors as an economic necessity (eg oil companies subcontracting maintenance services on oil rigs) or, in the case of the public sector, statutory requirements to contract out (ie privatisation of local government services).

Another test to be developed was the Entrepreneurial Test, first identified in the case of *Short v Henderson*,[40] where the presiding judge Lord Thankerton highlighted four criteria for establishing whether or not

---

37 (1880) 6 QB 530.
38 (1951) 2 KB 343.
39 (1967) 1QB 156.
40 (1946) SC HL 24.

a person was an employee: (1) The power of selection of servants to do the work (employers have this with employees but not with independent contractors); (2) Method of payment eg a salary would indicate a contract of employment; (3) right of suspension or dismissal; and (4) the right of control (but it was not the sole factor as before).

However, in *Market Investigations v The Minister for Social Security*,[41] the company was involved in market research. In addition to its permanent staff it employed interviewers to carry out around 8000 interviews a year, who worked as and when called upon. The issue was whether these interviewers were employees, in which case the employer was liable to pay National Insurance contributions on their behalf. The position of one interviewer was used as a test case and it was held they were employees. Justice Cooke in this case said the real question to be asked was 'Is the person who has engaged themselves to perform these services performing them as a person in business on their own account?' Factors which may be important in determining an answer to this are – is the person providing their own equipment, hiring their own helpers, undertaking a degree of financial risk and responsible for investment and management? If not, they are an employee.

The test which has proven to be the most important, and is still in use, is the multiple factor test.

This simply involved employment tribunals looking at all the facts in the case before reaching a decision and not being influenced by a single factor. The first case to utilise this test was *Ready Mixed Concrete v Minister of Pensions*.[42] The facts were that lorry drivers that were previously employed by the respondents agreed to change to self employed status. They were subject to a high degree of control but they owned their own vehicles and carried the risk of profit or loss. The two factors were sufficient to make them non-employees. Justice McKenna stated that:

> 'A contract of service exists if these three conditions are fulfilled. (i) The servant agrees that, in consideration of a wage or other remuneration, he will provide his own work and skill in the performance of some service for his master. (ii) He agrees, expressly or impliedly, that in the

---

41   (1969) 2 QB 173.
42   (1968) 2 QB.

performance of that service he will be subject to the other's control in a sufficient degree to make that other master. (iii) The other provisions of the contract are consistent with it being a contract of service.'[43]

This test has been relied on in many modern cases and has evolved to meet the changing needs and practices of the modern workplace. The three parts of the test must be passed in order to establish that a contract of employment exists and indeed the first two parts have been described as the irreducible minimum of a contract of service.[44]

Part a) of McKenna J's test contains 2 elements – 'mutuality of obligation' and 'personal service'.

Mutuality of obligation

4.20 This is often difficult to discern in a contract and has been the subject of many cases. What follows is a description of the leading cases dealing with mutuality of obligation and how this quality (of a contract of service) has been interpreted by the courts.

It is possible for a casual worker to acquire sufficient mutuality of obligation to pass this part of the test, however in order for this to happen there must be some expectation that they will continuously accept work from the employer and that the employer will continuously provide work throughout the duration of the contract. In *O'Kelly v Trust House Forte plc*,[45] where the Grosvenor Hotel in London employed Mr O'Kelly and others as regular casuals. They only worked when the hotel needed them and it suited them to work. However, they worked under the control of the hotel management and had to wear their uniform. When the hotel dispensed with their services they claimed unfair dismissal. They were unsuccessful, as were held to be self-employed. There was a lack of mutuality of obligation in the work arrangements, as neither the employer had to provide, or worker to do, the work and this was inconsistent with a contract of service. Similarly in *McLoud v Hellyer Brothers Ltd, Wilson v Boston Deep Sea Fisheries*,[46] five trawlermen based at the port of Hull

---

43   Supra at 515.
44   *Montgomery v Johntone Underwood Ltd* [2001] ICR 819.
45   [1983] IRLR 369.
46   [1987] IRLR 232.

were treated as working as independent contractors on the basis of lack of mutuality of obligation. The men were able to, and did, work for other employers during their periods of leave. As they were not working under a contract of employment during their leave they were not entitled to redundancy pay when their contract was not renewed.[47] In *Clark v Oxfordshire Health Authority*,[48] a women was employed as a bank nurse[49] and worked when required at three hospitals. She had no fixed hours of work and would be offered work as and when a temporary vacancy occurred. She could be asked to fill any vacancy she was appropriately qualified or experienced for. Ms Clark received a document entitled 'statement of employment' which set out her name, job title, grade and scale of remuneration. It also stated that 'employment will be on a day-to-day basis, consequently there can be no guarantee of work being available to suit individual requirements.' It also referred to conditions of service in the Whitely Council Regulations which defined bank nurses as follows: 'Bank Nurses are not regular employees and have no entitlement to guaranteed or continuous work.' She claimed unfair dismissal when the employer terminated her employment. The Court of Appeal held that there was a total lack of obligation in this case and the arrangement was a contract for services.

Similarly in *Carmichael and another v National Power plc*,[50] two women were employed as guides at Blyth Power Station in Northumberland on a casual as required basis. They ended up working an average of 25 hours per week, but only by invitation, and only when they chose to work. Their remuneration was paid after the deduction of income tax and National Insurance at an employed person's rate. They were provided with uniforms and when they were unable to work a replacement was found. They did not receive sick pay or holiday pay or a pension and were not covered by the grievance and disciplinary procedure. They brought a complaint against their employer when he refused to provide them with written particulars. The House of Lords held that the correct approach by tribunals is to look at documentary evidence to determine intentions, and failing this

---

47 For current position see *Cornwall CC v Prater* [2006] IRLR 362.
48 (1998) IRLR 125.
49 Required to fill in when employees were unavailable due to sickness etc.
50 (2000) IRLR 43.

any oral exchanges and the conduct of the parties. They can also ask the parties themselves what they construed the relationship to consist of. The court held that the employment tribunal had correctly concluded that the applicant's case 'founders on the rock of absence of mutuality to create a contract of service.

In contrast, in *Cornwall CC v Prater*,[51] Ms Prater had been engaged by the local authority as a home tutor, under their out of schools service, to teach children who were unable to attend school. The local authority offered work to Ms Prater in respect of particular children who were taught by Ms Prater at the pupil's home. The authority was under no obligation to offer her work and she was under no obligation to accept pupils. In fact Ms Prater never refused work and worked for the authority for a 10-year period. The duration of the individual engagements varied from a few months to several years. Tax and national insurance contributions were deducted at source from the money paid to her by the authority and at the end of each financial year Ms Prater received a form P60. She claimed that her individual engagements were contracts of service. The Court of Appeal dismissed the appeal and held that during the 10-year period Prater had had a number of work contracts with the local authority. They were contracts of service because, while they lasted, she was obliged to teach the pupil and the local authority was obliged to pay her for doing so. By virtue of s 212 of the Employment Rights Act 1996 she had continuity of employment because the gaps between contracts were regarded as temporary cessations of work. Following this decision, where companies frequently call on the same person to perform sequential assignments which are accepted by that person, there is a possibility that the gaps between assignments will be treated as a temporary cessation of work and that each assignment will be joined up to provide a period of continuous employment. Depending on the circumstances, this may render the individual eligible for various statutory rights, including the right not to be unfairly dismissed, the right to statutory redundancy pay and maternity pay. For more see chapter 6 which deals with continuity of employment.

A worker will not be self employed simply because he is paid only for work done. In *Nethermere St Neots v Gardiner*,[52] workers were paid

---

51   (2006) IRLR 362.
52   [2001] ICR 819.

to stitch the pockets into trousers. They could refuse work if they did not want it and were paid per pair of trousers. Nevertheless there was held to be sufficient mutuality of obligation to amount to a contract of service. In the case of *Four Seasons (Inn on the Park) Ltd v Hamarat*,[53] the EAT held that a regular casual who had worked as a wine waiter for seven years was an employee. He was only paid for the hours that he worked and received no sick pay or holiday pay. However, the Industrial Tribunal found that there was sufficient mutuality of obligation between the parties for him to be treated as an employee.

Personal service

4.21 According to McKenna J an important part of this part of the test was 'did the person undertake the work they do personally?' and, related to this, is an issue that has emerged in a number of cases concerning the effect of substitution clauses in a contract (allowing for other people to carry out the work under the contract in circumstances that the worker cannot). Is this type of clause incompatible with a contract of service, which is underpinned by the concepts of personal service and *delectus personae*? In *Express and Echo Publications Ltd v Tanton*,[54] Mr Tanton worked for the appellants as an employee until he was made redundant. He was then re-engaged as a driver on an ostensibly self-employed basis. His contract provided that 'in the event the contractor is unable or unwilling to perform the service personally, he shall arrange for another suitable person to perform the service.'

Mr Tanton found the agreement unacceptable but continued to work for the employer and, on the odd occasion, did provide a substitute driver. He claimed he was entitled to written particulars and invited the tribunal to consider his status. He was required to follow a set route, use a company vehicle and wear a company uniform. There was also a degree of control exercised by the company over Tanton's work. The Court of Appeal held that, where a person who works for another is not required to perform his services personally, as a matter of law, the relationship between the worker and the person he works for is not that of employer and employee.

---

53   EAT 369/84.
54   (1999) IRLR 367.

A right to provide a substitute is inherently inconsistent with the existence of a contract of employment.

The implication is that to insert a substitution clause in a contract will ensure it is treated as a contract for services as personal service is a legal minimum for a contract of service. However, in a decision of the EAT in *McFarlane v Glasgow City Council*,[55] the EAT attempted to circumvent this decision. The applicants were qualified gymnastic instructors who worked at recreational and sports centres. If one of them couldn't take a class he could arrange for a replacement from a register of coaches maintained by the Council. Occasionally the Council arranged replacements and they paid any substitutes. The Council tried to change the instructors contracts making them self-employed. McFarlane and the other gymnastic instructors declined to accept the new contract and resigned claiming constructive dismissal. The EAT accepted that the substitution clause was not necessarily incompatible with an employment contract. 'Properly regarded Tanton does not oblige a tribunal to conclude that under a contract of service an individual has always and in every event, however exceptional, to personally provide his or her services.'

In *Stevedoring and Haulage Services Ltd v Fuller*,[56] the employment tribunal had concluded that there was to be implied a term providing for an irreducible minimum of obligation on each side. The claimants were employees of the respondent under contracts of service. The dockers were employed under a contract, which stated expressly that there was 'no obligation on the part of the company to provide such work for [them] nor for [them] to accept any work so offered.' The tribunal found that mutuality of obligations is as much a part of the irreducible minimum for a contract of service as the element of personal service. The EAT upheld that decision on appeal, however, the Court of Appeal did not, pointing out that the implied term applied by the Tribunal was entirely inconsistent with the express written term. That decision was reached having considered the House of Lords' speeches in *Carmichael*. In other words where an express term covers the situation this will prevail in these circumstances.

---

55   (2001) IRLR 7.
56   [2001] IRLR.

The impact of the *Tanton* decision was illustrated in the case of *Real Time Civil Engineering Ltd v Mr D Callaghan.*[57] The EAT Chairman in this case said:

'I regret to say that in the light of higher authority I am again driven to uphold the employer's submission. In all ways, this appears to be a contract of service. Mr Callaghan worked regularly for the Respondent, driving their lorry for five years. After his break in 1999 he worked regular hours on a work and finish basis and plainly passed the business integration and control tests for a contract of service. But he entered into a written contract which, in my judgment, contrary to Ms Reed's submissions, was not found to be a sham. If not a sham this clause must prevail.'[58]

It is not necessary for both parties to have intended to mislead, for a substitution (or any other) clause in the contract to be rejected, because the tribunal finds it does not truly represent the relationship between the parties. The tribunal should have regard to all the evidence, including the conduct of the parties, to ascertain whether the words of the written contract represent the true intentions or expectations of the parties, or whether it is a sham.[59]

In *Redrow Homes (Yorkshire) Limited v Buckborough and Sewell,*[60] Mr Buckborough was a bricklayer who worked under a contract that required him to provide sufficient labour to ensure sufficient progress was made with the building works. The contract included a clause that explained, for the avoidance of doubt, that the obligation to perform the work was not personal to Mr Buckborough and that his obligations could be performed by other labour. Mr Buckborough claimed that he was a worker, (rather than an employee), and so entitled to annual leave under the Working Time Regulations. The claim succeeded before both the tribunal and EAT on the basis that the substitution clause was a sham, because neither of the parties intended that it should govern their relationship. However, the Tribunal had also held that Mr Buckborough's claim would have succeeded even if

---

57   2005 WL 3719519 also reported at [2006] ALL ER (D) 222.
58   Paragragh 13 Judge Peter Clark.
59   *Autoclenz v Belcher* [2009] EWCA Civ 1046, [2010] IRLR 70.
60   (2008) UKEAT 0528_07_1010.

the substitution clause was not a sham (and so binding upon the parties), despite the fact that, to establish he was a worker, Mr Buckborough would have to show that he had undertaken 'to do or perform personally any work or services.' The EAT considered that while Mr Buckborough might not have been obliged to do the work for Redrow personally he was, nevertheless, personally obliged to perform a service for them to find other labour.

What this case shows is that, even where a substitution clause is in place in a contract, this does not exclude a worker from obtaining rights under the legislation that applies to them.

Once mutuality of obligations has been established there must be sufficient control of the 'employer' over the 'employee'. Whilst the cases already mentioned as relevant to the old control test remain relevant in the context of the multiple test, it is clear from the case law that it is the legal right to control, rather than *de facto* control, which is important. In *Motorola Ltd v Davidson*,[61] Mr Davidson, was employed as a temporary employee under a contract for services with an employment agency to work at Motorola's plant. He was dismissed following a disciplinary hearing. He decided to bring an unfair dismissal claim against Motorola. In considering whether Mr Davidson was an employee of Motorola the control test featured prominently. The EAT said there were a number of factors which indicated that Motorola had effective control over Davidson as: he used their tools; wore their uniform and had to raise any grievances through Motorola. Also Motorola had suspended Davidson and then went on to terminate their relationship. Motorola argued that the key issue was whether they had the legal power to control Davidson. The EAT stated that, under the terms of Davidson's contract, he was obliged to attend work at Motorola's request. Although, the agency he worked for had similar or greater powers of control over Davidson, this did not mean Motorola did not have sufficient control over him to satisfy the 'control' test. Davidson was an employee of Motorola and they were liable for his unfair dismissal.

As can be seen from this case, control is a factor which can be particularly important in the case of agency workers. If the end user has

---

61   [2001] IRLR 4.

the right to exercise too much control over the worker then a contract of service may be implied with the end user becoming an unwitting employer.

As well as mutuality of obligation and personal service, there are other factors consistent with a contract of service. There is no exhaustive list of factors which the tribunal will take into account, but factors which may be relevant are: the provision of tools and equipment,[62] payment of tax and national insurance,[63] more than one 'employer',[64] payment of indemnity insurance. At this stage the courts and tribunals may also apply the entrepreneurial[65] or organisational tests discussed above.

Using the tests outlined it can be seen that many professionals are considered to be employees, as are some office bearers.[66] A group of workers whose employment status has proven particularly difficult to define are ministers of religion. In *Percy v Church of Scotland Board of National Mission*,[6767] the House of Lords decided that Ms Percy was an employee of the Church of Scotland for the purposes of the wider test employed by the Sex Discrimination Act 1975, but they were not required to decide whether she was an employee for unfair dismissal purposes. The courts will, in determining if office holders can also be employees, need to have regard to all the facts and circumstances of each case with varying results. In *New Testament Church v Stewart*,[68] a minister of the New Testament Church was held to be an employee, whereas a minister of the Presbyterian Church of Wales[69] and a minister of the Free Presbyterian Church in Scotland have been held not to be an employee.[70] The position of office holders of the Church of England has traditionally been that they are not employees,[71] although they now enjoy certain employment rights

---

62   *Willy Sheidegger Swiss Typewriting School (London) Ltd v Minister of Social Security* (1968) 5 KIR 65.

63   *Davis v New England College of Arundel* [1977] ICR 6.

64   *WHPT Housing Association Ltd v Secretary of State for Social Services* [1981] ICR 737.

65   *Hall v Lorimer* [1992] 1 WLR 939.

66   *Miles v Wakefield District Council* [1987] ICR 368.

67   [2005] UKHL 73, [2006] ICR 134.

68   [2007] IRLR 178.

69   *Davis v Presbyterian Church of Wales* [1986] ICR 280.

70   *Rev Allan MacDonald v Free Presbyterian Church* [2010] All ER (D) 265 (Mar).

71   *Diocese of Southwark and Ors v Coker* [1998] ICR 140.

by virtue of the Ecclesiastical Offices (Terms of Service) Regulations 2007.[72] The House of Lords in the *Percy* decision seems to have decided in favour of the conclusion that ministers of religion can be both office holders and employees for certain purposes at the same time.

The question as to whether a worker is an employee or not is a question of fact. As such, unless the tribunal has misdirected itself in law or made a decision which is wholly unreasonable, the courts will not intervene in their decision.[73]

INTERPRETATION OF CONTRACT

4.22 As we have seen above, any terms which are contained in documents or conversations which may form part of the negotiations of the parties leading up to the contract being formed, but are not in the offer, and unconditional acceptance, are not usually regarded by the courts a part of the contract itself, but may be used as guidance in determining the intentions of the parties.[74] The extent to which a tribunal may examine negotiations of the parties to assist interpretation of the contract has been considered in many cases including *Carmichael v National Power* where the tribunal had regard to the advert and to the conduct of the parties in order to determine the meaning of the written contract. Whether or not the written contractual documents were intended by the parties to contain the entire agreement between the parties is a matter of fact and therefore a matter for the tribunal. If this was not the intention of the parties, the tribunal will look at other relevant circumstances.

The tribunal will interpret the provisions of the contract in light of the facts and circumstances at the time.[75]

Written Statement of Particulars of Employment

4.23 Under ss 1 and 3 of the ERA 1996, as amended by ss 33-38 of the EA 2002, it states that no later than two months after the beginning of

---

72 SI 2009/2108.
73 *Lee v Chung and Shun Shing Construction and Engineering Co Ltd* [1990] IRLR 236.
74 *Butler Machine Tool Co Ltd v Ex – Cell-O Corp* [1979]1WLR 401 see also *Uniroyal v Miller & Co* 1985 SLT 101.
75 *Beattie v Age Concern* EAT/580/06.

an employee's employment with an employer the employer shall give a written statement to the employee which shall contain particulars of:

(a)   Name of employer and employee

(b)   Date when employment began (and date when continuous employment began taking into account work with previous employer)

(c)   Scale and rate of remuneration, the intervals at which paid etc.

(d)   Terms and conditions relating to hours of work. Working Time Regulations 1998

(e)   Provisions relating to holidays and public holidays etc Working Time Regulations 1998.

(f)   Sick pay provisions.

(g)   Pensions and pension schemes.

(h)   Notice provisions on both sides.

(i)   Where the employment is not intended to be permanent, the period for which it is expected to continue or, if it is a fixed term, the date when it is to end.

(j)   The place of work and extent of mobility.

(k)   Job title and/or job description.

(l)   Collective agreements which affect terms and conditions.

(m)   Grievance procedures, see *W A Goold (Pearmak) Ltd v McConnell* discussed above, under implied terms.[76]

(n)   Disciplinary agreements (see ACAS Code of Practice).

While undoubtedly the written particulars are valuable evidence of the contractual terms, they are not contractual (unless they are incorporated into a contract of employment), and are not legally binding and therefore, the rights set out in statement are not legally enforceable. The following quote is taken from a case where the status of the written statement of particulars was decided. 'It seems to us, that in general the status of the statutory statement is this. It provides very strong prima facie evidence

---

76   (1995) IRLR EAT 516.

of what were the terms of the contract between the parties, but does not constitute a written contract between the parties.'[77]

TERMS AND CONDITIONS IN THE CONTRACT

4.24 The difference between a 'term' and a 'condition' is that a term is a bilateral binding part of the contract, which should not be varied by one party, without the consent of the other. A condition, on the other hand, is unilateral and can be varied by one party. An example of a term is that the employee will be paid £300 per week. A condition would be that the payment is paid by electronic transfer into the employee's bank account on the last Thursday of each month. The employer may not vary the former provision without the consent of the employee, but will be able to vary the latter. The dangers of having matters which should be conditions as terms in the contract are illustrated in *Harlow v Artemis International Corporation Ltd.*[78] The employee handbook was incorporated into the employee's contract and he was therefore entitled to the enhanced redundancy package specified in the handbook at the date of incorporation, despite the fact that the handbook had, since that date, become web pages and had changed considerably.

There are various sources of contractual terms which require consideration and some degree of explanation. These fall into 3 categories:

(a)   express terms;

(b)   implied terms; and

(c)   incorporated terms.

(a) Express terms

4.25 An express term is one which is specifically negotiated between the parties. Express terms are often written in the primary contractual documents namely, letters of appointment, written contracts, letters of acceptance etc. However, express terms can also be oral, but where there is conflict between written and oral term the former prevails.

---

77   *System Floors v Daniel* [1981] IRLR 475 EAT.
78   [2008] EWHC 1126, (QB), [2008] IRLR 629.

'The contracting parties (or one of them) having considered a matter relative to their dealings, consciously and deliberately gives expressions to their agreement by specific writings or words.'[79] Express terms may also be incorporated into the contract from elsewhere (see incorporated terms below). Where there are express terms they will usually override implied terms,[80] but occasionally the implied terms will take precedence. In particular the statutorily implied terms, such as the implied term of equality under the Equal Pay Act 1970, of trust and confidence and that the employer will take reasonable care for the safety of his employee.[81] It is also possible that the express term terms will have been varied by implication.

The Courts will normally uphold the application of express terms, unless evidence can be led which suggests they do not represent what was agreed,[82] or that they are not being applied reasonably see *United Bank v Akhtar*.[83] In this case Mr Akhtar worked in the Leeds branch of the bank as a junior clerk. In his contract he had a mobility clause which stated that the bank had the power to transfer employees to any place of business the bank had in the UK, either temporarily or permanently. He was given three days notice to transfer to Birmingham and he asked for this to be suspended for three months for personal reasons but was refused. He then asked if he could take leave to sort out these matters but there was no reply, although his employer suspended his pay. He resigned and claimed contractive dismissal. The EAT held that, even if there is an express term in a contract, an employer must behave responsibly in implementing it. In this the manner of implementation of the express term was unreasonable and consequently this behaviour breached the implied term of trust and confidence.[84]

---

79 Craig, V. Miller, K. Walker S *Employment Law in Scotland* 3ed. (2004) Bloomsbury Professional p 57.
80 *Morrish v NTL Group Ltd* [2007] CSIH 56.
81 *Johnstone v Bloomsbury Health Authority* [1992] ICR 269.
82 *Tanton; Autoclenz v Belcher* supra.
83 [1989] IRLR 507, EAT.
84 *Rank Xerox Ltd v Churchill* [1988] IRLR 280, *Johnstone v Bloomsbury Health Authority* [1991] IRLR 118, CA.

However, the courts will normally enforce express terms if they are clear and mutually agreed. A case in point is *Nelson v BBC*,[85] where Mr Nelson's contract with the BBC included a clause that stated he could be required to work where and when the corporation required (mobility clause). The Caribbean service where Nelson worked closed down and Nelson was told by his employer to work elsewhere, but he refused claiming he was only employed to work in the Caribbean and he was therefore redundant. The Court of Appeal held that the contract had unrestricted language (express term) and Nelson could be expected to work anywhere, therefore he was not redundant.

Restrictive covenants and garden leave clauses

4.26 Restricting the use of secret or confidential information by employees after their term of employment has ceased can be vital to an employer to protect their market position. An employer may seek to protect the use of this information through the inclusion of a restrictive covenant in employees' contracts of employment at the commencement of their employment relationship. A restrictive covenant is a clause in the contract which prohibits an ex-employee from: competing with his ex-employer, or from soliciting customers of the business.

Restrictive covenants are regarded as contracts in restraint of trade and contrary to public policy. As such they will not be enforceable if they are unreasonably wide or restrictive[86] however, if the ex-employer can convince a court that the covenant is designed to protect his legitimate business interests and that it extends no further than is reasonably necessary to protect those interests, then it will be enforced.[87]

The standard types of restrictions which can be used by employers are:

- restrictions on the former employee working for a competitor;

---

85 (1977) ICR.

86 The breadth of the geographical area of any restriction and length of time of the post termination restriction must be justified. It is unlikely that a wide geographical area will be justified generally a restriction for more than six months will be difficult to justify.

87 *Cyrus Energy Ltd v Stewart, Xyrex Ltd v McTurk* [2009] CSOH 53.

- non-solicitation covenants which prevent poaching clients/customers of the former employer;
- non-dealing covenants which prevent a former employee from dealing with former clients/customers, regardless of which party approached the other.

The type of interest that is being protected will be important so information such as trade secrets may be granted a wider area of protection than information regarding confidential information, eg customer details. It is advisable to draft each part of the clause separately from others in the contract so that, should one part of the clause fail for lack of reasonableness, it may be severed from the other restrictions which are regarded as reasonable and they may stand alone and remain enforceable.[88]

Protection of trade secrets after the employment has ceased is provided for a reasonable time after the contract has ended under the implied term of good faith,[89] but the employer may also include restrictive covenants and both are enforceable by interdict.

Garden Leave

4.27 With respect to garden leave, this is compulsory home leave taken while employee is working his notice and it stops (usually senior) employees from leaving without proper notice, working for a competitor and divulging trade secrets.

The same principles which apply to restrictive covenants apply to garden leave clauses so, if an employer can convince a court that the clause is designed to protect his legitimate business interests and that it extends no further than is reasonably necessary to protect those interests, then it will be enforced. On the other hand they will not be enforceable if they are unreasonably wide or restrictive.

An example of a garden leave clause is: 'If this contract is terminated by notice of termination been given to you, the Company will require that you not to attend work or make contact with work colleagues, customers

---

88 *Mulvein v Murray* 1908 SC 528.
89 *Faccenda Chicken Ltd v Fowler* [1986] IRLR 69 *Evening Standard v Henderson* (1987) ICR 588.

or any other commercial connections of this Company for the duration of your period of notice.'

Even in the absence of an express garden leave clause the employer is often not obliged to provide work for the employee to do and can, therefore, send him home for the duration of his notice period.[90] A clause which in effect is imposing a period of compulsory idleness can be enforced by interdict[91] (see below).

Liquidate damages clauses

4.28 Another clause which is usually declared void on grounds of public policy is the penalty or liquidate damages clause. This is a clause in the contract which sets out the amount of damages which will be payable on a breach of contract. Such clauses will be considered unlawful unless they are a genuine pre estimate of loss rather than merely punitive.

In *Tullet Prebon Group Ltd v El Hajali*,[92] a clause which provided for damages in the event of the employee failing to show up to start a new job, was upheld by the court.

(b) Implied terms

4.29 Implied terms may come from various sources.

Terms implied by statute

4.30 There are not many examples of 'terms implied by statute' but the most widely known is provided under ss 73 and 74 of the Equality Act 2010 which introduces a 'maternity equality clause' into all womens' contracts. Section 73 (1) states: 'If the terms of the woman's work do not (by whatever means) include a maternity equality clause, they are to be treated as including one.' This ensure that a women on maternity leave has a contractual right, implied by law, not to lose improvements in her pay, or other terms, and conditions she would have got from her employer,

---

90   *SBJ Stephenson Ltd v Mandy* [2000] IRLR 233.
91   *Euro Brokers Ltd v Robey* [1995] IRLR 286.
92   [2008] EWHC, 1924 (QB), [2008] IRLR 760.

had she been at work. Another example is the implication of rights into the contracts of workers by the Working Time Regulations. In the case of *Barber v RJB Mining*,[93] it was held that the Working Time Regulations had implied into every persons contract of employment (in the absence of contrary written agreement) the right not to work more than 48 hours.

Terms implied by the actions of the parties

4.31 The tribunal or court may look at all the circumstances of the relationship, including the actions of the parties to ascertain whether there is an implied term in the particular contract.[94]

Often trade usage or custom may have a role to play in filling a gap in the express terms of a contract of employment, or perhaps in the interpretation of a particular term.[95]

In *McColl v Norman Insurance Co Ltd*,[96] a practice of employing workers in one particular place was held to override the employee's undertaking in his application form that he would be prepared to work anywhere in the UK. It was held that the job concerned, though not originally restricted geographically, had acquired a particular location as a result of practice. The employee in this case gained the contractual right not to relocate.[97] In a more recent case *British Association for Service to the Elderly v Lawton*,[98] BASE was a charity with whom Mrs Lawton had been employed since 1989. A new Chief Executive was appointed in October 2004 tasked with rectifying the decline of the charity. He discovered that the staff had no contracts of employment or statements of terms and conditions of employment. The terms on which Mrs Lawton was in practice employed, arising from a combination of custom and practice and policy documents, were regarded by BASE as too favourable particularly in relation to holiday entitlement, working hours and sick

---

93 (1999) IRLR 308, QBD.
94 *Mears v Safecar Security Ltd* 1983 QB 54 but see *Eagland v British Telecom plc* [1993] ICR 644.
95 *Maclea v Essex Lines Ltd* (1933) 45 LL Rep 254; *Stevenson v Teeside Bridge and Engineering Ltd* (1971) 1 All ER 296.
96 (1969) ITR 285.
97 *Marshall v English Electric Co Ltd* (1945) 1 ALL ER 653 CA.
98 2008 WL 2976649.

pay. Her employer tried to vary her contract and substantially reduce her contractual entitlements in the face of custom and practice, and she raised grievances to complain to no avail. When she refused to accept the changes she was dismissed. The employment tribunal decided the dismissal was unfair on the basis that the employer had failed to follow relevant dismissal and disciplinary procedures. This decision was upheld by the EAT on appeal.

In *Sagar v Ridehalgh & Son Ltd*,[99] it was held that the established trade custom of deducting money from wages because of poor workmanship had given rise to an implied term in the contract to that effect.

In order to succeed in persuading a court or tribunal that a term is implied into the contract in this way, evidence must be led to establish that the custom and practice is 'reasonable, certain and notorious', and is therefore capable of creating a contractual right.[100] It must be reasonable for the custom and/or practice to be treated as contractual, such as in the *McColl* case, where the employee was extended the right not to relocate. It must be certain, and therefore not ambiguous, and well established, such as the right to be paid a Christmas bonus or be given tea breaks. It must be notorious in the sense that the custom or practice is widely known about. In *Cunliffe-Owen v Teather & Greenwood*,[101] the judge stated that certain means it is a clearly established practice. When the parties to the contract or Employment Tribunals are dealing with a particular employment issue there may be no express contractual term covering the matter. In such a case it might be necessary for them to consider and uphold what has happened under custom and practice in the workplace.

Common Law Implied Terms

4.32 A frequent source of litigation are those terms implied by common law into every contract of employment. In the absence of express terms dealing with the matter are incorporated automatically into every contract

---

99 [1931] 1 Ch 310.
100 *Henry v London Transport Services Ltd* EAT/1397/97, EAT/177/98 & EAT/210/99, *Singh v British Steel Corporation* [1974] IRLR 131.
101 [1967] 1 WLR 1421.

of employment.[102] They usually have the effect of providing rights and obligations on both the employer and employee, and they may take the form of duties. Some of the most common issues in employment contracts relate to common law implied terms. They are derived from judges' decisions in legal cases and apply to all employment contracts. There are two common justifications put forward for judges intervening in contractual relations in this way. The 'Of Course' justification whereby the reasoning is the parties would have included these terms in the contract had they thought of them. 'Occasionally the courts and tribunals are prepared to imply a term into a contract in circumstances where the parties did not expressly insert a term to meet a particular contingency. The theory adopted is that the term was so obvious that the parties did not see the need to express it.'[103] So terms may be implied by the courts to reflect the presumed, but unexpressed, intention of the parties where contracts are silent on particular issues. This is sometimes referred to as the officious bystander test.

A court will also imply a term into the contract if it is necessary to make the contract effective (business efficacy) and it is easy to see how some of these terms can help with this, eg implied duty to obey a reasonable and lawful order, duty to cooperate with the employer. This is a test based on necessity rather than reasonableness. The question is: is it necessary to imply a term in order to make this contract work ie to give it business efficacy?

Duties imposed on employees towards their employer

4.33 Implied duties, which are owed by the employee to the employer, include the following:

Duty to do whole work under contract

4.34 This duty includes a duty not only to carry out the work which is specified in the contract, but also any work which is reasonably incidental

---

102 *Morrish v NTL Group Ltd* [2007] CSIH 56.
103 Selwyn, *N Selwyn's Law of employment*. 16th ed (2011) OUP p 97.

to the contract.[104] A refusal without justification to obey a reasonable and lawful order, within the scope of an employee's employment, is a breach of the contract. In *Pepper v Webb*,[105] a gardener was told by his employer's wife, and then his employer, to plant some flowers. He responded by swearing at his employer and refusing to do the task. He was dismissed and it was held that he had breached his contractual duty to obey a reasonable order and his dismissal was justified. However the breach may not always be so fundamental as to justify a dismissal. It is also justifiable to refuse an order where to follow it would put the employee in a position of danger,[106] or where the order is to do something which is unlawful. A refusal to comply with a request, rather than an order, does not constitute a breach of the implied term.

This duty does not require the employee to obey orders which are completely out with the scope of his normal duties.[107] In *Bull and Anor v Nottinghamshire and City of Nottingham Fire and Rescue Authority*, it was held that 'co-responding', ie attending to the injured until paramedic assistance arrived, was out with the duties which could be ordinarily be expected of a fireman and therefore a refusal to co-respond was not a breach of the contract of employment. The employee's duties include anything which the employer could reasonably ask him to perform and (particularly in exceptional circumstances) are not restricted to those specified.[108] The employee is expected to co-operate with the employer in his carrying out of contractual duties. This could extend to cooperation with the introduction of new technology, as was the case in *Cresswell v Board of Inland Revenue*[109] where an employee refused to work with a new computer system which was introduced in to the workplace by the Inland Revenue. It was held that by refusing to cooperate with the introduction of new technology in the work place the employee was in breach of their contract. In the case of *Ticehurst v British Telecommunications plc*,[110] a manager's refusal to sign an undertaking that she would work normally

---

104 *Redbridge London Borough Council v Fishman* [1978] ICR 569, EAT.
105 [1969] 1 WLR 514.
106 *Ottoman Bank v Chakarian* [1930] AC 272.
107 *O'Brien v Associated Fire Alarms Ltd* [1969] 1 All ER 93.
108 *Luke v Stoke on Trent County Council* [2007] EWCA Civ 76.
109 [1984] IRLR 190.
110 [1992] IRLR 219.

during a period of industrial action, was a breach of the duty to cooperate under his contract. In fact any kind of industrial action such as a strike,[111] 'go-slow',[112] or 'work-to-rule'[113] will amount to a breach of contract at common law.

Duty of care

4.35 The employee must carry out his duties with reasonable care and, if he carries out his duties negligently, he will be liable in damages to his employer and third parties for any loss occasioned by his failure. This duty includes a duty to take reasonable care of his employer's property.[114]

Duty of Good Faith and Loyalty

4.36 There is a duty of good faith placed on employees which includes, firstly, a duty not to disclose trade secrets, secondly, a duty not to make secret profits and, thirdly, a duty not to compete with the employer. In *Faccenda Chicken v Fowler*,[115] the Court of Appeal held that there were two types of confidential information. The first consists of trade secrets or information of such a highly confidential nature that it should be treated as if it were a trade secret. The second is information which is confidential, in that for the employee to use it for their own purposes, or disclose it to someone else while employed, would represent a breach of their contract but which they would be entitled to use after leaving. While the former type of confidential information will be protected by the implied term after the employee has left the employer's service, the latter will not,[116] unless it is covered by a restrictive covenant and, only then, where its use is subject to reasonable restriction.

---

111 *Simmons v Hoover Ltd* 1977 ICR 61.
112 *General Engineering Services Ltd v Kingston and St Andrew Corp* [1988] 3All ER 867.
113 *Miles v Wakefield Metropolitan District Council* [1987]ICR 368; *Secretary of State for Employment v ASLEF & Ors (no2)* [1972] ICR 19.
114 *Lister v Romford Ice and Cold Storage Co Ltd* (1957) 1 All ER 125.
115 (1986) ICR 297.
116 *Brooks v Olyslager OMS (UK) Ltd* [1998] IRLR 590.

In some industries it is common practice that employees will receive tips and benefits from other parties. If this is not the case then the employee will be in breach of contract for receiving them and must account for them to his employer (see below).

There is a duty on employees not to work for competitors of their employers in own time, when it is likely to lead to them disclosing trade secrets. An employee is not in general prohibited from doing another job in his or her spare time, however he or she must not work for a rival employer where the effect of this will be to seriously damage their principal employer's business. In the case of *Hivac Ltd v Park Royal Scientific Instruments*,[117] the employee was banned by an injunction from working with a competitor in the evenings because he could have disclosed trade secrets regarding the production process for miniature valves.

Duty to account/indemnify

4.37 There is duty for employees to account to employers for secret profits and benefits which they receive from third parties as a result of their employment, and for any profit made by competing with their employer. The liability to account is separate from the liability to pay damages for the breach of duty and the applicant should be careful to choose the remedy which will be most advantageous. Unlike damages (see below) the pursuer need not take action to mitigate loss in an action of accounting. Similarly there is no need to prove loss. The pursuer will simply be entitled to the profits made by the employee, whether or not the employer could have taken advantage of the opportunity which the employee exploited.

The employee is also under a duty to indemnify the employer against any loss they incur for the employer in the context of their employment.[118]

Duty of trust and confidence

4.38 This duty is the reflection of the duty of trust and confidence owed by the employer to the employee. The employer is entitled to be able to

---

117 (1946) Ch D 169.
118 *Lister v Romford Cold Storage and Ice Co* [1957] AC 555.

trust his employee and this duty will be breached if the employee conducts himself in such a way as to destroy that trust. Acts of misconduct, such as dishonesty and negligence, amongst others will amount to a breach of this duty. Although an employee has a duty to report misconduct of other employees, he may, in certain circumstances, be expected to make a report of his own wrongdoing. In a leading case[119] where the employee Fassihi had breached his fiduciary duty as director, it was established he had breach the duty of good faith. In her leading judgment, the appeal court judge made the following comment:

> 'One route by which it might be concluded that Fassihi had a duty to disclose his own wrongdoing, is that no logical distinction can be drawn between a rule that an employee must disclose his own wrongdoing and a rule that he should disclose the wrongdoing of fellow employees, even if that involves disclosing his own wrongdoing too.'[120]

Where he is a senior employee this duty to report would always extend to the misconduct of others and his own wrongdoing.[121]

Duties imposed on employers towards employees

Duty to Pay Wages

4.39 The employer must pay wages at the contractual rate, but where no rate is specified for pay in the contract, must pay the *quantum meruit* (market rate for the job). As long as the employees are willing to work an employer must pay them wages even if no work is available, unless their contract says otherwise. The consideration for pay is for being available for work rather than actually performing it, unless a specific provision in the contract provides otherwise. However, the onus is on the employer to show that there is a term relieving the employer of the normal obligation to pay: see the decision of the EAT (Lord Johnston presiding) in *Beveridge*

119 *Software UK Ltd v Fassihi* [2004] IRLR 928.
120 *Item Software (UK) Limited v Fassihi and others* [2004] EWCA Civ 1244.
121 This principle was affirmed in *Sybron Corporation v Rochem Limited* [1983] 2 All ER 707 and in the more recent cases of *British Midland Tool Limited v Midland International Tooling Limited and others* [2003] All ER (D) 174. *Tesco Stores Ltd v Pook & Ors* [2004] IRLR 618.

v KLM Ltd.[122] Pay is subject to statutory regulation in respect of equality of pay between men and women, eg Equal Pay Act 1970, unlawful deductions (Wages Provisions in Employment Rights Act 1996) and requirement for a minimum wage (National Minimum Wage Act 1998).

Duty to provide work

4.40 There is no general duty on employers to provide work to employees provided that an employer continues to remunerate them. This is made clear in the case of *Collier v Sunday Referee Publishing Co*,[123] where it was stated that 'it is true that a contract of employment does not necessarily, or perhaps normally, oblige the master to provide the servant with work. Provided I pay my cook her wages regularly she cannot complain if I choose to take any or all of my meals out.'[124] The following quote from the Citizens Advice Bureau in a statement from their website is a bit more ambiguous about this: 'your employer has a duty to pay your wages and provide work. As long as you are willing to work, your employer must pay your wages even if no work is available, unless your contract says otherwise.'[125]

This only applies where the implied duty to be ready and willing to work is met by the employee. However, there are exceptions to this rule. In the case of a skilled employee, for example, the courts may be prepared to make an exception to the general rule and imply a duty to provide a reasonable amount of work in order that the employee maintains his or her particular skills (eg workers in dynamic and highly specialised professions).[126]

Other exceptions to this rule are where pay is dependent on someone working, (eg commission only work, piece rate work),[127] or where an employee must work to maintain their public reputation, (eg actors).[128]

---

122 [2000] IRLR 765 para 9.
123 (1940) 2 KB 647.
124 *Collier v Sunday Referee Publishing Co* [1940] 2 KB 647.
125 http://www.adviceguide.org.uk/index/life/employment/contracts_of_employment. htm
126 *William Hill Organisation v Tucker* [1999] ICR 291.
127 *Devonald Rosser and Son*; [1906] 2 KB 728; *Baumann v Hulton Press Ltd* [1952] 2 All ER1121; *Breach v Epsylon Industries* [1976] ICR 316.
128 *Herbert Clayton and Jack Waller Ltd v Oliver* [1930] AC 209.

Duty of Trust and Confidence

4.41 It has been generally recognised that the most important implied term in the employment contract is the implied term of mutual trust and confidence. Indeed it has been described as the 'overarching duty' in the contract of employment.[129] One reason for its prominence is that it is framed in general terms, so it can be applied to most situations. It has strengthened the position of employees by filling gaps in the law not covered by legislation or the common law, so that employers can no longer rely on the absence of legal rules in the contract of employment to protect them if their conduct is so unreasonable or intolerable it undermines the employment relationship. This is an important, wide-ranging duty of the employer not to do anything that will jeopardise the position of trust and confidence between him and his employees.

In *Robinson v Crompton Parkinson*,[130] the employee was an electrician of many years standing who was wrongly, unfairly and improperly accused of theft from his employer. After he was acquitted in a criminal court he sought an apology from his employer. When it was not forthcoming he left and claimed unfair dismissal. Justice Kilner Brown stated that 'In a contract of employment and in conditions of employment, there has to be mutual trust and confidence between master and servant. Where the employer has behaved in a way which is contrary to that mutual trust ... it seems to us to say that there is conduct which amounts to repudiation of that contract.'

In *Post Office v Roberts*,[131] a senior official wrote an unfair report on an employee judging her to be unfit for promotion. This was written without proper consideration of the employee's record of employment. It led to her being refused a transfer to another branch. The reason for the refusal was not made known to her for some time. She left and an industrial tribunal found she had been constructively dismissed because of her employer's breach of her trust and confidence.

---

129 Brodie, D The Heart of the Matter: Mutual Trust and Confidence (1996) Industrial Law Journal Vol. 25 p 121; Brodie D The Employment Contract; Legal Principles, Drafting and Interpretation (2005) OUP.
130 (1978) ICR 401 EAT.
131 (1980) ICR 347 EAT.

In the leading case of *Malik v BCCI SA*,[132] the employee had his future job prospects materially damaged because of his employment and association with BCCI, a fraudulent bank. They had breached the term of trust and confidence in his contract. He claimed and was awarded stigma damages, which is a remedy that reflects extreme injury to reputation and is only available in England and Wales. The House of Lords decided in this case that the employee's contract contained an implied term that the bank would not, without reasonable and proper cause, conduct itself in a manner likely to destroy or seriously damage the relationship of confidence and trust between employer and employee.

The House of Lords extended the duty of trust and confidence to include a positive obligation on the employer to take all steps which are necessary to achieve the purposes of the employment relationship. In assessing whether there has been a breach of the duty, what is significant is the impact of the employer's behaviour on the employee, rather than what the employer intended. It was decided in *BG plc v O'Brien*,[133] that if the employee's behaviour is intolerable enough to amount to repudiation of contract there is no obligation on an employer to act reasonably or treat employee in a reasonable manner.

Following *Malik v BCCI*, it is not necessary for the behaviour complained of to be targeted at the victim. An employee need not know of the employer's trust destroying conduct while still employed. For example, an employee may find out after he has resigned that his manager was regularly making unwarranted, unfavourable comments about him in meetings. He could then, based on the breach of the implied term, bring a claim against his employer for breach of contract or constructive dismissal.

A failure to support an employee (particularly when they are in a opposition of authority) can amount to a breach of the duty of trust and confidence. In the leading case of *Wigan Borough Council v Davies*,[134] Miss Davies, formerly the 'third in charge' at a nursing home, sided with the warden in a dispute with the care assistants. After a local authority enquiry she returned to work as a care assistant, but she was sent to Coventry by the other staff and they refused to co-operate with her in her

---

132 (1997) IRLR 462.
133 (2001) IRLR 406.
134 (1979) IRLR 127.

work. Her employer was aware of this. She left and claimed constructive dismissal. The EAT held that the employer's duty of trust and confidence includes enabling the employee to carry out her duties without disruption or harassment from fellow employees, accordingly the duty had been breached.

In *Whitbread plc t/a Thresher v Gullyes*,[135] an employee was promoted to a position for which she lacked experience, and was promised support and resources which were not forthcoming. The EAT held the employer to be in fundamental breach of the implied term that the employer should not act so as to prevent the employee from being able to carry out her part of the contract.

It is an implied term of the employment contract that an employer will give employees a reasonable opportunity to obtain redress of grievances. In *W A Goold (Pearmak) Ltd v McConnell*,[136] the EAT held that the failure of an employer to give employees a reasonable opportunity to obtain redress of grievances was a breach of the implied term of trust and confidence entitling the employee to resign and claim constructive dismissal.

Although the duty imposes a broad range of obligations upon the employer it does not go as far as imposing a duty on an employer to advise an employee that by retiring early due to ill health he would lose entitlement under a health insurance scheme.[137] The House of Lords in *Scally v Southern Health and Social Services Board*,[138] states that an employer will however be expected to advise his employees of contractual benefits if the employee cannot reasonably be expected to be aware of them. In that case the employee had not been aware of his right to purchase additional years to enhance his pension. The House of Lords held that where 1) the terms of an employee's contract of employment had not been negotiated with the individual employee, but resulted from negotiations with a representative body or were otherwise incorporated by reference, 2) a particular term of the contract made available to the employee a valuable right contingent upon his taking action to avail himself of its benefit and 3)

135 1.7.94 EAT 478/92.
136 [1995] IRLR 516.
137 *Crossley v Faithful and Gould Holding Ltd* [2004] EWCA Civ 293, [2004] 4 All ER 447; *University of Nottingham v Eyett* [1999] IRLR 87.
138 [1992] 1 AC 294.

the employee could not, in all the circumstances, reasonably be expected to be aware of the term unless it was drawn to his attention, there was an implied duty on the employer to take reasonable steps to make the employee aware of his contractual rights.

If an employer treats an employee less favourably than another for no good reason, or on a capricious whim, then that treatment may amount to a breach of this duty.[139]

Duty to take reasonable care for employee's safety

4.42 Employers are under a duty to take reasonable care for the safety of all their employees. There is an almost identical delictual duty (under the law of negligence) which employees are more likely to utilise. Employers must provide a safe place of work, a safe system of work, safe plant and appliances and safe and competent fellow workers.[140] If an employer fails to take reasonable care to protect an employee from a foreseeable injury, by failing to provide any of the above, he or she could be found to have breached the 'duty of care'. The standard of care is that of the reasonable employer,[141] and the reasonable employer will take more care of more vulnerable employees, such as the young and inexperienced or the disabled.[142]

Under the implied duty to provide a safe working environment, employers are under an implied obligation to provide and maintain so far as is reasonably practicable, a working environment that is suitable for the performance of the contractual duties of employees. This duty may be breached, for example, where an employee is being bullied at work by fellow employees or exposed to passive smoking. In *Waltons & Morse v Dorrington*,[143] the claimant was a non-smoker who had to work alongside smokers for a number of years. When her office was moved the problem escalated and she complained to her employer. They made some changes, but the situation was not much improved. She made further complaints and

---

139 *Hira Company Ltd v Daley* 2011 WL 2748076
140 *Wilson & Clyde Coal Company v English* [1938] AC 57.
141 *Latimer v AEC Ltd* [1952] 2 QB 701.
142 *Paris v Stepney BC* [1950] 1KB 320.
143 (1997) IRLR 488.

then eventually resigned and claimed constructive dismissal. In finding in her favour, the EAT held that there was an implied term that the employer will ensure employees work in an environment reasonably suitable for the performance by them of their contractual duties. In this case a reasonably practical step would have been to ban smoking in the building. In the earlier case of *Dryden v Greater Glasgow Health Board*,[144] a smoker, in the face of a smoking ban in the workplace tried to claim he a contractual right to smoke and when he was refused permission to continue smoking in the workplace he left. The EAT held that the introduction of a new non-smoking policy amounted to a 'works rule' which had no contractual effect, and therefore could not be used as a foundation for a constructive dismissal claim. It considered that employers are entitled to make rules for the conduct of employees that work within the scope of the contract and the introduction of a new works rule did not breach the implied term of trust and confidence. It also held that there was no implied term in the employees' contract that smoking was permissible.

The duty to take reasonable care now extends to taking reasonable care not to cause employee's psychiatric harm through bullying or harassment or through the nature or the quantity of the work they have to undertake.

There is a more in depth analysis of this duty in chapter 13.

Duty to indemnify

4.43 Employers are under a duty to indemnify employees for reasonable expenses and liabilities incurred by him in the course of his employment. This duty is not problematic in most cases because employers accept that they have to reimburse their employees for out of pocket expenses and other costs which they necessarily incur in the course of their employment.

Duty to provide references

4.44 An employee is unlikely to have an express right under the contract to receive a reference from his employer. The right could be established by custom and practice where references have been provided widely to employees by the employer over a considerable time. Failure to provide

---

144 (1992) IRLR 469 EAT.

a reference in these circumstances could be a breach of contract. There are certain industries where the giving of a reference is a requirement of a professional body, eg Life Assurance and Unit Trust Regulating Organisation (LAUTRO) rules in the financial services industry, and failure to provide a reference may lead to disciplinary action being taken by that body.

However, the rules governing references are not primarily contractual but derive from the law of delict in Scotland.[145] There is normally no obligation under statute or the common law for the employer to provide a reference to his employees, but when he does he is under a duty of care to ensure it is accurate, and any failure in this respect could give rise to a delictual action.

This was confirmed in the case of *Lawton v BOC Transhield*,[146] where it was held that employers owe employees a duty to take reasonable care to ensure that the opinions contained in a reference are honestly held and based on accurate facts.

The leading case on references was *Spring v Guardian Assurance plc*,[147] where the House of Lords held that an employer providing a reference in respect of a former employee is under a duty to take reasonable care in the preparation of that reference, and would be liable to the employee in negligence if the reference was inaccurate and the employee suffered damage as a result. The importance of this case was that for the first time it provided a delictual remedy to employees which could be pursued on the basis of the employer's negligent misstatement. Previously an employee would be unlikely to succeed in a case involving an inaccurate reference which had been compiled without due care and attention, because they would need to bring a case of defamation which required the employee to prove malice which was considered to be unduly onerous.

In *Bartholomew v London Borough of Hackney*,[148] the Court of Appeal, held that, although it would be imposing too high a burden to

---

145 Middlemiss, S The Truth and Nothing but the Truth? Legal Liability of Employers for Employee References, Industrial Law Journal Oxford University Press, March 2004 Vol. 33 p 59.
146 [1987] IRLR 404.
147 [1994] IRLR 460.
148 [1999] IRLR 246.

say employers had a duty to be 'full and comprehensive' in providing a reference , there is a duty on employers to ensure that references are true and accurate and fair in substance. However in *Cox v Sun Alliance Life Ltd,* the Court of Appeal held that as long as the reference is accurate and fair it need not report on all the material facts concerning the individual.

In a Scottish case *Sutherland v British Telecommunications plc,*[149] it was held that no action could be taken for defamation in circumstances where a reference is provided without malice and given in good faith, as the defence of qualified privilege will apply. This defence applies where a person communicates, or has an interest, or a legal/social/moral duty, to communicate something to another who has a corresponding interest or duty to receive the communication. So qualified privilege protected communications such as references given by employers. This protection, however, will be lost if the reference is passed on to another person with whom there is no mutuality of interest. It is important for an employer to ensure that where a reference is given it should not fall into the wrong hands, namely anyone who is not the subject of the reference or the prospective or current employer of the subject who with the subject's permission has requested and received the reference.

In *Coote v Granada Hospitality Ltd,*[150] an employer refused to give a reference because the employee in question had complained of sex discrimination in the past, and this refusal to provide a reference amounted to 'victimisation' under s 4 of the Sex Discrimination Act 1975 (SDA 1975). The EAT in its decision held that while employers are not forced to give former employees references, they simply cannot selectively refuse to write a reference for the sole reason that the employee had carried out a protected act.[151]

---

149 [1989] SLT 531.

150 (1999) ICR 942.

151 Under the Data Protection Act 1998 a confidential reference sent to the prospective employer is exempt from disclosure by the employer who prepared it under schedule 7. However, the exemption does not apply to the prospective employer who receives the reference, so an unsuccessful candidate could try to obtain disclosure by way of a data subject access request from the prospective employer. This is not to say that the reference must be disclosed by the prospective employer to the unsuccessful candidate because the reference may contain third party data.

So there is normally no obligation under statute or the common law for the employer to provide a reference to his employees, but when he does he is under a duty of care to ensure it is accurate and fair (including any important facts about the employee) and any failure in this respect could give rise to a contractual or delictual action. Some employers insist that references are not given by their employees or, when they are given, are restricted to confirming the basis facts about the employee eg employment dates, job title. The temptation to give a particularly good reference (which is unwarranted) about an employee in order to get rid of them should be avoided because, the recipient of the reference (the employer employing them on the basis of the reference) would be able to sue for negligent misstatement in these circumstances.[152]

Incorporated terms

4.45 Incorporated terms are made part of the contract of employment by being referred to in the contract of employment, but not repeated verbatim there. Common examples include collective agreements, disciplinary and grievance procedures and pension scheme rules.

An employer should consider the consequences carefully when deciding to incorporate such documents in the contract of employment, as it can result in employees enjoying additional rights such as enhanced redundancy rights which he might not otherwise have been contractually entitled to. It is also important to note that employers who include disciplinary and grievance procedures as contractual terms risk substantial claims for damages if these are not followed and a dismissal results.[153]

Collective Agreements

4.46 The collective bargain is the outcome of collective bargaining between unions and employers. It is normally a voluntary agreement that is generally not enforceable by the union or employer, and as the

---

152 Middlemiss, S Koyabashi, T, The legal and human resource issues for employers providing references (2006) Irish Law Times Part 1 Vol. 24, No 10 p 156 and part 2 Vol 24 No11 p 172.
153 *Edwards v Chesterfield Royal Hospital NHS Foundation Trust* 2010 EWCA 571.

individual employee is a third party, and not privy to the agreement, it will not generally be enforceable by them; *see Burton Group Ltd v Smith*.[154] Under s 179 of the Trade Union Labour Relations (Consolidation) Act 1992 (TULR(C)A) 'any collective agreement shall be conclusively presumed not to have been intended by the parties to be legally enforceable unless the agreement (a) is in writing and (b) contains a provision which (however expressed) states that the parties intended that the agreement shall be a legally enforceable contract.'

So although collective agreements, and any terms and conditions agreed under it, are not normally part of the contract, a term may be incorporated into a contract of employment from a collective bargain expressly where the parties agree verbally or in writing that all or part of a particular collective agreement shall be binding upon them.[155] It may also become incorporated by implication where the parties behaviour imply an agreement between them that the agreement should become incorporated into the contract.[156] It may be difficult for the courts to be convinced that incorporation has come about in this way.

In workplaces where collective agreements apply they do still have importance as a direct or indirect source of contractual terms. However, the significant decline in trade union membership over the last twenty years has meant the influence and scope of collective bargaining and collective agreements has diminished. This has had more impact in the private sector where many traditional industries that were heavily unionised have largely disappeared (eg mining, shipbuilding) or industries where the staff were almost exclusively trade union members have been replaced by non-unionised labour (eg printing). For more on trade unions and the law see chapters 15 and 16.

VARIATION OF CONTRACTUAL TERMS

4.47 Once an employment contract is agreed between the parties and takes legal effect why would employers or (less likely) employees want to vary the terms of a contract?

---

154 (1977) IRLR 351.
155 *NCB v Galley* (1958) 1 WLR 16 CA.
156 *Alexander v Standard Telephones and Cables* (No2) [1990] ICR291.

Employers may want to vary the terms of the contract for a variety of reasons but it will often be to gain more flexibility in uncertain times brought on by changed market conditions or economic circumstances.

A contract of employment can only be varied with the agreement of both parties. This agreement could be reached with employees on an individual basis or as a group through the auspices of a collective agreement.

Employers are generally not able to unilaterally change employees' contractual terms without facing certain legal consequences (see below, eg actions under common law, or statute for breach of contract). However, employers could be able to require changes in the way employee's work where either these alterations are conditions rather than terms or even if terms, fall within the scope of the employees' implied duty of co-operation[157] or where the employer is permitted by an express contractual term to have flexibility in their work arrangements.[158]

An employer who is wishing to make changes to an employee's contract of employment should fully consult with the employee or their representative[159] and discuss any reasons for change. Agreement needs to be reached verbally or in writing (preferably recorded in writing) before variation of the contract can take place. Where a variation in the contract has been agreed, and the changes affect the terms and conditions in the written statement of particulars of employment,[160] the change must be included in the written statement and the employer should give written notification of the change to the employee within one month of the change taking effect.[161]

A contract may contain express terms which allow an employer through flexibility clauses (eg mobility clause) to make future changes in working conditions. The contract may therefore be drafted to introduce clauses that permit changes to be made within the lifetime of the contract to the

---

157 *Cresswell v Board of Inland Revenue* (1984) IRLR 190, Ch D.
158 *United Bank Ltd v Akhtar* (1989) IRLR 507, EAT, *White v Reflecting Roadstuds Ltd* (1991) IRLR 331, EAT.
159 *Rigby v Ferrodo* [1988] ICR 29.
160 Sections 1–2 of the Employment Rights Act 1996.
161 Section 4 of the Employment Rights Act 1996.

terms of the existing agreement. These clauses will only be upheld by the tribunals and courts where they are deemed to be reasonable by them.[162]

An individual contract can be varied by a collective agreement where an employer and a trade union expressly agree to it that relevant changes in terms and conditions negotiated with a trade union are incorporated.

Increasingly, employers try to introduce flexibility into express terms to allow them to make unilateral change to contractual terms in the future eg mobility clauses. If they wish to do this they must make sure that they do so in unambiguous terms.[163] If this is done then the courts are likely to enforce the clause subject to the restrictions of the implied duty of trust and confidence.[164]

A unilateral attempt by an employer to force through contractual change in the absence of agreement on the part of his or her employee would amount to a breach. What are the options for the employee in these circumstances? Where the employee fails to respond or take action (eg continues to work without objecting to the change) acceptance can be inferred from the employee's conduct.[165] Alternatively the employee can reject the new terms but continue to work under protest and then make a claim for breach of contract through the Courts. Where the contract is terminated because of an employee's refusal to accept changes to his contractual terms he can bring a claim for breach of the contract to an Employment Tribunal.[166] An employee with sufficient continuity of employment can also reject the changes, resign and perhaps claim

---

162 Employment Tribunals and courts may refer to implied terms which they believe authorise or prevent alterations of working conditions eg it would be usual for an employee to be expected to work within reasonable daily travelling distance of his or her home *Bass Leisure Ltd v Thomas* (1994) IRLR 101, EAT.

163 *Security & Facilities Division v Hayes and others* [2001] IRLR 81.

164 *Hussman manufacturing v Weir* [1998] IRLR258; *Bateman &ors v ASDA Stores Ltd* UKEAT/0221/09/ZT.

165 *Bainbridge v Circuit Foil (UK) Ltd* CA 1997 ICR 541, CA.

166 The Industrial Tribunals Extension of Jurisdiction (Scotland) Order 1994 No. 1624 To make a breach of contract claim through an Employment tribunal the contract must have been terminated. Also there is a cap of £25,000 on what a tribunal can award and restrictions on the types of claim that can be made. In addition the claim must be made within three months of the breach.

constructive dismissal. Lastly, where the change relates to a reduction in his wages he could also bring a claim under the wages legislation.[167]

In *Bateman and others v Asda Stores Ltd*,[168] Asda decided that all store staff should be on the same pay structure. This involved changing the method of remuneration of around 18,000 staff who worked under the old pay structure to payment under a new pay structure which was applicable to the vast majority of store staff. Prior to introducing the change, Asda had commenced an extensive consultation process after which 9,300 employees affected voluntarily agreed to move to the new structure, whilst the remaining (approximately 8,700) employees had their pay terms unilaterally changed.

Asda ensured that no employee suffered a reduction in pay as a result of the new structure. As justification for imposing this change without consent, Asda relied on a provision in the staff handbook which included the following statement under the heading of 'Your Contract': 'The Company reserves the right to review, revise, amend or replace the content of this handbook, and introduce new policies from time to time to reflect the changing needs of the business...' The handbook also provided that some sections of it, including those relating to pay and right to change terms, were part of the employees' contracts of employment.

When the changes were introduced 700 employees brought Employment Tribunal claims for the unlawful deduction of wages, breach of contract and in a few cases, unfair dismissal.

The EAT upheld the Employment Tribunal's decision that Asda were entitled to introduce new pay terms without the consent of their employees because they had been given the right to make changes under a statement in the staff handbook which reserved a right for Asda to make unilateral variations to the terms of contracts of employment of their employees.

The importance of this decision is that it underlines the fact that flexibility clauses that become incorporated into the contracts of employees' can be upheld provided they are applied reasonably. In this case there was consultation before the changes were introduced there was no reduction in wages resulting from the change, and the employees

167 Section 13 of the Employment Rights Act 1996.
168 [2010] IRLR 370.

had agreed to be bound by a term incorporated into their contracts which allowed the variation.

FRUSTRATION OF THE CONTRACT

4.48 Frustration occurs, or is caused, when the contract comes to an end because of circumstances which are not the fault of the parties to the contract. Examples of frustrating events include incarceration of the employee or supervening impossibility including long term illness. The rules dealing with are covered in chapter 7.

TERMINATION AND BREACH OF CONTRACT

4.49 The difference between a breach of contract and termination of a contract, is that a breach is caused by one party failing to perform his obligations, whereas in the case of termination one party, usually the employer, has intentionally brought the contract to an end. Where a breach of contract will allow the innocent party to seek a remedy at law for breach however, at common law no remedy is available when a contract is terminated unless a breach of contract has occurred by the employer such as the failure to give contractual notice where the remedy would be an action for wrongful dismissal.

Remedies for breach of contract – Employment Tribunal or Court

Employment Tribunal

4.50 Breach of contract claims can be brought before Employment Tribunals under the Industrial Tribunal Extension of Jurisdiction (Scotland) Order 1994.[169] An employment tribunal can only hear a breach-of-contract claim if the claim arises, or is outstanding, on the termination of the employee's employment. The claim must also not relate to: (a) personal injury, (b) a term imposing an obligation of confidence, (c) a term which is

---

169 SI 1994, No 1624.

a covenant in restraint of trade, (d) a term relating to intellectual property, eg copyright, moral rights, design rights, registered designs, patents and trademarks, or (e) a term either requiring you to provide the employee with living accommodation or imposing a duty relating to the provision of living accommodation.

These restrictions apply to both employee claims and employer counter-claims.

The tribunal may award an employee damages for their loss, eg a payment of arrears of wages, holiday pay or pay in lieu of notice. Any award for damages is limited to £25,000.

Otherwise a claim can be brought to Employment Tribunals under the Wages Legislation in the Employment Rights Act 1996 (as per ss 28, 64 & 135).

Court

4.51 For an employee to bring a claim while they are still employed they would normally go through the Sheriff Court (possibly under the small claims procedure, but more usually an the ordinary action in the Sheriff Court). The disadvantages are the formality and cost of a court action, but the benefits often outweigh this. As well as the fact that there is no upper limit to the damages which can be awarded by a court in an ordinary action, an important benefit is that the time limit for making a claim of breach of contract to a civil court is 5 years,[170] whereas the time limit for complaining to an Employment Tribunal is generally 3 months.[171] There are also remedies available to the court which are not available to a tribunal (see below).

In the event that an employer wants to sue his employee/s for damages, he would normally bring a claim before the Sheriff Court. However,

---

170 Prescription & Limitation (Scotland) Act 1973 introduces the concept of short negative prescription which states in general terms, an obligation (whether arising under contract or in respect of delict or breach of statutory duty) which has subsisted for a period of five years from the 'appropriate date' without any claim being made and without the subsistence of the obligation being acknowledged, is extinguished. The limitation period for bringing a similar claim in England and Wales is six years under the Limitation Act 1980.
171 Eg Action for Unfair Dismissal and unlawful deduction of wages.

employers would be able to make an application to an Employment Tribunal when it is a counterclaim in response to a breach of contract claim brought by their employee/s under the jurisdiction. Damages are only awarded for employer's actual financial loss, which may be difficult to quantify, but could include costs incurred through failure to give proper notice, eg costs of replacement staff, or loss of revenue resulting from an employee's untimely departure. Even in these circumstances employees would still have the right to be paid wages they had earned before leaving or outstanding holiday pay.

Civil Court Remedies for Breach of Contract

4.52 It is important to remember that a party can usually only enforce the terms of a contract if he himself has 'clean hands' and is prepared to abide by the contract. If a pursuer is himself in breach of contract then he may lose the right to enforce its terms against the other party.

Specific Implement and Interdicts

4.53 The primary remedy for any breach of contract in Scotland is specific implement or interdict. An order of specific implement is an order by the court ordering a party to perform an act in compliance with the contractual terms (see pension example below). An interdict is an order restraining a party from performing an act which is contrary to the contractual terms, eg acting in breach of a restrictive covenant. Specific implement is specifically excluded for certain kinds of actions. Although this restrictive measure is introduced under trade union legislation it has general application. Under s 236 of the Trade Union Labour Relations (Consolidation) Act 1992 (TULR(C)A 1992), it provides: 'no court shall, by way of (a) an order for specific implementation of a contract of employment, or (b) an interdict restraining a breach … of such a contract, compel an employee to do any work or attend any place for doing any work.' Although specific implement will not be granted to force the employee to work, or force the employer to continue to employ someone, it remains an important remedy because it can be used to force performance of other obligations under the contract of employment for example an employer could be forced to make pension contributions.

In recent years, interdicts have become an increasingly important remedy in the employment field. The courts may award an interdict or injunction to restrain a wrongful dismissal, where the trust and confidence of the employer in the employee's ability to do their job has not been harmed.

In *Pearce v City of Edinburgh Council*,[172] the Court of Session held that an employee who was suspended pending the outcome of disciplinary proceedings was entitled to seek an interdict restraining his employer from proceeding in accordance with new disciplinary procedures which were in breach of his existing contract of employment. He successfully argued earlier disciplinary arrangements were applicable in his case.

Similarly in *Anderson v Pringle Scotland*,[173] the Outer House of the Court of Session granted an interdict to prevent application of an improper disciplinary procedure and dismissal in contravention of a redundancy procedure.[174]

Interdicts are commonly granted to restrain employees from working for competitors in their own time, or restrain breaches of restrictive covenants after the employment has ceased, where failure to do so may lead to disclosure of trade secrets or confidential information.

The use of injunctions in England to restrain unlawful industrial action has become commonplace and are discussed in Chapter 16.

Interdicts take two forms, interim interdicts and final interdicts. An interim interdict is a provisional order of the court which can be granted at very short notice provided a *prima facie* case is established by the pursuer. The pursuer can ask the court for this order as soon as the writ is warranted, even before the court action has been served on the defender and the motion for interim interdict will usually be heard in chambers the same day. Unless the defender has lodged a caveat with the court, the initial hearing will be held out with the defenders presence and interim interdict will be granted if the court is satisfied that, on the balance of convenience, it is better to grant it than not (eg where an employee is being dismissed under the wrong disciplinary procedure). The interdict takes effect as soon as the defender is served with it and, after 1 week,

---

172 [1999] IRLR 417.
173 [1998] IRLR 64.
174 See also *Hughes v London Borough of Southwark* [1998] IRLR 55, QBD.

the defender has the opportunity to have the interdict recalled. This time the hearing is before both parties in front of the sheriff in chambers. Once again the test is the balance of convenience test. In a case involving breach of the implied term of good faith or a restrictive covenant, the rights of the employer A to protect his trade secrets or confidential information against his employee B, will be balanced against the B's right after leaving A's employment to earn a living working for a competitor. Whether or not the interim interdict is recalled or continued, final interdict is granted after a full hearing of the case which may not be until several months later. Often the case is settled on the basis of the decision of the court at the interim stage. A breach of interdict is a contempt of court which may result in a civil fine or, in extreme cases, imprisonment.

Dismissal and constructive dismissal

4.54 A remedy for a serious breach of contract is recission which allows the innocent party to set the contract aside. In the context of the employment relationship this means that if the employee is in serious breach of contract the employer can dismiss him without notice (summary dismissal). If the employer is in serious breach of contract, the employee can resign and claim constructive or wrongful dismissal. A wrongful dismissal is a dismissal which is a breach of contract. Both of these remedies are almost always combined with a claim for damages. This is discussed in detail in chapter 7.

Damages

4.55 Both employers and employees can be in breach of a contract of employment so either can claim damages as recompense for their loss. Damages are intended to put the claimant back in the position he would have been in if the breach had not occurred. The damages that are recoverable are those flowing naturally from the breach, provided that it is reasonable at the time they made the contract the parties would have been aware that such damages were the likely consequence of such a breach. Damages are intended to be compensatory rather than punitive, therefore it is important that the pursuer can prove real financial loss, eg failure to pay wages or other economic loss. The pursuer is expected to take action to mitigate loss, eg by looking for another job. General damages are any damages which were reasonably foreseeable at the time the contract was entered into. Special damages are only recoverable if the other party was made aware of them being payable prior to the contract being entered into. Damages for breach of contract in an employment case are often limited to wages or loss which would have been incurred during the contractual period of notice (or statutory period of notice if greater), because the parties could have terminated the contract lawfully by giving notice at any time. This is not always the case. There are many situations where the parties will be able to recover losses in excess of this and some examples are considered below.

A breach of disciplinary or grievance procedures which form a contractual term will amount to a breach of contract and, in *Edwards v Chesterfield Royal Hospital NHS Foundation Trust*,[175] the court decided that damages were not restricted to the notice period but could include damages for damage to the employees reputation and career which in this case amounted to over £4 Million.

If the employee is in breach of contract, for example by negligent performance of his duties, then the employer (and indeed a third party who has suffered loss) will be entitled to any damages which were foreseeable. Similarly, breach of a restrictive covenant or duty of loyalty may result in substantial damages.

It is also possible for a breach of contract (usually the duty to take reasonable care for the employee's safety) to result in physical or psychiatric injury, and solatium will be awarded if this is the case.

Double recovery is not possible. It is not possible to recover damages for the manner of dismissal as common law does not imply into the contract of employment that the employer will act fairly when dismissing the employee. Unfair dismissal is a statutory creature and has a specific statutory remedy.[176] It is possible to recover damages for conduct which amounts to a breach of contract where there is also a dismissal, but only if the breach of contract can be separated from the dismissal itself in which case a claim for breach of contract can be made.[177] Examples could be a

---

175 [2010] EWCA Civ 571.
176 *Johnson v Unisys* [2001] ICR 480.
177 *Eastwood v Magnox Electric plc* [2004] ICR 1064.

breach of the implied term of trust and confidence where the employee has been subjected to a campaign of bullying resulting in psychiatric damage before a constructive dismissal took place, or a breach of contractual disciplinary procedures resulting in damage to reputation or career prospects before the final dismissal.

Lien and retention

4.56 At common law a party who is owed money by someone in connection with a contract can, without going to the trouble of obtaining a court order, exercise personal remedies against the other party. Therefore, an employee who is owed money by his employer can retain any property belonging to his employer which is lawfully in his possession (lien). The employee can also withhold any payments due by him to the employer in terms of the contract until his employer performs his contractual obligations. These remedies are not usually available to the employer because they would amount to an unlawful deduction from wages.

Declarator

4.57 Often sought in conjunction with legal remedies a declarator is simply a judgment of the court deciding and declaring the factual or legal position.

Chapter 5

Legal Rights of Atypical Workers

5.1 The tests applied by the tribunal, or court, to determine if someone is an employee or not are discussed in chapter 4. These tests apply to atypical workers and therefore this chapter should be read in conjunction with chapter 4. We will now go on to look in more depth at the issues raised by atypical working, and the application of the tests to such workers and the statutory protections afforded specifically to them. It should also be borne in mind that the majority of atypical workers are women and, therefore, to treat someone less favourably because of their atypical status may, in certain circumstances, amount to discrimination on the ground of sex. This is a topic which is discussed more fully in chapter 8.

ATYPICAL EMPLOYMENT

5.2 'Atypical employment' is an umbrella term[1] that is used by commentators to describe employment practices which deviate from traditional, standard, forms of contract in employment. Atypical work refers to employment relationships not conforming to the standard, or 'typical', model of full-time, regular, open-ended employment with a single employer over a long time span. The latter, in turn, is defined as a socially secure, full-time job of unlimited duration, with standard working hours, guaranteeing a regular income and, via social security systems geared towards wage earners, securing pension payments and protection against ill-health and unemployment.

As the following research results show, full-time employment is still the predominant type of arrangement that applies in the UK, but it looks unlikely this will always be the case. In the 2009 Labour Force Survey, employment status amongst workers in the UK was made up as follows: All persons in employment were 28,927,000 and, of these, 24,844.000

---

1 Sometimes referred to as marginal or precarious employment.

were employees and, of those, 18,327, 000 were full-time employees. There were 7,664,000 part time employees/workers, and there were 107,000 Government trainees.

Atypical working arrangements can differ from standard employment in: the number of hours worked; the place of work; the contracted term of work, or the way work is allocated, and controlled. Many casual or atypical workers are excluded from legal protection, because of the contract under which they work. 'Employees' have better rights than 'workers' who, in turn, have better rights than the 'self employed'. Groups such as casual workers, sessional workers, agency workers, homeworkers, and others, are vulnerable to exploitation under this system.

> 'The development of 'complex employment relationships', which flourish on the theoretical freedom of the people in the labour market to make contracts of their choice, has added to the difficulty of deciding whether an individual, doing paid work for another, does so under a contract of service…'[2]

Background to use of atypical workers

5.3 Globalisation, the spread of information technology, the shift from the manufacturing sector to the service sector, and the desire of employers for more casual and responsive ways of working, have created a new economy that emphasizes flexibility in the marketplace, and in employment relationships. These influences have resulted in the increase of women in the workplace, as well as the rise in atypical work. In 1997/98 the Labour Force Survey found that there were 1.7 million temporary workers (6.5% of all workers); 868,000 fixed term (3.3) 324,000 in casual employment (1.2) 222,000 agency supplied temp workers (0.9) 180,000 zero hours workers (0.7) 621,000 homeworking (2.4) and 3.2. million self-employed. Some of these figures are now much higher. For example in 2005/6 there were 7, 324,000 part time workers, and of those 1,668,0000 were men and 5, 655,000 were women. At the same time there were only 1,409,000 temporary workers.[3] In 2011 there was a total of 29,119,000

---

2   Mummery LJ in *Dacas v Brook Street Bureau* (UK) Ltd (2003) IRLR 190.
3   Source ONS Labour Force Survey 2006 www.ons.gov.uk.

people in employment and of those 24,790,000 were employees. There were 7,848,000 people working part-time and of those 6,580,000 were employees. Of people in part-time employment 1,459,000 were men and 5,120,000 were women. Finally there were 1,553,000 temporary workers.[4]

Types of atypical workers

5.4

- Casual Workers
- Temporary Workers
- Agency Workers
- Fixed-term Workers
- Part-time Workers
- Trainees

Employment status

5.5 Many organisations engage a variety of workers under different forms of contract. These include: (a) employees engaged under 'traditional' contracts of employment, (b) contractors engaged directly by the 'employer', who are designed as self employed, and paid gross on a 'day rate' basis, (c) individuals who provide their services through their own limited companies primarily for tax purposes, and (d) agency workers who are not contracted directly but rather to a third party agency, who in turn enters into a commercial arrangement with the end user etc. Businesses may have very good reasons for engaging individuals under different forms of arrangement and, indeed, there may be advantages to the worker.

Legal protection of atypical workers

5.6 From an employment law perspective, the key issue is the status of individuals who are engaged in atypical working arrangements. Although workers may be engaged using different forms of contract, the employer, for good business reasons, will often integrate such workers into the

---

4   Source ONS Labour Force Survey 2011 www.ons.gov.uk.

organisation, and manage and control them in the same way as it does with its direct employees. This makes it difficult to recognise the workers true legal status.

The crucial issue is whether or not an individual working on these basis is or is not an employee, as many employment rights apply to employees only (eg right to claim unfair dismissal or redundancy). The definition of employees and workers in s 230 (1) of the Employment Rights Act 1996 are not very helpful.[5] More recent legislation has extended rights, to workers, although there is still a lack of clarity over who is entitled to them.[6] The term 'worker' covers employees, but also covers individuals who do not have a contract of employment but who, nevertheless, contract to supply their services to the employer and to some degree, are economically dependent on the employer's business. What follows is detailed consideration of the way in which the tests, considered in chapter 4, have been applied to the various forms of atypical worker, starting with the most contentious, agency workers.

AGENCY WORKERS

5.7 Until the Agency Workers Regulations, that were introduced in the UK in 2010,[7] there was little law that covered this category of worker. What statute law there was, namely, the Employment Agencies Act 1973; Conduct of Employment Agencies and Employment Businesses Regulations 1976 and Conduct of Employment Agencies and Business Regulation 2003,[8] failed to address the key issues surrounding this type of employment. The Agency Workers Regulations that were introduced, in compliance with EU requirements,[9] will have some impact through

---

5 Powers were given to the Secretary of State under s 23 of the Employment Relations Act 1999 to extend coverage of employment rights beyond employees or workers but to date these are unused.

6 Examples are the National Minimum Wage Act 1998, Working Time Regulations 1998.

7 SI 2010/ 93.

8 Under the Conduct of Employment Agencies and Business Regulation 2003 agencies must provide clients with a warranty of competency for temporary staff. There is sometimes a need for screening or assessing skills preparation for health and safety for certain jobs and this is incumbent on agencies.

9 Directive on Temporary Agency Work 2008/104/EC.

introducing new rights for agency workers. But, what has proven to be the thorny issue is the status of these workers, and who their employers are, and this has not been dealt with by the Regulations. It has accordingly been up to the judiciary (most significantly the Court of Session in Scotland and the Court of Appeal in England), through their decisions in various cases, to try and resolve this issue.

Status and nature of employment of agency workers

5.8 A case that illustrates the difficulty is *Motorola Ltd v Davidson.*[10] Mr Davidson was placed by an agency to repair mobile phones for Motorola and he worked for them for two years. He was then suspended, and had his contracted terminated, over a disciplinary issue. He claimed unfair dismissal citing Motorola as his employer. There was a high degree of control exercised over Mr Davidson's work by them, and he was subject to Motorola's disciplinary procedures. The Employment Tribunal upheld his claim, and the EAT rejected the employer's appeal. In a case with similar facts, *Montgomery v Johnson Underwood Ltd,*[11] the Court of Appeal reached the same conclusion as the EAT in *Motorola*. In *Dacas v Brook Street Bureau Ltd,*[12] Ms Dacas was registered with BSB for six years and, during that time, worked for a single client. Her contract stipulated it was not to be treated as an employment relationship. The employment tribunal held she was not an employee of either employer however, on appeal to the EAT, it was decided she was an employee of BSB. The case went on appeal to the Court of Appeal,[13] where it was held that Dacas was not an employee of the agency. However, they also held it was not credible to find that an agency worker was not an employee of either the agency or the client. The court was of the opinion that, in most cases, agency workers will be employed by the client/end user under an implied contract of service. In *Franks v Reuters CA,*[14] Franks was supplied as a driver through an agency to Reuters for a period of six years. The employment

---

10 (2001) IRLR 4.
11 (2001) IRLR 269.
12 (2003) IRLR 190.
13 *Dacas v BSB* (2004) IRLR 358.
14 (2003) IRLR 423.

tribunal held he was not an employee of Reuters. However, the Court of Appeal decided he could be an employee of Reuters, and remitted the case back to the employment tribunal. There was the possibility of an implied contract of employment between Franks and Reuters and documentation, or a lack of documentation, in place (as in this case) was only one factor to be considered. Also they held that the background circumstances, and how parties operate in practice, could be important. In *Muscat v Cable & Wireless*,[15] the applicant was employed by a company, but was treated as a contractor, and required to provide services through an agency, and the agency paid the claimant's salary. The Court of Appeal, following *Dacas*, said there was an implied contract of employment between the worker and the client company.

In *Craigie v Haringey*,[16] Justice Bean declined to follow the Court of Appeal's decision in the *Dacas* case, on the ground that he preferred to focus on the more traditional 'necessity' test for implying a contract. He upheld the tribunal's decision that there was no 'necessity' to imply a contract of employment between the agency worker and the end-user. The EAT commented that the law on agency workers was unsatisfactory but, that it needed legislation to change it. The EAT, in two separate judgments,[17] deconstructed the Court of Appeal's reasoning in *Dacas* and the other agency worker cases. First, in *Heatherwood & Wexham Park Hospitals NHS Trust v Kulubowila & ors*,[18] the EAT pointed out that: 'It is not enough to form the view that because the Claimant looked like an employee of the Trust, acted like an employee and was treated like an employee, the business reality is that he was an employee and the employment tribunal must, therefore, imply a contract of employment'. It was held that, where the affairs of the parties are as consistent with the express arrangement (ie a triangular agreement), it cannot be said that it is necessary to infer a contract of service between end-user and worker. In *Astbury v Gist*,[19] the EAT convincingly demonstrated the error implicit in the comment of Lord Justice Sedley in *Dacas*, that: 'the conclusion

---

15 (2006) EWCA Civ 220.
16 Appeal No UKEAT/0556/06/JOJ.
17 Both decisions of HHJ Peter Clark.
18 [2007] UKEAT 0633_06_2903 (29 March 2007).
19 (2005) All ER (D) 165 (Apr).

of the employment tribunal that Mrs Dacas was employed by nobody is simply not credible'. HHJ Peter Clark demonstrated precisely how the statutory framework does allow for someone in Mrs Dacas's position to be employed by nobody.

The significant change needed in the law came about in *James v Greenwich Borough Council*,[20] when the Court of Appeal tried to resolve the question of whether agency workers can became employees of the client or end-user. A large number of tribunal cases were stayed pending this decision, pursuant to the President's Practice Direction. However, the Court of Appeal had not grappled with what many believed to be the conflicting authorities on this. Instead, it asserted that no conflict exists and that all the authorities point the same way. The correct approach, according to the Court, is for an employment tribunal to decide, as a question of fact, whether it is necessary to imply a contractual relationship between agency worker and end-user. As a question of fact, it should not be reviewed by an appellate court unless a clear error of law exists. Is it necessary to imply a contractual relationship between agency worker and end-user? The mere passage of time is not sufficient to require any such implication. Tribunals should only imply contracts in situations when it could point to 'some words or conduct' to show that the worker was working 'not pursuant to the agency arrangements but, because of mutual obligations, binding worker and end user which are incompatible with those arrangements.' Thus, there would need to be, in the employer's choice of agency worker, a demonstrable need for their particular attributes or skills (*delectus personae*).

This decision, in this case, was generally regarded as a definitive statement on this aspect of the law, but must now be read in light of the decision of the Supreme Court in *Autoclenz Ltd v Belcher*,[21] which is discussed in chapter 4.[22]

---

20 (2008) EWCA Civ 35.
21 [2011] UKSC41; [2011] IRLR 820.
22 Middlemiss, S Legal Impact on Employers where there is a *Sham* Element in Contracts with their Workers, International Journal of Law and Management, (2012) Vol. 54 3 Published May 2012.

Directive on Temporary Agency Work

5.9 The implementation in the UK of Directive 2008/104/EC, on Temporary Agency Work, was achieved through the Agency Workers Regulations 2010/93.[23] The main purpose of the Agency Worker Directive (AWD) was to ensure the appropriate protection of temporary agency workers, through the application of the principle of equal treatment, and to address unnecessary restrictions and prohibitions on the use of agency work. Under the Directive, 'equal treatment' relates only to basic working and employment conditions of temporary agency workers (eg pay, working time). However, the Directive does not affect the employment status of temporary workers.

Agency Workers Regulations 2010/93

5.10 The Agency Worker Regulations, apply when one organization supplies labour to another organization in return for a fee, based on the work performed by the agency worker for the 'hirer'.[24] The agency is engaged in the economic activity of supplying workers for temporary assignments (whether or not for profit), so the agency supplies labour rather than an end product. The Regulations would not apply to organisations, such as recruitment agents, who provide an introductory service by matching job applicants to job vacancies.

Under Regulation 3(1), the meaning of an agency worker is defined as an: individual who (a) is supplied by a temporary work agency to work temporarily for, and under, the supervision and direction of a hirer; and (b) has a contract with the temporary work agency which is (i) a contract of employment with the agency, or (ii) any other contract to perform work and services personally for the agency. The Regulations do not apply where the agency is, in fact, a client of the individual worker.

---

23 The European Commission estimated that over three million temporary agency workers currently working across the EU will benefit from better protection of their working conditions.

24 Under Regulation 2 'hirer' means a person engaged in economic activity, public or private, whether or not operating for profit, to whom individuals are supplied, to work temporarily for and under the supervision and direction of that person.

Equal rights

5.11 Under Regulations 5 and 6 it affords agency workers two categories of rights to equal treatment. Firstly, those rights that apply from the first day they are placed with the hirer (Day 1 Rights) and, secondly, those rights that apply after they have accrued 12 weeks' continuous service with the hirer (Week 12 Rights).

Day 1 Rights

5.12 From the first day that an agency worker is assigned by the agency to the hirer, the hirer must, under Regulation 12, provide the agency worker with (i) access to on-site collective facilities and amenities (such as use of the: canteen, rest rooms, on-site gym etc) and, under Regulation 13, (ii) information about all relevant vacancies in the hirer's organisation.

Week 12 Rights

5.13 If an agency worker has worked for the same hirer for 12 calendar weeks,[25] he qualifies for equal treatment with individuals directly hired by the hirer as regards relevant terms and conditions. Under Regulation 6 (1), 'relevant terms and conditions' means terms and conditions relating to (a) pay;[26] (b) the duration of working time; (c) night work; (d) rest periods; (e) rest breaks; and (f) annual leave.

The definition of pay under Regulation 6 is wide, and includes bonuses that relate to performance or quality of work. However, under Regulation 6 (3), certain types of payments are not included. Those payments or rewards are: (a) any payment by way of occupational sick pay; (b) any payment by way of a pension, allowance or gratuity in connection with the worker's retirement, or as compensation for loss of office; (c) any payment in respect of maternity, paternity or adoption leave; (d) any payment referable to the worker's redundancy; (e) any payment or reward, made pursuant to a financial participation scheme; (f) any bonus, incentive

---

25 The 12 week period applies to the agency worker working for the hirer, regardless of what agency supplied the worker so two or more agencies could have supplied their services over the 12 week period.
26 As defined at length in Regulation 6.

payment or reward which is not directly attributable to the amount or quality of the work done by a worker, and which is given to a worker for a reason other than the amount or quality of work done, such as to encourage the worker's loyalty, or to reward the worker's long-term service; (g) any payment for time off; (h) a guarantee payment under s 28 of the 1996 Act; (i) any payment by way of an advance under an agreement for a loan, or by way of an advance of pay; (j) any payment in respect of expenses incurred by the worker in carrying out the employment; and (k) any payment to the worker otherwise than in that person's capacity as a worker.

Some breaks within the 12-week period restart the accrual process for establishing the continuity of service needed for entitlement to these rights, eg if the worker moves to a substantively different role within the hirer's organisation, or the worker is supplied to a different hirer.[27] An agency worker, who accrues the requisite 12 weeks' service, may claim equal pay with a comparable individual who was directly hired by the employer.

The Week 12 rights are enforceable, under Regulation 14, by workers against the agency not the hirer. As a result agencies are likely to contractually oblige hirers to monitor the periods for which individuals are placed within their organisations, regardless of whether those individuals are supplied by that particular agency for the whole period of their work for the hirer. This could also mean that agencies increase the fees they charged to cover the risks to them of claims under the Regulations, and agencies are likely to require hirers to indemnify them for any such risk.

In order to aid agency workers in enforcing these rights, Regulation 16 imposes an obligation on both the agency and the hirer to supply information to the agency worker (within 28 days of his request), regarding terms and conditions of directly-hired workers in the hirer's organisation, whose work is comparable to that performed by the agency worker.

Regulation 17 makes provision in relation to the right not to be unfairly dismissed or subjected to a detriment for a reason relating to these Regulations. Regulation 18 provides remedies for individuals, including compensation, by way of proceedings in employment tribunals. Regulation

---

27 Regulation 8.

18 includes provision for a minimum award of two weeks' pay, and for an additional award of up to £5,000 where Regulation 9 applies.

Some hirers may decide that in order to get around the Regulations, they will only use agency workers for less than 12 weeks where this is feasible. However, repeating such practices, or moving workers between different jobs, will not pose a viable means of avoiding the Regulations, because of Regulation 9. Any 'structure of assignments', such as placing agency workers on a series of 11 week contracts or varying their roles every few weeks, is prohibited and may also attract additional financial penalty in the form of a fine of up to £5,000.

Liability

5.14 The hirer is liable for breaches of Day 1 Rights, and he has a defence if he can show that the difference in treatment was objectively justified. As already noted the agency is liable for breaches of Week 12 Rights, and it can defend this action by calling into question whether the directly engaged worker, chosen as a comparator by the agency worker, is actually doing comparable work. Secondly, it can show that it took 'reasonable steps' to obtain relevant information from the hirer about employment terms, ordinarily included for the hirer's comparable, directly-engaged workers but was refused. In the latter case, the liability would then shift to the hirer.

Where Week 12 rights have been breached, agency workers can choose to bring claims for damages in the employment tribunal against either the agency or the hirer, because, they might not know whether the liability for these Week 12 rights has shifted. In determining any award, the tribunal will consider matters such as the seriousness of the breach, and any financial loss caused to the agency worker. Besides awarding compensation, the tribunal can also make declarations or recommendations for action to be taken by the party at fault.

Unfair dismissal and the right not to be subjected to detriment

5.15 Under Regulation 17(1) an agency worker who is an employee and is dismissed shall be regarded as unfairly dismissed if the reason (or, if more than one, the principal reason) for the dismissal is a reason specified in paragraph (3). Also under Regulation 17 (2), an agency worker has the right not to be subjected to any detriment by, or as a result of, any act, or any deliberate failure to act, of a temporary work agency or the hirer, done on a ground specified in paragraph (3).

Paragraph (3) reasons or, as the case may be, grounds are stated as follows:

> '(a) that the agency worker (i) brought proceedings under these Regulations; (ii) gave evidence or information in connection with such proceedings brought by any agency worker; (iii) made a request under Regulation 16 for a written statement; (iv) otherwise did anything, under these Regulations, in relation to a temporary work agency, hirer, or any other person; (v) alleged that a temporary work agency or hirer has breached these Regulations; (vi) refused (or proposed to refuse) to forgo a right conferred by these Regulations; or (b) that the hirer or a temporary work agency believes or suspects that the agency worker has done, or intends to do, any of the things mentioned in sub-paragraph (a).'

CASUAL OR TEMPORARY WORKERS

5.16 With respect to casual and temporary workers, employment law does not recognise such categorisations. The considerations that apply here are, are they employees or sub contractors? In *O'Kelly v Trust House Forte plc*,[28] involving the employment of casual labour the lack of mutuality of obligation between the parties was a key element in that case. Following this decision; home workers, agency workers, zero-hours contract workers and workers in casualised trades or occupations, have been held not to be employees due to lack of mutuality of obligation. In *Clark v Oxfordshire Health Authority*,[29] a bank nurse who had no fixed or regular contact hours was only offered work when temporary work arose. The relevant conditions of service stipulated that bank nurses were not regular employees and had no right to guaranteed or continuous work

---

28 (1983) IRLR.
29 (1998) IRLR 125.

(zero-hours worker). The Court of Appeal held that she was not working under a contract of service, because of the lack of mutual obligation.

In circumstances where employees are working under a series of contracts, with substantial gaps between them, they may struggle ever to get the continuous employment necessary to qualify for certain employment rights. 'Even if an individual can show that he or she was employed as an employee for the purposes of a particular task or job, or for a particular period of time, they may be unable to show they have a global or umbrella contract which spans the gaps between periods of work'.[30]

However, in *North Wales Probation Area v Edwards*,[31] the claimant was placed on a list of relief hostel workers, after signing a document entitled 'Relief Hostel Worker Contract' which set out terms and conditions, under which, the respondent offered 'sessional employment'. Relief hostel workers could decline to work any particular shift, or could make arrangements for another relief hostel worker to cover the shift for them. The EAT held that the Tribunal Chairman did not err in law in finding that, when the claimant worked a session, she did so pursuant to a contract of employment for that session. But, not during the periods when Mrs Edwards did not attend work. Mrs Edwards was, therefore, an employee for the purposes of the Disability Discrimination Act 1995, and could bring a claim for disability discrimination, for which no continuity of employment is required.

The following quote neatly summarises the position of casual or seasonal workers under the law.

'Many casual or seasonal workers, such as waiters or fruit pickers or casual building labourers, will periodically work for the same employer, but often neither party has any obligations to the other in the gaps or intervals between engagements. There is no reason in logic or justice, why the lack of worker status in the gaps should have any bearing on the status when working. There may be no overarching or umbrella contract and, therefore, no employment status in the gaps, but that does not preclude such a status during the period of work. If casual and seasonal workers were to be denied worker status when actually

---

30 The Employment Status of Individuals in Non Standard Employment, Burchell, Deakin and Honey, March 1999 para 2.4, see www.bis.govuk
31 UKEAT/0468/07/RN.

working, because of their lack of any such status when not working, that would remove the protection of minimum wage and other basic protections from the groups of workers most in need of it.'[32]

DEPENDENT SELF-EMPLOYED

5.17 'Dependent self-employed' are ostensibly self employed, but only work for one employer and are dependent on them for work. What kind of status do these people have? They could fall within the statutory definition of 'worker' for the purpose of various pieces of legislation. Dependent self-employed could be freelance workers, sole traders, home workers and casual workers of various kinds.

SELF-EMPLOYED CONTRACTOR

5.18 A requirement of personal service is essential in an employment contract and therefore a contract which permits a substitute to undertake the work (unless a sham clause) could not be a contract of employment and therefore would have to be a contract for services, or a consultancy agreement. A 'self-employed' contractor would be expected to work autonomously and not be integrated into the organisational structure. Self-employed contractors are not normally part and parcel of the organisation, and would normally work for a number of customers. They usually carry out self-contained tasks and undertake work that is ancillary to the main activities of the employer and not similar to the work of other employees. Therefore, a self-employed contractor, who has previously been an employee of an organisation, and is returning to carry out the same role in a 'consultancy capacity', which often happens, is very unlikely to be genuinely self-employed.[33] Where appropriate, self-employed contractors provide their own equipment and tools and possibly have their own premises. They often incur financial risk of profit or loss, and the method of their receiving pay and being taxed would be relevant factors.

---

32 *James v Redcats (Brands) Ltd* (2007) IRLR 296 Justice Elias, Para 84.
33 This is common in legal profession.

FIXED TERM WORKERS

5.19 The Council Directive on Fixed Term Work 99/70/EC was implemented in the UK by the Fixed Term Employees (Prevention of Less Favourable Treatment) Regulations.[34] The Regulations came into force in July 2002 and, prior to this, there was no statutory regulation of these contracts.

What is fixed term contract? It is one that provides a specified term of employment and terminates automatically at the end of that term. It can still be a fixed term contract even if there is a term in the contract that allows the parties to terminate by giving notice before the full term expires.[35] If the contract contains no right to prior termination (before the fixed term is complete) where employer does so summarily, the worker has the right to claim damages for breach of contract. Also under s 95 (1) of the Employment Rights Act 1996, it states that where an employee is dismissed when fixed term expires, without being renewed, they may be able to claim unfair dismissal where it is reasonable to continue the contract and the employer fails to do so. They can also claim redundancy pay, provided they have two year continuous employment with the same employer.[36] Contracts for a specific task, purpose or event are extended the same rights as workers on permanent contract and fixed term workers, and termination of these kind of contracts may entitle the worker (with sufficient continuous service) to make a claim for unfair dismissal.

The Fixed Term Employees (Prevention of Less Favourable Treatment) Regulations,[37] aimed to establish minimum requirements and general principles which should apply to fixed term work. Under Regulation 2, it is unlawful to subject to less favourable treatment any part time worker in respect of the terms of his contract, or him being subjected to any other detriment by any act or failure to act by his employer. The right not to be treated less favourably than others is not absolute, but employers must

---

34 SI 2002/2034.
35 *Dixon v BBC* (1979) ICR 281(CA).
36 Redundancy waiver was abolished under the Regulations by repeal of s 197 of the Employment Rights Act.
37 SI 2002/2034.

justify different treatment on objective grounds.[38] The comparators are those employed by the same employer as a permanent employee and engaged in same, or broadly similar, work, at the same establishment. Importantly, permanent staff must not enjoy preferential treatment for promotion or redundancy, unless objectively justifiable. If a fixed-term employee feels less favourably treated because of their employment status, or believes their rights have been infringed, they can request a written statement from an employer that should detail the reasons for the difference. This must be produced within 21 days of the request. It is unfair dismissal if the principal reason for dismissal was one set out in Regulation 5(4) namely that: fixed term employee has brought proceedings; has requested a written statement of reasons, or has alleged that the employer has infringed the Regulations. Under Regulation 8, the use of successive fixed term contracts beyond four years is unlawful unless it can be objectively justified, or a workplace or collective agreement has agreed otherwise. If a fixed term contract is renewed in breach of the limitation, the term of the contract limiting it to fixed term will be invalid, and the contract will be regarded as permanent.

In *Impact v Minister for Agriculture and Food (Ireland),*[39] the ECJ handed down an important judgement dealing with fixed term contracts. They decided that non-discrimination rules in the Fixed Term Workers Directive have direct effect, meaning they can be enforced directly irrespective of the national laws.[40] They also decided that the rules protecting against the abuse of fixed term workers by the use of successive fixed term contracts, do not have direct effect but the national law should be interpreted consistently with the Directive, if at all possible.[41] Finally, they decided that the principle of non discrimination against fixed term workers extends to pension entitlement. This will cause difficulty for employers who have, in the past, treated fixed term employees differently for pension purposes, or excluded them from their pension schemes altogether.

---

38 Less favourable treatment will be justified on objective grounds if you can show that it is necessary and appropriate to achieve a legitimate and genuine business objective.
39 (2008) IRLR 552.
40 Paras 59–68.
41 Para 80 and para 104.

PART TIME WORKERS

5.20 The Part-time Workers (Prevention of Less Favourable Treatment) Regulations 2000,[42] introduced new rights for part-time employees and workers. Part-time workers represent a sizeable part of the workforce. In Apr-Jun 2006 there were 7,339,000 persons in part-time employment in the UK. With the recession, and cuts in employment, the size of the population of part time workers looks set to increase (see para 5.3).

Under a contract of employment, they have pro-rata contractual rights. The Part-time Workers Regulations 2000 ensured that Britain's part-timers are not treated less favourably than comparable full-timers in their terms and conditions, unless it is objectively justified. This means part-timers are entitled, for example, to the same: hourly rate of pay; access to company pension schemes, entitlements to annual leave, and maternity/parental leave, on a pro rata basis, entitlement to contractual sick pay, and no less favourable treatment in terms of access to training, promotion and redundancy rights. Under the Part-Time Workers Regulations,[43] individual part-timers were allowed to compare themselves to a full-time colleague, irrespective of whether either party's contract is permanent or fixed-term. However, the EAT has handed down its decision in *Carl v The University of Sheffield*,[44] which is the authority for the following propositions. A claimant seeking to establish unlawful less favourable treatment under the Regulations, must be able to point to a real comparator who amounts to a 'comparable full-time worker' under Regulation 2(4). Under clause 3.2 of the Part Time Worker Directive 97/81/EC, it was not a requirement that a hypothetical comparator is available to claimant who is a part-time worker. Also they found that it is not necessary that the treatment was only on the ground of part-time status.[45] The EAT held that part-time working must be the effective and predominant cause of the less favourable treatment complained of, but need not be the only cause.[46] This case has reinforced,

---

42 Implemented the Part Time Work Directive 97/81/EC.
43 From 1 October 2002.
44 EAT/0261/08.
45 Rejecting the approach in *Gibson v Scottish Ambulance Service* EATS/0052/04 (which focused on the presence of the word 'solely' in the Directive) and preferring the decision in *Sharma v Manchester City Council*, (2008) IRLR 336)
46 Para 42

and confirmed, the position that part-time workers must be able to point to an actual full-time worker as a comparator. This will present an unfair challenge for part-time workers in small organisations because identifying a full-time worker carrying out the same or broadly similar work will be difficult. However, once a claimant has identified an actual comparator, an employment tribunal panel may take into account hypothetical comparators in considering why the claimant was treated less favourably. Since the Part-Time Workers Regulations (unlike the Fixed-Term Regulations) apply, both to employees and to non-employees/workers, the new possibilities of comparison under the Part-Time Regulations are available to both categories of individual. In 2002, of the six million part-timer workers in the United Kingdom at that time, only one million had a full-time equivalent working under the same type of contract.[47] With respect to enforcement of the Regulations, an employer, or agent of the employer, will be liable for anything done by an employee in the course of his employment. There is a defence for an employer if they can establish they have taken all reasonable steps to prevent the worker doing the act in the course of his employment. There is the right not to be dismissed or suffer a detriment as a result of exercising any rights under the legislation, and to receive written reasons from employer for less favourable treatment. The tribunal can award damages, although not for injury to feelings, and employment tribunals can make recommendations for action by the employer to correct any fault on their part.

TRAINEES

5.21 Where trainees are 'relevant trainees', in other words working under a government sponsored, or government supported, training scheme,[48] they are treated as workers for the purposes of certain legislation, eg Working Time Regulations, National Minimum Wage Act, although they are not entitled to other employment rights. Other trainees, such as students on a course at university undertaking a placement (sandwich course), have

---

47 *England v Governing Body of Turnford School* (2003) All ER (D) 105 (May).
48 Eg Work Based Learning for young people (aged 16–18), the Apprenticeship Programme and the New Deal.

limited employment rights,[49] as they are deemed to be working under a contract of training. However all trainees will have some protection under health and safety legislation, eg s 3 of the Health and Safety at Work Act 1974, which imposes a duty on the occupier or controller of premises to take care of the safety of everyone present in the workplace. In Apr-Jun 2006, there were 95,000 Government trainees and in 2011 there were 96,000. With respect to the National Minimum Wage trainees, working under Government employment programmes may not be entitled to the NMW if the government employment programme is meant to provide the trainee with training, or work experience, or to help them to obtain or look for work.[50]

VOLUNTARY WORKERS

5.22 Voluntary Workers are in a similar position to casual workers, whereby their contractual status depends on the nature of the agreed terms and conditions. They may or may not work under a contract of service or be treated as a worker. In *Gradwell v Council for Voluntary Service*,[51] where someone was employed subject to a 'volunteer agreement', it was held that a contract had not been created. In *South-east Sheffield CAB v Grayson*,[52] an EAT decision was that, for the purposes of the Disability Discrimination Act 1995,[53] volunteers should not be considered to be employees. The crucial question in this case was whether the volunteer agreement imposed a contractual obligation upon the CAB to provide work for the volunteer to do and, upon the volunteer personally to do the work, such that if this did not happen, a breach of contract situation were theoretically possible. The work expected of the volunteers was voluntary and there was no contractual remedy against them if they withdrew their labour. Therefore, they were not employed within the meaning of

---

49 They could have protection against the various types of discrimination under the Equality Act.
50 Middlemiss, S The Legal Liability of Employers for Trainees, Journal of Education and Law, Vol 15, No 2/3 2003 p 115.
51 (1997) COIT 2404314/97.
52 (2004) IRLR 253.
53 Now the Equality Act 2010.

the Disability Discrimination Act 1995.[54] In *X v Mid Sussex CAB*,[55] the EAT ruled that volunteers were not covered by the term 'occupation' in the European Framework Directive, for the purpose of protection from disability discrimination. The Claimant was a volunteer part-time advisor at the CAB. She had no contract and left in circumstances which, she alleged, amounted to discrimination on grounds of her disability. She argued she was protected by the EU Directive, and that the DDA 1995 should be 'read down' to provide that protection.

Burton J, in the EAT, held that her claim should be struck out. He held that 'employment' in the Directive requires a material contract between the parties. He observed there was no jurisprudence to suggest that 'occupation' meant unpaid employment. Also, he held that the Directive offered protection only in relation to 'access' to occupation. He held the Directive was not intended to protect volunteers in the Claimant's position, and declined to make a reference to the ECJ on the point. As can be seen, mutuality of obligation can be a key element for tribunals in deciding on the rights of voluntary workers.

If a voluntary worker is accepted by a tribunal as an employee or worker, they would be entitled to normal statutory rights applicable to their status. Otherwise rights will not be available to them. If voluntary workers are undergoing a high level of training, they could be working under a contract for training. Importantly voluntary workers are an exempt category of worker for purposes under s 44 of the National Minimum Wage. As volunteers are not entitled to be paid the National Minimum Wage, they should receive no more than limited expenses[56] and benefits in kind. Volunteers' expenses are free of tax and examples of expenses which volunteers could receive (but which the Revenue would not allow for employees, because they would fail the test of s 198, of the Income and Corporation Taxes Act 1988), include babysitting costs, costs of enablers for the disabled while on volunteer duty, holiday cancellation costs, and long service awards (when paid outside of the exemption

---

54 In *X v Mid Sussex CAB* [2010] IRLR 722 the EAT ruled that volunteers were not covered by the term 'occupation' in the European Framework Directive for the purpose of protection from disability discrimination.

55 (2010) IRLR 722.

56 Including expenses for home-to-office travel.

available to employees). In *Migrant Advisory Service v Chaudri*,[57] Chaudri the applicant was paid 'expenses' of £25 per week rising to £40 per week, regardless of whether she worked or was on holiday or off sick and regardless of the fact that she incurred no actual expenses. This was considered to be 'consideration' and gave rise to a contract of employment entitling the individual to make a claim for unfair dismissal. It would also have enabled the volunteer to claim the minimum wage. In *Melhuish v Redbridge CAB*,[58] the EAT clarified this when they held that an unpaid volunteer working for the CAB, who had no obligation to attend work, was not an employee and, therefore, was unable to claim unfair dismissal.

However, on the more positive side organisations have a duty of care towards volunteers under the law of delict, and a duty, under s 3 of the Health and Safety at Work Act, to protect their Health and Safety. The protection against disclosures, under the Data Protection Act 1998, covers information on volunteers. Finally volunteers could retain copyright in the work they produce whilst working.

It is generally recommended that employers have Volunteer Agreements that can make it clear; what the volunteer and the organisation will be doing; and that the agreement does not involve an employment contract. They should be informal, particularly in the language that is used, avoiding words like duty, rights or obligations.

CONCLUSIONS

5.23 There is still a substantial amount of ambiguity in the status of the various atypical workers we have looked at.[59] While self employed persons will have very limited employment rights, dependant self employed persons may qualify as workers and get some rights. This issue is picked up in the following quote: 'while some degree of uncertainty in the operation of the law in this area is probably inevitable, a situation in which a substantial proportion of the workforce is unsure of its legal

---

57 (1998) EAT/1400/97. See Industrial Law Journal [1999] Vol 28 Part 3, p 249 for review.
58 (2005) IRLR 419.
59 Middlemiss, S Legal Rights of Atypical Workers Irish Law Times, Volume 23 (9) June 2005 p 132.

position would give rise to concern.'[60] This touches upon the fact that many atypical workers may have no, or little, idea what their status is, and even less idea what employment rights if any they have. Employers may avoid their obligations by a number of means, including exploiting the atypical workers' lack of awareness of their entitlement. Agency workers, and zero-hours workers, rarely exercise their legal right to turn down work and, genuinely, self employed and freelance workers may have to take work due to economic dependence. All the classes of atypical workers will have some protection extended in respect of enforcement of health and safety, under s 3 of HASAW 1974, and risk assessment requirements under the MHSW Regulations 1999. There is now the possibility of a civil action against employers for breach of statutory duty, where they fail to consider them in their health and safety arrangements implementing the Regulations.[61] There are other potential for legal actions under the equality legislation, although the success rate for these actions to date has been pretty limited (as seen in the case of voluntary workers). Of course part-timers, who are clearly the largest group of workers, have some degree of protection. However, there are some concerns being raised by commentators about its value.

The division between employed and self employed status is causing problems, as the following quote suggests: 'More generally evidence of the individual's experience of non-standard work suggests that the legal division between employment and self-employment does not correspond to perceptions of a clear divide between these different forms of work. In the context of non-standard work there is considerable ambiguity in the notions of control, autonomy and mutuality of obligation used as guidelines by the courts in assessment of employment status.'[62]

The commercial advantage of using agency workers is now questionable after agency workers were extended various rights under the Agency Workers Regulations 2010/ 93. UK business groups are concerned the new law will damage the temping industry, as the essence of agency work is

---

60 The Employment Status of Individuals in Non Standard Employment, Burchell, Deakin and Honey, March 1999 www.dti.govuk now www.berr.govuk.
61 An action for breach of duty of care under the law of delict where the employer's negligence has led to the worker suffering physical or mental harm could apply.
62 Supra 59.

that employers rely on hiring staff according to peak and trough demands in their business, which may be made more difficult when agency workers get certain employment rights from the outset of being hired. Employers have also argued the equality measures in the Regulations could be hard to implement, because it is often difficult to define a temporary worker's role or compare them with permanent employees.

There is a new underclass of workers who are asylum seekers, or immigrants. Many migrant workers are employed through agencies or by, gangmasters,[63] and are at particular risk of poor treatment at the hands of contractors. Recent research, published by the Health and Safety Executive (HSE 2007), found that migrant workers are more likely to be working in sectors or occupations where there are health and safety concerns, and that their status as new workers may place them at added risk. It found that few checks were made on migrant workers' skills and qualifications for undertaking the work they were doing, and this is discussed further in chapters 14 and 17.

---

63 Gangmasters (Licensing) Act 2004 and The Gangmasters (Licensing Conditions) Rules 2009/304 were legislative attempts by the last Government to control the activities of gangmasters employing casual and immigrant labour.

Chapter 6

Continuity of Employment and Transfer of Undertakings

CONTINUITY OF EMPLOYMENT

6.1 The concept of continuous employment in the Employment Rights Act 1996 (ERA 1996) is very important in employment law in the UK because an employee, to be eligible for certain statutory rights, eg unfair dismissal or redundancy, must complete a minimum period of continuous employment with his employer. Also the length of continuous employment is often an important factor in assessing compensation which may be due to an applicant in a statutory claim (eg redundancy payment). On the first point redundant employees have a number of rights, the most important being the right to receive statutory redundancy pay. However, in order to qualify for this they must have at least two years' continuous service with the same employer. Also under the Employment Rights Act 1996 (ERA 1996) a person is entitled to claim unfair dismissal provided they have continuous employment of one year with the same employer. This will include any weeks during which an employee is absent from work on account of a temporary cessation of work.[1] The statutory concept of continuity of employment is defined by ss 216–219 of the ERA 1996.

Calculating continuity of employment

6.2 Continuity of employment is achieved where an employee works for an employer continuously without a break, or only with short breaks, for a continuous period.[2] Under s 210(5) of the ERA 1996 there is statutory presumption in favour of continuity. The onus is therefore on the employer to prove that continuity has been broken. So where

---

1 For a list of the statutory rights that employees need periods of continuous service before qualifying go to www.businesslink.gov.uk
2 *Cornwall City Council v Prater* (2006) IRLR 362.

continuity is an issue in employment tribunal proceedings the tribunal will assume the employment was continuous until it is shown otherwise.[3] An employee's period of continuous employment begins with the day on which he starts work.[4] Thereafter any week 'during the whole or part of which an employee's relations with his employer are governed by a contract of employment' counts in computing the employee's period of employment.[5] Variation in the contractual terms and condition, no matter how significant, will not affect the continuity of employment. To determine the length of continuous service an employee has had with his employer it is necessary to establish the qualification date. This date is defined differently for different employment rights. In unfair dismissal cases this is the effective date of dismissal, and in redundancy cases the relevant date. Once the qualification date has been established the tribunal will need to count back from that date to the time they started working for the employer to determine the period of continuous employment. For the purposes of continuity a week runs from Sunday to Saturday.

Normally when an employee moves his employment from one employer to another this breaks the continuity of employment and they must start again to build up continuous employment to qualify for employment rights. However, for some employees the time working with a previous employer can sometimes be taken into account in determining the period of continuous employment with the present employer, particularly where that person is employed in the public sector. Any continuity of service earned at previous employment which can be counted for these purposes must be mentioned in the written particulars of employment of employees provided under s 1(3) of the ERA 1996. Within the period of continuous employment there could be periods which don't count towards total length of service but don't break the continuity, eg days when an employee is taking part in industrial action. In these circumstances, the starting date is treated as postponed by that number of days. The starting date is not, however, postponed by periods of lockout, ie where the employer prevents employees going to work. An employee can be treated as retaining continuous employment even where his or her employment has come

---

3   ERA 1996 s 210(5) and see *Wood v York City Council* (1978) ICR 840, CA.
4   ERA 1996 s 211(1)(a).
5   ERA 1996 s 212(1).

to an end (albeit temporarily). So continuity of work is protected for an employee who is absent from work due to the following: maternity or paternity leave; sickness absence; absence due to injury; temporary cessation of work and a break in employment due to custom and practice. See s 212(3) of ERA 1996.

Career breaks

6.3 One somewhat contentious issue is should career breaks taken by employees, for whatever reason, affect his or her continuity of employment. The current position, supported by the Court of Appeal's decision in the case of *Curr v Marks and Spencer*,[6] is that the period of the break does not count for continuity purposes. Ms Curr believed that her service before and during the career break she took would count towards her redundancy entitlement. Marks & Spencer thought it only needed to pay for the years Curr had worked after her return from the break. The Employment Appeals Tribunal (EAT) looked at matters pragmatically, and 'in the round', to find that there was no intended effect on Curr's continuity of employment as a result of the career break and decided in her favour. However, the Court of Appeal rigorously analysed the relevant provisions of the ERA 1996 to find that employment had been broken and restored the decision of the original employment tribunal, namely that the period before and during the rest break should not count towards continuity of employment.

Changes to the business not affecting continuity

6.4 However, some types of change do not break continuity. So, for example, continuous service before the change in ownership of a business still counts if a trade or business, or part of one, is transferred to another employer (see below). Also where the employer dies and their personal representatives or trustees continue to employ the employee, continuity is preserved. Lastly, where the employee moves from one employer to another when, at the time of the move, the two employers are both

---

6   (2003) ICR 443.

associated employers.[7] An absence from work will not affect continuity (and count automatically) for the following reasons: sickness, maternity, paternity, adoption and parental leave, temporary lay-off and annual leave, provided the contract continues throughout.[8]

Casual or Umbrella Contracts

6.5 There will be no continuity of employment if the work (whether full or part time) is simply a series of short self-contained engagements with gaps in between, during which there is no 'mutuality of obligation'[9] between the employer and the employee. However, where there is mutuality of obligation it is likely that, even where there are substantial gaps between contracts, the courts will find that continuous employment applies. This is illustrated by the case of *Cornwall County Council v Prater*[10] where a teacher had been employed by a local authority under a number of contracts of different type and duration over a ten-year period. The question arose as to whether this could be regarded as continuous employment. The Court of Appeal held that there was mutuality of obligation in the individual contracts between the Council and Mrs Prater; that they were contracts of service; and that, by virtue of s 212 of the ERA 1996, she was to be regarded as an employee of the Council continuously throughout the period 1988 to 1998. To sum up, the legal position between the Council and Mrs Prater was as follows: the Court held, amongst other things, that it made no difference to the legal position that she was engaged to teach the pupils out of school on an individual basis under a number of separate contracts running concurrently or successively.

---

7 In *Da Silva Junior v Composite Mouldings and Design Ltd* UKEAT/0241/08 the EAT held that continuity of employment was preserved where an employee of a company that was in voluntary liquidation subsequently went to work for a company with the same majority shareholder.

8 Periods of absence from work for normal holidays or otherwise by 'arrangement or custom' (as well as periods of absence because of temporary cessation of work and periods of absence of up to 26 weeks when the employee is incapable of work in consequence of sickness or injury are treated as weeks of employment for the purposes of computing a period of continuous employment under s 212(3)(c) of the Employment Rights Act 1996.

9 *Carmichael & anor v National Power plc* (1999) ICR 1226, HL.

10 [2006] IRLR 362.

They held further:

> 'nor does it make any difference to the legal position that, after the end of each engagement, the Council was under no obligation to offer her another teaching engagement or that she was under no obligation to accept one. The important point is that, once a contract was entered into and while that contract continued, she was under an obligation to teach the pupil and the Council was under an obligation to pay her for teaching the pupil made available to her by the Council under that contract. That was all that was legally necessary to support the finding that each individual teaching engagement was a contract of service.[11] Section 212 took care of the gaps between the individual contracts and secured continuity of employment for the purposes of the 1996 Act.'[12]

Except in redundancy cases, in determining questions relating to ascertaining the length of continuous employment of an employee, the calculations are not directly affected by whether employment is in Great Britain or overseas (ERA 1996 s 215(1)). The exception to this is redundancy cases where a week does not count for the purpose of calculating statutory redundancy pay if any part of it was spent in employment outside Great Britain, unless national insurance contributions were payable for that week.[13]

Temporary cessation of work

6.6 The continuous employment rules set out in the ERA 1996 say that any week during which an employment contract is in force counts towards continuous employment. Under s 212, when calculating continuity of employment, tribunals can include any week in which an employee has a contract of employment with his employer. A week's gap in the employment breaks the continuity unless the employee: cannot work due to sickness or injury; is absent due to a temporary cessation of work; or is absent in circumstances that are treated as not breaking continuity, see s 212(3).

---

11 Dacvies, ACL, Casual Workers and Continuity of Employment (2006) Industrial Law Journal Vol 35 Issue 2 p 196.
12 Paragraph 40(5).
13 ERA 1996 s 215(2).

In *Flack v Kodak*,[14] the Court of Appeal held that where an industrial tribunal has to consider the effect of gaps in employment of employees engaged in work where the seasonal demand varies, the proper course is not to conduct a mathematical exercise, such as determining the percentages of gaps and employment over the period, but rather to examine and consider the whole period of the employee's employment, looking at all the circumstances.[15]

The Court of Appeal held, that the tribunal had been wrong simply to carry out the mathematical exercise of calculating the lay-off periods, as compared with the periods of employment. The correct approach was to look at the entire history of the applicants' employment with Kodak, and all the circumstances surrounding their employment.

The case of *Hussain v Acorn Independent College Ltd*[16] involved the 'temporary cessation of work' exception. The EAT ruled in the case that, on being dismissed from his post as a teacher, Mr Hussain had more than one year's continuous employment, in spite of a break in his employment of seven weeks. Although this particular case was concerned with whether Mr Hussain could claim unfair dismissal, the decision has a broader application to any situation where continuity of employment is an issue, including employment rights such as entitlement to statutory redundancy pay and statutory maternity/adoption/paternity pay. The facts were that Mr Hussain was employed in the spring term for a period of 12 weeks under a fixed-term contract, covering for a sick teacher. The contract ended at the start of the summer break. The sick teacher resigned at that point, and during the summer holidays Mr Hussain was offered and accepted a permanent position from the start of the next term. When he was later dismissed it was argued that he had not been employed for long enough in the permanent job to make a claim for unfair dismissal. However, if the calculation of continuity of service for the two periods of his employment included the 7-week Summer holiday break of employment his full period

---

14 (1986) IRLR 255.

15 Flack and the other applicants were employed by Kodak in a department where the workload varied with the seasons; when light they were dismissed, and when heavy they were re-employed. The length of time during which each was employed, when compared with the lay-off periods, varied. Eventually the department was closed and all the applicants were dismissed.

16 [2010] UKEAT 0199_10_0809.

of employment would be more than one year's service. In explaining his decision, that the seven week period was a 'temporary cessation of work', the EAT made the following points: there is no requirement in the legislation that there be an expectation of further work when the first contract ends; the two contracts do not have to be the same type of contract; in education (also in the case of agricultural and seasonal work) there are periods when employees are not required to be at work, the first contract had ended as a result of the cessation of work, and that same work resumed at the start of the new term and the interval was short and temporary.

Strikes and transfers

6.7 Workers who take part in industrial action will not break their continuous service unless they commence a permanent post with another employer during the industrial dispute. However, working days lost to the employer through an employee taking industrial action will not count towards the total length of his continuous service.[17] These days of absence due to industrial action are discounted from the calculation of continuity of employment under s 216 of the ERA 1996 where it states that: (1) in calculating the length of a period of continuous employment the beginning of that period is postponed only by the days of strike or lockout; and (2) continuity of employment is not fractured by a strike or lockout.

In a TUPE situation (as described below) after the relevant transfer of the business the transferee is seen as stepping into the shoes of the transferor, and thus, the continuous service of existing employees is preserved and carried over to the new employment with the transferee.

Agency workers

6.8 When the Agency Workers Regulations 2010 came into effect from 1 October 2011, agency workers were for the first time given rights to a form of equal treatment with employees. This right was not retrospective and agency workers in employment on 1 October 2011 could not claim they had already satisfied the required qualification period of 12 weeks

---

17 www.direct.gov.uk-continuous employment.

for entitlement to rights. As the starting point for the calculation of the 12 week period ran from 1 October 2011 the earliest date for qualification was the week commencing 25 December 2011. The Regulations are designed to ensure that after a qualifying period of 12 weeks in a given role with the same hirer (irrespective of how many hours are worked in a week), the agency worker must receive no less favourable terms and conditions than he/she would have been entitled to if hired directly by the organisation for which he/she is working. The general rule is that any break of six weeks or less between assignments shall not break 'continuity' for qualification purposes. This means that if a worker returns to a role with a hirer within six weeks of his/her previous assignment, the previous assignment will count towards qualification. Continuity is also preserved in cases of sickness (of up to 28 weeks), temporary cessation of work, shutdown due to holidays, jury service, time off relating to a statutory contractual entitlement (eg emergency time off for dependants) or strike – the clock is 'paused' during the absence. The position is different for pregnancy and maternity related absence, maternity leave, adoption leave and paternity leave.

In such circumstances, the qualifying period is not paused but is deemed to continue to run for the original intended duration of the assignment or likely duration, whichever is longer.

TRANSFER OF UNDERTAKINGS

Introduction

6.9 The Transfer of Undertakings (Protection of Employment) Regulations 2006 (TUPE) protects employees' terms and conditions of employment when a business is transferred from one owner to another. Under these Regulations employees of the owner of the business that is selling, leasing or transferring to another business (transferor) will, when the business changes hands, automatically become employees of the new employer (transferee) on the same terms and conditions of employment. Their continuity of service and any other rights, including wages and pensions, are all preserved. Both the transferor and transferee are required to inform and consult employees affected directly or indirectly by the transfer.

The Transfer of Undertakings (Protection of Employment) Regulations 2006[18] entirely replaced the Transfer of Undertakings (Protection of Employment) Regulations 1981.[19] So it is now the main piece of legislation governing the transfer of an undertaking, or part of one, to another employer.[20] The TUPE 2006 regulations were introduced to comply with relevant European Union Directives concerning transfers of undertakings. The main Directives are: the Acquired Rights Directive (77/187/EC) the Acquired Rights Directive (98/50/EC) and the Acquired Rights Amendment Directive (2001/23/EC).

Relevant Transfers

6.10 TUPE 2006 only provide rights to employees who are involved in a relevant transfer. What is a relevant transfer of undertaking? In *Allen v Amalgamated Construction*,[21] the European Court of Justice usefully defined a relevant transfer as 'a change in the natural or legal person responsible for carrying out the business, who by virtue of this acquires the obligations of an employer vis-a-vis employees of the undertaking, regardless of whether or not ownership is transferred'. Relevant transfers may occur in a wide variety of situations, although the two broad categories are business transfers and service provisions changes. Some transfers will be both a business transfer and a service provision change.

Under Regulation 3 of TUPE 2006 relevant transfers are defined as: 3(1)(a) a transfer of an undertaking, business or part of an undertaking or business situated immediately before the transfer in the United Kingdom to another person where there is a transfer of an economic entity which retains its identity. Under s 3(2) an economic entity means an organised grouping of resources which has the objective of pursuing an economic

---

18 SI 2006/246.
19 SI 1981/1794.
20 Other statutes and regulations which have an impact on TUPE transfers are. The Collective Redundancies and Transfer of Undertakings (Protection of Employment) (Amendment) Regulations 1995 (SI 1995/2587) The Collective Redundancies and Transfer of Undertakings (Protection of Employment) (Amendment) Regulations 1999 (SI 1999/1925) The Pensions Act 2004, especially sections 257 and 258 and The Transfer of Employment (Pensions Protection) Regulations 2005 (SI 2005/649).
21 (2000) IRLR 119.

activity, whether or not that activity is central or ancillary. The questions for employment tribunals is whether or not there is a transfer of an economic entity, does it retain its identity after the transfer, and is there a 'stable economic entity' that is capable of being transferred?

To decide these issues the following factors have to be considered:

(1)   Is the type of business being conducted by the transferee (incoming business) the same as the transferor's (outgoing business)?

(2)   Has there been a transfer of tangible assets such as building and moveable property (although this is not essential)?

(3)   What is the value of the intangible assets at the time of the transfer?

(4)   Have the majority of employees been taken over by the new employer?

(5)   Have the customers transferred from the transferor to the transferee?

(6)   What is the degree of similarity of the activities carried on before and after the transfer?

(7)   If the answer to some, most, or all, of the above questions is affirmative then it is likely to be a relevant transfer of a stable economic entity. The absence of a profit-motive is not a determinative factor and voluntary and public sector bodies can be covered.[22]

Legal tests

6.11 In what is now regarded as a leading case on TUPE 2006, *Spijkers v Gebroeders Benedik Abbatoir CV*,[23] the ECJ stated that in determining what is a relevant TUPE transfer, a key question is does the business retain its identity after the transfer (points (1) and (6) above)? They set out the aspects which need to be considered in answering that question at paragraph 13 as follows:

---

22 Daddy's Dance Hall (1985) IRLR 315.
23 (1986) 2 CMLR 296.

in order to determine whether those conditions are met, it is necessary to consider all the facts characterizing the transaction in question, including the type of undertaking or business, whether or not the business's tangible assets, such as buildings and movable property, are transferred, the value of its intangible assets at the time of the transfer, whether or not the majority of its employees are taken over by the new employer, whether or not its customers are transferred and the degree of similarity between the activities carried on before and after the transfer ... it should be noted, however, that all those circumstances are merely single factors in the overall assessment which must be made and cannot therefore be considered in isolation.'

Later in the case of *Ayse Süzen v Zehnacker Gebäudereinigung GmbH Krankenhausservice*[24] (*known as the Suzen case*), the ECJ stated that when applying the important test of whether there is a transfer of an economic entity retaining its identity, it is necessary to analyse whether a function being transferred is either labour-intensive (in which case the importance is to be attached to whether there is a transfer of the workforce), or asset-reliant (where the determining factor may be whether assets have transferred).[25] The problem with this two-fold analysis is that some transfers are not easily categorised into either labour-intensive or asset-reliant.

In the UK, the courts prefer to take into account additional material to the two tests highlighted in *Suzen* on the basis that the multifactorial aspect of the *Spijkers* test allows an employment tribunal to draw on these additional factors where appropriate. This is illustrated in the case of *Scottish Coal Company Ltd v McCormack*.[26] In this case the Court of Session queried whether it is necessary to characterise a function as, strictly, either asset-reliant or labour-intensive to the exclusion of other possibilities. Scottish Coal held a contract with Crouch Mining Ltd, under which Crouch carried out mining activities at an opencast mine

---

24 (1997) ICR 662.
25 See *RCO Support Services Ltd v UNISON* [2002] ICR 751 (labour-intensive case) and *P & O Trans European Ltd* [2003] IRLR 128 and *GEFCO UK Ltd v (1) Oates (2) Car and Delivery Co Ltd* (EAT/0014/05) (both asset-reliant cases).
26 (2005) CSIH 68.

in Ayrshire. They owned the coal deposits in the area and arranged with Crouch to mine it. The operations required the use of extremely heavy and expensive plant, which was provided by Crouch, and took the form of large excavating plant, each unit servicing around four or five large dumper trucks. In total there were four excavators and 15 dumper trucks, along with ancillary equipment. The value of this plant was in excess of £2m. In addition to this plant, Crouch had erected on the site a workshop and office buildings, with a canteen and shower area for the use of employees, and the tribunal noted in evidence that the structures were worth around £150,000. In April 2001, Scottish Coal took over Crouch's activities at the site. Although Scottish Coal paid a relatively small sum for various fittings and fixtures left behind on site when Crouch departed, Scottish Coal did not acquire Crouch's expensive plant, as Crouch did not wish to sell it on to Scottish Coal. The majority of Crouch's employees were hired by Scottish Coal, carrying on the same mining activities they had carried out prior to the changeover. The employment tribunal found that there was the transfer of a stable economic entity from Crouch to Scottish Coal. It found that the workforce was specifically and permanently assigned to the task of mining, and there was a sufficiently autonomous structure, and that there was a transfer of an undertaking. The EAT upheld the employment tribunal's decision. On appeal to the Court of Session it held that whether an operation is asset or labour intensive is not a primary test of a transfer having taken place. The Court said that when deciding if a transfer has taken place, the guidance given by the ECJ in *Spijkers* (considered above), on determining whether an economic entity has retained its identity for the purpose of deciding whether a 'relevant transfer' has taken place, is still to be followed. No single factor is likely to be decisive. The later ECJ judgments in *Suzen* (see above), and *Oy Likenne*,[27] do not set out a rigid primary test that an economic undertaking must first be characterised as 'asset reliant' or 'labour intensive' or that these categories are mutually exclusive.

---

27 (2001) IRLR 171 is an example of the asset-reliant case.

Effect of a relevant transfer

Automatic Transfer of Rights and Obligations

6.12 The contract of employment of employees transferring from their present employer (who is the transferor) to the employer taking over the business (the transferee) will automatically be continued. Regulation 4(1) states that: '...a relevant transfer shall not operate so as to terminate the contract of employment of any person employed by the transferor and assigned to the organised grouping of resources or employees that is subject to the relevant transfer, which would otherwise be terminated by the transfer, but any such contract shall have effect after the transfer as if originally made between the person so employed and the transferee'. It is not just contracts of employment that continue but any other rights under statute or the common law etc. This is covered by Regulation 4(2) as follows: '...on the completion of a relevant transfer (a) all the transferor's rights, powers, duties and liabilities under or in connection with any such contract shall be transferred by virtue of this regulation to the transferee; and (b) any act or omission before the transfer is completed, of or in relation to the transferor in respect of that contract or a person assigned to that organised grouping of resources or employees, shall be deemed to have been an act or omission of or in relation to the transferee'

The transferee takes over the liability for all statutory rights, claims and liabilities arising from the contract of employment, for example, liabilities in tort (delict) (including personal injury claims), unfair dismissal, equal pay and discrimination claims. The exception to this is criminal liability of the transferor (eg for breach of health and safety statutes) which cannot transfer to the transferee.

In *Bernadone v Pall Mall; Martin v Lancashire County Council*,[28] the Court of Appeal had to decide in the face of conflicting cases whether a transferee under TUPE inherits liability for workplace accidents or diseases occurring before the transfer to staff who had transferred. The Court of Appeal's found that liability in tort (delict) transfers under Regulation 5(2)(a) of the 2001 TUPE Regs, as it arises in connection with an employee's contract of employment. The transferor would cease

---

28 (2000) IRLR 487 (Court of Appeal).

to be liable even although that employer would have employer's liability insurance covering the accident. The transferee would become liable but, his insurers would not be liable to indemnify for accidents arising before the transfer. However the Court of Appeal concluded that the benefit of the old employer's indemnity under the insurance policy, in respect of liability for the accident, also transfers. This means that the new employer is sued in legal proceedings, but the insurance company for the old employer remains liable to pay out.

However, in *Parkwood Leisure Ltd v Alemo-Herron and others*,[29] the Court of Appeal held that following the TUPE transfer of employees whose contracts contained a term that their pay was negotiated in accordance with collective arrangements, the transferee employer who was not a party to those arrangements was not bound by agreed pay rises made under the collective agreement and applying after the date of transfer.

Objecting to the transfer

6.13 The employee has the right under the TUPE Regulations to object to the automatic transfer of his contract from the transferor to the transferee. This right applies under Regulation 4(7) of TUPE 2006. This could be the result of a number of factors, such as where the employee would not work for the new employer, or where the worker has arranged other means of employment rather than continue post-transfer. This regulation acts to prevent the automatic transfer laid out in Regulation 4(1). Regulation 4(8) states that objection 'shall operate so as to terminate his contract of employment with the transferor but he shall not be treated, for any purpose, as having been dismissed by the transferor'. As such there would be no form of redress for the employee if they exercise this right of their own free will.

This is treated as a resignation, so he would not be entitled to claim unfair dismissal or redundancy rights. This was confirmed in the case of *The University of Oxford v Humphreys and Associated Examining Board*.[30] The Court of Appeal had to consider what happens when an employee objects to transferring under a TUPE transfer. They decided that the Regulations provide that where an employee objects to transferring simply because

---

29 [2010] EWCA Civ 24, [2010] ICR 793.
30 (2000) IRLR 183 (Court of Appeal).

they do not wish to work for the new employer, they do not transfer, but they lose any right to claim unfair dismissal or redundancy. However, the Regulations also say that if the objection is because the transfer would involve a substantial change to an employee's working conditions to his detriment, he can treat his contract as terminated by the employer, and claim unfair dismissal. The Court of Appeal held that this is so whether the employee leaves before or after the transfer. In *Capita Health Solutions v BBC and McLean*,[31] the EAT said that an employee's objection to a TUPE transfer was not valid, where the employee had objected to the transfer but then worked for the transferee for six weeks following the transfer. The EAT held that on the facts, Mrs MacLean had not objected to the transfer; instead, she had simply insisted that she would only transfer her employment for a limited period of time. Therefore, there had been a TUPE transfer of her employment to Capita for that period. The dangers of accepting a secondment are illustrated here and if employees do not wish to transfer their employment on a TUPE transfer, they must object to the transfer and act accordingly. As referred to above under Regulation 4(9) of TUPE 2006 it states that where there is a 'substantial change in working conditions to the material detriment of a person whose contract of employment is or would be transferred' that worker may treat the contract as terminated and therefore dismissed by their employer.

What kind of arrangements does TUPE cover?

6.14 There are a number of different business transactions that are covered by TUPE. One of the most common examples are mergers, where two businesses are combined through the sale of one business to another to form a new business. Other transactions leading to a relevant transfer are: the sales of a business by the sale of its assets, where all or part of a sole trader's or a partnership's business is sold or otherwise transferred; transfer through the execution of a will and the inheritance of a business; or the contracting out of services and a change of contractors. Even a change of licensee in a public house or other licensed premises or a change in franchisee (holders of a franchise from another company) will be covered.

---

31 UKEATS/0034/07/MT.

Relevant Transfers

6.15 There are two broad types of transfers that are protected under TUPE: 'business transfers' and 'service provision changes'. In this context business transfers occur when a business, undertaking, or part of a business or undertaking, is transferred from one employer to another. For the employees to be protected by TUPE during a business transfer the identity of their employer must change.

A service provision change is more common in work contracts for office cleaning, workplace catering, or security. It normally happens in one of three situations, when a service previously undertaken by an employer is awarded to a contractor (called 'contracting out' or 'outsourcing') who won the tender; a contract is assigned to a new contractor during a re-tendering process; and a contract ends with the service being performed 'in house' by the former client (referred to as 'contracting in or insourcing').

However, it is important to point out that TUPE does not apply to: transfers of control of the business by share take-over; the transfer of a contract to provide goods or services where this does not involve the transfer of a business or part of a business; the supply of goods for sale by another business, a very common transaction; the transfer of assets of the business only (property or plant); and transfers of undertakings situated outside the United Kingdom although the territorial application of TUPE in 2006 was extended so that overseas employees may also be caught by the transfer.

A service provision change will occur most commonly in industries where it is required by statute for employers to tender for contracts on a regular basis (eg local government or civil service) or it is the recognised standard of behaviour in an industry (eg oil and gas, construction). It happens when a client who engages a contractor to do work on its behalf either: reassigns the contract (whether by contracting out, outsourcing or re-tendering), or brings the work back 'in-house' (where a contract ends with a contractor the service thereafter is performed in-house by the client themselves).[32]

---

32 It will not be a service provision change if: the contract is wholly or mainly for the supply of goods for the client's use, or the activities are carried out in connection with a single specific event or a task of short-term duration.

Consequences of Breach of the TUPE regulations

6.16 If an employee is offered less favourable terms by the transferee than he had with the transferor prior to the transfer, this will be treated as an unfair dismissal, or if someone is dismissed for a reason connected with the transfer this will also be an unfair dismissal. Where the terms and condition are more favourable after the transfer then there is no breach of the law. In *Power v Regent Security Services Ltd*,[33] the EAT held that in a transfer situation, the TUPE Regulations do not prevent the employee relying upon an agreement reached with the transferee to vary their contract where the variation is to their advantage. The Regulations only render a variation void if the transferee seeks to change the contract by reason of the transfer where the variation is to the employee's detriment.

Unfair Dismissal

6.17 Subject to a one-year qualifying period, a transfer related dismissal will be automatically unfair for a reason connected with the transfer unless it is for an 'economic, technical or organisational' (ETO) reason, considered below.

Due to conflicting case law and an element of confusion surrounding the meaning of the TUPE Regulations, the Government decided under the 2006 Regulations to update and clarify the effect of the Regulations in relation to dismissals and changes to terms and conditions of employment. Their aim was to set out clearly how dismissals or variations of contract are to be treated in three different sets of circumstance.

- dismissals or variations for which the sole or principal reason is the transfer itself or a reason connected with the transfer that is not an economic, technical or organisational reason (an 'ETO' reason) entailing changes in the workforce will be unlawful;
- dismissals or variations for which the sole or principal reason is not the transfer itself, but is a reason connected with the transfer that is an ETO reason (considered below) will be potentially lawful

---

33 UKEAT 0499/06.

- dismissals or variations for which the sole or principal reason is unconnected with the transfer will be potentially lawful.

In the first of these situations, if there is such a reason, and it is the cause or main cause of the dismissal, the dismissal will only be fair as long as an employment tribunal decides that the employer acted reasonably in the circumstances in treating that reason as sufficient to justify dismissal and the employer met the other requirements of the general law on unfair dismissal, which is unlikely. In *London Metropolitan University v Sackur*,[34] the EAT held that it was automatically unfair for the transferee to dismiss and re-engage a group of employees on harmonised terms and conditions (with their existing workforce) following a TUPE transfer. The decision to harmonise terms and conditions following a TUPE transfer cannot be a valid economic, technical or organisational reason that could potential justify the dismissals. So TUPE protects the worker by ensuring that the transfer does not disadvantage them in any way, and it does this by preventing variations to the employment contract. Regulation 4(4)(a) renders all variations void if the sole or principal reason is in connection with the transfer itself. Additionally any variation will be void where it is connected with the transfer but does not amount to an 'economic, technical or organisational (ETO) reason entailing changes in the workforce', Regulation 4(4)(b).

The second kind of dismissal referred to above, is a dismissal for an ETO reason which is now explained.

ETO Reason

6.18 The onus lies on the employer dismissing the employee (transferor or transferee) to show that the dismissal falls within the ETO exemption to the automatic unfairness rule.

There is no statutory definition of this term, the legislators of both the UK legislation and the EU Acquired Rights Directive failing to define what an ETO reason is. The courts and tribunals in interpreting what they believe it is have not generally tried to distinguish between the three ETO reasons, but have treated them as a single concept. However, to qualify as an ETO reason an economic, technical or organisational explanation must

---

34 UKEAT/0286/06/ZT.

be one 'entailing changes in the workforce.' It is difficult to be precise about what an 'economic, technical or organisational' reason is, because of the lack of a statutory definition and case authority on this point, but the following are examples of possible ETO defences:

- a reason relating to the profitability or market performance of the new employer's business (ie an economic reason);

- a reason relating to the nature of the equipment or production processes which the new employer operates (ie a technical reason); or

- a reason relating to the management or organisational structure of the new employer's business (ie an organisational reason).

Also, if the dismissal occurred by reason of redundancy, then the usual redundancy arrangements will apply, and the dismissed employee could be entitled to a statutory or contractual redundancy payment. Dismissals on the grounds of redundancy are permitted by TUPE as they will often be for an ETO reason, however, the transferee employer will need to make sure that the redundancy is fair within the rules of employment legislation, eg selection for redundancy is not simply based on the fact that the person is a transferred employee. Dismissed employees will be entitled to a redundancy payment if they have been employed for two years or more. An employee's entitlement to redundancy payments will not be affected by the failure of any claim which they make for unfair dismissal compensation. Where there are redundancies, and it is unclear whether the Regulations apply, it will also be unclear whether the transferor or transferee employer is responsible for making redundancy payments. In such cases employees should consider whether to bring claims against both employers at an employment tribunal. In the case of *Hynd v (1) Armstrong and (2) Bishop Solicitors*,[35] the Court of Session held that where a transferor employer seeks to rely on an ETO reason for effecting redundancies in a TUPE situation, it must have its own reason for doing so, and cannot rely on a reason of the transferee. The facts were that a law firm, Morison Bishop, had offices in Glasgow and Edinburgh. Mr Hynd was one of two corporate lawyers working in the Glasgow office. The Morison Bishop partnership

---

35 (2007) IRLR 338.

was to be dissolved, with the Glasgow partners establishing a new firm, Bishops, and the Edinburgh partners establishing a new firm, Morisons. As Bishops did not intend to focus on corporate law, it was made clear that, going forward, it would have a reduced requirement for corporate lawyers. Hynd was made redundant on the date of dissolution of Morison Bishop. The Court of Session held that the dismissal was automatically unfair. It reached that decision because the dismissal had been carried out pre-transfer by Morison Bishop, it could only be fair if that firm could demonstrate that at the time of the dismissal it had an ETO reason.

The third category of dismissal mentioned above are dismissals or variations for which the sole or principal reason is unconnected with the transfer. These will not be covered by TUPE and will be potentially lawful or, if unlawful, will be subject to the normal unfair dismissal provisions in the Employment Rights Act 1996.

Duty for Transferor to Provide Information to Transferee

6.19 From 6 April 2006, transferors became obliged to give the transferee written information about the employees who are to transfer and all the associated rights and obligations towards them. This information includes, for example, the identity and age of the employees who will transfer, information contained in the employees' written particulars of employment under s 1 of the ERA 1996, and details of any legal or non-legal (eg wages) claims that the transferor reasonably believes might be brought. So the transferor employer must provide the new employer with a specified set of information which will assist him to understand the rights, duties and obligations in relation to those employees who will be transferred. This should help the new employer to prepare for any claims, legal or otherwise, that the transferred employees have against them. The employees transferring will benefit from their new employer being made aware of his inherited obligations towards them.

The information that must be provided is:

(i)   the identity of the employees who will transfer;

(ii)   information contained in the written statements of employment particulars concerning those employees;

(iii) the age of the employees;

(iv)   information relating to any collective agreements which apply to those employees;

(v)   instances of any legal actions taken by those employees against the transferor in the previous two years, and instances of potential legal actions which may be brought by those employees where the transferor has reasonable grounds to believe such actions might occur;

(vi)   details of any disciplinary actions or grievances concerning those employees over the preceding two years.

If any of the specified information changes between the time when it is initially provided to the new employer and the completion of the transfer, then the transferor is required to give the new employer written notification of the changes. The information must be provided in writing or in other forms which are accessible to the new employer. This information should be provided at least two weeks before the completion of the transfer, however, if special circumstances make this not reasonably practicable, the information must be supplied as soon as is reasonably practicable.

If the transferor does not provide this information, the transferee may apply to an employment tribunal who, if satisfied that there has been a breach of TUPE, can award such an amount of compensation as it considers just and equitable. Compensation starts at a minimum of £500 for each employee in respect of whom the information was not provided or was defective.

Informing and Consulting Employees and Their Representatives

6.20 There is also a requirement in the Regulations on both the new and transferor employers to consult representatives of the affected workforce before the relevant transfer takes place. The Regulations place a duty on both the transferor employer and transferee employer to inform and consult representatives of their employees who may be affected by the transfer or measures taken in connection with the transfer. The 'affected employees' will include: those individuals who are to be transferred; their colleagues in the employment of the transferor employer who will not transfer but whose jobs might be affected by the transfer or their new colleagues already in employment with the transferee whose jobs might be affected by the transfer.

Employers must inform the representatives about the following matters in sufficient time before a relevant transfer to enable them to consult with the employees affected:

- that the transfer is going to happen,
- the approximate date when,
- the reasons why;
- any legal, economic and social implications of the transfer for the affected employees;
- whether the employer envisages taking any action in connection with the transfer which will affect the employees, and if so, what action is envisaged;

Where the transferor is required to give the information, he or she must disclose whether the prospective new employer envisages carrying out any action which will affect his employees transferring and, if so, what. The transferee must give the transferor the necessary information so that he is able to meet this requirement. If action is envisaged which will affect the employees, eg reorganisation of the business, the employer must consult the representatives of the employees affected about the action and the consultation must be undertaken with a view to seeking the agreement of the employee representatives to the intended measures. During the consultations the employer must consider and respond to any representations made by the employee representatives and, if he rejects these representations, he must state the reasons. Where the employees affected by the transfer are represented by an independent trade union recognised for collective bargaining purposes, the employer must inform and consult an authorised official of that union. Where the employees are not represented by a trade union, the employer must inform and consult other appropriate representatives of those employees who may be either existing representatives or representatives elected for the purpose. So the transferor has a responsibility to conduct a full and meaningful consultation with employees at the earliest practicable time. A failure by them to conduct the consultation results in their liability for the payment of compensation, which may be up to 13 weeks' pay. The transferor and transferee are both liable for any award of compensation made by an employment tribunal for failure to inform and consult.

Pensions

6.21 Occupational pension rights earned up to the sale or disposal of the business are protected by social security law and pension trust arrangements. Transferee employers are required to offer pension provision to transferred employees on transfer. This applies where the employees had access through the transferor to an occupational pension scheme with an employer contribution before the transfer. Specifically ss 257 and 258 of the Pensions Act 2004 do apply to transfers, and this means in effect that the TUPE regulations apply to pension rights. In essence, if the previous employer provided a pension scheme then the new employer has to provide some form of pension arrangement for transferred employees who were eligible for, or are members of, the transferors' scheme. It will not have to be the same as the arrangement provided by the transferor but will have to be of a certain minimum standard specified under the PA 2004.

An employer can opt to provide an occupational pension scheme or a stakeholder pension scheme. If an employee chooses a stakeholder or a defined contribution scheme they will have to match the employee's contributions by up to 6 per cent. This can be increased if both parties agree.

TUPE and insolvency

6.22 TUPE 2006 provide greater flexibility when applying the Regulations to transfers of insolvent businesses to make them more attractive for potential buyers to rescue those businesses and save jobs. It also places greater emphasis on the rescue and sale of businesses as a going concern.

Whether employees will transfer to a buyer under TUPE, will depend on the type of insolvency proceedings the organisation undergoes. In the case of companies that have no hope of continuing as a going concern, bankruptcy and any analogous insolvency proceedings set out to liquidate company assets, the insolvency proceedings will be carried out under the supervision of an Insolvency Practitioner. However, employees will not automatically transfer to the buyer of the business under TUPE and employment rights for affected employees will be limited. The debts owed to employees will be guaranteed by the Secretary of State and will include 'some arrears of pay, notice periods, holiday pay and any basic award for unfair dismissal compensation. Other debts owed to employees will transfer.'[36]

In the recent case of *Oakland v Wellswood (Yorkshire) Limited*,[37] the EAT decided that, on the facts of the particular case, rescue of the business had never been considered a realistic outcome, with the administrators' efforts always focused on the secondary aim of achieving a better result for creditors. Therefore, Regulation 8(7) applied, and the claimant's employment did not transfer to the buyer of the assets. The EAT held that, because parliament had declined to spell out in TUPE which particular insolvency proceedings should be considered as being 'with a view to liquidation', this was a question for employment tribunals to decide. The decision in *Oakland* is an important EAT case because the judge decided that a pre-pack administration business sale did not result in automatic transfer of employees under Regulation 4 of TUPE, as the transferor was in 'bankruptcy proceedings or… analogous insolvency proceedings… instituted with a view to the liquidation of assets.' This case suggests that the question of whether TUPE will operate or not operate in an insolvency situation will be one of fact for a tribunal to decide in each case, having regard to the position envisaged by the parties at the time the insolvency proceedings were instituted. This leaves the position for insolvency practitioners, potential buyers and employees unhelpfully unclear.

More significantly under Regulation 8(6), where the business is doing badly but is capable of being saved, called 'relevant insolvency proceedings', the insolvency will also take place under the supervision of an Insolvency Practitioner. However, these proceedings are initiated with the aim of helping the business emerge as a going concern and, in these circumstances, TUPE will apply and employees will transfer to the new owner with their employment rights intact.

---

36 Lewis, D Sargeant, M Essentials of Employment Law 10 ed (2009) CIPD p 277.
37 (2009) IRLR 250.

SUMMARY

6.23 This is a complicated area of employment law and we have endeavoured to explain it in straightforward terms. While the change to the law in 2006 has brought much needed clarity to some aspects of the law dealing with transfer of undertakings, other areas require further clarification.

While there will undoubtedly be problems for employer's transferring employees (possibly on a regular basis) at least they have the reassurance of knowing that their contractual and statutory rights are protected. Employers taking on an existing business are now in a much better position to know the full extent of their liabilities in taking on the transferor's employees.

FURTHER READING

References on Transfer of Undertakings

Department Of Trade And Industry. (2007) Employment Rights on the Transfer of an Undertaking: A Guide to the 2006 TUPE Regulations for Employees, Employers and Representatives. DTI. Available at: http://www.berr.gov.uk/files/file20761.pdf

Incomes Data Services. (2007) Transfer of Undertakings. Employment law handbooks. IDS.

Journal articles

Brettle, O. (2007) The EU Acquired Rights Directive and its impact on business transfers. Benefits and Compensation International. Vol 37, No 4, pp 7–8, 10, 12–13.

Cole, K. (2008) Is TUPE a safety net or a tricky act to follow? People Management. Vol 14, No 1, p20.

McMullen, J. (2007) Don't be caught out by TUPE agency rules. People Management. Vol 13, No 22, p21.

McMullen, J. (2008) Stay the right side of cross-border rules. People Management. Vol 14, No 2, p24.

Chapter 7

Termination of the Contract

INTRODUCTION

7.1 In this chapter we will look at the ways that the contract of service can be terminated under the law. There are various ways in which a contract can come to an end, for example in fixed term contracts or contracts for a particular purpose (considered below) the contract will normally come to end when the term expires or the purpose is fulfilled and the employer dismisses the worker. The contract may also be terminated by the employee's resignation or dismissal by the employer. We will examine the legal consequences of the various methods of termination of the contract of employment from the perspective of the law of contract and then in relation to the statutory protection from unfair dismissal.

PERFORMANCE

7.2 Some contracts of employment end on performance of a specific task, or on reaching a certain point in time (fixed term contract). The expiry of contracts such as these is without legal consequence in terms of the law of contract, but a failure to renew such a contract will be regarded as a dismissal in terms of the legislation relating to unfair dismissal (see below).

DEATH OF A CONTRACTING PARTY

7.3 The death of a party to a contract generally terminates the contract. In the case of the contract of employment however there are certain statutory provisions in place to protect employees in the event of their employer's death. In the event that an employer dies then there are various entitlements for employees. If business does not carry on after the employer's death this is deemed to be redundancy.[1] If the deceased employer's business is carried on by his personal representatives, the employee's contract of employment continues.

Where the business is carried out by a limited company, the death of a member of the senior management team or a director will not bring about cessation of business because of the concept of separate legal personality.[2] The business entity is regarded as a separate legal personality from the directors, shareholders and other people who make up the business and continues irrespective of anyone's death, so an employee will continue in employment. A similar situation exists where the employer is a limited liability partnership.[3] In a partnership the death of a partner will bring a partnership to end unless the partnership agreement provides otherwise.[4] The contracts of employment of employees would be terminated unless provision is made for continuance of the firm after the death of a partner in the partnership agreement. Termination would be by reason of redundancy, and qualifying employees would be entitled to a redundancy payment. Employees would also be entitled to payments in lieu of notice and holiday pay.

Where an employee dies during the course of the contract of employment their executors may be entitled to various rights related to unpaid wages, pensions etc, but the contract comes to an end. Any pending proceedings before an employment tribunal at the time of death can be continued by the deceased employee's representatives.

DISSOLUTION OF THE ENTERPRISE

7.4 Where there is a dissolution of a business this will normally result in dismissal and will be treated as redundancy under s 139 Employment Rights Act 1996. Where there is a compulsory winding up ordered by court then this order serves as notice of dismissal.[5]

---

1   Employment Rights Act 1996 s 139.
2   *Salomon v Salomon & Co Ltd* [1897] AC 22.
3   Limited Liability Partnerships Act 2000.
4   The Partnership Act 1890 s 33.
5   *Day v Tait* (1900) 8 SLT 40, OH.

Where the business is bankrupt or insolvent, what wages or other benefits employees are due at the time bankruptcy is declared will be payable as preferential debts so there is a degree of protection, but only where the business has sufficient funds to meet these debts. When there are insufficient funds available in the business after liquidation of the company assets to meet the costs of redundancy, or pay in lieu of notice, then they will be met (through application to the Secretary of State) by the National Insurance Fund.[6] If the business continues through the auspices of the liquidator, the employee will enter into a new contract with them under which the liquidator will be responsible for payment of wages etc.

FRUSTRATION OF THE CONTRACT

7.5 In contract law, frustration of a contract occurs where a supervening event during the currency of the contract makes it impossible for the purpose of the contract to be fulfilled. So frustration occurs when some reasonably unforeseeable event occurs which makes the contract impossible or illegal to perform, or radically different from what the parties originally intended. When such a contract is frustrated, at common law it comes to an end without a dismissal on the part of the employer, or a resignation on the part of the employee. So if, for example, the contract was for the hire of a boat and the boat sank in an unprecedented storm then the contract would be frustrated. Although this example is not drawn from employment law it does illustrate the concept well. From the point that the event occurs which renders the contract illegal, impossible, or pointless to perform, the contract is deemed void and no further rights can be extended to either party. So the employee can obtain his rights up to the point of frustration, but cannot obtain any benefit from the employer beyond that point which would cessate his pension entitlement, lead to loss of future earnings etc. Because of this the courts may be reluctant to accept that frustration has occurred. Many instances of frustration of contract will be regarded as a dismissal for the purposes of unfair dismissal legislation for example where the employer terminates the contract because the employee no longer has permission to work in the UK. At common law

---

6   ERA 1996 s 166.

this would be frustration, however it is regarded merely as a dismissal for a potentially fair dismissal under the Employment Rights Act 1996 (ERA 1996). Similarly, a case of long term sickness may be regarded as a dismissal for the potentially fair reason relating to capability. So whilst the common law may impose no liability on the employer where the contract is frustrated, he must still comply with the provisions of the ERA 1996 to ensure a fair dismissal.

The normal requirement for frustration of contract is that neither party is responsible for the frustrating event (no fault rule) although, as will be seen, this rule has been relaxed somewhat in the area of employment law.

Long term sickness

7.6 The first area to consider is long term sickness which is seen as a factor responsible for frustration of the contract of employment. In theory a long term inability to perform the contract will frustrate the contract. The difficulty is in deciding at what point, if any, frustration occurs in these circumstances. In the case of *Marshall v Harland & Wolff Ltd*,[7] Sir John Donaldson set out factors that should be considered by an employment tribunal when considering if there has been frustration namely:

(a) the terms of the contract including any provisions regarding sick pay;

(b) how long employment was likely to last in the absence of his sickness (a temporary or specific hiring is more likely to be frustrated);

(c) the nature of the employment in particular whether the employee was in a key post which had to be filled permanently if his absence was prolonged;

(d) the nature of the illness, how long it has continued and the prospects for recovery;

(e) the period of past employment, a relationship of long standing is not so easily destroyed as one which has a short history.

---

7   [1972] 1 WLR 899 at 903.

The difficulties with frustration in this context were highlighted in the case of *Egg Stores (Stanford Hill) Ltd v Leibovici*,[8] where some guidance was offered as follows:

> 'It may be a long process before one is able to say whether the event is such as to bring about frustration … But there will have been frustration even though at the time of the event the outcome was uncertain …if one can say at some point …matters have gone on so long and prospects for recovery so poor …it is no longer practical to regard the contract as subsisting'.[9]

Frustration of the contract occurs by operation of the law and is independent of the intention of the parties. In *Collins v Secretary of State for Trade and Industry*,[10] the employee had severely injured his hand and had not worked for some years. Although both the parties thought the contract was continuing and acted accordingly, as a consequence of frustration the employee was not entitled to redundancy pay when the company went into receivership.

Interestingly, in *Hogan v Cambridgeshire County Council*,[11] it was held that frustration had occurred even although the ill-health termination procedure (sickness scheme) in the contract of employment had not been brought to its conclusion. Frustration occurs regardless of the actions or intentions of the parties. An employment contract may be frustrated by long-term sickness even in cases where the contract expressly foresees such an eventuality and provides a remedy for it.

Imprisonment

7.7 Another area of frustration that applies in employment law is imprisonment. Where the employee is in prison it is difficult or impossible for him to continue to fulfil his contractual duties under the contract of employment, and frustration of the contract may occur freeing the employer from further obligations under the contract. The difficulty with

---

8   (1977) ICR 260.
9   Phllips J at 265.
10   30.1.01 EAT 1460/99.
11   26.7.01 EAT 382/99.

regarding this as frustration of the contract is that imprisonment is usually a consequence of the fault of the employee and the doctrine of frustration assumes that no fault should lie on either party. This was resolved by the Court of Appeal in *FC Shepherd & Co Ltd v Jerrom*.[12] They held that the rule against self-induced frustration only meant neither party could rely on his *own* misconduct to establish the defence of frustration. As the employer was relying on the employees fault, that requirement was satisfied and frustration could succeed: to hold otherwise would allow a party at fault to benefit from his own misdeeds which would not be tolerated. Therefore an innocent party can rely on frustration arising from the blameworthy conduct of the other.

MUTUAL TERMINATION

7.8 If termination of the contract is by mutual agreement, the employment relationship will usually end without liability on either side. Often, however, the employee has agreed under duress. If the employer's behaviour has forced the employee to agree to the contract ending then this will be a constructive dismissal, rather than a mutual termination of the contract, as the employer may be in breach of the implied term as to trust and confidence. There are other areas where mutual termination applies and most notable of these is voluntary redundancy where, in return for a redundancy package provided by the employer, the employee agrees to give up their job and be made redundant. Retirement is another form of mutual agreement where an employee, in return for a pension, will agree to terminate his contract on a set date.

TERMINATION BY THE EMPLOYEE

7.9 Where an employee resigns his job, whether by giving the appropriate amount of notice or not, then this will end the contract. With resignation, provided the employee concerned complies with the notice requirements, this will not be dismissal. In *Harvey v Yankee Traveller Restaurant*,[13] a pregnant employee agreed to resign after arrangements which the

---

12   (1986) IRLR 358 CA.
13   (1976) IRLR 35.

employer offered her were not acceptable. It was held that she was not dismissed. If however, the employee is forced to resign by the employer's behaviour, the resignation will be treated as constructive dismissal.

Where an employer invites an employee to resign this could be a dismissal, as could offering an employee the opportunity to resign as an alternative to facing disciplinary proceedings.[14]

An employee should give his contractual notice or, if there is no express contractual provision, one weeks notice is required unless a different period can be implied eg by the custom and practice of the particular trade or industry. If an employee resigns without giving the correct notice the employer's only remedy is to sue in the civil court for damages for loss resulting from the breach, as it is not possible to enforce contracts of personal service by specific implement. The loss will generally be the extra cost of hiring a replacement worker for the notice period and such actions are extremely unusual.

DISMISSALS AT COMMON LAW

7.10 If a dismissal is carried out in accordance with the contractual provisions, including those relating to notice and disciplinary procedures, there will be no right of action against the employer at common law since the common law remedies relating to dismissal are based on breach of contract. The statutory provisions relating to unfair dismissal are superimposed onto the contractual position and separate from it and they rely on concepts of reasonableness and procedural fairness. Unfair dismissal will be considered separately later in this chapter.

Wrongful dismissal

7.11 Wrongful dismissal should not be confused with unfair dismissal as they are very different rights for an employee that has been dismissed. An action for wrongful dismissal is based in contract law, and unfair dismissal is a statutory remedy (considered below). Any claim for wrongful dismissal will, therefore, involve examining the employee's employment contract to see if the employer has breached its terms. A

---

14   *Elliot v Waldair (Construction) Ltd* (1975) IRLR 104.

situation which amounts to a wrongful dismissal may or may not amount to an unfair dismissal under the ERA 1996 (and vice versa). If it is both wrongful and unfair the remedy should be chosen carefully, bearing in mind the advantages and disadvantages of bringing a case before the court or tribunal respectively. These are discussed in chapters 2 and 4.

The most common breach is where the employee is dismissed without notice or the notice given to the employee is too short. Of course either party in the employment relationship can bring the contract to an end if they give the necessary notice.[15] For employees this will either be the legal minimum under statute[16] or the period of notice stated in the employee's contract. However, an employee can be summarily dismissed (ie dismissed without notice) in situations where the employer is entitled to treat the contract as repudiated and dismiss the employee without notice. This will only occur in serious circumstances where an employee is guilty of gross misconduct eg a serious case of dishonesty, intoxication, or violence at work etc. If an employee is behaving in such a seriously bad manner that a reasonable response on the part of the employer is to dismiss the employee instantly then it is a form of common law dismissal known as 'dismissal for cause' as it involves serious misconduct on the part of the employee which entitles the employer to dismiss him without notice.

The essential question is 'has the employee disregarded the essential conditions of his employment contract.'[17] If so, his employer can dismiss him without notice. Another possible example of wrongful dismissal is a failure by the employer to follow correctly a contractual disciplinary procedure.[18]

Wrongful dismissal claims, since they are based on a common law claim for breach of contract, would be pursued in the courts (usually the Sheriff Court). However, there are now claims under statute for breach of

---

15 Under s 86(2) of the Employment Rights Act 1996 an employee must give an employer one week's notice.
16 Under s 86(1) of the Employment Rights Act 1996 after a month's service the employees is entitled to a week's notice for the first two years and thereafter one week for every year of service up to a maximum of 12 weeks.
17 *Lord Evershed in Laws v London Chronicle Ltd* (1959) 1 WLR 698.
18 *Dietman v Brent London Borough Council* (1987) ICR 259, *Boyce v London Lambeth Borough Council* (1995) IRLR 50.

an employment contract, arising on termination of the contract that can be brought before an employment tribunal.[19]

Damages

7.12 Damages for breach of contract claims in the court can only be awarded where the employee can prove that the employer's action represents a breach of the contract which has led to his wrongful dismissal. In *Ridge v Baldwin*,[20] the House of Lords quoted Lord Denning in the Court of Appeal who summarised the position thus:

> 'The law regarding master and servant is not in doubt. There cannot be specific performance of a contract of service and the master can terminate his contract with the servant at any time and for any reason or none. But if he does so in a manner not warranted by the contract he must pay damages for breach of contract.'

The case of *Addis v Gramophone Co Ltd*[21] was instrumental in ensuring that compensation would be limited only to actual losses incurred by the dismissal, eg loss of notice or wages in lieu of notice, and not extend to other forms of harm suffered. So employees would not be compensated for the manner in which dismissal was carried out, or the effect dismissal had on obtaining future employment. In *Boardman v Copeland Borough Council*,[22] an employee who was wrongfully dismissed was not entitled to recover compensation at common law either for damage to his health and reputation flowing from his dismissal, the manner of that dismissal, or compensation for his inability to obtain new employment.

In practice, damages in wrongful dismissal cases are usually insubstantial for the following reason: the employer has the right to terminate the contract without due notice and doesn't need a good reason or any for doing so. Any damages for the failure to give notice will be limited by the requirement to mitigate loss and employees can only claim

---

19 Industrial Tribunals Extension of Jurisdiction (England and Wales) Order 1994 and Industrial Tribunals Extension of Jurisdiction (Scotland) Order 1994.
20 [1964] AC 65.
21 [1909] AC 488.
22 [2001] EWCA Civ 888, [2001] All ER (D) 99 (Jun), CA.

damages for a clear contractual entitlement. Since, in most cases, an employee is only entitled to remain in employment until the end of the notice period, damages will be limited to a sum representing net salary for the notice period only. However, where the employee in question is very highly paid and has a long period of notice, compensation can be substantial. In the case of *Gregory v Wallace and another,*[23] the employee was entitled to 2 years notice. Similarly in *Shove v Downs Surgical plc,*[24] the pursuer was a chairman and managing director who was sacked when he became ill and successfully sued for loss of salary for 30 months allowed under the contract, loss of company car, loss of BUPA membership and pension rights etc, and was entitled to £60,729 in damages.

In *Gogay v Hertfordshire County Council,*[25] the Court of Appeal had allowed damages to be awarded to Ms Gogay for psychiatric illness resulting from the employer's breach of contract (implied term of trust and confidence) resulting from her suspension from work, but subsequent case law makes it clear that it is not possible to claim damages for breach of contract relating to the manner of dismissal because the only remedy for such complaints is the statutory remedy of unfair dismissal.

In the leading case of *Johnson v Unisys Ltd,*[26] Mr Johnson commenced employment in 1971 and at the end of 1985 suffered psychological illness brought on by work-related stress. In 1994 he was dismissed for an alleged irregularity. He brought a claim for unfair dismissal and was successful. However, 2 years later he brought an action against the company in the county court for damages arising from a breach of contract or negligence. He claimed he was dismissed in breach of various implied terms, including the duty to maintain trust and confidence. The manner of dismissal (without a hearing and in breach of company's disciplinary procedure) and the fact of his dismissal meant he suffered a mental breakdown which affected his family life and made it impossible for him to find work. The Court of Appeal found that Mr Johnson had no cause of action at common law. The House of Lords dismissed the appeal on the basis that 'there is no common law contractual remedy for financial

23   (1998) IRLR 387.
24   (1984) IRLR 17.
25   (2000) IRLR 703 CA.
26   [2001] ICR 480.

or other loss allegedly flowing from the manner or circumstances of the dismissal'. Lord Hoffman summarised the reasoning for this conclusion thus: 'for the judiciary to construct a general common law remedy for unfair circumstances, attending dismissal would be to go contrary to the evident intention of Parliament that there should be such a remedy, but it should limited in its application and extent.'[27]

In cases following on from *Johnson v Unisys*, employees have successfully attempted to distinguish claims for loss, injury, and damage arising from the manner of dismissal, from loss, injury, and damage arising from breach of contract in the run up to the dismissal itself. In the latter situation, damages will be recoverable at common law. Therefore, in *Eastwood Magnox Electric Ltd*,[28] the employee made a claim in respect of damages for psychiatric injury which arose from events leading up to his dismissal from a teaching position, following allegations of inappropriate sexual conduct. He recovered damages for financial loss resulting from psychiatric illness caused by the failure by the employer to investigate the allegations against him and to conduct the disciplinary proceedings properly, since this failure could be shown to have preceded and been independent of the dismissal.

The House of Lords in *Johnson v Unisys* also made it clear that employee would only receive 'stigma' damages for loss of reputation and loss of employability flowing from a breach of contract in exceptional cases. An exception to this rule can be seen in *Malik v BCCI SA*,[29] where it was stated 'employers must take care not to damage their employees future prospects by harsh or oppressive behaviour or by any form of conduct which is unacceptable today as falling below the standards set by the implied trust and confidence term'. A claim for stigma damages was upheld to compensate an employee working for a bank with corrupt and illegal practices, on the basis of breach of his trust and confidence, which adversely affected his opportunities for continuous employment (future employment). He was entitled to leave employment and, on the basis of breach of implied term, claim wrongful dismissal. This decision qualified part of *Addis* decision mentioned above.

---

27   [2001] ICR 480 at 500.
28   [2004] ICR 1064.
29   (1997) 3 ALL ER 1, HL.

In an important combined appeal relating to this issue, *Edwards v Chesterfield Royal Hospital NHS Foundation Trust* and *Botham v Ministry of Defence*,[30] the Supreme Court held that the reasoning in *Johnson v Unisys Ltd* was a bar to a claim for damages by an employee for loss arising from the unfair manner of his dismissal for gross misconduct in breach of an express term of his employment contract. Edwards had been a consultant surgeon summarily dismissed after a complaint that he had inappropriately examined a female patient. He found himself unable to find another consultants position. He claimed that the dealing with his dismissal was not properly constituted and the employer was, therefore, in breach of his contractual disciplinary procedures. He had been awarded damages by the Court of Appeal in respect of loss of reputation arising from his dismissal which he claimed would not have occurred if the contractual procedures had been followed. The Supreme Court decided that this situation did not fall within the exception to *Johnson v Unisys* and overturned the decision of the lower court. Botham was a youth worker dismissed following allegations of inappropriate conduct towards two teenage girls. Following his dismissal he was placed on a list of persons unsuitable to work with children. His claim for breach of contract was unsuccessful but, in light of the *Edwards* case, an appeal was allowed. His appeal was unsuccessful. In view of these decisions an employee concerned that an employer is failing to follow procedures might consider seeking an interdict to prevent dismissal in breach of these procedures. Otherwise the only remedy available will be a claim of unfair dismissal.

Interdicts

7.13 While damages would be the normal remedy in wrongful dismissal cases there could be circumstances where an interdict might be a possible remedy particularly:

(1)   Where the employer has failed to observe contractual disciplinary procedure;[31]

---

30   [2011] UKSC 58, [2012] 2 WLR 55.
31   *Dietman v Brent London Borough Council* [1987] ICR 259, *Boyce v London Lambeth Borough Council* [1995] IRLR 50.

(2)   Where courts are willing to restrain certain breaches of contract by the employer.[32]

In *Irani v Southampton and South-West Hampshire Health Authority*,[33] an employee had been dismissed because the working relationship with his superior had broken down, however, they had not followed correct disputes procedure in dismissing him and he successfully sought an injunction stopping the dismissal taking effect until the dispute procedure was followed. This remedy is discussed further in Chapters 2 and 4.

STATUTORY CLAIM FOR BREACH OF CONTRACT/ WRONGFUL DISMISSAL

7.14 Under the Industrial Tribunals Extension of Jurisdiction (Scotland) Order 1994,[34] employment tribunals were extended the jurisdiction to hear claims for breach of an employment contract, or any other contract connected with employment, including a claim for any sum due under such a contract, and a claim for recovery of any sum in pursuance of any enactment relating to the terms or performances of such a contract. It provided that the claim must be outstanding on the termination of the employee's contract and the maximum award in respect of any claim is £25,000. There are exceptions which are (a) damages for personal injuries, (b) a term relating to intellectual property, (c) a term imposing an obligation of confidence, and (d) a term requiring the employer to provide living accommodation for the employee. The nature of this remedy was summarised in the case of *Sarker v South Tees Acute Hospitals NHS Trust*[35] as follows:

'The purpose of the 1994 order ... it is intended to avoid the situation where an employee .. is forced to use both a tribunal and a court of law to have all his or her claims determined. In simple terms, the purpose of the extension of the jurisdiction was to enable an industrial tribunal to deal with a claim for unfair dismissal and a claim for damages for

---

32   See for example *Powell v Brent London Borough Council*, (1987) IRLR 466.
33   (1985) IRLR 203.
34   Industrial Tribunals Extension of Jurisdiction (England and Wales) Order 1994.
35   (1997) IRLR 328, EAT.

breach of the same employment contract. Two sets of proceedings are now avoided.'

The significance of tribunals having a limit of £25,000 on the amount of compensation that can be awarded for wrongful dismissal is that the most sensible route for a claimant may be to pursue an unfair dismissal claim[36] before an employment tribunal or a wrongful dismissal claim before the Sheriff Court or the Court of Session. In saying this, breach of contract claims are currently the third most common type of claim for employment tribunals.

UNFAIR DISMISSAL

7.15 A qualifying employee has the right not to be unfairly dismissed by his employer. Unfair dismissal is a purely statutory creature which was created by the Industrial Relations Act 1971 but, after considerable amendment since then,[37] the rules are now contained in the Employment Rights Act 1996 ss 94-98. The remedy for unfair dismissal is provided by this statute and consist of an application to an employment tribunal within three months of the effective date of the dismissal.

Entitlement to protection

7.16 Not every worker is protected from unfair dismissal. The person bringing a claim must be an 'employee' defined in section of the Employment Rights Act s 230 (1) as 'an individual who has entered into or works under (or, where the employment has ceased, worked under) a contract of employment' and under s 230(2) 'contract of employment' means 'a contract of service or apprenticeship, whether express or implied, and (if it is express) whether oral or in writing'.

The various tests which the employment tribunal will use to ascertain whether a worker meets this definition are discussed in chapter 4.

The employee must not be excluded from protection against unfair dismissal, except in the following circumstances:

---

36   With compensatory damages well in excess of £60,000.
37   The Employment Act 2008 repealed an earlier provision requiring employers to have statutory disciplinary and dismissal procedures.

(a)   Employees who work abroad. Employees who work wholly out with Great Britain may still be protected in exceptional cases where, despite the workplace being abroad, there are other relevant factors so powerful that the employment relationship has a closer connection with Great Britain than with the foreign country where the employee works.[38] Factors which will be relevant in deciding whether the connection is close enough will be whether the employer is based in Britain, whether the contract is governed by British Law, and whether the terms and conditions of the contract are entirely those of British Law[39] (see chapter 2).

(b)   Employees of foreign governments and those employers with diplomatic immunity (unless immunity is waived). An employer will not have diplomatic immunity if the contract was made in the UK or the work is to be wholly performed in the UK, unless at the time the claim is made the claimant was a national of the relevant state, or at the time when the contract was made he was not a UK national or habitually resident in the UK.[40]

(c)   Members of the armed forces.[41]

(d)   Persons who serve as members of a constabulary maintained by virtue of an enactment, or who have the powers or privileges of a constable.[42]

(e)   Share fishermen.

(f)   Merchant seamen on ships registered out with Great Britain, or whose employment is wholly out with Great Britain, or who are not ordinarily resident in Great Britain.

38   *Lawson v Serco Ltd* [2006] UKHL 3, [2006] 1 All ER 823.
39   *Duncombe v Secretary of State for Children, Schools and Families* [2011] UKSC 36; [2011] 4 All ER 1020; [2011] ICR 1312.
40   State Immunity Act 1978.
41   www.businesslink.gov.uk.
42   Employment Rights Act 1996 s 200 British Transport police are included in this exclusion *Spence v British Railways Board* [2001] ICR 232.

(g)   An employee who is obliged to submit any dispute to arbitration under the ACAS arbitration scheme.[43]

(h)   Employees who work in an employment which is covered by a designated dismissals procedure agreement which has been agreed between the employer and an independent trade union approved by the Secretary of State.[44] At the moment there are no such schemes in existence.

Employees on oilrigs or platforms are included in the protection provided they work on installations in UK Territorial Waters or in the area designated as Continental shelf.[45] Prison officers are also included in the protection.[46]

Qualifying service

7.17 In order to make a claim for unfair dismissal the employee must usually have qualifying service with the employer of at least one year calculated at the effective date of termination. For employees starting new employment on or after 6 April 2012, the qualifying period for the right to claim unfair dismissal will be two years and the right to request a written reason for dismissal will be two years.

This continuous service requirement does not apply where the reason for the dismissal is an automatically unfair reason (see later).

The date of dismissal can be important in view of the short timescale for lodging an application and necessity for having one years continuous service.

A dismissal is only effective once it has been communicated to the employee.[47] In a departure from the usual rules of contract law, if an employee is notified of dismissal by letter then the dismissal is effective when the letter is read, not when it is delivered. In *Brown v Southall and*

---

43   TULR(C)A s 212A.
44   Employment Rights Act 1996 s 110 and s 203(2)(8).
45   Employment Protection (Offshore Employment) Order 1976 and Continental Shelf Act 1964.
46   Criminal Justice and Public Order Act 1994 s 126.
47   *Widdicombe v Loncombe Software Ltd* [1998] ICR 710; *Gisda CIF v Barratt* [2009] ICR 1408.

Knight,[48] an employee was on holiday when the letter arrived and did not read it until his return a week later. The EAT overturned the decision of the tribunal and held that the dismissal was effective from the date he read the letter resulting in him narrowly achieving sufficient service to make an claim.[49] A dismissal will not be effective until the employee has read the letter or had a reasonable opportunity of doing so.

The date of termination is a matter of fact and can be agreed retrospectively between the parties in contrast to the definition of continuity of employment which was stipulated by statute and could not be varied by agreement.[50] Continuity of employment is considered further in chapter 6.

The employee must have been dismissed

7.18 In order to make a claim the employee must firstly demonstrate that he has been dismissed. The fact of dismissal is not always easy to prove. In most cases it will be clear whether the employer has terminated the employee's contract particularly where he has put it in writing. A warning of future dismissal does not amount to a dismissal.[51] There are sometimes situations where it is not clear whether the employee has been dismissed, the contract has been frustrated or indeed the employee has resigned *(see Harvey v Yankee Traveller Restaurant)*,[52] or has resigned in circumstances which amount to constructive dismissal. (See above for a discussion of frustration and constructive dismissal). An employee who has resigned in the face of an ultimatum (ie resign or be dismissed) has been dismissed for the purposes of the legislation.[53] That is not to say, however, that an employee who resigns rather than face a disciplinary hearing has been dismissed.[54]

---

48   [1980] ICR 617.
49   (1980) IRLR 130.
50   *Lambert v Croydon College* [1999] ICR 409.
51   *Doble v Firestone Tyre and Rubber Co Ltd* [1981]IRLR300; *Rai v Somerfield Stores Ltd* [2004] IRLR124.
52   (1976) IRLR 35.
53   *Robertson v Securicor Transport Ltd* 1972 IRLR104 *East Sussex County Council v Walker* (1972) 7ITR 280.
54   *Martin v Glynwed Distribution Ltd* [1983] ICR511.

Another situation where problems can arise is where ambiguous oral statements are made by the employer or his representative, often in the heat of the moment, that leave the employee unsure if he has been dismissed or not. In *Craig v Costley & Costley Ltd*,[55] a housekeeper was due to finish her shift at 5pm but around 3pm she was waiting at the reception desk for customers to leave so she could finish her cleaning duties. Her manager, Mr Poggi, remarked that the applicant was standing doing nothing. She remarked flippantly that she might as well leave, and his response was 'f**k off and don't come back'. She remarked to a colleague that 'I think I have been sacked.' She then left her employment, but her employer didn't know until she asked for her P45. The EAT upheld the appeal against the employment tribunal's decision that there was no dismissal here stating that, in these circumstances, it was up to employer to clarify the position which he had failed to do in this case. This was a slight departure from the position in *Futty v D & D Brekkes Ltd*,[56] where it was held that it is for a reasonable listener to determine if there was a dismissal or not. Whether or not an employee has been dismissed by unclear language depends on the circumstances of the case including the type of employment and the language commonly used in the workplace. In the case of *Futty*, the employee was a fish filleter and the language used was not unusual in that work environment so the expression did not amount to a dismissal. In another case, the employee's brother who was a partner in the firm employing him as an insulation engineer told him to 'f**k off and play with your shop'. When the employee returned an hour later for his cards and money, his brother said 'You can have the f**king things now if you want them'. The tribunal held that although his brother may not have intended to dismiss him, a reasonable man would have interpreted his words as a dismissal. Accordingly it was held that he had been dismissed.[57]

Words uttered in anger and withdrawn promptly may not amount to a dismissal,[58] but generally if an employer tells an employee to go he is in danger of being found to have dismissed him. The words used by

---

55   EAT No 376/00, 9.10.01.
56   (1974) IRLR 130.
57   *Kendricj v Aerduct Productions* [1974] IRLR 322.
58   *Martin v Yeomen Aggregates* [1983] ICR 314; [1983] IRLR 49.

the employer must be given their ordinary meaning and construed in their context, and only if then there is ambiguity will it be necessary to consider whether a reasonable employer might have understood them to be tantamount to dismissal.[59] Examples of statements which have been held to amount to dismissals include telling the employee he has been taken off the payroll,[60] telling the employee to 'f**k off and p**s off'.[61] An example of a statement which was held not to amount to a dismissal was 'if you are not satisfied you can f**k off',[62] because in that case it was thought that the employee was merely being invited to resign if he was not happy. When an employer has spoken words in anger they may held not to be a dismissal.

In *Tanner v Kean*,[63] the employer told the employee not to use the company van outside working hours. The employer lent him £275 to buy a car and was annoyed to find that he was still using the van. The employer said 'What's my f**king van doing outside; you're a tight bastard. I've just lent you £275 to buy a car and you are too tight to put juice in it. That's it, you're finished with me.' The EAT held that the tribunal was entitled to find that the employers words were spoken in annoyance and not to have been a dismissal. If the employer's words amount to a dismissal they cannot usually be retracted and the employee reinstated without his consent, since reinstatement cannot occur unilaterally.[64]

Similar principles apply to resignations and, where unambiguous words are used, the tribunal is likely to find there has been an effective notice even though it may have been done in haste and later regretted.[65] An employer is therefore entitled to act on the employee's unambiguous words of resignation, even if uttered in haste.[66]

---

59 *Stern (J & J) v Simpson* [1983] IRLR 52.
60 *Kirklees Metropolitan Council v Radecki* [2009] ICR1244.
61 *King v Webbs Pultry Products (Bradford) Ltd* 1975 IRLR 135.
62 *Davy v Collins (Builders) Ltd* [1974] IRLR 324.
63 [1978] IRLR 110.
64 *Chesham Shipping v Rowe* [1977] IRLR 391; CF *Capital v Willoughby* [2011] IRLR 985.
65 *BG Gale Ltd v Gilbert* [1978] ICR 1149.
66 *Greater Glasgow Health Board v MacKay* 1989 SLT 729.

If an employee is summarily dismissed with pay in lieu of notice the date of termination is the date the employee receives notification of the dismissal rather than the date on which the notice would have expired.[67]

The circumstances in which an employment tribunal would be prepared to extend the time limit are discussed in chapter 2.

Constructive dismissal

7.19 A constructive dismissal occurs where the employee terminates his contract with or without notice in circumstances as such that he is entitled to terminate it without notice by reason of the employer's conduct. In order for there to be a constructive dismissal the conduct of the employer must have been more than unfair or unreasonable[68] it must have amounted to a material breach of contract going to the root of the contract of employment, in other words a repudiation of the contract by the employer. In the case *Western Excavating (ECC) Ltd v Sharp,*[69] Lord Denning stated:

> 'If the employer is guilty of conduct which is a significant breach going to the root of the contract of employment or shows that he no longer intends to be bound by one of the essential terms of the contract, then the employee is entitled to be discharged from any further performance. If he does so then he terminates the contract by reason of the employer's conduct and he is constructively dismissed.'

In *Bournemouth University Higher Education Corp v Buckland,*[70] the Court of Appeal made it clear that when considering whether an employer was in fundamental breach of contract, an objective test applies rather than the range of reasonable responses test which is applied to determine whether the dismissal was fair. Furthermore, an employer who had committed a fundamental breach could not retract, cure or make amends for the breach prior to acceptance of the breach by the employee.

An employee must show that the employer must be in actual or anticipatory breach of an express or implied term of the contract, eg a

---

67 *Dedman v British Building & Engineering Appliances* [1974] ICR 53; *Robert Cort & Son Ltd v Charman* [1981] ICR 816; [1981] IRLR 437; EAT.

68 *Wadham Stringer Commercials (London) Ltd v Brown* [1983] IRLR 46.

69 (1978) QB 761, CA.

70 [2010] ICR 908.

delay in payment may not amount to repudiation of contract,[71] nor will a genuine dispute about a contractual provision,[72] but a refusal to pay or a reduction in pay without agreement will.[73] Other examples of repudiation of contract include forcing an employee to accept unreasonable changes to his conditions of employment, for example a change in status,[74] or change in hours.[75] A breach of the employers implied duties under the contract of employment is just as likely to give rise to a constructive dismissal as a breach of any of the express terms. Breaches of the implied duty of trust and confidence occur when an employer acts in a way which is calculated, or likely to damage or destroy, the relationship of trust and confidence between the parties.[76] This may include unfair investigatory procedures, failure to investigate complaints about health and safety[77] bullying or harassment, or permitting violence against an employee, failing to provide an employee with a safe system of work,[78] or making him work in dangerous conditions without his agreement.[79] It should be noted that a breach of the implied duty of trust and confidence at any time during the contract of employment, including during investigatory proceedings, will amount to repudiation of the contract,[80] but once the decision to dismiss has been made there is no room for an implied term of trust and confidence.[81] See above and chapter 4 for other examples of breaches of this duty.

The employer's underlying motive or the reasonableness of his conduct are not factors that can legitimately be taken into account when seeking to determine whether there had been a repudiatory breach of contract.[82] The breach must be sufficiently serious to justify the employee resigning or

---

71   *Adams v Charles Zub Associates Ltd* [1978] IRLR 258.
72   *Frank Wright and Co Ltd v Punch* [1980] IRLR 217.
73   *Hill(RF) v Mooney* [1981] IRLR 258; *Cantor Fitzgerald International v Callaghan* ICR 639.
74   *Hilton v Shiner Ltd* [2001] IRLR 727.
75   *Simmonds v Dowty Seals Ltd* [1978] ICR 211.
76   *Malik v BCCI SA* [1997] ICR 606.
77   *British Aircraft Corpn v Austin* [1978] IRLR 332.
78   *Dutton & Clark Ltd v Daly* [1985] ICR 780.
79   *Graham Oxley Tool Steels Ltd v Firth* [1980] IRLR 135.
80   *King v University of St Andrews* [2002] SLT 439.
81   *Johnson v Unisys Ltd* [2001] ICR 480.
82   *Hilton v Shiner Ltd* [2001] IRLR 727.

be last in a series of incidents which taken together, justify the employee leaving (ie the last straw principle).[83]

The employee must resign in response to the breach and not for any unconnected reason, and if he wishes to assert that he has been constructively dismissed the employee must make it clear that he is resigning because of the employer's breach of contract. In *Logabox Ltd v Titherley*,[84] the employer had delayed paying commission. Titherley resigned to take up new employment but his letter to his former employers stated that there was no question of a resignation or termination of the employment by himself, the contract had simply expired. The EAT held that, even if the employers' conduct in refusing to pay commission was a repudiation of the contract of employment, the employee had failed to accept and act on that refusal. In *Holland v Glendale Industries Ltd*,[85] a parks foreman received more responsibility, doing the job of a charge hand, and received higher pay, when the responsibility for parks was outsourced. Five years later he was told that this work was to be done by a younger man and the extra payments would stop. He resigned because of this but told his employer that he was resigning to take 'early retirement', therefore it was held that he had not been constructively dismissed.

The employee must not delay too long in terminating the contract in response to the employer's unreasonable behaviour, otherwise he or she may be deemed to have waived the breach and affirmed the contract.

A party in breach of contract may not rely on the terms of that contract,[86] therefore, in *Aberdeen City Council v McNeill*,[87] the EAT held that the claimant who was in a senior position of Sports and Leisure Manager had been in repudiatory breach of the contract of employment, in particular the implied term of trust and confidence, because he had harassed and bullied a junior colleague. It followed that since he was in prior repudiatory breach he was not entitled to terminate the contract on the basis that the

---

83   *Lewis v Motorworld Garages Ltd* [1986] ICR 157; *Wishaw and District Housing Association v Moncrief* UKEATS/0066/08.
84   [1977] ICR 369.
85   [1998] ICR 493.
86   *RDF Media Group Plc v Clements* [2008] IRLR 207.
87   [2010] IRLR 374.

local authority had itself then breached that implied term, therefore he was not entitled to claim constructive dismissal.

It must be noted that once a constructive dismissal has been proved the usual provisions regarding unfair dismissal apply in order to determine whether that dismissal was fair or unfair.

Just because an employee has been constructively dismissed that does not mean that he has been dismissed unfairly, for example in *Hilton v Shiner*[88] a demotion which constituted a repudiatory breach of contract was because the employer had suspicions that the employee was not trustworthy and the dismissal was ultimately held to be fair.

Non-renewal of fixed-term or completion of a specific task contract

7.20 Under s 95 of the Employment Rights Act 1996, where the employee is employed under a contract for a fixed term or to perform a specific task and the contract expires without being renewed under the same terms, this will be a dismissal.

Employees with at least one year's service (2 years service if they started their employment on or after 6 April 2012) have the right to a written statement of reasons for this dismissal (ERA 1996 s 92(1)(c)) and the right not to be unfairly dismissed. If the employee qualifies to make a claim of unfair dismissal, the employer will have to demonstrate that there was a potentially fair reason for the dismissal eg redundancy, that he acted reasonably, and the procedures followed were fair and reasonable. On completion of a specific task, or expiry of a fixed-term, the employer should offer the employee suitable alternative work if available. The assumption is that a fixed-term contract should terminate on the date specified, however, a fixed-term contract should only be terminated if there is no longer a requirement for that particular job to be done. This will normally arise where there is a cessation or reduction of an activity, or as the result of the funding underpinning the appointment being expended. Since the introduction of the Fixed Term Employee (Prevention of Less Favourable Treatment) Regulations 2002, there have been very few cases concerning fixed-term contracts. These Regulations made it unlawful to

---

88   [2001] IRLR 727.

treat a fixed-term employee less favourably than a comparable employee on a permanent contract.

However, in *Department for Work and Pensions v Webley*,[89] the Court of Appeal restored the employment tribunal decision that where the only act of less favourable treatment is the failure or a refusal of an employer to extend or renew a fixed-term contract, then termination of the contract at the end of that fixed term period cannot, of itself, be less favourable treatment in terms of the 2002 Regulations.

Reasons for dismissal

7.21 Employees with at least one year's service (two years for employees whose employment commenced on or after 6 April 2012) have the right to a written statement of reasons for this dismissal (ERA 1996 s 92(1)(c) and the right not to be unfairly dismissed. There are three categories of reasons for dismissal namely discriminatory reasons, automatically unfair reasons and potentially fair reasons.

Once the employee has proved a dismissal has occurred, the onus shifts to the employer to prove that the reason for the dismissal was one of the listed in ss 98(1)(b) and (2) of the Employment Rights Act 1996 (the potentially fair reasons). If it is a potentially fair reason then, under s 98(4) the employer must also prove that he has acted reasonably in treating it as a sufficient reason for dismissal and that he has followed fair procedures before reaching the decision to dismiss.

Under s 98 ERA 1996, there are only 5 potentially fair reasons for dismissal namely:

- Capability;
- Conduct;
- Redundancy;
- Illegality; and
- some other substantial reason.

If dismissal is not for one of these reasons it will be unfair.

---

89   [2005] IRLR 288.

In addition there are certain reasons which will be automatically unfair. If the employer dismisses for an automatically unfair reason, the dismissal will always be unfair no matter how reasonable the employer has been.

The tribunal will hold the dismissal of an employee to be automatically unfair if they are dismissed or selected for redundancy for the following reasons:

- for having sought, in good faith, to assert a statutory employment protection right;

- for exercising, or seeking to exercise, their right to be accompanied at a disciplinary or grievance hearing, or to accompany a fellow worker at such a meeting;

- for reasons relating to jury service;

- on grounds relating to pregnancy, childbirth or maternity, or for taking, or seeking to take, maternity leave, paternity leave, adoption leave, parental leave;

- for taking, or seeking to take, time off for dependants;

- for taking, or proposing to take, certain specified types of action on health and safety grounds;

- because, subject to certain conditions, the employee was a shop worker or a betting worker and refused to work on Sundays or gave, or was proposing to give, an 'opting-out' notice to their employer;

- for performing, or proposing to perform, any duties relevant to their role as an employee occupational pension scheme trustee for exercising, or for seeking to exercise, the right to be accompanied at a meeting to consider a request not to retire, or for exercising, or seeking to exercise, the right to accompany a fellow employee at such a meeting;

- for performing, or proposing to perform, any duties relevant to their role as an employee representative or as a candidate to be such representative or as a participant in the election of such a representative;

- for making a protected disclosure;

- for reasons relating to the national minimum wage;

- for requesting flexible working arrangements;
- on grounds related to the Part-time Workers (Prevention of Less Favourable Treatment) Regulations 2000 or the Fixed-term Employees (Prevention of Less Favourable Treatment) Regulations 2002 or for reasons relating to the Working Time Regulations 1998;
- for reasons relating to the European Public Limited-Liability Company Regulations 2004;
- for reasons relating to the Information and Consultation of Employees Regulations 2004;
- for reasons relating to the Occupational and Personal Pension Schemes (Consultation by Employers and Miscellaneous Amendment) Regulations 2006;
- for reasons relating to the European Cooperative Society (Involvement of Employees) Regulations 2006;
- for reasons relating to the Companies (Cross-Border Mergers) Regulations 2007.[90]

In the case of automatically unfair reasons, the employer need not comply with continuous service requirement in order to make a claim. In addition there are, in some cases, additional remedies available (see below).

---

90 Reasons related to industrial relations are: (i) because of their trade union membership, trade union non-membership, trade union activities or proposed activities, or use or proposed use of trade union services (2) because they failed to accept an unlawful inducement from an employer to give up their trade union rights or to disapply a collective agreement (3) because they failed to accept an offer made by an employer to induce them to become a trade union member (4) because they refused to make a payment in lieu of union membership, or objected to their employer deducting a sum from their wages or salary to make such a payment (5) for exercising or seeking to exercise rights relating to trade union recognition procedures (6) for taking lawfully organised official industrial action lasting 12 weeks or less (or more than 12 weeks in certain circumstances) for reasons relating to the Transnational Information and Consultation of Employees Regulations 1999.

Discriminatory reasons for dismissal

7.22 To dismiss for a reason which is a protected characteristic under s 9 of the Equality Act 2010 will usually amount to direct discrimination which cannot be justified (except where the protected characteristic is age), also some methods of selection for redundancy may amount to indirect discrimination which will be unfair if the employer cannot show that the provision, criterion or practice applied in the selection method was a proportionate means of achieving a legitimate aim.

If a dismissal amounts to discrimination then the employee will make a claim under the Equality Act 2010. There is no qualifying service required and no upper limit to compensation.

Potentially fair reasons and fair dismissals

7.23 We have already identified the five potentially fair reasons for dismissal. In *Abernethy v Mott*,[91] the Court of Appeal made it clear that although the employer may initially apply the wrong legal label to the dismissal, provided there is evidence that that the dismissal did relate to a potentially fair reason, the dismissal could be fair. In that case, the employer dismissed for redundancy when in fact the dismissal related to capability. It is often the case that more than one potentially fair reason is pled as a reason for dismissal.

Whether or not a potentially fair dismissal is actually fair depends on whether the employer has acted reasonably, and whether the procedures followed have been fair and reasonable. These two factors are often interlinked. Let us examine firstly the general requirements of reasonableness including procedural fairness, and secondly how these requirements apply to the individual potentially fair reasons for dismissal.

Reasonableness

7.24 The employer must have acted reasonably in treating the potentially fair reason as sufficient reason to dismiss the employee. This requirement on the employer is set out in s 98(4) Employment Rights Act 1996, which

---

91   [1974] ICR 323.

states that: 'the question is whether the employer acted reasonably or unreasonably in treating the reason as sufficient reason for dismissing the employee, and will be decided in accordance with equity and the substantial merits of the case.' In deciding this an important factor will be the procedures applied by the employer in reaching the decision to dismiss and these are considered below. The test for reasonableness is the same in each case, but how it applies will depend on the type of reason for dismissal and the facts and circumstances of the case. The test was set out in *Iceland Frozen Foods Ltd v Jones*:[92]

> '(1) the starting point should always be the words of [the section] themselves; (2) in applying the section an industrial tribunal must consider the reasonableness of the employer's conduct, not simply whether they (the members of the industrial tribunal) consider the dismissal to be fair; (3) in judging the reasonableness of the employer's conduct an industrial tribunal must not substitute its decision as to what was the right course to adopt for that of the employer; (4) in many, though not all, cases there is a band of reasonable responses to the employee's conduct within which one employer might reasonably take one view, another quite reasonably take another; (5) the function of the industrial tribunal, as an industrial jury, is to determine whether in the particular circumstance of each case the decision to dismiss the employee fell within the band of reasonable responses which a reasonable employer might have adopted. If the dismissal falls within the band the dismissal is fair: if the dismissal falls outside the band it is unfair.'

Although the test was doubted in subsequent cases, it was reaffirmed in *HSBC v Madden Foley v Post Office*.[93] In that case the Court of Appeal confirmed that the tribunal will not substitute its decision for that of the employer,[94] therefore the amount of latitude available to the employer is considerable. The dismissal may therefore be fair, even though another employer or indeed the tribunal would not have dismissed in these circumstances. The decision as to whether a dismissal was fair is one of

---

92 [1983] ICR 17 Lord Bridgewater at 24.
93 [2000] ICR 1283.
94 See also *Grundy (Teddington) Ltd v Willis* [1976] ICR 323; DB *Schenken Rail (UK) Ltd v Doolan* EAT (Scot) 13 April 2011.

fact for the tribunal to decide and the EAT will only interfere with this decision if the tribunal has applied the wrong test in law or the decision was perverse.[95] Recently in *North West London Hospitals NHS Trust v Bowater*,[96] the Court of Appeal made it clear that this should happen only rarely. In that case the employment tribunal considered whether the sacking of a nurse for making a lewd comment whilst trying to restrain a patient fell within the band of reasonable responses. The employment tribunal found that the comment could be described as lewd, but that most people would consider it to be merely humorous. It held that the decision to dismiss B fell outside the band of reasonable responses a reasonable employer could have adopted. The EAT overruled this decision but the Court of Appeal stated the EAT should not have interfered with the employment tribunal's decision since an appeal to the EAT only lay on a point of law and the EAT was not to substitute its own judgment under the guise of a charge of perversity.

The tribunal will make its decision on the facts known to the employer at the time the decision becomes effective and when considering whether an employee has been unfairly dismissed it is necessary to take account of the whole process of dismissal, and events occurring during the notice period are not excluded from consideration.[97] All the factors known to the employer at the time are relevant, including the employers' economic difficulties and the seriousness of breaching nationally negotiated agreements, and it is for the tribunal to balance these factors.[98]

An employer may not rely upon information which comes to light after the employee's dismissal to justify the dismissal, however such conduct may be taken into account in assessing compensation.[99]

Procedural fairness

7.25 A reasonable employer will have employed fair procedures before deciding to dismiss an employee and a failure to follow fair procedures

---

95 Iceland Frozen Foods supra 92.
96 [2011] EWCA Civ 63, [2011] IRLR 331.
97 *Stacey v Babcock Power Ltd* [1986] ICR 221.
98 *Kent County Council v Gilham* [1985] ICR 227.
99 *W Devis & Sons Ltd v Atkins* [1977] AC 931.

will, therefore, make the decision unfair unless it would have made no difference and the employee would have been dismissed anyway.[100] The exact nature of fair procedures will vary from case to case depending on the circumstances of the case and the reason for dismissal, however generally the employer must follow his own procedures (or risk being in breach of contract)[101] and in cases where the dismissal is for reasons relating to capability or conduct, he should follow the ACAS Code of Conduct on Discipline and Grievance.[102] Following the Gibbons Report,[103] the mandatory three step statutory procedure for discipline and grievance procedures was repealed and replaced[104] with the ACAS Code. The Code is not mandatory but if the employer unreasonably fails to follow it then an employment tribunal can increase any award it makes against the employer on a finding of unfair dismissal by up to 25%. Also, if an award has been made in favour of an employee who has unreasonably failed to follow the ACAS grievance procedures the tribunal may reduce the award by up to 25%.

It is also important to remember that the employee has the statutory right to request that he be accompanied by a work colleague or representative of an independent trade union (which need not be recognised), or representative of a trade union who has been trained in acting as a companion, to any disciplinary or grievance hearing under s 10 of the Employee Relations Act 1999.

This right applies to any disciplinary or grievance meeting, other than an investigative meeting or a meeting where the only outcome is an informal warning.

The right is to be accompanied and the companion may address the meeting to put the employee's case and to sum up, but cannot answer questions on the employee's behalf. There is no statutory right to legal representation, however, the contractual procedures may allow for this.

In situations where the result of the disciplinary procedures may be that the employee is barred from practising his trade or profession the

---

100 *Polkey v AE Dayton Services Ltd* [1988] CR 142.
101 But see *Edwards v Chesterfield* supra 30.
102 http://www.acas.org.uk/index.aspx?articleid=2174.
103 M Gibbons. A review of employment dispute resolution in Great Britain, March 2007
104 And s 199 of the Trade Union and Labour Relations (Consolidation) Act 1992.

employees rights under Article 6 of the European Convention of Human Rights (right to a fair trial) are engaged and, consequently, the failure to allow legal representation will render the dismissal unfair. This situation applies in professions where an employee may be struck off by his professional body or put on a list of persons unsuitable to work in certain fields. In *Kulkarni v Milton Keynes Hospitals NHS Trust*,[105] it was suggested that a doctor's Article 6 rights were engaged in disciplinary hearings relating to improper conduct towards a female patient since he could be struck off as a result of the proceedings, in any event it was decided he had this right under the contractual provisions. In *R v Governors of X School*,[106] a schoolteacher was accused of inappropriate behaviour with a young person who was at the school on work experience. The outcome of proceedings could have resulted in the teacher being placed on a list of persons unsuitable to work with children and vulnerable adults, therefore he was entitled to legal representation.

Article 6 does not apply where the outcome of proceedings will only involve loss of a particular job rather than the right to practice a trade or profession. The question is whether the outcome would have a substantial influence or effect on the determination of that right.[107] It remains to be seen whether these rights apply to workers in the private sector.

Dismissal for Capability or Qualifications of the employee

7.26 An employer may dismiss an employee for the reason of capability if the employee is failing to perform the work to the required standard. What the employer must do to comply with the requirements of reasonableness and procedural fairness will depend on the cause of the incapability. In cases of dismissal for capability or conduct reasons, the ACAS Code of Practice on Discipline and Grievance applies (see below), and the employer should follow the Code and his own procedures giving preference to the Code if the two are incompatible. The case law regarding

---

105 [2010] ICR 101.
106 [2010] IRLR 222.
107 *R (on the application of Puri) v Bradford Teaching Hospitals NHS Foundation Trust* [2011] IRLR 582; [2011].

procedures prior to dismissal should therefore be read in the light of the Code and any contractual requirements.

The reason for the incapability may result from a wide range of circumstances. The most common of these are:

(1)   The employee inherently lacks the physical or mental capacity to perform the work to the required standard.

(2)   The employee has become mentally or physically unable to do the work to the required standard because of illness.

(3)   The employee is failing to perform the work to the required standard because of deliberate or neglectful incompetence.

(4)   The employee cannot perform the work to the required standard because the nature of the work or the way of doing the job has changed and he cannot adapt to the change.

(5)   The employee does not have the formal qualifications required to do the work.

Let us examine each of these causes in more detail.

(1) Inherent inability

7.27 If the employee lacks the necessary mental or physical ability to do the job, the reasonable employer would be expected to be sympathetic, in so far as he would be expected to identify the ways in which the employee was failing and to provide suitable support and training. In approaching a case involving dismissal on grounds of lack of capability, the employment tribunal should clearly distinguish in their own minds whether the case in point is one of sheer incapability due to incapacity to function, or one of failure to exercise to the full such talent as is possessed. In the latter case, this would be incapability due to deliberate or neglectful incompetence. In *Abernethy v Mott Hay and Anderson*,[108] an employee's 'inflexibility' and 'lack of adaptability' came within his 'aptitude and mental qualities' and therefore within the statutory definition of 'capability'.

In the situation where the employee is simply incompetent, the reasonable employer will provide supervision and training. An employer

---

108 (1974) IRLR 486 EAT.

will be expected to support an employee and provide clear instructions and training. In *Davidson v Kent Meters Ltd*[109] the employee was dismissed when she failed to assemble approximately 500 components in the right order. The supervisor denied having shown her how to do this and her dismissal was held to be unfair because if he had not shown her how to do it he should have.

If supervision and training do not result in an improvement, the employer should consider alternatives to dismissal, transfer or, as a last resort, demotion. If an employee is performing poorly they should usually be warned that their work is unsatisfactory and given a chance to improve before any further action is taken. 'In the case of incapacity, an employer will normally not act reasonably unless he gives the employee fair warning and the opportunity to mend his ways and show that he can do the job.'[110] If a warning would have avoided the need for a dismissal, then the failure to warn will render the dismissal unfair.[111] However, warnings and a chance to improve are not always required where they would make no difference.[112] A lack of warning does not necessarily make the dismissal unfair. The strict procedural requirements of dismissal for misconduct do not apply to cases of dismissal for lack of capability and the correct question is whether the employee's incapability warranted dismissal, and whether he might have been able to improve following a warning.[113]

Where the incompetence is extremely serious it is not necessary to issue warnings, and the employee can be dismissed for the first incident of incompetence. In *Taylor v Alidair Ltd*,[114] a pilot who was negligent in landing a plane was deemed fairly dismissed by reason of his incapability of doing the job to the required standard.

(2) Mental or physical inability due to illness

7.28 Ill health can cause the employee to be incapable of doing the job either on a temporary or permanent basis. Illness is not normally a form

---

109 [1975] IRLR 145.
110 *Lord Bridge in Polkey v AE Dayton Services.*
111 *Winterhalter Gastronom Ltd v Webb* [1973] ICR 245.
112 *AJ Dunning (Shopfitters) Ltd v Jacomb* [1973] ICR 448.
113 *Littlewoods Organisation Ltd v Egenti* [1976] ICR 516.
114 (1978) IRLR 82.

of misconduct so it should be not be treated as such, unless the absences for ill health are in effect unauthorised absenteeism. Often the employer cannot obtain a prognosis for intermittent unrelated absences. In such a situation the employer may set an acceptable attendance standard and, if the standard is not met, follow the relevant disciplinary procedures and ultimately dismiss the employee. With respect to long term ill health this could frustrate the contract and, if so, this may mean the contract is terminated but there is no dismissal. In the case of long term ill health which does not amount to frustration, although the employer is still entitled to dismiss, he must try to get medical reports[115] and consult[116] the employee about their condition first. The employee should be consulted and alternatives considered. The employee is expected to cooperate in providing information and a failure to do so may make a dismissal fair.[117]

If consultation would have made no difference then a failure to consult will not make the dismissal unfair. In *Taylorplan Catering Scotland v McInally*,[118] following six months' illness, the employee was seen by a company medical officer who advised that he was medically unfit to continue his employment. His own GP had agreed. He was informed of this advice rather than consulted and sent a letter dismissing him. The tribunal held that since discussion would only have delayed the dismissal by two weeks, the failure to consult did not make the dismissal unfair.

Once the employer has made investigations and consulted the employee, he then has to decide how long he is willing to wait for recovery.

In cases where the capability of the employee is affected by long term sickness, the tribunal will consider whether a reasonable employer would have dismissed the employee taking into account all the circumstances of the case. The factors which will be taken into consideration include the length of service of the employee, the length of the job, the nature of the job, the expected length of absence and prognosis, the effect of his absence on the employer's business, and the resources available to the employer. An employer is not expected to hold the sick employee's job

---

115 *East Lindsey District Council v Daubney* [1977] IRLR 181.
116 *A Links & Co v Rose* [1991] IRLR 353.
117 *McGivney v Portman Mansions Management Ltd* [2011] All ER (D) 74 (Jan), EAT.
118 [1980] IRLR 53.

open indefinitely,[119] or to go to unreasonable lengths to accommodate the employee. What is reasonable is a matter for the tribunal to decide and if an employee is not fit for night shift it may decide that a reasonable employer would have moved him to day shift if there was an available position.[120]

The fact that the employer may be responsible for the employee's illness does not prevent a fair dismissal where the employee is incapable of performing the work.[121]

Persistent absenteeism may be regarded as reason for dismissal even though all the illnesses appear to be short term and unrelated.[122]

In *Lynock v Cereal Packaging Ltd*,[123] the EAT gave guidance to the employer contemplating dismissal because of persistent absenteeism. They stated that factors to be taken into account included the nature of the illness, the likelihood of a recurrence, and length of absences and periods of 'good spells', the need of the employer to have the work done, impact on other employees, the adoption and carrying out of the sickness policy, and the fact that the employee has been warned of the consequences of continued absence from work, and the likelihood of dismissal.

Obviously in dealing with dismissal for illness related incapability the provisions of the Equality Act 2010 relating to disability discrimination, in particular the employer's duty to make reasonable adjustment must be considered where the illness amounts to a disability in terms of s 6 of this Act (see chapter 9).

(3) Deliberate or neglectful incompetence

7.29 In cases where a person has not come up to the required standard through his own carelessness, negligence or idleness, they are much more appropriately dealt with as cases of misconduct rather than of capability (see below). In such cases support and training may be less appropriate but the employee will generally be entitled to receive warnings prior to

---

119 *Coulson v Felixstowe Dock and Railway Co Ltd* [1975] IRLR 11.
120 *Garrick Caterers Ltd v Nolan* [1980] IRLR 259.
121 *Royal Bank of Scotland Plc v McAdie* [2008] ICR 1087.
122 *International Sports Limited v Thomson* [1980] IRLR 340.
123 (1988) ICR 670.

dismissal unless the first incidence of incompetence is so serious that it justifies summary dismissal,[124] or if the employer can no longer be expected to have trust and confidence in the employee.[125]

(4) The nature of the work or the way of doing the job has changed and the employee cannot adapt to the change

7.30 An employee who refuses to adapt to a new way of doing the job will be in breach of the implied term as to obedience.[126] If the employee simply cannot adapt or attend training,[127] then he may be dismissed due to incapability. The reasonable employer would identify the particular areas in which the employee was deficient and would provide supervision and training coupled with a series of warnings as to what is likely to happen if the employee's performance does not improve. If the nature of the work, or the way in which it is done, has changed substantially it may be that the employer has a diminished need for the particular type of employee and that he is in fact redundant.[128]

(5) Lack of necessary formal qualifications

7.31 In a situation where obtaining a qualification is a prerequisite for a job (eg HGV licence) or is a requirement arising within employment (eg accountancy, banking), a failure to possess or obtain the qualification may well justify dismissal. In order to dismiss an employee under the capability ground for failing to have a qualification, it must be an implied term of the contract that it was essential to hold the qualification in order to do the job. In *Tayside Regional Council v McIntosh*,[129] the EAT held that it was an implied term of the contract of employment as a vehicle mechanic that the employee should have a valid driving licence. When he was disqualified from driving his subsequent dismissal was fair.

---

124 *Taylor v Alidair Ltd* [1978] IRLR 82.
125 *Cook v Thomas Linnell and Sons Ltd* [1977] ICR 770.
126 *Cresswell v Inland Revenue Commissioners* [1984] ICR 508.
127 *Coward v John Menzies (Holdings) Ltd* [1977] IRLR 428.
128 *North Riding Garages v Butterwick* [1967] 2 QB 56; [1967] 2 WLR 571 but see *Hindle v Percival Boats* [1969] 1 WLR 174.
129 [1982] IRLR 272.

Even if the qualification is a necessary requirement the employer must act reasonably, for example by finding suitable alternative employment or giving the employee more time and support to obtain the qualification. In *Sutcliffe & Eaton Ltd v Pinney*,[130] a trainee hearing aid dispenser failed to pass the necessary exams and was dismissed. It was held that this was an unfair dismissal because she could have been given more time to re-sit them.

A failure to have the requisite qualification may also make it illegal to continue to employ the employee in that particular role.

Conduct

7.32 The term conduct covers a wide variety of behaviour ranging from minor faults, eg bad time-keeping, absenteeism, and breaching a dress code,[131] to serious misconduct, eg being drunk at work. Persistent minor misconduct may eventually justify dismissal after appropriate disciplinary procedures have been applied. Where less serious forms of misconduct are involved, informal counselling and a series of warnings should be given before dismissing an employee, but gross misconduct on the part of an employee will give his employer good reason to dismiss him without notice. Examples of gross misconduct include dishonesty,[132] fighting, taking drugs, abusive behaviour, and using the internet for accessing pornography, and unauthorised use of a computer to access confidential information.[133] The contract of employment or the employer's policies and procedures may cite behaviour which will be regarded as gross misconduct. Conduct need not actually be reprehensible to amount to the potentially fair reason.[134]

In determining if the employer acted reasonably the tribunal will consider if they have followed fair procedures in the dismissal. It is important an employer investigates any accusations of misconduct thoroughly and satisfy themselves that the employee is responsible for

---

130 (1977) IRLR 349.
131 *Atkin v Enfield Hospital Management Committee* [1975] IRLR 217.
132 *Parkers Bakeries v Palmer.*
133 *Denco Ltd v Joinson* [1991] ICR 172.
134 *Royal Bank of Scotland v Donaghay Scottish* EAT 11 November 2011.

the conduct complained of. Where there is an accusation of dishonesty, the employer does not need absolute proof of it but there must be strong evidence of the dishonesty for them to dismiss the employee. In *BHS Ltd v Burchell*,[135] it was decided that where an employee is dismissed because the employer suspects or believes they are guilty of misconduct, the employment tribunal in determining the fairness of the dismissal has to be satisfied that the employer entertained a reasonable suspicion amounting to a belief in the guilt of an employee of the misconduct at that time. This involves three elements: firstly there must be a genuine belief, secondly there must be reasonable grounds on which to sustain that belief, and thirdly the employer must have carried as much investigation into the matter as was reasonable in all the circumstances of the case.

The Court of Appeal has stated that the employer's investigation process should be looked at, as a process in itself, and must be reasonable.[136] The band of reasonable responses test applied by the tribunal, applies to the investigation process, and therefore to procedure, as much as it does to the substantive decision to dismiss the employee.[137]

In *Panama v London Borough of Hackney*,[138] the approach taken in *British Home Stores v Burchell* was reaffirmed as correct by the Court of Appeal. Here an employer failed to carry out adequate and reasonable investigation into the conduct of an employee before dismissing her. Although the employer believed in the guilt of the employee, and thus satisfied the first of the *Burchell* requirements, it failed to comply with the second and third of the *Burchell* requirements, which are to have reasonable grounds for its belief and to have carried carry out as much investigation into the matter as was reasonable before taking the decision to dismiss the employee.

It is not therefore sufficient that the employer genuinely believed that the employee had committed misconduct. The genuine belief must be based on reasonable grounds,[139] and it the reasonableness is assessed on the facts in possession of the employer at the time the dismissal was

---

135 (1978) IRLR 379 EAT.
136 *Whitbread plc v Hall* [2001] IRLR 275.
137 *Sainsbury (J) Ltd v Hitt* [2003] ICR 111.
138 (2003) IRLR 278, CA.
139 *Porter v Oakbank School* CSIH 19/3/04.

carried out.[140] It is not always necessary to wait until a finding of guilt in court,[141] but a thorough investigation must be carried out. In *Securicor Guarding v Rouse*,[142] the employer dismissed a security guard facing criminal charges involving sexual offences against children without seeking the views of the relevant client he was working for and this was held to be an unfair dismissal. It is possible for an employer to use covert surveillance to investigate misconduct provided its use is proportionate.[143] If it is not proportionate it will be considered a breach of the employee's human rights, under Article 8 of the European Convention of Human Rights, and the dismissal will be unfair.

It is the knowledge of the person who is carrying out the dismissal which is important, not the knowledge of other senior employees,[144] but other factors may be considered such as the HR resources of the employer.[145]

An employer may not rely upon misconduct by an employee which comes to light after his dismissal to justify the dismissal. Such conduct may only be taken into account in assessing compensation.[146]

Where there is more than one employee involved in a misconduct the employer should act consistently, although it is possible to differentiate between employees for relevant reasons such as prior good/bad disciplinary record, or status within the company. Where it is not possible to identify which of a group was the wrongdoer it may be fair to dismiss all of them.[147]

In deciding whether the decision to dismiss was within the band of reasonable responses test factors such as the nature of the misconduct, the employee's position in the organisation is relevant, eg was he in a position of trust, his length of service and his previous good record.

---

140 *Carr v Alexander Russell Ltd* [1979] ICR 469.
141 *Harris & Shepherd v Courage (Eastern) Ltd* [1982] ICR 509.
142 [1994] IRLR 633.
143 *McGowan v Scottish Water* [2005] IRLR 167; *Corus UK Ltd v AM Mainwaring* EAT 22/6/07.
144 *Orr v Milton Keynes Council* [2011] EWCA Civ 62, [2011] IRLR 317.
145 *Sakharkar v Northern Foods Grocery Group Ltd (t/a/Foxes biscuits)* EAT 18/3/11.
146 *W Devis & Sons Ltd v Atkins* [1977] AC 931.
147 *Monie v Coral Racing Ltd* [1980] IRLR 464.

In *Pepper v Webb*,[148] a gardener was asked to plant some flowers in a greenhouse in his employer's garden. He was rude to his employer's wife when first asked, and then when his employer asked him his response was to say to his employer 'I couldn't care less about your bloody greenhouse and your sodding garden' and to walk off. It was held that this behaviour represented a repudiation of the employee's contract and the employer was entitled to terminate it.

Another matter which is relevant is whether the employer has considered alternatives to dismissal such as suspension (with or without pay), transfer or training. Also, where the dismissal is based on conduct, has the employer considered if there are mitigating circumstances[149] for the employee's behaviour (see *Taylor v Parson Peebles* above). The employment tribunal will also consider if he has applied his disciplinary rules in accordance with rules of equity and natural justice. With respect to equity all employees should be subject to the same disciplinary action for the same type of misconduct. In *The Post Office v Fennel*,[150] it was held that 'the word equity … comprehends the concept that employees who behave in much the same way should have meted out to them the same punishment. Where this is not done and an employee is treated unduly harshly this amounts to unfair dismissal.'

Natural justice requires the employer to endeavour to ensure that the process of disciplining or dismissing the employee is not tainted by breaches of natural justice. In *Khanum v Mid-Glamorgan Area Health Authority*,[151] it was held that there are only three basic requirements of natural justice which have to be complied with during the proceedings of a domestic disciplinary enquiry. Firstly that the person should know the nature of the accusation against him, secondly, that he should be given an opportunity to state his case, and thirdly, that the tribunal should act in good faith.[152]

---

148 (1969) 2 ALL ER 216, CA.
149 Eg exemplary work history, personal problems underlying behaviour etc.
150 (1981) IRLR 221 CA.
151 (1978) IRLR 215, EAT.
152 *Tehrani v United Kingdom Central Council for Nursing, Midwifery and Health visiting* (2001) IRLR 208.

In *Ladbroke Racing Ltd v Arnott*,[153] it was held that the standard of acting reasonably ... requires an employer to consider all the facts relevant to the nature and the cause of the breach, including the degree of its gravity. They held that where there is a rule prohibiting a specific act for which the stated penalty is instant dismissal, an employer does not satisfy the requirement of acting reasonably if he imposes that penalty without regard to any facts or circumstances other than the breach itself.

The tribunal will consider whether the employer followed the ACAS Code of Practice on Discipline and Grievance.[154] They will also consider whether the employer followed his own disciplinary procedures. Every employer must have a disciplinary and grievance procedure[155] and in *Stoker v Lancashire County Council*[156] it was stated that a reasonable employer can be expected to comply with the full requirements of the procedure in his own disciplinary code. In *West Midlands Cooperative Society v Tipton*,[157] it was decided by the House of Lords that, where the contract specifies that employees entitled to a right of appeal against dismissal, failure to offer right of appeal will lead to a finding of unfair dismissal.[158]

Rigid and inflexible application of contractual procedures may not always be fair, and even where misconduct is cited as gross misconduct justifying dismissal in the employer's disciplinary procedure, it may not be sufficient to justify dismissal where mitigating circumstances apply. In *Taylor v Parsons Peebles*,[159] a tribunal was found by the EAT to have erred in law in finding that the employer's acted reasonably in dismissing an employee with a long service of good conduct for striking a fellow worker, simply because the company's disciplinary rules laid down that such behaviour would lead to a dismissal.

The ACAS Code on Discipline and Grievance applies to dismissals for incapability, or misconduct. It does not apply to failures to renew fixed term contracts, dismissals due to redundancy, or illegality. Although

---

153 (1983) IRLR 154, CS.
154 At www.acas.org.uk see Disciplinary and grievance procedures.
155 *W A Goold (Pearmak) Ltd v McConnell* (1995) IRLR 516.
156 (1992) IRLR 75, CA.
157 (1986) ICR 192 HL.
158 *Post Office v Mearney* (1990) IRLR 170 EAT.
159 (1981) IRLR 82.

the provisions of the Code are not compulsory, if it is not followed the tribunal may increase any awards for compensation for employees can be adjusted upwards by up to 25%. For the first time, it is necessary for employers to inform employees of their right to be accompanied and, if the employer fails to do so, it's a breach of the ACAS Code and so could lead to a potential uplift in compensation.[160] Employees will no longer need to lodge a written grievance with their employer before they can bring a tribunal claim. However, their failure to do so may mean that any compensation they are awarded is reduced. The new Code sets out a framework for conducting grievance and disciplinary proceedings fairly and resolving workplace disputes.

The main general points of the Code are:

•   employers and employees should raise and deal with issues promptly and without unreasonable delay.

•   employers should carry out all necessary investigations to establish the facts.

•   employers and employees should act consistently.

•   Employers should inform employees of the basis of any problem and allow them an opportunity to put their case before any decision is made.

•   Employees have a statutory right be allowed to be accompanied to any formal disciplinary or grievance meeting by a co worker or trade union representative.

It should be noticed that there is no right to be represented (legally or otherwise) at a disciplinary or grievance hearing unless there is a possibility that the outcome of the procedure will be not only dismissal but the employee may lose his right to practise his trade or profession (see above).

The ACAS Code on Disciplinary Procedures would expect employers to follow a typical procedure set out by them. Normally disciplinary action would commence with an informal investigatory meeting first between a

---

160 Under previous law it had just been required that the employee could not be unreasonably refuse a representative now they've got to be told of their right to be accompanied as well.

manager and his employee to establish facts, where no disciplinary action would be taken. Where there was a failure after a given time to improve, this would be followed by a formal disciplinary hearing where an oral warning can be delivered. Where again there is no further improvement over the given time, this would normally be followed by a written warning (and possibly final written warning following that) and then the dismissal (could be a hearing at this stage). Employees should be allowed to appeal against any formal decision to dismiss.

Grievances are concerns, problems, or complaints that employees raise with their employers. If an employee resigns and claims constructive unfair dismissal without following the ACAS Code on Discipline and Grievance, or if the tribunal feels the failure to follow the Code on the part of the employee (perhaps by failing to turn up or other refusal to participate in the procedures) contributed to the dismissal, they may reduce any award by up to 25%.

It is irrelevant to the question of reasonableness that if the employer had followed the correct procedures the dismissal would have occurred anyway. It is the employer's action in dismissing the employee which is to be characterised as reasonable or unreasonable. The leading case on this point is *Polkey v Dayton Services Ltd.*[161] Although the reason for dismissal in this case was redundancy, it applies also to dismissals for conduct. The facts of the case were that the company employed four van drivers, including the applicant. It was decided to replace the four drivers with two van sales people. Only one of the existing drivers was thought capable of carrying out the selling as well as driving function, so the other three were made redundant. The first that Polkey knew of any of this was when he was called into the office, told that he was redundant and sent home. There was no warning, consultation or discussion with the employees. The case went all the way to the House of Lords who set a new precedent for unfair dismissal cases. With respect to lack of consultation they stated that 'thus in the case of a failure to give an opportunity to explain, except in the rarest of cases (where a reasonable employer could properly take the view on the facts known to him at the time of the dismissal that no explanation or mitigation could alter his decision to dismiss) an industrial

---

161 (1988) AC 344 HL.

tribunal would be likely to hold that the lack of equity inherent in the failure to consult, would render the dismissal unfair.' The House of Lords rejected the employer's argument that since consultation would not have made any difference to his decision to dismiss the employee the dismissal was fair. Overruling *British Labour Pump v Byrne*,[162] the House of Lords held that this argument was irrelevant for deciding whether a dismissal is fair or unfair, although it is relevant in assessing compensation.[163] The effect of *Polkey* has been a renewed emphasis on the importance of using correct procedures in relation to all kinds of dismissal.[164] However, where a dismissal is unfair purely on procedural grounds, a tribunal can reduce the compensation to the claimant, or eliminate it completely, in proportion to the likelihood that the dismissal would have gone ahead even if the correct procedure had been followed. This reduction is known as the 'Polkey reduction'. It applies only to the compensatory award.

Conduct out with the workplace

7.33 The general rule is that if the conduct does not relate to the employment relationship then the dismissal will be unfair.[165] In *Bradshaw v Rugby Portland Cement Co Ltd*,[166] the employee was dismissed when he was convicted of incest with his daughter. The dismissal was held to be unfair because the offence did not relate to or affect his employment as a quarryman.

Conduct will relate to the employment relationship if there is a connection between the conduct and the employment, eg an offence of dishonesty where the employee is in a position of trust. In *Moore v C&A Modes*,[167] a manager in a store who had 20 years service was dismissed when she was suspected of shoplifting in another store. She signed a form

---

162 *British Labour Pump Co Ltd v Byrne* [1979] ICR 347, EAT.
163 An unfair dismissal for conduct can be unfair purely on the basis of a procedural failure but if the tribunal is satisfied that the employee's conduct was such that they would have been dismissed in any event they may apply *Polkey* and reduce the compensatory award.
164 See in particular Lord Bridges comments.
165 *Thomson v Alloa Motor Co Ltd* [1983] IRLR 403.
166 [1972] IRLR 46.
167 [1981] IRLR 71.

admitting taking goods without paying, but later protested her innocence. It was held that her employers were entitled to dismiss her as they had a reasonable suspicion of her dishonesty.

In *Matthewson v RB Dental Laboratory Ltd*,[168] the employee was fairly dismissed after being arrested for possession of cannabis in his lunch hour.

In *Gardiner v Newport County Borough Council*,[169] a lecturer at an art college was convicted of gross indecency with another man in a public lavatory. His dismissal was fair as his behaviour was unacceptable in someone who had responsibility for students aged 16-18 years old.

Indeed, anything which seriously affects the employer's trust or confidence in the employee is likely to allow the employer to dismiss, In the case of *Richardson v City of Bradford*[170] a senior meat inspector, was fairly dismissed after admitting thefts of money from a rugby club bar.

An employee's conduct out with the workplace may also entitle the employer to dismiss if it affects the employer's interests, including his financial interests, including breach of the duty not to compete with the employer,[171] or to make secret profits.[172]

In recent years, employers have increasingly dismissed employees who they felt conducted themselves in ways which affected the employer's reputation, for example by posting unflattering comments on Facebook. It will not always be fair to dismiss in such cases if no actual damage is done to reputation. In *Whitham v Club 24 Ltd (t/a Ventura)*,[173] the employee's comments were only available to friends and, although damage could have been done to the employer's relationship with an important client, no actual damage was done and in these circumstances the tribunal felt the dismissal was unfair.

There is of course some tension between the employer's interests and the employee's rights to privacy under Article 8, and freedom of expression under Article 10, of the European Convention of Human Rights. In *Pay v UK*,[174] the European Court of Human Rights considered

---

168 [1988] IRLR 512.
169 [1974] IRLR 262.
170 *Richardson v City of Bradford Metropolitan Council* [1975] IRLR 296.
171 *Hivac Ltd v Park Royal Scientific Instrument* [1946] Ch 169.
172 *Neary v Dean of Westminster* [1999] IRLR 288.
173 *Whitham v Club 24 Ltd (t/a Ventura)* Unreported 2011 (ET).
174 [2009] IRLR 139.

the dismissal of a probation officer for conduct in his private life. Part of his duties included the supervision and rehabilitation of sex offenders. His employers dismissed him when they discovered that he was appearing on the internet and in private members clubs advertising his business which sold sadomasochistic and bondage equipment. They felt that this behaviour undermined their credibility and affected their reputation. The dismissal was held by the tribunal to be fair and proportionate. The EAT upheld this decision. He brought a case against the UK claiming that his right to privacy under Article 8 and his right to freedom of expression under Article 10 had been infringed. The Court held that sexual orientation and sexual life were important elements of the personal sphere protected by Article 8. However, his rights under Article 8 were not engaged in respect of that part of the conduct which had appeared on the internet and was therefore no longer private. Article 8 was engaged in respect of the conduct in private members clubs where there was a reasonable expectation of privacy, and his rights under Article 8 had been infringed in this respect. As he was dismissed as a consequence of his expression of aspects of his sexual identity, Article 10 was also engaged and had been interfered with. However, in both instances the interference was considered necessary in a democratic society to protect the interests of others namely his employers. While the dismissal of a specialist public servant was a very severe measure, it was important that Pay maintained the respect of the offenders placed under his supervision and also the confidence of the public in general, and victims of sex crime in particular. Therefore, given that he had not accepted that his activities could be damaging the nature of his work with sex offenders and the fact that the dismissal resulted from his failure to curb even those aspects of his private life most likely to enter into the public domain, the dismissal measure was not disproportionate.

In *X v Y (Employment: Sex Offender)*,[175] the Court of Appeal held that the interpretative duty imposed by s 3 of the Human Rights Act 1998 applied to the same degree in legislation which applied between private parties, as it did in legislation which applied between public authorities and individuals. Therefore, when Convention rights are engaged, an employer will be able to dismiss an employee for behaviour which affects

---

175 [2004] ICR 1634.

his interests, but the interpretation of reasonableness under s 98 of the Employment Rights Act 1996 will include consideration of whether the dismissal is proportionate in order to protect these interests.

In *A v B*,[176] a public authority dismissed an employee who had been accused of paedophile activity in Cambodia, even though the Cambodian court had acquitted him. He did not work with children but the EAT held that where an employer had taken reasonable steps to assess the reliability of unproven allegations of paedophile activity made by the police against its employee, it was entitled to treat that information as reliable and to dismiss the employee to avoid potential reputational damage and that his lack of openness with his employer about what happened in Cambodia justified summary dismissal.

Redundancy

7.34 Redundancy is a potentially fair reason for dismissal and is discussed below.

Illegality

7.35 It is a potentially fair reason to dismiss an employee if it would be illegal to continue to employ them, for example if they lost their work permit or right to reside in the UK, were disqualified from driving, or were in breach of health and safety legislation. Where there is statutory restriction on employing, or continuing to employ, someone then the employer would be entitled to dismiss them particularly, if the employer would otherwise be in breach of the civil or criminal law. However, the employer should check whether the situation can be made legal before dismissing the employee. He should also offer alternative employment if that would be legal.

The employer is expected to find an alternative solution if it is reasonable to do so, but what is reasonable will depend, amongst other things, on the resources of the employer. It may be unfair for an employer to dismiss an employee who had been disqualified for driving but who had

---

176 [2010] IRLR 844.

offered to pay for a chauffer at his own expense.[177] However, in *Appleyard v Smith (Hull) Ltd (2)*,[178] because of the size of the firm the employer found it impracticable to find alternative employment for a mechanic who was disqualified from driving because of a traffic conviction.

Some other substantial reason

7.36 This pertains if the reason for the dismissal is fair but does not fall within any of the preceding categories. This is very wide and is used to cover other possible reasons for dismissal where the other categories do not apply. It is often pled along with another potentially fair reason.

This ground for dismissal is often used where there has been a breach of trust. If an employer can show that the reason for dismissal of an employee was a 'substantial reason of a kind such as to justify the dismissal of an employee holding the position which that employee held (commonly referred to as 'some other substantial reason' or 'SOSR') then the dismissal is, in effect, *prima facie* (on the face of it) fair.[179]

Another example might be where an employee does not agree to a reorganisation or restructuring of the work, for example a change in working hours.[180] Providing it can be shown that such changes are necessary, eg for sound business reasons,[181] it will be a fair dismissal if an employee refuses to accept them.[182]

The employer is once more entitled to protect their financial interests and, in *Foot v Eastern Counties Timber Co Ltd*, the claimant was fairly dismissed because she had access to confidential information and he husband worked for a rival company.[183] In *RS Components v Irwin*,[184] a salesman was fairly dismissed when he refused to sign a restrictive covenant which was reasonable in its terms. In *Henderson v Connect*

177 *Mathieson v WJ Noble* [1972] IRLR 76.
178 [1972] IRLR 19.
179 ERA 1996 s 98(1)(b).
180 *Muggeridge and Slade v East Anglia Plastics Ltd* [1973] IRLR 163.
181 *Hollister v National Farmers Union* [1979] IRLR 238, CA.
182 *Scott & Co v Richardson* [2005] All ER (D) 87 (Jun), EAT.
183 [1972] IRLR 83.
184 [1973] ICR 535.

(South Tyneside) Ltd,[185] an employee was a coach driver who was fairly dismissed when a client refused to have him work for them because of allegations of sexual abuse which had been held to be unfounded. The fact that the client was acting unjustly did not make the dismissal unfair.

This potentially fair reason for dismissal can sometimes 'fill the gap' left by other potentially fair reasons. A genuine but mistaken belief by employers that to continue to employ a Turkish employee would be unlawful under immigration law, constituted 'some other substantial reason' justifying his dismissal.[186] If the reason for dismissal is that the employer has reasonable concerns about the employee's likely future conduct, it is not appropriate to dismiss for reasons relating to conduct but may be appropriate to dismiss for some other substantial reason.[187] If two employees simply don't get on and their behaviour is disrupting the harmony of the workplace, it is fair to dismiss one of them provided the employer has exhausted all other possibilities such as alternative work.[188] It may be impossible to prove which of a group of workers committed an act of dishonesty and, therefore, inappropriate to dismiss any of them for conduct, but the employer may dismiss all of them for some other substantial reason.[189] It may even be appropriate to dismiss some, but not all, provided there is justification for treating them differently. In *Frames Snooker Centre v Boyce*,[190] the employer suspected employees of being involved in a theft from the safe. He could not prove which of them had done it but one of them was his daughter, who he trusted and so it was fair to dismiss the other two but not her.

In all cases the employer must still have acted reasonably including, where appropriate, carrying out a thorough investigation, consulting the employee following fair procedures, and considering alternatives.

---

185 [2010] IRLR 466.
186 *Bouchaala v Trusthouse Forte Hotels Ltd* [1980] ICR 721.
187 *O'Brien v Prudential Assurance Co* [1979] IRLR 140.
188 *Gorfin v Distressed Gentlefolks Aid Association* [1973] IRLR 290; *Turner v Vesteric Ltd* [1980] ICR 528.
189 *Parr v Whitbread & Co PLC* [1990] ICR 427.
190 [1992] IRLR 472.

Remedies for unfair dismissal

7.37 The employee must bring a claim within three months of the effective date of dismissal. The tribunal has the power to extend this period where it believes it was not reasonably practicable for the applicant to present the claim within this time. This will be a question of fact for the tribunal, although they tend to adopt a strict approach, so lack of knowledge of the legal rules will not suffice, nor will the failure of a representative to take the appropriate action. Time limits and continuous employment are discussed in chapter 2.

In the event that it finds that the dismissal was unfair, the tribunal has several remedies available to it.

Reinstatement and reengagement

7.38 Reinstatement and reengagement are remedies for unfair dismissal,[191] and both involve re-employment of the dismissed employee. The tribunal must explain its powers to make such an order, although if it does not do so, the other orders it makes will remain valid unless the employee was prejudiced by the failure.[192]

Reinstatement is re-employment of the employee in the role that he was dismissed from and treated as if the dismissal had never occurred. Reengagement is re-employment of the employee into a different role to the one he was dismissed from, on terms and conditions as close as is reasonably practicable to those he was dismissed from. In either case the continuity of employment is preserved. The latter remedy is particularly useful where relations between the employee and his supervisor or colleagues has broken down. The tribunal may specify the terms and conditions relating to the re-engagement. In circumstances where an employment tribunal makes a finding of unfair dismissal in favour of an employee, it must ask him whether or not he wishes to be reinstated or reengaged. If the employee expresses the desire to be reinstated or reengaged, then the employment tribunal has complete discretion as to whether or not to make such an order. The tribunal will take into account

---

191 Section 113 Employment Rights Act 1996.
192 *Cowley v Manson Timber Ltd* [1994] ICR 252.

whether it is practicable for the employee to return to work for the employer and, where the employee was partly to blame for the dismissal, whether or not it would be just and equitable to make such an order (see below). In practice employment tribunals rarely order reinstatement or reengagement because, after the dismissal and what follows (disciplinary procedure and employment tribunal case), the relationship between the employer and the dismissed employee is often left beyond repair and only in rare cases will the tribunal conclude that the relationship remains workable. If the tribunal does order reinstatement or reengagement, then it is open for the employer to refuse to take the employee back, however, the refusal by an employer to comply with the order will give rise to the employee being awarded increased compensation,[193] unless the employer can satisfy the tribunal that it was not practicable to comply.

In deciding whether to make an order for reinstatement or re-engagement, the tribunal will consider:

- The employee's wishes;
- Whether it is practicable for the employee to return to work; and
- Whether it would be just for the employer to re-employ the employee, in cases where the employee was partly to blame for the dismissal.

In judging whether or not it is practicable for the employee to be reinstated or re-engaged, the tribunal must apply the reasonable responses test and must not substitute its views for that of the employer. Factors which will be taken into consideration include the size and resources of the employer,[194] whether the position no longer exists due to reorganisation,[195] whether reinstatement or re-engagement would result in another employee's

---

193 Tactically, requesting reinstatement/reengagement may be a good idea for an unfairly dismissed employee because an employer's failure to comply would entitle the employee to be compensated in full for all his loss of earnings from the date of the dismissal to the date of reinstatement/reengagement and the statutory limit on the compensation (outlined below) would not apply. Therefore, if the employee's losses to the date of the hearing exceed the statutory limit then reinstatement/reengagement will be seriously considered.

194 *Enessy Co SA v Minoprio* [1978] IRLR 489.

195 See *Thamesdown Borough Council v Turrel* EAT 459/97.

redundancy[196] whether the claimant is fit for work,[197] whether there is animosity with employer or co-workers,[198] or lack of trust and confidence between employer and employee,[199] and whether the employer is likely to comply with any order.[200]

Compensation

7.39 Sections 117-127A of the ERA 1996 set out the types of compensation available. Compensation generally consists of basic award, compensatory award and additional award. In certain circumstances, it is also possible to make an interim award or a protective award. The compensation may be increased or reduced if either party failed to follow the new ACAS Code of Practice 1: Disciplinary and Grievance Procedures.[201] It would also be reduced if the employee's behaviour contributed to the dismissal. If the employer's failure to follow procedures would have made no difference to the outcome and the employee would have been dismissed anyway, the compensatory award may be reduced (see Polkey Reduction above)

Basic award

7.40 The basic award applies automatically if there is a finding that the dismissal was unfair, and unlike the compensatory award is not dependent on loss.[202] There is, therefore, no requirement that the claimant mitigate his loss.[203]

A basic award is calculated in a similar way to a redundancy.

The employee receives:

---

196 *Cold Dawn Tunes Ltd v Middleton* [1992] ICR 318.
197 *Rao v Civil Aviation Authority* [1992] ICR 503.
198 *Wood Group Heavy Industrial Turbines Ltd v Crossan* [1998] IRLR 680.
199 *Central & London NHS Trust v Abimola* EAT 3 April 2009; *Nothman v London Borough of Barnet* [1978] ICR 336.
200 *ILEA v Gravett* [1988] IRLR 497.
201 www.acas.org.uk
202 *British United Shoe Machinery Co Ltd v Clarke* [1978] ICR 70; *Cadbury Ltd v Doddington* [1977] ICR 982.
203 *Locke v Connell Estate Agents* [1994] ICR 983.

- A half weeks pay for each years service below the age of twenty one
- One weeks pay for each year's service between the ages of 22 and 40 inclusive
- One and a half weeks pay for each year's service above the age of 41.

A maximum of 20 years service is taken into account (the most recent 20 years). The rate of weekly pay is calculated on what the employee should have received after deduction of National Insurance. The amount of weekly pay to be taken into account is capped, and the cap is currently £430, therefore, the maximum basic award is $20 \times 1.5 \times £430 = £12,900$.

This award will be subject to reduction if the tribunal thinks it is just and equitable to do so because the employee's conduct prior to his dismissal contributed to his dismissal, and indeed it can be reduced to zero. Conduct during the notice period will only reduce the compensatory award. There will be no reduction due to contributory conduct if the dismissal was for reason of redundancy, unless the minimum basic award applies. If the minimum award applies, then that part of the basic award which makes up the difference between the normal basic award and the minimum award can be reduced.[204]

The basic award may also be reduced if the employer has offered to reinstate the employee on the same terms and conditions and the offer is unreasonably refused. If the offer is made on different terms and conditions, only the compensatory award can be reduced.

If the employee has received a redundancy payment, the amount of that payment will be deducted from the basic award unless the reason for dismissal was not redundancy.

If the employee is reengaged or his contract renewed under new terms and conditions, and he or the employer terminate the new contract during the trial period (of 4 weeks), he will be regarded as dismissed from the date his previous employment ended and, if the reason for that dismissal is redundancy, he will be entitled to a *minimum* award of two weeks pay.[205]

---

204 Section 122(3) ERA 1996.
205 Section 121(a) ERA 1996.

Where the employer offers to reengage the employee or renew the contract on the same terms as the old contract, or on different terms which constitute an offer of suitable alternative employment in a redundancy situation, the employee is not entitled to a redundancy payment if he unreasonably refuses the offer, but he will be entitled to an award of two weeks pay.[206]

A minimum basic award (currently £5,300) will apply if the dismissal or selection for redundancy is found to be because:

–   His trade union membership or activities[207]

–   He was a health and safety representative or was designated to carry out health and safety activities[208]

–   He was a workforce representative under the Working Time Regulations[209]

–   He was an occupational pension scheme trustee[210]

–   He was an employee representative for consultation purposes[211]

Compensatory award

7.41 Under s 123 Employment Rights Act 1996, a tribunal may make such compensatory award as it thinks just and equitable to compensate the employee for the financial losses incurred as a result of his dismissal, up to a current maximum of £72,300.

The limit does not apply in limited circumstances, eg where an employee is dismissed or selected for redundancy because he made a protected disclosure,[212] or acted as a health and safety representative.[213]

Interest will be due on the financial award 42 days after the date the decision is recorded and sent to the parties. The rate of interest is currently

---

206 Section 121(b) ERA 1996.
207 TULR(C)A 1992 s 152.
208 ERA 1996 s 100(1).
209 ERA 1996 s 101A(d).
210 ERA 1996 s 103.
211 ERA 1996 s 103.
212 ERA 1996 s 103A.
213 ERA 1996 s 100.

11 % per annum.[214] Interest will run on any aspect of the award which relates to injury of feeling (which is only recoverable in discrimination cases) and will run from the date the act of discrimination occurred.[215]

The employee must prove his loss, and this is likely to include actual loss of past earnings up until the date of the tribunal, future loss (this will be based on speculation) expenses (eg money spent looking for other jobs), loss of statutory rights (usually a small amount), and loss of pension rights.

There is no maximum weekly wage which will be awarded, the claimant will be awarded his actual loss of earnings and an estimate of future loss. Any earnings in a new job, or benefits paid, will be offset against this loss. Any such earnings will not be offset against pay he should have received during his statutory notice period.

In the joint appeal of *Dunnachie & Kingston-upon-Hull City Council*,[216] it was confirmed by the EAT that there can be no compensation in a statutory unfair dismissal claim for injury to feelings, distress, anxiety, pain, suffering, and loss of amenity, or any other non-economic loss.[217] This decision was overturned by the Court of Appeal,[218] but on appeal to the House of Lords reaffirmed the correctness of the EAT decision.[219]

The employee has a duty to mitigate his loss, eg by looking for paid alternative work, and should produce evidence of any mitigation or attempts to mitigate.

He is entitled to any bonuses or overtime, which would normally be paid by the employer,[220] that he was likely to have received.[221] He is not entitled to 'tips' which he would have received from persons other than the employer.[222]

---

214 Act of Sederunt (Interest in Sheriff Court Decrees or Extracts) 1975/948.
215 Employment tribunals (Interest Order) 1990.
216 EAT/0848/02/RN, EAT/1036/02/RN.
217 *Johnson v Unisys* (2001) IRLR 279 wrongful dismissal claim on basis of above grounds thrown out by House of Lords.
218 [2004] EWCA Civ 84
219 [2004] IRLR 727 Lord Steyn's Judgment para 22–29.
220 *Mullet v British Electrical Machines Ltd* [1977] ICR 829.
221 *Palmanor Ltd v Cedron* [1978] ICR 1008.
222 Employment Protection (Recoupment of Jobseekers Allowance and Income Support) Regulations 1996.

Where the employee has actually gained from the situation by finding better employment, the tribunal may make a deduction from the compensatory award to reflect this.

Jobseekers allowance is deducted from the award and later recouped from the employer.[223] There is an incentive for the claimant to reach an out of court settlement if he has received this allowance, because it is not recouped in that situation.

The tribunal makes an award based on the gross earnings during the period from dismissal until the hearing date, and this is withheld from the claimant whilst the Secretary of State services a notice on the employer to pay this amount to the relevant department. The Secretary of State will pay this sum to the claimant after deduction of jobseekers allowance.

Reduction of Compensatory Award

7.42 The award can be reduced to take account of a failure by the employee to mitigate his loss (eg take reasonable steps to find other employment). In the case of *Prestwick Circuits Ltd v McAndrew*,[224] the Court of Appeal clarified that the duty of an employee to mitigate his loss only arises after he has been dismissed by the employer. 'The EAT had correctly held that conduct before dismissal is not relevant to the question of mitigation of loss. Also the onus is on the employer to show failure in this respect'.

The award of compensation can also be reduced to take account of the employee's contribution to his own dismissal, however, the employee must be blameworthy. The reduction will be by the amount that the tribunal believe is just and equitable. In the case of *Campbell and Others v Dunoon & Cowal Housing Association Ltd*,[225] the unwillingness of staff to take action in response to a threat to their continued employment led to their compensation being reduced by 75%. In extreme cases the employment tribunal can make a nil award.[226] The rules relating to

---

223 (1990) IRLR 191.
224 (1993) IRLR 496.
225 *Kristapaitis v Thistle Seafood Ltd* EAT (Scotland) 29 October 2009.
226 [1997] IRLR 147.

remoteness of damage or loss applies so that the employment tribunal will only compensate employee for the loss to them caused by the employer's conduct. In *Simrad Ltd v Scott*,[227] the EAT held that the fact that the dismissed employee had chosen to retrain as a nurse was too remote to be attributable to the employer's conduct. Part of the reason for this decision was the decision to change career, [which] was too remote in time from the dismissal.

A Polkey Deduction may be made from this award (see above) and an increase or decrease of the award of up to 25% may be made, if the tribunal thinks this is just and equitable in the light of the employer's failure to follow the ACAS Code on Discipline and Grievance in capability or conduct dismissals, or an employee's failure to follow the grievance procedures (see above). This type of reduction or increase should be made immediately before any reduction relating to failure to mitigate loss or relating to the employees conduct.

Under ERA 1996, s 123(7), if the employee has received an enhanced redundancy payment from his employer then this will be deducted from the compensatory award.

Additional Award

7.43 The *additional award* is used to compensate employees who have been unjustifiably refused reinstatement or reengagement.[228] The tribunal can award a minimum of 26 weeks pay (the maximum weeks pay is currently £430 therefore the minimum award is currently £11,180) and a maximum of 52 weeks pay (currently £22,360).[229] This limit can be exceeded in limited circumstances.[230]

---

227 Section 117 Employment Rights Act 1996.
228 Section 124(3) ERA 1996.
229 See s 124(3).
230 Sections 128–132 Employment Rights Act 1996. An application for interim relief has to be made within seven days of the dismissal.

Interim relief

7.44 In special cases employees can urgently apply[231] to the courts for an order of interim relief[232] to reinstate them pending the main hearing of their case. This will be appropriate where the reason for dismissal was because of membership of a trade union or involvement in health and safety activities; acting as a pension fund trustee; acting as an employee representative for the purposes of TUPE or the Working Time Regulations; acting in relation to union recognition; or exercising rights to be accompanied to a disciplinary or grievance hearing.

Payment in lieu of notice

7.45 In *Morrish v NTL Group Ltd*,[233] the appellant was entitled to 12 months notice under contract. He brought an action for breach of contract on the basis that he should have been allowed to work his notice and payment in lieu of notice was insufficient to meet the terms of the contract. It was observed by the Inner House that: 'The court had said ... that it had strong reservations as to whether, in the 21st century, there was any scope for the implication into employment contracts of an entitlement in favour of the employers to dismiss without notice or paying wages and other contractual entitlements in lieu.

REDUNDANCY

7.46 Employees are usually made redundant because their employer needs to reduce the workforce or because the job they do is no longer necessary. Redundancies often happen because an organisation is cutting costs and needs to reduce staff numbers, or because new systems or technology have made a job unnecessary. It could be because the employee's job no longer exists or because the business is closing down or moving. Redundancy is one of the most traumatic events an employee may experience. Announcement of redundancies will invariably have an adverse impact on morale, motivation and productivity of the workforce. The law plays an

---

231 Interim interdict.
232 [2007] CSIH 56.
233 [1967] 2 ITR 20.

important part in ensuring that the impact the redundancy has is minimised by providing various rights. There have been statutory rights related to redundancy since 1965 and the passing of the Redundancy Payments Act 1978 however, since then, the law has gone through considerable changes. The redundancy rights now available are: compensation, suitable alternative employment, notification and consultation, and time off to look for work, or to arrange training. All of these rights will be considered, as will other aspects to the law of redundancy such as unfair redundancy, sex discrimination and the legal effect of reorganisation.

Part XI of the Employment Rights Act 1996 relates to redundancy and redundancy payments. Redundancy is also a potentially fair reason for dismissal under s 98 ERA 1996 and will be fair only if the employer has acted reasonably in treating redundancy as a sufficient reason for dismissal and followed fair procedures.

Collective redundancies are dealt with under s 188-198 of the Trade Union and Labour Relations (Consolidation) Act 1992.

According to s 139 ERA 1996, dismissal is by reason of redundancy only if one of the following situations applies:

If the dismissal is 'wholly or mainly attributable to:

(a)   the fact that his employer has ceased or intends to cease:

    (i)   to carry on the business for the purposes of which the employee was employed by him, or

    (ii)   to carry on that business in the place where the employee was so employed, or

(b)   the fact that the requirements of that business:

    (i)   for employees to carry out work of a particular kind, or

    (ii)   for employees to carry out work of a particular kind in the place where the employee was employed by the employer, have ceased or diminished or are expected to cease or diminish.'

In other words, the reason for dismissal is only redundancy if it is caused:

(a)   by the business or part of the business closing down;

    (b)   the business or part of the business is moving; or

    (c)   the employer has surplus labour of a particular kind.

A failure to renew a fixed-term contract could amount to a redundancy.

Business closing down

7.47 Even a cessation of the business (or part of the business) for a relatively short period will result in a redundancy. In *Gemmell v Darngavil Brickworks Ltd*,[234] the business ceased trading for 13 weeks and the employees were held to be redundant. Section 139 defines two sets of circumstances where dismissal will take place on the ground of cessation of business. It occurs where '...the employer has ceased, or intends to cease, to carry on the business for the purpose of which the employee was employed by him, or to carry on the business in the place where the employee was so employed...'. In *Bass Leisure Ltd v Thomas*,[235] Ms Thomas worked from the company's depot in Coventry. Her employer decided to close the depot and move to a suburb of Birmingham, 20 miles way. She worked at the new depot for a short while but resigned because the additional travelling time did not fit in with her domestic arrangements. She claimed constructive dismissal by reason of redundancy. The employers argued that she had not been constructively dismissed because of the mobility clause in her contract which referred to redundancy pay. There was a mobility clause in her contract giving the right to the employer to transfer employees. The EAT upheld the decision of the tribunal that she was indeed constructively dismissed for redundancy. They stated that: 'An employee's refusal to move as required does not prevent the dismissal being for redundancy.'[236] The place where she was employed was Coventry. Her place of employment was a question of fact and the determination of 'place' could not be extended to any place where an employee may be contractually required to work.

    This attitude to a mobility clauses can act against the employee as well as in his favour. The Court of Appeal confirmed this approach in

---

234 (1994) IRLR 104 EAT.
235 Supra 5 p 235.
236 [1998] ICR 409.

High Table v Horst and Others.[237] High Table was a catering company providing catering services for one client. The employees in this case were waitresses who had all worked for several years at one client's premises. Their contracts of employment contained a mobility clause obliging them to work at other clients premises if required. High Table issued redundancy notices when the client at whose premises they worked required less service. The employees complained that since they could be required to work at any clients premises their place of employment was with High Table rather than at the client's premises. The Court of Appeal held that an employee's place of work for redundancy purposes had to be determined primarily by reference to the factual situation existing prior to the dismissal, and not by reference to the contract of employment alone. The fact that an employee had a mobility clause in her contract should not be regarded as widening the location of her employment for the purposes of the business, when she had in fact worked in only one place. To do so could have the effect of encouraging the use of mobility clauses to defeat genuine redundancy claims.

Therefore, if an employee only works in one place and the business at that place has ceased, he will be redundant irrespective of a mobility clause in his contract. If the employee has actually worked in different places then the mobility clause becomes more important, as it can be used as an aid to deciding what the factual situation was.

That is not to say that an employer cannot use a mobility clause when it wishes to close down premises and move to another. In *Home Office v Evans*,[238] the Court of Appeal were of the opinion that if the employer invokes the mobility clause before redundancies are announced in order to avoid them, then there is no redundancy. If redundancies have been announced then it becomes too late to invoke the mobility clause because a redundancy situation exists.

The proper approach to the question of where somebody is employed for the purposes of redundancy, is to determine that issue as a question of fact in the light of the evidence before the tribunal, and the determination of whether a person ordinarily worked abroad, for the purpose of

---

237 [2008] ICR 302.
238 *Pitman v Foreign and Commonwealth Office* [2003] ICR 699.

determining jurisdiction of the employment tribunal, does not decide the issue of place of employment for the purpose of s 139 ERA 1996.[239]

Business is moving

7.48 Whether or not a move of place of business is far enough to amount to a redundancy, depends on the facts and circumstances of each case. In *Managers (Holborn) Ltd v Hohne*,[240] a move from Holborn to Regent Street was not sufficient to amount to a repudiation of contract as both places were in central London.

Surplus labour

7.49 Under s 139 (1) (b), dismissal will be deemed to be by reason of redundancy where it is wholly or mainly attributable to: 'the fact the requirements of that business for employees to carry out work of that particular kind ... have ceased or diminished or are expected to cease or diminish.'

The employer may require fewer employees to do the same work,[241] or there may be less work for existing employees.

In *Safeway v Burrell*,[242] the EAT's view was that the correct approach for determining what is a dismissal by reason of redundancy in terms of s 139(1)(b), involves a three-stage process: (1) was the employee dismissed? If so, (2) had the requirements of the employer's business for employees to carry out work of a particular kind ceased or diminished, or were they expected to cease or diminish? If so, (3) was the dismissal of the employee caused wholly or mainly by that state of affairs? The EAT also held that at the second stage, the work of a particular kind was not necessarily defined in terms of the employee's employment contract. In the case the contractual requirements for the new job was quite different from the old although the duties performed in fact were virtually the same. However, there was arguably a redundancy situation, in that the employers' requirements for

---

239 [1977] IRLR 230.
240 *Delanair v Mead* [1976] ICR 522.
241 (1997) IRLR 200 EAT.
242 (1999) IRLR 562.

managers had diminished (fewer were employed than before). So where the employment tribunal is considering whether there has been a diminution or cessation in the employers requirement for employees to carry out work of a particular kind, it is appropriate to consider the reduction in the work overall and not to focus on the work of the individual applicant.

The House of Lords held in *Murray v Foyle Meats Ltd*,[243] that if a dismissal was attributable to diminution of the 'employer's need for employees', then it is irrelevant to consider either the contractual obligations or the functions which the employees performed.

Once dismissal is established on either of these grounds, under s 139, the burden shifts onto the employer to disprove it was for reason of redundancy (s 163 (2)).

Work of a particular kind should not be qualified as work for which the employee was employed, and the tribunal must consider the contract and the work actually being done by the employee.[244]

In light of these cases, transferred redundancy (or bumping) is a perfectly acceptable form of redundancy. This occurs when an employer requires to decrease the size of his workforce and retains the employees who are most valuable to him in terms of skills, experience and other qualities. This may have the result that an employee is made redundant when another employee who is retained fills his position.

Redundancy as a fair dismissal

7.50 If the dismissal is for a redundancy reason, the employee will be entitled to a redundancy payment provided he meets the qualifications outlined below.

Redundancy is a potentially fair reason for dismissal and the dismissal will be fair only if the employer's decision to dismiss falls within the band of reasonable responses test, discussed above.

Where an employer acts unfairly in the way a redundancy dismissal is carried out, or in the choice of who is made redundant, he may face a claim of unfair dismissal. An employer cannot use redundancy as an excuse for getting rid of staff.

---

243 *Shawkat v Nottingham City Hospital NHS Trust (Remitting)* [1999] ICR 780.
244 (1982) IRLR 83 EAT.

In *Williams and Others v Compair Maxam Ltd*,[245] the EAT set out guidelines for employers to try and ensure a fair dismissal in the context of redundancy.

- The employer will seek to give as much warning as possible of impeding redundancies as to enable the unions and employees who may be affected to take early steps to inform themselves of the relevant facts, consider possible solutions and, if necessary, find alternative employment in the undertaking or elsewhere.

- The employer will consult the union as to the best means by which the desired management result can be achieved (the union and employer decide on criteria for selection, and jointly consider if criteria complied with).

- Objectively justifiable criteria for selection of redundant employees should be used by employer, (eg attendance record, efficiency at job, experience or length of service).

- The employer will ensure selection is made in accordance with appropriate criteria and should consider representations of union.

- The employer should try and find alternative employment rather than dismissal.

Warnings and consultation

7.51 In addition to any notice and consultation requirements which are required in relation to collective redundancies (detailed below), individual employees must be warned and consulted in connection with their own position, and a failure to do so may make the dismissal unfair.

In *Langton v Cranfield University*,[246] Mr Langton was employed as a research assistant under a series of fixed-term contracts. When his final contract expired without being renewed he was dismissed on the grounds of redundancy. He claimed unfair dismissal on the basis there was a lack of consultation and no attempt to find alternative employment for him.

---

245 (1998) IRLR 173.
246 [1987] IRLR 503.

The EAT held that there are three elements to the reasonableness test set out in the dismissal provisions which needed to be considered in redundancy dismissals. They are unfair selection for redundancy, lack of consultation, and failure to offer alternative employment. Normally an employer is expected to lead evidence as to the steps they took to ensure these aspects were applied reasonably.

A similar conclusion was reached in *Polkey v A E Dayton Services Ltd*,[247] where the House of Lords held that, in the case of redundancy, an employer will be deemed to have acted unreasonably unless he: warns and consults any affected employees (or their representatives); adopts a fair basis on which to select for redundancy; and takes such steps as may be reasonable to avoid or minimise redundancy by redeploying potentially redundant employees within its own organisation. However, possibly more importantly, they underlined the importance of following the correct procedure in redundancy which has at its heart consultation with the employee affected.

Each case will depend on its own facts and circumstances, and in the case of *Azko Coatings plc v Thomson and others*,[248] the EAT decided it was not always required of employers to follow the guidelines set down in the *Williams* case above. 'It will be immediately apparent that the tribunal had slavishly applied the Williams approach to selection for dismissal of redundancy to the way in which the company dealt with the possibility of alternative employment. This is a misdirection in law and the present case illustrates the dangers of misapplying guideline cases.' It is clear that the EAT, in this case, believed that the crucial factor in these cases is the reasonableness of the employer rather than the application of either agreed selection criteria for redundancy, or the application of objective criteria.

This case was followed in *Ralph Martindale and Company Limited v Harris*,[249] where the EAT held:

> 'that the procedures for the allocation of alternative employment following a redundancy selection were unfair and that they could not accept the submission that a tribunal was not entitled to rely on its own

---

247 1996 EAT Unreported.
248 UKEAT/0166/07 .
249 [1975] IRLR 73.

sense of what good industrial practice was. The tribunal had also been entitled to find that inviting applications for alternative employment from the entire workforce, before deciding whether any potentially redundant employee was suitable for a new role, did not reflect the current industrial relations practice of a reasonable employer.'

The EAT recognised that tribunals, having heard the evidence, develop a 'feel' for the cases before them which is relevant to their consideration of whether or not a dismissal is fair, having regard to the requirements of fairness under s 98A(4) of ERA 1996. This decision emphasised that tribunals may take a more interventionist approach when it comes to assessing the fairness of the redundancy procedures adopted by an employer.

Fair selection

7.52 A failure to use a fair and transparent selection procedure will render a dismissal unfair.

There may be a selection procedure agreed with the trade union, perhaps in a collective agreement. This agreement does not inevitably make the procedure fair, but the tribunal is likely to be satisfied. A failure to consult the trade unions, where it is not reasonable to do so, will not make the selection procedure unfair. In *Guy v Delanair (Car Heater) Ltd*,[250] one of the employer's major customers reduced its custom and the employer stopped operating a night shift and made all night shift workers redundant. The tribunal held that in this case this method of selection for redundancy was reasonable, and failure to consult with unions and employees was also reasonable in view of the urgency of the decision. Even if the union has been consulted about the selection procedure, the employer need not involve disclosing the detail to them in its implementation.[251]

The tribunal will not substitute its view of what should be in a fair selection procedure but the employer must lead evidence to show how, by whom, and on what basis, the employee was selected for redundancy.[252]

---

250 *Clyde Pipeworks v Foster* [1978] IRLR 313.
251 *Bristol Channel Ship Repairers Ltd v O'Keefe* [1978] ICR 691.
252 Section 138 Employment Rights Act 1996.

Factors which may be taken into account include length of service, skill and experience, and matters which should not be taken into account include any factors which could be considered to be discriminatory, and disciplinary records which should have expired.

In *John Brown Engineering v Brown*, the EAT held that what is required is a fair process, where an opportunity to contest the selection of each individual is available to the individual employee. Individual consultation is not essential in every case, an individual's opportunity to contest his selection can be achieved through his trade union, a policy decision to withhold all markings in a particular selection process may result in individual unfairness if no opportunity is thereafter given to the individual to know how he has been assessed. In the instant case, the tribunal was entitled to conclude that the withholding of the actual marks from each employee once the assessment had taken place, did render the appeal system a sham and, as such, constituted unfairness in the manner in which the agreed and acceptable criteria were being applied.

Automatically unfair selection

7.53 Section 105 of the ERA 1996 contains a list of reasons which if they are the reason for selection for redundancy, will render the dismissal automatically unfair. In these cases there is no qualifying service required to make a claim. The automatically unfair reasons include:

–   health and safety reasons;
–   the employee is an employee representative or occupational pension trustee;
–   the employee is a protected or opted out shop worker;
–   the employee had made a protected disclosure;
–   asserting a statutory right;
–   exercising rights to maternity and paternity, parental leave and emergency leave for dependents;
–   employee is pregnant;

–   employee is trying to enforce rights under the National Minimum Wage Act.

Suitable alternative work

7.54 Under s 141 ERA 1996, where an employer offers an employee during the notice period for redundancy suitable alternative employment on different terms and conditions, they should try the job out for a trial period of four weeks, and refusal to offer a trial period may be grounds for a claim of unfair dismissal.[253]

If an offer of suitable alternative work is made, and the employee unreasonably refuses it, he will lose his right to a redundancy payment.

An offer of suitable employment must take into account all the relevant details, including the nature of the work, the hours, the pay, conditions, qualifications and experience of the employee. The suitability of alternative work should be judged objectively, however subjective issues can be taken into account such as an employee's personal problems from making the change, availability of educational facilities for children, travel facilities and loss of friends. In the leading case of *Taylor v Kent County Council*,[254] the applicant had been the headmaster of a boy's school which was merged with a girl's school, and his appointment was therefore terminated. He was offered a post as one of a pool of mobile teachers to be sent out to schools as and when required, and his salary remained the same. He refused this job and claimed redundancy pay. The council opposed his claim for redundancy pay on the ground of his refusal to accept this offer. The leading judge clarified the position by stating that 'by the words suitable employment, suitability means employment which is substantially equivalent to the employment which has ceased ... conditions of employment which are reasonably equivalent to those under the previous employment. It does not mean, employment of an entirely different nature, but in respect of which the salary is going to be the same.[255] Mr Taylor was accordingly entitled to his redundancy pay.

---

253 (1969) 2 QB 560.

254 Lord Parker CJ.

255 The range of reasonable responses test does not apply *Hudson v George Harrison Ltd* [2003] All ER (D) 381.

Whilst the suitability of the work is assessed objectively, whether or not an employee's refusal is reasonable is assessed subjectively,[256] and personal circumstances relevant to a particular employee may be taken into account such as family needs, including education of the employee's children,[257] concerns about being able to cope with the new post,[258] and loss of status.[259]

The employee's refusal must be more than a whim and in *Fuller v Stephanie Bowman*[260] when a claimant had rejected the offer of alternative employment, because the new job was based in Soho rather than Mayfair, where her old job was based. The tribunal had to consider whether her view was reasonable, and that question had to be answered by reference to whether someone in her particular circumstances could reasonably have taken the view she did, This was held to be an unreasonable refusal and she was not entitled to a redundancy payment.

In *Bird v Stoke-On-Trent Primary Care Trust*,[261] a physiotherapist who managed 25 other physiotherapists refused alternative employment, as she felt it was lower status, and had a different balance of clinical and managerial responsibilities. The EAT held that by considering for itself whether her acceptance of the new post involved a demotion, and by concluding that her view was irrational, the tribunal had substituted its own view for hers. The tribunal should have considered whether her view was reasonable, and that question had to be answered by reference to whether someone in her particular circumstances could reasonably have taken the view she did. The case was remitted to a different tribunal.

Situations which do not amount to redundancy

7.55 An employer is entitled to reorganise his business. The employee's terms and conditions may be changed by a reorganisation, and the change may amount to a repudiation of the contract by the employer, resulting in a constructive dismissal, or an employer can legitimately dismiss an

---

256 *Paton Calvert & Co Ltd v Westerside* [1979] IRLR 108.
257 *Spencer v Gloucester County Council* [1985] 233.
258 *Cambridge & District Cooperative Society Ltd v Ruse* [1993] IRLR 156.
259 1977] IRLR 87.
260 EAT 21 July 2011.
261 [1977] ICR 235.

employee if he or she will not accept changes in his terms and conditions resulting from a reorganisation. Provided the employer can establish that these changes are necessary to the continued management and efficiency of the business, and the employee's refusal to comply would justify his dismissal. A dismissal in these circumstances may amount to a dismissal for some other substantial reason rather than redundancy.

A change in terms and conditions which does not amount to repudiation of the contract will not result in a redundancy. In *Lesney Products & Co v Nolan*,[262] the reorganisation of shifts following a change in routine after a fall did not necessarily give rise to a redundancy situation.

It is sufficient for an employer to show the reorganisation is for sound business reasons which require a change in an employee's terms and conditions.

In *Johnson v Notts Combined Police Authority*,[263] the Court of Appeal dismissed a claim of two clerical workers that they had been made redundant as a result of changes in their working week to shifts whereby they would work from 8am to 3pm for six days one week, and from 1pm to 8pm the following week. In this case the police authorities proved that the change in hours of work was not due to a redundancy situation, but to a reorganisation in the interests of efficiency

In *Robinson v British Island Airways*,[264] it was decided that where there was a genuine re-organisation which displaces an employee (they cannot be fitted into the reorganised business) it must be open to the employer to dismiss him. But in those circumstances he will usually be redundant, and thus entitled to redundancy pay.

COLLECTIVE REDUNDANCIES

7.56 In addition to the requirement to act reasonably, which gives rise to the need to inform and consult individual employees, there are specific provisions regarding notification and consultation the event of collective redundancies. These are set out in ss 188 – 198 of Trade Union and Labour Relations (Consolidation) Act 1992 (TULR(C)A 1992), as amended

---

262 (1974) ICR 170 CA.
263 [1978] ICR 304.
264 (2008) IRLR 4.

by the Trade Union Reform and Employment Rights Act 1993, and the Collective Redundancies and Transfer of Undertakings (Protection of Employees) (Amendment) Regulations 1995 and 1999.

Consultation

7.57 Where there are collective consultations with recognised trade unions or elected representatives must start:

- at least 90 days before notification of redundancies for redundancy dismissals of 100 or more employees,
- at least 30 days before notification of redundancies for 20–99 employees.

In cases where collective consultation is required, it must be completed before notice of dismissal is given to any of the employees concerned. The law requires meaningful consultation with recognised trade unions, or elected representatives, it is not enough only to inform them. Where the employer fails to comply with these requirements, the employment tribunal can award the representatives a protective award and the maximum compensation that can be awarded, if an employer fails to consult, is 90 days pay per person covered by the award.

Under s 188(2) TULR(C)A 1992, the employer is required to divulge certain information to the representative which includes: the reason for proposals, the number and description of employees being dismissed, the total number of those category of employees in the workplace, the proposed method of selection for redundancy, eg last in first out (LIFO), and the proposed method of undertaking dismissals.

Consultations must be carried out with recognised trade unions or, where this is not appropriate, employee representatives where they have been elected by employees in the workplace. The Collective Redundancies and Transfer of Undertakings (Regulations) Act SI 1995/2587 and Collective Redundancies and Transfer of Undertakings (Protection of Employment) (Amendment) Regulations SI 1999/1925 set up a mechanism for appointment of employee representatives. In

UK Coal Mining Ltd v NUM,[265] the EAT handed down a very important decision dealing with collective consultation obligations in redundancy cases. Overturning previously binding authority, the EAT held that there is a duty on employers to consult the trade union over the reason for making redundancies in the first place (in this case the closure of a mine) previously something which had always been an area in which tribunals would not interfere.

Employers are under no specific legal obligation to consult employee representatives, or notify the BIS Department, in cases where redundancies fall below twenty. However, if they fail to warn and consult individual employees who are to be dismissed in such cases, they may be at risk of successful unfair dismissal claims. In *Polkey v Dayton Services Ltd*,[266] the House of Lords held that 'in the case of redundancy, the employer will not normally act reasonably unless he warns and consults any employees affected, or their representative, adopts a fair basis on which to select for redundancy, and takes such steps as are reasonable to avoid or minimise redundancy by redeployment within his own organisation.'[267] Accordingly, individuals who are not given this consideration by their employer can claim unfair dismissal. However, the court went on to point out that if the consultation would have made no difference and the employee would still have been dismissed, then the dismissal may still be fair.

Under s 189 of the Trade Union and Labour Relations (Consolidation) Act 1992, if the employer fails to meet the requirements regarding consultation the trade union, a trade union official, or in any event an affected employee can make application to the employment tribunal for a protective award. The tribunal will make a declaration that consultation should have taken place and did not and make a protective award. The protective award will be made in respect of employees who have been dismissed as redundant (or it is proposed to dismiss as redundant) and in respect of whom the employer has failed to comply with the consultation requirements. It consists of remuneration for each employee for such period of the 'protected period' as the tribunal considers just and equitable.

---

265 (1987) IRLR 13.
266 Lord Bridge.
267 Section 191.

The 'protected period' begins with the date on which the first of the dismissals to which the complaint relates takes effect, or the date of the award, whichever is the earlier, and is of such length as the tribunal determines to be just and equitable in all the circumstances, having regard to the seriousness of the employer's default in complying with any requirement of s 188. The maximum length of the protected period is 90 days.

If an employee is fairly dismissed during the protected period. or unreasonably refuses an offer to reengage or of suitable alternative employment within the protected period he may lose his right to the protective award.[268]

Notification for collective redundancies

7.58 Under s 193 (1) and (2) of the TULR(C)A 1992,[269] notice must given to the Secretary of State (Department of Business Innovation and Skills (BIS)) before giving notice to terminate the employees' contracts. The notice which must be given to the Secretary of State is as follows:

- at least 90 days notice , if proposing to dismiss as redundant 100 or more employees at one establishment, within a period of 90 days, or

- 30 days notice if proposing to dismiss as redundant between 20 and 99 employees.

- Where there are fewer than 20 employees being made redundant, no notification to BIS is required.

The date of notice is the date the notification is received. Failure to notify BIS without good cause can lead to legal proceedings and on conviction up to a fine of £5,000 on summary conviction, for the company and/ or an officer of the company. An employer is only entitled to carry out collective redundancies after concluding the consultation procedure and after notification is made before any notice of dismissal has been issued.

---

268 The Collective Redundancies (Amendment) Regulations 2006.
269 Trade Union and Labour Relations (Consolidation) Act 1992, ss 188–192.

The employer must send a copy of this notification to the representatives of the employees.

Rights on redundancy

7.59 There are various legislative measures that apply here, but the main rules can be found in the ERA 1996.[270]

To qualify for most of the redundancy rights, the person making a claim must: be an employee, have at least 2 years continuous service, and not be expressly excluded on various grounds. See ss 139-141 of the Employment Rights Act 1996 for exceptions.[271] There are now no age restrictions on who can claim a redundancy payment, however, there are some workers who are specifically excluded from making a claim. These are:-

– employee's dismissed for misconduct;

– redundant employees who refuse suitable alternative employment (see above);

– fixed term contract workers of more than 2 years who have renounced their redundancy rights in agreements made before 10 July 2001.

The burden of proof for establishing the right to claim redundancy payment initially lies with the employee who has to establish they have been dismissed by reason of redundancy (as defined in s 139(1) of the ERA 1996.

A claim for a redundancy payment must be made within 6 months of the effective date of termination of the contract. If the employee wishes to make a claim of unfair dismissal relating to the redundancy, the usual time limit of three months applies to that part of the claim.

---

270 Collective Redundancies and Transfer of Undertakings (Protection of Employees) (Amendment) Regulations 1995, (SI 1995/2587) & 1999, (SI 1999/1925). The Collective Redundancies (Amendment) Regulations 2006 (SI 2006/2387).

271 Some jobs are exempt from redundancy payments and these include: some members of the Armed Forces, House of Lords and House of Commons staff, apprentices whose service ends at the end of their contract, domestic servants who are members of the employer's immediate close family, some fishermen, crown servants or employees in a public office and employees of the Government of an overseas territory.

For each year's continuous employment below the age of 22, an employee is entitled to receive a half weeks pay for each years continuous employment. Between the ages of 22 and 40 he will be entitled to one weeks pay for each year's employment for each year's continuous employment. Above the age of 40 he will receive one and a half weeks pay for each year's continuous employment.

The maximum number of years which will be taken into account is 20, and the maximum rate of pay £430 per week, therefore the maximum statutory redundancy payment is $20 \times 1.5 = £12,900.$[272]

Time off

7.60 An employee who has two years continuous service, and who has been served with notice of redundancy, is entitled to reasonable paid time off for training and to seek employment.[273] The remedy for failure to allow time of, or for refusal to pay, is to make a claim to the tribunal within three months of the refusal. The tribunal will award the pay up to a maximum of two fifths of a weeks pay.

Redundancy and insolvency

7.61 Under Part X11 of the Employment Rights act 1992 employees may write to the Secretary of State to apply for payment of debts owed to them by the employer from the National Insurance Fund (NIF).

The Secretary of State will need to be satisfied that the employer is insolvent, the employee's employment has been terminated, and the employee is entitled to be paid whole or part of the debt.[274] Employees will only receive a payment if they can show they are working under a contract of service and their job with the insolvent employer had ended. They do not need to have worked for their employer for a certain time and there are no age limits. If the employer is insolvent, the employee might be able to claim the following from the NIF:

- Redundancy pay

---

272 http://www.direct.gov.uk/redundancy.dsb
273 Section 52 Employment Rights Act 1996.
274 For detailed rules see Sargeant M, Lewis D, *Employment Law* 3 ed. pp 376–378.

- Wages – up to a maximum of eight weeks[275]
- Holiday pay – up to a maximum of six weeks
- Pay in lieu of statutory notice – 1 week after one calendar month's service, rising to 1 week per year of service up to a maximum of 12 weeks

If employees are still owed any pay after their claim from the National Insurance Fund has been settled, they will only entitled to receive a further amount if enough funds are released from the sale of the company assets although some debts, including holiday pay and wages, will be a preferential debt.

Redundancy and discrimination

7.62 It is unlawful for an employer to select employees for redundancy based on their: age, disability, sex, race, religion, pregnancy, or sexual orientation. If the reason for selection for redundancy is one of the protected characteristics under the Equality Act 2010, the dismissal will be unlawful. No continuous service will be required to make a claim and there is no limit on the compensation which may be awarded.

When selecting employees for redundancy, employers must use a method which is fair and which does not discriminate against employees. In *Clarke v Eley (Kyoch) Ltd*,[276] Mrs Clarke and another employee were employed part-time at a munitions factory in Birmingham. They were among 60 part-time women made redundant, 20 full-time males and 26 full-time women were also dismissed. The redundancy policy of company agreed with the trade union, allowing for the dismissal of part-time employee before full timers. It had been possible to convert from part-time to full-time, but Mrs Clarke hadn't done it. It was held: that choosing part timers for redundancy before full timers was indirect discrimination on the ground of sex. The Court of Appeal in *Chagger v Abbey National Plc & another*,[277] reviewed a decision of the EAT where they had found that the applicant's selection for redundancy was influenced by race, and awarded

---

275 There is a limit of £430 per week on the amount claimed for weekly pay.
276 (1982) IRLR 482.
277 [2009] EWCA Civ 1202, [2010] IRLR 47.

him £2,794,962 (plus interest) in compensation for this treatment. The Court of Appeal decided to send the case back to the tribunal to reconsider the size of the award. This case illustrated that if an employer selects an employee for a redundancy dismissal on the basis of a discriminatory ground, then the consequences for them in terms of the compensation they can pay can be severe.

FURTHER READING

Journal articles

Bradley, 'Crime in the employment context'. 2011 Emp. L. Bulletin.

Brodie, 'Mutual trust and confidence: further clarification'. (2011) Emp. L. Brief, 102, 2.

Cloke, 'Mobility clauses: Home Office did not "dodge" redundancy law.' Emp. LJ 2008, 87, 5.

'Compensatory awards – Polkey reductions'. IDS Emp. L. Brief 2010, 912, 13-18.

McMullen, Adopting the right course. NLJ 2011, 161(7469), 795.

Williamson, '*High Table v Horst*: Are Mobility Clauses Redundant?' 1998, 142(17), 394.

Chapter 8

Equality Law

INTRODUCTION

8.1 This chapter examines the law of equality in employment in Scotland in so far as it relates to the protected characteristics under the Equality Act 2010. The equality clause which applies to terms and conditions of the contract is mentioned here but considered in more detail in Chapter 11. Disability Discrimination is discussed in chapter 9. Equality laws apply throughout the United Kingdom and therefore do not have a particular Scottish dimension, however, many of the most important cases in this area have been Scottish and the Scottish courts and tribunals have been extremely influential in the development of equality law.

Each area of discrimination law falling within the scope of equality law (except disability discrimination which is dealt with in a separate chapter) will be explained and given separate consideration. The rules relating to maternity and equal pay will be considered here only insofar as they relate to discrimination. Other aspects of these areas will be considered in the chapters on family friendly rights and wages respectively. The legal rules provided by statute will be analysed from a historical perspective and examined in their current context and the case law from Scotland, England and Wales brought under the different pieces of legislation will be considered. This chapter will provide an invaluable overview of the equality rules applying in the United Kingdom and knowledge of these is essential to an understanding of the subject as it impacts on most areas of working life.

THE ROLE OF THE LAW

8.2 It is outwith the remit of this book to examine in detail the desirability or otherwise of an equal society,[1] and the role of law in the struggle to

---

1 For an interesting discussion as to whether it is necessary to create an equal society at all see Cavanagh M *Against Equality of Opportunity* (2003), Clarendon Press.

achieve a fair and equal society.[2] We will confine ourselves to a brief look at the historical development of equality legislation.

There were clear trigger points for the increase of both sex and race discrimination in the workplace. The starting point for sex discrimination within employment in the United Kingdom is commonly identified as the Industrial Revolution, when for the first time the home was separated from the place of work,[3] and women were expected to stay at home and out of the workplace.[4]

> 'The fact is that where women were brave enough to enter employment in the face of a general opposition, they were regarded by paternalistic employers as second class workers. They were consequently restricted to low paid and unskilled occupations,[5] required to work for long hours in bad working conditions and often subjected to sexual harassment.'[6]

With respect to race discrimination, this is clearly related to the large scale introduction into British Society of immigrants. There was a substantial influx of Irish immigrants in the 19th century onwards. From the end of the 19th century there was immigration by large numbers of Jews and small numbers of black communities grew up around British seaports, but none of these developments instigated the level and degree of racism experienced in post second world war Britain. The large scale influx of racial and ethnic minorities into the United Kingdom started with recruitment of cheap migrant labour from the New Commonwealth territories such as the West Indies, India and Pakistan, and other countries in Europe in the 1950's and 1960's. These immigrants were used to fill the labour shortages caused by post-war industrial expansion in the United

---

2   See Barnes (2003) 32 ILJ 200 and Bell (2004) 67 MLR 465 in this context.
3   In the agrarian society prior to the Industrial Revolution men and woman worked alongside each other on an equal basis and the place of work, the farm, was also their home. The process of alienation of work from home brought about by changing work patterns caused by the process of industrialisation has become known amongst sociologists as the 'social division of labour'.
4   Durkheim, E *The Division of Labour in Society* 1997, The Free Press.
5   Resulting from the sexual division of labour and job segregation where employment of women was restricted to low skilled and low paid occupations.
6   Ed. Sargeant *Discrimination Law* (2004) Pearson Longman, Middlemiss, S Chapter 4, Sex and Race Discrimination.

Kingdom. 'Migrants to Britain of the 1950's and 1960's ...experienced a high degree of exploitation, discrimination and marginalisation in their economic and social lives. Despite the need for their labour their presence aroused widespread hostility at all levels.'[7]

Unfortunately the law cannot by itself bring about the fundamental changes needed within society to create a fair and equal workplace. Often discriminatory attitudes are deeply instilled in individuals in childhood and then throughout their adult life, and what is needed is something which can engender change in their views and consequent behaviour at work. The law can play its part, but employers must be the change agent here encouraging through example and educating people away from workplace discrimination and disciplining those that choose to break the rules. The law, or the threat of legal action for breach of the law, often represents the impetus to employers to bring about this change.

Usually the law intervenes in the free market only where there is social or economic pressure to do so. It has proven necessary to legislate in a number of areas because of a general failure within society and, more particularly within employment, to apply rules and standards. of treatment fairly to everyone. The European Union has played a pivotal role in influencing legal developments in this area in its Member States (including the United Kingdom) since 1973. Where the UK legislators or judiciary have in the past or in more recent times tried to depart from the European model they have been subject to legal challenge.

The development of legislation to deal with discrimination started properly in 1970,[8] with the Equal Pay Act 1970 (EPA 1970) which was an attempt[9] to deal with the inequality between men and women's pay, where men and women were doing the same work or work of equal value. The next landmark was the Sex Discrimination Act 1975 (SDA 1975) which was designed primarily to provide protection against the discriminatory practices of employers directed against women. This not only extended rights to female (and male) employees in work not to be discriminated against on the grounds of sex or marital status, but also to job applicants,

---

7   Solomos, J Back, I *Racism and Society* 1996, Macmillan pp 67–69.

8   There was a Race Discrimination Act passed in 1968 but this largely ineffective and was repealed and replaced by the Race Discrimination Act 1975.

9   As it turned out a somewhat ill-fated attempt see Chapter 8.

workers and even if, on a limited basis, to the self employed. The following year the Race Discrimination Act 1976 (RRA 1976) was passed which largely mirrored the provisions in the SDA 1975 except in respect of the basis for a claim (nationality, colour, ethnic origin, race) and the nature of the genuine occupational requirements which allowed discrimination in recruitment and selection in limited circumstances.[10] Another difference was the right under the RRA 1976 for someone to claim discrimination if they had been instructed to discriminate by their employer.

The next landmark was around twenty years later when the Disability Discrimination Act 1995 (DDA 1995) was passed. There were similarities between this Act and the earlier Acts particularly, the definition of direct discrimination[11] and the unlawful activities of employers covered by the Act. However, it also differed from them as it was construed and applied around a complex definition of disability and did not offer the opportunity for the physically or mentally impaired to claim for indirect discrimination.[12] Also the DDA 1995 introduced the concept of reasonable adjustment, which created an expectation that employers would make changes in the workplace (physical or operational) to accommodate the opportunity of entering employment, or maintaining continued employment, for the disabled.

---

10 The GOQ in the SDA 1975 now in the Equality Act 2010 covered issues such as the need for particular physiological characteristics or where a particular sex was needed because of privacy issues.

11 Direct discrimination (1)A person (A) discriminates against another (B) if, because of a protected characteristic, A treats B less favourably than A treats or would treat others see s 13 of Equality Act 2010.

12 This was changed by the Equality Act 2010 and indirect discrimination is defined by s 19 of that Act as where: (1) A person (A) discriminates against another (B) if A applies to B a provision, criterion or practice which is discriminatory in relation to a relevant protected characteristic of B's. (2) For the purposes of subsection (1), a provision, criterion or practice is discriminatory in relation to a relevant protected characteristic of B's if (a) A applies, or would apply, it to persons with whom B does not share the characteristic, (b) it puts, or would put, persons with whom B shares the characteristic at a particular disadvantage when compared with persons with whom B does not share it, (c) it puts, or would put, B at that disadvantage, and (d) A cannot show it to be a proportionate means of achieving a legitimate aim.

The European Union was instrumental[13] in the introduction of laws in the UK in 2003 to deal with sexual orientation discrimination[14] and religion and belief discrimination[15] and in 2006 age discrimination[16] and in amending existing areas of discrimination law, to bring it in line with EU law.[17]

It is perhaps not surprising that the three Regulations dealing with sexual orientation, religion and belief, and age, followed broadly similar lines to the legislation dealing with sex and race except when it comes to the grounds for discrimination and genuine occupational requirements. Age is different from them all however, in respect of various exemptions for employers that are involved. There have been some difficulties with application and enforcement of this recent legislation, which will be discussed later in the chapter.

The most recent development in UK equality law commenced in June 2008 when the labour government's policy document entitled Framework for a Fairer Future – The Equality Bill was presented to Parliament. It commenced with an aspirational statement that the government's commitment to equality was based on the belief that equality was necessary for the individual. That it was a basic right to be free from prejudice and discrimination; that an unequal society can't be at ease with itself, an equal society gives greater social cohesion; equality was necessary for our economy – a modern economy thrives in a culture of equality which brings employers the widest labour pool, which sees all participate in the labour market rather than some being marginalised and excluded and recognises that diversity makes us outward facing and helps us compete in a global economy.

The driving force for this particular piece of legislation can therefore be seen as both social and economic.

The intention of the Equality Bill was to 'declutter' the existing law which comprised 8 major pieces of legislation, and over a hundred

---

13   Framework Directive 2000/78/EC.
14   Employment Equality (Sexual Orientation) Regulations SI 2003/1661.
15   Employment Equality (Religion or Belief) Regulations SI 2003/1660.
16   Employment Equality (Age) Regulations SI 2006/1031.
17   Directive 2000/43 EC implementing principle of equal treatment on grounds of race or ethnic origin, Directive 2002/73/EC amending Directive 76/207/EC on equal opportunities for women and men etc.

statutory instruments, and replace it with one statute. When the Equality Act 2010 (EA 2010) was finally passed it also codified some of the existing case law. The main aims of the Act were stated to be to:

(1)   Introduce a new equality duty on the public sector

(2)   End age discrimination

(3)   Require transparency particularly in payment systems

(4)   Extend the scope of positive action

(5)   Strengthen enforcement of equality law

SOURCES OF DISCRIMINATION LAW

United States Law

8.3 The only areas of UK discrimination law that were directly influenced by the discrimination law in the United States were the statutes covering sex and race discrimination but, given that most discrimination law passed since the SDA [1975] and RRA [1976] replicates their main provisions (except Disability Discrimination), then the general impact of the US rules on UK equality law should not be underestimated.

The United Kingdom had already joined the European Community (EC) when the Sex Discrimination Act was introduced in 1975 but, despite this, little or no account was taken of the equality law of the European Commission at the time. 'It is doubtful too, whether the EEC Directive had much influence upon the structure of the UK Act.'[18]

The Equal Treatment Directive 76/207 clearly came into being after the SDA [1975] was enacted, although the detail of what it contained was available to the legislators and could easily have included by them in its main provisions. They chose to largely ignore the Directive because the major influence on the legislators was the law of the United States. 'The main foreign influence on the UK Legislation was clearly from the

---

18   Ed. McCrudden, C (1987) *Women, Equality and European Equality Law*, Eclipse
     Publications, p 36.

United States.'[19] The ideas that were borrowed from their legal system included the concept of indirect discrimination[20] and the role of the Equal Opportunities Commission.[21]

As the legal provisions in the SDA 1975 and the RRA 1976 were very similarly constructed,[22] the latter Act also included concepts borrowed from the US. In discrimination cases, reference to American discrimination cases has been generally deemed relevant by the courts in the United Kingdom and in the European Court of Justice (ECJ).[23]

European Union Law

8.4 Although perhaps not influential in the early days, undoubtedly the most direct source of equality law in recent years has been the legislation and case law of the European Union.

The most relevant sources of European law will be discussed later in the chapter but in summary they are:

Article 141 of the EC Treaty (was formerly Article 119 of the Treaty of Rome)

Directive 75/117/EEC (Equal Pay)

Directive 76/207/EEC (Equal Treatment)

Directive 79/7/EEC (Equal Treatment in Social Security Matters)

Directive 79 EEC (Equal Treatment in Occupational Pension Schemes)

Directive 86/613/EEC (Equal Treatment for the Self Employed)

Directive 97/80 EC (Burden of Proof in Sex Discrimination Cases)

Directive 2000/78/EC (Equal Treatment in Employment and Occupation)

---

19   Ibid p37.
20   As defined by the United States Supreme Court in *Griggs v Duke Power Company* 401 US 424 [1971].
21   Based on the role of the Employment Equal Opportunities Commission (EEOC) in the United States.
22   Since then the Acts have been interpreted together so any change in the law through legislation or case law affecting one Act has also affected the other Act in the same way.
23   *Jenkins v Kingsgate* [1981] IRLR 228, ECJ.

Directive 2000/43/EC (Equal Treatment between Persons irrespective of Racial or Ethnic Origins)

Framework Directive 2000/78/EC (Employment)

Directive 2000/43/EC (Race)

Directive 2006/54 that amended the Equal Treatment Directive 76/207/EEC and introduced for the first time statutory protection against harassment and sexual harassment Article 2(1) (c) & (d)

Each of the legal measures highlighted above will be considered in the context of the area of discrimination law being covered.

Although, as seen, this area of law was not influential in the early stages and, in particular, the original format of the law, however the legislation and case law of the European Union has become the most direct source of UK equality law.

While there are various Directives and a Treaty that covers discrimination law in the European Union the most important and long standing of these is the Equal Treatment Directive 76/207 EEC.

This deals with sex discrimination and Article 5 of the Directive introduces the principle of equal treatment to working conditions, including the conditions governing dismissal which means that men and women shall be guaranteed the same conditions without discrimination on the grounds of sex.

It is interesting to note that race discrimination in employment was not part of the agenda of the EU until very recently. In the past however, where changes in the legislation dealing with sex discrimination came about through EU legislation or case law, the UK Government tended to introduce equivalent changes to legislation dealing with race discrimination shortly after (eg Race Relations (Remedies) Act 1994).

The Amsterdam Treaty[24] introduced the power to adopt a Directive to implement the principle of equal treatment on grounds of race or religion.[25]

---

24   It was signed on 2 October 1997, and entered into force on 1 May 1999 and it made substantial changes to the Treaty on European Union.

25   Council Directive 2000/43/EC prohibiting discrimination in employment on the grounds of race or ethnic origin.

The power to adopt measures to deal with discrimination is now contained within Article 13 of the EC Treaty.[26]

The need for the EU to legislate to protect victims of discrimination on the basis of sexual orientation, religion and belief, and age became apparent when various attempts to utilise existing law to extend protection to those suffering discrimination on these grounds were unsuccessful.[27] The European Commission introduced the European Employment Framework Directive (2000/78/EC) which provided that discrimination on these grounds should be treated as unlawful. The United Kingdom Government have consequently introduced the Employment Equality (Sexual Orientation) Regulations 2003 SI 1661, Employment Equality (Religion or Belief) Regulations 2003 SI 1660, Employment Equality (Age) Regulations 2006 SI 1031, to implement the Directive into UK law.

The European Charter of Fundamental Rights

8.5 The Charter of Fundamental Rights of the European Union has introduced certain political, social, and economic rights for European Union (EU) citizens and residents, into EU law. The European Charter of Fundamental rights includes a very wide ranging provision regarding discrimination, namely Article 21(1), which states:

> 'Any discrimination, based on any ground such as sex, race, colour, ethnic or social origin, genetic features, language, religion or belief, political or any other opinion, membership of a national minority, property, birth, disability, age, or sexual orientation shall be prohibited.'

It was drafted and officially proclaimed in 2000, but its legal status was uncertain and it did not have full legal effect until the entry into force of the Treaty of Lisbon on 1 December 2009. In the negotiations leading up to the signing of the Lisbon Treaty, Poland and the United Kingdom secured a protocol to the treaty relating to the application of the Fundamental Rights Charter in their respective countries. The protocol contains two substantial provisions. The first, Article 1(1), precludes both the domestic

---

26 Guild E The EC Directive on Race Discrimination: Surprises, Possibilities and Limitations Industrial Law Journal Volume 29, December 2000 p 416.

27 *Smith and Grady v The United Kingdom* [1999] IRLR 794.

courts in Poland and the UK, and the EU's courts from finding that laws, regulations or administrative provisions, practices or action in the countries to which it applies are inconsistent with the Charter. The second, Article 1(2), says that the Title IV of the Charter, which contains economic and social rights, does not create justiciable rights. So, although the EC charter of Fundamental Rights will not apply in the UK to provide legal rights to workers the European Convention for Human Rights applies (see below) and can be enforced by individual employees in the public sector before the UK Courts.

Human Rights

8.6 One of the most important influences on UK equality law is the European Convention of Human Rights.

Article 14 of the European Convention of Human Rights 1950 iterates the anti-discrimination theme when it states: The enjoyment of the rights and freedoms set forth in this Convention shall be secured without discrimination on any ground such as sex, race, colour, language, religion, political or other opinion, national or social origin, association with a national minority, property, birth or other status.

Since the passing of the Scotland Act 1998 all legislation of the Scottish Parliament requires to be Convention compliant and, since the coming into force of the Human Rights Act 1998 on 2 October 2000, convention rights have been directly enforceable in the UK courts and tribunals. (See chapter 3 for a detailed explanation of the methods by which human rights can be enforced in the domestic law.)

The International Labour Organisation and the International Covenant on Civil and Political Rights

8.7 There are various sources of international law affecting UK equality law, including the International Labour Organisation (ILO) and the UN International Covenant on Civil and Political Rights (ICCPR).[28] The

---

28   Other international influences on UK Equality Law are the International Covenant on Economic, Social and Cultural Rights and the Convention on the Elimination of All Forms of Discrimination.

International Labour Organisation was established in 1958 and the ILO Convention No 111 on Discrimination prohibits the behaviour, and defines it as 'a distinction, exclusion or preference made on the basis ... of sex ... which has the effect of nullifying or impairing equality of opportunity or treatment in occupation or profession.' While the influence of this Convention, and others dealing with discrimination, is hard to evaluate they have undoubtedly played a part in fashioning the legislative agenda of signatory States and the EU. In theory there is no real enforcement mechanism for the provisions of the ILO conventions but recent case law from the European Court of Justice mentions these measures, and is influenced by them, thereby implementing them indirectly.

The UN International Covenant on Civil and Political Rights (ICCPR) has an equality clause which again establishes the principle of equality of treatment under the law and guarantees protection against it. Under Part II of the Covenant, Article 2, in furtherance of one of the aims of the Covenant (to ensure accordance with the principles proclaimed in the Charter of the United Nations recognition of the inherent dignity and of the equal and inalienable rights of all members of the human family) states the following:

(1) Each State Party to the present Covenant undertakes to respect and to ensure all individuals within its territory and subject to its jurisdiction get the rights recognized in the present Covenant, without distinction of any kind, such as race, colour, sex, language, religion, political or other opinion, national or social origin, property, birth or other status.

(2) Where not already provided for by existing legislative or other measures, each State Party to the present Covenant undertakes to take the necessary steps in accordance with its constitutional processes and with the provisions of the present Covenant, to adopt such legislative or other measures as may be necessary to give effect to the rights recognized in the present Covenant.

(3) Each State Party to the present Covenant undertakes: To ensure that any person whose rights or freedoms as herein recognized are violated shall have an effective remedy ...provided for by the legal system of the State. It is clear that the expectations set out in the Covenant do not represent a challenge to the UK Government

(as a State Party) as they are in compliance with its expectations in respect of most of the forms of discrimination highlighted.

The Equality Act 2010

8.8 The Equality Act 2010 received Royal Assent on 8 April 2010 and its core provisions came into force on 1 October 2010. The Public Sector Equality duty came into force on the 5 April 2011 but the Public sector duty regarding socio-economic inequalities and Dual Discrimination Protection did not come into force and there is currently no intention on the part of the Government to bring them into force. The ban on age discrimination in provision of goods, facilities, services and public functions in 2012, and Private and Voluntary Sector Gender Pay Transparency Regulations (if required) and political parties publishing diversity data will happen in 2013. Whether the Act will achieve the aims set out in the policy document remains to be seen.

Protected Workers

8.9 The protection of the EA 2010 does not extend to all workers. It extends to those who are employed 'under a contract of service or apprenticeship or a contract personally to do work'.[29]

The definition of employee is therefore wider than that used to confer rights to redundancy payments and the right not to be unfairly dismissed which we have already discussed in Chapter 7. The definition is similar to that used by the Sex Discrimination Act 1975 s 82(1) and the case law relating to that section remains relevant. For example in *Mirror Group of Newspapers v Gunning*,[30] it was held that the tribunal must consider whether the 'dominant purpose' of the contract is to execute the work or labour personally. In that case which involved a contract for distribution of newspapers, it was held that it was not. Sub postmasters, held not to be employees since the notion of work or labour implied physical activity, could not be extended to mean acceptance of responsibility.[31] GPs were

---

29   Section 83(2).
30   1986 1 WLR 546.
31   *Chohan v Logan* EAT 29/8/02.

not considered to be employed by the Local Health Authority.[32] A man who engraved pens at a booth in a department store was an employee of that store, since he had to do the work personally and could not send a substitute.[33] A taxi driver was held not to be an employee of the taxi company, because the dominant purpose of the contract was that he provide his services as a self employed person, and also that there was insufficient mutuality of obligation since, provided he paid for his radio hire, he did not actually have to work.[34] A three year franchise between a solicitor and the Legal Aid Board was not a contract of employment because there was no requirement to do the work personally.[35]

DEFINITION OF DISCRIMINATION AND PROTECTED CHARACTERISTICS

8.10 Put at its simplest, discrimination occurs where someone, because of their nature, characteristic or background, is treated less favourably than someone without that nature, characteristic or background, and they suffer because of it.[36]

Most of the Equality Act 2010 came into force in October 2010,[37] and replaces the pre existing anti discrimination legislation, with one piece of legislation covering all 9 of the protected characteristics which are:

(1)   Age

(2)   Disability

(3)   Gender reassignment

(4)   Marriage and Civil Partnership

(5)   Pregnancy and Maternity

(6)   Race

(7)   Religion or belief

---

32   *Wadi v Cornwall and Isles of Scilly Family Practitioner Committee* [1985] ICR 492; *Essex SHA (formerly North Essex HA) v David-John* EAT 15/8/03.
33   *Quinnen v Hovells* 1984 ICR 525.
34   *Mingeley v Pennock* [2004] ICR 727.
35   *Patterson v Legal Services Commission* [2004] ICR 312.
36   Section 13 of the Equality Act.
37   The Equality Act 2010 (Commencement No. 4, Savings, Consequential, Transitional, Transitory and Incidental Provisions and Revocation) Order 2010.

(8)   Sex

(9)   Sexual orientation[38]

In order for a discrimination claim to be successful it must first be shown that there was less favourable treatment experienced by a person with a protected characteristic, compared to a person who did not share that protected characteristic (or because they are perceived to have the characteristic, or are discriminated against because of their association with some with that characteristic).

It should be noted that the protection offered in respect of each protected characteristic varies and we shall examine each in turn. The comparator is an important part of this process and is considered in detail below.

The reason for that less favourable treatment or disadvantage must be the protected characteristic. Not all inequality of treatment within the workplace will be unlawful, for example, in *Bahl v the Law Society*,[39] the Court of Appeal upheld the decision of the EAT that the reason for less favourable treatment was not the applicant's sex or race, but the fact that, because of her behaviour, the persons treating her in this way held her in disdain and were trying to protect their own jobs.

Nevertheless, if the reason for the treatment is a protected characteristic, the motive for that treatment is irrelevant.[40]

The Equality Act 2010 (EA 2010) refers to disadvantage rather than detriment, which is the term used by previous legislation. It is possible that it will be easier for an applicant to demonstrate a disadvantage than a detriment. The case law relating to the previous legislation makes it clear that the detriment suffered by the applicant had to be more than trivial.[41] It is likely that this will remain the position under the new legislation. It is possible to treat men and women differently because of their sex but, for the treatment not to amount to a disadvantage (see the dress code cases below for an example of this).

---

38   Equality Act 2010 ss 5–12.
39   [2004] IRLR 799.
40   *James v Eastleigh Borough Council* [1990] ICR 554, HL, *Porcelli v Strathclyde Regional Council* (1986) IRLR 134, Ct Sess.
41   *Jeremiah v Ministry of Defence* [1979] IRLR 436.

Types of Prohibited Conduct – Sex Discrimination

8.11 The 2010 Act identifies various types of 'prohibited conduct.'[42] Both men and women are protected against discrimination, although the legislators clearly anticipated that women would need the protection most.

Some types of prohibited conduct relate only to a particular protected characteristic so we will first examine those types of prohibited conduct which relate to the majority of protected characteristics, namely, direct discrimination, and indirect discrimination. Victimisation and harassment also apply to most of the protected characteristics and are discussed below. We shall examine the types of prohibited conduct primarily in the context of sex discrimination and later we will look at the differences which apply to the other protected characteristics. An action or incident may amount to more than one type of discrimination. It is important when raising a claim that the type of discrimination suffered is clearly specified, as it is difficult, if not impossible, to subsequently amend the ground of the claim. In *Ali v Office of National Statistics*,[43] the Court of Appeal held that a claim alleging direct discrimination will not necessarily include a claim for indirect discrimination.

Under s 11 of the Equality Act 2010, the ground of sex in relation to discrimination law is defined as (a) a reference to a person who has a particular protected characteristic is a reference to a man or to a woman; (b) a reference to persons who share a protected characteristic is a reference to persons of the same sex.

Where the protected characteristic is sex, no account is to be taken of special treatment afforded to a woman in connection with pregnancy or childbirth. Which is dealt with separately under s 18.

The Equality Act formally introduced the concept of associative discrimination into statute law. This applies where an individual is directly discriminated against, or harassed, for association with another individual who has a protected characteristic (although this does not cover harassment because of marriage and civil partnership, and pregnancy and maternity). It also provides that perceptive discrimination is covered. This is where an individual is directly discriminated against, or harassed, based on a

---

42   Sections 13–18.
43   (2005) IRLR 201.

perception that he or she has a particular protected characteristic when he or she does not, in fact, have that protected characteristic (although this does not cover harassment because of marriage and civil partnership, and pregnancy and maternity).

Prior to the Act it was unlawful for a person to instruct or induce someone to discriminate against, harass or victimise another person, or attempt to instruct or induce someone to do so, because of sex, race and disability only. However, the Act harmonises the law in this area by extending this protection to all protected characteristics. It also extends the definition to include instructing including, and/or causing, someone to discriminate against another person. There is also a separate course of action included where the individual who has been instructed to carry out the discrimination has been subjected to a detriment as a result of the conduct of the person giving the instructions, even if the instructions were not carried out.

Direct discrimination

8.12

> 'A person (A) discriminates against another (B) if, because of a protected characteristic, A treats B less favourably than A treats or would treat others.'[44]

and

> 'if the protected characteristic is sex …in a case where B is a man no account is to be taken of special treatment afforded to a woman in connection with pregnancy or childbirth.'

Direct discrimination is therefore a relatively straightforward concept whereby an employer directly, and often blatantly, discriminates against persons of one sex in terms of their process of recruitment and selection in their employment policies, or general treatment of prospective and actual employees. In direct discrimination cases the motive or intention of the discriminator in carrying out his discriminatory act is irrelevant. So this

---

44   Section 13(1).

will not be considered in a clam, as decided by the House of Lords in *James v Eastleigh Borough Council*.[45] Mr and Mrs James, both aged 61, went for a swim in Eastleigh Borough Councils baths. Mrs James was allowed in without paying because she had reached the 'pensionable age' of 60, while Mr James had to pay 60p because he had not yet reached the pensionable age for men of 65. Mr James, with the support of the Equal Opportunities Commission, brought a claim of direct sex discrimination under s 1(1)(a) of the SDA 1975. In this case, Lord Bridge said, 'pensionable age' is a convenient shorthand expression that refers to 60 for women and 65 for men. Thus, this is a case of direct discrimination – which is in breach of s 1(1)(a) of the SDA 1975 – and, but for the fact that Mr James was a man, he could swim free of charge in Eastleigh Borough Council's baths. The House of Lords in *James v Eastleigh BC*[46] underlined the importance of the 'but for' test that asks 'but for the fact that the victim of the discrimination was a women would she have been discriminated against?' They also confirmed that laudable motives of an employer in introducing a practice, measure or rule are of no significance in determining if the employer is guilty of direct discrimination. In order to establish direct discrimination, the complainant must show that he has been treated less favourably by the discriminator than the discriminator treats, or would treat, other persons in the same circumstances. However, in certain cases, the comparison need not be demonstrated by evidence as to how a comparator was, or would be, treated, because the very action complained of is in itself less favourable treatment on sexual grounds.[47]

There may be the situation where there is an absence of a suitable male comparator in a case and in these circumstances the employment tribunal may have to consider the treatment of a hypothetical male comparator.[48]

One of the main aims of the legislation is to combat stereotypical assumptions about women and make unlawful behaviour by an employer that is based upon such assumptions. In *Skyrail Oceanic v Coleman*[49] an

---

45 (1990) IRLR 288 HL.
46 Ibid.
47 *Sidhu v Aerospace Composite Technology Ltd* (2000) IRLR 602 CA.
48 This process is not necessary in maternity/pregnancy discrimination cases as no comparator is required in such cases.
49 [1981] ICR 864.

assumption that a man was the 'breadwinner' in a marriage resulting in the dismissal of a female employee was held by the Court of Appeal to be discriminatory. In *Hurley v Mustoe*[50] the employer's general assumption that employees with young children were unreliable was held to be directly discriminatory against women and also indirectly discriminatory on the grounds of marital status.[51]

Most employers are now familiar with the expectations of the law and consequently will be particularly unlikely to directly discriminate against women in their employment practices, because it can never be justified.[52]

Indirect discrimination

8.13 Indirect discrimination can be less obvious than direct. The definition is more complex, and the evidential difficulties in successfully pursuing a case of indirect discrimination have given rise to a multitude of cases over the years.

As defined in s 19 of the 2010 Act:

(1)   'A person (A) discriminates against another (B) if A applies to B a provision criterion or practice which is discriminatory in relation to a relevant protected characteristic of B's

(2)   …a provision criterion or practice is discriminatory in relation to a relevant protected characteristic of B's if -

(a)   A applies, or would apply, it to persons with whom B does not share the characteristic,

(b)   it puts, or would put, persons with whom B shares the characteristic at a particular disadvantage when compared with persons with whom B shares the characteristic at a particular disadvantage when compared with persons with whom B does not share it,

(c)   it puts, or would put, B at that disadvantage, and

(d)   A cannot show it to be a proportionate means of achieving a legitimate aim.'

---

50   [1981] IRLR 208.
51   See also *Horsey v Dyfed County Council* [1982] IRLR 395.
52   *Moyhing v St Barts NHS Trust* [2006] IRLR 860.

It should be noted that the list of protected characteristics which are relevant for indirect discrimination does not include pregnancy or child birth. The definition of indirect discrimination encourages the tribunals and courts to consider the impact of the discriminatory behaviour firstly on a group, and then on the individual claimant.

In *Price v Civil Service Commission*,[53] the issue in dispute was the ability of women to comply with a length of experience requirement for eligibility to apply for the position of executive officer in the Civil Service, as opposed to that of men in the same position. Mrs Price applied for a job as an executive officer in the Civil Service but she was told that she was too old at 32, as the age requirement for candidates was between 17 and 28. She claimed that this requirement represented indirect discrimination, as less qualified individuals in the job market would be able to comply with it, whereas many women were absent from the sphere of work during this time bringing up their families compared to men. It was held, on appeal, that it was a case of indirect discrimination that was not justifiable and the Civil Service was liable for damages. The Civil Service altered its age requirements for executive officer posts following this decision.

The requirement of many employers that employees work full-time, and an insistence on non-flexible working practices, often amounts to indirect discrimination. In the case of *Home Office v Holmes*,[54] the facts were that Mrs Holmes had previously worked full-time for the civil service but after returning to work after her maternity leave, she found full time work difficult and asked her employer for part-time work. Her employer refused to employ her part-time on the basis that all their posts at that time were full-time. She claimed indirect discrimination on the basis that it was more difficult for women to comply with the full time requirement than men, given that women are more likely to have primary childcare responsibility. A comparison was undertaken by the employment tribunal between males and females working in a specific department of Civil Service to discover the relative discriminatory impact of having to work full time on both groups. It was held in this case that there was indirect discrimination. The tribunal at the initial stage of the legal process summarised the position as follows 'it is still a fact that the raising of children tends to place a greater

---

53   [1978] ICR 27.
54   [1984] IRLR 299, EAT.

burden on women than it does on men.' The EAT however took the view that this ruling was not to be treated as a precedent that women are entitled to work part-time in all such circumstances. Whether or not a woman would be entitled to be offered part-time employment, would depend on the circumstances in the case. The nature of an indirect discrimination claim usually brought by an individual, but based on their experience as part of a group, is summarised in the following quote.[55]

> '...although the focus on groups rather than individuals and inequality of results underlies indirect discrimination, the concept stays short of insisting on a strict pattern of equality. This ensures that indirect discrimination continues to operate as an individual rather than group concept. The individual's right does not depend on others in the group although the individual may be classified as part of a group, making a claim because of his membership of that group and is claiming that the wrong is the disparate impact of conduct or decision on that group.'[56]

Issues in indirect discrimination cases

8.14 Particular issues which can arise in all kinds of claim for indirect discrimination are:

(a) 'Provision Criterion or Practice'

8.15 In considering the behaviour of the employer leading to the alleged discrimination, the original definition of indirect discrimination contained in the Sex Discrimination Act 1975 required the claimant to show she was subjected to a 'requirement or condition' by the employer. The meaning of the term 'requirement or condition' was clarified in *Falkirk Council v Whyte*,[57] where these terms were broadly interpreted by the EAT. In that case, three women raised a claim of indirect discrimination after they were refused employment in a managerial post at Cortonvale Prison. The job

---

55 This is unlike a class action in the United States where a group of people take a complaint forward to the courts or the EEOC.
56 Bamforth, N et al Discrimination Law Theory and Context Text and Materials (2008) Thomson/Sweet and Maxwell p 191.
57 [1997] IRLR 560.

specification stated that management training and supervisory experience were desirable qualities. It was clear that possession of these qualities was a decisive factor in being selected for the job. It was more difficult for women than men to comply with this factor, as all women were employed at basic grades.[58] It was held that a 'desirable quality' could be a requirement or condition in this case.

This definition was amended by the Sex Discrimination (Indirect Discrimination and Burden of Proof) Regulations SI 2001/2660 (considered below). Under these Regulations, the terms 'requirement' or 'condition' were replaced with the much broader terms of 'provision, criterion or practice' for certain important ss of the Act. This made it easier for claimants in indirect discrimination cases to establish that they have been subjected to inequality of treatment by their employer. This wording has been retained in s 19 of the EA 2010.

'Provisions, criteria or practices' (PCP's) can be written or unwritten, formal or informal, explicit or implicit. What is required is that some differentiating factor is applied that has an impact upon the complainant. 'It may even be sufficient to amount to a provision if the conduct complained of has happened on only one occasion'.[59] Common examples of PCP's include insistence on full-time work,[60] refusal to allow a job share, imposition of shift patterns which made it difficult to arrange childcare,[61] method of recruitment (by word of mouth). A refusal to allow flexible working may amount to indirect sex discrimination.

(b) The Pool for Comparison

8.16 The norm is that either the person as an individual is discriminated against because of the particular characteristic he has, or more likely, he is discriminated against because he is part of particular group. In the latter situation it will often be necessary for the claimant to produce statistical

---

58 A very different conclusion was reached in a race discrimination case *Perera v Civil Service Commission (No 2)* [1983] IRLR 166, where it was stated that for a requirement or condition to be treated as discriminatory it must be an absolute bar to the employee gaining equal rights with their comparator.

59 *British Airways Plc v Starmer* [2005] IRLR 863.

60 *Hardys & Hansons Plc v Lax* [2005] ICR 1565.

61 *London Underground v Edwards* [1999] ICR 494.

evidence to support the fact that they have been disadvantaged. They will often need to produce a pool for comparison made up of persons who are members of a different group, and consequently not disadvantaged to substantiate their claim. It is important that in deciding the relevant 'pool' for comparison, for the purposes of an application, the claimant should try and anticipate the pool that the employment tribunal will choose. In *Jones v University of Manchester*,[62] the claimant had been excluded from employment as a careers adviser at the university. The employer wanted someone closer to the age of the students for the post and had restricted eligibility to graduates aged 27–35. The claimant was 46 years of age. The basis of her claim was that the requirement was indirectly discriminatory, as female mature students tended to be older than male mature students, and by definition fewer women could comply with the age requirement than men.

The Court of Appeal rejected this argument claiming that the appropriate comparators were all persons (irrespective of age) meeting the relevant criteria. 'It is, in effect, the total number of all those persons, men and women, who answer the description contained in the advertisement, apart from the age requirement. Here, that means all graduates with the relevant experience.'[63] In the event that a claimant chooses a pool for comparison which is incorrect he or she loses the case.[64] The relevant pool is a matter of fact for the employment tribunal to determine[65] but, as illustrated in the *Jones* case, the employment tribunal often prefers to choose a broad pool (eg all women in UK eligible to apply for a job). It will often expect statistical evidence to be produced and led to support assertions of indirect discrimination. One solution is to provide statistical evidence for a number of different pools to allow the employment tribunal, if deemed appropriate, to decide which statistical evidence is most apt, and accept that as evidence of discrimination. Nowadays, and particularly since the Employment Equality (Sex Discrimination) Regulations 2005 were introduced, it might be the case that statistical evidence of indirect discrimination is not required by the employment tribunal. There may be

62   [1993] IRLR 193.
63   Evans LJ pp 228–291.
64   *Pearce v City of Bradford Metropolitan Council* [1988] IRLR 378 EAT.
65   *Kidd v DRG (UK) Ltd* [1985] IRLR 190, EAT.

less reliance on workplace statistics as tribunals are more willing to rely on national statistics and 'common knowledge', eg that women have primary responsibility for childcare.[66] However, statistics remain one important way of proving particular disadvantage, along with evidence from experts or other witnesses.

The Women and Equality Unit[67] produced a guide that highlights the usefulness of statistics in establishing particular disadvantage: 'This may be apparent from a comparison of the statistics of male or female workers or applicants who are at a disadvantage, ie that a larger proportion of one sex experiences a detriment. Statistics can be helpful in ascertaining relative disadvantage, however they are not essential.'[68]

(c) Disadvantage

8.17 It is not enough to show that the claimant cannot comply with the provision criterion or practice. The claimant must show that her inability to meet or comply with the provision, criterion or practice caused her to suffer a disadvantage as per the EA 2010. The word used and standard applied under previous legislation was detriment. Interestingly in the case of the *Ministry of Defence v Jeremiah*,[69] the Court of Appeal in attempting to define the term 'detriment' (under the SDA 1975) said it was merely placing someone at a disadvantage. Since then, a few discrimination cases have mentioned disadvantage but have tended to treat it as synonymous with a detriment.[70] In the case *of Eweida v British Airways plc*,[71] a Christian employee who had been suspended from work for wearing, with her uniform, a small, visible cross in breach of her employer's staff dress code, which forbade the wearing of visible neck adornment, had not suffered unlawful indirect discrimination.

---

66 *London Underground v Edwards* [1997] IRLR 364 CA.
67 http://www.gender-equality.webinfo.lt/results/uk.htm
68 'Changes to Sex Discrimination Legislation in Great Britain: Explaining the Employment Equality (Sex Discrimination) Regulations 2005'.
69 [1979] IRLR 436, CA.
70 *Chief Constable of West Yorkshire v Khan* [2001] IRLR 830.
71 *Eweida v British Airways plc* [2010] EWCA Civ 80 [2010] IRLR 322, CA, *Shamoon v Chief Constable of the Royal Ulster Constabulary* [2003] UKHL 11, [2003] IRLR 285.

Lord Justice Sedley made reference to disadvantage in the following quote

> 'I am bound to say that … I have considerable difficulty in seeing how [the Tribunal] could hold that a previously unobjectionable rule had somehow become disproportionate once the claimant had raised the issue, even on the assumption that it was a rule that disadvantaged Christians as a group within the workforce.'

As neither Ms Eweida, nor any witness on her behalf, suggested that the visible wearing of a cross was more than a personal preference on her part, there was no proof that her religious belief called for her to wear a cross.

The EA 2010 does not list the ways in which discrimination may be practiced and, therefore, all that is required now is to prove disadvantage. It remains to be seen whether this will be less onerous for the claimant.

(d) Proportionate means to achieving a legitimate aim

8.18 Even if it has been shown by the claimant that they have been the victim of indirect discrimination, it is a defence to such a claim under s 19 of the EA 2010 for an employer to show that the types of discriminatory activity undertaken by him was a proportionate means of achieving a legitimate aim. The question is, when can an otherwise discriminatory provision, criterion or practice be shown to be a proportionate means of achieving a legitimate aim? What is a proportionate means of achieving a legitimate aim? There is some guidance on the defence in the codes of practice. A 'legitimate aim' should be legal, should not be discriminatory in itself and must represent a real, objective consideration. As regards what amounts to proportionate treatment, treatment is proportionate if it is an appropriate and necessary means of achieving a legitimate aim. A balance has to be struck between the discriminatory effect of the treatment and the need to apply it, taking into account all the relevant facts.

In this context proportionate means that: what the employer is doing is actually achieving its aim; the impact of the discriminatory behaviour should be significantly outweighed by the importance and benefits of the legitimate aim; and the employer should not have a reasonable alternative to the action he is taking. If the legitimate aim can be achieved by another less discriminatory route then the employer must then opt for that route.

The meaning of legitimate may vary depending on the characteristic being considered, but it could be economic factors or the need for the efficient running of the business.

In the recent case *Woodcock v North Cumbria Primary Care Trust*,[72] the EAT held that the dismissal of a Chief Executive of a Primary Care Trust was discriminatory on the grounds of age, as notice to terminate his employment was accelerated so as to expire before his 50th birthday, although the EAT went on to find that the discrimination was justified as it was a proportionate means of achieving a legitimate aim which, primarily was the avoidance of a significant financial cost to the organisation concerned.

In *Clarke v Eley (IMI) Kynoch Ltd*,[73] it was held not to be justifiable to choose part-timers for dismissal before full time staff under a redundancy procedure. It seems certain it would not be regarded as a proportionate means of achieving a legitimate aim. In *Ojutiku v MSC*,[74] the Court of Appeal said that the standard for proving a justifiable reason, other than sex, should be 'what was acceptable to right thinking people as sound and tolerable reasons for adopting the practice in question.'[75] This was not a very helpful definition for employment tribunals and the ECJ in *Bilka-Kaufhaus*[76] provided more clarification of the standard of proof required.

The employer must demonstrate objectively justified factors which are unrelated to discrimination based on sex. The employer must show that there is real business need for the discriminatory outcome, and the means chosen to achieve the outcome are suitable and necessary.[77]

In *Allonby v Accrington and Rossendale College*,[78] the Court of Appeal held that the justification must be based on a real need of the employer which outweighs the impact it has on the claimant/s in the case. In

---

72   [2011] IRLR 119.
73   [1982] IRLR 482 EAT.
74   [1982] IRLR 418 CA.
75   In *Rainey v Greater Glasgow Health Board* [1987] IRLR 26, HL the House of Lords held that the concepts of justification in indirect discrimination and equal pay cases should be interpreted in the same way.
76   *Bilka-Kaufhaus GmbH V Weber Von Hartz* [1986] ECR 1607.
77   Anderman S Chapter 8 pp 103–109 Dine, J Watt, B Discrimination Law Concepts, Limitations and Justifications (1996) Longman.
78   [2001] IRLR 364.

Hampson v Department of Education and Science,[79] the test was described as objective and it was differentiated from the range of reasonable responses test used in unfair dismissal cases.[80]

In *Elias v Secretary of State for Defence*,[81] the Court of Appeal set out 3 questions for the court to consider in determining whether there is sufficient justification, namely: (1) is the objective sufficiently important to justify limiting a fundamental right? (2) is the measure rationally connected to the objective? and (3) are the means chosen no more than are necessary to accomplish the objective?

One provision criterion or practice which employers often try to impose and justify (and is equally often subject to controversy), is the length of service criteria applied to pension schemes, promotion policies and redundancy selection criteria.

In *Gerster v Freistaat Bayern*,[82] the Bavarian State Civil Service had a length of service component in their policy for eligibility for promotion. Part-time worker's years of service were calculated in proportion to the fraction of full time hours which they worked. If they worked less than ½ of full-time hours, then they were not eligible at all. If they worked between ½ and ⅔ of full time hours they were treated as having ⅔ of full time service, and if they worked more than ⅔ of full-time hours they were treated the same as full-timers. The ECJ held that this rule was unlawful indirect discrimination, unless it could be objectively justified, for example if it could be proved that part-timers took longer to acquire job-related skills than full-timers. Obviously there will come a point where a worker is not acquiring many new skills in a job, so shorter periods of eligibility will be easier to justify than excessively long periods.

Other justification defences which have been tried and failed, have been health and safety[83] and cost. Cost implications may succeed as a justification if the employer is in the private sector,[84] provided a detailed

---

79   (1991) ICR. 511.
80   *HSBC v Madden* (2000) ICR 1283 CA.
81   [2006] IRLR 934 CA.
82   [1998] ICR 327.
83   *Cross and ors v British Airways plc* [2005] IRLR 423.
84   Ibid.

analysis is provided to the tribunal,[85] but this argument is unlikely to succeed where the employer is a public body.[86]

Harassment

8.19 Sexual harassment was originally actionable only under the provisions of s 6(2) of the Sex Discrimination Act 1975 relating to direct discrimination. In *Strathclyde Regional Council v Porcelli*,[87] Mrs Porcelli was subjected to a campaign of harassment by two male colleagues to force her to leave her job, including sexual comments, sexual innuendoes and threatening gestures. She applied for, and was given, a transfer and claimed that the behaviour constituted sex discrimination under SDA 1975. It was considered that to subject someone to sexual harassment was to submit them to 'any other detriment' under the terms of this section. Behaviour was discriminatory, as a man similarly placed who was equally disliked would not have suffered the same fate. Treatment was therefore on grounds of the women's sex. Sexual harassment by itself, without any accompanying threat to terms and conditions of employment, was sufficiently detrimental to be treated as sex discrimination. While it was originally believed that harassment must involve a continuous mode of conduct this was refuted by two cases. *Bracebridge Engineering Ltd v Darby*,[88] where a single incident of harassment (a serious assault by the claimant's supervisor and another) was capable of constituting sufficient detriment; and *Insitu Cleaning Co Ltd v Heads*,[89] where a single verbal comment of a sexist nature made to a female manager by a fellow male manager at a meeting was sufficient detriment to amount to sexual harassment which was contrary to s 6 (2)(c) of the Sex Discrimination Act.

However, the use of the provisions relating to direct sex discrimination to combat harassment was unsatisfactory, because of the general difficulty in establishing sufficient 'detriment' as can be seen from the

---

85 *Hardy and Hansons plc v Lax* [2005] ICR 1565.
86 *Schonheit v Stadt Frankfurt am Main* [2003] ECR I–12572 and *Steinicke v Bundesanstat fur arbeit* [2003] Case C-77/02 [2003] IRLR 892.
87 [1986] IRLR 134 CS.
88 [1990] IRLR 3 EAT.
89 [1995] IRLR 4 EAT.

case of *British Telecommunications v Williams*,[90] where an interview by a male manager of a female job applicant in a very confined space was not treated as sex discrimination as there was insufficient detriment. The requirement to claim direct discrimination was also unsatisfactory when used in a situation where both sexes would be similarly disadvantaged, as can be seen in *Stewart v Cleveland Guest (Engineering) Ltd*,[91] where pornographic images displayed in the workplace were not deemed to be discriminatory against women, because working in an environment tainted by pornography was gender neutral (a man would have been equally offended).[92]

In order to implement the Equal Treatment Directive 2002/73/EC, a separate provision regarding harassment was introduced into the SDA 1975. Effective from 1 October 2005, the new s 4A involved the creation of a distinct type of statutory unlawful conduct of harassment. The original definition of harassment was where, 'on grounds of her sex, he engages in unwanted conduct'.[93] This definition required to be amended from 6 April 2008[94] to 'he engages in unwanted conduct that is related to her sex or that of another person'. This was a much wider definition which applies to sex related harassment as well as sexual harassment. This wider protection is retained by the current definition which is contained in s 26(1) of the EA 2010. It states that: A person (A) harasses another (B) if A engages in

---

90   [1997] IRLR 668 EAT.

91   [1994] IRLR 440 EAT.

92   In *Moonsar v Fiveways Express Transport Ltd* [2005] IRLR 9, Ms Moonsar worked in an office where, male members of staff downloaded pornographic images on to screens where they were all working. The images were not circulated to Ms Moonsar, but she worked in close proximity to them and so was aware of what was happening. The EAT held that, viewed objectively, this behaviour clearly had the potential effect of causing an affront to a female employee working in a close environment, and as such would be regarded as degrading or offensive to an employee as a woman. It was clearly potentially less favourable treatment and a detriment clearly followed from the nature of the behaviour. There was evidence before the ET that the claimant found the behaviour unacceptable. The fact she did not complain at the time was not a defence where the behaviour was so obvious, as in the present case.

93   Linda Clarke, Harassment, sexual harassment, and the Employment Equality (Sex Discrimination) Regulations 2005. Legislative Comment, Industrial Law Journal 2006, Vol. 35(2), p 161.

94   The Sex Discrimination Act 1975 (Amendment) Regulations 2008.

unwanted conduct related to a relevant protected characteristic which has the purpose or effect of violating B's dignity or creating an intimidating, hostile, degrading or humiliating or offensive environment for B. Under the Equality Act, this form of harassment does not just apply to the protected characteristic of sex. It applies to all the protected characteristics with the exception of marriage and civil partnership. Specific provision is made in relation to sexual harassment. Under s 21 (2) it is also harassment if A engages in any form of unwanted verbal, non-verbal or physical conduct of a sexual nature that has the purpose or effect of violating B's dignity or creating an intimidating, hostile, degrading or humiliating or offensive environment for B. Finally it is also harassment if because of B's rejection of or submission to conduct (whether or not of A), A treats B less favourably than A would treat B if B had not rejected or submitted to the conduct.

The provisions relating to harassment under this provision are more advantageous to claimants than those relating to Direct Discrimination as there is no need for a comparator. It is not necessary for conduct to be sexually motivated to constitute harassment. It is sufficient if it is sex related.

It is possible to claim harassment by association, because harassment can be because of a protected characteristic of someone other than B. Accordingly, individuals who are friends as well as colleagues of another employee, who is subjected to the unwanted sexual harassment, may also receive protection if, for example, that it can show as friend of the victim it is offensive to them or it has created an unwelcome working environment. The case law relating to the previous statutory harassment provisions was unclear as to whether the test to be applied in deciding whether conduct amounted to harassment was subjective or objective. In *Reed v Stedman, Bull Information Systems v Stedman*,[95] the EAT suggested that tribunals should not use an objective test to determine whether an employee had suffered a detriment in sexual harassment cases. However, other cases favoured a more objective test. In *Driskel v Peninsula Business Services*,[96] the EAT stated that the tribunal should assess the matter objectively, but take into account the woman's subjective attitude to the incidents. The

---

95   [1999] IRLR 299.
96   (2000) IRLR 151, EAT.

EAT also said it was important to remember that sexual banter by a man towards a woman often had a wholly different effect on the recipient, than banter between members of the same sex.

The 2010 Act makes it clear that, in deciding whether the conduct of A has the purpose or effect of violating B's dignity or creating an intimidating, hostile, degrading or humiliating or offensive environment for B, account must be taken of:

(a)   the perception of B;

(b)   the other circumstances of the case;

(c)   whether it is *reasonable* for the conduct to have that effect.[97]

It remains to be seen what weight the court or tribunal will give to each of these factors, but it appears that, although the tribunal will take into account the feelings of the harassee it is possible that less serious incidents may not amount to harassment unless the harassee has given notice to the harasser that he/she finds such behaviours offensive. It is possible that we will see the development of a constructive knowledge test, ie that the harasser knew or ought to have known that the harassee would find the behaviour offensive.

It is important to look at the circumstances of the case as a whole, rather than at isolated incidents. In the *Driskel* case the EAT said that the tribunal should look at the incidents as a whole to assess whether conduct amounted to harassment. Therefore, it is possible that, although each incident taken separately may not amount to harassment the incident when looked at in the context of other incidents may be regarded as harassment. The demeanour, attitude and lifestyle of the claimant will continue to be relevant in determining whether she has been harassed and also determining the extent of injury to her feelings. In *Snowball v Gardner Merchant Ltd*,[98] evidence relating to the woman's attitude towards sexual matters was admitted as relevant in the case. In *Wileman v Minilec Engineering Ltd*,[99] the amount awarded for sexual harassment, where a woman was in the habit of wearing scanty clothing was a nominal £50. The assumption made by the employment tribunals in these cases was

---

97   S 24(4).
98   (1987) IRLR 397, EAT.
99   (1988) IRLR 144, EAT.

that a claimant's sexual attitude or behaviour was relevant in determining whether the claimant had suffered a detriment and this was problematic for the victim.

Liability of the Employer for Harassment

8.20 Under s 109 of the Equality Act 2010 it deals with the liability of employers and principals and states that:

• Anything done by a person (A) in the course of A's employment must be treated as also done by the employer.[100]

• It does not matter whether that thing is done with the employer's or principal's knowledge or approval.

• In proceedings against A's employer (B) in respect of anything alleged to have been done by A in the course of A's employment it is a defence for B to show that B took all reasonable steps to prevent A (a) from doing that thing, or (b) from doing anything of that description.

So the person who has primary responsibility for the harassment is of course the harasser who may be the claimant's supervisor or colleague. However, under s 109, the employer will be vicariously liable for all acts of discrimination committed by his employee (the harasser) in the scope of his employment unless the employer took all reasonable steps to prevent such conduct (see below).

Third Party Harassment

8.21 In certain situations conduct out with working hours or outwith the workplace will be considered to be within the scope of employment. However in *HM Prison Service and others v Davis*,[101] the EAT held the employment tribunal had erred in law by finding that acts between two off-duty prison officers (namely the unwanted sexual attentions of Mr

---

100 (2) Anything done by an agent for a principal, with the authority of the principal, must be treated as also done by the principal.

101 EAT/1294/98.

Randall) in a social setting (in Miss Davis' home) occurred in the course of employment.

The law concerning this aspect of harassment has undergone substantial changes recently so attention will be restricted to development within the last ten years. There were various cases where the employer was held vicariously liable for harassment perpetrated against their employees by third parties. A case in point was *The Chief Constable of the Lincolnshire Police v Stubbs*[102] where the employer was held liable under s 41 of the SDA 1975 for discriminatory act perpetrated outside the workplace. On two occasions outside work a female police officer socialising with her colleagues was sexually harassed physically and verbally by a fellow officer. A question arose concerning the liability of the employer for these acts. It was held by the EAT that the employer was liable because 'these incidents are connected to work and the workplace. They would not have happened but for the applicants work. Work related functions are an extension of employment and we can see no reason to restrict the course of employment to purely what goes on in the workplace.'

In the joined appeals of *Pearce v Mayfield School* and *MacDonald v Advocate General for Scotland*,[103] the House of Lords decided that the tribunal should consider whether in fact there were any effective steps which the employer could have taken to prevent the harassment by the third party. If no act by the employer would have made any difference the tribunal should not hold an employer liable for the act of the third party. Since the House of Lords decision in *Pearce*, employers have not generally been held vicariously liable for discriminatory acts or omissions of a third parties such as visitors, contractors, customers or suppliers. However, the Labour Government issued new regulations amending the law in this respect. The Sex Discrimination Act 1975 (Amendment) Regulations 2008, changed the rules relating to liability for third party actions. The Regulations overturned the *Pearce* decision in respect of sex, sexual, and gender reassignment harassment. It stated that an employer will be liable for harassment if a third party subjects a woman to harassment in the course of her employment and the employer has failed to take reasonably practicable steps to prevent the harassment. The employer must also have

---

102 [1999] IRLR 81.
103 [2003] ICR 937 (HL).

known that the woman had been subjected to harassment in the course of her employment on at least two other occasions by a third party. These provisions would apply equally to harassment suffered by a man. This was an important extension of employer liability and affected all employers that have employees fulfilling a role involving interaction with customers, contractors or members of the public. However, the requirement for three separate incidents of harassment to have occurred limited its impact, even although it was not necessary to show they all related to the same person.[104] Under s 40 of the Equality Act, the rules in the 2008 Regulations are simply restated as follows. Under s 40 (1) An employer (A) must not, in relation to employment by A, harass a person (B) (a) who is an employee of A's; (b) who has applied to A for employment. (2) The circumstances in which A is to be treated as harassing B under subsection (1) include those where (a) a third party harasses B in the course of B's employment, and (b) A failed to take such steps as would have been reasonably practicable to prevent the third party from doing so. However, this is qualified by the provision that Subsection (2) does not apply unless A knows that B has been harassed in the course of B's employment on at least two other occasions by a third party; and it does not matter whether the third party is the same or a different person on each occasion.

Under the Equality Act harassment of an employee related to a protected characteristic under the Equality Act 2010 (other than marriage and civil partnership, and pregnancy and maternity) by third parties, for example clients or customers are covered. The rules that already applied to third-party harassment only applied to sex discrimination, however, the Act extended them to cover age, disability, gender reassignment, race, religion or belief and sexual orientation.

Common law rules on harassment and vicarious liability

8.22 In addition to liability, under the EA 2010, if an act of harassment is committed within the scope of the perpetrator's employment this can amount to a civil wrong or delict, eg an assault and the employer can be vicariously liable under the common law. In *Waters v Commissioner for*

---

104 Middlemiss, S Employers Liability for Third Party Harassment, 2009, International Journal of Discrimination and the Law (2009) Volume 10, Number 1 p 39.

Police of the Metropolis,[105] a female police officer was sexually assaulted by a colleague outside working hours in her home. She reported the incident to her employer but after an enquiry no action was taken against the harasser. She then experienced victimisation (explained below) by her employer and made a claim (under s 4 of the SDA 1975). It was held that since no legal action could be taken against the employer under the Act for the assault, as they were not vicarious liable because the harasser was acting outside the scope of his employment, it was impossible to find that there had been victimisation. This was because victimisation was dependant on the action complained of following a complaint under s 41 of the SDA 1975. However, the case eventually went to the House of Lords where it upheld Ms Water's claim that the employer's failure to offer her support, and to permit harassment and victimisation of her, amounted to breach of their duty of care under the law of contract and delict.[106]

> 'If an employer knows that acts being done by employees during their employment may cause physical or mental harm to a particular fellow employee and he does nothing to supervise or prevent such acts, where it is in his power to do so, it is clearly arguable that he may be in breach of his duty to that employee. It seems to me that he may also be in breach of that duty if he can foresee such acts may happen, and if they do, that physical or mental harm may be caused.'[107]

The employer should have anticipated Ms Waters persistent complaint about the assault by a fellow officer would lead to retaliatory action.

> 'I consider the person employed under an ordinary contract of employment can have a valid cause of action in negligence against her employer if the employer fails to protect her against victimisation and harassment which cause physical or mental injury. This duty arises both under the contract of employment and under the common law principles of negligence.'[108]

---

105 [1995] IRLR 531.
106 *Waters v Metropolitan Police Commissioner* [2000] IRLR 720.
107 Ibid Lord Slynn
108 Ibid Lord Hutton

The advantage of suing in a civil court under common law is that the definition of scope of employment is very wide and, under the common law, there is no defence available to the employer as liability is strict (see below for a more detailed discussion of vicarious liability).[109]

Victimisation

8.23 It is important not to confuse victimisation and harassment. Victimisation only occurs in certain restricted circumstances, described in s 27 of the 2010 Act. This provision is designed to prevent an employer taking action against someone who has brought proceedings against the employer under the Act, or who had assisted someone else in bringing such proceedings. Under this section it is unlawful for someone (A) to subject a person (B) to a detriment, because B does a protected Act or because A believes B has done or may do a protected act. A protected act is defined in s 27(2) and includes the bringing of proceedings under the Act, giving evidence or information in connection with proceedings under this Act, doing any other thing for the purposes of, or in connection with, the Act or making an allegation (whether or not express) that A or another person has contravened the Act. The act will cease to be protected if the evidence allegation or information is false and made in bad faith.[110] A claim for victimisation is relatively narrow, compared with other kinds of discrimination claim, restricted as it is to combating discriminatory behaviour relating to a proposed or actual sex discrimination claim before an employment tribunal.

Post termination actions

8.24 In *Coote v Granada Hospitality Ltd (No 2)*,[111] a woman who had left her employment claimed she had been subjected to victimisation by her employer because they refused to provide her with a reference. This matter was referred to the ECJ by the EAT to determine if she had

---

109 There is also the possibility of liability for an employer under the civil provisions of the Protection from Harassment Act 1997 but it is out with the scope of this chapter.
110 S 27(3).
111 C-185/97 [1998] IRLR 656, ECJ.

a right of action under European Law. The ECJ ruled that Article 6 of the Equal Treatment Directive did provide a right to bring an action for discrimination after the contract had come to an end. The EAT decided it could give effect to the ECJ judgement without distorting the language of the SDA 1975 and it was possible to construe the Act in a way that it conformed with the Directive.[112]

The application of the Equality Act 2010 to discrimination and harassment, and relationships which have come to an end, is dealt with by s 108. (1) A person (A) must not discriminate against another (B) if (a) the discrimination arises out of and is closely connected to a relationship which used to exist between them, and (b) conduct of a description constituting the discrimination would, if it occurred during the relationship, contravene this Act. S108 (2) states that: A person (A) must not harass another (B) if (a) the harassment arises out of and is closely connected to a relationship which used to exist between them, and (b) conduct of a description constituting the harassment would, if it occurred during the relationship, contravene this Act.

Unlawful activities

8.25 The previous legislation[113] specified what type of discriminatory activities should be treated as unlawful. These applied to all characteristics of discrimination and covered discriminatory practices in recruitment and selection, within employment and dismissal. These have been reintroduced, under the Equality Act Section 39. Section 39 (1)[114] of the Equality Act 2010, states that:

An employer must not discriminate against a person

(a) in the arrangements A makes for deciding to whom to offer employment;

(b) as to the terms on which A offers B employment;

(c) by not offering B employment.

---

112 The legislation introduced to implement the Race Discrimination and Framework Directive makes it unlawful for an employer to discriminate against a former employee where the discrimination is closely connected to the employment relationship.

113 Section 6 Sex Discrimination Act 1975 (as amended).

114 Similar provision is made in relation to victimisation in s 39 (2).

These are relevant as examples of discriminatory behaviour that is unlawful rather than as an exhaustive list of ways in which an employer may be found to discriminate. Section 39(1) (a) in the arrangements A makes for deciding to whom to offer employment. In *Brennan v Dewhurst*,[115] the EAT held that it was irrelevant that the employer did not intend to discriminate and clarified that 'in all stages in applying for and obtaining employment a woman should be on an equal footing with a man.'

Discriminatory questions at an interview directed only at female candidates, discriminatory advertisements, eg which create the impression that female claimants are unwanted or even the location where the interview is carried out (eg where it is a tight space that requires female claimant to brush up against male interviewers), may all be examples of discrimination.

Section 39 (2) states that an employer (A) must not discriminate against an employee of A's (B):

(a)   as to B's terms of employment;

(b)   in the way A affords B access, or by not affording B access, to opportunities for promotion, transfer or training or for receiving any other benefit, facility or service;

(c)   by dismissing B;

(d)   by subjecting B to any other detriment.

Although inequality in pay and other terms and conditions between men and women in employment is covered by the equality clause contained in Chapter 3 of the Act, where the inequality applies to terms and conditions offered at the *selection stage* s 13 (Direct Discrimination) of the Equality Act 2010, applies. It would also apply where there was no opportunity to bring a case under the equality clause provisions for example where there was no suitable male comparator in the same employment.

Section 39(1) (c) Discriminating by refusing or deliberately omitting to offer her employment. This will be difficult to prove because the information needed to make a comparison is in the hands of the employer and the claimant needs to show that she is the best candidate and was

---

115 [1983] IRLR 357, EAT.

refused employment on the basis of her sex.[116] It is generally recognised that the employer has a managerial prerogative to decide who is chosen for employment and unless there is clear evidence of discrimination the employment tribunal may be reluctant to intervene

Section 39(2)(b) It will also be unlawful to discriminate in the way in which an employer affords a women access to promotion, transfer or training, or to any other benefits facilities or services or by refusing or deliberately omitting to afford access to them. This is a wide-ranging measure capable of covering most kind of discrimination arising within the employment relationship.

Section 39(2) (c) It is unlawful to discriminate by dismissing a woman (including failing to extend a fixed term contract where it is warranted) or subjecting her to any other detriment. The term dismissal here has been extended to cover constructive dismissal.[117]

The term detriment was interpreted by the courts as including sexual harassment (discussed above) although there is now a separate heading of liability for harassment under s 26 of the Equality Act 2010. Where a woman is dismissed on the ground of her sex, she may have a choice of bringing a claim under this part of the Act or for unfair dismissal.[118] The benefit of pursuing her claim under the discrimination legislation is that she will not need to establish that she has continuous service of one year with the employer (as required under the Employment Rights Act 1996) and the damages that she can be awarded are unlimited.

Vicarious liability

8.26 Under s 109 of the Equality Act the rules regarding liability of employers and principals for discriminatory act of their employees are largely the same as those originally in s 42 of the Sex Discrimination Act etc.

---

116 An order for the discovery of documents see *Nasse v Science Research Council; Vyas v Leyland Cars* [1979] IRLR 465 HL and a questionnaire procedure under s 74 of the SDA 1975 and s 65 of the RRA 1976 assisted the applicants in proving their case.
117 *See Derby Specialist Fabrication Ltd v Burton* [2001] IRLR 69 EAT.
118 Under s 95 of the Employment Rights Act 1996.

(1)   Anything done by a person (A) in the course of A's employment must be treated as also done by the employer.

(2)   Anything done by an agent for a principal, with the authority of the principal, must be treated as also done by the principal.

(3)   It does not matter whether that thing is done with the employer's or principal's knowledge or approval.

(4)   In proceedings against A's employer (B) in respect of anything alleged to have been done by A in the course of A's employment it is a defence for B to show that B took all reasonable steps to prevent A— (a) from doing that thing, or (b) from doing anything of that description.

This is a threshold requirement in discrimination cases and must establish that her/his employer was vicariously liable for the actions of the perpetrator of the discriminatory act. Where, for example, a female employee was refused promotion because her supervisor in the workplace did not like women, would the employer be vicariously liable under the Equality Act? Given the interpretation of vicarious liability rules under case law dealing with discrimination it seems highly likely.[119]

The employee could, in these circumstances, also sue the perpetrator of the discriminatory act or persons that assisted him. Under s 110 of the Equality Act it deals with liability of employees and agents as follows:

(1)   A person (A) contravenes this section if—(a) A is an employee or agent, (b) A does something which, by virtue of s 109(1); or

(2)   is treated as having been done by A's employer or principal (as the case may be), and (c) the doing of that thing by A amounts to a contravention of this Act by the employer or principal (as the case may be).

(3)   A does not contravene this section if (a) A relies on a statement by the employer or principal that doing that thing is not a contravention of this Act, and (b) it is reasonable for A to do so.

---

119 *Jones v Tower Boot Co Ltd* (1997) IRLR 168.

So a person who knowingly aids another person to commit an act which is unlawful under the Act shall be treated as himself doing an unlawful act of the like description.

In *Hallam and Smith v Avery and Lambert*,[120] the Court of Appeal held that it is not enough that the person assisted with a complete act of discrimination. It must be established that they knew that the perpetrator was treating or was about to treat someone less favourably on the ground of sex and proceeded to provide them with aid.[121] In *Anyanwu and another v South Bank Student Union and another*,[122] the House of Lords held that a person aids another to do an unlawful act under the RRA 1976 if he or she helps or assists that other. Liability will extend to them whether or not their help is substantial and productive, provided it is not negligible.

Remedies

8.27 The remedies that can be awarded by employment tribunals in successful claims for discrimination are provided by s 124 of the Equality Act 2010: (1) This section applies if an employment tribunal finds that there has been a contravention of a provision referred to in s 120 (1)(2). The tribunal may (a) make a declaration as to the rights of the complainant and the respondent in relation to the matters to which the proceedings relate; (b) order the respondent to pay compensation to the complainant; or (c) make an appropriate recommendation. (3) An appropriate recommendation is a recommendation that within a specified period the respondent takes specified steps for the purpose of obviating or reducing the adverse effect of any matter to which the proceedings relate (a) on the complainant; (b) on any other person.

---

120 [2001] ICR 381.
121 For some background to this provision see Middlemiss, S Aiding a Discriminatory Act of the Employer, (*AM v WC and SPF* [1999] IRLR 410) *Scots Law Times*, Issue 1, 7 January 2000 pp 1–4.
122 [2001] IRLR 305.

Declaratory Order

8.28 A declaratory order from the employment tribunal sets out the rights and obligations of the parties in relation to the act which the complaint relates.[123]

Compensation

8.29 Compensation is the most common remedy sought by and awarded to claimants. employment tribunals are given the power to order 'the respondent to pay compensation that is unlimited as a consequence of the ruling of the *ECJ in Marshall v Southampton and South West Hampshire Health Authority (No 2)*,[124] and the Sex Discrimination and Equal Pay (Remedies) Act 1993.[125] In some instances the amount of damages awarded have been considerable as unlimited damages may be awarded and can include compensation for injury to feelings, whether or not they include compensation under any other head. The headings of financial loss which the complainant can be compensated for by way of restitution include injury to feelings (solatium), loss of earnings (including future earnings), loss of pension rights, interest due on the award and expenses associated with the legal claim.

The compensation should recompense in full for the loss actually sustained by the applicant.[126] There is the possibility the compensation awarded will be reduced to reflect the contributory negligence of the claimant. In the case of *Way and another v Crouch*,[127] the EAT held that as a matter of law the award of compensation in a sex discrimination case (and in other discrimination claims) was subject to the Law Reform (Contributory Negligence) Act 1945, which allows for reduction in compensation in claims where the claimant's conduct itself amounts

---

123 For a critique of the remedies see Lustgarten, L *Racial Inequality and the Limits of the Law*, Modern Law Review Vol 49 1986 68.

124 [1993] IRLR 445.

125 The limit on compensation previously originally contained in s 65 (2) of the SDA 1975 was removed by the Sex Discrimination and Equal Pay (Remedies) Regulations 1993.

126 *Marshall v Southampton and South West Hampshire Area Health Authority* (No.2) [1993] IRLR 445 ECJ.

127 [2005] IRLR 603.

to negligence or breach of a legal duty and contributed to the damage suffered by claimant. It was held in this case that there was no basis on the facts for a finding of contributory negligence.

Recommendations

8.30 Recommendations can be made by a tribunal, recommending that an employer take action to remove the discriminatory effect of their behaviour on the complainant. This might consist of transferring a harasser away from his victim, introducing training for managers on equal opportunities policies and procedures, changing procedures for recruitment and selection to ensure equality of treatment and providing a fair and accurate reference to someone that is dismissed because of their sex. When an employer fails to comply with the recommendation without reasonable justification, then the amount of compensation they have been required to pay to the complainant can be increased or where no provision for compensation has been made then an order for compensation can be issued against the employer.

Although employment tribunals have a wide discretion to make recommendations it is not unlimited and recommendations cannot be made that would have the effect of discriminating unlawfully against someone else. In *The Scottish Agricultural College v O'Mara,*[128] the EAT held that an employment tribunal did not have the power to make a recommendation that the claimant, who had been discriminated against on the grounds of her sex by the failure to promote her, be promoted to grade II within a year of its decision. The EAT said that the SDA 1975 does not allow positive discrimination and the effect of the recommendation would be to prefer the claimant over other applicants who might have superior qualifications.[129]

The recommendation needs to relate to the original complaint brought by the applicant and this was upheld by the EAT in *Fishy v Greenwich*

---

128 Unreported, EAT 441/91.

129 In a similar case brought under the equivalent provisions in the Race Relations Act 1976 (RRA 1976), *British Gas plc v Sharma* [1991] IRLR 101, the EAT held that the ET did not have power to make a recommendation that the claimant be promoted to the next suitable vacancy.

LBC,[130] where they decided that an ET cannot make a recommendation unless it obviates or reduces the adverse effect on the claimant of the act to which the complaint relates and not some other act or acts to which the complaint does not relate. However, the law has changed and under s 124 of the Equality Act, tribunals will be able to make recommendations that benefit the whole workforce, rather than just applying a remedy to the individual that brought the claim (S 124(3)). For example, it could recommend that an organisation introduces or revises its harassment or bullying policy, or introduces equality training for its staff. Where a recommendation is made and, without reasonable justification, the respondent fails to comply with it then the employment tribunal may, when it thinks it is just and equitable, award further compensation (S 124(7)).

Positive or affirmative action[131]

8.31   The equality legislation prior to the Equality Act 2010 made provision for positive action for groups who were underrepresented in terms of employment, training or promotion. However, most commentators agreed that the provisions were inadequate as a positive force for combating inequality.[132] The provisions in equality law encouraged two types of positive discrimination. To encourage more persons in a disadvantaged group (usually women) to apply for jobs and to provide such groups with the opportunity to gain such skills and experience to allow them to compete for these jobs.[133] Positive discrimination in favour of one characteristic would not apply unless it could be shown that the group it is sought to discriminate in favour of are shown to be under-represented. Namely, where no one had been employed in a particular job for the previous 12 months or the number of persons doing that work was comparatively small.[134] Under sex discrimination law, in determining whether the number of employees in a particular job is comparatively

---

130 EAT/1078/99, Unreported.
131 These terms can be used interchangeably.
132 Townshend–Smith R J *Discrimination Law: Text, Cases and Materials*, 1998 but for the contrary view see Ed. Hepple B Szyszcak E *Discrimination: Limits of the Law* Chapter 15, Parekh B, *A case for positive discrimination*, 1993 Mansell p 261.
133 Ibid Chapter 19 Sacks V, Tackling Discrimination Positively in Britain, pp 357–383.
134 Section 37(1) of the RRA 1976.

small, the comparator with be all women in a population. The issues related to this are highlighted in the following quote.

There are changes to the law dealing with this aspect of equality law which have been brought in by the Equality Act 2010. Where an employer reasonably believes that people with a protected characteristic are disadvantaged, have different needs or are disproportionately under-represented, they may take proportionate measures to enable or encourage persons with the relevant characteristic to overcome that disadvantage, to meet their needs, or to enable or encourage their increased participation. Section 158 states that:

(1) this section applies if a person (P) reasonably thinks that (a) persons who share a protected characteristic suffer a disadvantage connected to the characteristic, (b) persons who share a protected characteristic have needs that are different from the needs of persons who do not share it, or (c) participation in an activity by persons who share a protected characteristic is disproportionately low.

(2) This Act does not prohibit them from taking any action which is a proportionate means of achieving the aim of (a) enabling or encouraging persons who share the protected characteristic to overcome or minimise that disadvantage,(b) meeting those needs, or (c) enabling or encouraging persons who share the protected characteristic to participate in that activity. Under s 159 positive action is allowed in limited circumstances for recruitment and promotion of disadvantaged staff. Under s 159 (3) that action is treating a person (A) more favourably in connection with recruitment or promotion than another person (B) because A has the protected characteristic but B does not.

The Act will also require private sector employers with at least 250 employees to publish information about differences in pay between male and female employees. However, this will not come into force until April 2013 at the earliest.

THE BURDEN OF PROOF IN DISCRIMINATION CASES

8.32 It is normally incumbent on the applicant to show (that within the balance of probabilities) their employer has discriminated against them (directly or indirectly) on the ground of sex, to their detriment. This burden of proof was not changed by the Sex Discrimination (Indirect Discrimination and Burden of Proof) Regulations 2001 which came into force on 12 October 2001. These Regulations reiterated the existing position under UK law which is where a *prima facie* case is established against an employer then the burden of proof moves from the claimant to the respondent to show justification for discrimination. Where they fail to justify their discriminatory act the employment tribunals should uphold a claim for discrimination.

In *Igen v Wong*,[135] the Court of Appeal provided guidance on when the inference of discrimination could be drawn in discrimination cases thereby allowing the burden of proof to shift.[136]

(1)   The claimant has to prove, on the balance of probabilities, facts from which the tribunal could conclude, in the absence of an adequate explanation, that the respondent has committed an unlawful act of discrimination.

(2)   At this stage a tribunal should consider what inferences could be drawn from these facts and must assume that there is no adequate explanation for them and must not take into account the employer's explanation at this stage.

(3)   If the claimant has proved facts from which conclusions that the respondent has treated the claimant less favourably could be drawn, then the burden of proof moves onto the respondent.

(4)   It is then for the respondent to prove, on the balance of probabilities that the treatment was in no sense whatsoever on the grounds of sex, race, disability, religion or belief, sexual orientation or age.

This is now dealt with by s 136 of the Act which states: (1) This section applies to any proceedings relating to a contravention of this Act. (2) If there are facts from which the employment tribunal could decide, in the absence of any other explanation, that a person (A) contravened the provision concerned, the court must hold that the contravention occurred.

---

135 [2005] 3 ALL ER 812.
136 This was a joint appeal with two other cases which were *Chamberlin and anr v Emokpae and Webster v Brunel University* [2004] IRLR 592.

(3) But subsection (2) does not apply if A shows that A did not contravene the provision. (4) The reference to a contravention of this Act includes a reference to a breach of an equality clause or rule.

Time limits

8.33 Under s 123 (1), proceedings on a complaint may not be brought after the end of

(a) the period of 3 months starting with the date of the act to which the complaint relates, or

(b) such other period as the employment tribunal thinks is just and equitable.

PROTECTED CHARACTERISTICS OTHER THAN SEX

1. Discrimination on the ground of pregnancy and maternity

8.34 There has been protection for pregnant women and women with newly born children since the Employment Protection Act was brought in in 1975, and this Act introduced many of the maternity rights which are around today under the Equality Act 2010.[137] Developments in the law since 1975 have been substantial and varied and largely influenced by developments in the European Union.

Under the Equality Act, where the protected characteristic is sex, no account is to be taken of special treatment afforded to a woman in connection with pregnancy or childbirth. There is now a separate protected characteristic of pregnancy and maternity. The EA 2010 also provides for two separate protected characteristic of 'pregnancy and maternity non-work' and 'pregnancy and maternity work'. We shall deal only with work related discrimination.

It should be noted that in Scotland the Breastfeeding Scotland Act 2005 imposes certain duties on employers. In particular to make it an offence to

---

137 Employment Rights Act 1996 which sets out rights to health and safety, time off for antenatal care, maternity leave and unfair dismissal.

prevent or stop a person in charge of a child, who is otherwise permitted to be in a public place or licensed premises, from feeding milk to that child in that place or on those premises.

It should be noted that discrimination on the grounds of pregnancy can now under the Equality Act 2010 only be direct.

Direct discrimination

8.35 The simplest example of direct discrimination would be for an employer to refuse to employ women of child-bearing age. Other examples might be harassment of a woman because she is pregnant or not considering a female employee for promotion who is on maternity leave. Employees are protected from discrimination on the ground of pregnancy from the beginning of their pregnancy but, only until the end of statutory maternity leave or their return to work, whichever is the sooner. There is no defence under 2010 Equality Act for unlawful discrimination because of this characteristic (an employer treating a woman unfavourably because of her pregnancy, because of a pregnancy related illness, or because of maternity leave during the protected period). However, the unfavourable treatment will only be unlawful if the employer knows, believes or suspects that a woman is pregnant whether he is informed by formal notification or through informal means, such as the office grapevine. As there is no defence to direct discrimination, even if an employer is suffering substantial financial problems this does not justify discrimination on this basis. In the case of *Decker v Stitching Vormingscentrum voor Jong Volwasswnen (VJV Centrum) Plus*,[138] Mrs Dekker applied for a job and was identified as the most suitable candidate for the post, but was not appointed because she was pregnant. The employer said the reason she was not recruited was that he would not have been able to recover the cost of her maternity pay under his insurance policy, and so he could not afford to recruit a replacement for her during maternity leave. The European Court of Justice held: 'As employment can only be refused because of pregnancy to a woman, such a refusal is direct discrimination on grounds of sex. Such discrimination cannot be justified by the employer showing they would suffer a financial detriment in such a case.'

---

138 [1991] IRLR 27, ECJ.

Less favourable treatment on the ground of an employee taking maternity leave is also sex discrimination. Maternity leave is the period of leave that only an employee is entitled to under the Employment Rights Act 1996.[139] A real or hypothetical male comparator is not required.

After the maternity leave is finished it is still possible to argue that there has been less favourable treatment on the ground that the woman had exercised a right to maternity leave. Any less favourable treatment, whenever it occurs, on the ground that the woman has been on maternity leave will be discrimination.[140] However, in *Brown v Rentokil Ltd*,[141] it was decided by the ECJ that when a woman's illness continued after her maternity leave had finished this would dealt with in the same way as a man would be dealt with who was absent for the same duration due to incapacity to work.

A woman does not need to compare her treatment to that of a male colleague, because there can be no comparison between a pregnant woman, or a woman on maternity leave, and a man. In the leading case of *Webb v EMO Air Cargo (UK) Ltd*,[142] the ECJ ruled that the use of a hypothetical male comparator in discrimination cases based on pregnancy was not appropriate. The ECJ stated that there can be no question of comparing the situation of a woman who finds herself incapable by reason of pregnancy of fulfilling the task for which she was employed with that of a man similarly incapable for medical or other reasons. Their position

---

139 The Agency Workers Regulations (AWR) become law in October 2011. Under them an agency worker should not be treated less favourably or refused work because she is pregnant or have asserted one of her rights, such as the right to time off for ante-natal care or the right to a health and safety risk assessment. The duty not to discriminate against an agency worker extends to both the agency and the organisation she is working for. Agency workers do not have the right to maternity leave in that there is no right to return to the same job. An agency worker is under no obligation to take work from the agency so she can take as much time off as she likes. When she is ready to return to work she will be in the same position as anyone else asking the agency to find work for them. However, she must not be refused work because she has been pregnant or away from work due to the birth of her child.
140 The normal time limit of three months from the time of the discriminatory act applies here see s 123 of the Equality Act.
141 [1998] ECR 1-4185.
142 [1994] IRLR 482 ECJ.

was that if a woman was treated unfavourably because she was pregnant or in a way that undermined her maternity rights under national or EC law that would amount to sex discrimination under the Equal Treatment Directive 76/207, regardless of how a man would have been treated in similar circumstances.

The comparison since *Webb* is 'how would the employer have treated the woman had she not become pregnant?' This is similar to the 'but for' test. Examples are: dismissing or disciplining a woman who is absent with a pregnancy related illness; failing to promote a woman because she is pregnant or on leave; cutting short a woman's probationary period on grounds of pregnancy, or by reason of her absence on maternity leave; and demoting or dismissing an employee because she is pregnant, is absent with pregnancy related illness or is on maternity leave.

If a woman on maternity leave returns to work only to find that her terms and conditions are less favourable than when she left or do not properly reflect changes that should have been made to her contract during the leave period (eg pay increases, holiday entitlement) she can claim constructive dismissal. In the Scottish case of *MacFadden v Greater Glasgow Passenger Transport Executive*,[143] Mrs McFadden was employed at the same grade (a grade CG3 clerk) before and after maternity leave, but after she was employed as a supernumerary rather than as part of the established staff. She no longer had her own desk and was not certain of getting a full days work. Her supernumerary status was a lower status than her previous job and subsequently she was at more risk of being made redundant. The employment tribunal concluded that the employee's conditions of employment were less favourable than previously and she had, therefore, been denied her statutory right to

The new pregnancy discrimination is to be found at s 18 of the Equality Act and it sets out the basis for protection namely '(2) A person (A) discriminates against a woman if, in the protected period in relation to a pregnancy of hers, A treats her unfavourably (a) because of her pregnancy ...' Section 18 at sub-section (7) disapplies 's 13, so far as

---

143 [1977] IRLR 327.

relating to sex discrimination' where the complaint concerns unfavourable treatment because of pregnancy during a protected period.[144]

So in respect of direct discrimination a woman claiming discrimination in these circumstances does not have to find a comparator if she can establish that her unfavourable treatment was because of her pregnancy or exercising her maternity rights.

Indirect discrimination

8.36 Under s 19 of the Equality Act 2010, pregnancy and maternity are specifically excluded from protection for indirect discrimination. The reasons behind this are uncertain although it has been suggested that it is because the majority of claims can be brought under direct discrimination.[145] It is submitted that this is not always the case and under the old legislation there were instances of indirect discrimination on this ground. Often such situations will also amount to indirect discrimination in respect of sex. Where a woman is refused part-time work after maternity leave, or treated less favourably in any way as a result of taking maternity leave, then this could be indirect sex discrimination. It could also occur, for example, where an employer places a requirement for a period of continuous service on employees before they are eligible for promotion. In *Lewen v Denda*,[146] a woman on parental leave was not given a Christmas bonus. The European Court of Justice held that the employer's failure to pay a bonus to a woman on parental leave may be indirect discrimination as female workers were more likely to be on parental leave. In the UK 35% of women but only 2% of men were estimated at the time (by the Department of Trade and Industry) to be taking parental leave. Although *Lewen* was a case under Article 141 of the Treaty of Rome 1957, relating to pay, the same principles would have applied to other less favourable treatment, such as dismissal or denial of access to promotion or training.

---

144 Under s 13 it defines direct sex discrimination as follows '(1) A person (A) discriminates against another (B) if, because of a protected characteristic, A treats B less favourably than A treats or would treat others.' The protected characteristics are listed in s 4 of the Act and include sex and also pregnancy and maternity.
145 Claims for harassment on those grounds are also excluded.
146 [2000] IRLR 67 ECJ.

Victimisation

The same principles apply as for the protected characteristic of sex in relation to victimisation.

2. Race discrimination

8.37 As already stated the legal rules relating to sex, are largely identical except for the characteristics and the Genuine Occupational Qualifications. Historically much of the interpretation placed on the statutory rules by case law in sex discrimination cases also applied to rules relating to race discrimination and vice versa. This had led to the rules in these areas now contained in the Equality Act 2010 and the other areas of discrimination law (considered below) now being largely the same. For the first time, race relations was included as part of the remit of the EU in the EU Race Discrimination Directive.[147] This was the first Directive to provide protective rights against race discrimination to employees in member states. Under the Directive, definitions of direct and indirect discrimination were altered to comply more closely with the earlier Burden of Proof Directive.[148]

As a consequence of the changes introduced by the Directive member states introduced new legislative rules that modified the existing legislation. In the UK this took the form of the RRA 1976 (Amendment) Regulations.[149]

Section 9 (1) of the Equality Act 2010 defines Race as including: (a) colour; (b) nationality; (c) ethnic or national origins. Under subsection (2): In relation to the protected characteristic of race (a) a reference to a person who has a particular protected characteristic is a reference to a person of a particular racial group; (b) a reference to persons who share a protected characteristic is a reference to persons of the same racial group.[150]

---

147 2000/43/EC.

148 97/80/EC.

149 SI 2003/1626.

150 (3) A racial group is a group of persons defined by reference to race; and a reference to a person's racial group is a reference to a racial group into which the person falls. (4) The fact that a racial group comprises two or more distinct racial groups does not prevent it from constituting a particular racial group.

DIRECT DISCRIMINATION

8.38 The provisions of s 13 relating to direct discrimination relate to race in much the same way as they do to sex. Under s 13 of the Equality Act 2010 associative discrimination (direct discrimination against someone because they associate with another person who possesses a protected characteristic) will extend to racial discrimination where it is particularly relevant. Also under this section racial segregation will always be discriminatory.

As in sex discrimination cases the motive of the employer is irrelevant. It is enough to show that the employee suffered less favourable treatment.[151]

The assumption is that the applicant will cite a comparator of a different racial group in a similar position to them who has been given (or would have been given) preferential treatment by the employer. In the event they cannot find a comparator in the workplace they are allowed to refer to a hypothetical comparator.[152]

The less favourable treatment may be on the ground of the race of a third party. In *Zarzynska v Levy*,[153] a female barperson was dismissed when she refused to follow an order not to serve drinks to persons of a particular racial group. It was held that this represented direct discrimination as per s 1 (1) (a) of RRA 1976.

In *Weathersfield Ltd t/a Van and Truck Rentals v Sargent*,[154] the employee had been instructed to discriminate on racial grounds and as a result she resigned because of the intolerable position in which she had been placed. The resignation was held to be constructive dismissal, and therefore fell within the RRA 1976 s4(2)(c). The appropriate comparator was someone who was prepared to go along with the employer's instructions.

The law of the European Union on sexual and racial equality operates alongside domestic legislation in these areas and, in many instances, offer more protection for victims of sex and race discrimination.

---

151 *James v Eastleigh Borough Council* [1990] IRLR 288.
152 *Balamoody v United Kingdom Central Council for Nursing, Midwifery and Health Visiting* [2002] IRLR 288.
153 [1978] IRLR 7, EAT.
154 [1998] IRLR 14, EAT.

INDIRECT DISCRIMINATION

8.39 Under s 19 (1), indirect discrimination is defined as where: (1) A person (A) discriminates against another (B) if A applies to B a provision, criterion or practice which is discriminatory in relation to a relevant protected characteristic of B's.

Section 19 (2) states that for the purposes of subsection (1), a provision, criterion or practice is discriminatory in relation to a relevant protected characteristic of B's if:

(a) A applies, or would apply, it to persons with whom B does not share the characteristic, (b) it puts, or would put, persons with whom B shares the characteristic at a particular disadvantage when compared with persons with whom B does not share it, (c) it puts, or would put, B at that disadvantage, and (d) A cannot show it to be a proportionate means of achieving a legitimate aim.

Race is one of the protected characteristics under s 4 of the Act and is defined under s 9 of the Act as detailed above. The evidential aspects of the definitions are best illustrated by consideration of indirect discrimination cases.

In *West Midlands Passenger Transport Executive v Singh*,[155] the applicant was a Sikh who had been denied promotion as a senior inspector and claimed racial discrimination and asked for a discovery of documents consisting of statistics relating to the ethnic origins, qualifications and experience of all applicants applying for senior inspector posts over a two year period. The Court of Appeal held that:

> 'The suitability of candidates can rarely be measured objectively; often subjective judgements will be made. If there is evidence of a high percentage rate of failure to achieve promotion at particular levels by members of a particular racial group, this may indicate that the real reason for the refusal is a conscious or unconscious racial attitude which involves stereotyped assumptions about members of the group. We are satisfied that the statistical material ordered is relevant to the issues in this case...'

---

155 [1988] ICR 614, CA.

Another case which illustrates the impact of indirect discrimination in this context is *Hussein v Saint Complete House Furnishers*,[156] where an employer made it part of the specification for a job that applicants could not be residents in the city centre of Liverpool. Evidence was led which showed that 50% of the population of the city centre were black, whereas only 12% of the residents in the acceptable area were black. There was no justification for this discriminatory requirement. It was held that this was indirect discrimination.

The employer or service provider etc has a defence to an indirect race discrimination case if an employer shows his conduct is a 'proportionate means of achieving a legitimate aim' (s 19 Equality Act 2010). In *Singh v Rowntree Macintosh Ltd*,[157] a 'no beard' rule was found to be indirectly discriminatory against Sikhs, however, it was justified on the ground of health and safety.

Unlawful activities

8.40 As in the case of sex discrimination the previous legislation specified what type of discriminatory activities should be treated as unlawful. These applied to all characteristics of discrimination and covered discriminatory practices in recruitment and selection, within employment and dismissal. Under s 39 of the Equality Act 2010 the type of unlawful activities are set out in detail.

Harassment

8.41 The first case of harassment to be brought under the RRA 1976 was *De Souza v Automobile Association*.[158] The employee was of Asian origin and overheard a conversation between the two managers where she was referred to in a discriminatory manner. In claiming racial discrimination on the basis of racial harassment she had to prove she had suffered a detriment for the purposes of s 4(2) (c) RRA 1976.

---

156 [1988] IRLR 399.
157 [1979] IRLR 199, EAT.
158 [1986] ICR 514 CA.

In *Jones v Tower Boot Co Ltd*,[159] an employee was racially harassed at work having to suffer severe physical and verbal abuse from his colleagues. He was burnt by a hot screwdriver slapped with rubber welt across the leg etc. The employer argued the acts were not committed in the course of the harasser's employment and therefore they had no liability for them.

The Court of Appeal said that the words 'in the course of employment' as set out in s 32 of RRA 1976 and s 41 of SDA 1975 should be given a purposive construction and interpretation should be on the basis of everyday speech. On this interpretation of course of employment the employer was held liable.

There is no requirement anymore for an applicant to produce a comparator in racial harassment cases.[160] In the recent case of *Richmond Pharmacology Ltd v Dhaliwal*,[161] the appellant employer (R) appealed against a decision upholding the claim of the respondent employee (D) for racial harassment contrary to s 3A of the Race Relations Act 1976 .

Ms D was of Indian ethnic origin and had resigned her job. While she was working her notice the co-owner of the business (L) commented that their paths would probably continue to cross, unless D was 'married off in India'. R, the employer, argued that the tribunal had not properly applied the test in s 3A of the Act, had found that L's remark had had the effect of violating D's dignity without saying what it was about the remark that had had that effect, and was mistaken in finding that the remark could reasonably be regarded as violating D's dignity. The employer's appeal was dismissed.

'Not every racially slanted adverse comment would constitute the violation of a person's dignity: while it was very important that employers and tribunals were sensitive to the hurt that could be caused by racially offensive comments or conduct, it was also important not to encourage a culture of hypersensitivity. The facts in the instant case were close to the borderline, but the tribunal had been entitled to hold that what L had said had fallen on the wrong side of the line.'

---

159 [1997] ICR 254, CA.
160 *Reed and another v Bull Information Systems Ltd* [1999] IRLR 299.
161 [2009] ICR 724.

As indicated above, under s 26 of the 2010 Act it provides that, in deciding whether the conduct of A has the purpose or effect of violating B's dignity or creating an intimidating; hostile degrading or humiliating or offensive environment for B, account must be taken of: (a) the perception of B; (b) the other circumstances of the case; (c) whether it is reasonable for the conduct to have that effect.[162] Under the EA 2010, employees will now be able to complain of harassment even if it is not directed at them, if they can demonstrate that it creates an offensive environment for them. So people working in an environment tainted with racial harassment or bullying would be able to pursue an action in their own right against their employer.

Victimisation

The same principles apply as for the protected characteristic of sex in relation to victimisation.

3. Sexual orientation

8.42 Employees or workers shouldn't be treated less favourably (for example, being refused employment) because of their sexual orientation or because an employer thinks they are of a certain sexual orientation.

If an employer gives benefits to the unmarried heterosexual partners of its employees (eg the employee's partner is able to drive the company car), refusing the same benefits to same-sex partners could be discrimination.[163]

Sexual orientation is widely defined under s 12 of the Equality Act.[164]

S12 (1) Sexual orientation means a person's sexual orientation towards:

(a)   persons of the same sex, (eg homosexuals)

(b)   persons of the opposite sex, (heterosexuals) or

(c)   persons of either sex. (bisexuals).

---

162 S 24(4).

163 Since December 2005, same-sex couples can register a civil partnership and in respect of employment a civil partner is entitled to the same benefits as a married person (for example, survivors benefits under a company pension scheme).

164 Formerly Regulation 2 of the Employment Equality (Sexual Orientation) Regulations 2003.

(2) In relation to the protected characteristic of sexual orientation:

    (a)   a reference to a person who has a particular protected characteristic is a reference to a person who is of a particular sexual orientation;

    (b)   a reference to persons who share a protected characteristic is a reference to persons who are of the same sexual orientation. This means that homosexuals, heterosexuals and bisexuals are potentially protected under the legislation provided the basis of the discrimination against them is their sexual orientation.

'They cover discrimination on grounds of perceived as well as actual sexual orientation (ie assuming – correctly or incorrectly – that someone is lesbian, gay, heterosexual or bisexual). The Act also covers association, ie being discriminated against on grounds of the sexual orientation of those with whom you associate (for example, friends and/or family).'[165]

It is only sexual orientation which is covered and not sexual preferences or fetishes.

In research carried out on behalf of the Trade Unions Congress into cases dealing with religious and sexual orientation discrimination it was found by the researcher that at the time of reporting, in June 2007, there had been no cases of indirect discrimination brought on these grounds.[166] [167]

This is undoubtedly a surprising outcome however it should be considered against the background that very few cases (much less than anticipated) had been brought at that time on the grounds of sexual orientation and religion or belief since the legislation was passed in 2003. There is evidence available that showed that there had been a relatively small number of cases brought under the new equality law. In the period 2004/2005 the combined number of cases constituted only 0.2% of the total number of employment tribunal claims registered. There are a number of possible reasons for this.

---

165 DTI website, http://www.dti.gov.uk/er/equality/eeregs_a.html now BERR website
166 [2008] EWCA Civ 1421.
167 Sexual Orientation and Religion or Belief Cases. A report prepared by Barry Fitzpatrick for the TUC 4 June 2007.

Firstly, employees in some workplaces or professions are still likely to be reluctant to tell people at work about their sexual orientation for fear of ridicule or victimisation, even in circumstances where they are already discriminated against because of their personal characteristics, mannerisms or dress. Secondly, there is inevitably a gap between the date the legislation is introduced and when workers are aware of it and their specific rights. This lack of awareness is exacerbated by poor publicity of new legislative developments. Thirdly there had, until 2006, been no body that provided advice, legal representation and support to parties experiencing this type of discrimination and considering making a claim to an employment tribunal. This problem was addressed by the Equality Act 2006 which came into effect in February 2006 and created the Commission for Equality and Human Rights a single equality commission covering all aspects of equality law. The number of cases are gradually increasing with 580 cases in 2007/08, 600 cases in 2008/09, and 710 in 2009/10 however it is still not a significant amount in relation to the total number of cases brought.[168] In a IDS publication they highlighted the fact 'that a high proportion of sexual orientation claims have involved harassment'.[169]

The Court of Appeal, in *English v Thomas Sanderson Ltd*, held by a majority,[170] that the Sexual Orientation Regulations 2003 protect a heterosexual man who is repeatedly tormented by homophobic banter when (a) he is not gay, (b) he is not perceived or assumed to be gay by his tormentors, and (c) he accepts that they do not believe him to be gay. The banter arose purely because he had attended a boarding school and lived in Brighton. Perceptive and associative discrimination is now included under s 13 of the 2010 Act.

The Equality Act 2010 extended protection against sexual orientation discrimination beyond the workplace to cover the provision of goods and services to consumers

---

168 Statistics available at www.justice.gov.uk.

169 Editorial from IDS Employment Law Brief 795, December 2005 Religion, belief and sexual orientation discrimination – the story so far…

170 [2009] IRLR 206 (CA).

4. Gender reassignment

8.43 Most provisions relating to the protected characteristic of sex apply to the protected characteristic of gender reassignment. A person will have this protected characteristic if is proposing to undergo, is undergoing or has undergone a process (or part of a process) for the purpose of reassigning the person's sex by changing physiological or other attributes of sex. Section 16 prevents an employer treating the employee less favourably in relation to absence from work in connection with his gender reassignment treatment than he would normally treat an employee who had the same absence for a reason not related to this protected characteristic.

5. Marriage or civil partnership

8.44 Most provisions relating to the protected characteristic of sex apply to the protected characteristic of marriage or civil partnership. The protection is only available where discrimination occurs because the person is married or has a civil partner. It does not apply of the reason for the discriminatory treatment is that they are single. Also there is no provision regarding associative discrimination in respect of this protected characteristic

6. Discrimination on grounds of religion or belief

Direct Discrimination

8.45 'A person (A) discriminates against another (B) if because of a protected characteristic A treats B less favourably than A treats or would treat others.'[171] So it is less favourable treatment 'on grounds of the employee's religion or belief'. However, this covers not only less favourable treatment on the grounds of a person's actual religion or belief but also treatment based on the discriminator's perception of a person's religion, or on a person's association with people of a particular religion.

 Discrimination by religious employers, against those of other faiths or no religious faith, is acceptable to a limited extent: whereby religious

---

171 Section 13(1).

ethos organisations can discriminate even where the job is not determined by its religious character. However, the maintenance of a religious ethos is not lawful if it results in direct discrimination on grounds of sex, sexual orientation or any other unlawful ground

Prior to the Employment Equality (Religion and Belief) Regulations[172] discrimination on grounds of religion or belief had not been covered by UK law, unless it could be treated as a form of indirect race discrimination[173] or where a religious group was also a separate ethnic group.[174]

The Employment Equality (Religion and Belief) Regulations 2003 SI No 1660 implemented the EC General Framework Directive 2000/78/EC and came into force on 2nd December 2003. It is now covered by the Equality Act 2010 and s 10 defines religion or belief as follows: (1) Religion means any religion and a reference to religion includes a reference to a lack of religion. (2) Belief means any religious or philosophical belief and a reference to belief includes a reference to a lack of belief. (3) In relation to the protected characteristic of religion or belief (a) a reference to a person who has a particular protected characteristic is a reference to a person of a particular religion or belief; (b) a reference to persons who share a protected characteristic is a reference

The terms religion and belief is loosely defined and tribunals are having to develop principles for determining the scope of these terms. It might be thought that guidance could be derived from the case law on Article 9 of the European Convention of Human Rights (which specifically deals with religious freedom and equality). However, to date the case law tends to support a fairly traditional view of what constitutes a religion. What is clear is that most forms of political beliefs are not covered, but non-religious beliefs (such as scientology, spiritualism; humanism or a belief in global warming) are likely to be covered. Section 77 of the Equality Act 2006 amended the Regulations by removing the word *similar* so it is no longer necessary to show belief equates which a religious belief and the effect of this might be to place strongly held political or philosophical beliefs within the definition above.

---

172 2003 SI No.1660.

173 *JH Walker v Hussain* [1996] IRLR 11.

174 *Mandla v Lee* [1983] IRLR 209.

There will continue to be much debate as to what kind of non-religious beliefs are covered. The legislators[175] seem keen that a distinction is drawn between certain beliefs (atheism and humanism) which are covered, and others which, without further explanation, are not protected (communism, Darwinism, fascism and socialism). This is contrary to the views expressed by the EAT in the case of *Grainger Plc and ors v Nicholson*.[176] There, the EAT accepted that a belief is not disqualified from being a philosophical belief simply because it is based entirely on scientific conclusions. The EAT gave the example Darwinism, which, it said, 'must plainly be capable of being a philosophical belief'. The EAT also added some comments on political beliefs.

Burton J stated that '(i) The belief must be genuinely held. (ii) It must be a belief and not, as in *McClintock v Department of Constitutional Affairs*,[177] an opinion or viewpoint based on the present state of information available. (iii) It must be a belief as to a weighty and substantial aspect of human life and behaviour. (iv) It must attain a certain level of cogency, seriousness, cohesion and importance. (v) It must be worthy of respect in a democratic society, be not incompatible with human dignity and not conflict with the fundamental rights of others'.[178]

Although the EAT accepted that support of a political party would not meet the description of a philosophical belief, it noted that that does not mean that a belief in a political philosophy or doctrine, such as Socialism, Marxism, Communism or free-market Capitalism, would not qualify. This part of the EAT's judgment is not legally binding and in *Greater Manchester Police Authority v Power*[179] it was held that a belief in spiritualism was capable of amounting to a philosophical belief.

Indirect discrimination

8.46 What kind of activity could be indirect discrimination on this ground? Certainly inflexibility on working hours could impact on members of

---

175 Expressed in the explanatory notes to the Bill.
176 [2010] ICR 360.
177 [2008] IRLR 29.
178 [2010] ICR 360 at 370.
179 EAT 12 November 2009.

religious groups who have strict worshipping times or the requirement to wear certain clothes or have a certain kind of appearance (eg unshaven) introduced under dress or grooming codes could be discriminatory.

In the case of *Joseph Estorninho v Zoran Jokic t/a Zorans Delicatessen,*[180] the complainant had agreed to work as a chef for a delicatessen in April 2005 on the basis that, as a devout Catholic, he could not work on Sundays, although he would attend Sunday staff meetings. When another chef who had only two years experience was promoted to Head Chef over him (with 18 years experience as a chef) he complained to the employer. The tribunal accepted that the refusal of promotion was not connected to the complainant's religious beliefs, however, the main issue turned out to be his refusal of Sunday working. As a result at a meeting with the employer he was told he should finish at the end of the month.

On the issue of Sunday working the tribunal decided a non-Christian comparator would have been required to work on Sundays and hence there was no direct discrimination. However, on the issue of indirect discrimination, the tribunal concluded that the complainant had suffered a 'particular disadvantage' because practising Catholics are required to attend church on Sunday and the employer's 'provision criterion or practice' of Sunday working placed him at a particular disadvantage compared to non-Catholics. The tribunal did consider whether there was evidence of an increased need for Sunday working and concluded that there was not. It also concluded that the employer had not considered other ways of arranging Sunday working without infringing the complainant's religious beliefs and practices and, accordingly, had not adopted proportionate means.

With respect to dress or appearance codes in the case of *Azmi v Kirklees Metropolitan Council,*[181] a teacher was told she could not wear the hijab in school classrooms while teaching children as it inhibited non verbal communication. On appeal, the EAT decided that although banning garments that cover the face was a form of indirect discrimination on religious grounds the reason for the policy (not inhibiting non verbal communication) was a proportionate means of achieving a legitimate aim. The discrimination was therefore lawful due to this defence. However,

---

180 Case No 2301487/06.
181 [2007] IRLR 484.

she received an award of £1,100 because of the employer's failure to deal with her grievance and because the Tribunal upheld her complaint about victimisation.

In *Harris v NKL Automotive Ltd & Matrix Consultancy UK Ltd*,[182] a Rastafarian male Mr Harris brought a claim for direct and indirect discrimination on the grounds of his philosophical beliefs under the Employment Equality (Religion and Belief) Regulations 2003. He had worked as an executive driver from April 2004 to February 2006 and worked on a regular basis between October 2005 and February 2006. The company had a dress code which provided that drivers 'should have a smart professional haircut and should ensure hair is tidy'. In February 2006 the company expressed concerns to the agency they had used to engage Mr Harris, saying his hair was untidy and that he did not represent them well.

Shortly after these concerns were raised with Mr Harris he complained to the agency about not being allocated work. He was also not transferred to the company on a permanent basis, unlike many other drivers from the agency. He said he believed he was being discriminated against because of his hair and notified the agency he was signed off from work for a month because of stress. After raising a grievance with both the company and the agency he issued proceedings in the employment tribunal.

It was accepted by the EAT that Rastafarianism constitutes a religious belief under the Regulations, however, the EAT accepted that it was legitimate for the Company to have rules requiring tidy hair to maintain a professional appearance to customers. It was for this reason, and not for the fact Mr Harris was a Rastafarian, that he was disadvantaged and his appeal failed.

In order to fall within the protection afforded to a religion under this section the PCP complained of must be a requirement of the religion rather than simply a preference of the individual. In *Eweida v British Airways plc*,[183] the tribunal held that the disadvantage suffered by the claimant because the employers no jewellery policy meant she could not wear a cross did not amount to indirect discrimination because she could not identify a group disadvantage rather than a personal disadvantage.

---

182 UKEAT 0134/07.
183 [2009] ICR 303.

Harassment

8.47 The EAT recently held in *Saini v All Saints Haque Centre*,[184] that Regulation 5(1)(b) of the Employment Equality (Religion or Belief) Regulations 2003 (now s 26 of the Equality Act 2010) will not only be breached where an employee is harassed on the ground that he holds certain religious beliefs but also where he is harassed because of someone else's religious beliefs. In reaching this conclusion, the EAT concluded that Regulation 5(1) requires conduct 'on grounds of religion or belief' and, as such, does not require the unwanted conduct to be on the grounds of the employee's own religious beliefs, and such an interpretation was consistent with the aims of the EC Framework Directive.

Victimisation

The same principles apply as for the protected characteristic of sex in relation to victimisation.

7. Age discrimination

8.48 The regulations covering age discrimination were called the Employment Equality (Age) Regulations[185] and came into force on 1 October 2006. The Regulations created new obligations for employers, providers of vocational training, trade unions, professional associations, employers' organisations and trustees and managers of occupational pension schemes. They will apply irrespective of the size of the organisation.

These measures have largely been re-enacted by s 5 of the Equality Act. which states that:

(1) In relation to the protected characteristic of age (a) a reference to a person who has a particular protected characteristic is a reference to a person of a particular age group; (b) a reference to persons who share a protected characteristic is a reference to persons of the same age group.

---

184 UKEAT/0227/08/ZT.
185 SI 2006/1031.

(2) A reference to an age group is a reference to a group of persons defined by reference to age, whether by reference to a particular age or to a range of ages.

The legislation is designed to protect a wide range of individuals which includes, not only older people, but younger workers and potentially persons of any age,[186] and to offer legal protection to individuals who are discriminated against, harassed or victimised on the ground of age.

Direct discrimination

8.49 The provisions of s 13 relating to direct discrimination apply differently in relation to the protected characteristic of age in that in the case of age (unlike all the other protected characteristics) direct discrimination can be justified if it can be shown that it is a proportionate means of achieving a legitimate aim.

The impact of the provisions on age equality to date has been *inter alia*; there is now no statutory upper age limit on the right to claim unfair dismissal or to receive redundancy payments and no compulsory retirement age.[187] The Equality Act also introduced a new ban on age discrimination by those providing services and exercising public functions, building on the existing law which banned age discrimination at work.

Following the ECJ's decision in *Coleman v Attridge*,[188] direct discrimination by association has been prohibited under the Equality Act which is important as the Employment Equality (Age) Regulations 2006 had not afforded protection from direct discrimination by association in the context of age.

In the case of most protected characteristics it has always been unlawful to discriminate against someone because they are (wrongly) perceived to

---

186 Unlike the legislation covering age in the United States which only applies to workers over forty under the Age Discrimination in Employment Act 1967.
187 Although the Government is removing the Default Retirement Age, it will still be possible for individual employers to operate a compulsory retirement age, provided that they can objectively justify it. Between 1 April 2011 and 1 October 2011, it will still be possible to compulsorily retire employees if the statutory notification process has been completed before 1 April 2011 and the due date of retirement falls before 1 October 2011.
188 Case C-303/06 in the Court of Justice of the European Communities.

possess the characteristic or because they associate with someone else that possesses that characteristic. The Equality Act extends this approach to the protected characteristic of age.

Indirect discrimination

8.50 There will only be limited circumstances when a difference of treatment on grounds of age is lawful. Namely, where the employer has demonstrated the existence of a legitimate aim. However, they must demonstrate that the provision, criterion or practice was proportionate. The ECJ has explained that such proportionality requires that the means used to achieve an aim must not exceed the limits of what is appropriate and necessary to achieve that aim.[189]

This will be achievable where the employer who wants to apply an age-related rule or practice can offer 'objective justification' for doing so or, alternatively, the practice in question falls within one of the exemptions set out in the Act.

In the absence of any justification for it a provision, criterion or practice which imposes a requirement that you must have a particular length of service or experience in an area before you are eligible to apply for a job or promotion or get access to a particular benefit would be indirect discrimination. Also indirect discrimination could occur under the Act where an employer's policy or procedure unjustifiably put individuals in a certain age group at a disadvantage (requiring all employees to undergo a strict health and fitness test, where people that are older would be less likely to pass than then their younger colleagues, or imposing a dress code which strongly favours younger staff).

Harassment

8.51 Unwanted conduct related to age under s 26 of the Equality Act 2010 that has the purpose of violating a person's dignity or creating an intimidating, hostile, degrading, humiliating or offensive environment for that person; or is reasonably considered by that person to have the effect of violating his or her dignity or of creating an intimidating, hostile,

---

189 *R v Maff ex parte NFU* [1998] ECR I-1211.

degrading, humiliating or offensive environment for him or her, even if this effect was not intended by the person responsible for the conduct. The wording in the Equality Act 2010 means that employees can complain of behaviour that they find offensive even if it is not directed at them. There were already rules on third-party harassment applying to sex but the Equality Act 2010 extends this to other forms of discrimination including age.

Victimisation

The same principles apply as for the protected characteristic of sex in relation to victimisation.

Exceptions

8.52 The Regulations made provision for a series of specific exceptions from the scope of the prohibition on age discrimination: the use of certain age-based or age-linked criteria. In some specified circumstances, treating people differently on the grounds of age would be possible but, employers must be able to justify doing so by reference to specific aims set out in legislation (see below), and only if it was appropriate and necessary in the particular circumstances. Employers would have to be able to produce supporting evidence if challenged on their use of the specific aims which are:

(1) Health, welfare, and safety for example special rules for the protection of younger workers

(2) Facilitation of employment planning, eg where a business has a number of people approaching retirement age at the same time

(3) The particular training requirements of the post in question. An example might be air traffic controllers who have to have high levels of health and fitness and concentration and have to undergo extensive training.

(4) Encouraging and rewarding loyalty

The various exceptions contained in the Age Discrimination Regulations are repeated in the Act.

In some specified circumstances, treating people differently on the grounds of age will be possible, but employers must be able to justify doing so by reference to specific aims set out in legislation (see below), and only if it is appropriate and necessary in the particular circumstances.

Employers will have to be able to produce supporting evidence if challenged on their use of the specific aims.

Specific aims include:

- Health, welfare, and safety, for example, the protection of younger workers.

- Facilitation of employment planning, for example, where a business has a number of people approaching retirement age at the same time.

- The particular training requirements of the post in question, for example, air traffic controllers, who have to have high levels of health and fitness and concentration, and who have to undergo extensive training.

- Encouraging and rewarding loyalty.

In *Live Nations (Venues) UK Ltd v Hussain*,[190] the EAT gave some guidance as to the conduct which may justify a finding of age discrimination:

- an employer that genuinely believes an employee is guilty of age discrimination against another employee and dismisses them for that reason, cannot be said to be discriminating against employee on the grounds of his or her age

- an unjustified or unreasoned belief that an employee has ageist tendencies may render a dismissal unfair

- if an employee's dismissal for suspected ageism justified an inference of age discrimination by the employer, it might restrict an employer in dealing with a suspected discriminator for fear that they would be found to be discriminating

- reference to an employee being 'too old to change' could, in an appropriate case, provide some basis for inferring age discrimination.

---

190 UKEAT/0234/08/RN.

8. Disability

8.53 Disability Discrimination is dealt with in detail in Chapter 9

Employer's defences to a discrimination claim

8.54 The Genuine Occupational Qualifications available as a defence to an employer under the previous anti discrimination legislation have been replaced by the 'Occupational Requirements' part 1 of Schedule 9 to the Equality Act 2010. If an employer can show that treatment which seems to be discriminatory is because of one of these requirements then there will have been no contravention of the Act in respect of the provisions relating to discrimination in the workplace (s 39(1)).

Paragraph 1 of part 1 contains a general occupational requirement which applies to all the protected characteristics where the employer shows that, having regard to the nature or context of the work—the requirement relating to a protected characteristic:

(a)   is an occupational requirement, and

(b)   the application of the requirement is a proportionate means of achieving a legitimate aim, and

(c)   the person to whom the employer applies the requirement does not meet it (or the employer has reasonable grounds for not being satisfied that the person meets it).

Paragraph two makes special provision where employment is for the purposes of an organised religion and the requirement relates to the protected characteristics of sex, marriage , gender reassignment civil partnership and sexual orientation the nature or context of the employment, the requirement is the requirement is applied so as to comply with the doctrines of the religion and to avoid conflicting with the strongly held religious convictions of a significant number of the religion's followers.

Paragraph 4 relates to the armed forces and also makes certain exceptions in relation to age discrimination for example for the purposes of the National Minimum Wage Act 1998.

PUBLIC SECTOR DUTIES

1. Socio Economic Duty

8.55 Under Part 1, s 1, of the Equality Act 2010 would have imposed a public sector duty on various public authorities in England regarding socio-economic inequalities but this measure will not now be implemented.

2. Public Sector Equality Duty

8.56 Under Part 11 chapter 1, Public Sector Equality Duty, s 149 states that (1) a public authority[191] must, in the exercise of its functions, have due regard to the need to (a) eliminate discrimination, harassment, victimisation and any other conduct that is prohibited by or under this Act; (b) advance equality of opportunity between persons who share a relevant protected characteristic and persons who do not share it; (c) foster good relations between persons who share a relevant protected characteristic and persons who do not share it.

Subsection 3 provides that the authority must have due regard to the need to advance equality of opportunity between persons who share a relevant protected characteristic and persons who do not share it involves having due regard, in particular, to the need to (a) remove or minimise disadvantages suffered by persons who share a relevant protected characteristic that are connected to that characteristic; (b) take steps to meet the needs of persons who share a relevant protected characteristic that are different from the needs of persons who do not share it; (c) encourage persons who share a relevant protected characteristic to participate in public life or in any other activity in which participation by such persons is disproportionately low. Under s 156 a failure in respect of a performance of a duty imposed by or under this Chapter does not confer a cause of action at private law. However, the existing race, disability and gender equality duties on public sector bodies will continue to apply.

---

191 It will apply not only to public sector bodies (such as government departments, local authorities, NHS Trusts etc) but also to organisations in the private and third sectors that carry out 'functions of a public nature'.

3. Equal pay

8.57 The Equal Pay Act 1970 was, repealed by the Equality Act 2010.[192] But the Equality Act maintains the distinction between discrimination on the grounds of sex and unequal pay because of sex. Part of the Act deals with claims which would have been regarded as equal pay claims under the old legislation. It obviously applies to claims for equality in terms and conditions relating to pay and the concept of 'pay' is a broad one. In *Defrenne v Belgium*[193] the ECJ held that the concept of pay comprises any consideration, whether in cash or in kind, whether immediate or future, provided that the worker receives it, albeit indirectly, in respect of his employment from his employer. Under Article 141 of the EC Treaty, the concept of 'pay' is not restricted to contractual entitlements; it may include indirect benefits and non-contractual bonuses, see eg *Lewen v Denda*.[194]

Thus, Article 141 has been held to cover complaints about voluntary bonuses, travel facilities,[195] occupational pensions,[196] severance payments,[197] and compensation for unfair dismissal.[198]

There are various stages in an equal pay claim and these remain unchanged under the new legislation The claimant firstly (a) identifies a male comparator in the same employment as her and (b) proves that he is employed on; like work (the same or similar), work rated as equivalent (under a valid job evaluation scheme (JES)) or work of equal value ('equal work') to her but that (c) one or more of the terms of his contract is more generous. If this is established a rebuttable presumption of sex discrimination arises.

The second stage is that the burden then shifts to the employer to explain the difference in terms by showing that the variation is genuinely due to a material factor which is not the difference of sex between the

---

192 Sections 64–69.
193 C-80/70 [1971] ECR 445 at 541.
194 [2000] ICR 648 ECJ.
195 *Garland v British Rail Engineering Ltd* [1982] ICR 420 ECJ.
196 *Warringham and Humphreys v Lloyds Bank Ltd* [1981] ICR 558 ECJ.
197 *Kowalska v Freie und Hansestradt Hamburg* [1992] ICR 29 ECJ.
198 *R v Secretary of State for Employment ex parte Seymour-Smith and Perez* [1999] ICR 447 ECJ.

claimant and her comparator. This could be achieved by establishing material differences between the situation of a woman and a man in the workplace (genuine material factor),[199] or that a gender neutral explanation for the difference applies. The third stage is that the claimant may argue that although the explanation for the difference in terms is apparently that it is because of a material difference of a man and woman's position, or is gender neutral, it operates in a discriminatory way or has a discriminatory impact. Fourthly, if this is established, the employer is required objectively to justify the difference in terms. If the employer fails to do this, liability is established.[200] Fifthly, if she is successful, the claimant (and possibly the entire category of female employees she falls under)[201] is entitled to damages for breach of contract for any period during which (in broad terms) in the 5 years prior to proceeding she was paid less than her comparator/s (six years in England). The difference between the two jurisdictions here is due to the law of prescription in Scotland restricting certain civil claims to five years after the unlawful event.[202]

It has been shown that pay discrimination remains one of the most persistent forms of inequality in the UK, with female workers earning on average 17% less than men. A range of measures brought in by the Equality Act 2010 are designed to target this, largely through encouraging transparency over pay. The Act outlaws secrecy clauses in employment contracts that relate to pay and employers can no longer discipline staff for discussing and comparing their pay with others in the workplace where this may be linked to discrimination. Monitoring and reporting on gender pay by employers is encouraged, under the Act, with the expectation that larger organisations will do so voluntarily.[203]

As a result of the Act individuals may get greater access to information about pay within their workplaces. There has over the last few years, and continues to be, an unprecedented volume of equal pay litigation in employment tribunals, to the extent that the large number of what

199 *Rainey v Greater Glasgow Health Board* [1987] ICR 129 HL.
200 *Ratcliffe v North Yorkshire County Council* [1995] IRLR 439, HL.
201 *Enderby v Frenchay Health Authority* [1994] ICR 112.
202 Prescription and Limitation (Scotland) Act 1973 s 6 and schedule 1 paragraph 5 year rule applies to ....1d) to any obligation arising from liability (whether arising from any enactment or from any rule of law) to make reparation.
203 There is a possibility that this duty will become compulsory in four years time.

are usually multiple claims, have clogged up the employment tribunal system. The vast majority of these claims are in the local authority and National Health Service sectors. One of the reasons for the huge number of claims in both local government and the health service sectors is that these employers are undertaking large-scale job evaluation and re-grading exercises,[204] the results of which have proven unpopular and led to legal cases being pursued. Equal pay is discussed in more detail in chapter 11.

FURTHER READING

Websites

http://www.homeoffice.gov.uk/publications/equalities/equality-act-publications/equality-act-guidance/equality-duty?view=Binary

---

204 An E-Reward survey in 2007 indicated that 60% of private sector and 80% of public sector organisations used job evaluation as the basis for grading and pay structures. www.e-reward.co.uk

Chapter 9

Disability Discrimination

9.1 Since the Industrial Revolution, social policies have been created and sustained by successive Governments that have discriminated against disabled people (until recently) and ensured they were excluded from society and employment in UK workplaces. Disabled people were excluded from the full rights of citizenship because they were deemed marginal to the labour market. There were various attempts to legislate in this area, particularly in the 1940's and 1950's, eg Disabled Persons (Employment) Acts 1944 and 1958 but these had limited or no success. Various lobby groups representing disabled people have since the second world war utilised their own and others personal experience of disability and institutional life, to illustrate that it wasn't their impairments which caused the problem, but the way in which society failed to make any allowances for their differences and chose to exclude or ignore them instead. In the UK, following extensive activism by disabled people over several decades, the Disability Discrimination Act 1995 (DDA 1995) was passed. This Act made it unlawful to discriminate against people with disabilities in relation to employment, the provision of goods and services, education and transport.

There are two main models that have influenced modern thinking about disability and these are the medical model[1] and the social model.[2] Under the classic medical model, disabled people are seen as the problem and the expectation is that they need to change and adapt to circumstances that are presented to them, with no acceptance or understanding that it is society that needs to change. This is clearly unhelpful and outdated. In contrast, the social model has been developed by disabled people for whom disability

---

1 Ainscow, M; Tweddle, D, (1979) *Preventing Classroom Failure: An objectives approach*, Chichester, Wiley.
2 Burchardt, T, (2004), Capabilities and Disability: The Capabilities Framework and the Social Model of Disability, Disability and Society, Vol. 19, 7, pg 735–751.

is caused by the barriers that exist within society and the way society is organised. Thus the social model of disability acknowledges how society discriminates against people with impairments and excludes them from involvement and participation. This 'social model of disability' explains disablement as the result of any behaviour or barriers which prevent people with impairments choosing to take part in the life of society. It does not attempt to deny the existence of differences caused by physiological or mental impairments, on the contrary it addresses them without attaching value judgements to them, such as normality.

The Disability Discrimination Act 1995 was been devised utilising the social model of disability, as can be seen by the introduction of the concept of reasonable adjustments into the Act (considered below).

Since the House of Lords decision in *L B Lewisham v Malcolm*,[3] disabled employees have had to prove that they have been treated less favourably than a non-disabled employee who is otherwise in the same circumstances. This severely curtailed some rights to claim for disability discrimination. This decision led to the two concepts of direct discrimination (less favourable treatment 'on the grounds of' disability) and disability-related discrimination becoming virtually indistinguishable. This significantly weakened the protection that was available under the law to disabled employees.

An example would be that disability-related discrimination claims often arose where an employee was dismissed for lengthy sickness absence relating to a disability. After the *Malcolm* case, an employer could defeat such a claim by showing that a non-disabled employee who was absent for the same length of time would also have been dismissed.

The new Equality Act prohibits employers from discriminating against disabled employees because of something arising as a consequence of their disability. Importantly for them, disabled employees are not required to establish that their treatment is less favourable than that experienced by other employees. They must simply establish that they have experienced unfavourable treatment, and that this is because of something connected with their disability.

---

3   (2008) IRLR 700 HL.

Under the Equality Act 2010, for the first time employers are prevented from asking candidates questions about their health that are unrelated to the job role. It will mean those with mental health issues, a medical condition or a disability will not be forced to disclose their condition prior to the offer of employment, unless it hinders their ability to do the job.

The Act also extends the law on direct disability discrimination to include discrimination by association and perception, introduces the concept of indirect discrimination for the first time (see below), and replace disability-related discrimination with 'discrimination arising from disability (see below).

The original Act was a companion piece of legislation to the Sex Discrimination Act 1975 and the Race Relations Act 1976, but differed from them in certain key respects. These differences have largely been removed by the Equality Act 2010 which is the current legislation applicable to discrimination. The Equality and Human Rights Commission provides support for the Act, and equivalent legislation in Northern Ireland, which is enforced by the Northern Ireland Equality Commission. Further guidance can be found in the codes of practice which can be found on the Equality and Human Rights commission website[4] and are:

- The Duty to Promote Disability Equality: Statutory Code of Practice: England and Wales
- The Duty to Promote Disability Equality: Statutory Code of Practice: Scotland
- Code of Practice: Employment and Occupation
- Revised Code of Practice: Trade Organisations, Qualifications Bodies and General Qualifications Bodies
- Guidance on matters to be taken into account in determining questions relating to the definition of disability

---

4   www.equalityhumanrights.com

THE EQUALITY ACT 2010

Unlawful activities

9.2 Section 39 of the Equality Act 2010 specifies the type of behaviour which is unlawful: The employer must not have discriminated on grounds of disability.

(a)   In the arrangements he made for the purpose of determining to whom he should offer employment s 4(1)(a).

(b)   In the terms on which he offered employment.

(c)   By refusing to offer, or deliberately omitting to offer employment.

(d)   In the opportunities which he afforded him for promotion, a transfer, training or receiving any other benefit.

(e)   By refusing to afford him or deliberately not affording such an opportunity.

(f)   By dismissing him or subjecting him to any other detriment.[5]

The definition of disability

9.3 This is fundamental to determining the scope of the legislation, even though the majority of potential applicants will be disabled under any other definition.

'A distinction must be drawn between chronic or handicapping conditions and temporary or minor maladies. The statutory definition adopted ... is highly complex. It is to be found in the main text of the statute, as amplified by Schedule 1. In addition, the meaning is further expanded by Regulations and Guidance on matters to be taken into account in interpreting the definition.'[6]

---

5   Under current rules, 'detriment' excludes unlawful harassment (Equality Act 2010 s 212(1)(5) However, 'detriment' perhaps will still be relevant for behaviour falling short of harassment as defined.

6   Townsend-Smith, RJ Discrimination Law: Text Cases and Materials, 1998, p 584.

Disability is a protected characteristic under s 6 of the Equality Act 2010 which states

(1)   A person has a disability if (a) someone has a physical or mental impairment, and (b) the impairment has a substantial and long-term adverse effect on their ability to carry out normal day-to-day activities.[7]

(2)   A reference to a disabled person is a reference to a person who has a disability.

(3)   In relation to the protected characteristic of disability:

    (a)   a reference to a person who has a particular protected characteristic is a reference to a person who has a particular disability;

    (b)   a reference to persons who share a protected characteristic is a reference to persons who have the same disability.

(4)   This Act applies in relation to a person who has had a disability, as it applies in relation to a person who has the disability etc.[8]

It should be noted that as a consequence of section 6 (4) a person who previously had a disability will continue to enjoy the protection of the Equality Act 2010 once he recovers.

In order for a condition to amount to a physical or mental disability a person's impairment must have a substantial effect on his abilities to carry out normal day-to-day activities. Whether or not a person is disabled is a question of law rather than medical opinion.[9]

In considering the definition reference should be had to section 6 of the Act, Schedule 1 of the Act which contains additional provisions, guidance

---

7   Further clarification can be found in Schedule 1 of the Act which provides supplementary provisions covering the determination of disability, the Disability Discrimination (Meaning of Disability) Regulations 1996 and the revised Guidance on matters to be taken into account in determining questions relating to the definition of 'disability'. The Guidance is available on the EHRC website at www.equalityhumanrights.com/en/publicationsandresources/Pages/Guidanceondefinitionofdisability.aspx

8   Previously under s 3A (5) of the DDA 1995.

9   *Abadeh v British Telecom* [2001] ICR 156; *McKechnie Plastic Components v Grant* [2009] All ER (D) 121, EAT.

and examples as to what will be considered a disability, the Equality Act (Disability) Regulations 2010/2128 and the relevant case law.

In *Goodwin v The Patent Office*,[10] an employee suffered from schizophrenia and as a result experienced difficulties in concentrating and communicating, was a disabled person within the meaning of the Act. In this case the EAT gave important guidance for tribunals on dealing with issues arising from the definition which were inter alia:

(a)   Tribunals should adopt an inquisitorial role prior to hearing, clarify issues, if necessary hold pre-hearing meeting to inform parties of medical evidence required.

(b)   Specific regard should be given to guidance to relevant statutory provisions in the Guidance Notes and Code of Practice

(c)   In considering 'adverse effect on abilities' focus should be on things a person cannot do or can only do with difficulty.[11]

Physical impairment

9.4 Determining what is a physical impairment is often not an issue in most disability discrimination cases because all serious illnesses will represent a disability and the eligibility of most less serious ones to be covered have been considered and settled by the courts. For example in the case *O'Neill v Symm & Co*,[12] ME was recognised as a disability for the purposes of the Act, although the EAT qualified this by saying it will only apply in the individual circumstances if it affects someone's ability to carry out their day-to-day activities. 'We have to look at the matter not generically, but in relation to the applicant and the impairments relative to her.'

Cancer, Multiple Sclerosis and HIV are all regarded as falling within the definition from the date of diagnosis.[13]

---

10 [1999] IRLR 4.
11 The EAT expanded on these principles in *J v DLA Piper* EAT 15 June 2010.
12 [1998] IRLR 233.
13 Para 6 Schedule 1.

Often it is not obvious whether an impairment is physical or mental. Provided there is an impairment this can be a physical impairment due to psychological causes[14] so long as it is not purely imaginary.[15]

Severe disfigurement can amount to a disability[16] and a person who is certified as blind, severely sight impaired, sight impaired or partially sighted by a consultant ophthalmologist is regarded as having a disability (Regulation 7).

Hay fever is excluded from the definition as is severe disfigurement arising from ear piercing and tattoos.[17]

Mental impairment

9.5 To show that an employee suffered from a mental impairment it was necessary, until recently, to show that the impairment resulted from, or consisted of, a mental illness which was a clinically well recognised illness. In other words recognised by the World Health Organisation classification or US classification etc as a mental illness. However, under s 18 of the DDA 2005 the need to show that a mental impairment falls within a medically well recognised classification of mental illness was removed.

The definition does include a wide range of impairments relating to mental functioning including what are known as learning disabilities.[18] In cases brought under the Equality Act 2010 mental impairment has included clinical depression, bi-polar affective disorder and bulimia nervosa. In *Dunham v Ashford Windows*[19] it was held to include the claimants general learning difficulties mainly difficulties in reading and writing which were not attributable to a particular condition, 'Mental impairment' does not include addiction to, alcohol, nicotine, or any other substance, unless dependency originally resulted from taking drugs which are medically

---

14 *College of Ripon and York v St Johns Hobbs* [2002] IRLR 185.
15 *McNicol v Balfour Beatty Rail Maintenance Ltd/Rugamer v Sony Music Entertainment UK Ltd* [2002] ICR 1498.
16 Para 3 schedule 1 Equality Act 2010.
17 Equality Act 2010 (Disability) Regulations 2010/2128 regulation 4 and 5.
18 *Patterson v The Commissioner of Police of the Metropolis* [2007] IRLR 763.
19 [2005] ICR 1584.

prescribed,[20] also tendencies to start fires, steal, physically or sexually abuse, exhibitionism and voyeurism are excluded.[21] If a claimant has a physical or mental condition which has resulted from an addiction this condition may be regarded as a disability although the original condition is excluded. The attitude of the courts and tribunals to this situation has been unpredictable. In *Power v Panasonic UK Ltd*,[22] the claimants depression was caused by alcoholism which is an excluded condition. The EAT held that the tribunal had erred in considering what had caused the depression but should have considered whether the depression was a disability in its own right. Similarly, in *Murray v Newham*[23] the Citizens Advice Bureau had refused Murray employment because of his record of violence which was caused by his schizophrenia. The EAT overruling the tribunal held that these were freestanding conditions which could be considered separately and that the excluded condition did not necessarily preclude the claimant suffering from a disability namely schizophrenia. However in the case of *Edmund Nuthall Ltd v Butterfield*[24] the claimant was sacked when he exposed himself to women. Voyeurism is an excluded condition but in his case it was caused by an underlying depression. His dismissal was held not to be discriminatory. In light of the Nuthall case the question which should be asked is whether it is the depression or the excluded activity which has resulted in the less favourable treatment.

Long-Term Adverse Effect

9.6 The impairment must have lasted for at least 12 months. This will often have to be determined by an employment tribunal through reference to medical opinion. Most cases involve consideration of the issue of whether the medical condition is likely to last for more than 12 months or can reasonably expected to last 12 months or more. In *SCA Packaging Ltd v Boyle*[25] the House of Lords (Northern Ireland) held that the proper

---

20 Equality Act 2010 (Disability) Regulations 2010/2128 regulation 3.
21 Equality Act 2010 (Disability) Regulations 2010/2128 regulation 4.
22 [2003] IRLR 151.
23 CAB [2003] ICR 643.
24 [2006] ICR 77.
25 [2009] ICR 1056; followed in *Anwar v Tower Hamlets College* EAT 23 July 2010 and *Grant v McKechnie Plastic Components* [2010] All ER (D) 194 (Feb), EAT.

test as to whether a claimant's medical condition was 'likely' to have a substantial adverse effect if medical treatment ceased was whether 'it could well happen' and not whether it was probable that it would.

Substantial Adverse Effects

9.7 For the effect to be substantial it must be more than minor or trivial. In assessing the effect, both the time taken to carry out the activity and the way in which it is carried out, should be taken into account. Both direct and indirect effects of an impairment should be assessed. Persons qualified to bring an action under the Equality Act 2010 do not lose the protection of the legislation because they have been successful in controlling or correcting a disability. It is treated as continuing to be an impairment where it would be likely to have an adverse effect on the person's ability to carry out normal day-to-day activities but for the medical treatment. Where the employee has a progressive condition this will be covered by the Act when their state of health adversely affects ability to carry out day-to-day activities and the tribunal should concentrate on what the claimant cannot do, as in the case of *Leonard v Southern Derbyshire Chamber of Commerce*.[26] In *Abadeh v British Telecommunications plc*,[27] it was decided it is not the task of the medical expert to tell the tribunal whether an impairment was or was not substantial. That is a question the tribunal itself must answer.

Normal Day to Day Activities

9.8 Previously a claimant had to show that their impairment affected their ability to carry out normal day to day activities and this would have been established if the impairment affected one of the following: (a) Mobility, (b) Manual Dexterity, (c) Physical Co-ordination, (d) Continence, (e) Ability to lift, carry or otherwise move everyday objects, (f) Speech, hearing or eyesight, (g) Memory or ability to concentrate, learn or understand, and (h) Perception of the risk of physical danger. It is no longer necessary to show the impairment falls into one of these categories.

---

26 [2001] IRLR 19 EAT.
27 [2001] IRLR 24.

In *Cook v Kitchen Range Foods Ltd*,[28] the applicant suffered a back injury as a result of an industrial injury and was unable to stand for more than two hours at a time or lift heavy objects. He was dismissed for no longer being able to do his job as a production operative. It was held he was not disabled for purposes of the Act. The term 'normal day-to-day activities' is not intended to include activities which are normal only for a person or group of people. It was decided that standing for a considerable length of time is not a normal day-to-day activity.[29]

The tribunal must look beyond the workplace or job in question or the particular applicant to determine whether disability affects normal day-to-day activities.[30]

However, in *Patterson v The Commissioner of Police of the Metropolis*,[31] the EAT took a more realistic approach to this issue. In this case the EAT held that the employment tribunal had misdirected itself in law in concluding that a dyslexic chief inspector of police was not disabled. His DDA 1995 claim alleged that the respondent had failed to make a reasonable adjustment for him in relation to an examination he wished to undertake for promotion to the rank of superintendent, in circumstances where expert evidence indicated that because of his disability it would take him 25% additional time to complete the paper. The employment tribunal had held that taking a high-pressure assessment or examination was not a normal day-to-day activity within the meaning of the DDA 1995. The EAT disagreed and stressed that what is normal cannot sensibly depend upon whether the majority of people do it. Rather 'normal' is best understood as the opposite of something that is unusual or abnormal.[32] The EAT held that s 1 DDA 1995 could be read in a way that gave effect to EU law by interpreting 'normal day-to-day activities' as including 'the activities which are relevant to participation in professional life' (see paragraph 67).

In *Ekpe v Commissioner of Police of the Metropolis*,[33] the EAT held that instead of asking what proportion of society undertakes the activity

---

28 Case No 1501064/97.
29 See *Vicary v British Telecommunications plc* [1999] IRLR 680.
30 *Abadeh v British Telecommunications plc* [2001] IRLR 24.
31 [2007] IRLR 763.
32 *Ekpe v Commissioner of Police of the Metropolis* [2001] ICR 1084.
33 [2001] ICR 1084.

what it should ask if it was an unusual one. The claimant was disabled because she could not put on her make up with her right hand.

Direct discrimination – s 13

9.9 Under s 13 of the Equality Act 2010, there is a definition of direct discrimination which states: (1) A person (A) discriminates against another (B) if, because of a protected characteristic, A treats B less favourably than A treats or would treat others.

Under s 13 (3): If the protected characteristic is disability, and B is not a disabled person, A does not discriminate against B only because A treats or would treat disabled persons better.

This legislation is asymmetric in operation as it only protects people who are disabled or have been disabled in the past. The intention of the legislation was to facilitate the integration of disabled people into the workforce. This differs from the old definition by virtue of the words 'because of' (instead of the old terminology 'on grounds of'). This is intended to significantly widen the scope of the law by allowing claims to be brought based on association (ie where the discrimination is because a person is associated with someone else who has a protected characteristic), or perception ie where an individual is treated less favourably because of another's perception of their having a protected characteristic.

However, the Equality Act 2010 aims to shift the position back to a more balanced approach, giving disabled people wider rights, but subject to the employer etc being able to 'justify' its conduct. This is being achieved by the introduction of new ways to claim for disability discrimination called 'discrimination arising from disability' and 'indirect discrimination'.

Direct discrimination arises when an employer treats someone less favourably because they have a disability. Direct discrimination requires the knowledge of the employer that the person has a disability but motive is irrelevant. Direct discrimination can never be justified. An example would be where an employer dismissed an employee for being HIV positive.[34] If the reason was simply because he was HIV positive (ie prejudice against someone with his condition) this will be direct discrimination and cannot be justified. If the reason is that the employee works in an

34 See *High Quality Lifestyles Ltd v Watts* [2006] IRLR 850.

industry such as food processing or in the care industry it may be that the employer dismisses him not because he is HIV positive but because the employer fears transmission to other people. The latter situation is not direct discrimination but may be discrimination arising from disability (see below).

DISCRIMINATION BY ASSOCIATION AND PERCEPTION

9.10 Direct discrimination or harassment based on association or perception are made unlawful, or in some cases more clearly unlawful. This might apply, for example, where a friend of a disabled person is harassed, or where an impairment does not actually have a substantial effect but someone thinks it does. This change implemented a European Court decision in *Coleman v Attridge Law*.[35] In this case Coleman claimed she was forced to quit her job at Attridge Law after she requested time off to look after her four-year-old disabled son. The question put to the ECJ was whether the European Union's discrimination law covered not just people who are disabled (or have a particular sex, race, religion, belief and age), but people who suffer discrimination because they are related or connected to disabled people. They ruled that able-bodied people can be covered by the Disability Discrimination Act 1995 and this change to the law was included in the Equality Act 2010. This has ramifications, not just for carers and friends and colleagues of disabled employees, but for employees connected to people covered by other discrimination legislation such as sexual orientation, religion and age.

Discrimination arising from disability – s 15

9.11 Under s 15 discrimination arising from disability arises where: (1) A person (A) discriminates against a disabled person (B) if (a) A treats B unfavourably because of something arising in consequence of B's disability, and (b) A cannot show that the treatment is a proportionate means of achieving a legitimate aim. Subsection (1) does not apply if A shows that A did not know, and could not reasonably have been

---

35 (2007) IRLR 88.

expected to know, that B had the disability. As can be seen in the case of discrimination arising from disability employers will be able to defend *all* claims of disability if they can show they did not know or could not reasonably be expected to have known that the employee was disabled, or if they can establish that the treatment was a proportionate means of achieving a legitimate aim.

In the example used above the employer may demonstrate that his treatment of the HIV positive employee was a proportionate means of achieving a legitimate aim (protection of other people from transmission) but in deciding whether or not dismissal is a proportionate response the tribunal will take into account whether the employer has fulfilled his duty to make reasonable adjustments (eg by supplying gloves etc).

Indirect discrimination – s 19

9.12 Under s 19 indirect discrimination arises where: (1) A person (A) discriminates against another (B) if A applies to B a provision, criterion or practice which is discriminatory in relation to a relevant protected characteristic of B's. (2) For the purposes of subsection (1), a provision, criterion or practice is discriminatory in relation to a relevant protected characteristic of B's if (a) A applies, or would apply, it to persons with whom B does not share the characteristic (b) it puts, or would put, persons with whom B shares the characteristic at a particular disadvantage when compared with persons with whom B does not share it (c) it puts, or would put, B at that disadvantage, and (d) A cannot show it to be a proportionate means of achieving a legitimate aim. What are 'provisions, criteria and practices'? 'Provisions, criteria and practices' encompasses the concept of 'arrangements', which was the previous formulation used in the DDA 1975, and which was held to be very wide. See, for example, *Archibald v Fife Council*[36] and *Nottinghamshire County Council v Meikle*.[37] So where it is reasonable to do so, an employer will be required to modify (or even disapply) any provision, criterion or practice which causes more than a minor or trivial disadvantage to a particular disabled employee, to the extent needed to remove the disadvantage. For example, an employer

---

36 [2004] IRLR 651 HL.
37 [2004] IRLR 703 CA.

might have to vary a rule under which all employees have to work from 9am to 5pm to allow a disabled employee to work flexible hours to enable them to have additional breaks to overcome fatigue arising from the disability.[38]

Duty to make reasonable adjustments – s 20

9.13 Under s 20, there is a duty to make reasonable adjustments to accommodate disabled persons. Section 20 (2) states that: the duty comprises the following three requirements:

S 20 (3) The first is a requirement, where a provision, criterion or practice of A's puts a disabled person at a substantial disadvantage in relation to a relevant matter in comparison with persons who are not disabled, to take such steps as it is reasonable to have to take to avoid the disadvantage.

(4) The second is a requirement, where a physical feature puts a disabled person at a substantial disadvantage in relation to a relevant matter in comparison with persons who are not disabled, to take such steps as it is reasonable to have to take to avoid the disadvantage.

(5) The third is a requirement, where a disabled person would, but for the provision of an auxiliary aid, be put at a substantial disadvantage in relation to a relevant matter in comparison with persons who are not disabled, to take such steps as it is reasonable to have to take to provide the auxiliary aid.

Where the first or third requirement relates to the provision of information, the steps which it is reasonable for A to have to take include steps for ensuring that in the circumstances concerned the information is provided in an accessible format (eg Braille for blind employees).

A person (A) who is subject to a duty to make reasonable adjustments is not (subject to express provision to the contrary) entitled to require a

---

38 The case of *Environment Agency v Rowan* [2008] IRLR 20 provided a renewed reminder of the importance of goingthrough each of the steps required under the reasonable adjustments provision of the DDA 1995.

disabled person, in relation to whom A is required to comply with the duty, to pay to any extent A's costs of complying with the duty.

In relation to the second requirement above, a reference in this section to avoiding a substantial disadvantage includes a reference to:

(a)   removing the physical feature in question,

(b)   altering it, or

(c)   providing a reasonable means of avoiding it.

A reference in this and other sections,[39] to a physical feature, is a reference to:

(a)   a feature arising from the design or construction of a building,

(b)   a feature of an approach to, exit from, or access to a building,

(c)   a fixture or fitting, or furniture, furnishings, materials, equipment or other moveable property, in or on premises, or

(d)   any other physical element or quality.

What is reasonable in the circumstances is an objective test. Factors which may be relevant include the size and financial resources of the employer,[40] operational needs of the employer and the interests of other employees[41] and the availability of other work. The employer is not expected to make adjustments which are not related to performance of the work.[42] Some examples of adjustments that can be made, other than to premises, are: allocation of some of disabled person's duties to another employee, altering their hours of work, changing their place of work, special arrangements for providing them with training or increased supervision, modifying equipment or instructions. In *Fu v London Borough of Camden*,[43] the EAT held that in deciding whether the employers met the pre-dismissal obligations in the context of their ill-health procedure to make reasonable adjustments ... the tribunal erred by failing to consider the extent to which, if at all, adjustments could have overcome her medical symptoms

---

39 Section 21 or 22 or an applicable Schedule.
40 *O'Hanlon v Commissioners for HMRC* [2007] ICR 1359.
41 *Chief Constable of Lancashire Police v Weaver* EAT 19 March 2008.
42 *Kenny v Hampshire Constabulary* [1999] ICR 27.
43 [2001] IRLR 186.

which otherwise prevented her return to work. In *Ridout v TC Group*,[44] Ms Ridout suffered from photosensitive epilepsy and claimed that the respondent had failed to make reasonable adjustment to the interview room thereby exposing her to bright fluorescent lights. It was not reasonable for the employer to know of the effect of this (given that it is a rare medical condition) and was up to the applicant to inform them.

Section 20(7) of the Equality Act 2010 clarifies that a person required to make a reasonable adjustment is not entitled to require the disabled person to pay any of the costs of complying with the duty.

Harassment – s 26

9.14 Under s 26 of the Act harassment is unlawful where (1) A person (A) harasses another (B) if (a) A engages in unwanted conduct related to a relevant protected characteristic, and (b) the conduct has the purpose or effect of: (i) violating B's dignity, or (ii) creating an intimidating, hostile, degrading, humiliating or offensive environment for B.

So under this provision, under the Equality Act 2010, harassment need no longer be 'for a reason' which relates to disability, as was previously required by the Disability Discrimination Act 1995. The harassment need only be related to the disability. This should be an easier requirement to comply with for the victim of harassment and means a claim can relate to someone else's disability (see harassment by perception or association above). For example, harassment could relate to the disability of a friend/ colleague or of one's child.

Under the Equality Act 2010 (s 40) employers are now liable for disability harassment by third parties in some circumstances, eg harassment by customers or suppliers. The liability for third parties only applies if the employer knew that the employee had been harassed in the course of his employment on at least two other occasions by a third party (it could be a different third party on each occasion). If the employer had this knowledge, the employer is liable for disability harassment where a third party harasses an employee because of his disability in the course of his employment and the employer failed to take such steps as would have been reasonably practicable to prevent the third party from doing so.

---

44 [1999] IRLR 628.

Victimisation – s 27

9.15 This is where the worker is essentially treated badly by the employer for raising a grievance or making a claim relating to a protected characteristic. The Equality Act 2010 goes further than previous law and includes a new definition of victimisation. This provides that an employer would victimise a worker if he subjects them to a 'detriment' because they have done a protected act. It also covers such treatment where the employer only believes that the worker has done, or may do, a protected act. A protected act would include bringing proceedings under the Act, giving evidence or information in connection with proceedings under the Act, doing any other thing for the purposes of or in connection with the Act, making an allegation (whether or not express) that the employer or another person has contravened this Act, or making a 'relevant pay disclosure' for the purposes of ascertaining if discrimination is occurring in relation to pay. Under the old law, an individual claiming victimisation had to indentify either an actual or hypothetical comparator. This requirement has been removed by the Act. An example would be if the colleague of a disabled member of staff gave evidence at a tribunal in support her colleague in respect of a complaint against the employer for disability discrimination, in respect of discriminatory behaviour by their supervisor. When that friend suddenly experienced non-cooperation or obstruction in her job by her supervisor, then this would be sufficient detriment for it to amount to victimisation.

PRE-EMPLOYMENT ENQUIRIES ABOUT DISABILITY AND HEALTH

9.16 Under s 60 of the Act, a person to whom an application for work is made must not ask about the health of the applicant before work is offered to him either on a conditional or unconditional basis. However. there are excepted situations where health related enquiries can be made namely, where they are for the purposes of: making reasonable adjustments to enable the disabled person to participate in the recruitment process; finding out whether a job applicant would be able to participate in an assessment to test his suitability for the work; finding out whether a job applicant would be able to undertake a function that is intrinsic to the job, with reasonable adjustments; for monitoring diversity in applications for jobs; supporting positive action in employment for disabled people and enabling an employer to identify suitable candidates for a job where there is a genuine occupational requirement for the person to be disabled. This section also allows questions to be asked where they are needed in the context of national security vetting.

It is the role of the Equality and Human Rights Commission to enforce a breach of this provision but, where the employer asks questions which are not allowed by this section and rejects the applicant, if the applicant then makes a claim of direct discrimination to the employment tribunal it will be for the employer to show that he has not discriminated against the candidate.

THE WORK OCCUPATIONAL REQUIREMENT EXCEPTION

9.17 The Work Occupational Requirement Exception is set out in Schedule 9 paragraph 1 of the Equality Act and provides a new exception to what would otherwise be direct disability discrimination. This applies where being disabled is an occupational requirement for work. Where a person does not meet that requirement it will not be discriminatory to reject that person. The requirement must be a proportionate means of pursuing a legitimate aim and the burden of showing that rests on those seeking to rely on it. As an example it could apply where an organisation for the teaching of the deaf might legitimately stipulate as a requirement that applicants are deaf persons who have experience of using British Sign Language in their work as a teacher.

Positive action

9.18 Under part 11, chapter 2, s 159 of the Act it deals with 'positive action' in respect of recruitment and promotion. It allows an employer to take disability into account when deciding who to recruit and promote where disabled people are at a disadvantage or are under-represented. This action can only be taken where candidates (disabled and non-disabled) are equally qualified, which is a matter of judgement taking into account all the criteria used for selection. It does not allow employers to have an automatic policy preferring disabled candidates and each case must be considered on its merits and any action must be a proportionate means of addressing such a disadvantage or under-representation.

Objective justification test

9.19 For some types of discrimination, an employer has a defence if it can 'justify' how it treated the disabled person. The different tests previously used are replaced by a single objective 'justification' test, namely the organisation must show that its conduct was a 'proportionate means of achieving a legitimate aim'. In employment, this could prove be a higher evidential challenge than the previous justification test and employers will not find it easy to justify less favourable treatment of employees. In *Callagan v Glasgow City Council*,[45] it was decided there must be a causal connection between the discriminatory act and the justifying circumstances. The justifying circumstances must be material in the sense of relevance and substantial. In this case it was his sickness record, his failure to respond to correct reporting procedures, his employer's various attempts to accommodate him and the fact he was not fit for work and it was uncertain he ever would be. There is some guidance given on the objective justification defence in the Codes of Practice which is a 'legitimate aim' should be legal, should not be discriminatory in itself, and must represent a real, objective consideration. So the health, welfare and safety of individuals could qualify as a legitimate aim for disallowing disabled people to work in a potentially dangerous workplace. Also business needs and economic efficiency might be legitimate aims in this context. However, an employer introducing discriminatory measures against disabled people simply to try and cut costs or improve their competitiveness will not satisfy the test.

A proportionate response is an appropriate and necessary means of achieving a legitimate aim. This means it must be reasonably necessary to achieve it. It does not have to be the only possible way of achieving the legitimate aim but the treatment will not be proportionate if less discriminatory measures could have been taken to achieve the same objective. A balance needs to be struck between the discriminatory effect

---

45 [2001] IRLR 724.

of the treatment and the need to apply it, taking into account all of the relevant facts.

As a consequence of the various changes brought in by the Equality Act 2010 it should be easier for the claimant's situation to fall within the definition of disability, and for him/her to successfully bring a claim for disability discrimination. This is in part because some of the key areas of difficulty, eg disability related discrimination claims, restricted meaning of day to day activities have been removed from the legislation and new concepts introduced, eg indirect discrimination, discrimination by association and perception and discrimination arising from disability, which have broadened the scope for claims.

Chapter 10

Family Friendly Rights

10.1 This chapter will consider the various statutory rights which have been introduced to benefit parents and their children. This is an area of law subject to constant change and improvement in the rights of employees. These rights originate in European Directives such as the Equal Treatment Directive 76/207; EEC; Protection of Pregnant Women at Work Directive 92/85; Parental Leave Directive 96/34 and the Framework Agreement on Parental Leave, and are implemented by the Employment Rights Act 1996 (as amended) and its associated Regulations.

There is a considerable overlap with issues of equality, which are considered in chapter 8.

HEALTH AND SAFETY

10.2 Under the law on health and safety at work, specifically the Management of Health and Safety at Work Regulations 1999,[1] all employers have a duty to protect female employees of child bearing age and expectant mothers working for them, and their babies. The Regulations confer a civil right of action and an employer who fails to implement them may be sued for damages in the civil courts in respect of any loss injury or damage resulting from the failure. This would be in addition to any other right to sue for damages for breach of contract, or sex discrimination, which will also result from such a failure. A failure by the employer to fulfil his duties in respect of health and safety could also result in a claim for constructive unfair dismissal.

---

1   The Management of Health and Safety at Work Regulations 1999 implement the health and safety measures in the Pregnant Workers Directive.

If the work is of a type which could involve a risk to the health and safety of an expectant mother, or an unborn baby, the employer must carry out a risk assessment.[2]

An employer has a further duty of care to carry out a specific risk assessment for employees who are pregnant, have given birth within the last six months, or are breastfeeding. It will review every area of their working conditions and recommend the appropriate course of action to protect an expectant mother, and the baby, against illness or injury. The Regulations require employers to take action to remove, reduce, or control risks where individual risk assessments reveal them. Where the assessment reveals a risk the employer's initial obligation is to take whatever preventative or protective measures is required. Where such action would not avoid the risk then, if it is reasonable to do so the employer must alter the woman's working conditions or hours of work. Where it is not reasonable to alter conditions or hours of work to avoid the risk then the employer must consider whether it would be possible to offer the woman suitable alternative work. Where an employee is suspended from work for safety reasons she must be offered suitable alternative employment (suitable to her and appropriate in the circumstances).[3] If no suitable alternative work is available, the women must be suspended from work for as long as necessary to avoid the risk.[4] These requirements will not be imposed on the employer unless the employee notifies them that they are a new or expectant mother. The employer can request medical evidence and where this is not provided these requirements need not apply.

If a registered medical practitioner or midwife certifies that the employee should be absent from work then in the absence of suitable alternative work the employer must suspend her. She must also be suspended in the absence of suitable alternative work if this is recommended in any HSE Approved Code of Practice. What is suitable will depend on the

---

2   Management of Health and Safety at Work Regulations 1999 Regulation 16.
3   Section 67 Employment Rights Act 1996.
4   Under the Control of Lead at Work Regulations 2002/2676, the Ionising Radiations Regulations 1999 SI 1999/3232 and the Control of Substances Hazardous to Health Regulations 2002 SI 2002/2177 it is provided that pregnant employees should be suspended from work where this proves necessary to safeguard their health and safety.

circumstances of each case and the terms and conditions must be no less favourable than those which apply to her usual job.[5]

If a woman is offered suitable alternative work during a period of medical suspension, and unreasonably refuses it, then she loses the right to be paid under ERA 1996 s 68.

During the period of suspension the employee is entitled to a weeks pay in respect of each week of suspension. Pay is at her normal hourly rate, averaged over the 12 weeks prior to the start of the period of suspension.

An employee who is not paid during the period of suspension may complain to an employment tribunal within three months of the failure or such other period as the tribunal feels is reasonable. The tribunal will make an award of compensation equivalent to the amount of pay which should have been received.

Regulation 25 (4) of the Workplace (Health, Safety and Welfare) Regulations 1992/3004 states that suitable facilities shall be provided for any person at work who is a pregnant woman or nursing mother to rest.

The Breastfeeding (Scotland) Act 2005 provides that it is a criminal offence for a person in charge of a public place or licensed premises to prevent a child being fed milk whether by breast or bottle. The employer has vicarious liability in respect of offences committed by his employees or agents unless the employer took such steps as were reasonably practicable to prevent the employee from committing such an offence in the course of the employee's employment.

MATERNITY RIGHTS

10.3 It is important to note that an employee's contract may often provide rights which are more favourable than the statutory minimum rights which are covered here. Maternity rights can generally be found in part of the Employment Rights Act 1996 and part II of the Maternity and Parental Leave Etc Regulations 1999/3312.

5   *Iske v P&O European Ferries (Dover) Ltd* [1997] IRLR 401, *British Airways (European Operations at Gatwick) Ltd v Moore and Botterill* [2000] ICR 678.

Time off for antenatal care

10.4 The Employment Rights Act 1996 ss 55 to 57, provides that any employee who is pregnant shall not be unreasonably refused paid time off work to attend antenatal care. The right applies to all pregnant employees, except share fishermen, or members of a constabulary, regardless of length of service, number of hours worked or size of employer. The right is extended to agencies workers by virtue of s 57 ZA. An employee who has undergone vitro fertilisation is regarded as pregnant from the time that the fertilised embryo is implanted in her womb.[6]

The term antenatal care will be construed widely, and includes relaxation classes and possibly also parent craft classes,[7] but the appointment must be made on the advice of a registered medical practitioner, registered midwife or registered health visitor. The employer may require proof of pregnancy.

Time off is with pay,[8] and the employer may not ask the woman to make up the hours if leave is granted, however, leave may be refused if it the refusal is reasonable and an employee who takes unauthorised leave may be disciplined for misconduct.[9]

If leave is unreasonably refused, or the employer does not pay her, the employee may make a complaint to the Employment Tribunal within 3 months of the date of the appointment, or such other date as the tribunal deems reasonable.[10] The tribunal may make a declaration and award her the remuneration which she should have received. She may also claim compensation (including damages for hurt feelings).[11] She is also afforded protection from detriment or dismissal and this is discussed in further detail below.[12]

---

6   *Mayr v Backerei und Konditerei Gerhard Flockner* OHG ECR I-1017, [2008] IRLR 387.
7   *Gregory v Tudsbury Ltd* [1982] IRLR 267.
8   Section 56 Employment Rights Act 1996.
9   *Gough v County Sports (Wales) Ltd* unreported.
10   Section 57(1) Employment Rights Act 1996.
11   Section 57(2) Employment Rights Act 1996 and Regulation 19 Maternity and Parental Leave etc Regulations.
12   Section 57(2) Employment Rights Act 1996 and Regulation 19 Maternity and Parental Leave etc Regulations.

Maternity leave

10.5 There are three periods of maternity leave to be considered, namely, compulsory maternity leave, ordinary maternity leave and additional maternity leave.

Compulsory Maternity leave

10.6 Under s 72(1) of the Employment Rights Act 1996, employers are prohibited from allowing an employee from returning to work until 2 weeks have elapsed from the date of childbirth. To allow an earlier return to work is a criminal offence and subject to a fine not exceeding level two on the standard scale. In addition, it is a criminal offence to allow a woman to return to work in a factory within 4 weeks of the date of childbirth and that offence is subject to a fine not exceeding level one of the scale.[13] No deduction from bonuses, which would otherwise have been payable, can be made in respect of the period of compulsory maternity leave.

Ordinary and Additional Maternity Leave

10.7 All pregnant employees, with the exception of members of the armed forces, share fisherman, and members of the constabulary, are entitled to 26 weeks Ordinary Maternity Leave followed by 26 weeks Additional Maternity leave regardless of length of service, hours worked, or size of employer.[14] In order to exercise this right, the woman must notify her employer of her pregnancy and her expected week of childbirth and the date on which she intends to start her ordinary maternity leave. She must give this notice no later than the end of the 15th week before the expected week of confinement, unless it is not practicable to do so.

The woman chooses the date her leave starts, however the date must be any time from the beginning of the 11th week before the expected week of childbirth. If she gives birth or is off work because of a pregnancy related illness after the beginning of the last 4 weeks before the expected date of childbirth, then leave will commence automatically from the day after

---

13   Factories Act 1961 Schedule 5.
14   Section 71(3) Employment Rights Act 1996.

the date of either of these events.[15] If this happens, the usual notification requirements outlined above do not apply but the woman must notify the employer as soon as is reasonably practicable. The EAT held in *Kwik Save Stores Ltd v Greaves*,[16] that where an employee had not returned to work on the date she said she would return, the right to return is accomplished when the notice requirements are complied with. The employee does not need to physically appear at work.

The employee may change the date on which she intends to start her leave by giving at least 28 days notice to her employer or, if that is not practicable, by notifying her employer of the change of date as soon as it is reasonably practicable to do so. The 28 days is 28 days before the date on which she originally intended to start leave or 28 days before the new date, whichever is earlier. The employer can require her to give this notice in writing.

On receipt of the woman's notice of the day on which it is intended leave should start, the employer must issue, within 28 days, a note of the day on which her leave will end. He should assume that she will take all the leave to which she is entitled, including additional maternity leave. If the employer fails to issue this notice he loses the right to complain if she returns to work too early or too late.

Since 1st April 2011, it has been possible for parents to 'share' leave. If a woman chooses to return to work her partner may be eligible for additional paternity leave and pay (see below).

'Keeping in Touch'

10.8 The employee may work up to 10 days during the period of maternity leave.[17] She will be paid for these days at the usual rate. These days must take place within the existing period of leave, rather than before or after leave begins, and may include training days and anything which would normally be considered part of her contract of employment. These days, and any other meetings or contact to ensure that employer and employee keep in touch, will not interrupt the leave period or affect entitlement to

---

15   Section 72(1)(b) Employment Rights Act 1996.

16   [1997] ICR 629.

17   Regulation 12A.

statutory maternity pay (SMP). There is no obligation on the employee to work or to keep in touch during the leave period but the employer may require to contact the employee in order to full the employer's obligations under the contract of employment, for example to notify of job vacancies[18] and to consult about the return to work.[19]

The Contract of Employment during Ordinary Maternity Leave and Additional Maternity Leave

10.9 The distinction between Ordinary and Additional Maternity Leave was formerly more important, however, as a result of case law from the Court of Justice of the European Union, the Maternity and Parental Leave Etc Regulations 1999[20] were amended in 2008. The effect of this amendment was that most contractual and non contractual terms, conditions and benefits, now continue throughout the period of ordinary and additional maternity leave. The main exception to this is remuneration. The right to remuneration does not continue but is replaced with statutory rights to pay or specific contractual rights to occupational maternity pay. Apart from remuneration, the woman is treated as if her contract applies throughout the period of statutory maternity leave. 'Remuneration' includes sick pay, so to refuse to pay a woman sick pay when she is on maternity leave does not amount to an unlawful deduction from wages.[21]

Bonus payments which would have been payable are perhaps the most contentious issue. In *Lewen v Denda*,[22] the European Court of Justice held that although a woman is entitled to any bonus payments which would have been payable during the year, the employer is entitled to make a deduction pro rata for any part of the bonus which relates to the woman's period of absence on maternity leave (apart from compulsory maternity leave). Following this case, in *Hoyland v Asda*,[23] the Inner House of the Court of Session held that, except for the two week period of compulsory maternity leave, an employer was permitted to make a pro rata deduction

---

18   *Visa International Service Association v Paul* [2004] IRLR 42.
19   *Blundell v St Andrews Catholic Primary School* [2007] IRLR 652.
20   SI 1999/3312.
21   *Department of Work and Pensions v Sutcliffe* EAT 10 October 2007.
22   [2000] ICR 648.
23   2006 SC 550.

in bonus payments from a discretionary bonus where, whether or not to make a bonus payment was not discretionary, but the amount paid was.

Leave entitlement continues to accrue during all periods of maternity leave. It cannot be taken during maternity leave but must be taken either before or after the leave.[24]

Pension rights do not continue to accrue throughout additional maternity leave.

The implied duties under the contract of employment continue to apply and, therefore, the employee is bound by duties of loyalty, including confidentiality, and the employer continues to be bound by the implied duty of trust and confidence. A failure on the part of the employer to inform the employee of suitable vacancies or promotions may amount to discrimination and a breach of the duty of trust and confidence.[25]

Return to work

10.10 A failure to allow a return to work will be an automatically unfair dismissal, unless the reason is redundancy and there is no suitable post available to offer her.[26]

The right to return to work varies depending whether the woman is returning after Ordinary Maternity Leave or Additional Maternity Leave. If she returns after Ordinary Maternity Leave she has the right to return to her original post,[27] whereas the right to return after Additional Maternity Leave is the right to return to the original post or, if that is not reasonably practicable, to a suitable post.[28]

Even if returning after Ordinary Maternity Leave, despite the fact that her contractual terms and conditions continue to apply, she cannot expect to find things exactly as she left so long as the work offered is the same nature and on the same terms as her original job and any differences are not fundamental changes to her contract of employment.[29] In *Blundell v*

24 *Merino Gomez v Continental Industrias del Caucho* [2004] ECR I-2605.
25 *Visa International Service Association v Paul* [2004] IRLR 42.
26 Section 99 Employment Rights Act 1996, The Maternity and Parental Leave Etc Regulations 1999 Regulation 10.
27 The Maternity and Parental Leave Etc Regulations 1999 Regulations 18(1),18A(1) and 10.
28 Regulations 18(2) and 18A(2).
29 *Edgell v Lloyd's Register of Shipping* [1977] IRLR 463.

St Andrews Catholic Primary School,[30] a primary school teacher was not entitled to return to teach the reception class which was the class she had been teaching when she left to go on leave. She could be asked to teach year two because her contract was as a primary school teacher and the work was that of a primary school teacher at the same location. She had however been discriminated against in that she had not been allowed to express a preference.

If she returns after Additional Maternity Leave, the woman is entitled to return to her old job including status, pay responsibilities and no less favourable terms and conditions than would have applied had she not taken leave.[31] If it is not reasonably practicable for her to return to her old job then she must be offered a suitable post. Continuity of employment is not interrupted for purposes of statutory rights, but the period of additional maternity leave may not count towards other service related matters such as eligibility for promotion. Pension contributions are suspended during the period of additional leave.

The right to return is accomplished when the notice requirements are complied with. The employee does not need to physically appear at work.[32]

There is no specific right to insist on working part-time after the woman returns to work. The usual principles regarding indirect discrimination apply however and it is likely that a woman who seeks to work part-time or flexibly to allow her to care for a child will suffer indirect sex discrimination if that request is refused.[33] This issue and the right to request flexible working are considered in more detail below.

A failure to allow the employee to return to work will amount to an automatically unfair dismissal.

Pregnancy and maternity related Redundancy, Dismissal and Detriment

10.11 A female employee who is dismissed whilst pregnant or on maternity leave or on her return for maternity leave is entitled to be given

---

30 [2007] IRLR 652.
31 Regulation 18(2), 18A(2).
32 *Kwik Save Stores Ltd v Greaves* [1997] ICR 629.
33 *Hardys and Hanson plc v Lax* [2005] ICR 1565.

written reasons for dismissal without having to request them.[34] Section 99 of the Employment Rights Act 1996, gives all employees the right not to be dismissed on grounds of pregnancy or childbirth, regardless of their length of service.

It is automatically unfair if the reason or principal reason for dismissal is: (a) she is pregnant or any reason connected with pregnancy; (b) she has given birth to a child or any reason connected with her giving birth to a child and dismissal occurred during her maternity leave period; (c) she took or availed herself of benefits of maternity leave; (d) she was suspended from work on maternity grounds; or (e) she was made redundant during the MLP but not offered suitable alternative employment.[35] In *George v Beecham Group Ltd*,[36] where an employee was dismissed due to an absence caused by a pregnancy-related illness the employer could not justify her dismissal by referring to her unauthorised absences which had been the subject of warnings previous to the pregnancy. These absences were held to be irrelevant.

The protected period against unfair dismissal lasts from the start of the pregnancy until the end of maternity leave period.

In *Caledonia Bureau Investment & Property v Caffrey*,[37] the dismissal of the applicant who had failed to return to her work after her maternity leave, because of post-natal depression, was dismissal for reasons connected with her pregnancy within the meaning of s 99.

The issue of pregnancy related dismissals has been the subject of many cases in the Court of Justice of the European Union who have taken a stringent approach to implementation of the Pregnant Workers Directive. In *Webb v EMO Air Cargo (UK) Ltd*,[38] Mrs Webb was employed by EMO Cargo (UK) Ltd (EMO) as cover for an employee who was soon to be on maternity leave. However, it was envisaged that if Mrs Webb successfully completed a probationary period she would be offered employment when the fixed period she was initially employed for came to an end. Mrs Webb began working for EMO, but within two weeks of

---

34 Employment Rights Act 1996 section 94 (4) and4(A).
35 Regulation 20(3).
36 (1977) IRLR.
37 (1998) IRLR 110.
38 (1994) IRLR 482 ECJ.

starting she discovered she was pregnant and immediately informed her employer. She was dismissed a short time later. Mrs Webb complained to a tribunal alleging direct discrimination on the grounds of sex, and in the alternative, indirect discrimination. Mrs Webb was unsuccessful in her claim both at the tribunal and later in the Court of Appeal. The case went on appeal to the House of Lords, who referred the case to the ECJ. They held that: 'the protection afforded by Community law to a woman during her pregnancy and after childbirth cannot be dependant on whether her presence at work during maternity is essential to the proper functioning of the undertaking in which she is employed. Any contrary interpretation would render ineffective the provisions of the Pregnant Workers Directive.' Also, that if a women is treated unfavourably because she is pregnant or in a way that undermines her maternity rights under national or EC law that amounts to sex discrimination under the Equal Treatment Directive, regardless of how a man would have been treated had his employment had similar consequences.[39] The ECJ rejected the hypothetical comparator defence that the treatment of a pregnant woman could be compared with the treatment a hypothetical man who was long term sick.

Provided the tribunal is satisfied that the employer knew of or believed in the pregnancy,[40] a dismissal due to pregnancy will, therefore, be automatically unfair and impossible to justify even if the pregnancy means the woman will be unavailable for work during most of a fixed term contract.[41]

In *Dekker v Stiching Vormingscentrum voor Jong Volwasswnen (VJV Centrum) Plus*[42] (known as the *Dekker* case), Mrs Dekker applied for a job, and was identified as the most suitable candidate for the post, but was not appointed because she was pregnant. The employer said the reason she was not appointed was that he would not have been able to recover the cost of her maternity pay under his insurance policy, and so he could not afford to recruit a replacement for her during maternity leave. The ECJ held that: as employment can only be refused because of pregnancy to

---

39   *Larsson (1997) IRLR 643 ECJ, Brown v Rentokil Ltd* (1998) IRLR 445 ECJ, *Handels Case* (1991) IRLR 31, ECJ.
40   *Ramdoolar Ltd v Bycity Ltd* [2005] ICR 368.
41   *Tele- Danmark A/S v Handels (HK) per Brandt-Neilsen* [2004] ICR 610.
42   (1991) IRLR 27, ECJ.

a woman such a refusal is direct discrimination on the ground of her sex and such discrimination cannot be justified by the employer showing they would have suffered a financial detriment in such a case.

Although a woman cannot be dismissed due to pregnancy related illness during the protected period (the period of Ordinary Maternity Leave), once this period is over she may be dismissed for absences due to pregnancy related illness provided similar sickness absence would have resulted in the dismissal of a man.[43]

Dismissals due to pregnancy related illness differ depending on the date the dismissal takes place. After the protected period of Ordinary Maternity Leave ends, it is possible for the employer to fairly dismiss a woman who continues to be absent due to sickness which began during the pregnancy.

Failure to let a woman return to work after maternity leave is ground for automatic unfair dismissal.[44]

A woman who returning to work after her maternity leave period is entitled to return on the same terms as those to which she would have been entitled to if she had never been absent.[45] Where she is refused the right to return to work, she can make a complaint of unfair dismissal to an Employment Tribunal. If her return is on substantially different terms to those she had prior to the leave commencing, then she may be regarded as having been dismissed.

In *MacFadden v Greater Glasgow Passenger Transport Executive*,[46] Mrs McFadden was employed as a grade CG3 clerk before and after her maternity leave. However, after returning to work she was employed as a supernumerary, rather than as part of the established staff. She no longer had her own desk and was not certain of getting full days' work. Her supernumerary status was a lower status than her previous job and she was more liable to be made redundant. The tribunal concluded that the employee's conditions of employment were less favourable than previously, and she had, therefore, been denied her statutory right to return to work and had been dismissed.

---

43   *Brown v Rentokil Ltd* C-394 *Handels-og Kontorfunktionaerernes Forbund i Danmark v Dansk Arbejdsgierforening* 1992 ICR 332.
44   Employment Rights Act 1996 s 99.
45   Employment Rights Act 1996 s 71.
46   (1977) IRLR 327.

If an employee is selected for redundancy, and the reason for selection for redundancy is pregnancy or childbirth, the dismissal will be unfair.[47] This does not prevent a pregnant woman from being made redundant and being entitled to a redundancy payment as the usual rules regarding redundancy and unfair dismissal apply (see chapter 7).

A woman who is made redundant whilst on maternity leave has certain additional rights. She is entitled to be given written reasons for her dismissal without requesting them and, if it is not reasonably practicable for her to be given back her job, she is entitled to be offered a suitable available alternative position with her employer or an associated employer.[48] A job will be considered available despite economic considerations.[49]

It is not necessary to accord to the woman treatment which is more favourable than that accorded to her male colleagues, beyond that which is reasonably necessary to remove the disadvantage caused by her pregnancy. In *Eversheds Legal Services v De Belin*,[50] the claimant was selected for redundancy instead of his female colleague. The selection procedure had been applied to him on the basis of his actual performance. She had been on maternity leave for part of the period and was given a notional 100% for an aspect of the selection procedure, whilst he was judged on his actual performance and received a lower score. His selection was held to be discrimination on grounds of sex and his dismissal unfair.

Section 47C Employment Rights Act 1996, and Regulation 19 of the Maternity and Parental Leave Etc Regulations 1999, provide protection from detrimental treatment on grounds that the employee is pregnant; has given birth to a child; took, sought to take or availed herself of the benefits of, ordinary maternity leave or additional maternity leave; failed to return after a period of ordinary or additional maternity leave in a case where the employer did not notify her of the date on which the period in question would end, and she reasonably believed that that period had not ended, or the employer gave her less than 28 days' notice of the date on which the period in question would end, and it was not reasonably practicable for her to return on that date. (See detriment and dismissal below).

---

47 Regulation 20(2).
48 Regulation 10.
49 *Community Task v Rimmer* [1986] ICR 491.
50 [2011] ICR 1137.

Statutory Maternity Pay and Maternity Allowance

10.12 The Statutory Maternity Pay (General) Regulations 1986 (as amended), regulate the payment of Statutory Maternity Pay and its recoupment by the employer. To qualify for statutory maternity pay, a woman must be an 'employed earner' and must be able to produce medical evidence of her expected week of confinement (the anticipated week the baby will be born). She must also give her employer a minimum of 21 days notice before her absence from work due to pregnancy is about to begin. For the purposes of SMP, 'employed earner' includes employment under a contract of service and or holding an office where earnings are liable to taxation under Schedule E.

All female employed earners who are pregnant, have twenty six weeks continuous service and have worked until the 15th week before the week the baby is due, earning at least the lower earnings limit for National Insurance (currently £102 per week) (averaged over the eight weeks ending with the last pay day before the end of the qualifying week) are entitled to statutory maternity pay (SMP). The rate of SMP is 90% of their average gross weekly earnings for the first six weeks (with no upper limit) followed by the lower of 90% of their average gross weekly yearnings for the first six weeks or £128.73 (to rise to £135.45 from 1 April 2012) for the next 33 weeks. However, under the Work and Families Act 2006, during the last remaining 13 weeks of the leave the statutory maternity pay allowance (and statutory adoption pay) is available from the job centre or social security office. The previous Government had plans for SMP to be extended to 52 weeks by date of the last election but this never transpired. Women without the 26 weeks service will simply be paid 39 weeks at the SMP rate and this will apply from day one of their employment.

If a woman does not qualify for SMP, her employer should issue a form SMP1 which she can use to support a claim for Maternity Allowance (MA).

A woman who does not qualify for SMP, including the employed and self employed paying class 2 NI contributions (or who have a small earning exemption certificate), may qualify to claim for Maternity Allowance of £128.73 a week (to rise to £135.45 from 1st April 2012) or 90 per cent of gross average weekly earnings whichever is less for 39 weeks.[51]

---

51   Maternity Allowance (Social Security Contributions and Benefits) Act 1992.

The employee may work up to 10 'keeping in touch' days but if she works any more than 10 days she will lose a weeks SMP or Maternity Allowance for each week in which she works.[52]

If a woman becomes entitled to a pay rise during her maternity leave, the employer must recalculate her benefit entitlement.

There are exclusions which apply in the case of SMP and MA to women who are in custody or who go out with the European Economic area.

If the woman does not qualify for SMP or MA then she may qualify for other means tested benefits.[53]

PATERNITY RIGHTS

10.13 Since December 2002 under the Paternity and Adoption Leave Regulations 2002, employees have had right to paternity leave and pay, and to leave and pay on adoption of a child. Paternity leave is available not only to fathers, or indeed not only to men, but is available to a range of employees who have responsibility for newborn infants.

In order to qualify for paternity rights the employee must be the father, spouse, partner or civil partner of the child's mother and if he is the father he must expect to have responsibility for the upbringing of the child. If the employee is the spouse, partner or civil partner, but not the father, he/she must expect to have the main responsibility (apart from the mother) of the upbringing of the child.

Basic Paternity Leave

10.14 In order to qualify for basic paternity leave, the employee must have 26 weeks continuous service with the employer at the end of the week immediately preceding the 14th week before the start of the week when the baby is due. He /she must also still be employed by the employer that week. In order to exercise the right the employee must give the employer notice 15 weeks before the expected week of childbirth.

---

52   Statutory Maternity Pay (General) Regulations 1986 Reg 9A.
53   Detailed guidance and a benefit calculator is available on dti.gov.uk.

If the child dies or is stillborn after 24 weeks of pregnancy the right to basic paternity leave is not lost and if there is a multiple birth only one leave can be exercised.

A qualifying employee is entitled to 2 weeks basic paternity leave. It must be taken in blocks of one or two weeks and must be taken after the child is born and within 56 weeks of the first day of the Expected Week of Childbirth (or within 56 days of the actual date of childbirth if the child is born earlier than the 1st day of the EWC). If the leave is not to commence on the date the child is born, or the first day of the EWC, the employee must give notice of the date the leave will commence.

Additional Paternity Leave

10.15 The Work and Families Act 2006, introduced 26 weeks Additional Paternity Leave and, therefore, permits fathers, spouses and civil partners to take leave equivalent to the period of Additional Maternity Leave, to take over the care of the child if the mother returns to work at the end of Ordinary Maternity Leave. Rights to additional paternity leave can be found in the Additional Paternity Leave Regulations 2010 and, once again, the right is not only available to fathers. The right applies to fathers, spouses, partners and civil partners, the mother of a child due/born on or after April 2011. In order to qualify for additional paternity leave the employee must have 26 weeks continuous service with the employer at the end of the 25th week before the start of the week when the baby is due. He must also still be employed by the employer that week and similar provisions apply regarding responsibility for the care and upbringing of the child, as apply for basic paternity leave. He must be responsible for the care of the child, and the mother must make a written declaration that he is the person entitled to additional paternity leave. The employee must give eight weeks notice before the start of the leave period. He can change the start date by giving the employer notice but if he gives less than six weeks notice of the change of date the employer can defer the start date until six weeks notice has been given if it is not reasonably practicable to accommodate the change.

The Additional Paternity Leave can be taken between 20 weeks and one year after the child is born. This leave can be taken only for the purpose of caring for the child and the child's mother, and the child's mother must have been entitled to Statutory Maternity Leave, Statutory Maternity Pay or Maternity Allowance. She must have returned to work so that Statutory Maternity Pay or Maternity Allowance has stopped. The employer of the employee taking Additional Paternity Leave can request information on the mother's employment details and check that she has returned to work.

The contract of employment continues during this period in the same way that the contract of employment continues during Additional Maternity Leave (see above) the most notable exception being the right to remuneration. The right to return to work after Additional Paternity Leave is to the same job or if that is not reasonably practicable to a suitable job.

Paternity Pay

10.16 In order to qualify for basic Statutory Paternity Pay (SPP) the employee must qualify for and take basic paternity leave, and his/her average earnings in the eight weeks preceding the 14th week before the expected week of childbirth must be at least the lower earnings limit for National Insurance Contributions (currently £102 per week before tax). Paternity pay is paid for the basic 2 weeks paternity leave at the lower rate of statutory maternity pay (currently £128.73 to rise to £135.45 from 1 April 2012) or 90% of the employee's average earnings whichever is lower.

If an employee who is entitled to Additional Paternity Leave is employed and earns at least the lower earnings limit for National Insurance Contributions (currently an average of £102 before tax per week) at the end of the qualifying week mentioned above, he will be entitled to Additional Statutory Paternity Pay. This is calculated in the same way as maternity pay during the period of additional maternity leave. Additional Paternity Pay is only payable during the remainder of the 39 weeks that SMP or MA would have been payable.

Additional Paternity Leave may be taken as unpaid paternity leave where the employee qualifies for leave but not Additional Paternity Pay.

If an employer fails to allow an employee to exercise his right to paternity leave the employee may complain to an employment tribunal. Fathers are protected from detriment or dismissal whilst taking additional paternity leave and have the right to return to work to the same job and on no less favourable terms and conditions.

STATUTORY ADOPTION LEAVE AND PAY

10.17 In the case of an adoption, the couple elect which of them is taking adoptive rights, which are the equivalent of maternity rights, and the other has entitlement to adoptive paternity rights. Either party has the right to parental leave. Entitlement to maternity and paternity leave and pay then operates in the same way as detailed above with a few modifications, in particular, qualification periods run from the date the adopter is notified of a match (Maternity and Paternity Leave) or from the date of adoption (in the case of parental leave).

In the case of children adopted from within the UK, the Adoption Leave (Paternity and Adoption Leave) Regulations 2002 allow an adopter who has not less than 26 weeks continuous service ending with the week in which he/she was notified that a match with a child had been made to take Ordinary Adoption Leave of 26 weeks and Additional Adoption Leave of a further 26 weeks. The employee must advise the employer of the date on which the child is expected to be placed for adoption, and the date leave is due to start, and provide evidence of entitlement to leave. The effect of Ordinary Adoption Leave and Additional Adoption Leave on the contract of employment and the right to return to work are the same as for Ordinary Maternity Leave and Additional Maternity Leave, respectively. There are also similar provisions regarding keeping in touch days.

An adopter who has 26 weeks qualifying service and, in the eight weeks prior to the date the adopter is notified of a match with a child, has earnings which are at or above the lower limit for National Insurance Contributions (currently £102 per week) is eligible for Statutory Adoption Pay which is equivalent to Maternity Pay.

The employer is entitled to recoup these payments in the same way as for SMP or SPP.

The Paternity Leave (Paternity and Adoption Leave Regulations) 2002 allow the spouse, partner or civil partner, of an adopter to take up to two weeks paternity leave in respect of a child who is aged under 18. In order to qualify, the employee must have 26 weeks continuous service ending with the week in which the adopter is notified of a match with a child. The leave must be taken in blocks of one week and must be taken by within 56 weeks of the date of the adoption. The Additional Paternity Leave

Regulations 2010 apply to adopters and the additional leave can be taken any time at least 20 weeks after the child's placement for adoption.

The Additional Paternity Leave (Adoptions from Overseas) Regulations 2010 allow spouses partners and civil partners of adopters to take additional paternity leave of between 2 weeks and 26 weeks in the first year after the child enters the UK.

The Parental Leave (Maternity and Parental Leave) Regulations 1999 make provision for Parental Leave to be exercised by adopters (see below).

PARENTAL LEAVE

10.18 The Parental Leave Directive (96/34/EU) made provision for the parents of young children to be entitled to take leave to care for them, and the Employment Relations Act 1999, and Part III of the Maternity and Parental Leave etc Regulations 1999, and the Employment Act 2002, implement that Directive. Both parents are entitled to parental leave, and unused parental leave cannot be transferred between them. The major drawback with parental leave is that it is unpaid.

In order to qualify for parental leave, the employee must have continuous employment for a period of not less than a year and have, or expect to have, responsibility for a child. The purpose of the leave must be to care for that child.[54]

'Persons who have responsibility' for the child includes anyone who has parental responsibilities for the child under the Children (Scotland) Act 1995 or has been registered as the child's father.

The maximum leave which may be taken is 13 weeks, or 18 weeks in respect of a child who is entitled to disability living allowance. (As from 12 March 2012 the basic 13 week period is likely to be increased to 4 months in line with the new European Directive). In the case of part-time workers leave is calculated pro rata. Leave must be exercised by the child's 5th birthday or, in the case of an adopted child, before the 5th anniversary of the date on which the placement for adoption began, or the child's eighteenth birthday whichever is earlier. In the case of a disabled child it must be exercised before the child's eighteenth birthday.

---

54   Maternity and Parental Leave etc Regulations 1999 Regulation 13.

There are exceptions to these time limits in Schedule 2 of the Regulations and in situations where the employee was not able to take the leave because the employer postponed the leave

Employer and employee are free to agree the manner in which leave is taken, however, if they do not or cannot agree, the default position is that 21 days notice must be given of intention to take leave, leave must be taken in blocks of one week and that no more than 4 weeks can be taken at once. Unless the employee is seeking to take leave from the EWC, or date of adoption, the employer can delay the date leave commences for up to six months if he considers that the operation of his business will be unduly disrupted. If the employee believes that the postponement is unreasonable he may complain to an employment tribunal within three months of the date of refusal, and the tribunal may award such leave as it considers just and equitable.[55] The default scheme is inflexible and does not provide for the situation where an employee simply wishes to take a days leave for the care of a child, eg if child care arrangements fall through.[56] Such leave must be taken as emergency leave for dependents (see below).

The contract of employment continues during the period of parental leave but many of the terms and conditions, including pay, are suspended whilst the employee is on parental leave. The terms which continue are the implied terms as to confidentiality, loyalty, trust and confidence, discipline and grievance procedures and notice periods. The employee has the right to return to the same job if leave is exercised in a block of four weeks or less, but if more than four weeks are taken in a row the employee has the right to return to the same job or if that is not reasonably practicable to a suitable job and appropriate job.[57]

If the employer unreasonably postpones or prevents or attempts to prevent the employee from taking parental leave the employee may complain to an employment tribunal within 3 months of the matters complained of (or within such further period as the tribunal considers reasonable if it is satisfied that it was not reasonably practicable for the complaint to be presented before the end of that period of three months).[58]

---

55   Employment Rights Act 1996 s 80.
56   *Rodway v South Central Trains Ltd* [2005] ICR 1162.
57   Maternity and Parental Leave etc Regulations 1999 Regulation 18.
58   Employment Rights Act 1996 s 80.

CHILD BENEFIT

10.19 Child Benefit[59] is a tax free payment, currently £20.30 in respect of the eldest child and £13.40 per week for each additional child. It is received by the person who has care of the child under 16 and under 18 if in full-time non advanced education. At the time of writing it is not means tested but there are proposals to means test this benefit.

THE EQUALITY ACT 2010

10.20 The original drafting of the Equality Bill prohibited an employer or service provider from treating a woman 'less favourably' for a reason related to pregnancy or maternity. 'Less favourable treatment' was defined as meaning 'being treated less favourable than is reasonable' which in effect would have created a defence of reasonableness in discrimination claims. The relevant clauses in the Equality Act 2010 have been redrafted to prohibit 'unfavourable' (rather than less favourable) treatment on pregnancy or maternity-related grounds. The word 'unfavourable' mirrors the approach in EC law, which does not recognise a defence of reasonableness to discrimination claims.

FLEXIBLE WORKING

10.21 On its introduction in April 2003, the right to request flexible working was restricted to qualifying employees seeking to care for a child under the age of six or a disabled child under the age of 18. From 6 April 2007, the right was extended to those qualifying employees wishing to care for a disabled adult,[60] and from 6 April 2009 it was further extended to encompass those seeking to care for a child under the age of 17.

The right to apply for flexible working, under ERA 1996, applies equally to male and female employees. It is expressly provided that the right to request flexible working does not extend to agency workers.[61] The right is only available to those employees having responsibility for the care of a dependent who falls within the scope of the provisions, ie a

---

59   Child Benefit Act 2005.
60   Ie an adult entitled to disability living allowance.
61   This is an important exclusion since the majority of agency workers are female.

child aged under 17, a disabled child aged under 18 or for the care of a disabled adult.[62] Additionally, the employee must demonstrate he has the prescribed relationship with the child or adult he is seeking to care for.[63]

The employee must have 26 weeks continuous service with the same employer in order to make an application to work flexibly.[64] This means that an employee who anticipates the need to request flexible working arrangements before commencing work, or from the start of his or her employment, is not entitled to request flexible working from the start of the employment.

The provisions confer a right to request a change to contractual terms and conditions to allow a change to hours of work, times of work and the place the employee is required to work (the choice being between his home and the employer's place of business). The provisions do not, by any means, provide a right to insist on working flexibly.

The employee must make the request in writing[65] and follow the procedures set out in the legislation. The employee must detail the likely effect of the request on the employer's business and specify any action which could be taken to mitigate this effect.[66] A further request cannot be made by an employee if a request has been made during the previous year (even if that request has been granted), so, even if circumstances change during the course of the year, the employee is unable to make a further request under these provisions.

Once a valid request is made the employer is obliged to follow the procedures and consider the request. The employer is however, not obliged to grant the request.

On receipt of the request, the employer must either agree the request or hold a meeting within 28 days of the request. The employee making the request is entitled to be accompanied by a co worker. If the request is refused, the employee has the right to appeal within 14 days and a further meeting must be held within 14 days of the date the appeal is lodged.

---

62 S80F(7) Employment Rights Act 1996.
63 Reg 3(1)(b) Flexible Working (Eligibility, Complaints and Remedies) Regulations 2002 SI 2002/3236.
64 Reg 3(1)(a) Flexible Working (Eligibility, Complaints and Remedies) Regulations 2002 SI 2002/3236.
65 Flexible Working (Procedural Requirements) Regulations 2002 SI 2002/3236.
66 S80F(1)(c) Employment Rights Act 1996.

Reasons must be given for the refusal and the grounds on which an employer can lawfully refuse a request are exhaustively listed in s 80G (1) (b) of the Employment Rights Act 1996 (ERA 1996) (as amended), and are:

(i)   the burden of additional costs;

(ii)   detrimental effect on ability to meet customer demand;

(iii)   inability to reorganise work amongst existing staff;

(iv)   inability to recruit additional staff;

(v)   detrimental impact on quality;

(vi)   detrimental impact on performance;

(vii)   insufficiency of work during the periods when the employee proposes to work;

(viii) planned structural changes; and

(ix)   such other grounds as the Secretary of State may specify by regulations.[67]

While some of these are clearly designed to exempt those employers with limited resources, others are extremely broad and will offer exemptions to all employers irrespective of size or resources. Under the Employment Rights Act 1996 there are extremely limited grounds for challenge of a refusal of a flexible working application, namely, that the employer has failed to comply with the correct procedures[68] or a reason has been given for the refusal which is not listed in s 80G(1)(b).[69]

There is no ground of challenge that the employer, although refusing for a lawful reason, is nevertheless acting unreasonably. An employer may, therefore, state that the reason for a refusal is the burden of a minimal additional cost. If that is shown to be the case the tribunal may not interfere with the decision on the basis that that it would be unreasonable for a large multinational company not to absorb this cost.

If an employer follows the correct procedure, and selects a section 80G (1) (b) reason as a ground for refusal, the employee has very little hope of forcing a reluctant employer to agree to a change in their working

---

67   Section 80G Employment Rights Act 1996.

68   Ie the procedures set out in s 80G(1) Employment Rights Act 1996 and the Flexible Working (Eligibility, Complaints and Remedies) Regulations 2002 SI 2002/3236.

69   Section 80H Employment Rights Act 1996.

practice, however, in the case of *Commotion Ltd v Rutty,*[70] the EAT stated that the tribunal was entitled to investigate the evidence to see whether the decision was based on incorrect facts and to look at the ground which the employer asserts is the reason why he had not granted the application to see whether it is factually correct. They also suggested that the tribunal is entitled to enquire what the effect of granting the application would have been, whether it could have been coped with without disruption, what were the feelings of the other staff and whether the time could be made up.[71]

In the event that a tribunal finds that there has been an unlawful refusal, it can make a declaration to that effect and order the employer to reconsider the request and it can award compensation, but the financial award is restricted to a maximum of 8 weeks pay and the maximum weeks pay is £430 (at this time),[72] so the maximum award possible is therefore £3,440.[73]

An employee who has been unlawfully refused the right to work flexibly may resign and claim unfair dismissal, since the unlawful refusal will amount to repudiation of the contract by the employer.[74] Similarly a refusal, without good reason, where other employees have been granted flexible working will be a breach of the implied term of trust and confidence. The onus will be on the employer to show that the reason for dismissal was one of the potentially fair reasons for dismissal in terms of the Employment Rights Act 1996, s 98. The reason for the dismissal will be the employee's inability to work full-time and under non flexible conditions. This will fall under the potentially fair reasons of capability, or some other substantial reason,[75] and the test which the tribunal will use to ascertain whether the dismissal was fair is whether the dismissal was within the range of responses which a reasonable employer might have adopted.[76]

---

70 [2006] ICR290.

71 [2006] ICR290 Judge Burke QC at 38.

72 £430 a week from February 2012.

73 The Flexible Working (Eligibility, Complaints and Remedies Regulations 2002 SI 2002/3236 reg 7).

74 *Commotion v Rutty* supra.

75 Section 98 Employment Rights Act 1996.

76 *HSBC v Madden* [2000] ICR 1283, *Iceland Frozen Foods v Jones* [1982] IRLR 439.

This remedy is superior to that available for a refusal of a flexible working request as it is possible to award a far higher level of compensation.

A refusal to allow flexible working because of the sex of the person making the request is direct discrimination. If an employer allows a female employee to work flexibly, but refuses a request from a male employee in the same position because he is male, this would be direct sex discrimination. If (and only if) there is no real female comparator a hypothetical comparator could be used.[77] Therefore, to refuse a man the opportunity to work flexibly in circumstances where a woman would have been granted a request (even where one has never been made) could also amount to direct sex discrimination. The protection against direct discrimination is equivalent in the case of both a male employee and a female employee. If an employee is successful in establishing direct discrimination then the employer will not be able to use the defence of justification which applies in cases of indirect discrimination. If however an employer refuses flexible working requests from all employees regardless of sex then there will be no discrimination against the man (regardless of whether the requests are lawful or not under the ERA 1996 provisions). The female employee is in a far better position to challenge this refusal since she has probably suffered indirect discrimination.[78]

In order to establish indirect sex discrimination, the female employee will have to show that the employer has imposed a provision criterion or practice (PCP) by refusing her request *or by some other means*. A refusal to allow most forms of flexible working is capable of constituting a 'provision criterion or practice', for example a refusal to allow part time working,[79] refusal to allow job share,[80] imposition of shift patterns[81] and refusal to allow working from home.[82] The same arguments will apply to other forms of flexible working.

---

77 *Shamoon v Chief Constable of The Royal Ulster Constabulary* [2003] UKHL 11, [2003] ICR 337, *Balamoody v United Kingdom Central Council for Nursing, Midwifery and Health Visiting* [2002] IRLR 288.
78 Equality Act 2010 s 19.
79 *Home Office v Holmes* [1985] 1WLR 71.
80 *Hardy and Hanson Plc v Lax* [2005] ICR 1565.
81 *London Underground v Edwards (No2)* [1998] IRLR 364.
82 *Lockwood v Crawley Warren Group Ltd*[2001] Emp LR 322.

Since the protection is extended to the terms on which the job is offered,[83] a woman who is offered a job on a non flexible basis does not qualify to make an ERA 1996 flexible working request, she may still claim indirect sex discrimination if the employer refuses to offer her the job on more flexible terms.

Once a PCP has been identified, the employee will have to show that this PCP places one sex at a particular disadvantage compared to the other. In earlier cases the courts seemed willing to accept that it was common knowledge that women would be less able to comply with such a PCP.[84] Some tribunals however look for statistics to back up this assertion including an accurate identification of the correct pool of comparators.[85] Statistical evidence is likely to shows that the majority of carers of disabled adults are women.[86] Therefore a female employee refused the option of working flexibly to look after a disabled adult will also have the option of claiming indirect sex discrimination.[87]

A male employee refused flexible working will not win a claim of indirect sex discrimination under the Equality Act 2010, as he will be unable to satisfy this element of the definition of indirect discrimination. A woman whose flexible working request is refused will not automatically be able to claim indirect discrimination. In order to succeed in a claim for indirect discrimination, the woman will additionally need to demonstrate that the refusal causes her *personally* a detriment.[88] The woman will, therefore, have to show that the detriment is more than mere inconvenience, therefore a PCP which makes it slightly more difficult to care for a child or adult dependent may not be sufficient. She must also show that the

---

83   Equality Act 2010 s 39.
84   *Home Office v Holmes* [1985] 1 WLR 71.
85   *Pearce v City of Bradford Metropolitan Council* [1988] IRLR 378 EAT, *Kidd v DRG (UK) Ltd* [1985] IRLR 190, EAT.
86   According to Census Carers UK 2001 across the UK 58% of carers are female compared with 42% of men, and according to Central Statistics Unit (2004) Community Care Statistics 2002 Scottish Executive Edinburgh, in Scotland the percentage of female carers is even higher 62% compared to 38% male carers.
87   Since certain ethnic communities have higher proportions of male carers than others it is also theoretically possible that in some circumstances a man refused flexible working will be able to claim indirect race discrimination.
88   *MacMillan v Ministry of Defence (Royal Navy)* EAT (Scotland) 22 September 2004.

detriment does not result from personal choices she has made, rather than the imposition of the PCP of non flexible working.

The category of persons protected by the Equality Act 2010 is much broader and includes office holders,[89] self employed, and agency workers who are required to provide personal service and, unlike the 26 weeks continuous service required under the flexible working provisions of ERA 1996, a woman requires no service at all to qualify under the equality provisions. Unlike the ERA 1996 provisions there are no particular procedural requirements and the request can be made at any time, even if a previous request has been refused. The request need not be in writing and, indeed, she may not actually have made a request at all. The PCP may have been imposed, for example, by the employer advertising a job as full-time or stating a general policy that employees are expected to work full-time, or that they must not work from home. It is not necessary to show a general policy of refusing to allow flexible working, as a refusal on one occasion will be sufficient to amount to a PCP.[90]

Obviously the right to work flexibly is not absolute even under the Equal Treatment Directive but, unlike the exhaustive list of lawful grounds for refusal available under the ERA 1996, the employer will only be able to refuse flexible working if he can show that his PCP is 'a proportionate means of achieving a legitimate aim'.[91] The test which he must satisfy is an objective test[92] which is a reformulation of the decision in *Bilka-KaufhausGmbH v Weber von Harz*.[93]

Because of the requirement of proportionality, it is more difficult for an employer to refuse to allow a woman to work flexibly under the equality legislation. The employer, when giving reasons for a refusal, must realise that he does not only have to meet the limited requirements of ERA 1996 but, in the case of a *female* employee who is likely to claim indirect sex discrimination, the onus is on the employer to justify his decision and he must be able to show that:

89 *Percy v Church of Scotland Board of National Mission* [2005] UKHL 73, [2006] 2AC28.
90 *British Airways v Starmer* [2005] IRLR 863.
91 Equality Act 2010 section 1992 (d).
92 *Hardy and Hanson v Lax* [2005] ICR 1565.
93 [1986] IRLR 317.

(1)   the objective is sufficiently important to justify limiting a fundamental right;

(2)   the refusal to all the employee to work flexibly is rationally connected to the objective;

(3)   the measures chosen are no more than is necessary to accomplish the objective.[94]

Each of the grounds listed in s 80 G (1) (b) of ERA 1996 is likely to be considered, in the context of anti-discrimination law, to be a real need of the organisation and, as such, a legitimate aim for imposing a PCP but, whereas under the ERA 1996 provisions reasonableness and proportionality are not considered, under discrimination legislation, the employer must also establish that the imposition of the PCP is a proportionate response to that need. Therefore, although an employer may use a small additional cost as a reason to refuse a request under ERA 1996, this will be open to challenge under the Equality Act 2010 because, although keeping costs down may be a legitimate aim, the employer's refusal may not be a proportionate means of achieving that aim. Depending on the size and profit margins of the organisation, the employer may be expected to absorb that expense.[95] Health and safety is not specifically listed as a ground for refusal under s 80G (10(b) ERA 1996 but might be accepted as a possible justification of indirect discrimination.[96]

Detrimental impact on quality and detrimental impact on performance are both valid grounds for refusal of a flexible working application according to s 80G (1) (b) ERA 1996, but they will not automatically be accepted as justification in a claim of indirect discrimination.[97]

It is clear that it is more difficult for an employer to refuse flexible working under the anti-discrimination provisions than under ERA 1996 and if a discrimination claim is successful the remedies conferred under this legislation are much more satisfactory than the ERA 1996 remedies

---

94   *R (on the application of Elias) v Secretary of State for Defence* [2006] IRLR 934.

95   *Schonheit v Stadt Frankfurt am Main* 2003 ECR I-12572 and *Steinicke v Bundesanstadt fur arbeit* Case C-77/02 [2003] ECR I-9027. *Cross v British Airways plc* [2005] IRLR 423.

96   *Sing v British Rail Engineering* [1986] ICR 22 *but see British Airways v Starmer* [2005] IRLR 863.

97   *Craddock v Cornwall County Council and anor* [2005] UKEAT 0367 05 1912.

for refusal of a flexible working request or unfair dismissal. The tribunal can make a declaration that there was unlawful discrimination, it can make recommendations of courses of actions to be followed by the employer and it may award compensation[98] but, most importantly, in this case, there is no upper limit to compensation and compensation may be awarded for hurt feelings.[99]

TIME OFF FOR URGENT FAMILY REASONS

10.22 Another right which derives originally from the Parental Leave Directive (96/34/EU) is the right to time off for urgent family reasons. It was implemented by the Employment Relations Act 1999 which amended the Employment Rights Act 1996. Under s 57A of the Employment Rights Act 1996, an employee is entitled to be permitted by an employer to take a reasonable amount of time off work during the employee's working hours in order to take action which is necessary:

(a)   to provide assistance where a dependant falls ill, gives birth or is injured or assaulted;

(b)   to make care provisions for ill dependant;

(c)   to make arrangements in the event of a death of a dependant;

(d)   to deal with unexpected disruption or termination of care arrangement for a dependant; or

(e)   an unexpected incident which involves a child of the employee at school etc

A dependant for these purposes is a spouse, child or a parent or person living in the same household.[100] In relation to (a) above 'dependant' includes anyone who relies on the employee for assistance. This is a wide definition and includes friend and neighbours. Emergency leave is unpaid and the employee cannot be asked to work the time later. The employee should give such notice as is reasonably practicable in the circumstances.[101]

---

98   Equality Act 2010 s 124.

99   Equality Act 2010 s 124 (6). For guidance on the quantification of such damages *Vento Chief Constable of West Yorkshire* [2002] EWCA Civ 1871, [2003] IRLR 102.

100   Section 57A (3)–(5) ERA 1996.

101   Section 57A (2) ERA 1996; *Truelove v Safeway Stores Plc* [2005] ICR 589.

What is considered reasonable will depend on the facts and circumstances of each case but emergency leave is intended to be for situations which arise unexpectedly, although not necessarily suddenly[102] and not intended as a long term solution. Therefore, if a child is off sick for any length of time the employee will be expected to make arrangements for care or use another form of leave.[103] The emergency leave in connection with a death is for the purpose of making funeral and other immediate arrangements, but not for coming to terms with the death.[104] Where leave is unreasonably refused, an employee can make a complaint to the employment tribunal within three months of the date of refusal (or within such further period as the tribunal sees fit if it was not reasonably practicable to present the complaint within 3 months).[105] The tribunal can make a declaration and award the amount of compensation it feels is just and equitable, having regard to:

(a)   the employer's default in refusing to permit time off to be taken by the employee, and

(b)   any loss sustained by the employee which is attributable to the matters complained of.

There is also the right not to suffer a detriment[106] as a consequence of taking time off work and it will be automatically unfair to dismiss someone for exercising this right. The employer must, therefore, make enquiries before disciplining or dismissing anyone who has taken unauthorised absence to ensure that he/she is not exercising this right.

DETRIMENT AND DISMISSAL RELATED TO THE EXERCISE OF FAMILY FRIENDLY RIGHTS

10.23 Dismissal and detriment related to the exercise of family friendly rights generally is governed by part V of the Employment Rights Act 1996. Section 47C provides that an employee has the right not to be

---

102 *Royal Bank of Scotland Plc v Harrison* [2009] ICR 116.
103 *Qua v John Ford Morrison Solicitors* [2003] IRLR 184; *Cortest Ltd v O'Toole* UKEAT/0470/07/LA.
104 *Forster v Cartright Black* [2004] IRLR 781.
105 Employment Rights act 1996 s 57B.
106 Section 47(C) ERA 1996.

subject to any detriment by any act, or any deliberate failure to act, by his employer done for a reason relating to:

(a)   pregnancy, childbirth or maternity,

(b)   maternity leave,

(c)   adoption leave,

(d)   parental leave,

(e)   paternity leave, or

(f)   time off for dependents.

Section 47 (e) provides similar protection from detriment on the ground that the employee has made or proposed to make an application for flexible working, exercised a right relating to flexible working brought proceedings against the employer in relation to a refusal to allow flexible working, or alleged the existence of any circumstance which would constitute a ground for bringing such proceedings.

If subjected to such a detriment the employee may complain to the employment tribunal within three months of the act (or the decision not to act in the case of an omission), the last act in the case of a series of continuing acts or such other further period as the tribunal considers reasonable in a case where it is satisfied that it was not reasonably practicable for the complaint to be presented before the end of that period of three months.[107]

If the tribunal finds the claim well founded it shall make a declaration and award such compensation as it considers just and equitable. There is no upper limit to the compensation which may be awarded. The claimant is expected to mitigate his loss and the award may be reduced in respect of any contributory action by the complainant.[108]

---

107 Employment Rights Act 1996 s 48.
108 Employment Rights Act 1996 s 49.

Chapter 11

Wages

11.1 This chapter will be concerned with covering the legal rules derived from statute law controlling the payment of wages to employees and workers including the national minimum wage, unlawful deductions of wages and equal pay (excluding discrimination in terms of pay which is dealt with in the chapter on equality law).

THE NATIONAL MINIMUM WAGE

Background

11.2 Although prior to the National Minimum Wage Act 1998 there had been examples of minimum wage levels in the UK, particularly in low paid industries, there was no universal minimum wage.[1] The Trade Boards Act of 1909 created four bodies (trade boards) that set minimum wages, which varied between industries, for a number of sectors where collective bargaining was not well established. This system was extended considerably after the Second World War, in 1945, when the Trades Boards became Wages Councils.[2] These bodies set minimum wage standards in many sectors of the economy including the service sector and manufacturing. The Wages Councils were finally abolished in 1993 as they were viewed by the Conservative Government at the time as acting in opposition to their social policy and they had by this time fallen into decline due, in large part, to the opposition to the Trade Union movement.[3] There then followed a period without any statutory minimum wage

---

1   The Fair Wage Resolutions (FWR) were introduced in 1891 in an attempt to eliminate unfair competition for public sector contracts based on undercutting recognised pay rates. These FWRs were in place for ninety years.
2   It peaked with coverage of 3.5 million workers in 1953.
3   A lower limit of pay, or 'pay floor' was regarded as threatening the voluntary system of collective bargaining favoured in the UK.

(except in agriculture) which operated until the introduction of the new minimum wage in 1998 following a change of Government.

National Minimum Wage Act 1998

11.3 This Act extends rights to workers and provides a definition of Worker under ss 1(2), 3 and 54(3). It defines a worker as a person who works under a contract of employment (including an apprenticeship), or any other contract, whether express or implied, and if it is express, whether oral or in writing, whereby the individual undertakes to perform personally any work or services for another party to the contract whose status is not by virtue of the contract that of a client or customer of any profession or business undertaking carried on by the individual

This covers a wide range of working relationships including employees; apprentices; agency workers; casual workers; homeworkers and crown employees. The National Minimum Wage Act (Amendment) Regulations 1999 extended coverage of s 3 of the Act to include workers under relevant training schemes eg New Deal and workers undertaking training, NVQ etc.

The Act, as amended by the NMWA (Amendment) Regulations 1999, specifies the type of work covered: (a) time work, paid in relation to the time actually worked; (b) output work (paid on piecework or commission basis); (c) non-hours work (e.g. those working on premises available 24 hours a day); and (d) salaried hours work which attempts to include those people covered by payment systems which provide for the workers to be paid the same amount in each pay period regardless of fluctuations in the amount of work carried out.

Basic principle

11.4 The basic principle underlying the Act is that all workers in the United Kingdom who are above compulsory school leaving age and not exempted by one of the ways specified by the Act (e.g. voluntary workers), and detailed in the Regulations (see below), are entitled to be paid at an hourly rate which is at least that recommended by the Low Pay Commission and set by the Secretary of State each year.

Those affected most by the introduction of the National Minimum Wage (NMW) were women, part-time workers, 'atypical' workers (for example, seasonal or casual workers), younger employees, workers with disabilities or those working for small employers (under 25 employees). Also most of those persons work in certain parts of the private sector (especially hospitality, retail, social and personnel services, and healthcare). Persons that are genuinely self-employed are not entitled to receive the NMW.

Rate of pay

11.5 Initially in 1998 the minimum wage was £3.60 an hour for workers 22 years old or more, which normally increases in October of each year. It increased to £5.35 from October 2006, from 1 October 2007 the national minimum wage was £5.52 per hour and from October 2009 it was £5.80 per hour. The rate is uniform and applies regardless of occupation, size of the employers business, location or employment sector. The three levels of minimum wage rates that applied from 1 October 2010 were: £5.93 per hour for workers aged 22 years and older; a development rate of £4.92 per hour for workers aged 18–21 inclusive and £3.64 per hour for all workers under the age of 18, who are no longer of compulsory school age. From October 2011 the hourly rate will be £6.08 for workers aged 22 or over, for workers aged 18–21 will be £4.98 and for those under 18 who are no longer of compulsory school age £3.68.

Exemptions and restrictions

11.6 The following workers are exempt from the Act or have restricted rights:

(a)   Apprentices – The Act specifies that apprentices under age 19 will not qualify for the national minimum wage, and for apprentices over 19 but in the first 12 months of their apprenticeship will not qualify;

(b)   Workers who are participating in a scheme under which shelter is provided in return for work are exempted;

(c)   Voluntary workers as defined by s 44 of the Act;

(d)   Students who are on a work experience scheme of not more than one year (eg teacher training, sandwich course) are excluded from its coverage;

(e)   If someone is working a company director as an 'office holder' they are not entitled to receive the National Minimum Wage for the work they do in this capacity

(f)   Certain government schemes at pre-apprenticeship level – If someone is taking part in one of the these schemes they are not entitled to the National Minimum Wage and in Scotland the schemes are Get Ready for Work or Skillseekers Led Apprenticeships.

Others who are exempt are:
- the genuinely self-employed
- residents of certain religious communities
- prisoners
- members of the armed forces
- share fishermen.

Pay reference period

11.7 The pay reference period is one month, or where a worker is paid at a shorter interval then that period. The NMW applies to all monies paid by the employer to the worker in that period.

Excluded from pay

11.8 The following are not include in the calculation of pay:
(a)   allowances (eg dirty work allowance, danger money, responsibility allowance, attendance allowance;[4]

(b)   benefits in kind (such as luncheon vouchers);

(c)   loans or advance of wages, pension payments, payments awarded by tribunals etc.

---

4   See *Aviation & Airport Services Ltd v Bellfield and others* 16.3.00 EAT194/00 where a weekly allowance payable to employees subject to full attendance in a given week was not attributable to the performance of the worker in carrying out his work. It was therefore not remuneration counting towards the minimum wage.

Deductions

11.9 The following must be subtracted from total pay:

(a)   any payment in current Pay Reference Period (PRP) which relates to previous PRP;

(b)   any payment made when worker was absent from work (extends to rest breaks, not to travelling in connection with work and training).

(c)   any payments made over and above normal hourly rate (eg overtime, shift allowance),

(d)   any allowances,

(e)   service charges, tips, gratuities, and

(f)   reimbursement of expenses.

In *Wright v Scottbridge Construction Ltd,*[5] a night watchman was required to be present on the employer's premises for up to 14 hours per day and was held to be entitled to be paid NMW for whole 14 hours. He was only required to fulfil tasks for four hours after which time he could sleep. However, as there was no set hours for sleeping specified in the contract the situation was not covered by regulation 15(1) which allows employer not to pay for the hours that an employee is asleep.

Record keeping

11.10 Employers must keep records sufficient to establish they are paying workers at a rate at least equal to the NMW. If a worker has reasonable grounds for suspecting that he is being paid less than the NMW he can require his employer to produce records (showing his compliance with NMW in respect of his pay) to receive a copy of them and to inspect or examine them. A failure in this respect by the employer gives workers the right to complain to an employment tribunal. They have the power to declare rights and can award up to 80 times the national minimum wage. There are also criminal penalties for employers failing to keep records or falsifying records.

---

5   2003 SC 520.

Enforcement by individual workers

11.11

(a) If a worker does not receive his contractual entitlement to the NMW he can take an action to the Sheriff Court for breach of contract.

(b) He can also treat the shortfall as an unauthorised deduction and bring an action before an employment tribunal on that basis as a breach of Part 11 of the Employment Rights Act 1996 (wages provisions)

(c) The legislation provides protection to workers against being subjected to a detriment because they are enforcing rights under the Act.

(d) It will be an automatically unfair dismissal where the employer dismisses a worker because he is asserting his statutory rights.

Any attempt to reduce an allowance in order to circumvent payment of the minimum wage or unilaterally reduce wages, could give rise to an action under the Act and/or under the wages legislation.[6]

Enforcement by officers

11.12 Enforcement Officers who work for the Inland Revenue and are appointed by the Secretary of State enforce the legislation. They have the right to inspect and examine employers' records, seek an explanation of them, to be given additional information and to enter premises at all reasonable times. They can also serve an enforcement notice which requires an employer to pay an employee the NMW. Under the National Minimum Wage (Enforcement Notices) Act 2003, there is a requirement to pay the NMW to current or former workers. Although there is a six year limit so enforcement notices must not relate to payments made more than six years in the past.

The sanctions for non-compliance with the enforcement notice are to make a complaint on behalf of the worker to an employment tribunal or civil court. They can serve an employer with a notice which requires them

---

6   *Laird v AK Stoddart* (2001) IRLR 591.

to pay a financial penalty to the Secretary of State. This is a civil fine of twice the amount of NMW for each day the employer does not comply. However there is a right of appeal to the Employment Appeal Tribunal.

In *Inland Revenue Wales & Midlands v Bebb Travel PLC*,[7] it was held that enforcement notices under s 19 of the NMW Act 1998 must relate to current or future failures to pay minimum wage as a notice only relates to pay reference periods ending on or after date of service of notice.

Criminal penalties

11.13 It is an offence to refuse or wilfully neglect to pay the National Minimum Wage to any worker who qualifies or to obstruct an officer, fail to keep proper records etc

In the first criminal prosecution for breach of the national minimum wage legislation a London nursery owner was fined £3,000 for paying his workers below the national minimum wage.[8] Also Torbay Council was fined £1,000 for not providing correct national minimum wage information to the HM Revenue and Customs.[9]

Research

11.14 Research was undertaken to determine the effectiveness of the NMW Act in controlling low wages.[10] The research findings were that awareness of the main NMW rate was limited and complexities of the lower development rate at the time meant that knowledge of it was very low amongst employers and workers. There was a lower number of persons benefiting from Act than was anticipated. Although the legislators thought 1.9 million workers would benefit from the NMW each year it actually only benefitted 1.3 million workers in 2001 and only 1.2 million workers benefitted in 2003. The researchers found that generally there was a low level of awareness amongst workers concerning the levels of pay they were entitled to. They also found that when Inland Revenue

---

7   (2002) IRLR 783.
8   Berry, M Personnel Today, 29 August 2007 www.personneltoday.com.
9   Ibid.
10   Bob Simpson, The National Minimum Wage Five Years On: Reflections on Some General Issues, Industrial Law Journal, Vol. 33, March 2004 pp 22–41.

inspectors were informed by workers that they were suffering detrimental treatment at the hands of the employer they were not willing to pass the fact onto ACAS or other interested parties. Interestingly from 1999–2003 out of the 83 cases that went to an employment tribunal involving appeals against enforcement and penalty notices and actions to enforce worker's rights where enforcement notice not complied with, revenue officers were successful in 77 of these cases. Over the years 2002 to 2006 the adult minimum wage was increased by 27.4% while average earnings increased by only 17%. More recently only 0.9 million workers benefitted from changes in the NMW. In 2005, 3.6 million workers benefited in 2006 and in 2008/09 around 1 million workers benefitted.

Low Pay Commission

11.15 They have identified ten industrial sectors of the economy in which low pay is common. Together they provide over eight million jobs, nearly a third of all jobs in the economy.

The two largest sectors are retail and hospitality accounting for nearly two-thirds of jobs in the low-paid workforce. Of course many of the jobs in both these sectors are paid at a level well above the minimum wage.

Current issues

11.16 In January 2007, the Previous Government announced its plan to review the minimum wage in relation to voluntary workers. It carried out a consultation in 2007 which resulted in *no* change to the law see www.berr.gov.uk for the Previous Government's response. The Previous Government's also desired to strengthen the enforcement regime as they believed there was no effective deterrent to non-compliance and no real disincentive for firms not to comply with Act see below. Approximately one million workers benefitted when the national minimum wage (NMW) increased to £5.73 per hour on Wednesday 1 October according to the TUC. Two-thirds of the beneficiaries were women, reinforcing the NMW's positive role in narrowing the gender pay gap.

From 1 October 2009, tips, service charges, gratuities and cover charges can no longer be used to make up the National Minimum Wage. This means that eligible workers will receive at least the National Minimum Wage in base pay with any tips being paid on top. Additional measures are being introduced through a voluntary code of best practice to improve the information to customers and workers. It provides practical guidance on how to operate in a fair and transparent way and should ensure that businesses are able to provide their customers with sufficient information to make an informed choice before they leave a tip or gratuity or pay a service charge.

From 6 April 2009, employers face a penalty if HM Revenue and Customs (HMRC) discover they have failed to pay the national minimum wage, and workers are entitled to have arrears of wages repaid at current rates. These changes were brought in by the Employment Act 2008. The Act also gave HMRC compliance officers new inspection powers, and strengthened the criminal regime for national minimum wage offences. If HMRC find that there has been an underpayment of the national minimum wage, in an investigation that is ongoing from 6 April 2009, they may issue a notice of underpayment requiring the employer to repay arrears to the workers and to pay a financial penalty to the Secretary of State. Employers are able to appeal against the notice of underpayment to the employment tribunal. The Employment Act 2008 gave HMRC the power to use the search and seize powers in the Police and Criminal Evidence Act 1984 when investigating criminal offences, under the National Minimum Wage Act 1998. The Act also made changes to the way that criminal offences under the National Minimum Wage Act 1998, are investigated and enforced: in particular, with effect from 6 April 2009, the most serious cases are can be tried in the Crown Court in England and Sheriff Court in Scotland. This means that employers who deliberately fail to pay the minimum wage may face stiffer penalties.

WAGES LEGISLATION

11.17 The legal rules controlling unlawful deduction of wages were originally provided by the Wages Act 1986, and can now be found in the Employment Rights Act 1996 (ERA 1996). These statutory provisions provide various definitions which spell out in detail the scope of the law.

Definition of wages

11.18 Section 27(1) of ERA 1996 defines wages as:

(a) any fee, bonus, commission, holiday pay, any other emolument referable to his or her employment.

(b) statutory sick pay under Part XI of the Social Security Contributions and Benefits Act 1992,

(c) statutory maternity pay under Part XII of that Act,

(d) ordinary statutory paternity pay or additional statutory paternity pay under Part 12ZA of that Act,

(c) statutory adoption pay under Part 12ZB of that Act,

(d) a guarantee payment (under s 28 of Employment Rights Act 1996),

(e) any payment for time off under Part VI of the Employment Rights Act 1996 or s 169 of the Trade Union and Labour Relations (Consolidation) Act 1992 (payment for time off for carrying out trade union duties etc),

(f) remuneration on suspension on medical grounds under s 64 of the Act, and remuneration on suspension on maternity grounds under s 68 of the Act,

(g) any sum payable in pursuance of an order for reinstatement or re-engagement under s 113 of the Act,

(h) any sum payable in pursuance of an order for the continuation of a contract of employment under s 130 of the Act or s 164 of the Trade Union and Labour Relations (Consolidation) Act 1992, and

(j) remuneration under a protective award under s 189 of the Act.

Exclusion from wages

11.19 Section 27(2) set out various payment which will be excluded from wages namely:

(a) Any payment by way of an advance of wages

(b) Any payment to the worker otherwise than in his capacity as a worker

(c)   Any payment in respect of expenses incurred by the worker in carrying out his/her employment

(d)   Any payment referable to a workers redundancy

(e)   Any payment by way of pension, allowance or gratuity in connection with the workers retirement or as compensation for loss of office

(f)   Any payment to the worker, otherwise than in his or her capacity as a worker.

In *Delaney v Staples*,[11] Mrs Delaney brought a claim in respect of her employer's failure to pay her commission and accrued holiday pay on the termination of her employment. In addition she claimed £82 in respect of her employer's failure to pay her in lieu of notice.

Regarding this latter claim, the Industrial Tribunal ruled that it did not constitute wages under s 7 of the Wages Act 1986 (now ERA 1996) as was in effect a claim for damages for wrongful dismissal. The House of Lords[12] upheld the tribunal ruling, finding that a payment in lieu of notice was not wages where it relates to a period after the termination of employment. There is only one situation where the wages legislation applies to termination of employment, which is garden leave, ie where an employee does not work his notice, but stays at home and cannot work for a competitor and the employer gives him wages attributable to that period. In the other situations involving payment in lieu of wages, employees can make a claim before an employment tribunal under the breach of contract jurisdiction or as a basis for case of wrongful dismissal in the ordinary courts.

In *Kent Management Services v Butterfield*,[13] an employee, Butterfield was told that in addition to his salary he would be able to participate in commission and bonus schemes, although they would be *ex gratia* and discretionary. On his dismissal he was paid all due salaries to him, but was told he would not receive the amount of outstanding commission as the company were exercising their discretion to refuse it. The EAT held that, although the commission was discretionary and non-contractual, it was… commission… referable to his employment, whether payable under

---

11   (1991) IRLR 191 (HL).

12   *Delaney v Staples* (1992) IRLR 191 (HL).

13   (1992) IRLR 394.

his contract or otherwise... Therefore it was a sum payable to him in connection with his employment, a wage, and he was entitled to receive the amount which he had already earned.

Definition of deductions

11.20 Deductions are not defined in the Act but, s 13(3) of the ERA 1996 provides that, where the total amount of wages that are paid on any occasion by an employer to any worker employed by him is less than the total amount of the wages that are properly payable to him on that occasion then, the amount of the deficiency is to be treated as a deduction made by the employer from the worker's wages.

Deductions excluded from application of the Act are set out under s 14 of the 1996 Act are considered below.

Authorised deductions

11.21 The underlying principle of the legislation in s 13(1) of ERA 1996 is that an employer must not make any deductions from the wages of any worker he employs unless they are: (a) authorised or required by statute; (b) authorised by a provision in a worker's contract; or (c) a worker has previously signified in writing his agreement or consent to the deduction.

In *Pename Ltd v Patterson*,[14] it was held that an employee's oral agreement to a deduction from his wages was not sufficient to justify it as per s 13 ERA 1996.

It was decided in *Kerr v The Sweater Shop (Scotland) Ltd*,[15] regarding notification of deductions from wages authorised by the contract under s 13(2)(b) of ERA 1996, that it is not enough to place a notice in a factory, the employer must inform all workers individually.

The employer clearly has to communicate individually any deduction from wages even if they are authorised. However, if deductions are mutually agreed between employers and trade unions (but subject to review), and contractually binding, then the trade unions and their members may lose

---

14   (1989) IRLR 195.
15   (1996) IRLR 424 EAT.

the right to be consulted about future changes brought in by the employer. In *Airlie and others v City of Edinburgh District Council*,[16] it was held that an incentive bonus scheme which was mutually agreed to by the employer and a trade union, and which had become incorporated into employee's contracts, was able to be changed without the agreement of trade unions and employees affected. It was enough that trade unions had agreed that this aspect of wages should be subject to regular review.

In *Potter v Hunt Contracts Ltd*,[17] a payment of fees by an employer made on behalf of an employee for a training course they attended was accompanied by a letter which the employee signed stating that he agreed that, in the event he left the company, he would repay the fees. It was held this was not an authorised deduction from wages, as it was not clear in the letter that the money would be deducted through wages, and it was therefore an unlawful deduction.

The issue in these cases does not always involve a straightforward analysis of whether pay has been unlawfully deducted. In *Greg May (CF & C) Ltd v Dring*,[18] the employer refused to pay accrued holiday pay to an employee on dismissal. An express term of the employee's contract provided that accrued holiday pay would not be paid if the employee was dismissed for gross misconduct. The employment tribunal in this case investigated the claim that the employee was guilty of gross misconduct. They held the behaviour did not constitute misconduct and the holiday pay was properly payable.

The following are excepted deductions, under s 14 of the ERA 1996, so s 13 does not apply to:

(1)   a deduction from a worker's wages made by his employer where the purpose of the deduction is the reimbursement of the employer in respect of:

(a)   an overpayment of wages, or

(b)   an overpayment in respect of expenses incurred by the worker in carrying out his employment, made (for any reason) by the employer to the worker.

---

16   (1996) IRLR 516.
17   (1992) IRLR 108.
18   (1990) IRLR 19.

(2)   a deduction from a worker's wages made by his employer in consequence of any disciplinary proceedings if those proceedings were held by virtue of a statutory provision.

(3)   a deduction from a worker's wages made by his employer in pursuance of a requirement imposed on the employer by a statutory provision to deduct and pay over to a public authority amounts determined by that authority as being due to it from the worker, if the deduction is made in accordance with the relevant determination of that authority (eg tax and national insurance).

(4)   a deduction from a worker's wages made by his employer in pursuance of any arrangements which have been established:

(a)   in accordance with a relevant provision of his contract to the inclusion of which in the contract the worker has signified his agreement or consent in writing, (eg car parking fees), or

(b)   otherwise with the prior agreement or consent of the worker signified in writing, and under which the employer is to deduct and pay over to a third person amounts notified to the employer by that person as being due to him from the worker, if the deduction is made in accordance with the relevant notification by that person (eg council tax).

(5)   a deduction from a worker's wages made by his employer where the worker has taken part in a strike or other industrial action and the deduction is made by the employer on account of the worker's having taken part in that strike or other action.

(6)   a deduction from a worker's wages made by his employer, with his prior agreement or consent, signified in writing, where the purpose of the deduction is the satisfaction (whether wholly or in part) of an order of a court or tribunal requiring the payment of an amount by the worker to the employer.

Variation of Contract

11.22 If the variation in contract is as a result of a unilateral change to the contract by the employer, then any resulting reduction in wages may contravene s 13 of the ERA 1996.

In *McCree v London Borough of Tower Hamlets*,[19] an employer introduced a new bonus system which absorbed a supplement previously paid to an employee. The unilateral abolition of the supplement was a breach of legislation as it was an unlawful deduction. In *Bruce v Wiggins Teape (Stationery) Ltd*,[20] Mr Bruce had been employed on a rolling night shift in January 1989 with an agreement for an enhanced overtime rate. In November 1992 his employer varied this term of his contract by reducing the pay to the normal level of pay without consulting the employee or his trade union. Bruce continued to work under protest but claimed that the reduction amounted to an unlawful deduction under the Wages Act 1986. The EAT held on appeal that the Industrial Tribunal had erred in law holding that a reduction in pay was not a deduction.

Remedies and procedure

11.23 The initial expectation would be that where a worker suffers a deduction from his pay and his employer has not followed the rules for making deductions then this should be raised as a grievance with this employer. If the problem cannot be sorted out informally, then the worker has the right to go to an employment tribunal and reclaim from his employer the deduction in his wages.

A complaint under ss 23–26 of the Act, that the employer made an unlawful deduction must be presented within 3 months, beginning with the date of payment of wages from which the deduction complained of was made, or the date when a payment was received. If there are a series of deductions the worker must complain no later than three months from the date of the last deduction.

A worker's remedy for an unlawful deduction from their wages is to make a claim to an employment tribunal under s 23(1), ERA 1996. If the tribunal upholds the claim, then under s 24 it must make a declaration to that effect and order the employer to pay (or repay) to the worker the amount unlawfully deducted or received.

---

19   (1992) IRLR 56.
20   (1994) IRLR 536.

Where the unlawful deduction represents a breach of the contract, eg unilateral variation of contract, the employee affected could also make a breach of contract claim where they can also try to reclaim any money they have lost.

If an employee is dismissed for complaining that unlawful deductions have been made, this will count as 'asserting a statutory right' and if they can prove that was the reason why they were dismissed, the dismissal will be automatically unfair. So where an employee is dismissed because they brought a claim under the wages legislation this will be automatically unfair dismissal requiring no continuity of service.

Wages claims

11.24 There were 21,285 applications to tribunals in 1999/2000 which amounted to 20% of all tribunal cases which was a 27% increase over the previous year. In 2003/2004 there were 20,853 claims of which 6,847 were conciliated, 5,923 withdrawn and 3556 were successful at tribunal. In 2005/06 the most common claims were for unfair dismissal (41,832), breaches of the working time directive (35,474), and unauthorised deduction of wages (32,330). In 2008/09 the top three complaints before employment tribunals number of cases were unfair dismissal 52,711, unauthorised deductions 33,839 and breach of contract 32,829.

The number of wages claims has steadily increased over the years and these type of claims have oscillated between being the second or third most common kind of claim brought before employment tribunals. Interestingly this growth has not been significantly affected by the extension of the jurisdiction of employment tribunals to deal with breach of contract cases.[21] A reason for this is that the two type of claim complement each other, eg breach of contract claims deal cover most situations where payment is made in lieu of notice (see the Delaney case). Another possible

---

21   Employment Tribunals Extension of Jurisdiction (Scotland) Order 1994 No. 1624
     Employment Tribunals Extension of Jurisdiction (England and Wales) Order 1994
     No. 1623.

reason is that the statutory claim for breach of contract is limited to cases where the contract has terminated unlike wages claims.

Recent cases

11.25 In *Key Recruitment v Lear*,[22] the President of the EAT, sitting alone, provided some useful guidance on the application of the protection of wages rules. The facts were that Mr Lear received a commission payment of £1,831 in June 2006 for introducing a new client. When he left his employment in April 2007 the employer deducted the full amount of the commission from the termination payments, on the basis that the client had subsequently defaulted on payments. An employment tribunal agreed with Mr. Lear's claim that the deduction was unlawful because the employer could have recovered the commission payment earlier, and the amount deducted meant that he received no monies on termination. The employer appealed the decision, arguing that the tribunal had wrongly applied the provisions of ss 13 and 14 of the ERA 1996. The EAT agreed that the tribunal had erred in its decision and remitted the case to be heard by a fresh tribunal. The two issues discussed in the EAT's decision are helpful in understanding the application of these provisions. It was held there is no limitation in the legislation to the amount that may be recovered or to the period of time within which any recovery of overpayment must be made.

A commission payment, if paid at the time in accord with contractual provisions, does not become an overpayment unless there is also a contractual provision allowing it to be recovered in defined circumstances and, in fact, in this case those circumstances had arisen.

In a more important decision of the House of Lords in the case of *HM Revenue and Customs v Stringer and others*,[23] they overturned the decision of the Court of Appeal in the case[24] and found that claims for

---

22 [2008] UKEAT 0597/07.
23 [2009] UKHL 31, [2009] IRLR 677.
24 This case was the culmination of several years of litigation which began with claims in the Employment Tribunal by five employees of the Inland Revenue for holiday pay that was due while they had been on long term sick leave. Mr Ainsworth, one of the claimants, made a claim for statutory holiday pay which he asserted was outstanding on termination of his employment, even though he had, until termination, been on long term sick leave. The Employment Tribunal and the Employment Appeal Tribunal (EAT) upheld his claim but it was overturned by the Court of Appeal (CA) in 2005.

unpaid statutory holiday pay, and accrued statutory holiday pay, on termination, can be made as an unlawful deduction from wages under the Employment Rights Act 1996 as well as under the Working Time Regulations 1998. This means that workers can take advantage of the more favourable time limits which apply under the ERA 1996, which could potentially allow them to claim unpaid holiday pay on termination of their employment going back several years, provided they bring their holiday pay claim within three months of their employer's most recent failure to pay them holiday pay. The only issue which the House of Lords addressed in its judgment was whether workers can bring claims for holiday pay only under the Working Time Regulations, or whether they can also use the more favourable regime under the ERA 1996 which applies to unlawful deductions from wages, and they decided they could. So they decided that holiday pay which has accrued during the holiday year in which the employment terminates is payable, and any claim in respect of such sum must be brought within three months of termination. But they also decided that claims for unpaid holiday in respect of the previous holiday year can also be brought under the ERA 1996 as an unlawful deduction of wages, provided this claim is made within three months of the date of the deduction or, in the case of a series of deductions, the last in that series. This decision has opened the possibility that workers will be able to claim for holiday pay accrued over the current and the preceding holiday year.

EQUAL PAY

11.26 Inequality of pay has been a feature of UK workplaces for many years and there are a number of underlying reasons for this. The following quote highlights the more important of these:

> 'Such challenges are fundamental to tackling the part of the gender pay gap which is associated with the segregation of women workers into low paying, predominantly part-time workplaces … The reasons for this are many and complex, and include historical notions about men being the 'breadwinner' in a family, higher value being accorded to jobs requiring traditionally 'male' qualities, the concentration of women in certain job roles, the concentration of women in part-time

roles, childcare requirements, and women missing out on promotion opportunities due to maternity leave.'[25]

It is outwith the scope of this book to give these matters detailed consideration and other commentators who have done so can be referred to.[26] What the quote above doesn't mention is that, unlike male workers, women workers who were brave enough to enter the world of work were subjected to inequality in most things, but most notably pay, and they were until relatively recently[27] largely unrepresented by trade unions.

> 'The campaign for equal pay has a long history; one which is still ongoing. It is a demand which was not always supported by the trade union movement and in some instances was actively resisted by sections of it. As a movement it does not have a continuous history, reflecting the fact that although a constant part of the labour force in Industrial Britain, women were often a marginalised sector of it...'.[28]

Current position

11.27

Although the position of women has dramatically improved in terms of pay equality since the Equal Pay Act in 1970, it is still an issue for many women.

> 'What this act highlighted is that which has been apparent throughout the history of women's paid employment in the 19th and 20th centuries; namely that the real cause of women's low and unequal pay is the issue of job segregation and the consequential undervaluing of "women's skills".'[29]

---

25 www.cipd.co.uk.
26 Boston, S (1987) *Women Workers and the Trade Unions*, Lawrence and Wishart 13–14. Pinchbeck, I (1969) Women Workers and the Industrial Revolution, Frank Cass & Co. Ltd.
27 Only in the last fifty or sixty years have women been fully represented by trade unions.
28 An Historical Introduction to the Campaign for Equal Pay by Mary Davis www.unionhistory.info/equalpay/
29 Ibid.

According to the Office for National Statistics (ONS) recently the gender pay gap for full-time workers, based on mean hourly earnings excluding overtime, has fallen from 17.4 per cent in 2008 to 16.4 per cent in 2009. The inequality is even more pronounced for female part time workers when compared with their male equivalents.

Equal Pay Legislation

11.28 There were formerly various statutes in the UK covering equal pay but these have now been replaced by the provisions of the Equality Act 2010 (see below). Equal pay has been at the forefront of the social policy of the European Union since it began and the European Union has influenced the development of the equal pay law in the UK since joining it in 1973. The legislation of the EU that applies is (a) Article 119 of the EEC Treaty (now article 141) application of the principle that men and women should receive equal pay for equal work (b) Equal Pay Directive (75/117/EEC).

The Equality Act 2010

11.29 Section (1) of Equal Pay Act 1970 introduced the equality clause which was a statutory implied term which incorporated into all womens' contracts a clause that provided the right to equal pay and other contractual terms with men (and vice versa). The Act required that the contract of employment of all women shall be deemed to include an equality clause. This operated where women were undertaking 'like work' or 'work rated as equivalent' or work of 'equal value' to that of a man within the same employment. Under s 66 of the Equality Act 2010, this has been replaced by a sex equality clause which applies in similar circumstances. When this applies then any term (not only pay) in a women's contract which is less favourable than that in a man's contract will be modified so as to not be less favourable (and vice versa). Of course this means that employers acting in breach of this term, breach the contract of employment of his employees, which will give the employee the right to sue for breach of contract. However, it is more likely that the person would bring an action under the Act for equal pay.

A claimant must bring their case within six months of leaving their employment or from the end of a particular contract.[30] In the case of part-time workers employed under a series of contracts, they must bring their claim within 6 months of a particular contract coming to an end.

The Equality Act 2010 provides that the provisions apply to terms of a person's employment which are 'in the person's contract of employment, contract of apprenticeship or contract to do work personally.'[31] Therefore, workers and employees are included whether they work full-time or part-time. Self employed persons can also be included under the provisions, as in *Quinnen v Howells,*[32] where a self-employed man could be included because he was being paid less than two fellow self-employed female workers who were doing similar work at a department store. Men and women are entitled to equal pay if they are employed 'in the same employment' under s 79 (3). The equivalent term under the Equal Pay Act 1970 was broadly interpreted by the employment tribunals and courts. For example in *Leverton v Clwyd County Council,*[33] nursery teachers were held to work in common with clerical workers for the purposes of the Act as they were governed by the same collective agreement. They were on different hours, with different holiday entitlement and different pay scales. Similarly in a Scottish case *South Ayrshire Council v Morton,*[34] the applicant, Ms Morton, was a school head teacher employed by South Ayrshire Council who named as her comparator a male secondary school head teacher employed by Highland Council. The salaries of both employees and all head teachers were determined by the Scottish Joint Negotiating Committee (SJNC). This case involved one of around 600 claims by primary school head teachers who compared themselves and claimed equal pay with secondary head teachers. 'In our view the material considerations are that the applicant and the comparators are in the same branch of public service and are subject to a uniform system of national pay and conditions set by a statutory body whose decision is binding on both their employers. It seems reasonable to us to refer to them being

---

30   See *Preston v Wolverhampton NHS Trust* (1998) IRLR 197 HL.
31   Equality Act 2010 s 80.
32   *Quinnen v Howells* (1984) ICR 525.
33   [1989] ICR 33.
34   [2002] IRLR 256, Ct of Sess.

in the same service'. This was the case even though they worked several hundred miles apart. This approach was continued by the ECJ (now the CJEU) in *Lawrence v Regent Office Care.*[35]

Where a woman (or man) brings a claim for equal pay the starting point is to find a suitable comparator/s of the opposite sex, and there are three methods that can be used set down under s 65 of the Equality Act 2010. The bases for comparison between men and women for equal pay are (a) Like Work, (b) Job Rated as Equivalent, and (c) Work of equal value. Each of these bases for comparison will be considered in some detail. The Equality Act 2010 provisions apply when a person is being employed to do work that is equal to work being done by a comparator of the opposite sex working for the same or an associated employer. Although the Equality Act 2010 still requires an actual comparator under s 64(2) the comparator need not be working contemporaneously with the claimant. The benefit of using a hypothetical comparator may be lost if an employee cannot prove their case to a high enough level. The provisions are also limited to cases of direct sex discrimination and, therefore, equal pay cases involving indirect sex discrimination would still require an actual comparator.

Like work

11.30 This term 'like work' means that the work being undertaken by the women is of the same, or broadly similar nature as that of a man in the same employment. In *Capper Pass v Lawton,*[36] Mrs Lawton worked as a director's cook and she cooked 10–20 lunches per day. She sought equal pay with two male assistant chefs who prepared 350 meals a day for the factory canteen. She worked a 40-hour week they worked a 45-hour week. Despite this the EAT held she was entitled to equal pay on basis of like work.

To defend a claim the employer must show that there is a difference of practical importance in the jobs being compared. In *Thomas v National Coal Board,*[37] women canteen assistants compared themselves with one male assistant that worked at night and was paid more. It was found the

35   C-320100
36   [1977] 2 QB 852.
37   [1987] IRLR 451 EAT 1500.

difference was he worked alone without supervision and, therefore, had more responsibility which justified the pay difference.

In *Shields v E Coomes (Holdings) Ltd*, Lord Bridge[38] said in determining if this defence applies there are three questions to be asked. Firstly, was the work of the comparators the same or of a broadly similar nature? Secondly, if so, were the differences between the jobs of practical importance? Thirdly, can the employer show that a material factor accounts for the difference in pay?

In *Eaton v Nuttall*,[39] responsibility was the issue at stake. Was the male comparator's added responsibility a material difference? The EAT rejected the employer's contention that the gravity of consequences where an error is made is a determinant of responsibility. The appropriate question was the same function done with the same degree of competence and, as the answer was yes, they rejected the argument that there was a practical difference between the jobs.

Job evaluation

11.31 Work rated as equivalent is concerned with job evaluation and whether an evaluation of pay under the scheme is discriminatory or not. Job evaluation can be defined as 'a method of determining on a systematic basis the relative importance of a number of different jobs.'[40] There are various types of evaluation schemes, however, for the purposes of the Equal Pay Act they are only valid if they are analytical and fair.

Points Rating – This is the most commonly used method. The key elements of each job, which are known as 'factors', are identified by the organisation and then broken down into components. Each factor is assessed separately and points allocated according to the level needed for the job. The more demanding the job, the higher the points value. The factors usually assessed include:

---

38   (1978) ICR 1159 CA.
39   (1977) IRLR 171.
40   ACAS (2008) Job evaluation: considerations and risks. Advisory booklet. London: Acas. Available at: http://www.acas.org.uk/index.aspx?articleid=682.

Knowledge and skills

- work experience
- qualifications
- external qualifications
- specialist training

Communication and networking

- social skills
- presentation skills
- diplomacy

Decision-making

- judgement
- initiative
- analytical ability

Impact and influence

- efficiency
- impact on customers
- responsibility
- results of errors

People management

- human relations skills
- ability to deal with work pressure
- supervisory responsibility

Freedom to act

- depth of control
- supervision received

Working environment

- knowledge of special working practices
- breadth of management skill required

Financial responsibility

- budgeting[41]

The other common method is factor comparison where the assessor chooses a smaller number of factors and examines these against key jobs (which are fairly paid) to determine the proportion of wage attributable to each factor and then a scale is produced. Finally there is a comparison of other jobs against the scale.

With respect to equal pay, it was decided in *Bromley v H & J Quick Ltd*,[42] that for a job evaluation scheme to be fair it must be objective. In

41   www.cipd.co.uk/subjects/pay/general/jobeval.htm.
42   (1988) ICR 623 CA.

other words, carried out using criteria which do not differentiate between the gender of employees (comparators), and must not have the effect of discriminating against one sex.

Under s 2A of the Equal Pay Act it had provided that a valid JES rating provides an absolute defence to an equal value claim if the claimant was rated lower than her/his comparator. However, this was amended by The Equal Pay Act 1970 (Amendment) Regulations 2004[43] as follows: 'It allows the employment tribunal to choose to determine the question of equal value itself, or to appoint an independent expert to prepare a report on that question. In a case where there has already been a job evaluation study which has given different values to the work of the claimant and the comparator, the employment tribunal must determine that the work is not of equal value, unless it has reasonable grounds for suspecting that the study discriminated on the grounds of sex, or there are other reasons why it is not suitable to be relied upon.' There is no objective right or wrong, so far as job evaluation is concerned.[44]

In practice, the evaluation will often depend upon the subjective value judgments of the person operating the scheme. The end result of a job evaluation is a hierarchy of jobs to which pay scales can later be allocated. The determination of actual pay is often a separate operation which is subject to negotiation between management and employees and their trade union representatives. Only the job is evaluated, not the person doing it. The effect of all of this is that, to a perhaps unexpected degree, JES and consequential pay and grading changes often have a corrosive effect on morale.

Work of equal value

11.32 This concept is derived originally from European Union Law and in particular Article 157 of the Treaty on the Functioning of the European Union. This provides that men and women should receive equal pay for equal work. Under the EC Council Directive on Equal Pay,[45] it states that: 'the principle of equal pay means for the same work or work to which

---

43   SI 2004/2352.
44   Explanatory Notes on the Regulations.
45   75/117.

equal value is attributed, the elimination of all discrimination on the grounds of sex with regard to all aspects and conditions of remuneration.'

The original Equal Pay Act failed to take account of the European legislation in this respect and the UK Government in 1982 were taken to the European Court of Justice (ECJ) and challenged on this failure. In *The Commission of EU v UK*,[46] the European Court of Justice (ECJ) were asked to consider allegations of the European Community (EC) Commission that the UK Equal Pay provisions did not comply with the requirements of EC law. The ECJ held that it did not comply. The law in the UK was brought in line with EU law in this respect by the Equal Pay (Amendment) Regulations 1983[47] which introduced, for the first time in the UK, the concept of equal pay for work of equal value. This meant that a woman's job could be compared with that of a male comparator who was doing completely different work provided she worked in the same organisation as him. If the woman's job was found to be of equal value to his, then her pay also had to be equal. Male workers could also compare their work with that of a woman on the same basis. In such a claim, the man is entitled to the same arrears of pay as was awarded to the woman.

Equal Value Procedure

11.33 The tribunal can carry out an investigation into equal value itself or instruct an independent expert to report on whether the work is of equal value except where: (1) There are no reasonable grounds for determining the work is of equal value;[48] (2) the work of the woman and the man have been given different values on a valid job evaluation study; or (3) at a preliminary stage the employment tribunal take the view that the employer has proved the variation in pay is genuinely due to a material factor.

In the first case to deal with equal value in the UK, *Hayward v Cammel Laird Shipbuilders Ltd*,[49] Mrs Hayward was employed as a canteen cook and she claimed equal pay with tradesmen (joiners, painters etc) in the shipyard who were paid a higher rate of pay. She had been paid the same

---

46   (1982) IRLR 333 ECJ.
47   SI 1983/1794.
48   *Adams v International Insider Publishing Co Ltd* 1 March 20001, 2202350/0.
49   (1988) IRLR 257, HL.

as them when she was an apprentice. It was held by the employment tribunal that she was entitled to receive the same rate of pay as the men. The Court of Appeal however, had overturned this decision, and held she was not entitled to equal pay because she got certain rights not available to the men (free meals, meal breaks, sickness benefit) which compensated for the difference in pay. However, the House of Lords overturned the Court of Appeal's decision. They held that differences in pay cannot be offset by other benefits for the purpose of showing equal value.

In another leading equal value claim, *Enderby v Frenchay Health Authority*,[50] a claim was brought by speech therapists. They argued that on the basis of equal value they should receive the same pay as senior clinical psychologists and pharmacists. The speech therapists were almost exclusively women while in the other two professions, while mixed at the lower grades, were predominantly male at the senior grades. The European Court of Justice clarified the law in this area by concluding: (1) the fact of pay disparity between two highly segregated jobs of equal value was sufficient to raise a *prima facie* case of discrimination, requiring the employer to show that there were objective reasons for the difference in pay. (2) The mere fact that the rates of pay were decided by separate collective bargaining processes did not preclude a finding of *prima facie* discrimination where the results show that the two groups with the same employer, and the same trade union, were treated differently. (3) The state of the employment market, which might lead an employer to increase the pay of a particular job in order to attract candidates, may constitute an objective justification for a pay discrepancy (market forces defence). They also stated that where a national court can determine precisely what proportion of the increase is attributable to market forces, it must accept that the pay differential is justified only to the extent of that proportion. As a consequence of the decision, more than 350 speech therapists shared £12 million to settle their long-running legal battle for equal pay (14 years), and they also got a revised grading structure which allowed employees at the top of the profession to earn an extra £20,000 per year. This was the highest ever settlement in an equal pay case.

---

50   (1994) ICR 112.

Material factor defence

11.34 A further equal pay provision that needs to be examined is the material factor defence. Under the previous legislation, the defence had been available when the employer could prove that the variation between a man and woman's pay was genuinely due to a material factor other than sex.[51] A genuine material factor was one that justified the reasoning behind what would otherwise have been indirectly discriminatory levels of pay provided to a woman.[52] A notable change brought in by the Equality Act 2010 in relation to this defence, is that the word genuine no longer appears and it is now simply known as a material factor defence. The Government omitted this word on the basis that it did not consider that the term genuine added anything to its meaning.[53] Although the sex equality clause is now implied into all employment contracts, it will not have any impact if the employer can show that the difference is in pay is due to a material factor, reliance on which: (a) does not involve treating the employee less favourably because of their sex than they treat the comparator and (b) it is a proportionate means of achieving a legitimate aim.[54] Therefore, if an employer can show that the difference is because of a material factor which is not related to the claimant's sex, this would provide them with a defence and the sex equality rule would have no effect.[55] There is no justification needed if the reason for the pay inequality is not gender related.[56] This was confirmed by the Court of Appeal in *Glasgow City Council v Marshall*[57] and *Redcar & Cleveland BC v Bainbridge & ors; Surtees & ors v Middlesbrough Council CA.*[58] However, when the pay disparity is sex related it is necessary to show that it was justified. The case law from the ECJ (now the CJEU) has highlighted that employers may need to show an objective justification for a difference in pay between workers of

---

51   Equal Pay Act 1970 s 1(3).
52   Supra 7 p 409.
53   Keen, S, Pre-employment health questions & equal pay', News Section, New Law Journal, October 2010 1327 at 1332.
54   Equality Act 2010 s 69 (1). The effect of part (b) remains to be seen.
55   Equality Act 2010 s 69 (4).
56   *Strathclyde Regional Council v Wallace* [1998] 2 WLR 259.
57   [2000] ICR 196.
58   [2008] EWCA Civ. 885, [2008] IRLR 776, CA see also *Armstrong v Newcastle upon Tyne NHS Hospital Trust* [2006] IRLR 124.

different sexes doing work of equal value. This can apply even where there is no evidence that the employer has intentionally discriminated against women in terms of pay and there are no apparent barriers to equal pay.[59] In *Enderby v Frenchay Health Authority and Secretary of State for Health*,[60] a female speech therapist claimed equal pay on the basis that it was an overwhelmingly female profession and that in other comparable NHS professions which were predominantly male, such as pharmacists the pay was higher. The ECJ stated that where there was a significant difference in pay between jobs of equal value and where one job was predominantly female and the other predominantly male, that a *prima facie* case of discrimination would be made out.[61] In *Sharp v Caledonia Group Services Ltd*,[62] the EAT held that employers must always objectively justify their use of the defence. The need to justify pay differences was affirmed in *Gibson and others v Sheffield City Council*,[63] when the Court of Appeal held that an employment tribunal was wrong to find that a pay differential between male street cleaners and gardeners and female carers that had been caused by a productivity bonus given to the cleaners but not the carers (as it was inappropriate due to the nature of the work) was not tainted by sex. As a result of these decisions, the test for the material factor defence, where the difference in pay is sex related, has become more strict. This is because an employer is required to show that the difference in pay is necessary and sensible rather than just genuine and this development is significant because it means that employers will not be in a position to establish a defence as easily. The most important of these is the market forces defence referred to by the ECJ in *Enderby*. In the case of *Rainey v Greater Glasgow Health Board*,[64] the Health Authority decided to set up its own prosthetic fitting service. In order to attract a sufficient number of qualified persons to get the service started, it was necessary to make a higher pay offer to those who came from the private sector. The applicant who came into the service direct from her training in the public sector claimed equal pay with a man

59 B Perrins et al, Harvey on Industrial Relations and Employment Law (2010), Issue 211, LexisNexis, at K-19 para 8.
60 [1993] IRLR 591.
61 Supra 88.
62 [2006] ICR 218.
63 [2010] EWCA Civ 63, [2010] IRLR 277.
64 [1987] ICR 129 HL.

on a higher salary who came from the private sector. The House of Lords held that the difference in pay was due to a genuine material factor other than sex. The reason the man was paid more was because of the need to attract qualified persons (of either sex) from the private sector, in order to form the nucleus of the new service. This is a good example of the market forces defence in operation.

In *Ratcliffe v North Yorkshire County Council*,[65] school catering assistants claimed equal pay with men in jobs such as road sweepers and gardeners, with whom they had been rated equivalent under the local government job evaluation scheme. However, because of compulsory competitive tendering they were given notice of dismissal and re-employed at a lower level of pay. They were told that, unless rates of pay were lower, the Authority would lose the schools meals contract to a cheaper private contractor. The House of Lords upheld the decision of the employment tribunal that the employers had failed to make out a defence of market forces. The women could not find suitable work and were obliged to take the wages offered if they were to continue with their work. This was direct discrimination on the ground of sex.

Other Genuine Material Factors

11.35 Other genuine material factors justifying differences in pay are: regional variations in pay and other conditions, eg London weighting, red circling, longer service resulting in incremental differences, different qualifications, the fact that the jobs are carried out at different times,[66] and the need to ensure the efficient carrying out of the business. In *Crossley v ACAS*,[67] the employment tribunal decided that seniority was only a valid genuine material factor, where the difference in pay because of seniority, was justified, for example the employer needed to show that the difference in experience had an impact of the way the job was carried out.

However, in *Cadman v Health and Safety Executive*,[68] the ECJ held that in normal circumstances an employer does not have to objectively

---

65   (1995) IRLR 439, HL.
66   *Dugdale v Kraft Foods* (1977) ICR 48 EAT.
67   20 December 1999 case no 1304774/98.
68   [2006] IRLR 969 ECJ.

justify the use of length of service as a criterion in determining pay levels, even where it leads to unequal pay between men and women. It is only in 'special cases' that specific justification may be required. Unfortunately, the ECJ did not provide detailed guidance on when the 'special cases' would occur, although undoubtedly the exception will be triggered where the employee can raise serious doubts that the experienced gained through length of service leads to improved performance.

Choice of Comparator

11.36 In *Pickstone v Freemans plc*,[69] the applicant was a warehouse operative who worked alongside other male warehouse operatives and received the same pay as them. She brought an equal value claim naming as her comparator a male checker warehouse operative who was paid at a higher rate. It was claimed by her employer that, because she was receiving equal pay with the men in her job, she could not bring an equal value claim with others. It was held by the House of Lords that she was entitled to succeed, under s2(1) c of the Act, as to hold otherwise would enable an unscrupulous employer to defeat equal value claims by ensuring that one man worked alongside women and were paid the same. In *McAvoy and Others v South Tyneside Borough Council and Others*,[70] the EAT held that a man is entitled to bring a 'piggyback' claim under the Equal Pay Act, comparing themselves to a comparator woman who works alongside him, where the woman has received a higher rate of pay as result of her own equal pay claim, using a higher paid male comparator, as was the situation in the Pickstone case. In *Allonby v Accrington and Rossendale College and others*,[71] Ms Allonby was originally employed by the college on a series of fixed-term contracts. However, in 1996 the college terminated her contract and offered her continued work as a self-employed worker through an agency. As a result her income fell and she lost pension benefits. Ms Allonby claimed equal pay with a male full-time lecturer working for the college.

---

69   [1988] All ER 803 HL.
70   UKEAT Case nos. 0006/08, 0057/08, 0058/08, 0168/08, 0276/08.
71   [2004] IRLR 224.

It was held by the ECJ that a female agency worker cannot make an equal pay claim with a male who works for the same employer. She was denied an equal pay claim as there was no single source (employer and agency) responsible for the inequality in pay. Formal classification as a self-employed person under national law can be disregarded if, in reality, the individual's independence is purely notional. The crucial factor is subordination to another person, if so they are a worker. Under s 71 of the Equality Act 2010, employees may bring sex discrimination claims, relying on hypothetical comparators, in circumstances in which it is impossible to identify actual comparators for the purpose of equal pay claims. The law is very recent, so it is difficult to know how the courts and employment tribunals will deal with cases brought under s71 of the Act.

Transparency of Pay

11.37 In *Handels-og Kontofunkionaevernes Forbund i Denmark v Dansch Arbejdsgiverforening (acting for Danfoss)*,[72] it was held that where the employer operates a pay structure which lacks transparency in respect of the criteria used for the payment of employees, the burden of proof is on the employer to show that his pay structure is not discriminatory. Transparency pay, or the lack of it, is a real issue for the European Union and the Equality Act 2010 (mentioned below) and has introduced a number of measures designed to increase transparency.

Remedies

11.38 Under s 2(5) of the Equal Pay Act 1970 it was stated that back pay was only available for a maximum of two years from the date that proceedings were started. However, this was challenged in various legal decisions including *Levez v TH Jennings (Harlow Pools) (No 2)*,[73] where the EAT, following a decision of the ECJ, held that an applicant was entitled to back pay for 6 years preceding date of complaint.[74] Now s 132(4) of the Equality Act 2010 provides that sums can be awarded

---

72 (1989) IRLR 532 ECJ.
73 (1999) IRLR 764.
74 See obiter comments by ET chairperson in *National Power v Young* (2001) IRLR 32.

back to the 'arrears date', which is now normally five years before the claim was made. It is six years back pay in England. Under the Employment Tribunals (Interest on Awards in Discrimination Cases) Regulations 1996/2803, interest is payable on an equal pay award from the day after the tribunal ruling. Under the Equal Pay (Amendment) Regulations 2003, a woman might be entitled to aggravated damages in compensation if the employer deliberately conceals information that would be relevant to bringing a claim (such as the pay and grading of a potential comparator). However, the revised Act takes such behaviour into account by allowing for the unlimited recovery of arrears, instead of the normal 6-year limit.

The *Employment Act 2002* brought in an 'equal pay questionnaire' which can be sent to an employer and their response can support a claim for equal pay.

> 'The purpose of introducing a questionnaire procedure was to formalise the drive to transparency by providing a route to obtaining information about relevant issues, such as details of pay schemes and job grading systems, and about the way in which skills and experience are reflected in the company's pay system.'[75]

The questions and any answers will be admissible as evidence in equal pay proceedings. An employer's deliberate failure to respond will enable the tribunal to draw appropriate inferences. The Secretary of State will prescribe a time by which the employer must respond.

Pension provisions had previously been excluded from the definition of pay but was given similar protection to equal pay protection by the Pensions Act 1995. This introduced an 'equal treatment rule' to occupational pensions provided by employers. Under s 67 of the Equality Act 2010 it provides that (1) If an occupational pension scheme does not include a sex equality rule, it is to be treated as including one. (2) A sex equality rule is a provision that has the following effect (a) if a relevant term is less favourable to A than it is to B, the term is modified so as not to be less favourable; (b) if a term confers a relevant discretion capable of being exercised in a way that would be less favourable to A than to B, the term is modified so as to prevent the exercise of the

---

75 Hansard (HC) Standing Committee, 17.1.02.

discretion in that way.[76] Under s 67(9) of the Equality Act 2010, a successful claim for access to an occupational pension scheme can result in the granting of retrospective access in respect of any period going back to 8 April 1976.[77] Under Schedule7 Part 2 of the Equality Act 2010, there is an exception to the sex equality rule that allows a difference in occupational pension contributions for women and men because of prescribed actuarial factors. For example, an employer may have to pay higher contributions for female than male employees because of their longer life expectancy.

Objective justification

11.39 In *Villalba v Merill Lynch*,[78] the EAT held that the employer did not have to prove that the difference in pay was objectively justified, where it had demonstrated that the reason for the difference was not based on sex. This re-stated the position of the House of Lords in the cases of *Glasgow City Council v Marshall*,[79] and *Strathclyde Regional Council v Wallace*,[80] that required the employer to show that the reason for the disparity was genuine and had caused the difference in pay. There was no requirement for further justification unless the factor relied upon was indirectly discriminatory or tainted by discrimination. However, the *Villalba* decision is at odds with the decision of another division of the EAT that held, in *Sharp v Caledonia Group Services*,[81] that objective justification was required in all equal pay cases not just those involving indirect discrimination. However, the decision in *Sharp* has been rejected by the Court of Appeal in *Armstrong v Newcastle Upon Tyne NHS Hospital Trust*,[82] which followed the earlier Marshall decision. So, in summary, provided an employer can produce for an employment tribunal a reason for pay disparity that is genuine, then nothing more is required

---

76 This section provides detailed descriptions of the terminology used.
77 Equality in pension benefits can only be claimed for service from 17 May 1990.
78 [2006] IRLR 437 EAT.
79 [2000] IRLR 272 HL.
80 [1998] IRLR 146 HL.
81 [2006] IRLR 4 EAT.
82 [2005] EWCA Civ 1608, [2006] IRLR 124 CA.

as a defence unless the reason itself is indirectly discriminatory or tainted by discrimination.

RECENT OR CURRENT TRENDS

11.40 There has recently been an unprecedented volume of equal pay litigation in employment tribunals, to the extent that the large number of multiple claims has clogged up the employment tribunal system. The vast majority of these claims are in the local government and health service sectors. The reason for the huge number of claims is that in both sectors, employers and employees, are in the throes of large-scale job evaluation and re-grading exercises which has thrown up serious issues concerning pay.

Secrecy Clauses

11.41 Under s 77 of the EA 2010, it is provided that a term which prevents or restricts an employee from disclosing, or seeking to disclose, information about the terms of his work is unenforceable.[83] Secrecy or 'gagging' clauses have become popular amongst employers with the Equal Opportunities Commission[84] finding that nearly a quarter of employers included such a clause in their employment contracts.[85] This provision is, therefore, important as it allows employees more of a chance to collect important pay-related information to assist them in raising an equal pay claim.[86] Otherwise an employee may not be aware of the variations in pay in relation to gender or he may fear disciplinary action for having breached a secrecy clause. However, the right only applies to a 'relevant pay disclosure' which is defined as one where the purpose of an employee disclosing or receiving the information is to ascertain whether, or to what extent, there is a connection between pay and gender.[87] This particular aspect of the provision has been criticised because it may be

---

83   Equality Act 2010 s 77 (1).
84   Successor called the Equality and Human Rights Commission.
85   'Equality Act 2010' Health & Safety at Work (2010) 16 (9) p 8.
86   'Will the Equality Act bring equal pay closer?' IDS Pay Report (2010) Issue 1059 p 12.
87   Equality Act 2010 s 77 (3).

hard to distinguish whether an employee is actually seeking information in relation to perceived discrimination against them or not.[88] An employer may not be certain as to the employee's intentions if they do not expressly state them. Therefore, this could cause confusion for an employer who may be uncertain as to whether or not the employee is protected by s 77. This negative aspect was most likely not intended by Parliament. However, it highlights another issue with the legislation that will need clarification by the employment tribunals and courts.

Gender pay gap reporting

11.42 The EA 2010, under s 78, requires employers with over 250 employees to publish information relating to the pay of their employees to determine if there are any differences between the pay for men and women. However, the Government announced in December 2010 that it would not implement the gender pay reporting measures while it is working with business to encourage the publication of equality workforce data on a voluntary basis. Organisations are being encouraged to voluntarily report on the pay gap between the level of pay between male and female employees. The Government does not intend to review this voluntary arrangement until 2013 at the earliest. They will then decide whether publication by employers of gender pay gap information will become mandatory.[89] It is clear that the provision will only be brought back in if voluntary disclosure proves to be unsuccessful.[90] The Coalition Government are not taking a strong stance with regard to tackling the gender pay gap through encouraging transparency. This is perhaps not surprising given the Conservative party's pro business stance and cost-cutting agenda. The Equality and Human Rights Commission (EHRC) has noted that to tackle the gender pay gap it needs to be identified and

---

88 Thomas, D 'Closing the gap' Employers' Law (2010) 7 July p 14.

89 'EHRC proposals for gender pay reporting' Equal Opportunities Review (2010) Issue 198, p 16.

90 R McDonald, S Buckley. 'Equal pay' Employment Law Bulletin (2010) Issue 96 (Apr), 8.

measured at an organisational level.[91] However, they believe that businesses can voluntarily change and embrace greater transparency on pay without the need for s 78 being brought back into force.[92] The Discrimination Law Review (DLR) is a governmental body that was set up to provide the framework for reforming equality laws in the UK. They were also against mandatory equal pay reviews, on the basis that they tackle only one cause of the gender pay gap, this being gender pay discrimination.[93] They recommended instead the spread of good practice, although there was some criticism of their view given that they had in reaching it ignored clear evidence of the ineffectiveness of voluntary measures.[94] It is clear that because of the current views of the Government and independent statutory bodies, such as the EHRC, gender pay reporting will remain voluntary for the foreseeable future and there is some indication that some companies have already decided to carry out voluntary reporting. Employers are now more appreciative of the need to tackle equal pay because shareholders, consumers and employees are increasingly more selective when choosing companies to contract or deal with, restricting their choice of companies to those that have a positive outlook on issues such as equality.[95] Some of the more progressive companies in the UK are already carrying out pay audits and adopting the Equal Opportunities Commission's model.[96] HBOS is an interesting example, as they are part of the finance sector which is the employment sector that has the largest gender pay gap in the UK. However, HBOS have been carrying out equal pay reviews since 2003. These audits had shown that, although they had no pay-related bias against women, they employed fewer women than men

---

91 EHRC. 'Proposals for promoting greater transparency in the public sector: a consultation on improving gender equality in the workplace' EHRC (2009) p. 9 http://www.equalityhumanrights.com/uploaded_files/consultations/gender_pay_consultation.pdf

92 Ibid p 9.

93 S Fredman. 'Reforming equal pay laws' Industrial Law Journal (2008) Vol. 37 Part 3 pp 193–218 at p 215.

94 Ibid p 215.

95 'EHRC proposals for gender pay reporting' Equal Opportunities Review EOR (2010) 198 p 9.

96 R Lewis, S Smee. 'Closing the gap: Does transparency hold the key to unlocking pay equality?' (2009) Fawcett Society p. 9 http://www.fawcettsociety.org.uk/?PageID=1022.

in higher-paid specialist or senior roles.[97] HBOS took the findings from their audit and formulated a plan to tackle equal pay.[98] It demonstrates that a large company can commit to tackling the gender pay gap and companies may find HBOS's actions a helpful model. Particularly, if they are keen to pre-empt the Government making this review process a legal requirement.[99] However, it is clear only a minority of companies are reporting voluntarily and the EHRC gathered evidence showing that 'few private sector companies are taking action to close the gender pay gap.'[100] Even if s 78 of the Act was enforced, the Fawcett Society[101] have identified that of the 4.7 million businesses in the UK only around 6000 have more than 250 employees. Thus, around 59% of employees would be unaffected by the provisions if reintroduced in their current form.[102] It is important that, in the unlikely event that this provision is brought into force, it should be amended to include businesses with fewer than 250 employees. A suitable example can be found in Sweden, where businesses with 25 or more employees have to carry out an equality action plan every three years. This has proved to be successful with a gender pay gap of only 3% in Sweden for women working in male dominated professions.[103]

The general equality duty in the public sector

11.43 The gender pay gap varies between the public and private sectors and one notable difference between them is that the gender equality duty

97 K Godwin. 'Equal pay reviews in action' Equal Opportunities Review (2008) 174, 8.
98 Ibid p 10.
99 The costs of gender pay reporting and equal pay audits are one of the main arguments against implementing section 78 – Minster for Equalities, Lynne Featherstone, stated that it may place a 'burden on business.' Will the Equality Act bring equal pay closer?' IDS Pay Report (2010) 1059, 12.
100 EHRC. 'Proposals for promoting greater transparency in the public sector: a consultation on improving gender equality in the workplace' EHRC (2009) http://www.equalityhumanrights.com/uploaded_files/consultations/gender_pay_consultation.pdf p 16.
101 The Fawcett Society is a charity in the UK who undertakes a campaign for womens' rights. Where there's an inequality gap between women and men they're working to close it.
102 Supra 96 p 9.
103 Supra 96 p 10.

that was introduced for public sector organisations only by the Equality Act 2006.[104] Under this Act, the public sector was subject to duties in relation to race, disability and gender. This duty was introduced in a bid to tackle discrimination in public sector organisations and it required them to promote equality and not just avoid discrimination. It also shifted the burden of taking action against discrimination from individuals to organisations.[105] This has now been replaced by a new more general duty, under s 149 of the Equality Act 2010, which extends to all areas of discrimination and provides that a public authority must have due regard to: ...eliminate discrimination... advance equality of opportunity between persons who share a relevant protected characteristic and persons who do not share it and foster good relations between persons who share a relevant protected characteristic and persons who do not share it.[106] This duty came into force under the Equality Act 2010, on 5 April 2011.[107] The Act also allows for the creation of what are known as 'specific duties' to be placed on public authorities. These duties help those bodies to fulfil their responsibilities under the general duty. Complying with the Gender Equality Duty means public authorities need to be proactive. Although the public sector now has more of a specific duty in relation to equality than the private sector, criticism has been raised in the past over the wording of the public sector duties. The new duty uses the phrase to have 'due regard', suggesting that an authority is only required to consider the need to eliminate pay discrimination rather than actually taking action to eliminate it.[108] However, specific duties were introduced in the UK which required all listed public bodies to produce a gender equality scheme that informs how they will fulfil both the general duty and the specific duties.[109]

---

104 Now the Equality Act 2010 s 149.
105 EHRC (2010) Background to the public sector duties http://www.equalityhumanrights. com/advice-and-guidance/public-sector-duties/background-to-the-public-sector-duties.
106 Equality Act 2010 s 149.
107 EHRC (2010) The new Public Sector Equality Duty http://www.equalityhumanrights. com/advice-and-guidance/public-sector-duty.
108 Supra 92 p 213.
109 EHRC (2010) Gender equality duty http://www.equalityhumanrights.com/advice-and-guidance/public-sector-duties/what-are-the-public-sector-duties/gender-equality-duty/

All public authorities in Scotland are subject to the general duty, but only some public authorities (for example, the Scottish Government, Local Authorities, Health Boards etc) are subject to the specific duties. However, the Scottish Government has decided to postpone its operation until later in 2011.[110] The Scottish specific duties will include a requirement for listed public bodies with 150 or more employees to publish an equal pay policy statement and report on it every three years.[111] The specific duties do appear clear in their aim to tackle the gender pay gap by requiring public authorities to report on it and provide statistics to back it up.[112] However, the impact of this requirement is unlikely to be significant unless the type of data to be reported is more clearly specified and the duty to provide it can be enforced. The exclusion of public bodies with less than 150 employees from undertaking the specific the duties should be overturned as an organisation should not be permitted to be less equality minded just because it is smaller. It has been identified that what is needed is as a move away from a remedial model to one of positive obligations imposed on organisations.[113]

Statutory Sick Pay

11.44 In the UK Statutory Sick Pay (SSP) must be paid by employers to all their employees[114] who are sick for a period longer than 4 consecutive days and up to 28 weeks. The current rate of SSP is £81.60 per week.

---

110 EHRC (2010) Interim advice on the Equality Act Scottish Specific Duties http://www.equalityhumanrights.com/scotland/scottish-news/interim-advice-on-the-equality-act-scottish-specific-duties/
111 Ibid.
112 At organisational level, relevant information would include sex-specific information on for example: numbers of employees, categories of employment, duration of employment contracts, proportions of part-time workers, wage levels, types of jobs, proportions in management positions, take-up of family leave policies, access to training. This information can be collected and analysed by the company management.
113 K Monaghan. 'The Equality Bill: a sheep in wolf's clothing or something more?' European Human Rights Law Review (2009) Vol. 4, p 515.
114 Employees include office holders, for example police officers, Members of Parliament, the judiciary and some company directors.

There is an SSP calculator available to help employers work out if employers are entitled to SSP and if so how much.[115]

Employees who are unable to work due to illness for longer than 28 weeks will not be entitled to SSP, but maybe entitled to Government support through the employment and support allowance.[116] Also SSP is not paid to a number of categories of employees, including those: over the age of 65; those who are paid less than the national insurance lower earnings limit;[117] pregnant employees already in receipt of Statutory Maternity Pay (SMP) or Maternity Allowance; in prison; on strike etc. To be eligible for SSP the employee must inform his employer of his illness and provide medical certification if requested. Employees can self-certify sickness up to a period of seven days but, thereafter, the employer is entitled to ask for medical certification.

Breach of Contract Claims

11.45 Employment tribunals can deal only with matters specifically assigned to them by or under statute. Until 1994, which was the date that the law changed, they had no jurisdiction to deal with common law claims, such as claims for breach of contract, even though the claim arose in an employment context. From 12 July 1994 an employment tribunal can only hear a breach-of-contract claim if the claim arises out of a contract of employment and is outstanding on the termination of the employee's employment. So to make a breach of contract claim through an employment tribunal, an employee's employment must have ended. The claim must also not relate to personal injury; a term imposing an obligation of confidence; a term which is a covenant in restraint of trade; a term relating to intellectual property eg copyright, rights in performances, moral rights, design rights, registered designs, patents and trademarks and a term either requiring an employer to provide the employee with living accommodation or imposing a duty relating to the provision of living

---

115 www.hmrc.gov.uk/paye/employees/statutory-pay/ ssp-overview.htm.
116 Formerly incapacity benefit.
117 Employees must earn an average of at least £102 a week to qualify for SSP. If they do not earn enough to qualify for SSP they can claim Employment and Support Allowance instead and the same applies to the self employed.

accommodation. These rules apply to both employee claims and employer counter-claims.

The claimant will only get damages of up to £25,000 if he can prove real financial loss, for example, if his employer does not pay him the correct wages eg a payment of arrears of wages, holiday pay or pay in lieu of notice.[118] This limit has applied since the 1994 Order was brought in and the Law Society of England is concerned that the current £25,000 cap for a breach of contract claim in the employment tribunal is too low, particularly for higher earners. The Society believes there should be no cap.[119] If an employee decides to take legal action for not getting proper wages, bonuses etc, he can either bring an action to an employment tribunal or a civil court.

It was thought an employee who wished to claim more than £25,000 could first seek the limit from an employment tribunal and then go on to seek the balance from a civil court. However, the case of *Fraser v HLMAD Ltd*,[120] illustrates the 'potential trap' for claimants who do this and bring a breach of contract claim in an employment tribunal and then seek to recover any excess over £25,000 in the High Court or County Court. The 'trap' appears because of rules that prevent claimants from re-litigating causes of action that have already been litigated in earlier proceedings (including employment tribunal proceedings). Mr Fraser brought an employment tribunal claim for unfair dismissal and wrongful dismissal (the latter being a breach of contract claim) in May 2004. In his ET1, Mr Fraser said that, although he was pursuing his claims in the employment tribunal, he intended to keep open the possibility of bringing proceedings in the High Court to recover any wrongful dismissal damages in excess of the statutory cap of £25,000. In December 2004, Mr Fraser took the precautionary step of starting an action for wrongful dismissal in the High Court with a view to recovering the excess of any award that he received in the employment tribunal. Mr Fraser did not withdraw his employment

---

118 There is no compensation allowed for distress or hurt feelings.
119 Law Society of England Employment Tribunal web survey Results of an online survey 19 March – 2 April 2009. Over two thirds of 87 respondents (70%) thought that the current £25,000 cap for breach of contract claims in Employment Tribunals should not be retained.
120 (2006) IRLR 687.

tribunal claim before doing this. Mr Fraser's employment tribunal claims were successful and his wrongful dismissal damages were assessed at £80,000. However, the employment tribunal awarded him only £25,000 for wrongful dismissal, in line with the statutory cap. His employer HLMAD applied to strike out Mr Fraser's High Court claim, on the basis that the matter had already been litigated in the employment tribunal and it could not also be pursued in the High Court. The Court of Appeal agreed with them, and said that Mr Fraser's employment tribunal claim had merged with his High Court claim and the fact that the claimant had expressly reserved his position in his ET1 did not change this position, and that once the claims had 'merged', there was no independent cause of action that Mr Fraser could pursue in the High Court for the excess of the wrongful dismissal damages. The Court of Appeal said that claimants wishing to bring high value breach of contract claims, should do so in the High Court or County Court, unless they are willing to limit their damages to £25,000. The Court also recommended that the Employment Tribunal Service amend its materials to clarify that wrongful dismissal claims worth over £25,000 should not be brought in employment tribunals. An employee has three months after the date of their termination of employment to make a breach of contract claim to an employment tribunal.

There has been a steady increase in the number of breach of contract (wrongful dismissal) claims being brought before employment tribunals since they have been given the jurisdiction to hear them. Wrongful dismissal is discussed in Chapter 17.

FURTHER READING

Journal articles

Dennis (2007) 'Employers' view on the national minimum wage' (1). IRS Employment Review. No 866, p 17.

'European minimum wage survey'. (2005) European Industrial Relations Review. No 379, p 17.

Various articles by Bob Simpson in the Industrial Law Journal eg (2009) 38 (1) p 57.

Chapter 12

Statutory Regulation of Working Time and Rights to Time Off Work

12.1 In this chapter we will examine the various statutory rules regulating working time and time off work.

WORKING TIME

12.2 Prior to legislation being introduced, working time was since the start of the modern system of employment relations (starting around the early part of the 20th century) only regulated through contractual provisions, voluntary agreement or by collective agreement. Some industries, such as engineering, set down a standard working week but usually only in response to trade union pressure.[1] In general, the parties to a contract of employment were free to negotiate whatever hours they wished, subject only to the implied duty of care.[2] It was not until the 1990's that legislation was enacted to regulate working time.

BACKGROUND TO REGULATIONS

12.3 The EU Working Time Directive (93/104/EC). was first drafted in 1993, and was introduced to improve the living and employment conditions of workers within the EEC. The most commonly known clause within the Directive is that dealing with the 48-hour maximum working week and the opt-out associated with it. The EC Working Time Directive, which required Member States to implement its provision dealing with working hours, should have been implemented in the UK by 23 November 1996. However, the Conservative Government at

---

1   Hakim, Catherine (1999) Working time in Britain: non-regulation and laisser faire policies. In Kravaritou, Yota, (ed) The regulation of working time in the European Union: gender perspectives. PIE-Peter Lang, Brussels, Belgium, pp 269-303.

2   *Johnstone v Bloomsbury Health Authority* [1991] ICR 269.

the time delayed implementation while it awaited the outcome of an (unsuccessful) challenge in the European Court of Justice. The Labour Government that came into power in 1997 implemented the European Working Time Directive in the UK, under the terms of the Working Time Regulations 1998 (SI 1988 No 1833), on 1 October 1998. It was classed as health and safety legislation and introduced measures relating to the organisation of working time including maximum weekly working hours, a statutory right to paid holidays. rest breaks and limits on how many hours of work certain persons can be required to work in a week, eg nightworkers.[3] This legislation has been subsequently updated by various pieces of legislation, most notably the Working Time (Amendment) Regulations 2003.[4]

The aim of the Directive is to ensure that workers are protected against adverse effects on their health and safety caused by working excessively long hours or having inadequate rest or disrupted work patterns. Whether or not legislative intervention has been successful in reducing working hours is unclear.

According to the Annual Report of the Employment Tribunal Services 2009/10,[5] of the 392,800 jurisdictional claims received in 2009-10, just under a quarter, 95,200, were Working Time Directive claims (largely multiple airline industry cases that are resubmitted every three months),[6] which was a vast increase on the number of cases related to working time in 2008/09, which was 23,976. Although the average weekly working hours of full-time workers dropped from 38.7 in 1996, to 37 in 2008,[7] this is only a slight improvement since the introduction of legislation. A labour force survey[8] carried out in 2002 (four years after the Working Time Regulations were introduced), found that around 4 million employees (around 16 percent of the total workforce) worked more than 48 hours per week compared to only 3.3 million employees working these hours

---

3   The Regulations also implemented aspects of the Young Workers' Directive.
4   SI 2003/1684.
5   Employment tribunal and EAT statistics 2009/10, Employment Tribunal Service.
6   The figures includesd over 10,000 claims from airline employees that had been resubmitted a number of times.
7   Office for National Statistics (2009) Labour Force Survey London ONS http://www. statistics.gov.uk/downloads/theme_labour_/LMS_FR_HS/WebTable08.xls
8   www.statistics.gov.uk

in the early 1990's. Nowadays, the UK has over 6 Million workers who work over 45 hours per week. The longest hours are typically worked by male workers in the private sector, aged 30-49 and women with children are least likely to work long hours.[9] Incidents of long working hours are generally higher in private sector rather than the public sector, particularly in the construction, transport, communication, agriculture, forestry and fishing industries. Managers, professionals, operatives and assembly workers are most likely to work unpaid overtime.[10]

There are health and safety aspects to working long hours, as the connection between employees working excessive hours and their suffering ill health is well established.[11] The types of medical problems it can lead to are often severe, such as mental health issues; cardiovascular or gastro-intestinal problems; cancer; and increased risk of accidents and injuries.[12]

The exact connection between working long hours and organisational performance has also been difficult to ascertain. The research cited earlier[13] found no conclusive evidence that long hours lead to lower levels of overall work or organisational performance, but they found that a decrease in hours often lead to improvements in productivity.

THE WORKING TIME REGULATIONS[14]

12.4 The EC Working Time Directive[15] and Young Workers Directive[16] were introduced, under Article 11a of the EC Treaty[17] as a health and

---

9   White J. and Beswick J. (2003) Working Long Hours Sheffield: Health and Safety Laboratory. http://hse.gov.uk/research/hsl_pdf/2003/hsl03-02.pdf

10 Kodz et al (2002) A review of the research literature, analysis of survey data and cross-national organisational case studies Employment Relations Research Series No 11 London DTI.

11 Cooper C, Dewe P, O'Driscoll M P, *Coping with Work Stress* (2010); Wiley; Vanitallie, T, *Stress: A Risk factor for serious illness* (2002) Elsevier.

12 Spurgeon, A Working time: Its impact on safety and health (2003) International Labour Office.

13 Supra 1.

14 SI 1998/1833

15 93/104/EC replaced by EC Working Time Directive 03/88/EC.

16 94/33/EC.

17 Now Article 137 EC.

safety measure to address concerns that working long hours would adversely affect workers' health. In particular, the Working Time Directive was intended to tackle issues of maximum weekly hours, rest breaks, paid annual leave, night workers and young workers.

The Working Time Regulations finally came into force on the 1 October 1998, however both the Directive and the Regulations suffered from a lack of clarity in their key provisions and the scope of their application. They have, therefore, been amended since their inception and the current UK legislation is contained in the Working Time Regulations as amended by the Working Time (Amendment) Regulations 2003.[18]

The main protective provisions of the Regulations can be summarised as follows:

Regulation 4 – maximum weekly working time

Regulations 5A and 6A – young workers

Regulation 6 – length of night work

Regulation 8 – monotonous work

Regulation 9 – record keeping

Regulation 10 – daily rest

Regulation 11 – weekly rest periods

Regulation 12 – rest breaks

Regulation 13 – entitlement to annual leave

PROTECTED WORKERS

12.5 The rights available under the Regulations are available to 'workers' which is a much broader category than 'employees'. The definition of worker is provided in Regulation 2 (1), which states that a worker is anyone who works under a contract of employment or any other contract, whether express or implied, and, if express, whether oral or in writing, whereby the individual undertakes to do or perform personally any work or services for another party to the contract whose status is not that of client or customer of any profession or business undertaking carried on by that individual. The definition will usually include people working under

---

18   SI 2003/1684.

a contract for services, where their duty is to provide personal service. Therefore, carpenters working exclusively for a company were held to fall within the definition of worker, despite the fact they were labelled self-employed and paid tax and National Insurance contributions as self-employed contractors.[19] The decision was influenced by the fact that they were obliged to give personal service and could only send a substitute with the express consent of the company. This attitude has been confirmed by subsequent case law.[20] There must, however, be a sufficient element of mutuality of obligation to amount to a contract of employment.[21]

If a worker is operating a business on their own account they will fall outside the scope of the Regulations even if they are obliged to provide personal service. Sub-postmasters and sub-postmistresses were therefore held[22] not to be entitled to paid annual leave under the Regulations because, although they were working for only one business, the Royal Mail, and had agreed to provide a certain amount of personal service, they were running a business of their own. After various, sometimes conflicting, decisions by employment tribunals in recent years it now seems to be finally settled that sub-postmasters (and sub-postmistresses) are self-employed and, as such, are generally outside the scope of employment protection legislation. The EAT has given a comprehensive ruling to the effect that sub-postmasters are not 'employees' of the post office (and so do not qualify for, for example, unfair dismissal rights) and that they are not 'workers' for the purposes of the Working Time Regulations and the National Minimum Wage rules. After various, sometimes conflicting, decisions by employment tribunals in recent years this approach seems to be final.[23]

The Regulations will also apply to workers employed under agency agreements[24] and people undertaking relevant training.[25] Either the principal or the agency will be responsible for implementation of the Regulations, depending on who has responsibility for paying the worker. If

19 *Byrne Brothers (Farmwork) Ltd v Baird and Others* EAT 542/01.
20 *Yorkshire Window Co Ltd v Parkes* EAT 2//05/10, *Cavil v Barratt Homes* EAT 1/0//03 and *JNJ Bricklaying Ltd v Stacey* EAT8/07/03.
21 *Cotswold Developments Construction Ltd v Williams* [2006] IRLR 181.
22 EAT 0524/01.
23 *Bacica v Muir* [2006] IRLR 35.
24 Regulation 36 and see *Giannelli v Edmund Bell & Co Ltd* EAT 6/09/05.
25 Regulation 42.

it is not obvious who bears that responsibility then the party who actually pays the worker will have liability under the Regulations.

The Regulations do not apply uniformly to all workers. Some categories of worker are excluded from the provisions completely, others are partially excluded and still others, such as young workers and night workers, have specific provisions which relate to them alone. We shall consider the main categories later.

PROTECTION UNDER THE REGULATIONS

Regulation 4 – Working time and the 48 hour working week

12.6 Under Regulation 4, there is a limitation of working time in the average working week. The limitation is not absolute. The employer must take all reasonable steps to ensure the limit is complied with in respect of each worker and must keep accurate records of workers to whom the limit does not apply.

The current limit is 48 hours including overtime. This is an average figure calculated over a reference period of 17 weeks.

'A worker's average working time for each seven days during a reference period shall be determined according to the formula:

$$\frac{A + B}{C}$$

Where:

A is the aggregate number of hours comprised in the worker's working time during the course of the reference period;

B is the aggregate number of hours comprised in his working time during the course of the period beginning immediately after the end of the reference period and ending when the number of days in that subsequent period on which he has worked equals the number of excluded days during the reference period; and

C is the number of weeks in the reference period'.[26]

---

26   Regulation 4(6).

Working time is defined as any period during which a worker is at his employer's disposal. This would include working lunches and mandatory training courses, but time travelling to and from work is not included as working time.

On-call time

12.7 One of the most contentious issues has been the applicability of the Regulations to on-call time.

In the two important cases of *Syndicato de Medicos de Asistencia Publica (SIMAP) v Valenciana*[27] and *Landeshaupstadt Kiel v Jaeger*,[28] the ECJ ruled that time spent on-call when physically present at work can be working time for the purposes of the Directive, eg doctors who are on-call but also required to be physically present in a medical centre.

The result is that an employee is working (and not on a rest break) if he is on-call at his employer's premises. This applies even if he is not been paid for this time. In *Anderson v Jarvis Hotels plc*,[29] the guest care manager was required to sleep over at the hotel on a regular basis. Although he was not paid for this time, he was disciplined if he left the hotel. The Scottish EAT held that this was working time and could not be regarded as a rest period. In *MacCartney v Oversley House Management*,[30] the resident manager of a care home was also held to be working when on-call even though she spent on-call time in her home, which was a tied house on the premises which was provided by her employer.

Time on-call in such situations will count as working time towards the 48 maximum working hours in a working week, and the worker will be entitled to rest breaks after the appropriate number of hours. Such time must also be paid at the national minimum wage (see chapter 11).

---

27 3/10/00 Case 303/98 [2001] ICR 1116, ECJ.
28 C-151/02 [2003] IRLR 804.
29 EAT (Scotland) 30/05/06.
30 [2006] ICR 510. See also *Hughes v Jones (t/a Graylyns Residential Home* EAT 3/10/08.

Time on-call spent at home where the employee is unlikely to be called out is not treated as working time.[31]

Regulation 5 – Individual employees opt-out

12.8 It is possible for workers to opt-out of the maximum working week and many employers request that they do so. A survey of 163 organisations,[32] which together employed nearly 500,000 people, found that 71% of employers surveyed asked at least some of their managers to sign an opt-out form releasing them from the protection of the Working Time Regulations. Also 70% of those organisations surveyed said they would ask new recruits to opt-out of the legal protections afforded by the Regulations at the beginning of the employment relationship. This figure rose to 90% in relation to managers.

Employers may not insist that workers opt-out, or subject them to dismissal,[33] or other detriment if they refuse to do so.[34]

During 2009, the individual right to opt-out was the subject of a negotiating process amongst members of the European Union. However, attempts to remove it failed and it continues to be possible for UK workers to opt-out of the 48 maximum working week.

It is important to note that the opt-out can only be made by the individual his/herself and not by a trade union (or anyone else) on their behalf.[35]

Regulation 5 sets out some requirements for an opt-out agreement. The agreement must:

(a)   Be in writing

---

31   Time spent on-call has been the subject of debate since *SiMAP v Conselleria de Sanidad y Consume de la Generalidad Valenciana,* see above and other ECJ cases. The ECJ held that all 'on-call' time constitutes working time if the employee is required to be in the workplace rather than at home, even if the worker is asleep (at the workplace) for some or all of that time.

32   Employment Relations Survey covered in Employers make liberal use of working time Regulations opt-out Crail, M Personnel Today, 26 November 2007.

33   Regulation 32.

34   Regulation 31.

35   Syndicato de Medicos de Asistencia Publica (*SIMAP v Valenciana* (C303/98)).

(b)   Specifically disapply the Regulations, rather than simply state the hours the employee is agreeing to work.

(c)   Specify its duration. The agreement may be indefinite but must state the employee has a right to bring it to an end by notice. The maximum notice period is 3 months and if there is no notice period specified, then the default position is 7 days notice.

Employers must keep up-to-date records covering all those exempted. The Regulations have been amended in respect of individuals who voluntarily opt-out of the 48-hour week. Employers must: (a) keep up-to-date records of all workers who have opted out under Regulation 4(2). No time limit is specified for the retention of records and the duty to keep records with regard to those employees is arguably less onerous than the duty on employers to keep records of the working time of employees who have not opted out; and (b) make records available to the HSE or other relevant enforcement authority on request.

The following example of an opt-out agreement is taken from the Direct Gov website:[36]

> I [name] agree that I may work for more than an average of 48 hours a week. If I change my mind, I will give my employer [amount of time – up to three months] notice in writing to end this agreement.
>
> Signed………....................................
>
> Dated………....................................

Rest

12.9 The Regulations specify periods for three types of rest namely daily rest, rest breaks and weekly rest. There are special provisions for young workers, night workers and workers undertaking monotonous work.

---

36   http://www.direct.gov.uk/en/Employment/Employees/WorkingHoursAndTimeOff/
DG_10029426.

and these are discussed separately. Workers who are excluded from the provisions relating to rest breaks are discussed below.[37]

Regulation 10 – Daily Rest – Under Regulation 10(1), adult workers are entitled to at least 11 hours consecutive rest in every 24 hour period.

Regulation 11 – Weekly Rest – Under Regulation 11, adult workers are entitled to at least 24 hours uninterrupted rest in a seven day period.

Regulation 12 – Rest Breaks – Regulation 12 provides that every six hours an adult worker is entitled to a break specified by workforce agreement or collective agreement but failing that a minimum of 20 minutes. He is entitled to spend it away from his workstation.

Regulation 8 – Monotonous work

12.10 The rules defined by regulation 8 are: 'where the pattern according to which an employer organises work is such as to put the health and safety of a worker employed by him at risk, in particular because the work is monotonous or the work-rate is predetermined, the employer shall ensure that the worker is given adequate rest breaks.'

There is no definition of the term monotonous used in the Regulations, however this provision would apply to staff who carry out a single task on a continuous basis,[38] or do not have the opportunity to leave their workstation or vary the manner in which the task is performed. These breaks should be additional to the normal rest breaks provided for in the Regulations.

Regulation 6 – Night workers

12.11 Night work under the Regulations means work during 'night time' which is defined as a period of not less than seven hours which includes the period between midnight and 5 am. In *R v Attorney General for Northern Ireland*[39] a worker who only worked one week out of three as a night worker could still be regarded as a night worker for the purposes

---

37   Regulation 21.
38   Sometimes historically referred to a piece workers.
39   (1999) IRLR 315.

of the legislation, since the phrase in the 'normal course' of work means nothing more than a regular feature.

Night workers (who regularly work at least three hours during night time) should not exceed an average of eight hours in each 24-hour period, averaged over 17 weeks.[40] The averaging period can be extended by agreement or in specified circumstances. Night workers whose work involves special hazards or physical or mental strain are limited to working eight hours in **any** 24-hour period during which he performs night work. There are some exemptions in health and public services (eg nursing homes).

Night workers cannot opt-out of the Regulations.[41]

Regulation 7 – Night work health assessments

12.12 Night workers are entitled to a free health assessment before being required to perform night work and such assessments should be repeated regularly.[42] Where a registered medical practitioner has advised an employer that a worker is suffering from health problems related to night work, the employer shall transfer the worker to other suitable work which is not night work.[43] It is not clear how long this requirement would last but seems likely it would be at the discretion of the employment tribunal to uphold the transfer for as long as the medical condition persists, or permanently where it is a permanent condition. This duty is qualified by the phrase 'where it is possible'. So the duty might be ignored when it is impossible to transfer the worker or he is not suited to the alternative duties available.

Regulation 5A and 6A – Young workers

12.13 In Scotland, a child who is by law required to attend school may not work more than 12 hours a week[44] and workers who are under school

---

40   Night workers in the transport industry are limited to ten hours in 24.
41   A night worker cannot opt-out of the night working limit. http://www.direct.gov.uk/ en/Employment/Employees/WorkingHoursAndTimeOff/DG_10029426.
42   Regulation 7.
43   Regulation 7(6).
44   Children and Young Persons (Scotland) Act 1937.

leaving age[45] are not entitled to annual leave under the Working Time Regulations.[46]

There are special provisions in the Working Time Regulations for 'young workers' who are under 18 but over compulsory school leaving age. Young workers must not work more than 8 hours a day and their maximum working week is limited to 40 hours a week.[47] Young workers are entitled to 48 hours consecutive rest each week.[48] Young workers are entitled to the same amount of annual leave as adults.

The standard position regarding rest breaks is that young workers are usually entitled to 12 hours rest in 24 hours[49] and a rest break of 30 minutes, if his daily work is more than 4 and ½ hours. Regulation 27 provides an exception to these rules if his employers require him to undertake work which no adult is available to perform and which is occasioned by either an occurrence, due to unusual and unforeseeable circumstances beyond the employer's control, or exceptional events, the consequences of which could not have been avoided despite the exercise of all due care by the employer. In such limited circumstances the work must be of a temporary nature, must be performed immediately, and the young worker must be allowed equivalent compensatory rest within the following three weeks.

An additional exception applies in the case of regulation 6A (maximum working time), where his employer requires the young worker to undertake work which is necessary to maintain continuity of service or to respond to a surge in demand for a service or product and no adult worker is available to perform the work and performing the work would not adversely affect the young workers education and training.

Young workers must not usually work during the restricted period of 10pm-6am,[50] or work at night between 10pm and 6am, or between 11pm

---

45   Compulsory school age is up to the end of the Summer term in the year someone's 16th birthday falls.
46   *Ashby v Addison and anor* (2003) ICR 667. The Employment Appeal Tribunal held that a 15 year-old paper boy was not a worker for the purposes of the Working Time Regulations. As such, he was not entitled to four weeks paid annual leave.
47   Regulation 5A.
48   Regulation 11(3).
49   Regulation 10 (2).
50   Regulation 6A.

and 7am if the contract of employment provides for work after 10pm. However, exceptions apply in limited circumstances, in the case of certain kinds of employment. Young workers may work throughout the night if they are employed in:

- Hospitals or similar establishments

or in any of the following activities:

- Cultural
- Artistic
- Sporting
- Advertising. Only applies if the circumstances described above in italics under Regulation 6A arise.

Young workers may work between 10pm or 11pm to midnight, and between 4am to 6am or 7am, if they are employed in:

- Agriculture
- Retail trading
- Postal or newspaper deliveries
- A catering business
- A hotel, public house, restaurant, bar or similar establishment
- A bakery

Under Regulation 7 (2) an employer (a) shall not assign a young worker to work during the period between 10 pm and 6 am ('the restricted period') unless (i) the employer has ensured that the young worker will have the opportunity of a free assessment of his health and capacities before he takes up the assignment; or (ii) the young worker had an assessment of his health and capacities before being assigned to work during the restricted period on an earlier occasion, and the employer has no reason to believe that that assessment is no longer valid; and (b) shall ensure that each young worker employed by him and assigned to work during the restricted period has the opportunity of a free assessment of his health and capacities at regular intervals of whatever duration may be appropriate in his case. (4) The requirements in paragraph (2) do not apply in a case where the work a young worker is assigned to do is of an exceptional nature.

Regulation 21 – Exclusions from rest breaks

12.14 Regulation 21(c) provides an exclusion from rest breaks where there is a need for continuity or there is a surge in activity. This exclusion has been construed narrowly by the Court of Appeal. It is the activities of the worker, rather than the employer, which must require continuity and a surge of activity means an exceptional level of activity which is out with the normal fluctuation of the working week or working day. The Court of Appeal in *Gallagher and others v Alpha Catering Services*[51] stated that an employee who is on-call and may be summoned at any moment is not enjoying a rest break. Downtime could not therefore constitute a rest break for the purposes of the Regulations: 'a rest break is an uninterrupted period of at least 20 minutes, which is neither a rest period nor working time, and which the worker can use as he pleases.'

Regulations 13 and 14 – Annual leave

12.15 Since April 2009, the minimum holiday entitlement for most full-time workers is 28 days paid leave per year.[52] Bank holidays will only be in addition to this if there is a contractual entitlement, as bank holidays are included within the annual leave entitlement under the Regulations. Part-time workers are entitled to the same leave as full-timers calculated on a pro rata basis.

The original entitlement to paid leave under Regulation 13 was only available after thirteen weeks continuous employment with the employer. However, as a result of the ECJ decision *R v Secretary of State for Trade and Industry ex parte BECTU*,[53] the Regulations were amended[54] and the qualifying period was removed so holidays now accrue monthly at the rate of 1/12th of the annual entitlement in the first year of employment.[55]

---

51 *Gallagher and ors v Alpha Catering Services Ltd* [2004] EWCA Civ 1559, [2005] ICR 673.
52 Regulation 13.
53 (C-173/99) [2001] IRLR 519.
54 Working Time (Amendment) Regulations SI 2001/3256.
55 Regulation 15A.

The parties may stipulate the start of the 'leave year' in the worker's contract or as part of a relevant agreement, otherwise the leave year will commence on the worker's start date.[56] The employer is entitled to stipulate when in the leave year holidays may be taken, but he must not be unduly restrictive or unreasonable. He must give the employee notice of the days on which he requires holiday to be taken. The notice given should be twice as long as the holiday he wants to be taken.[57] Likewise the worker must take the holiday at a reasonably convenient time and give reasonable notice. Again the notice given should be twice as long as the holiday he intends to take, eg two weeks notice of a week's holiday.[58] In most cases, annual leave must be taken in the leave year in which it accrues and it cannot be taken in the subsequent year.[59] It is not possible to pay a worker in lieu of his statutory holiday entitlement,[60] unless the employee cannot take all his leave because his employment has ended. A worker who leaves the employment during the leave year will be entitled to pay in lieu of any accrued leave which has not been taken.[61] It is not possible to contract out of the statutory entitlement to annual leave, even in circumstances where the employee is guilty of misconduct. Any such contractual provision will be void.[62] It is, however, possible for an employer to insist the holiday is taken during the notice period.[63]

The rate of pay is stated in Regulation 16 to be the workers normal rate of pay. It may be that a worker is contractually entitled to more than the statutory rate of holiday pay but if not then he is entitled to a weeks pay per week of statutory leave and, if his hours of work vary, a weeks pay will be calculated as his average weeks pay over the previous 12 weeks.[64] Overtime which is not contractually guaranteed will not count.[65]

---

56 Regulation 13(3).
57 Regulation 15(4)(a).
58 Regulation 15(1) and 15 (4)(a).
59 *Kigass Aero Components Ltd v Brown* 2002 ICR 697.
60 *Federatie Nederlandse Vakbeweging v Staat der Nederlanden* (C-124/05), [2006] IRLR 561.
61 Regulation 14(2).
62 *Whitley and District Men's Club v MacKay* [2001] IRLR 595.
63 Regulation 15.
64 *Sanderson & Anor v Excel Management* [2006] ICR 1337.
65 *Barnsey and Ors v Albon Engineering Ltd* [2004] ICR 1083.

If a worker leaves the employment having taken more than his entitlement to holidays, it is normally unlawful for the employer to deduct it from his pay. Employers wanting to deduct holiday pay in this situation must include the right in a relevant agreement with their employees. This agreement must be in writing and would give the employer the contractual right to make a deduction.[66] If an employer makes a deduction without a relevant agreement in force this could be an unlawful deduction under the Employment Rights Act 1996 (see chapter 11).

The question as to whether Article 7 of the Directive applies in relation to workers who have been absent due to sickness has resulted in considerable litigation. In *Stringer and others v HMRC*,[67] the House of Lords referred a case to the European Court of Justice (ECJ) for clarification about workers on long term sick leave and their entitlement to annual leave under the Working Time Directive.[68] The claimants were all previously employees of Her Majesty's Revenue and Customs (HMRC). One had requested to take annual leave during a period of sickness absence, which HMRC refused. The others were dismissed following long-term sickness absence, and they claimed payment in lieu of outstanding holiday entitlement. The European Court of Justice stated that workers are entitled to four weeks' annual leave (now 28 days), and a worker on sick leave for all or part of the annual leave year is entitled to any untaken annual leave when they return to work, which could be in the following leave year. The ECJ also held that where a worker's employment is terminated before he has had the opportunity to take his annual leave entitlement due to sickness, the worker must receive payment in lieu at the normal rate of pay. A worker who has been on sick leave during his holidays must be allowed to take the leave he missed after he recovers. It had been thought by many employers that the worker would simply lose their annual leave entitlement, however in *Pereda v Madrid Movilidad SA*,[69] the ECJ dealt with this issue. The ECJ held that the worker had the option to designate an alternative period of leave as annual leave. So a worker who falls ill during his period of annual leave may be entitled to reclaim the leave. The case also makes it clear

---

66   *Hill v Howard Chappell* [2003] IRLR 19.
67   [2009] UKHL 31.
68   EC Directive 2003/88.
69   [2009] IRLR 959.

that, although a worker can take annual leave whilst on sick leave, the employer cannot force him to do so.

Annual leave and maternity leave

12.16 A woman is entitled to her annual leave in addition to her statutory maternity leave (including compulsory maternity leave, ordinary maternity leave and additional maternity leave).

It makes sense for contracts of employment to provide for the accrual of annual leave during maternity leave, given that all contractual terms now subsist during ordinary maternity leave and additional maternity leave so that annual leave will continue to accrue during these periods. The difficult issue is often when is the time when a woman can take her accrued annual leave? It was held by the ECJ, in *Merino Gomez v Continental Industries del Caucho SA*,[70] that a woman is entitled to take the paid holiday that she has accrued during a period other than her maternity leave. In the ECJ's view, maternity leave is intended to protect a woman's health during and after pregnancy and her relationship with her child in the period immediately after birth. Given that the purposes of maternity leave and annual leave are different, a woman must be able to take annual leave during a period that is not a period of maternity leave (i.e. she cannot take two types of leave simultaneously, effectively sacrificing one type).[71]

Pay in lieu and Rolled-up holiday pay

12.17 For the purpose of paying holiday pay some employers have adopted the practice of 'rolling-up' holiday pay with normal salary, e.g. expressing a percentage of the amount a worker is paid as being for holiday so that when the worker takes holiday they are not paid during that time. The practice of using rolled-up holiday pay has been held to be unlawful in the UK since 2002, when the Scottish EAT[72] decided that it was inconsistent with the requirements of the European Working Time Directive and the

70 *Merino Gomez v Continental Industrias Del Caucho SA* (C-342/01) ECR I-2605.
71 The ECJ decisions potentially conflict with Reg 13(9)(a) of the Working Time Regulations 1998, which does not permit employees to carry over statutory annual leave that they are unable to take in the relevant leave year.
72 *MPB Structures Limited v Munro*, (2002) IRLR 601 EAT.

UK's implementation of that Directive in the Working Time Regulations 1998. The EAT's view, subsequently confirmed by the Court of Session,[73] was that holiday leave and pay is a single entitlement and that payment must be made at the time the holiday is taken. In April 2004, the Court of Appeal referred two cases to the ECJ, *Caulfield and Others v Marshalls Clay Products Ltd* and *Clarke v Frank Staddon Ltd*. In the *Marshalls Clay* case, the employer and trade union introduced rolled-up holiday pay under a joint agreement that applied to shift workers. In the *Staddon* case, Mr. Clarke's rate of pay did not increase when the rolled-up holiday agreement was introduced on the basis that it was already included in the daily rate of pay. In both cases, the EAT decided that the arrangements were lawful. The Court of Appeal's view was that these EAT decisions did not conflict with the WTD or WTR. However, it was unhappy that such a decision would mean that the two national appeal courts, the Court of Appeal and the Court of Session, had come to contradictory conclusions on the same issues. Accordingly, the Court of Appeal decided to refer a number of questions to the ECJ. Following the ECJ judgment,[74] and more recent judgments in UK courts, rolled-up holiday pay was judged to be unlawful and payment for statutory annual leave should be made at the time when leave is taken. However, a potential problem is that the Directive allows an employer to make genuine and transparent payments of holiday pay in addition to normal remuneration throughout the holiday year. The burden of proof on the employer is to show that such payments are genuinely additional to normal remuneration but, if the employer can show that they are then he is entitled to set off those payments against a worker's right to payment for annual leave.

EXCLUDED CATEGORIES OF WORKERS AND SPECIAL PROVISIONS

12.18 Under the original legislation, a broad category of workers were excluded from rights provided for by the Working Time Regulations 1998,

---

73 *MPB Structures Limited v Munro*, 2003 SC 485.

74 *Robinson-Steele v PD Retail Services, Clarke v Frank Staddon Ltd, Caulfield & Others v Hanson Clay Products Ltd (formerly Marshalls Clay Products Ltd)*, (C-131/04 and C-257/04), [2006] IRLR 386.

including adult workers in the air, rail, road, sea, inland waterway and lake transport sectors, sea fishing and other work at sea (including offshore platform workers), domestic workers and doctors in training. Most of these exclusions were removed in August 2003 by the Working Time (Amendment) Regulations 2003,[75] although mobile workers in the road transport sector had to wait until 2005 to be included in the WTR, and junior doctors experienced a phased reduction in working hours which should have been completed by 1 August 2009. The UK took advantage of an extension to the time limit and the maximum working week which is applicable to some categories of doctors in training is 48 hours from 1 August 2011.[76]

There are certain classes of workers that remain specifically excluded by the Regulations. Service activities such as the armed forces and the police are outside the scope of the Regulations in certain circumstances, which are discussed below. Sea fishermen and seafarers, such as those working on seagoing ships and on inland waterways (including hovercrafts),[77] mobile road transport workers,[78] mobile aviation workers,[79] and domestic servants in private households,[80] are all excluded.

---

75   SI 2003/1684.

76   Working Time (Amendment) Regulations 2009/1567.

77   The Seafaring week of 72 hours and 14 hours' rest in any 24 or a minimum weekly rest requirement of 77 hours and the Directive on the organisation of working time, concluded by the social partners provides for a maximum work hours in any 24-hour period. It also provides for 4 weeks' paid annual leave and health assessments. The Department for Transport implemented this Directive through the Merchant Shipping (Hours of Work) Regulations 2002 (SI 2002/2125) which came into effect in September 2002.

78   The Road Transport Directive (RTD) makes provision in respect of breaks, rest periods and working time for those subject to Council Regulation No. 3820/85 on the harmonisation of certain social legislation relating to road transport, otherwise known as 'the European drivers' hours Regulations'. The RTD was implemented in April 2005.

79   Mobile aviation workers are subject to the Civil Aviation (Working Time) Regulations 2004/756.

80   Regulation 19.

Emergency services

12.19 Regulation 18(2) (a), provides that the essential public services are exempt where characteristics peculiar to certain specific services such as the armed forces, or to certain specific activities in the civil protection services, inevitably conflict with the provisions of these Regulations. This Regulation does not confer a blanket exemption to emergency services. In *Bernard Pfeiffer and Others v Deutches Rotez Kreuz*,[81] the ECJ held it applied to them only in so far as their work could not be planned, for example if a major catastrophe had occurred.

Agricultural workers

12.20 There are special arrangements for agricultural workers in respect of leave and pay. They are governed by the Agricultural Workers Boards, although this arrangement is likely to be reviewed soon. In Scotland the relevant board is the Scottish Agricultural Workers Board.[82] The introduction of the National Minimum Wage Act 1998 allowed for the Agricultural Wages Boards for Scotland, England and Wales, and Northern Ireland to set minimum wage rates for agricultural workers provided that the hourly rates set were never less than the corresponding rate under the NMWA 1998. The Scottish Agricultural Workers Board also has to take account of the holiday provisions set out in the Working Time Regulations when fixing the holiday entitlement for workers in agriculture. The Agricultural Wages (Scotland) Order provides that the holiday year will cover the period 1 January to 31 December. A worker is entitled to 5 weeks holiday per year and a week is the equivalent to the number of days that an employee would normally be expected to work in the course of a regular working week. In addition they are entitled to four days special holidays which are set.[83]

---

81   C-397/01 to C-403/01, [2005] IRLR 137, ECJ.
82   The Agricultural Wages (Scotland) Order (No. 57) 2009.
83   In 2009/2010, each worker was entitled to 4 special holidays as follows: Christmas Day; New Year's Day; the first Monday in May; the first Monday in October.

Partial exemptions under Regulation 21

12.21 Under Regulation 21, various workers are exempt from Regulations 6 (length of night work), 10 (daily rest), 11(weekly rest period) and 12 (rest breaks).

This partial exemption applies where:

(a) the worker's activities are such that his place of work and place of residence are distant from one another, or his different places of work are distant from one another, including cases where the worker is employed in offshore work;

(b) the worker is engaged in security and surveillance activities requiring a permanent residence in order to protect property and persons;

(c) the worker's activities involve the need for continuity of service or production in relation to services relating to the reception, treatment or care provided by hospitals or similar establishments including the activities of doctors in training, residential institutions and prisons;

(d) the worker works at docks or airports etc;

(e) the work is in the press, radio, television, cinematographic production, postal and telecommunications services and civil protection services;

(f) the work is in gas, water and electricity production, transmission and distribution, household refuse collection and incineration;

(g) the work is in industries in which work cannot be interrupted on technical grounds; research and development activities;

(h) the work is in agriculture;

(i) the carriage of passengers on regular urban transport services;

(j) there is a foreseeable surge of activity, as may be the case in relation to; tourism; and postal services;

(k) the worker's activities are affected by an occurrence due to unusual and unforeseeable circumstances, beyond the control of the worker's employer; exceptional events, the consequences of which could not have been avoided despite the exercise of all due care by the employer; or an accident or the imminent risk of an accident;

(l)   other special cases specified under Regulations 23 and 27.

These workers will continue to be entitled to compensatory rest.[84] Regulation 24 provides that workforce or collective agreements can modify or exclude the requirements relating to night work, only if provision is made for compensatory rest to be provided to the workers who are affected. In general, where a worker is required to work during a period which would otherwise be rest period or rest break, the employer must (wherever possible) allow the worker to take an equivalent period of compensatory rest (Regulation 24(a)).

Also workers will continue to be protected by other provisions of the Working Time Regulations that are not exempted under Regulation 21.

Workers whose working time is wholly unmeasured

12.22 Workers who, because of the characteristics of work engaged in, cannot measure working time are excluded from the provisions relating to maximum working week, rest breaks and night working.[85] This exemption applies only to workers whose working time **as a whole** is not measured or predetermined or can be determined by the worker himself.[86]

Opted out workers

12.23 An agreement can be made between an employer and his workers to vary or exclude the application of the Regulations. There are several types of agreement:

(a)   Individual Opt-out Agreements under Regulation 5 which only apply to 48 hour limit (see above);

(b)   Relevant agreements which are defined as a workforce agreement or any provision of a collective agreement which forms part of the contract between employer and worker or any other agreement in writing which is legally enforceable.

---

84   Regulation 24.
85   Regulation 20.
86   Regulation 20(2).

The collective agreements providing for modification or derogation from the Regulations will be agreed upon by independent trade unions and employers or employers' associations or elected employee representative and employers. Workforce agreements apply to workers where no provision regarding modification or derogation from the Regulations is covered by a collective agreement. The workforce agreement must be in writing, have a specified length of less than five years and apply to all relevant members of a workforce or those in a particular group.

The provisions which can be modified or excluded by *relevant* agreements are Regulation 6 (length of night work), Regulation 10 (daily rest), Regulation 11 (weekly rest period) and Regulation 12 (rest breaks). Such agreements cannot exclude the maximum working week but may substitute an alternative reference period for the usual 17 weeks. The maximum period which can be substituted is 52 weeks.

Shift workers

12.24 Regulation 22 makes special provision for shift workers, who are workers whose work schedule is a part of any method of organising work in shifts whereby workers succeed each other at the same work stations according to a certain pattern, including a rotating pattern, and which may be continuous or discontinuous, entailing the need for workers to work at different times over a given period of days or weeks. Such workers may be unable to take their daily or weekly rest periods and, if this is the case, they will be entitled to the equivalent period in compensatory rest. If a shift worker works shifts which include 3 hours of night work in one week out of 3, then he will be a night worker. In the case of varying shifts holiday pay can be averaged.[87] An example would be where the total shift pay was calculated by multiplying the shift pay for each shift pattern by an agreed payment. This could then by divided by the number of weeks in that pattern to produce a weekly payment.

---

87   *British Airways plc v Noble & Forde* [2006] IRLR 533.

Offshore workers

12.25 Offshore workers were originally exempt from the Working Time Regulations, however, this exemption was removed from 1 August 2003.[88] Offshore work is defined[89] as work which is performed mainly on or from offshore installations (including drilling rigs), directly or indirectly in connection with the exploration, extraction or exploitation of mineral resources, including hydrocarbons, and diving in connection with such activities, whether performed from an offshore installation or vessel. The geographical area covered by the Regulations includes Great Britain and UK territorial waters. This was extended in 2006 to include the Continental shelf.

Typically offshore workers work a period of intense work offshore followed by a period of field break onshore when their contract does not actually require them to work. The 48 hour maximum working week applies differently to offshore workers, because their reference period is 52 weeks instead of 17 weeks.[90] Regulation 21 exempts oil workers from Regulations 6(1) and (2) and (7) which relate to length of night work, Regulations 10(1) which relates to daily rest, 11(1) and (2) relating to weekly rest and 12(1) relating to rest breaks. They will, however, be entitled instead to compensatory rest under Regulation 24.

One particularly contentious issue relating to offshore workers is whether entitlement to paid holidays, under Regulation 13, is in addition to field leave because it should be taken from the periods when they would normally be offshore. In 2009 the Scottish EAT held, in *Craig and Ors v Transocean International Resources Ltd and Ors*,[91] that this was not the case. Annual leave should be taken from onshore time. The Court of Session[92] agreed with the EAT in their conclusion that rest periods within a working week in which an employee actually works, as defined by the WTD, do not count towards his entitlement to annual leave. But they held there was nothing in the WTR's definition of 'rest period' which required

---

88   Working Time (Amendment) Regulations 2003 reg 3(b).
89   Regulation 2(1).
90   Working Time (Amendment) Regulations 2006.
91   [2009] IRLR 519.
92   *Russell and others v Transocean International Resources Limited and others* [2010] CSIH 82.

a working week, in which the employee does not work and is not required to work, to be treated as being a 'rest period'. Accordingly, the WTR definition of 'rest period' did not lead to the conclusion that field breaks should not be regarded as being capable of constituting annual leave. The Court also compared the present situation with that of teachers and other workers where holidays had to be taken at prescribed times and described the results which might occur if the oil rig workers won their case as absurd. This decision has now been affirmed by the Supreme Court.

ENFORCEMENT

12.26 Remedies for a breach of the Working Time Regulations are set out in regulation 30. Depending on which Regulation is being enforced the methods of enforcement are different. Some Regulations give rise to criminal sanctions, others can be enforced by the individual employee making a claim to an employment tribunal, while some may also result in a claim by the worker for enforcement in the civil courts.

Regulations 4 to 9, which include obligations regarding maximum average weekly working time, hours of night workers, night workers health assessments, rest breaks and records are enforced by the Health and Safety Executive, Local Authorities and other enforcement agencies. Failure to comply with these obligations is a criminal offence. Regulation 29(3) provides that an employer will be guilty of an offence liable to a fine on conviction of up to £5000 under summary conviction if they fail to comply with these provisions. In Scotland, inspection and enforcement is carried out by the HSE where the employer operates factories, mines, farms, chemical plants, schools or hospitals. The Environmental Health Department of the local councils deals with inspection and enforcement where the employer is engaged in retailing, offices, hotels, and catering etc. In the case of non mobile aviation workers the investigating authority is the Civil Aviation Authority, and in the case of non mobile transport workers, the Vehicle Operation Services Agency.

Enforcement officers, from whatever organisation they work for, have extensive powers of investigation which are set out in Schedule 3 of the Regulations. In addition to referring the matter to the Crown (procurator fiscal) for prosecution, they have the power to issue prohibition and improvement notices on the controller of any activities which in the inspector's opinion contravene the Regulations. An improvement notice orders the employer to suspend activities which are perceived to be a risk and a prohibition notice orders the cessation of any activities which pose a risk of serious personal injury. The employer has 21 days from the date of service to appeal to an employment tribunal in respect of such notices. The tribunal may cancel, affirm or amend the notice. Failure to comply with such a notice is a criminal offence and may result in a fine of up to £20,000 and or six months imprisonment on summary conviction, or an unlimited fine and two years imprisonment if convicted on indictment.

A breach of Regulations 10 to 17, which include the right to a rest period every 24 hours weekly (or fortnightly) daily rest periods and annual leave are actionable by the individual worker who can raise proceedings before an employment tribunal. The claim must be made to the tribunal within 3 months of the act complained of, (or the last act complained of if a continuing act) or the date payment was due in the case of a claim for holiday pay. The tribunal may make a declaration and order the employer to pay such compensation as is just and equitable having regard to the employer's default and the loss suffered by the worker as a result.[93]

Unpaid holiday pay may be claimed as an unlawful deduction from wages under s 13 of the Employment Rights Act 1996. If the employer has terminated the contract of employment of an employee he can bring a claim to a tribunal for breach of contract. A worker may enforce the statutory duty on the employer to observe the particular limits on working time (regulation 4) as a civil claim for breach of contract in the courts.[94] On the other hand, although the statutory duty can be enforced, there is no direct civil claim for damages for injury resulting from breach of the statutory duty.[95]

---

93 Employment Rights Act 1996 s101A.
94 In *Barber and others v RJB Mining Ltd* [1999] IRLR 308, High Court. It was held that following the WTD there was an implied term in every employee's contract of employment .that they should work a 48 hour maximum working week.
95 *Sayers v Cambridgeshire County Council* [2007] IRLR 31.

DISMISSAL AND DETRIMENT

12.27 Employees who are dismissed for reasons connected with the Working Time Regulations will have a claim for automatic unfair dismissal.[96] No period of qualifying service is required to make such a claim. In *Brown v Controlled Packaging Services Ltd*,[97] an employee was told his services were no longer required unless he signed an opt-out agreement. It was held by the employment tribunal that he had been unfairly dismissed. If the employee suffers a dismissal because he refuses to comply with a breach of the Regulations or refuses to forego a right, or to sign a workforce agreement, or because he is, or is seeking to be, a worker representative, such a dismissal will be automatically unfair and the worker will not require a period of qualifying service to make a claim.[98] In addition to the usual remedies for unfair dismissal there is a right to interim relief. It should be noted that in order to make a claim of unfair dismissal the worker will have to meet the definition of an employee and not just a worker.

All workers are protected against being subjected to a detriment connected with the Regulations.[99] Examples of detriment might include dismissal, selection for redundancy, refusal of access to promotion, or disproportionate deduction in pay as a result of a reduction in working time. The available remedies are declaration and compensation.

STATUTORY RIGHT TO TIME OFF

12.28 There are many situations in which the right to time off is guaranteed by statute. The right is usually available to those that meet the statutory definition of employees, rather than workers, and the amount of time must usually be reasonable and the time off may be paid or unpaid. As a general rule of thumb, time off is unpaid unless there is a connection with the employment. Family friendly rights such as the right to time off to care for dependents and maternity paternity and adoptive leave are

---

96 Employment Rights Act 1996 s 101A and 104(4)(d).
97 Case No. 1402252/98.
98 Employment Rights Act 1996 s 101A.
99 Employment Rights Act 1996 s 45A.

considered in Chapter 10, Time off work in relation to trade union duties and activities in Chapter 15, Time off for consultation in chapter 7 and Time off for a companion in disciplinary or grievance proceedings in Chapter 7.

EMPLOYMENT RIGHTS ACT 1996

12.29 There are various rights to time off under the Employment Rights Act 1996 and we shall consider them in turn.

Part IV Sections 50–51 Time off for public duties

12.30 Section 50 of the Employment Rights Act 1996 requires employers to permit employees who hold certain public positions reasonable time off to perform the duties associated with them.

An employee is entitled to unpaid time off work for the performance of their public duties if he is one of the following:

- a justice of the peace (sometimes known as a magistrate);
- a member of a statutory tribunal;
- a police authority;
- a member of the managing or governing body of an educational establishment
- a member of a school board in Scotland or school council in England and Wales;
- a member of the General Teaching Councils for England and Wales;
- a member of the Scottish Environment Protection Agency or the Environment Agency;
- in Scotland, a member of the prison visiting committees or in England and Wales a member of the prison independent monitoring boards; or
- a member of Scottish Water or a Water Customer Consultation Panel.

The amount of time which an employee should be permitted to take off to perform these public duties is defined as that which is reasonable in all the circumstances, having particular regard to how much time off is required overall to perform the duties and how much time off is required to perform the particular duty in question; how much time off the employee has already been permitted for this purpose, or for trade union duties and/or activities, and the circumstances of the employer's business and the effect of the employee's absence upon it. While there is nothing to prevent an employer from making payment to an employee for time off for public duties, there is no obligation for payment to be made to them.

Employees can complain to an employment tribunal if they are unreasonably refused time off for public duties (where the remedies discussed above for trade unionists apply) or are dismissed for asserting the right to time off for public duties.

Part IV Sections 52–54 Time off to look for work and make arrangements for training

12.31 This right to time off to look for work and arrange training for future employment, is enjoyed by employees who are have been given notice of redundancy provided they have 2 years continuous service at the date notice would expire or the statutory minimum period of notice would expire if relevant. In this case the entitlement is to reasonable time off and the right is to paid time off. The method of calculation of the amount of pay is set out in s 53, and will generally be one weeks pay divided by the normal working hours in a week. If the number of hours a week vary, the hourly rate will be the average over the preceding 12 week period. In the event of an unreasonable refusal by the employer or a failure to pay, complaints must be made to an employment tribunal within 3 months. The tribunal may make a declaration and order the employer to pay. If an employer unreasonably refuses to permit an employee to take time off from work as required by s 52, the employee is entitled to be paid an amount equal to the remuneration to which he would have been entitled if he had been permitted to take the time off. However, the employer only has to pay up to two-fifths of a week's pay for each week of time off his employee is entitled to.

Part VI Sections 58–60 Time off for Occupational Pension Scheme trustees

12.32 The trustee of a relevant pension scheme[100] is entitled to reasonable paid time off to perform his duties as a trustee or to undergo relevant training (whether on the employer's premises or elsewhere). Matters which may be taken into account include the purpose of the training, the occasions when it is taken, any conditions imposed on the taking of leave, the circumstances of the employer's business and the effect of the employee's absence on the running of that business.

Payment will be the employee's normal remuneration for the work he would ordinarily have been doing during that time or, where the employee's remuneration for the work he would ordinarily have been doing during that time varies, an amount calculated to the average hourly earnings for that work. This is dealt with by s 59 of the Employment Rights Act 1996. Under subsection (4) it provides that the average hourly earnings mentioned in subsection (3) are (a) those of the employee concerned, or (b) if no fair estimate can be made of those earnings, the average hourly earnings for work of that description of persons in comparable employment with the same employer or, if there are no such persons, a figure of average hourly earnings which is reasonable in the circumstances.

If the employer fails to allow time of or to make payment, the employee may present a complaint to an employment tribunal within 3 months of the failure. The tribunal may make a declaration and order payment of the sum due and any amount which it considers just and equitable having regard to the employer's default and any loss suffered by the employee.

Part VI Section 61 Employee representatives

12.33 An employee who is an employee representative for the purposes of redundancy consultation under Chapter II of Part IV of the Trade Union and Labour Relations (Consolidation) Act 1992 or TUPE or a candidate in an election to be an employee representative, is entitled to take reasonable paid time off to perform his functions as such an employee representative or candidate [or in order to undergo training to perform such functions].

---

100 Defined in s 1 of the Pension Schemes Act 1993 and established under a trust.

He is entitled to be paid at the rate of one week's pay divided by the number of normal working hours in a week. If his rate of pay varies then the hourly rate will be averaged over the preceding 12 weeks. If his employer has failed to allow him time off or payment then the remedy is to make an application to the employment tribunal within 3 months of the failure and the tribunal will make a declaration and order the employer to make payment of the sum which would have been due by way of remuneration.

Part IV Section 63 Time off for young person for study or training

12.34 An employee who is aged 16 or 17, who is not receiving full-time secondary or further education, and has not attained such standard of achievement as is prescribed by Regulations made by the Secretary of State, eg grades A* to C in five GCSE subjects[101] or equivalent in Scotland is entitled to reasonable time off during working hours in order to undertake study or training leading to an external qualification, the attainment of which would contribute to the attainment of the standard prescribed and would be likely to enhance the employee's employment prospects.

Under the Employment Rights Act, an employee aged 16 or 17 has a right to take time off work for study or training which leads to a relevant qualification. The amount of time that may be taken is that which is reasonable, taking into account the nature of the training or study and the needs of the employer. The rate of pay and remedy are the same as for employee representatives above.

Part VI Section 64D Time off for study and training

12.35 In April 2010, the new right to request paid time off for study and training was introduced by amendment into the Employment Rights Act 1996.[102] At the time of writing it is not fully in force. It currently applies to employees in organisations that employ more than 250 employees. On

---

101 Sections 63A to 63C of the Employment Rights Act 1996.
102 By the Apprenticeships, Skills, Children and Learning Act 2009.

1 April 2011, the right was extended to all employees. Agency workers are however not included.[103] It should be noted that the right is not a right to time off, but a right to request it and have it considered. It is fashioned on the right to request flexible working hours and much of the case law relating to flexible working will be relevant. In order to make a request the employee must have 26 weeks continuous service. He must put the request in writing stating details of the proposed study or training namely:

(a)   its subject matter:

   (i)   where and when it would take place;

   (ii)   who would provide or supervise it;

   (iii) what qualification (if any) it would lead to.

(b)   explain how the employee thinks the proposed study or training would improve:

   (i)   the employee's effectiveness in the employer's business; and

   (ii)   the performance of the employer's business.

(c)   contain information of any other description specified by the Secretary of State in Regulations.[104]

Once the application is received by the employer, the employer must arrange a meeting with the employee. The meeting must be held at a convenient time and place and the employee has the right to be accompanied by a trade union official or fellow employee. A decision must be given in writing within 14 days of the meeting. A further request may not be made within 12 months.[105]

If an application is granted the employee has certain duties. He must inform the employer if the employee:

(a)   fails to start the agreed study or training;

(b)   fails to complete the agreed study or training;

---

103 This right is not extended to agency workers under the Agency Workers Regulations.
104 The form of the request is set out in the Employee Study and Training (Eligibility Complaints and Remedies) Regulations 2010/156.
105 The procedures which are to be followed are set out in the Employee Study and Training (Procedural Requirements) Regulations 2010/156.

(c)   undertakes, or proposes to undertake, study or training that differs from the agreed study or training in any respect.

The permissible grounds for refusal are:

(a)   that the proposed study or training to which the application, or the part in question, relates would not improve:

    (i)   the employee's effectiveness in the employer's business, or

    (ii)   the performance of the employer's business;

(b)   the burden of additional costs;

(c)   that the proposed study or training would detrimental effect on the employer's ability to meet customer demand;

(d)   inability to re-organise work among existing staff;

(e)   inability to recruit additional staff;

(f)   detrimental impact on quality;

(g)   detrimental impact on performance;

(h)   insufficiency of work during the periods the employee proposes to work;

(i)   planned structural changes; or

(j)   any other grounds specified by the Secretary of State in Regulations.

An employee whose application has been refused, or refused in part, can make a complaint to an employment tribunal. The only possible grounds of complaint are that the employer has failed to follow the correct procedures or that the decision was based on incorrect facts. The complaint must be made within 3 months of the date of refusal or the date of breach of the procedures. There is no appeal on the basis that the decision was unreasonable. This means that if the employer does not want to grant time off work, there is very little the employee can do about it unless the employee can point to a procedural failure.

The employment tribunal may make an order for reconsideration of the application. In that case the date of the tribunal's order will be considered the date of application. The tribunal may also make an award of such compensation which it considers just and equitable in all the circumstances, but the maximum that can be awarded is 8 week's pay and a week's pay is capped at the maximum weekly pay for the purposes of the unfair dismissal basic award and redundancy payments, and is currently £430.[106] There is no obligation on the employer to pay for the time off.

DETRIMENT AND DISMISSAL

12.36 In relation to each of the statutory rights to time off under the Employment Rights Act described above there is a right not to be subjected to a detriment[107] because the employee has asserted the right to time off. Where a complaint has been made that an employee has been subjected to a detriment and the tribunal finds the complaint well-founded, it will make a declaration to that effect and may order the payment of compensation. It is for the tribunal to decide the appropriate award of compensation taking account of the loss suffered by the applicant.

Any dismissal where the principal reason for the dismissal was the assertion of a statutory right will be automatically unfair. In such cases there is no qualifying period of service to make a claim for unfair dismissal.

JURY SERVICE

12.37 There is no statutory entitlement to time off to allow the employee to serve on a jury however a failure to allow time off would be considered a contempt of court on the employer for not granting time off and/or the employee for not attending. An employee who is cited for jury service during his pre arranged holidays would not, therefore, be entitled to claim the time back from his employer. There is accordingly no right to payment from the employer during this period of absence. An allowance for lost earnings up to a maximum limit, including expenses and subsistence can be claimed from the Scottish Courts Service. More information can be obtained from the Scottish Court Service guidance note.[108] The employer will be required to complete and stamp the certificate on the citation form which the juror should then take to court with him. Self-employed workers will need a self-assessment tax return or certified accounts for the previous year. The system is currently subject to review and more details about the

---

106 Regulation 6 Employee Study and Training (Eligibility, Complaints and Remedies) Regulations 2010/156.
107 Employment Rights Act Part V.
108 http://www.scotcourts.gov.uk/courtusers/jurors/docs/jurorsallowances.pdf.

consultation can be obtained from the Scottish Government website.[109] Under s 98B of the Employment Rights Act, if an employee who has been cited for jury service (under the Court of Session Act 1988 or Criminal Procedure Scotland Act 1995) and is not allowed by his employer to return to work after jury service this will be treated as dismissal which will be automatically unfair. As such there is no requirement for continuous service. There is, however, an exception under s 98B (2) where the circumstances were such that the employee's absence was likely to cause substantial injury to the employer's undertaking, those circumstances were brought to the employee's attention by the employer and the employee unreasonably refused or failed to apply for excusal or deferral for jury service.

SUMMARY AND CONCLUSION

12.38 The rules relating to statutory regulation of working time and rights to time off work get more complicated over time as the legislation is amended to comply with EU requirements and the fact that increasing categories of person qualify for time off. There are undoubtedly going to be changes to the working time legislation in the future, although at this stage it is difficult to know what they are. The possibility of the removal of the opt-out for maximum working hours seems slight given the opposition of all political parties, although given that we are the only country in the EU that allows it there is always the possibility of a successful challenge.

FURTHER READING

Journal articles

Barnard, Deakin, Hobbs: 'Opting out of the 48 Hour Week: Employer Necessity or Individual Choice?' An empirical study of the operation of Article 18(1) (b) of the Working Time Directive in the UK, Industrial Law Journal, Vol. 32 No 4 (2003), pp 223-252.

Websites

http://www.berr.gov.uk/policies/employment-matters/rights/working-time

---

109 http://www.scotland.gov.uk/Publications/2008/09/17121921/8.

Chapter 13

Health and Safety, the Common Law

INTRODUCTION

13.1 There are three aspects of Heath and Safety law which are relevant to the employment relationship. Firstly, there are the civil/common law rules, derived from the law of contract and delict in Scotland, which provide civil remedies to those employees and other parties harmed by the breach of duty of an employer. Secondly, vicariously liability of employers to compensate other employees and third parties for harm caused to them by a wrongful act or omission, committed within the scope of the wrongdoer's employment. Finally, there is Health and Safety legislation which primarily imposes criminal liability, and sometimes also civil liability, on employers, and other persons, in breach of them.[1] We will examine the first two in this chapter and the statutory rules in Chapter 16.

THE COMMON LAW DUTY OF CARE

13.2 Under the law of delict, every person owes a duty to take reasonable care for those, whom it is reasonably foreseeable, will be affected by his actions.[2] According to the House of Lords, in *Caparo Industries v Dickman*,[3] a duty of care will exist if (a) the loss to the pursuer is reasonably foreseeable; (b) there is a close degree of proximity between the defender and the pursuer; and (c) it is fair just and reasonable to impose a duty of care.

It must be shown that the particular defendant stood in the required relationship to the claimant, such that he came under an obligation to use care towards him. This not an issue where the claimant is an employee,

---

1 Eg Health and Safety at Work Act 1972, Management of Health and Safety at Work Regulations 1999.
2 *Donoghue v Stevenson*, [1932] AC 562.
3 [1990]2 AC605.

because there is a contractual relationship between employee and employer which satisfies the 'proximity' requirement. Further, in every contract of employment, there is an implied term that requires all employers to take reasonable care for their employees' safety. Breach of this term by an employer, could give rise to actions being brought by employees against him for breach of contract. Such a material breach of contract by the employer, could result in a resignation by the employer in circumstances amounting to a wrongful or unfair constructive dismissal.

The duty of care is only one element in the delict of negligence. It must also be shown that, not only was the defendant under a duty towards the claimant to be careful, but also that he breached that duty and that breach of duty caused loss, injury and damage to the pursuer.[4]

EMPLOYER'S DUTY OF CARE

13.3 The duty of care is to take reasonable care for the employee's physical and psychiatric safety.[5] The duty is a personal duty, owed by the employer, and those acting on the employer's behalf, to each employee individually. It cannot be avoided simply by the employer appointing a health and safety specialist or agent, because it is a non delegable duty.[6] It is not possible to exclude liability for death or personal injury.[7]

Standard of care

13.4 The standard of care that must be exercised is that of an 'ordinary prudent employer' in the circumstances, ie reasonable care.[8] The reasonable employer will make a judgement balancing the likelihood of injury, likely seriousness of injury, and the disadvantage of using

---

4   *Rothwell v Chemical Insulating Co Ltd* [2007] UKHL 39, the House of Lords held that pleural plaques caused by negligent exposure to asbestos were not actionable neither was the risk of future disease of anxiety they caused. The Damages (Asbestos-related Conditions) (Scotland) Act 2009 was passed specifically to ensure that in Scotland the decision in this case is of no effect and such plaques were actionable.

5   *Barber v Somerset County Council* 2004 UKHL13.

6   *Wilson & Clyde Coal Co v English* (1938) AC.

7   Unfair Contract Terms Act 1977 s 2.

8   *General Cleaning Contractors v Christmas*

precautions.[9] The precise standard required will, therefore, vary according to the circumstances. These circumstances include the cost of introducing precautions[10] and the employee's particular susceptibilities and characteristics. So the standard expected of the employer will be higher where an employee is young and inexperienced, or where they have a pre-existing physical or mental condition which requires them to exercise a special standard of care. In *Paris v Stepney Borough Council*[11] a workman who was employed as a garage hand had only one good eye. He lost his good eye when a metal chip flew off the thing he was working on and lodged in his eye, leaving him blind. His employers had not provided him with goggles and he claimed damages. It was held that, although it was not customary to provide goggles for this type of work, the employer was negligent in failing to provide goggles for this particular employee because they had a special duty to take extra care for this particular employee, bearing in mind his existing disability.

Aspects of Duty of Care

13.5 Although the employer's duty is a general duty of care, in *Wilson and Clyde Coal Co v English*, the House of Lords[12] identified three main aspects of the duty, of namely, the duty to provide: (a) safe plant (machinery, vehicles etc), and equipment, and a safe place of work; (b) a safe system of work; and (c) reasonably safe and competent fellow employees. We will look at each of these in turn.

(a) The Duty to Provide Safe Plant and Equipment and a Safe Place of Work

13.6 An employer has a duty to take reasonable care to provide proper appliances and to maintain them in a proper condition. 'Equipment' is construed widely,[13] and in *Bradford v Robinson Rentals*,[14] a driver was

---

9 *Brisco v Secretary of State for Scotland* 1997 SC14.
10 *Latimer v AEC*, [1952] 2 QB 701.
11 [1951] AC 367.
12 [1938] AC 57.
13 *Knowles v Liverpool City Council* [1993] 4 All ER 321.
14 [1967] 1 WLR 337.

required, as part of his job, to drive in an unheated van on a 400 mile journey in the middle of winter. It was held the employer was liable for breach of his duty of care when the driver contracted frostbite. This part of the duty is overtaken somewhat by the strict liability provisions of s 1(1) of the Employers' Liability (Defective Equipment) Act 1969, which makes an employer liable if an employee suffers personal injury in the course of his employment in consequence of a defect in equipment provided by the employer, and the defect is attributable, wholly or partly, to the fault of a third party, whether identifiable or not. In other words the employer must ensure that the workplace and work environment are safe. This includes any place where the employee may be required to work, even if not the employer's own premises.[15] It also includes anything which is incidental to the work. In *PRP Architects v Reid*,[16] it was held that an employer has a duty to ensure the safety of his employees while at work or entering or leaving the workplace. In this case, an employee injured her hand while leaving her employer's office following the end of her day's work, by means of a lift which was within the same building as her office, but was not owned or controlled by her employer. The Court of Appeal directed that while the employee was in the lift she was still at work. The employer was liable for the employee's injury.

If an employer has a proper system of inspection and maintenance in place, this will usually provide evidence that he has fulfilled this part of the duty of care.

(b) Duty to Provide a Safe System of Work

13.7 The system of work is the way of doing the work. It is a question of fact whether a particular operation requires a system of work in the interests of safety, or whether it can reasonably be left to the employee charged with the task. This duty is usually applied to a regular work situation, where the employer is exercising managerial control over the method of working to his employees, and providing them with instructions on safety. It is usually insufficient to simply instruct employees to follow a safe

---

15 *Crombie v McDermott (Scotland) Ltd* 1996 SLT 1238; *Muir v North Ayrshire Council* 2005 SLT 963.
16 (2007) ICR 78, CA.

system, that system must be enforced (see *Bux v Slough Metals* below). Provided this is done, an employer will not be liable if a worker fails to make proper use of the equipment supplied, or follow the instructions of the employer. In *Charlton v Forrest Printing Ink Co Ltd*,[17] a senior employee was required to collect the firm's wages each Friday from the bank. There had once been a payroll snatch in the past, and the company gave instructions to him that the collection arrangements should be varied each week. However, contrary to these instructions, the employee started to follow the same route and was seriously injured in a payroll robbery. It was held that the employers were not liable for his injuries.

It is now well established that the obligation to provide a safe system of work also extends to an employee's mental health,[18] and protection from violent attacks by third parties.[19] If an employee suffers psychiatric harm as a result of stress, harassment, or overwork, or witnessing a shocking event (as a primary victim) for which his employer is responsible, then the ordinary rules for these claims apply. Where an employer has, in establishing a system of work, followed a general practice of a particular trade or industry, the claimant may have some difficulty in establishing that the practice was negligent.

The duty to provide a safe system of work is not absolute. It must be considered in the light of the circumstances of the particular case. The question which the court must answer is whether adequate provision was made for carrying out of the job at hand, under a) the general system of work adopted by the employer, or b) under some special system adopted to meet the special circumstances of the case.[20]

That said, the employer should not be complacent in the light of the decision in *General Cleaning Contractors v Christmas*,[21] where the court held that employers should know that employees become habitually careless, and where careless practices have become prevalent, the employer's duty requires them to take action to correct this, and not rely on individual employees to use precautions and devise safe systems.

---

17 (1978) 122 Sol J 730.
18 *Petch v Customs and Excise Commissioners* [1993] ICR 789.
19 *McGinnes v Endeva Service Limited* 2006 SLT 638.
20 *Winter v Cardiff Rural DC* [1950] 1 All ER 819.
21 (1953) 2 WLR 6.

It is now well established that, in some circumstances, it is not enough to tell employees about safety clothing and provide it. There is an expectation that the employer insist (using disciplinary measures if necessary) that safety clothing is worn or safety equipment is used. In *Bux v Slough Metals Ltd*,[22] it was summarised as 'the question of whether instruction or persuasion, or even insistence, in using protective equipment *(safety goggles in this case)* should be resorted to is therefore, at large, the answer, depending on the facts of the particular case. One of the most important of these is the nature and degree of risk of serious harm resulting if it is not worn.'[23] It must also be remembered, that if the individual employee is particularly vulnerable, a higher duty of care will apply.[24]

(c) Duty to provide safe and competent fellow employees

13.8 The employer has an obligation to select competent fellow employees, and a correlative duty to give them proper instruction in the use of equipment. If an employer knows, or can foresee, that acts being done by an employee might cause physical or psychiatric harm to a fellow employee,[25] it is likely that the employer could be in breach of their duty to that employee, if he did nothing to prevent those acts, when it was in his power to do so. In *Hudson v Ridge Manufacturing Co*,[26] an employee, who was a well known practical joker, went too far with a joke on one occasion, and injured a fellow employee. It was held that the employer was liable as, knowing of his behaviour, he should have taken steps to remove him from the workplace.[27]

In order to fulfil this part of the duty of care, an employer must check each employee's qualifications and references before employing them, and

---

22 [1974] 1 All ER 262.

23 In what is probably no longer a sound decision *MacWilliams v Sir William Arrol Ltd* [1962] 1 All ER 62 a steel erector fell from a scaffolding and was killed. Safety belts had been provided to him in the past but he had not used them and it was decided that the employer's negligence did not cause the accident which would have occurred even if the safety belts had been provided therefore they were not liable.

24 *Paris v Stepney BC*.

25 *Smith v Crossley Bros* (1951) 95 SJ 655.

26 [1957] 2 QB 348.

27 See also *Gibson v British Rail Maintenance* 1995 SC 7.

provide training and supervision. A failure to train or instruct employees, will result in a breach of duty.[28] Incompetent employees, and perpetrators of dangerous pranks, should be subjected to disciplinary procedures.

BURDEN OF PROOF

13.9 The burden of proof normally lies with the pursuer, to show that a breach of his employer's duty of care has occurred, and that this caused the physical or mental harm that he suffered. It is not necessary to prove that the exact injury was foreseeable, so long as some kind of injury was foreseeable.[29]

Where, on the basic facts, there is no explanation other than the defender's fault the principle of *res ipsa loquitor* (the thing speaks for itself) applies, the pursuer is freed of his burden of proof and the onus shifts to the defender to show that the damage occurred, without their negligence.[30]

DEFENCES

13.10 There are various defences that can be put forward by employers, in the face of a delictual claim by their employee. The first of these, is to deny the facts on which the claim is based, the second is the simple denial that the facts amount to a breach of the duty of care. This latter defence includes the situation where the employer can show they have done all they can do, in the circumstances, to avoid the harm suffered by the employee. In *Latimer v AEC Ltd*,[31] where a factory floor became slippery because of a combination of oil and water that was due to an unprecedented rainfall. The management had ordered that sawdust be spread around, but there was not enough to cover the whole factory floor. An employee slipped and was injured. It was held that the employer had done all he reasonably could do, in the circumstances, and they were not

---

28 *Pickford v ICI* [1996] ICR566.
29 *Smith v Leech Brain & Co* [1962] 2 QB 405 but see *Tremain v Pike* [1969] 1 WLR 1556.
30 *Cassidy v Ministry of Health* 1951 2 KB 343 and *Scott v London and St Katherine Docks* (1865) 3 H&C 596.
31 (1953) AC 643.

liable. The only alternative was to close the factory down, which was a step too far.

The employer may argue that, although there was a breach of duty, the pursuer's loss, injury and damage, was caused by a new intervening event *(novus actus interveniens)*. In *Horton v Taplin Contracts Ltd*,[32] the claimant was standing on an unsecured scaffolding tower. He was injured when the tower collapsed, after being pushed deliberately by a fellow workmate. The workmate's act was held to be a *novus actus interveniens*, which broke the chain of causation. The employers were, therefore, not personally liable for their employee's injury. Aggressive acts by third parties may be regarded as *novus actus interveniens*,[33] but an employer does have a duty to protect employees from foreseeable attacks by third parties.[34]

The employer may aver in his defence, that the injury suffered by their employee, was the employee's sole fault. Where an employee had gone somewhere in the workplace, and done something which was prohibited by the employer, and consequently suffered harm, then it may be seen to be attributable to their own fault, and the employer would not be liable.[35]

If the defender proves that the claimant failed to take reasonable care of their own safety, and that this failure was a contributing cause of the damage, or harm, they suffered, then the court will consider the extent to which the pursuer's negligence contributed to the loss, injury, or damage, suffered by the pursuer. Under the Law Reform (Contributory Negligence) Act 1945 (as amended), apportionment of liability, in the case of contributory negligence, is dealt with under s 1 as follows:

> 'where any person suffers damage as the result, partly of his own fault, and partly of the fault of any other person or persons, a claim in respect of that damage shall not be defeated by reason of the fault of the person suffering the damage, but the damages recoverable in respect thereof shall be reduced to such extent as the court thinks just and equitable having regard to the claimant's share in the responsibility for the damage. This is provided that (a) it shall not operate to defeat any

---

32 [2003] ICR 179.
33 *Yorkshire Traction Co v Searby* [2003] EWCA Civ 1856 148 SJLB 61.
34 *McGinnes v Endeva Service Limited* 2006 SLT 638.
35 *Kirby v NCB* 1958 SC 514; *Ammah v Kuehne & Nagal Logistics* [2009] EWCA Civ 11, {2009] All ER (D) 155 (Jan).

defence arising under a contract, (b) where any contract or enactment providing for the limitation of liability is applicable to the claim, the amount of damages recoverable by the claimant by virtue of this subsection shall not exceed the maximum limit so applicable.'

If contributory negligence is established, the current position is that the claimant will have their damages reduced by the court, in proportion to their own fault.[36]

Another complete defence is '*violenti non fit injuria*' (to the person willing no harm is done). The fact that an employee works in the knowledge of the existence of a danger, does not in itself amount to their consent to run the risk.[37] The requirements for a defence of *volenti non fit injuria* in a negligence action is a complicated matter however, it must be shown that the claimant acted voluntarily, in the sense that they could exercise a free choice. Some judges are of the opinion that there must be an express or implied agreement between the parties before the defence can operate. Another view is that, where the claimant has already come across a danger and continued to work in the knowledge that it's there, then the defence can operate. Where the defence is successful, it absolves the employer, and the claimant will recover no damages at all. This defence rarely succeeds in employment cases, however, in *ICI Ltd v Shatwell*,[38] the plaintiff and his brother were both experienced shot firers employed by the defendants. They jointly chose to ignore their employer's orders, and statutory safety regulations, by testing detonators without taking shelter. There was an explosion and the plaintiff was injured. He sued the defendants on the grounds of their vicarious liability for his brother's negligence and breach of statutory duty. The question for the House of Lords, was whether an employer who was under no statutory duty could be vicariously liable for an employee's breach of statutory duty to another employee. Had the plaintiff acted on his own, rather than in combination with his brother, no action would have lain. The House held that the plaintiff was *volens* to the risk of harm, and his action therefore failed. Had the plaintiff sued

---

36 Supra 9 the Bux case where it was held the employee was 40% to blame for refusing to wear safety equipment.

37 *Smith v Baker & Sons* [1891] AC 325 but see *Thomas v Marconi's Wireless Telegraph Co* (1965) 1 WLR 850.

38 (1965) AC 656.

his brother, then the action would have failed on the grounds of *volenti*. There had been no pressure brought by the employers to adopt the unsafe method of working, therefore, there was no reason why *volenti* should not succeed for the employer.

With respect to the duty of care there are particular issues which are worthy of mention.

OTHER ASPECTS OF THE DUTY OF CARE

13.11 We will now consider some of the more complicated issues commonly encountered in the employment field.

Repetitive strain injury

13.12 Repetitive strain injury, is a condition where repeated actions at work lead to muscular strains and other medical problems. The courts have not always considered RSI to be an injury. In *Mughal v Reuters Ltd*,[39] a newspaper sub editor that operated a Visual Display Unit claimed he was suffering from RSI as a result. Lord Prosser held that RSI was not a condition known to medical science, because it had no pathology, and no clinical symptoms. In other unreported cases around the same time, similar claims were successful. In *Lodge & McSherry v BT*,[40] an employee who had poor posture as a result of prolonged and repetitive keyboard work was successful in their claim for RSI.[41]

The difficulties in pursuing such a claim are illustrated in *Pickford v Imperial Chemical Industries plc*,[42] Miss Pickford was a secretary who had responsibility for organising her own work. Her typing duties gradually increased, so that 75% of her time at work was spent typing. She experienced pain in her wrists and doctors were unable to detect a medical condition. She claimed that she had RSI, because of long periods of typing without a break. The Court of Appeal found the employers to be in breach of their duty of care. The case went on appeal to the House of Lords, who were not satisfied that the medical evidence was conclusive, and that the

---

39 (1993) IRLR 571.
40 Unreported (1992).
41 See also *Bettany v Royal Doulton (United Kingdom) Ltd Unreported* (1993).
42 (1998) IRLR 435 HL.

employer was not under a duty to warn their employee to take rest breaks, because she was not required to type continuously, and she organised her own work, and should have known to take breaks. They overturned the Court of Appeal's decision.

Despite the decision in *Pickford,* in 2008 a checkout worker received a payout from her employer, the Co-op, after sustaining an arm injury while trying to reach for the chip and pin machine. The employer denied liability, but made a substantial out of court settlement to her.[43] This is fairly typical of recent cases, where repetitive strain injury is readily accepted by employers as a medical condition, and where it is established that it applies to the victim, the payment made to them (usually in the form of an out of court settlement) tend to be substantial.

Asbestosis, lung cancer, mesothelioma and pleural plaques

13.13 Many occupations involve exposure to hazardous materials, and exposure to asbestos fibres in particular was a risk in occupations such as shipbuilding, railway building, building and construction work, insulation and electricity generation industries.[44] Asbestosis is scarring of the lungs, caused by exposure to asbestos. It often results in lung cancer. Mesothelioma is cancer of the pleura, or covering of the lungs, caused by exposure to asbestos. All these diseases are serious, and often terminal. These diseases are actionable in Scotland and in rest of the UK. Pleural plaques, on the other hand, are patches of thickening on the pleura which are caused by exposure to asbestos. Pleural plaques usually cause no symptoms, and the link between these and asbestosis or mesothelioma is not proved, but their presence does indicate that there has been exposure to asbestos, and that the person may be likely to develop such diseases because of that exposure. The legal position in Scotland differs from that in the rest of the UK in respect of pleural plaques. In *Rothwell v Chemical Insulating Co Ltd,*[45] the House of Lords held that pleural plaques caused by negligent exposure to asbestos were not actionable, neither was the risk of future disease or anxiety they caused. The Damages (Asbestos-related

---

43 Peacock, L Personnel Today 11 December 2008 www.personneltoday.com
44 http://www.nhs.uk/conditions/Asbestosis/Pages/Introduction.aspx
45 [2007] UKHL 39.

Conditions) (Scotland) Act 2009 was passed specifically to ensure that, in Scotland, the decision in that case is of no effect and such plaques are actionable in Scotland.

Claims for psychiatric injury resulting from stress and overwork

13.14 Stress related illness appears to be on the increase, however in order to make a claim for work related stress, it must be shown that the employee has suffered a psychiatric injury as a result of the employer's failure to take reasonable care for his safety.

In *Walker v Northumberland County Council*,[46] a senior social services manager successfully claimed damages for psychiatric injury resulting from overwork. In that case his department's workload increased considerably over a period of years, but without any increase in staff. He complained, but was told he would have to make do with the resources he had. He suffered a nervous breakdown due to overwork. His employer assured him that, on his return to work, he would have a lighter workload. However, when he returned he found that his workload was as unmanageable as before, and he suffered a second nervous breakdown. Following his breakdown, he was unable to return to work and was dismissed on grounds of ill health. The court decided the second breakdown was foreseeable and, as the employer's response was inappropriate, they were found to be in breach of their duty of care. The relevant standard is that of a reasonable employer, and the court will measure the risk of injury against cost or practicality of preventive measures. In order to make a successful claim the employee must prove that the psychiatric damage was foreseeable. In Walker the clear indicators were that Walker and his department were overworked, and since he had already suffered mental illness, it was foreseeable he would suffer from stress-related illness. The employer did very little to prevent the risk of further injury. They argued that their inability to relieve the pressure of work was due to a shortage of staff and resources. Where the organisation has substantial resources this defence is unlikely to be successful.

The possibility of liability for psychiatric injury was also recognised by the Court of Session Outer House in *Cross v Highland and Island*

---

46 (1995) IRLR 35.

Enterprise.[47] Although the Outer House judge Lord McFadyen found, that in this case, the evidence did not support the contention that the employer was in breach of care, he did accept that the employer could be in a position to foresee the build up of stress and psychiatric illness over time, and take action to prevent it. Lord McFayden was under no doubt that the duty of care in actions based on physical and psychological harm should be the same, and he was quite clear that the employer is under a duty to take reasonable care not to subject the employee to working conditions that are reasonably foreseeable to cause him psychiatric illness.

> 'It would be unacceptable for the law to adopt a position which meant
> that an employer who knew, without doubt, that the working conditions
> in which he required an employee to operate were so stressful that it
> was objectively likely that, over time, the employees would succumb
> to psychiatric illness and who, nevertheless, continued to subject
> the employee to those conditions despite growing signs that he was
> developing such psychiatric illness, would incur no liability for the
> loss and damage suffered by the employee as a result of developing the
> psychiatric illness.'

In *Rorrison v West Lothian College,*[48] the Outer House demonstrated the Scottish courts' attitude to forseeability. The pursuer was a welfare nurse that claimed that, as a result of her line manager's behaviour, such as putting pressure on, and unjustified criticism of, her, and misunderstanding of her role, she had suffered psychological damage, in the form of severe anxiety and depression, panic attacks and loss of confidence and self-esteem. It was alleged she had experienced a nervous breakdown, although no medical evidence was led to confirm this. She was unsuccessful in her claim, primarily, because she failed to produce sufficient evidence of her medical condition to satisfy the court that the psychological harm she suffered was medically recognised under major diagnostic classification systems.[49] Where it is not a fully recognised psychiatric illness, but a respected body of psychiatric

---

47 2001 SLT 1060.

48 (1999) Rep LR 102 (OH).

49 Two of the major classification systems for mental illness are the American diagnostic and statistical manual of mental disorders or World Health Organisation's International Classification of Disease and Related Health Problems.

opinion believes it should be covered, then the employee may be able to recover damages. The judge in the Court of Session adopted a restrictive interpretation of foreseeability in this context, arguing that generally the employer, as an 'ordinary bystander', would not be in a position to foresee psychological harm being inflicted on their employees, unless there was a 'specific reason' to foresee it in a particular case.

The leading case on stress related injury is *Barber v Somerset County Council*,[50] where the House of Lords heard an appeal from a case, originally heard under a joint appeal heard by the Court of Appeal, reported as *Sutherland v Hutton*.[51] In the Court of Appeal, Hale LJ set out 16 points which were specifically approved by the House of Lords in *Barber*. These were:

(1)   There are no special control mechanisms applying to claims for psychiatric (or physical) illness or injury arising from the stress of doing the work the employee is required to do. The ordinary principles of employer's liability apply.

(2)   The threshold question is whether this kind of harm to this particular employee was reasonably foreseeable: this has two components (a) an injury to health (as distinct from occupational stress) which (b) is attributable to stress at work (as distinct from other factors).

(3)   Foreseeability depends upon what the employer knows (or ought reasonably to know) about the individual employee. Because of the nature of mental disorder, it is harder to foresee than physical injury, but may be easier to foresee in a known individual than in the population at large. An employer is usually entitled to assume that the employee can withstand the normal pressures of the job, unless he knows of some particular problem or vulnerability.

(4)   The test is the same whatever the employment. There are no occupations which should be regarded as intrinsically dangerous to mental health.

(5)   Factors likely to be relevant in answering the threshold questions include: (a) the nature and extent of the work done by the employee.

---

50 [2004] UKHL 13, [2004] IRLR 476.
51 [2002] EWCA Civ 76, [2002] IRLR 263.

Is the workload much more than is normal for the particular job? Is the work particularly intellectually, or emotionally, demanding for this employee? Are the demands being made of this employee unreasonable, when compared with the demands made of others in the same or comparable jobs? Or are there signs that others doing this job are suffering harmful levels of stress? Is there an abnormal level of sickness or absenteeism in the same job or the same department? (b) Signs from the employee of impending harm to health. Has he a particular problem or vulnerability? Has he already suffered from illness attributable to stress at work? Have there recently been frequent or prolonged absences, which are uncharacteristic of him? Is there reason to think that these are attributable to stress at work, for example, because of complaints or warnings from him or others?

(6)   The employer is generally entitled to take what he is told by his employee at face value, unless he has good reason to think to the contrary. He does not generally have to make searching inquiries of the employee, or seek permission to make further inquiries of his medical advisers.

(7)   To trigger a duty to take steps, the indications of impending harm to health, arising from stress at work, must be plain enough for any reasonable employer to realise that he should do something about it.

(8)   The employer is only in breach of duty if he has failed to take the steps which are reasonable in the circumstances, bearing in mind the magnitude of the risk of harm occurring, the gravity of the harm which may occur, the costs and practicability of preventing it, and the justifications for running the risk.

(9)   The size and scope of the employer's operation, its resources and the demands it faces, are relevant in deciding what is reasonable; these include the interests of other employees and the need to treat them fairly, for example, in any redistribution of duties.

(10)   An employer can only reasonably be expected to take steps which are likely to do some good. The court is likely to need expert evidence on this.

(11) An employer who offers a confidential advice service, with referral to appropriate counselling or treatment services, is unlikely to be found in breach of duty.

(12) If the only reasonable and effective step would have been to dismiss or demote the employee, the employer will not be in breach of duty in allowing a willing employee to continue in the job.

(13) In all cases, therefore, it is necessary to identify the steps which the employer, both could, and should, have taken before finding him in breach of his duty of care.

(14) The claimant must show that that breach of duty has caused, or materially contributed to, the harm suffered. It is not enough to show that occupational stress has caused the harm.

(15) Where the harm suffered has more than one cause, the employer should only pay for that proportion of the harm suffered which is attributable to his wrongdoing, unless the harm is truly indivisible. It is for the defendant to raise the question of apportionment.

(16) The assessment of damages will take account of any pre-existing disorder or vulnerability, and of the chance that the claimant would have succumbed to a stress related disorder in any event.[52]

On appeal, the House of Lords endorsed the principles and general guidance set out in *Sutherland v Hatton*. The standard of care is linked to what employers know, or should know. The House of Lords, whilst approving this part of the Court of Appeal judgement felt that in Barber's case his injury was foreseeable, and accordingly, his employer was liable. They concluded that the employer had failed to give adequate weight to the fact that Mr Barber had been off work, certified as due to stress and depression, for three weeks earlier in the year that he had suffered his mental breakdown. This should have put the employer on notice. The majority thought Mr Barber's condition should have been monitored and more proactive steps taken, if his condition did not improve.

The decision in *Barber* restricts liability for stress related illness to employers who had been informed of stress-related symptoms or illness,

---

52 Repeated in *Barber v Somerset Council* 2004 UKHL 13 para 6.

or those that should have reasonably known that their employee was suffering from them.

The onus is, therefore, on employees to tell their employees that they are suffering from overwork/stress and that it is affecting their health. They must keep their employer informed as to how their condition is developing, which may sounds simple, but often, employees don't want to admit they are suffering from undue stress or don't recognise that they are. The employer could also be liable in circumstances where they should have known (constructive knowledge) that stress related illness is a likely outcome of the employee's job.[53] Where, for example, they work overlong hours, or are overworked, and their productivity suffers or their absence rates increases. However, the Court of Appeal held that an employer would be entitled to assume that an employee could cope with their job, unless he or she complained about suffering undue stress, and it is unlikely that an employer would be held liable if the employee did not make it clear that work was affecting their health. In *Sayers v Cambridgeshire County Council*,[54] the High Court considered the case of Sayers, a senior operations manager, who had a heavy workload and was working 50 to 60 hours per week. In recorded incidents, Sayers had been tearful and upset at work, though these episodes could be seen as the natural reaction of a dedicated employee to confrontation, criticisms or a failure to achieve. Sayers had absences from work, but these were limited, and Sayers avoided any reference to her illnesses being caused by depression or symptoms of psychiatric illness. In the period leading up to Sayer's illness, three other employees working in similar posts had suffered psychiatric illness, though there was no discernible pattern to these incidents linking them to Sayer's illness. On these facts, the High Court held that Sayer's psychiatric injury was not reasonably foreseeable.

The courts have retreated somewhat from the extreme position taken in *Barber*, so that providing a free counselling service to employees will not automatically be regarded as relieving the employer of liability.[55] The guidelines approved in *Barber* must be applied with care, but it remains the case that no job can be regarded as inherently stressful,

---

53 *Barber v Somerset County Council* [2004] UKHL 13.
54 [2006] EWHC 2029 (QB), [2007] IRLR 31 HC.
55 *Daw v Intel Corp (UK) Ltd* [2007] EWCA Civ 70, [2007] IRLR 355.

and the onus remains on the employee to prove forseeability.[56] It will be easier to establish liability, where the employee is required to perform duties additional to his/her contractual duties.[57] There is a growing body of evidence that employees may be subject to great stress owing to the pressure of work. In all these cases, the employer owes a duty to reduce the likelihood of personal injury. However, there is sometimes difficulty for the pursuer in establishing a causal link between the actual harm they suffer (stress-related illness), and workplace causes. This is because other factors may be at play in causing stress related illness, unconnected with work.

The Scottish Law Commission have reviewed the operation of the law in Scotland in relation to psychiatric injury in delictual actions, and their proposals were an attempt to bring some clarity to this area of law.[58] They have not lead to a change in the law as yet.[59]

Under the Disability Discrimination Act 1995, the requirement that a mental impairment which consists of a mental illness must be clinically well-recognised was removed (now the Equality Act 2010), which could lead to people suffering from stress related illness bringing their case under the Act, rather than pursuing a common law action with its evidential difficulties. This will be particularly likely in Scotland.

Nervous shock

13.15 Nervous shock is a term used in the law to denote psychiatric illness, or injury, inflicted upon a person by intentional or negligent actions or omissions of another. It is most often refers to psychiatric illness triggered by witnessing an accident, for example, an injury caused to a close family member. The possibility of recovering damages for nervous shock, particularly caused by negligence is limited because of evidential obstacles placed in the way of the pursuer. The pursuer can recover damages for the nervous shock which they suffered as a result of

---

56 *Hartman v South Essex Mental Health and Community Care NHS Trust* [2005] ICR 782.

57 *Flood v University Court of the Universityof Glasgow* [2010] CSIH3.

58 On Damages for Psychiatric Injury Scottish Law Commission August 2004.

59 Christie, D, Psychiatric Harm and Occupational Stress: The Limit of Employer's Liability, Juridical Review (2003) Part 3 pp 233–246.

the defender's negligence, provided they can prove all the elements of a delictual action for negligence are present. Namely: the existence of a duty of care on the part of the defender not to inflict nervous shock upon the pursuer; a breach of that duty, through acts or omissions that fall below that expected from a reasonable person in the circumstances; a causal link between the breach and a psychiatric illness. It must be shown that the psychiatric illness caused by the nervous shock was not too remote a consequence of the breach.

The courts have been anxious to limit the circumstances where someone can claim compensation for the effects of nervous shock, to avoid a vast number of claims going through the courts. So they have restricted claims to those persons that are primary victims of the negligent act or omission. A primary victim is a person who was physically injured, or could foreseeably have been physically injured, as a result of another person's negligence. Their physical proximity to the harm causes them to suffer nervous shock. Primary victims can often include rescuers such as firemen, policemen, doctors or volunteers who regularly, as part of their job, put themselves in danger and suffer psychiatric shock as a result. In the employment context, a duty of care exists solely by reason of the relationship between employer and employee. The standard of care required of an employer in the discharge of that duty and the degree of proximity, would vary according to, inter alia, the degree of fortitude expected of the employee and the nature of the job being undertaken. So a rescuer, whether a member of the emergency services or a layman, might recover against an employer for physical or psychiatric injury caused in the course of his employment by their negligence.[60]

Another problem for primary victims witnessing a serious incident leading to death or personal injury of another person is that for them to succeed in an action they would normally have to establish they have a close tie with the victim eg usually need to be a blood relative of theirs. They would also need to show that they were directly involved in the incident causing them to suffer the nervous shock and not merely witnesses to the event.

---

60 The courts have is some cases taken the view that persons who are employed in this capacity cannot recover for nervous shock because their experience of witnessing a disaster etc is part and parcel of their job.

This last point is illustrated in an employment context by the case of *Robertson v Forth Road Bridge Joint Board.*[61] The facts were that, on an extremely windy day, two employees saw a close colleague being blown off the bridge and falling to their death while they were all in the process of removing some metal sheeting from the bridge. Despite the fact that they were able to establish the traumatic effect the incident had on them, they were unable to recover damages for nervous shock. They had argued that they were so directly involved in the accident as to be within the ambit of their employers' duty of care to them. This argument was, however, rejected by the Court of Session, who regarded the case not as one involving active participation in the event, but one where the pursuers were merely bystanders or witnesses. In which event the pursuers did not comply with the required degree of involvement in the case as claimants who were only witnesses, and their claim failed. This case provides authority for the fact that, in a claim by an employee against his employer for damages for psychiatric injury, arising from the death of or injury to another, the claim will fail if the claimant is simply a bystander who witnesses the event and is not an active participant in it.

Secondary victims

13.16 A secondary victim is someone who stands in a relationship of proximity with one or more of the primary victims. There are two aspects to this: firstly, there must be close physical proximity to the trauma that kills, injures, or threatens injury, to the primary victim(s); secondly, the secondary victim must have a close tie of love and affection with one or more of the primary victims. A secondary victim is a person who suffers nervous shock, possibly through witnessing an incident, or seeing it, or hearing it, from a distance without being exposed to any danger themself. The courts, in these cases, have been particularly reluctant to award damages to secondary victims for nervous shock. Nervous shock refers to a psychiatric illness caused by negligence, and the legal requirement is that the injury must be induced by a shock, usually via sight or sound. The secondary victim must perceive a shocking event with his own unaided senses, as an eye-witness to the event, or hearing the event in person, or

---

61 (1996) SLT 263.

viewing its immediate aftermath.[62] This would normally require their close physical proximity to the event and would usually exclude events witnessed by television, or informed of by a third party. The House of Lords, in *Alcock v Chief Constable of South Yorkshire Police*,[63] were the first to make the distinction between primary and secondary victims. This is the leading case on nervous shock and this case along with other important cases,[64] has lead to the development of a set of rules dealing with this area of law summarised as: the shock must be sudden and not a gradual assault on the claimant's nervous system; it must be reasonably foreseeable that a person of normal fortitude in the claimant's position would suffer psychiatric damage;[65] where the nervous shock is caused by witnessing the death or injury or another person, the claimant must show a sufficiently proximate relationship to that person. Once it is established that psychiatric damage was foreseeable to a person, it does not matter that the person was particularly susceptible to psychiatric illness, as the defender must take his victim as he finds him (known as the 'thin skull rule') and pay for all the consequences of nervous shock.

In *McFarlane v EE Caledonia Ltd*,[66] where the plaintiff's position was on a support vessel, some 550 yards away from the exploding Piper Alpha oil rig, it was said by the Court of Appeal that the plaintiff could not have reasonably feared for his own safety. It was held that the claimant was owed a duty of care on the ground that he was not a participant in an event, and had not reasonably been in fear for his life and safety, and the impact of the events that had caused the shock. The defendants appealed and it was held that the claimant was not entitled to damages in negligence as a primary victim as, whilst the vessel on which he was stationed was close to the danger, it was never actually in danger, which made the claimant's fear for his life unreasonable. He was no more than a mere bystander to the event, and a mere bystander can, in the vast majority of cases, not expect to receive compensation for psychiatric shock.

---

62 *Attia v British Gas plc* (1988) QB 304.

63 (1992) 1 AC 310.

64 *White v Chief Constable of South Yorkshire Police* (1999) 2 AC 455, *McLaughlin v O'Brian* (1982) 2 All ER 298, *Page v Smith* (1996) AC 155.

65 The closer the tie between the claimant and the victim, the more likely it is that he would succeed in this element.

66 (1994) 2 All ER 1.

Lord Steyn prophetically, in the case of *Frost v Chief Constable of South Yorkshire*,[67] summarised the difficulty with the law in this area as follows:

> 'The law on the recovery of compensation for pure psychiatric harm is a patchwork quilt of distinctions which are difficult to justify ... In reality there are no refined analytical tools which will enable the courts to draw lines by way of compromise solution in a way that is coherent and morally defensible. It must be left to Parliament to undertake the task of radical law reform.'

VICARIOUS LIABILITY

13.17 The second area of liability, which can be incurred by employers, is vicarious liability. If an employee commits a wrongful act which causes injury or damage to a third party, the employee will be personally liable. In addition, where the wrongful act or omission has been committed/omitted in the course of his employment, the employer will also be liable to compensate that third party. This type of liability requires no fault on the part of the employer, and is known as vicarious liability.

Various rationales have been put forward for this principle applying, even in circumstances where the employer is unaware of the wrongful act, and these are that:

(1)   An employer can delegate the task but not the responsibility.

(2)   An employer is in a better financial position than the employee responsible for the unlawful act to meet the cost of a damages claim (they will also have insurance cover).

(3)   *Respondeat Superior* (let the master be responsible).

An employer will be vicariously liable for wrongful acts of the employee in the following situations:

(a)   Where the employee does something he is authorised to do, and he does it in an authorised manner. This situation is straightforward. The employer will be vicariously liable, when the employee

---

67 (1992) AC 455 paragraph 500.

commits a wrong whilst doing his job the way he was meant to do it.

(b)   Where the employee does something which is reasonably incidental to his employment. This situation includes examples such as leaving the place of employment

(c)   Where the employee does something he is authorised to do, but does it in an unauthorised manner. The employer may have set out the way the employer has to do the work, or even prohibited certain ways of doing it, yet even though the employee fails to follow instructions, or even disobeys the employer's instructions, if he is still doing his job/acting for the employer's interests, the employer will be vicariously liable for his actions. Examples include:

(i)   Where the employee does something for his own interest, but it is so closely connected to his employment that it is fair to hold the employer liable. This type of situation is most complicated and there has been a great deal of litigation on the boundaries of vicarious liability. The leading case on the modern law of vicarious liability is *Lister v Hesley Hall*.[68] The House of Lords were asked to consider whether an action in tort could be sustained against an employer of a warden in a children's home, who had sexually assaulted his charges. It was held that the appropriate test is not whether the acts were carried out within the course of their employment, but whether the wrongful acts were so closely connected with their employment that it would be just to hold the employer liable. The court found that he did not merely take advantage of the opportunity which employment at a residential school gave him, but rather, he abused the special position in which the school had placed him to enable it to discharge its own responsibilities, with the result that the assaults were committed by the very employee to whom the school had entrusted the care of the boys.

---

68 (2001) UKHL 22.

> (ii)   The less stringent requirement of showing that the
>   wrongful acts were so closely connected with their
>   employment, that it would be just to hold the employer
>   liable, could result in employers being held vicariously
>   liable, in most cases, where harm to a third party results
>   from the actions of their employees. In *Dubai Aluminium
>   Co Ltd v Salaam*,[69] a fraud case, the court followed *Lister*
>   when it was stated that it is: 'important to concentrate
>   attention on the closeness of the connection between the
>   act of the employee and the duties he is engaged to do
>   broadly defined.'[70] The House of Lords held that it was
>   not necessary for there to be a duty owed by the employer
>   to the victim, in order for there to be a finding of vicarious
>   liability. Lord Millett said that vicarious liability may arise
>   even if the act of the employee is 'an independent act in
>   itself.' He underlined that the mere fact that the employee
>   was acting dishonestly, or for his own benefit, is seldom
>   likely to be sufficient to show that an employee was not
>   acting in the course of employment.

An example of how far the principle of vicarious liability can be stretched can be seen in *Mattis v Pollock*.[71] Pollock, a nightclub owner, was sued for injuries sustained by Mattis in a knife attack initiated by an unlicensed doorman, employed by Pollock. The employee had committed an assault on two customers, and Mattis had sought to intervene on their behalf. The doorman escaped from the nightclub with a number of customers in pursuit, and Mattis left the club and joined some customers outside. The doorman went home, got a knife and then returned and stabbed Mattis in the back, rendering him a paraplegic. The Court of Appeal considered whether the assault was so closely connected with what Pollock had expected of his employee, or authorised him to do in the performance of his employment, that it would be fair and just to find Pollock vicariously liable for damages. It was shown in evidence that Pollock had encouraged

---

69 [2002] UKHL 48, [2003] 2 All ER (Comm) 451.
70 Lord Millet.
71 [2003] EWCA Civ 887, [2003] IRLR 603.

his employee to use violence, and through applying the *Lister* test they found Pollock liable.

The intentional acts of employees are covered by the modern *Lister* definition of vicarious liability, even when they are of a criminal nature. Unfortunately for employers, the precise scope of actions which are so 'closely connected to someone's employment' will depend on the individual circumstances of a case, and is consequently difficult to predict.

When considering whether an employer is vicariously liable for the negligent acts of his employees, the question to ask is: was the employee's behaviour incidental to his or her work (even if prohibited) in which case the employer is liable? The policy purposes underlying the imposition of vicarious liability on employers are served only where the wrong is so connected with the employment, that it can be said that the employer has introduced the risk of the wrong.

Vicarious liability and employees

13.18 Vicarious liability generally only applies where there is an employer/employee relationship. Unlike the test for employee for other situations, such as for unfair dismissal, redundancy, and the duty of care, the emphasis when the test is being applied for vicarious liability purposes is based very much on control.

Independent contractors

13.19 Generally, where a person engages an independent contractor through the medium of a contract (*locatio operis*), that person is not liable for the negligence of the independent contractor. However, there are certain situations where employers can be vicariously liable for independent contractor's wrongful acts. These would be: (a) where the contractor is authorised or instructed to commit a delict by the employer; (b) where the employer instructs an incompetent contractor to do a job for him; (c) where the employer instructs the contractor to carry out an inherently dangerous operation (ie working on gas pipes, rock blasting); (d) where the employer is under a statutory duty to take care, they cannot escape liability by delegating it to an independent contractor; and lastly (e) where an employer is controlling and directing an operation, and the contractor is obeying instructions. An example of this last situation is *Marshall v William Sharp & Sons Ltd,*[72] where a contractor who was an electrician was called in by the employer to rectify an electrical fault, and the contractor negligently caused injury to an employee. It was held that the employer who had called him in was vicariously liable for the injuries to the employee, and this was so, even although the electrician was a person with special expertise, because he was under the supervision and control of the employer.[73]

Seconded employees

13.20 The issue here is what happens when an employer lends or rents out (seconds) the services of his employee to another employer, and that employee is negligent and causes harm to a third party. Which employer is liable in these circumstances?

The leading case on this, until relatively recently, was *Mersey Docks & Harbour Board v Coggins & Griffith Ltd.*[74] The harbour board loaned a crane and a driver to a firm of stevedores, the latter employer being responsible for the drivers wages. There was an accident, because of the driver's negligence. It was held that the Harbour Board was his employer for purpose of being held vicariously liable, as they had failed to discharge the burden of showing that he was no longer their employee. The court will look at the reality of the situation and, in particular, which employer exercises control over what the employee does. Lord Uthwatt in the *Mersey Docks* case summarised the position thus:

'The workman may remain the employee of his general employer but, at the same time, as a result of the arrangements, it may be that there is vested in the hirer a power of control over the workman's activities to attach to the hirer responsibility for the workman's acts and defaults and to exempt the general employer from that responsibility.'

72 (1991) SLT 114 (IH).
73 Middlemiss, S Employer's Liability for Non-Employees Institute of Occupational Safety and Health Journal, (1998) Vol. 2, Issue 1 pp 15–27.
74 (1974) AC 1.

It was easier for the courts to determine the issue in *Arthur White v Tarmac Civil Engineering*,[75] where there was an express agreement between the employers, that the employer benefiting from the services of the employee was liable for his negligence. It was held that this agreement was capable of shifting vicarious liability.

This matter was finally resolved in the case of *Viasystems (Tyneside) Limited v Thermal Transfer (Northern) Limited and others*,[76] when the court found that, in certain circumstances, two unconnected parties can be liable for the negligent act of an employee. This concept, that there can be dual vicarious liability, was an important departure from a longstanding legal tradition that this form of liability could not exist. Now that the principle of dual vicarious liability has been judicially approved, the potential exists for multiple claims by injured parties seeking to secure recompense from all the parties involved, or the defendant with the deepest pockets. This will be another issue for sub-contractors (and their insurers) to consider when negotiating contracts, particularly, labour-only arrangements. The possibility now arises that employers who previously wouldn't have thought themselves exposed to claims, could now find themselves facing full liability.

Liability therefore depends on the right to control the employee,[77] which can be distinguished from the right to merely supervise.[78]

DAMAGES

13.21 The purpose of damages is to compensate for loss.[79] In order to claim damages, the damages must naturally and directly arise out of the wrong done.[80] In most employers' liability cases, the injured party will be claiming for *solatium* (personal injury) and patrimonial loss. Any award of *solatium* will include past, present and future suffering, and awareness that

---

75 [1967] 1 WLR 1508.

76 [2005] EWCA Civ 1151, [2006] QB 510.

77 *Hawley v Luminar Leisure Ltd* [2006] EWCA Civ18 [2006] IRLR 817.

78 *Biffa Waste Services Ltd v Maschinenfabrik Ernst Hase GmbH* [2008] EWCA Civ 1257, [2009] QB 725.

79 For a discussion of damages generally see J. Thomson, *Delictual Liability* (4 Edn, Bloomsbury Professional, 2009) Chapter 16.

80 *Alan v Barclay* (1864) 2 M 873.

expectation of life has been shortened.[81] Patrimonial loss will include loss of income, including future loss of earnings,[82] and reasonable expenses. The latter includes the cost of necessary services rendered by a relative in consequence of the injuries suffered, and a reasonable sum to compensate for any gratuitous services which the employee is unable to render to his family.[83] Loss of pension rights[84] and loss of employability[85] are other items which may be included. Future loss of earnings is calculated by applying a multiplier to the loss of net earnings at the date of proof. It is assumed that the rate of tax and National Insurance contributions will not change, and the rate of return on investment of damages is 3%. It is also assumed that the injured party is expected to use up the capital and income from the damages by the time he/she dies.

Interest

13.22 In cases of any court decree, interest runs at the court rate from date of payment until date of decree. In addition to that type of interest, interest runs on past *solatium* at the average court rate from the date of injury, until the injury diminished, or the date of proof, whichever is later. Interest on patrimonial loss runs from the date of the accident for past losses, half the average court rate from the date of the accident to the date of proof. Interest is not applied to future patrimonial loss.

PRESCRIPTION AND LIMITATION

13.23 Under s 6 of the Prescription and Limitation (Scotland) Act 1973, the obligation to make reparation for a delict is extinguished after 5 years from the date of the delict. The date of the delict is the date the pursuer suffers harm. In addition under s 18B, the right to raise an action for personal injuries, death, defamation and harassment must be brought within 3 years of the date the injury occurred. If it was not reasonably

---

81 Section 9A Damages (Scotland) Act 1993.
82 Future loss of earnings includes earnings he would have made if his life expectancy had not been cut short – Damages (Scotland) Act 1976 ss 9(1) and (2).
83 Section 8 and 9 Administration of Justice Act 1982.
84 *Mitchell v Glenrothes Development Corporation* 1991 SLT 284.
85 *Hill v Wilson* 1998 SC 81.

practicable for the pursuer to be aware of his/her injuries at that time, then the 3 years start to run from the date on which it was reasonably practicable for the pursuer to be aware that the injuries were sufficiently serious to bring an action, and that the defender was responsible for an act of omission causing the injury or death. Any time during which the pursuer was under a legal incapacity (age or insanity) does not count towards the three years.[86] Under s 19A, the court may allow an out of date action for personal injuries or death proceed out with the time limit, if it is just and equitable to do so.

FURTHER READING

Books

Thomson. *Delictual Liability* (4th edn Bloomsbury Professional, 2009).

Journal articles

Baker, 'Employers and Vicarious Liability' (2010) ELN 94.
Case, 'Pushing at the boundaries of Vicarious Liability' (2011), PN 27(1), 42–45.
Case, 'Vicarious Liability for harassment' (2011), PN 27(1), 46–48.
Middlemiss, 'Employer, Liability for Death by Suicide or Stress and Overwork in the Workplace', (2009) Juridical Review Part 4 pp 245–263.
Patten, 'Employment defining harassment' (2010) 160 NLJ 331.
O'Sullivan, 'Nightclub Fight club' (2011) 161 NLJ 206.

---

86 Sections 17(3), 18(3), 18A(2), 22B(4) and 22C(3).

Chapter 14

Health and Safety – Statutory Duty

BREACH OF STATUTORY DUTY

14.1 This chapter outlines the statutory rules that apply to health and safety. The main aim of heath and safety legislation is to improve health and safety in the workplace, by imposing criminal liability on employers who are careless in their responsibilities towards the health and safety of their employees. The primary legislation in this area is almost entirely contained in the Health and Safety at Work Act 1974 (HASAW 1974). It sets out the main principles and delegates authority to the Secretary of State to make more detailed legislation in the form of regulations. There is no civil liability for a breach of the Health and Safety at Work Act, but some of the regulations impose civil liability for breach of their provisions. The provisions of the Act apply mainly to employees, including those working offshore within UK territorial waters and the continental shelf.[1] It also applies to police officers[2] and government sponsored trainees.[3] It does not apply to domestic workers. Some provisions of the Act protect third parties, who are affected by the activities of the business or undertaking. The Act also gives responsibility for enforcement of the Act to the Health and Safety Executive, and confers power to Health and Safety Inspectors to inspect workplace, and to issue improvement and prohibition notices.

European law has had an impact on the secondary legislation being introduced. The Framework Directive (98/391/EEC) resulted in the 'six pack' regulations coming into effect in the UK on 1 January 2003. These Regulations were the Management of Heath and Safety at Work Regulations 1992, now replaced by the 1999 Regulations (as amended), the Personal Protective Equipment at Work Regulations 1992, the Provision and Use of Work Equipment Regulations 1992, Workplace (Health, Safety and

---

1   Continental Shelf Act 1964.
2   Police (Health and Safety) Act 1997.
3   Health and Safety (Training for employment) Regulations 1999.

Welfare) Regulations 1992, the Manual Handling Operations Regulations, and the Health and Safety (Display Screen Equipment) Regulations 1992. The purpose of these is to make detailed provision for specific problem areas. Various other important Regulations have also been passed since then, and will be considered below.

THE HEALTH AND SAFETY AT WORK ETC ACT 1974

14.2 The Health and Safety at Work Etc. Act 1974 is an enabling Act and has introduced under its auspices numerous other pieces of (usually secondary) legislation.[4] Its objectives are set out in s 1 of the Act and are to: secure the health safety and welfare of all people at work; protect third parties from risks arising from the work activities; control the storage and use of flammables and explosives; and control emissions. The standard expected of the employer, and other persons with duties under the Act, is 'so far as is reasonably practicable.' The term is now generally interpreted to mean that whatever is technically possible, in the light of current knowledge, must be carried out. Although it is normally the employer that is liable for a breach of duty, under the Act individual directors or senior managers can be held personally liable. In *Armour v Skeen*,[5] a workman fell to his death while repairing a road bridge over the river Clyde. Mr. Armour was the Director of Roads for the Regional Council and, as such, the responsibility for supervising the safety of road workers was his. He had not produced a written safety policy for such work. He was prosecuted under s 37(1) of the Health and Safety at Work, etc Act 1974, which imposes personal liability on senior executives. His defence was that he was not under a personal duty to carry out the Council's statutory duties, one of which was the formulation of a detailed safety policy for the roads department. This was rejected. Section 37(1) imposed upon Mr. Armour the personal duty to carry out the Council's statutory duty to prepare a written policy. This he had failed to do and was, therefore, guilty of an offence.

---

4 Domestic Regulations which derive from the Framework and other European Directives.
5 1977 SLT 71; [1977] IRLR 310.

The level of fines for a breach of the Act seem to vary between Scotland and England, with Scottish courts traditionally imposing lower fines. Recent Scottish cases indicate a tendency toward increasing fines.

Section 2 Duty of employer to employees

14.3 Firstly, this section imposes a general duty on the employer to ensure, so far as is reasonably practicable, the health safety and welfare at work of his employees. It then lists the particular aspects of the duty which the employer must perform. In *R v Gateway Foodmarkets Ltd*,[6] the charge of breach of s 2(1) of the Act arose out of a fatal accident at the company's Broomhill supermarket at Sheffield. An employee Mark Finn, who was aged 22 years old, fell to his death through a trap door in the floor of the lift control room which was situated on the flat roof of the building.

In essence, the issue was whether the appellants could be held to have committed an offence under the section if their employee, Mr Finn, was exposed to the risk of injury, not by any act or omission of their own head office personnel or senior management who could be identified with the company itself, but by those of their employees at a lower level, specifically the store manager or the section managers, who had allowed the irregular system to grow up and who had implemented it in contradiction of their instructions from head office. The Court of Appeal upheld the ruling that the appellants could be liable under s 2(1), notwithstanding that at senior management or head office level they had taken all reasonable precautions to avoid the risk of injury to Mr Finn. Since, on the undisputed facts, there was a failure at store management level they held that the offence was made out.[7]

The five more particular duties are:

(a)   the provision and maintenance of plant and systems of work that are, so far as is reasonably practicable, safe and without risks to health;

---

6   (1997) ICR 382: also see *R v British Steel plc* [1995] 1 WLR 1356.
7   *HMA v Munro and Sons* [2009] SLT 233; LH *Access Technology Ltd v HMA* [2009] SCL622.

(b)   arrangements for ensuring, so far as is reasonably practicable, safety and absence of risks to health in connection with the use, handling, storage and transport of articles and substances;

(c)   the provision of such information, instruction, training and supervision, as is necessary to ensure, so far as is reasonably practicable, the health and safety at work of his employees. Some employees will, by reason of inexperience or other reason, require more intensive training and supervision than others. Information may have to be provided in more than one language[8] and also supplied to persons other than employees.[9]

(d)   so far as is reasonably practicable, as regards any place of work under the employer's control, the maintenance of it in a condition that is safe and without risks to health and the provision, and maintenance of means of access to and egress from it that are safe and without such risks;

(e)   the provision and maintenance of a working environment for his employees that is, so far as is reasonably practicable, safe, without risks to health, and adequate as regards facilities and arrangements for their welfare at work. This would include provision of toilets and washing facilities and a working environment which is suitably heated and free from noxious fumes.

Written Health and Safety Policy

14.4 The employer must prepare and revise a written statement of health and safety policy and bring it to the notice of all employees.[10] This duty does not apply where the employer employs fewer than 5 employees. A template is available on the Health and Safety Executive website.[11]

---

8   *Tasci v Peklap of London Ltd* [2001] ICR 633.
9   *R v Swan Hunter Shipbuilders Ltd* [1981] ICR 831.
10 Section 2(3).
11 http://www.hse.gov.uk/simple-health-safety/write.htm

Health and safety representatives

14.5 Under ss 2(4), (6) and (7), the employer must allow recognised trade unions to appoint safety representatives from amongst the employees (who may or may not be members of the trade union, provided they are within the category of employee in respect of which the trade union is recognised). If there is no recognised trade union the employer may consult with individual employees, or allow non-union representatives to be elected[12] and must consult any such representatives about health and safety policy and other issues including the introduction of new technologies into the workplace and the provision of information and training. If requested to do so by the safety representatives, the employer must establish, within three months, a safety committee to keep health and safety measures under review. The safety representative is entitled to reasonable time off with pay to perform his functions which, if he is appointed by the trade union, include:

- the investigation of possible hazards and dangerous occurrences in the workplace,
- the investigation of the causes of accidents in the workplace,
- the investigation of employee complaints relating to health and safety,
- representation to employers regarding health and safety generally, or specific hazards or incidents,
- the carrying out of inspections of the work place at least every three months with additional inspections in the event of a change in conditions or the occurrence of a notifiable incident (see RIDDOR below). The employer may insist on an employer's representative being present at any inspection, but otherwise must provide reasonable assistance and facilities to allow the inspection to be carried out, representation of employees in consultation with the employer and Health and Safety Inspectors and attendance at meetings of safety committees and reception of information from the employer.

---

12 Health and Safety (Consultation with Employees) Regulations 1996.

There is also, under s 2 (3), a requirement to prepare a written statement of Health and Safety Policy. It is the employer's responsibility to develop a comprehensive Statement of Health and Safety Policy and they must ensure that they provide exhaustive written details of their health and safety practices, and revise this as often as is necessary. There is, however, an exception to this; an organisation that comprises fewer than five employees is exempt from the requirement to provide a written Statement.[13] [14] A model safety policy is available from the Health and Safety Executive (HSE), although the employer, to fully comply with the law, should develop a tailor-made policy.

What is reasonable in terms of time off will depend on the facts and circumstances of each case.[15] Pay will be calculated in accordance with the employee's normal average hourly rate. A representative may complain to the employment tribunal if the employer fails to do so. The complaint must be made within three months of the failure, and may result in a declaration and an award of such compensation as the tribunal deems just and equitable.

The health and safety representative is protected from detriment and dismissal by his employer as discussed below.

Case law has shown that the statutory duty on employers to keep work places safe, so far as is reasonably practicable under s 2 of the Health and Safety at Work etc Act 1974, applies regardless of whether a particular danger was foreseen, provided it was ascertainable and should have been ascertained.[16] This is the cases regardless of whether or not senior management were responsible for the failure to maintain safety standards.[17]

---

13 *R v Gateway Foodmarkets Ltd* [1997] 3 All ER 78.
14 Although they must provide oral training.
15 *White v Pressed Steel Fisher* [1980] IRLR 176 EAT
16 *Mains v Uniroyal Englebert Tyres Ltd* (1995) Times Law Reports 29th September 1995 and *Baker v Quantum Clothing Group & ors* (2009) EWCA Civ 499.
17 *R v Gateway Foodmarkets Ltd CA* (1997) ICR 382.

Section 3 General duties of employers and independent contractors to third parties

14.6 Section 3 imposes a general duty on employers and self employed persons to conduct their undertaking in such a way as to ensure, in so far as is reasonably practicable, that people who are third parties (not employees) but who may be affected by their actions are not exposed to risks to their health and safety. Under this section, employers, therefore, have a duty to contractors (and their employees), visitors, customers, members of the emergency services, neighbours, passers-by and the public at large. Individuals who are self-employed operate under a similar duty, and must also take care of themselves.

The extent of liability for non-employees was demonstrated in *R v Swan Hunter Shipbuilder and Another*,[18] where a fire broke out on board a ship which was under construction by Swan Hunter Ltd. The fire was intense, because the atmosphere inside the vessel had become oxygen enriched, and eight men were killed. The oxygen had escaped from a hose left by an employee of a firm of subcontractors. Swan Hunter Ltd. had distributed a book of rules to their own employees for the safe use of oxygen equipment, but this was not distributed to subcontractors' employees, except on request. Swan Hunter were prosecuted, under the Health & Safety at Work Etc. Act 1974, for 'failure to provide a safe system of work' (contrary to s 2(2) (a)), 'failure to provide information and instruction to ensure the safety of their employees' (contrary to s 2(2) (c)), and 'failure to ensure that persons not in their employment were not exposed to risk' (contrary to s 3(1)). The trial judge ruled that all the above sections of the Act imposed a duty on Swan Hunter to inform or instruct the employees of contractors working alongside their own employees, with regard to all relevant safety matters. Swan Hunter Ltd appealed, and the Court of Appeal dismissed the appeal and upheld the trial judge's ruling. If, to ensure a safe system of work for an employer's own employees, it was necessary to provide to persons other than his employees with information and instruction as to potential dangers, then he was under a duty to provide such information and instruction, so far as was reasonably practicable.

---

18 (1982) IRLR 403.

In *R v Associated Octel Co Ltd*,[19] the defendant company engaged some contractors to carry out repairs of a tank during a shut-down period. A permit to work was issued by the defendant, but it proved to be inadequate and was not monitored. A contractor took a flammable liquid into the tank to clean the inner surface. However, a flash fire developed and the contractor was seriously burned. The HSE successfully prosecuted Octel, who were fined £25,000. The defendant appealed, first to the Court of Appeal who upheld the conviction, and then the House of Lords. The Lords held that if an employer engages a contractor who works on his or her premises then the employer, subject to reasonable practicability, must ensure the contractors' health and safety. The House of Lords appeal was concerned with the definition of the term 'undertaking', which it was held effectively includes any work carried out on the employer's premises. It was also held that the employer's actual control, or duty to exercise control, over the activity is not decisive in these cases. Even where an employer is not present on their site where a contractor is working, they can still be liable for a contractor's breach of the Act.

The employer, or self employed person, must conduct his undertaking in such a way as to ensure, so far as is reasonably practicable, that persons not in his employment, who may be affected by his undertaking, are not exposed to risks to their health or safety. This duty extends to providing the third party with information relevant to health and safety. For an indication as to the seriousness of a breach of section 3 and the level of fine which might be imposed see *HM Advocate v Munro & Sons (Highland) Ltd*.[20]

Section 4 General duties of persons concerned with premises to persons other than their employees.

14.7 The 'controller' of a building owes a duty to third parties, who are not their employees but are on their premises. The duty under this section is to take such measures, as it is reasonable for a person in his position to take, to ensure, so far as is reasonably practicable, that

---

19 (1996) ICR 972, HL.
20 [2009] HCJAC 10; 2009 SLT 233.

the premises, all means of access thereto or egress and any plant or substance in the premises or provided for use there are safe and without risks to health. The controller is usually the occupier of the premises either owner or tenant and will also have duties under the Occupiers Liability (Scotland) Act.

Section 6 Manufacturers' duty as regards articles and substances for use at work.

14.8 Any person who designs, manufactures, imports or supplies any article for use at work, or any article of fairground equipment must ensure, so far as is reasonably practicable, that it is designed and constructed so that it will be safe and without risks to health at all times when it is being set, used, cleaned or maintained by a person at work and to carry out maintenance and testing, and to provide persons supplied with the article with adequate information about its safe use.

Subsections 4 and 5 impose similar duties on the manufacturers, importers or suppliers of substances.

Designers and manufacturers have an additional duty to carry out research to lead to the elimination or minimisation of risk from such articles. Employers will have strict liability for defective work equipment, under the Employer's Liability (Defective Equipment) Act 1969.

Section 7 General duties of employees at work.

14.9 Employees must take reasonable care for their own health and safety and that of others, and must cooperate with the employer or other person to enable them to carry out any health and safety duties incumbent upon them.

Section 8 Duty not to interfere with or misuse things provided pursuant to certain provisions.

14.10 Section 8 provides that no person shall intentionally or recklessly interfere with or misuse anything provided in the interests of health, safety or welfare in pursuance of any of the relevant statutory provisions.

Section 9 Duty not to charge

14.11 The employer cannot charge an employee for anything done or provided in pursuance of any specific requirement of the relevant statutory provisions.

Standard of Care – Reasonably practicable

14.12 In contrast to the standard of the 'reasonable employer' which applies to the common law duty of care, the standard of 'reasonably practicable' applies in statutory Health and Safety law. In deciding what is reasonably practicable in terms of health and safety, it is necessary to balance the risk against the effort needed to offset it. So the courts will take into account, on the one hand, the danger or hazard or injury which may occur and balance it, on the other hand, with the cost, inconvenience, time and trouble which would have to be involved to counter it. If the former aspect outweighs the latter, then there will be liability and vice versa.

In considering what is reasonable practicable the courts will look at the industry standard of behaviour to determine is the employer acted reasonably. If he has acted in accordance with the industry standard this would point to him acting reasonably, but is not conclusive. In *Martin v Boulton & Paul Ltd*,[21] the Divisional Court held that the existence of a universal practice did not, by itself, lead to the conclusion there was no other reasonably practicable way of doing something. It is a factual matter to be taken into account along with all the other evidence.

Approved Codes of Practice

14.13 The Act provides for the production by the Health and Safety Commission of Approved Codes of Practice (ACoP).[22] The usual role of a Code of Practice is to provide a non-binding account of good practice which can be cited as evidence of good practice in court. ACoPs have a different legal status, in that a failure to observe an ACoP shall not,

---

21 (1982) ICR 366.
22 Section 17.

of itself, result in liability in civil or criminal proceedings; but in criminal proceedings the ACoP is not only admissible in evidence, but any proven breach of it shall be taken as proof of liability, and the onus shifts to the accused to show that he complied with the statutory provision.

Enforcement of the Act

14.14 The Health and Safety Commission (HSC) and the Health and Safety Executive (HSE) were established under the HSAWA to respectively decide upon, and implement, health and safety policy. These two bodies merged into a unitary body in 2008, but retained the name Health and Safety Executive. Investigations are carried out either by the Health and Safety Executive,[23] or the Environmental Health Department of a local authority in Scotland. The powers of health and safety inspectors (or other enforcement officers), when investigating an incident, are considerable (in some cases more extensive than the police), they include the power:[24]

(a) of entry without a warrant and, if necessary, accompanied by a police constable or other person authorised by the HSE at any reasonable time, and taking any necessary equipment or materials with him,

(b) to make such examination and investigation as may in any circumstances be necessary,

(c) to direct that premises or any part of them, or anything therein, shall be left undisturbed for so long as is reasonably necessary for the purpose of any examination or investigation,

(d) to take such measurements and photographs, and make such recordings, as he considers necessary,

(e) to take samples of any articles or substances found in any premises which he has power to enter, and of the atmosphere in, or in the vicinity of, any such premises;

---

23 For manufacturing, large construction or industrial sites the HSE (Health and Safety Executive) carries out inspections.
24 Section 20 (2).

(f)   to have articles which he considers to be a danger to health and safety to be dismantled and subjected to non-destructive testing,

(g)   in the case of any such article or substance as is mentioned in the preceding paragraph, to take possession of it and detain it for so long as is necessary for all or any of the following purposes, namely:

         (i)   to examine it and do to it anything which he has power to do under that paragraph;

         (ii)   to ensure that it is not tampered with before his examination of it is completed;

         (iii)   to ensure that it is available for use as evidence in any proceedings for an offence, under any of the relevant statutory provisions or any proceedings relating to a notice under s 21 or 22;

(h)   to require any person whom he has reasonable cause to believe to be able to give any information relevant to any examination or investigation to answer in private such questions as the inspector thinks fit to ask, and to sign a declaration of the truth of his answers. The person has the right to be accompanied by a person of his choosing. Any answer given by such a person shall not be admissible in evidence against that person or the spouse or civil partner of that person in any proceedings.

(i)   to require the production of, inspect, and take copies of or of any entry in:

         (i)   any books or documents which by virtue of any of the relevant statutory provisions are required to be kept; and

         (ii)   any other books or documents which it is necessary for him to see for the purposes of any examination or investigation under paragraph (d) above;

(j)   to require any person to afford him such facilities and assistance with respect to any matters or things within that person's control, or in relation to which that person has responsibilities, as are necessary to enable the inspector to exercise any of the powers conferred on him by this section;

(k)   any other power which is necessary

Nothing in s 20 compels the production of any document which that person would be entitled to withhold production of, on an order for the production of documents, in an action in the Court of Session on grounds of professional privilege.

Breach of any duty under the Act may result in prosecution under summary or solemn procedure. An additional method of enforcement is the power of Health and Safety Inspectors to issue either an improvement notice or a prohibition notice.[25]

An improvement notice is a notice served on the employer detailing the ways in which he is contravening, or likely to contravene, health and safety legislation, and giving him a time limit (not less than 21 days) in which to set matters right. A prohibition notice will be issued when the activity which is the subject of the notice is considered to constitute a serious risk of personal injury and, therefore, too dangerous to allow it to continue until remedial action is taken. Both notices may be appealed to the employment tribunal within 21 days. Breach of a notice is a criminal offence.

The Health and Safety Offences Act 2008 came into force in January 2009. It raises the maximum penalties that can be imposed for breaching health and safety regulations and the range of offences for which an individual can be imprisoned. It raises the maximum fine which may be imposed in the lower courts to £20,000 for most health and safety offences. It also makes imprisonment an option for more health and safety offences in both the lower[26] and higher courts,[27] and certain offences, which could previously only be tried in the lower courts, can now be tried in either the lower (Sheriff Court) or higher court (High Court of Justiciary).

SMOKING

14.15 One other piece of primary health and safety legislation in Scotland is the Smoking (Health and Social Care) (Scotland) Act 2005, which provides that all workplaces, clubs, pubs and restaurants etc. should be free from tobacco smoke. It creates an offence of smoking in non-smoking

---

25 Section 21 and section 22.
26 Maximum of 12 months imprisonment.
27 Maximum of 2 years imprisonment.

premises, which is liable to summary prosecution in the sheriff court, and on conviction to a fine not exceeding level 3 on the standard scale. It also creates the offence of knowingly permitting smoking in non-smoking premises. It includes the situation where the management of premises ought to have known the person was smoking. It is a defence for an accused to prove that he or his employer took all reasonable precautions and exercised all due diligence not to commit the offence; or (b) that there were no lawful and reasonably practicable means by which the accused could prevent the other person from smoking in the non-smoking premises. A breach will be prosecuted under summary procedure in the sheriff court. The penalty for breach of this provision is a fine on level 4 of the standard scale.

There is also provision for warning notices to be displayed, and the penalty for summary conviction is level 3 on the standard scale.

Fixed penalties may be issued as an alternative to prosecution, where the accused is a natural person. This Act does not impose civil liability for exposure to tobacco smoke.

HEALTH AND SAFETY REGULATIONS

14.16 Most of the other statutory measures covering health and safety are initially derived from EU Law and introduced to comply with EU Directives. Under Article 137 of the EC Treaty, there is a general commitment to improving health and safety and various Directives have been introduced towards this end. The most important is Council Directive 89/391, known as the Framework Directive, which has the objective of introducing measures to encourage improvements in the safety and health of workers at work. Under Article 6, the employer's general obligations are: take the measures necessary for safety and health of workers; prevention of occupational risks; information and training; provision of organisation; means to tackle health and safety; and adjusting to changing circumstances.

The general principles of prevention inherent in the objectives of the Framework Directive involve the following aspects: avoiding risks; evaluating the risks; combatting the risks at source; adapting the work to the individual; adapting to technical progress; replacing or lessening the dangerous task; and developing a coherent overall prevention policy.

Various domestic Regulations were introduced in the United Kingdom in 1992 to implement the Framework Directive, and these were: Management of Health and Safety at Work Regulations; Workplace (Health Safety and Welfare) Regulations; Provision and Use of Work Equipment Regulations; Personal Protective Equipment at Work Regulations; Manual Handling Operations Regulations and the Health and Safety (Display Screen Equipment) Regulations. Some of these Regulations have been substantially amended since 1992.

While breach of the Health and Safety at Work Act 1974 does not give rise to civil liability, under that Act (therefore claims will be brought under the common law duty of care), a breach of health and safety regulations will give rise to civil liability unless the regulation provides otherwise.

Health and Safety (Display Screen Equipment) Regulations 1992[28]

14.17 It now well established that working at IT workstations or with IT equipment can lead to medical problems, most notably pains in the back, neck, shoulder, or arms, extreme tiredness and eye problems.[29] According to the TUC the problem appears to be getting worse.[30]

This regulation gives effect to Directive 90/270EEC and provides that employers must carry out an analysis of workstations with a view to assessing any risk to health and safety.[31] The employer must reduce risks, to the extent which is reasonably practicable,[32] and review the arrangements when there is any change or reason to suspect the assessment is no longer valid. Display screen equipment (DSE) is classed as any work equipment that has a screen that displays information.[33] Regulation 1, plus the accompanying guidance, defines Display Screen Equipment

---

28 As amended by the Health and Safety (Miscellaneous Amendments) Regulations 2002.
29 These medical problems are often referred to as upper limb disorders (ULDs) or repetitive strain injuries (RSI).
30 Stress, overwork and office hazards top workers' safety concerns Friday 24 October 2008 www.tuc org.uk
31 Regulation 2.
32 Regulation 2(3).
33 Screens which show television or film pictures are excluded as are calculators, cash registers and most scientific and medical devices.

(DSE) users as employees who habitually use display screen equipment as a significant part of their normal work. The workstation must comply with the requirements set out in Schedule one of the Regulations which relate to the standard of equipment eg screen keyboard, desk and chair, the interface between the operator and the computer and the working environment. The employer must plan the activities of the user so that there are regular breaks.[34] The other Regulations apply to users who work: at their employer's workstation; at home or at another employer's workstation.

Users must be provided with training and information.[35] There is provision, under Regulation 5, for employers to pay for eye tests for regular users, but in Scotland annual eye tests are available free on the NHS

Management of Health and Safety at Work Regulations 1999 (as amended) (MHSW)

14.18 These Regulations replaced the 1992 Regulations of the same name, and are, arguably, the most important of the six legal measures introduced to implement the Framework Directive. It is important to note that breach of these Regulations could result in the civil liability for breach of Regulations to employees, but not third parties.[36]

All workers are covered by the Regulations, including mobile and home workers, excepting seafarers and young people performing temporary or short-term work in a family business, or domestic service (Regulation 2).[37] They provide for health and safety arrangements including emergency procedures and health surveillance[38] in the workplace, and for risk assessments[39] of the workforce and workplace. The Regulations make

---

34 Regulation 4.
35 Regulations 6 and 7.
36 Regulation 22.
37 The Regulations are published with an Approved Code of Conduct (ACOP) which has special legal status (courts will take account of adherence to the ACOP in prosecutions for breaches of health and safety law) and with Guidance (adherence to Guidance is not compulsory).
38 Regulation 6.
39 Regulation 3.

specific provision for risk assessment of young workers, who must have had a risk assessment prior to starting employment. Where young workers are concerned, the employer must protect them from risks associated with their lack of experience and maturity, and there are certain types of work involving specific risks which should not be given to young persons.[40]

Special provision is also made for pregnant women and all women of child bearing age including those who are new or expectant mothers or are breastfeeding.[41] The special provision includes provision regarding exposure to infectious or contagious disease and makes provision for medical suspension where necessary to protect the employee.

The most important aspect of the Regulations arise under Regulation 3, which provides for risk assessments to be carried out by employers as follows: (1) Every employer shall make a suitable and sufficient[42] assessment of (a) the risks to the health and safety of his employees to which they are exposed whilst they are at work; and (b) the risks to the health and safety of persons not in his employment, arising out of or in connection with, the conduct by him of his undertaking, for the purpose of identifying the measures he needs to take to comply with the requirements, and prohibitions imposed upon him by, or under, the relevant statutory provisions. Under Regulation 3(2) a similar duty is placed on self employed persons.[43]

The whole point of a proper risk assessment is that an investigation is carried out in order to identify whether the particular operation gives rise to any risk to safety and, if so, what is the extent of that risk, which of course includes the extent of any risk of injury, and what can and should be done to minimise or eradicate the risk.[44]

---

40 Regulation 19.
41 Regulation 16.
42 Employers are not instructed about the appropriate method of carrying out a risk assessment but it must be thorough and regularly reviewed.
43 (2) Every self-employed person shall make a suitable and sufficient assessment of (a) the risks to his own health and safety to which he is exposed whilst he is at work; and (b) the risks to the health and safety of persons not in his employment arising out of or in connection with the conduct by him of his undertaking, for the purpose of identifying the measures he needs to take to comply with the requirements and prohibitions imposed upon him by or under the relevant statutory provisions.
44 *Terence Joseph Griffiths v Vauxhall Motors Limited* (2003) EWCA Civ 412 CA.

Once the risk has been assessed the employer must record the findings if he employs more than 5 employees. All employers must then prevent or, if they cannot be prevented, minimise, the risks identified. In doing this the employer must bear in mind the principles of prevention set out in Schedule 1 to the Regulations:

(a)   avoiding risks;

(b)   evaluating the risks which cannot be avoided;

(c)   combating the risks at source;

(d)   adapting the work to the individual, especially as regards the design of workplaces, the choice of work equipment and the choice of working and production methods, with a view, in particular, to alleviating monotonous work, and work at a predetermined work-rate, and to reducing their effect on health;

(e)   adapting to technical progress;

(f)   replacing the dangerous by the non-dangerous or the less dangerous;

(g)   developing a coherent overall prevention policy which covers technology, organisation of work, working conditions, social relationships and the influence of factors relating to the working environment;

(h)   giving collective protective measures priority over individual protective measures; and

(i)   giving appropriate instructions to employees.

Risk assessments must be reviewed when there is any significant change in circumstances. It is also likely that, as a result of the general risk assessment of the workplace, issues will be identified which will require more specialised risk assessments, eg under the Manual Handling Operations Regulations 1992 or COSHH (both of which are discussed below). The Health and Safety Executive produce detailed guidance on the process in their booklet entitled Five Steps to Risk Assessment.[45] The five steps are:

Step 1 – Identify the Hazard

---

45 http://www.hse.gov.uk/pubns/indg163.pdf

Step 2 – Decide who might be harmed and how

Step 3 – Evaluate the risks and decide on precautions

Step 4 – Record your findings and implement them

Step 5 – Review your assessment and update if necessary

The Approved Code of Practice gives advice on the planning, organisation, control, monitoring and review of health and safety arrangements by employers.[46]

If there are more than 5 employees the employer must keep a record of the arrangements.

Regulation 13 states that employers must take into account their employee's capabilities, and ensure they are provided with appropriate training and information.

Regulation 14 imposes duties on employees to take care of their own safety, and that of others, and to cooperate with the employer in health and safety matters.

Under Regulation 5 there is a requirement on employers to carry out health surveillance. They are also encouraged to take into account the views of employees and safety representatives.

Employers must also make arrangements to ensure the health and safety of the workplace, including making arrangements for emergencies, adequate information and training for employees, and for health surveillance, where appropriate.

Employees must work safely in accordance with training and instruction given to them. Employees must also notify the employer, or the person responsible for health and safety, of any serious or immediate danger to health and safety, or any shortcoming in health and safety arrangements.[47]

Managers should be aware of relevant legislation, and should be competent to manage health and safety effectively,[48] and all employees, including senior management, should receive relevant training.[49] In selecting competent persons (those with sufficient knowledge, training and expertise of relevant health and safety factors) for the performance

---

46 Regulation 4.
47 Regulation 14.
48 Regulation 13.
49 Guidance Regulation 13.

of health and safety tasks, employers should give preference to people in their employment over competent persons not in their employment, such as consultants,[50] although external specialists can be used if required, or a combination of internal and external personnel may be appropriate.[51] Mistakes by competent persons do not free employers from liability for breaches of statutory duty.[52]

Since 2003, employers have been liable to employees in the civil courts for breach of these Regulations, however, not for breach of any Regulations intended for the protection of a third party, as third parties cannot sue for a breach of these Regulations.

These Regulations, and others mentioned below, are made under the Health and Safety at Work Act and breach of them can incur the same criminal liability as under that Act.

Manual Handling Operations Regulations 1992 (as amended) (MHO)

14.19 These Regulations govern manual handling operations and a breach of them generally does result in civil liability. Regulation 4 provides that an employer shall, so far as is reasonably practicable, avoid the need for employees to undertake any manual handling which involves a risk of injury and, where avoidance is not reasonably practicable, the employer will take steps to assess the risk and take steps to minimise the risk of injury. Whether an operation is regarded as a manual handling operation will be decided on a case by case basis, therefore, whilst the laying of grit was considered to be manual handling,[53] the manipulation of chicken carcases was not.[54] This Regulation confers a civil liability on the employer, and a claim for injury may more easily succeed under this provision than under the common law duty of care. This is because the common law duty of care requires that injury was reasonably foreseeable,

---

50 Regulation 7.
51 Approved Code of Practice; Regulation 7.
52 Regulation 21.
53 *King v RCO Support Services Ltd* [2001] I.C.R. 608; [2001] PIQR P15.
54 *Hughes v Grampian Country Food Group Ltd* [2007] CSIH 32; 2007 SLT 635; 2008 SCLR 157; [2007] Eu LR 719; 2007 Rep. LR 72; 2007 GWD 18-324; Times, June 4, 2007.

whereas in order to establish a breach of Regulation 4(1)(a), the operation must be a manual handling operation and involve a risk of injury. Regulation 4(1)(a) imposes a general duty to avoid the need for all manual handling carrying with it a risk of injury, and where a particular pursuer is injured when engaged in and as a result of such an operation, liability for breach of the Regulation will only be avoided if an employer had relevantly pled that it was not reasonably practicable to avoid the lifting operation.[55] In that case the onus moves to the employer to prove it was not reasonably practicable to avoid the need to lift.[56]

The risk need not be a probability, merely a foreseeable possibility,[57] which is something less than a likelihood of injury.

Even if the employer proves that it was not reasonably practicable to avoid the operation, he must then go on to prove that he assessed the risk and took steps to avoid the injury. Regulation 4(1)(b)(ii) provides that an employer must risk assess any manual handling operation and, in assessing risk, is obliged to consider the particular task in the context of where it is to be performed and the particular employee by which it is to be performed.[58]

In taking reasonable steps, the employer must provide information and training to the employee, and a failure to do so may result in civil liability for any injury suffered.[59] Employees must make full and proper use of any system of work provided by employer, and a failure to do so, or other carelessness on the part of the employee, may amount to contributory negligence.[60] What steps are reasonable in minimising the risk depends on the circumstance of the individual case, but the social utility of the

---

55 *Taylor v Glasgow City Council* 2002 SC 364; 2002 SLT 689.
56 *Anderson v Lothian Health Board* 1996 SCLR 1068; 1996 Rep LR 88 *Hall v Edinburgh City Council* 1999 SLT 744, 1999 Rep LR 26, 1998 GWD 37-1935.
57 *Cullen v North Lanarkshire Council* [1998] SC 451 at 455.
58 *Koonjul v Thameslink Healthcare Services* [2000] PIQR P123.
59 *O'Neill v DSG Retail Ltd* [2002] EWCA Civ 1139; [2003] ICR 222.
60 See for example *Egan v Central Manchester and Manchester Children's University Hospitals NHS Trust* [2008] EWCA Civ 1424; [2009] ICR 585 and *Koonjul v Thameslink Healthcare Services* [2000] PIQR P123; Times, May.

operation was taken into consideration in deciding that the lifting of a patient by an ambulance technician was not in breach of the regulations.[61]

Personal Protective Equipment at Work Regulations 2002 (PPE)

14.20 The employer is under a duty to provide personal protective equipment where there are risks at work which cannot be controlled in any other way. Personal protective equipment sold,[62] or supplied,[63] must be safe, or the person selling it or supplying it will be guilty of an offence. It shall be a defence to a charge, under Regulation 8 and 9, if that person was to show that he took all reasonable steps and exercised all due diligence to avoid committing the offence. If the defence involves an allegation that the commission of the offence was due to the act or default of another, or reliance on information supplied by another, then the accused must identify that person and it must have been reasonable in all circumstances for him to have relied on the information, having regard in particular:

(a)   to the steps which he took, and those which might reasonably have been taken, for the purposes of verifying the information; and

(b)   to whether he had any reason to disbelieve the information.[64]

Personal protective equipment includes all equipment (including clothing affording protection against the weather) which is intended to be worn or held by a person at work, and which protects him against one or more risks to his health or safety, except hearing and respiratory protective equipment which are subject to other regulations. In *Fytche v Wincanton Logistics Plc*,[65] the employer was only liable in respect of the risk for which steel toe capped boots were provided and was not liable when a tiny hole in the boots led to an employee developing frostbite, the employer was not liable

---

61 *King v Sussex Ambulance NHS Trust* [2002] EWCA Civ 953; [2002] ICR 1413; (2002) 68 BMLR 177; Times, July 25, 2002.
62 Regulation 8.
63 Regulation 9.
64 Regulation 19.
65 [2003] EWCA Civ 874; [2003] ICR 1582; [2004] PIQR P2; (2003) 147 SJLB 785.

under the Regulations, although it may be established he was under the common law duty of care.

Provision and Use of Work Equipment Regulations 1998 (PUWER)

14.21 These Regulations state that equipment provided for use at work must be suitable for the intended use; safe for general use, maintained in a safe condition and, in certain circumstances, inspected to ensure this remains the case. The equipment should be used only by people who have received adequate information, instruction and training, and it should be accompanied by suitable safety measures eg protective devices, markings, warnings.

Under Regulation 2 of PUWER, 'work equipment' means any machinery, appliance, apparatus, tool or installation for use at work. This term has been widely defined by the courts. In *Kelly v First Engineering Ltd*,[66] the House of Lords held that a bolt for securing fish plates in place was not an appliance but it was an apparatus. In *Beck v United Closure & Plastics plc*,[67] two heavy doors that were closed to allow machinery to start were work equipment, and in *Mackie v Dundee County Council*,[68] a folding table was also found to be work equipment when used at work.

Employees who use work equipment, and supervisors and managers of such equipment, must have available to them adequate health and safety information and, where appropriate, written instructions about the use of the equipment.[69]

Regulation 4 provides that every employer should ensure work equipment is so constructed or adapted as to be suitable for the purpose for which it is to be used or provided. In *English v North Lanarkshire County Council*,[70] the House of Lords decided it was not enough that a meat slicing machine was constructed so it could safely slice meat, it should also be safe to clean the machine after use. In *Crane v Premier*

---

66 [1999] SCLR 1025 OH.
67 [2001] SLT 1299.
68 [2001] Rep LR 62.
69 There is a corresponding general duty under s 2(2)c of HASAW 1974.
70 [1999] SCLR 310, OH.

Prison Services,[71] a failure by the employer to fit hand holds to the back of a van where people had to move around was a breach of the Regulations. Employers must also ensure work equipment is used only for operations for which it is suitable and work equipment must be maintained in an efficient state, in efficient working order and in good repair.

In *Barnett v Scottish Power*,[72] the employee was employed as a meter reader and she had requested the use of a ladder to read meters set high on the wall, but was refused. She, therefore, had taken to using a chair. A chair toppled over when she was on it and she fell, and was injured, and it was held this was a breach of Regulation 5.

Regulation 6 provides that every employer shall ensure that work equipment is maintained in an efficient manner. In *Stark v Post Office*,[73] the employee was a postman who was making deliveries on a work's bicycle. Without warning the front brake broke in two jamming the front wheel and causing the claimant to fall and be injured. It was accepted that the most rigorous of inspection systems would not have revealed the defect and that it could in no way be guarded against. Despite this, and accepting the employers were blameless, there was still a breach of Regulation 6.

The Regulations also contain specific rules about dangerous parts of machinery, eg Regulation 11, which sets out the requirement for protection against specific hazards, use of controls and control systems and maintenance requirements, and includes a duty to fence dangerous parts of machinery.

Workplace (Health, Safety and Welfare) Regulations 1992

14.22 These Regulations expand on the general duties contained in s 2 and 4 of the Health and Safety at Work Act 1974, and cover matters such as ventilation, temperature, lighting, cleanliness, space, toilets, washing facilities and eating facilities. Regulations 12(1) and (2) (condition of floors and traffic routes) are particularly relevant in cases of tripping and

---

71 [2001] CLY 3298
72 [2002] EWCA Civ 104, [2002] All ER (D) 345 (Jan).
73 [2000] ICR 1013

slipping.[74] The standard of care imposed on the employer is reasonable practicability.

Under Regulation 2(1), 'workplace' is given a wide definition and means any premises, or part of premises, which are not domestic premises and are made available to any person as a place of work including any place within the premises to which such person has access while at work and any room, lobby, corridor, staircase, road or other place used as a means of access to, or egress from, that place of work or where facilities are provided for use in connection with the place of work, other than a public road, but does not include workplaces involving construction work on construction sites, those in or on a ship, or those below ground at a mine, all of which are covered by other legislation.

The Reporting of Injuries, Diseases and Dangerous Occurrences Regulations 1995 (RIDDOR)[75]

14.23 These Regulations place a legal duty on responsible persons, namely, employers; self-employed persons and persons in control of premises to report: work-related deaths, major injuries or over-three-day injuries, work related diseases,[76] and dangerous occurrences (near miss accidents).[77] Reportable major injuries are: fractures (other than to fingers, thumbs and toes); amputation; dislocation of the shoulder, hip, knee or spine; loss of sight (temporary or permanent); chemical or hot metal burn to the eye or any penetrating injury to the eye; injury resulting from an electric shock or electrical burn leading to unconsciousness, or requiring resuscitation or admittance to hospital for more than 24

---

74 *Marks and Spencer Plc v Palmer* [2001] EWCA Civ 1528.

75 Statutory Instrument 1995 No. 3163.

76 Reportable diseases include: certain poisonings; some skin diseases such as occupational dermatitis, skin cancer, chrome ulcer, oil folliculitis/acne; lung diseases including: occupational asthma, farmer's lung, pneumoconiosis, asbestosis, mesothelioma, infections such as: leptospirosis; hepatitis; tuberculosis; anthrax; legionellosis and tetanus; other conditions such as: occupational cancer; certain musculoskeletal disorders; decompression illness and hand-arm vibration syndrome.

77 Gas safe registered gas fitters must report dangerous gas fittings they find and gas conveyors/suppliers must report some flammable gas incidents see http://www.hse.gov.uk/riddor/

hours; any other injury: leading to hypothermia, heat-induced illness or unconsciousness; or requiring resuscitation; or requiring admittance to hospital for more than 24 hours; unconsciousness caused by asphyxia or exposure to harmful substance or biological agent; acute illness requiring medical treatment, or loss of consciousness arising from absorption of any substance by inhalation, ingestion or through the skin; acute illness requiring medical treatment where there is reason to believe that this resulted from exposure to a biological agent or its toxins or infected material.

An over-three-day injury is one which is not usually a major one, but if it results in the injured person being away from work or unable to do their full range of their normal duties for more than three days, the employer must report it. This might arise where there is an accident connected with work (including an act of physical violence) and an employee or self-employed person working on their premises, suffers an over-three-day injury. They must report it to the enforcing authority, the Health and Safety Executive, or Environmental Health, within ten days. Breach of the regulations is a crime, punishable on summary conviction to a small fine and, if convicted on indictment in the High Court of Justiciary, an offender can be required to pay an unlimited fine. Either an individual or a corporation can be liable. However, it is a defence in proceedings against any person, for an offence under these Regulations, to prove that he was not aware of the event requiring him to notify or send a report to the relevant enforcing authority, and that he had taken all reasonable steps to have all such events brought to his notice. In April 2009, the Reporting of Injuries, Diseases and Dangerous Occurrences Regulations 1995 (RIDDOR) website was re-launched by the HSE with a new structure and style, as well as the addition of a number of new features. This site contains basic guidance on the reporting of such injuries and incidents.[78]

---

78 http://www.hse.gov.uk/riddor/index.htm. It is possible to make a report on-line.

Control of Substances Hazardous to Health Regulation (as amended) (COSHH)

14.24 Using chemicals or other hazardous substances at work can put people's health at risk, causing diseases including asthma, dermatitis or cancer. The COSHH Regulations require employers to control substances that can harm workers' health. This includes: chemicals, products containing chemicals, fumes, dusts, vapours, mists and gases, and biological agents (germs). It also covers asphyxiating gases.[79]

The HSE advice[80] is always to try and prevent exposure at source, for example: simply avoid using a hazardous substances, or use a safer process preventing exposure, eg using water-based rather than solvent-based products and, where something is hazardous, substitute it for something safer eg replace an irritant cleaning product for something milder. They further advise that where the employer can identify hazardous substances they need to: consider the task and methods of exposure; assess the risk; identify and institute control measures; provide control equipment; check and maintain it and monitor the health of workers; train, inform and consult the workers and keep records.[81] The COSHH Regulations require employers to implement a suitable management system in order to control risks to employees and non-employees, such as members of the public, who may be exposed to the hazardous substances or ultimately affected by the company's work activities. Action taken by an employer which would otherwise be regarded as discrimination on grounds of sex, to protect women of childbearing age from chemicals which are harmful to the unborn child, may be lawful if the employer was fulfilling his duties under health and safety legislation such as COSHH.[82]

79 COSHH covers germs that cause diseases such as leptospirosis or legionnaires' disease and germs used in laboratories.
80 www.hse.gov.uk
81 http://www.hse.gov.uk/coshh/basics.htm.
82 *Page v Freighthire Tank Haulage Ltd* [1981] 1 All ER 394; [1981] ICR 299; [1981] IRLR 13.

Control of Noise at Work Regulations[83]

14.25 These Regulations implement the Physical Agents (Noise) Directive (2003/10/EC) which tightens the legal requirements in relation to noise by lowering the exposure action values. The Regulations came into force on 6 April 2006 for most industries, but the music and entertainment industry had until 6 April 2008 to comply.

These Regulations shall have effect with a view to protecting persons against risk to their health and safety arising from exposure to noise at work. The HSE calculate that over one million employees in Great Britain are exposed to levels of noise that puts their hearing at risk.

Under Regulation 5 (1), an employer who carries out work which is liable to expose any employees to noise at or above a lower exposure action value, shall make a suitable and sufficient assessment of the risk from that noise to the health and safety of those employees, and the risk assessment shall identify the measures which need to be taken to meet the requirements of the Regulations. The Regulations cover not only the obviously noisy industrial premises and construction sites, but virtually all workplaces with few exceptions, including workplaces where the risk of the noise may not be immediately obvious.

In *Baker and Others v Quantum Clothing and Others*,[84] the case concerned the liability of an employer in the knitting industry of Derbyshire and Nottinghamshire for employees' loss of hearing caused by exposure to noise at a lower level than was previously recognised as giving rise to liability. The employee had worked for eighteen years with excessive noise levels without any protection before being provided with ear protection. The judge, in this particular case, found that ,although there was a clearly defined legal limit at which action to protect an employee's hearing from damage should have been taken and the noise levels experienced by her were slightly under this limit, there was still a moderate chance of noise-related hearing loss occurring. The woman in this particular case was awarded over £3,000 for her hearing loss. This will potentially open compensation claims to workers whose hearing has been damaged by moderate noise levels before the new lower noise levels

---

83 Statutory Instrument 2005 No 1643.
84 [2009] EWCA Civ 499, [2009] PIQR P332.

were introduced, although these claims will still require the employee to prove causation which could still represent a significant difficulty.

CORPORATE HOMICIDE

14.26 The offence addresses a key defect in the law that meant that, prior to the new offence, organisations could only be convicted of culpable homicide (or manslaughter in England) if a 'directing mind' at the top of the company (such as a director) was also personally liable. The reality of decision making in large organisations does not reflect this and the law, therefore, failed to provide proper accountability and justice for victims. Under the common law in Scotland an organisation including a corporation could be convicted of culpable homicide. In *Transco plc v HMA*,[85] Transco were fined £15million for health and safety breaches behind a fatal explosion in Larkhall in 1999. The criminal court of appeal held that it was competent to charge culpable homicide in such a situation. The court also held that in order to establish the necessary *mens rea* it was necessary to identify an individual, or group of individuals, who constitute the 'controlling mind' of the company. In other words, an individual or group with sufficient seniority and whose acts and state of mind represent that of the company. In such a case they must be found to be criminally responsible. The problem with the law prior to the recent Act was there was difficulty in identifying senior individuals responsible in complex structures, these structures change over time and individuals need to be the same throughout the commission of the offence. So, in practice, it is very difficult to prosecute complex organisations for culpable homicide, although prosecution was successful in the *Transco* case.

Because of this difficulty prosecutions were often taken under the statutory provisions of HASAW 1974 instead and fines under these provisions could be substantial.[86]

The Corporate Manslaughter and Corporate Homicide Act 2007 is a landmark in law, because the new offence of corporate homicide allows an organisation's liability to be assessed on a wider basis, providing a more

---

85 2004 SCCR 1.

86 *HMA v Munro and Sons* [2009] HCJAC 10, 2009 SLT 233; *LH Access Technology Ltd v HMA* [2009] SCL622.

effective means of accountability for very serious management failings across the organisation. For the first time, companies and organisations can be found guilty of corporate homicide in Scotland (or corporate manslaughter in England and Wales) as a result of serious management failures resulting in a gross breach of a duty of care. The Act came into force on 6 April 2008 and clarifies the criminal liabilities of companies, including large organisations, where serious failures in the management of health and safety result in a fatality. Prosecutions will be of the corporate body and not individuals, but the liability of directors, board members or other individuals under health and safety law, or general criminal law, will be unaffected. So the corporate body itself and individuals can still be prosecuted for separate health and safety offences under HASWA etc. An organisation will be guilty of the new offence if the way in which its activities are managed or organised causes a death, and amounts to a gross breach of a duty of care to the deceased. The juries in these cases will consider how the fatal activity was managed or organised throughout the organisation, including any systems and processes for managing safety and how these were operated in practice. A substantial part of the failure within the organisation must have been at a senior level. Senior level means the people who make significant decisions about the organisation or substantial parts of it. This includes both centralised, headquarters functions as well as those in operational management roles. An organisation guilty of the offence will be liable to an unlimited fine. The Act also provides for courts to impose a publicity order, requiring the organisation to publicise details of its conviction and fine. Courts may also require an organisation to take steps to address the failures behind the death (a remedial order). Corporate homicide cases will be prosecuted by the Procurator Fiscal in Scotland.

The first conviction under the 2007 Act was in *R v Cotswold Geotechnical Holdings Ltd*.[87] The company was fined £385,000 (to be paid over 10 years) when an employee was killed when an unsupported pit collapsed on him. The Court of Appeal upheld the amount of the fine even though it might result in the company going into liquidation.

---

87 [2011] EWCA Crim 1337, (2011) *Times*, 20 July.

DISMISSAL AND DETRIMENT

14.27 Safety representatives and members of safety committees enjoy no special status and may be dismissed for the same reasons as other employees,[88] however, dismissal for a health and safety related reason is automatically unfair under s 100 Employment Rights Act 1996. In such cases there is no upper limit on compensation and, in addition, if he is a health and safety representative, a member of a safety committee, or he has been designated to carry out health and safety functions, he may apply within seven days of effective termination of employment for interim relief.[89]

Section 44 of the Employment Rights Act 1996 makes it unlawful for an employer to subject his employee to a detriment for a heath and safety reason.

A health and safety reason will include dismissal of an employee or subjection to detrimental treatment because that employee:

(i)   has been designated a health and safety function and carried out or proposed to carry out that function,

(ii)   is a health and safety representative, or a member of a safety committee, and is performing or proposing to perform their functions or taking part in consultations as a safety representative or participating in an election for safety representative.

(iii)   in the absence of health and safety representatives or safety committee, or where it is not reasonably practicable to bring a matter to the attention of the representative or committee, brings the employer's attention to health and safety issues by reasonable means.[90]

(iv)   leaves or refuses to return to his place of work because of serious and imminent danger.[91]

(v)   takes reasonable and appropriate steps to protect himself or others from serious and imminent danger.

---

88 *Smiths Industries Aerospace and Defence Systems v Rawlings* [1996] IRLR 656.
89 Employment Rights Act 1996 ss 128–130.
90 *Balfour Kilpatrick Ltd v Acheson* [2003] IRLR 683.
91 *Harvest Press Ltd v McCaffrey* [1999] IRLR 778.

Where dismissal or detriment is for a health and safety reason described in iii), iv) or v), the question to be addressed by the tribunal is not whether the employee was in fact in any danger, but whether that employee held a genuine and reasonable belief that he or any third party was in serious and imminent danger. The employee must also have been acting in good faith.[92]

CONCLUSION

14.28 Despite all the common law rules and statutes dealing with health and safety, it is still a serious problem in UK workplaces. The health and safety statistics for 2008/09 produced by the Health and Safety Executive (HSE) showed that around 1.2 million people who worked during that year suffered from an illness (this included long standing as well as new cases) and 551 000 of these were new cases. During that year 180 workers were killed at work,[93] 131,895 other injuries to employees were reported under the (RIDDOR 1995). A total of 246 000 reportable injuries occurred and 29.3 million working days were lost overall. Of these 24.6 million was due to work-related ill health and 4.7 million due to workplace injury.

FURTHER READING

Books

Brown, *Safety, Health and Equality: A Guide for Union Reps.* (LRD Publications, 2008).
Health and Safety Executive. *Essentials of Health and Safety at Work* (4th edn HSE Books, 2006).
Peck, *Health and Safety Law* (LRD Publications, 2008).
Stranks, *Health and Safety at Work: An Essential Guide for Managers.* 8th edn (Kogan Page, 2008).
Tolley's Health and Safety at Work Handbook 2009 (Butterworths Law, 2008).

---

92 *Shillito v Van Leer (UK) Ltd* [1997] IRLR 495.
93 Middlemiss, S Employer's Liability for Death by Suicide or Stress and Overwork in the Workplace (2009) Juridical Review Part 4 pp 244–263.

Journal articles

Barrett, 'The Health and Safety (Offences) Act 2008: The Cost of Behaving Dangerously in the Workplace' (2009) Industrial Law Journal. Vol 38, No 1, pp 73–79.

Cook, 'Travellers' checks'. (2006) Occupational Safety and Health Journal. Vol 36, No 6, pp 18–22.

Morris, 'How to draw up a health and safety policy' (2001) People Management. Vol 7, No 10, pp 50–51.

'New safety laws on the statute book, but who will enforce them?' (2005) Workplace Report, No 27, pp 13–15.

Scotland (May) Comparative law; Fines; Health and safety offences; Scotland; Sentencing guidelines IHL 2011, 190, 55–56.

Websites

http://www.hse.gov.uk

Chapter 15

Trade Union Law

15.1 There is no doubt that an understanding of the historical background to labour law as it relates to trade unions in Britain is important. A unique feature of our trade union law, compared with other countries in Europe and the rest of the world, is that it does not provide positive rights to trade unions to engage in collective bargaining, take industrial action or congregate collectively in public to protest or promote their cause.

The history of trade unions will be covered in this chapter as will an examination of their legal status. The legal rules dealing with recognition of trade unions are considered, as well the law dealing with balloting. Finally, analysis of the future of trade unions from a legal perspective will be undertaken. Individual trade union rights and rights relating to industrial action are considered in Chapter 14.

HISTORICAL DEVELOPMENT OF TRADE UNIONS

15.2 Prior to the beginning of the 19th century, trade unions in their present form didn't exist. There were guilds made up of highly skilled workmen (eg master joiners) who could dictate terms and conditions to employers because of the scarcity and value of their skills. The low skilled and semi-skilled workers could not take collective action or form unions because they were viewed by the law as acting in restraint of trade. Anything they did was regarded as unlawful (set up for an unlawful purpose) and so they could not make enforceable contracts, or protect their property or their members. Any collective gathering to discuss issues such as wages or working conditions was viewed by the courts as a criminal conspiracy under the common law and any congregation of two or more persons, meeting for such a purpose, would suffer serious penalties. A most memorable crisis arose over the sentencing to transportation (to Australia) of five labourers in Tolpuddle, Dorset, for taking illegal oaths. There was a public outcry and questions about the legality of the sentence led to them being quashed in 1840. This was symptomatic of the widespread intimidation both by employers and the State towards union organisations in the first half of the nineteenth century. Member of criminal conspiracies could be banished, whipped or sent to prison.

This crime was given statutory form by Combinations Acts 1799 and 1800 which provided that holding any unauthorised meeting was a statutory offence. This was repealed in 1824, but the common law crime still existed. These Acts also applied in Scotland but they were never enforced, as the Guilds system began to be replaced by trade unions representing semi-skilled or low skilled workers and covering entire industries or occupations.

Industrial disputes were prevalent in the mid part of the 19th century, perhaps unsurprising given the extent of rapid change with new working practices and technologies being introduced. Most strikes began as unofficial affairs, later ratified by a sometimes reluctant national leadership. This is a feature of industrial action which is still evident today.

The unions in the 19th century were unincorporated associations which meant they had extremely limited legal status. They could do nothing in their own name and contracts were carried out by their members who had personal liability for any debts etc. More significantly they could not protect their own funds when they were embezzled by their members. If employers or the State wanted to sue trade unions for civil damages or bring criminal proceedings against them they needed to bring their action against individual members. Given the floating membership at the time it was very difficult for employers to know who to sue.

The move towards national and industrial unions who negotiated with employers or employers organisations, often on a national scale, began in the latter half of the 19th century. This development of trade unions was called 'new unionism' and was characterised by the establishment of the Trade Union Congress in 1868. In 1871, the Trade Union Act was passed which was an attempt to clarify the status of trade unions and give them some degree of protection. Combined with this was an attempt to make trade unions more legally accountable. Under this Act, trade unions no longer deemed to be acting in restraint of trade,[1] which meant they

---

1   Now contained in s 11 of the Trade Union and Labour Relations (Consolidation) Act 1992.

could enter into legally binding contracts and enforce them if necessary. Registered unions were, for the first time, entitled to purchase or lease land and the Act provided that trade unions' real and personal estate could be placed in the hands of trustees and they would be deemed to hold the property personally in legal proceedings. Lastly, trustees were given the right to bring or defend an action in their own name where action concerned the property rights of the union. This Act was closely followed by the Conspiracy and Protection of Property Act 1875, which provided various statutory offences which unions could be prosecuted for in the context of picketing, some of which still apply today. More significantly, trade unions were no longer to be treated as criminal conspiracies.

In *Taff Vale Railway Co v Amalgamated Society of Railway Servants*,[2] the union was sued in their own name by the employer for damages and an interdict in respect of industrial action they had undertaken. The employer successfully argued that, as a consequence of being given rights under Trade Union Act 1871, a trade union had sufficient status to be sued in their own name. The House of Lords agreed and imposed liability on trade unions in their own name in tort (delict). The House of Lords held: 'that whatever it's precise juristic basis a union is a creature known to the law and which can be sued.' The principle remains in force today that unions can be sued in their own name for delicts or breach of contract.

The Trade Union Congress lobbied the Government to provide protection for trade unions in this context. This was done by the Trade Disputes Act 1906 under which trade unions were given blanket immunity against any delictual actions pursued against them in their own name. Trade union officials (usually full-time employees of the union) were provided with limited immunity for specific delicts, eg inducing a breach of contract.

In 1965, a Royal Commission was set up under Lord Donovan to investigate the industrial relations system in the UK. They reported in 1968 that Britain had two systems of industrial relations. The first was the 'formal system' embodied in the official institutions, eg national collective bargaining between unions and employers. The other was the 'informal system' which was created by the actual behaviour of trade unions and

---

2   (1901) AC 426.

employers or employers' associations at plant level. Nationally agreed settlements were treated as the basis from which further local negotiations would take place. This resulted in vastly increased levels of pay awards (wages drift) and was a direct cause of inflation. The Commission also recognised a connection between the informal system and significant development of unofficial strike action which caused serious disruption in the workplace. The Donovan Commission, in their Report in 1968, recommended that the Government should formalise the informal system by making it a requirement to have written and binding collective agreements and also formalise the process of collective bargaining. They also recommended that trade unions should be given corporate status and stressed that legal intervention was unnecessary.

The response of the Conservative Government in 1971 was to largely ignore the Report and subject the industrial relations system to a set of strict legal controls. Under the Industrial Relations Act 1971, they removed all the immunities and effectively made unions and industrial action unlawful. A National Industrial Relations Court was established with powers to impose a 60-day cooling off period in major strikes, and to require unions to ballot members before strike action. Unions were required to register to get recognition and legal protection. This led to the non-cooperation of trade unions and employers, and eventually led to the imprisonment of individual strikers known as the 'Pentonville 5' who became martyrs in the eyes of the public.

This Conservative Government went out of power in 1974 and was replaced by a Labour Government that had fully reinstated the immunities by 1976. In 1978, there was a period known as the 'winter of discontent' when many of the largest unions went on strike for substantial periods. Britain experienced widespread power cuts, as the energy and transport workers took industrial action, and when the grave diggers and refuse collectors participated in strikes the chaos resulted in Labour losing power at the General Election in 1979.

Margaret Thatcher's Government was elected on an agenda of reforming the industrial relations law in the UK. The impact of the various legal changes this government introduced was considerable. It included the removal of the blanket immunity. They introduced a number of statutes that increasingly removed many of the rights and immunities possessed by unions. The Employment Acts of 1980 and 1982, made secondary strike action illegal and picketing lawful only if carried out by workers at their own places of work. Secret ballots were required for union elections, under the Trade Union Act 1984, and further Employment Acts of 1988 and 1990 made all closed shops illegal, and made unions responsible for unofficial actions by their members unless they disavowed them in writing. Unofficial strikers could be dismissed. The Trade Union Reform and Employment Rights Act 1993 tightened control over ballots for industrial action and required seven days' notice of a strike ballot to be given. The consequences of these changes was that the legal protection extended to trade unions and their officials was drastically reduced which led, in part, to a weaker trade union movement and a strong decline in its membership.

This law was consolidated in 1992 and largely remains in force today.

THE MODERN LAW AND INSTITUTIONS RELATING TO TRADE UNIONS

15.3 The modern law relating to trade unions is mostly, but not exclusively, contained in the Trade Union Relations (Consolidation) Act 1992 (TULR(C)A 1992). This statute makes provision for the legal status of trade unions, sets out statutory procedures for the recognition of trade unions, procedures for taking industrial action, provides protection for trade unions and their members in taking industrial action and sets out the limits of that protection.

We have already considered some of the institutions of the law relating to trade unions in Chapter 2 however it is useful to consider the role of the Central Arbitration Committee and the Certification Officer.

Central Arbitration Committee (CAC)

15.4 The Central Arbitration Committee arbitrates disputes between employer and trade unions with regard to matters such as the statutory recognition procedure[3] and adequacy of information provided to trade unions for collective bargaining purposes,[4] and to employees regarding

---

3   Part I of Schedule A1 to the Trade Union and Labour Relations (Consolidation) Act 1992 (TULR(C)A).
4   Section 181 of TULR(C)A.

Works Councils[5] and European Works Councils,[6] and other disputes relating to employee involvement in the workplace.[7]

It also provides an arbitration service relating to the ACAS arbitration scheme.[8] Each Committee is chaired by a chairman or depute chairman who are legally qualified, and two lay representatives – one experienced in representing employers' interests and one experience in representing employees' interests.

The Certification Officer

15.5 The responsibilities of the Certification Officer include:

i.   Maintaining a list of trade unions and employer's associations;

ii.   Certifying the independence of trade unions;

iii.   Receiving, ensuring compliance with statutory requirements and keeping available for public inspection annual returns for trade unions and employers' associations;

iv.   Determining complaints concerning trade union elections, ballots;

v.   Complaints regarding breach of trade union rules;

vi.   Ensuring observance of the statutory requirements governing mergers between trade unions and employers associations;

vii.   Overseeing the finances of trade unions and employers associations' including their political fund.[9]

LEGAL STATUS OF TRADE UNIONS

15.6 Trade unions are no longer regarded as unincorporated associations and their legal status is defined in S 10(1) of the Trade Union Labour

---

5   The Information and Consultations Regulations 2004.
6   The Transnational Information and Consultation of Employees Regulations 1999 came into force on 15 January 2000.
7   The European Public Limited-Liability Company Regulations 2004, The European Cooperative Society Regulations 2006, The Companies (Cross Border Mergers) Regulations 2007.
8   Section 212 of TULR(C)A 1992 SEE Chapter 18 for more detail.
9   http://www.certoffice.org/

Relations (Consolidation) Act 1992 (TULR(C)A 1992), which provides that a trade union is not a body corporate but:

(a)   It is capable of making contracts;

(b)   It is capable of suing and being sued in its own name whether in proceedings related to property or founded in contract or tort (delict) or any other cause of action; or

(c)   Proceedings for an offence alleged to have been committed by it or on its behalf may be brought against it in its own name.

Despite the clarity of these legal provisions the precise limits of the trade union's status are still uncertain. In *EETPU v Times Newspapers*,[10] the plaintiff trade union sued the defendants in libel for an article in their newspaper which allegedly injured their reputation. The defendants successfully argued that the commission of the tort (delict) of defamation depended on the existence of a legal personality and that, by virtue of s10 (1) of TULR(C)A 1992, the union was not a body corporate and could not be treated as if it were one. Therefore, as a mere unincorporated association it had no legal personality to protect.

TRADE UNION RECOGNITION

15.7 Recognition is important for a trade union because without recognition the union and its members will not enjoy the full array of rights and protections conferred by TULR(C)A 1992 and other legislation. Prior to the present scheme for recognition there were various statutory rights for independent unions which still apply regardless of recognition. Dismissal will be automatically unfair if the reason for dismissal is membership or non membership of an independent trade union (whether recognised or not),[11] or taking part in the activities of an independent trade union at an appropriate time.[12] Action short of dismissal taken for these reasons is unlawful and an employee can make a claim to an employment tribunal [13]

---

10   (1980) 3 WLR 96.
11   Section 152(1)(a) TULR(C)A 1992.
12   Section 152(1)(b) TULR(C)A 1992.
13   Section 146(1)(a) and s 146(1)(b) TULR(C)A.

Additional rights enjoyed by independent recognised trade unions include: information and consultation rights, right to continued recognition under the Transfer of Undertakings Regulations 1981, (all of which are discussed below), the right to appoint safety representatives (see chapter 16), the right to reasonable time off work for trade union officials and right to reasonable unpaid time off work for trade union members to participate in trade union activities.

Recognition

15.8 The statutory recognition procedure now in force is set out in Schedule A to of TULR(C)A 1992.

Recognition is defined by s 178(3) of TULR(C)A 1992, as 'Recognition by the employer to any extent for collective bargaining purposes'.

There is a difference between informal recognition, voluntary recognition and recognition under the statutory procedures. Informal recognition can be for any purpose and the parties are free to agree the negotiation procedures. There may be partial recognition or full recognition (covering all aspects of trade union activities). Some employers will recognise a trade union only for limited purposes, such as representation at grievance/disciplinary hearings, etc. In *NUGSAT v Albury Bros Ltd*,[14] Lord Denning ruled that recognition was so important to statutory union rights that, in the absence of an express agreement, it could not be deemed to be established unless there was clear and unequivocal evidence of conduct from which recognition could be inferred. In *NUTGW v Charles Ingram & Co Ltd*,[15] it was established that:

'Recognition plainly, we think, implies agreement which of course involves consent. That is to say it is a mutual process by which the employers recognise the union which obviously agrees to be recognised and it may come about in a number of different ways. There may be a written agreement that the union be recognised. There may be an express agreement not in writing. Or, as we think, it is sufficient if neither of those exist, but the established facts are such that it can be said of them that they are clear and unequivocal and give rise to the

---

14   (1978) IRLR 503 CA.
15   [1977] IRLR 147.

clear inference that the employers have recognised the union. This will normally involve conduct over a period of time'.[16]

The onus is on the trade union to show that there is an agreement that it is recognised for collective bargaining.[17] An agreement between an employer and a trade union which granted recognition for representation purposes only, is sufficient to prevent the trade union from being consulted about impending redundancies.[18] However, negotiations by one union member acting alone will not amount to recognition[19] and neither will representation of an employee in disciplinary proceedings by a union representative.[20]

Voluntary recognition applies where the process has been started for statutory recognition but the parties reach an agreement and the recognition becomes 'voluntary.' In this case, the recognition is for the purpose of negotiations relating to pay, hours and holidays only unless the parties agree otherwise.[21]

Statutory recognition applies to a bargaining unit for the purpose of negotiations relating to pay, hours and holidays only and, unless the parties can agree a procedure for collective bargaining, one will be imposed. Usually the procedure imposed will be that set out in Schedule 1 A to the Act.

The Statutory Recognition Scheme

15.9 Section 1 of the Employment Relations Act 1999 inserts Schedule A1 into TULR(C)A 1992 (Collective Bargaining Recognition). The scheme is restricted to employers with 21 or more employees. For most purposes, under these provisions, reference to collective bargaining means negotiations relating to pay, hours and holidays only,[22] unless the parties agree in a separate agreement that other matters should be the subject

---

16 Phillips J at 533.
17 *T&GWU v Dyer* [1977] IRLR 93.
18 *USDAW v Sketchley Ltd* (1981) IRLR 291.
19 *AUEW v Sefton Engineering* [1976] IRLR 318.
20 *T&GWU v Courtenam Products* [1977] IRLR 8.
21 Schedule A1 TULR(C)A 1992 (Collective Bargaining Recognition paragraph 3(2)(3)).
22 Schedule A1 TULR(C)A 1992 (Collective Bargaining Recognition paragraph 3(2)(3)).

of collective bargaining. 'Pay' should be interpreted to include pension contributions in defined contribution schemes and pension benefits in defined benefit schemes for the purposes of the statutory scheme.[23]

Independence

15.10 Independence is a prerequisite of recognition. A union is independent where:

(1)   it is not under the control of an employer; and

(2)   is not liable to interference by an employer (arising out of the provision of financial or material support or by any other means whatsoever) tending towards such control.[24]

The decision of the Certification Officer is conclusive, although he must give reasons for the decision.[25] There are various factors that the Certification Officer will consider in deciding if a union is independent, for example whether or not there is financial assistance provided to the union by employer, other assistance such as free accommodation and free mailing.[26]

Application for recognition

15.11 Recognition in respect of a bargaining unit can be requested by one or more independent unions. A pre-existing collective agreement in force in respect of the same bargaining unit with another union will prevent an application for recognition.

This rule applies even where the number of members of the union which held the collective agreement was small[27] and where the union making the application has demonstrably more support within the bargaining unit than that which has been recognised.[28] A collective agreement does not have

---

23   *UNIFI v Union Bank of Nigeria plc* (2001) IRLR 712.
24   Section 5 TULR(C)A 1992.
25   Section 6 TULR(C)A 1992.
26   *Squib UK Staff Association v Certification Officer* (1979) IRLR 75 CA, see also *Blue Circle SA v Certification Officer). (1977) IRLR 20.
27   *TGWU v Asda* [2004] IRLR 836.
28   *R (on application of NUJ) v CAC and MGN Ltd* [2006] ICR 1.

to be implemented to be 'in force.' It simply has to be unconditionally signed.[29]

The request must take the form of a formal written request to the employer; it must specify the union(s) and bargaining unit involved, and state that the request is made under schedule A1.

If the employer and the union fail to reach agreement at the end of the first period (or at the end of the second period if there has been an extension), then the union can make an application for compulsory recognition to the CAC.

Bargaining Unit

15.12 The union proposes the bargaining unit but this may be changed by the CAC who must be satisfied that it is compatible with effective management.[30] The primary decision making body is the CAC and the courts will only intervene if CAC exceeds its jurisdiction, acts unfairly or acts in contravention of the principles of natural justice.[31] The union must satisfy CAC that at least 10% of the bargaining unit comprises of union members and that the majority of workers in the bargaining unit are 'likely' to favour recognition.

The CAC need not provide reasons for its decision. There is no right of appeal against the CAC decision and the only means of challenge is to seek judicial review in the Court of Session. In *Fullarton Computer Industries Ltd v Central Arbitration Committee*,[32] the employer argued the CAC decision was ultra vires and a breach of natural justice. The court was not convinced and ruled against them.

Recognition ballot

15.13 If these conditions are satisfied then the CAC must order recognition unless it is required to hold a ballot, because:

---

29 *R (on application of NUJ) v CAC and MGN Ltd* [2006] ICR 1.
30 TULR(C)A Schedule A1 para 19B(2)(a).
31 *R v CAC, ex parte Tube Division Services Ltd* [1978] IRLR 183.
32 (2001) IRLR 752.

(i)   it has evidence that a majority of the union members in the bargaining unit are not in favour of recognition, or

(ii)   it considers that it would be in the interest of good industrial relations to hold a ballot.[33]

A Code of Practice on access to workers during recognition and de-recognition ballots was issued by the DTI and took effect June 2000.[34] A ballot must be conducted by a qualified independent person who must be (i) a solicitor who holds a practising certificate, (ii) a person qualified to act as a company auditor, or (iii) members of certain specified independent bodies.[35]

The CAC may order the ballot to be rerun if it was not properly conducted.[36]

If a ballot is held the CAC will issue a declaration of recognition when a ballot shows that a majority of those voting are in favour of recognition **and** that majority constitute at least 40% of workers in the bargaining unit.

During the course of the ballot both the union and the employer must refrain from unfair practices which are listed in s 7A (2) of Schedule A TULR(C)A 1002. These unfair practices include the situations where a party does the following actions with a view to influencing the result of the ballot,

(a)   offers to pay money or give money's worth to a worker entitled to vote in the ballot,

(b)   makes an outcome-specific offer to a worker entitled to vote in the ballot,

(c)   coerces or attempts to coerce a worker entitled to vote in the ballot to disclose-

(i)   whether he intends to vote or to abstain from voting in the ballot, or

---

33   TULR(C)A 1992 Schedule A1 para 22(4)(a).
34   The Code of Practice on Access and Unfair Practices During Recognition and Derecognition Ballots.
35   Recognition and Derecognition Ballots (Qualified Persons) Order 2000 SI 200/1306 by as amended by The Recognition and Derecognition Ballots (Qualified Persons) Order 2000 (Amendment) Order 2002, SI 2002/2268.
36   *R (Ultraframe (UK) Ltd) v CAC* [2005] ICR 1194.

(ii)   how he intends to vote, or how he has voted in the ballot.

(d)   dismisses or threatens to dismiss a worker,

(e)   takes or threatens disciplinary action against a worker,

(f)   subjects or threatens to subject a worker to any other detriment, or

(g)   uses or attempts to use undue influence on a worker entitled to vote in the ballot.

The remedy for a party complaining about an unfair practice is to complain to the CAC on or before the first working day after the date of the ballot (or last date of the ballot). The CAC may make a declaration and order any party to do a specific thing or order a secret ballot on recognition. Where the unfair practice consists of violence or dismissal of a union official or if the CAC has made an order under s 27 which has not been complied with, then under s 27D the CAC may order recognition if the unfair practice was committed by the employer or order that the union not be recognised if the unfair practice was committed by the union.

Effect of recognition

15.14 The union will be recognised for the purpose of collective bargaining, as described above. The Trade Union Recognition (Method of Collective Bargaining) Order 2000[37] specifies, for the purpose of certain provisions of Schedule A1 to TULR(C)A 1992, the method by which collective bargaining might be carried out. The specified method is required to be taken into account by the CAC when, following an application for trade union recognition under Schedule A1, it is required to specify a method by which the union and employer concerned are to conduct collective bargaining. The bargaining method imposed by the CAC has effect as if it were a legally binding contract between the employer and the union(s). If one party believes the other is failing to respect the method, the first party may apply to the court for an order of specific performance, ordering the other party to comply with the method. Specific performance is, however, the only available remedy. Failure to comply with such an order could

---

37   SI 2000/1300.

constitute contempt of court. Once the CAC has imposed a bargaining method, the parties can vary it (including the fact that it is legally binding) by agreement, provided that they do so in writing.

As a consequence of the decision of the European Court of Human Rights (ECtHR) in *Wilson and Palmer v UK*,[38] the small business exemption under these Regulations has less significance as trade unions will now have the right under Article 11 of the ECHR to go along and represent members in pay negotiation. This decision may also extend to the protection of workers rights when employers take retaliatory action in response to a recognition application. Although there is already some protection under statute, this may lead to stronger measures being introduced. *Wilson* and *Palmer* may also render the statutory procedure even less necessary by promoting a surrogate recognition facility which will be much cheaper and easier for unions to use.[39]

The three year rule

15.15 A failed application for recognition will prevent another attempt by that union within three years. Recognition will prevent another union from applying for recognition for the same bargaining unit. A voluntary agreement for recognition is made between the parties after a request for recognition has been made under the Schedule, the employer has to maintain that agreement for 3 years unless the union ends it before that time. This is known as semi-voluntary recognition.

Individual rights under the Recognition Scheme

15.16 A worker has the right not to be subjected to any detriment by any act, or any deliberate failure to act, by his or her employer, if the act or failure to act takes place on any of certain specified grounds relating to trade union recognition or derecognition.[40]

As to the effect on the contract of the collective agreement, see below.

---

38 (2002) IRLR 128.
39 Ewing, KD (2003) The Implications of Wilson and Palmer. Industrial Law Journal, vol 32, no 1, pp. 1–22.
40 Schedule A1 TULR(C)A 1992 paragraph 156(1).

Derecognition

15.17 Under the rules,[41] it may be claimed by the employer or the union that the bargaining unit is no longer appropriate and that application to the CAC is necessary for the decision as to what is an appropriate unit. This claim is not admissible unless the CAC decide that it is likely that the original unit is no longer appropriate by reason of any of the circumstances detailed below:

(1)   a change in organisation or structure of business;

(2)   a change in the business activities pursued by the employer; or

(3)   a substantial change in the number of workers employed in the particular unit.

(4)   the employer now employs fewer than 21 workers.

If the CAC is satisfied that one or more of these changes apply it can revoke the decision to allow recognition. Automatic derecognition occurs when a trade union loses its certificate of independence. An application will be inadmissible if made within 3 years of a previous application.

Conclusion on recognition rights

15.18 Trade union recognition is now the largest part of the workload of the Central Arbitration Committee (CAC) and 70 cases were processed in the first year of operation of the scheme.

Voluntary agreement is the prevalent method of resolving recognition dispute, with statutory procedure being last resort because employers prefer a voluntary option when there is union support for it, because they are better able to control the process and content of the agreement and they can avoid polarisation of positions and poor external publicity.

After 20 years of decline, trade union membership began to show a slight increase in 1999 and the number of undertakings in which a union was recognised as having bargaining rights also began to increase, particularly when the unions were given the statutory right to demand recognition came into force. In the first 5 years of the new statutory recognition regime, 444 applications for recognition were made, of which 116 ended

---

41   TULR(C)A Schedule A1, paragraphs 149–154,

in a declaration of recognition. As a result, within that first 5-year period, nearly 23,000 workers were covered by collective bargaining.[42]

Trade union information and consultation rights

15.19 An important consequence of recognition are the information and consultation rights enjoyed by the independent recognised trade union. The independent trade union has the right to be informed and consulted in the event of large scale redundancies and transfers of undertakings, and we consider these rights in chapters 7 and 6 respectively.

We will consider the ongoing rights to information and consultation later in this chapter.

EUROPEAN WORKS COUNCILS

15.20 The purpose of the European Works Council Directive[43] (EWC Directive) was to improve the right to information and to consultation of employees in transnational businesses, known as 'community scale undertakings' and 'community scale groups of undertakings'.

When the EWC Directive was passed, on 30 September 1994, the UK were not a party to it, but, following the end of the UK opt-out of the Social Chapter, a further directive was passed[44] and the provisions of the EWC Directive were extended to the UK.

Many multinational companies who operated in the UK were already covered by the Directive as far as their European workers were concerned because of their European activities, but about 100 further UK undertakings became subject to the provisions of the Directive.

The Works Council Directive was implemented in the UK by the Transnational Information and Consultation of Employees Regulations 1999[45] (TICER). These Regulations came into force on 15 January 2000.

The TICER Regulations apply to employers:

---

42 See CAC Annual Reports.
43 94/45/EC.
44 (97/74/EC).
45 SI 1999/3323.

A   1) whose central management is in the UK; or

2) where central management is outside the European Economic Area (EEA) but whose representative agent is within the UK; or

3) where central management is outside the EEA but there are more employees employed in a single establishment in the UK than are employed in any other establishment in a Member State.

and

B   who are considered to be either 'community scale undertakings' or 'community scale groups of undertakings'.

A 'community scale undertaking' (CSU) is defined as an undertaking which has:

(a)   more than 1,000 employees in total in the EEA (which includes the EU Member States, Iceland, Liechtenstein and Norway); and

(b)   at least 150 employees in each of two of these states.

A 'community scale group of undertakings' (CSGU) is defined as a group of undertakings which has

(a)   at least 1,000 employees within the EEA; and

(b)   at least two group undertakings in different Member States employing at least 150 employees.

An 'undertaking' includes any natural or legal person carrying on activities of an economic or commercial nature.[46]

If a business falls within these criteria then, according to the EWC Directive, the central management have a responsibility to create the means and conditions necessary for establishing the appropriate information and consultation mechanisms. The process of informing and consulting with the workers is to be carried out by the means of 'European Works Councils' (EWC) or by an information and consultation procedure (ICP).

The first step in the process is the establishment of a Special Negotiating Body (SNB), whose role is to represent the employees in negotiations with

46 *Hydrotherm Geratebau GmbH v Compact del Dott. Ing Mario Andreoli and CSAS* [1984] ECR 2999 para 10–12).

central management about the procedures which will ultimately be used for informing and consulting.

The process may be initiated by the employer but if the employer fails to do so, the employees or employee representatives may make a request under Regulation 5(1) for a SNB to be set up.

The request must be in writing and dated, and it must be by at least 100 employees, or their representatives, in at least two undertakings or establishments in at least two different Member States. The request may consist of one single request meeting this criterion, or separate requests which in total amount to it. The requests can be sent to the central or local management of the undertaking or group of undertakings.

On receipt of the request(s) the central management should take steps to set up a SNB.

The Directive states that the SNB should consist of one member representing each Member State in which the CSU/CSGU has an establishment or has its controlling undertaking or controlled undertakings, and additional members dependent upon the percentage of employees of the CSU/CSGU employed in that Member State.

Each Member State has its own Regulations for appointment of these members. The UK members of the SNB are appointed by a secret ballot of the UK employees. The central management must arrange the secret ballot, appoint a ballot supervisor and arrange for publication of the results. They also bear the cost of the ballot.

The ballot supervisor, if not satisfied, must issue an ineffective ballot report within 1 month of publication of the result.[47]

There is no need for a ballot if there is already a consultative committee in existence who nominate UK members to the SNB.

Once elected the SNB and central management will commence negotiations. The end result of these negotiations is usually the establishment of a EWC, but they may decide instead to establish an information and consultation procedure (ICP). If so, they must put this decision in writing.

Central management must pay the reasonable expenses of the SNB or ICP.

---

47   Regulation 12(3).

Regulation 17(4) governs the matters to be decided by the SNB. They must negotiate who is on the EWC, which employees/undertakings/ establishments are covered, how seats are allocated, the term of members, the procedure for informing/consulting, frequency of meetings, resources, terms of agreement and method of renegotiation. They have complete freedom to negotiate but there is a default procedure set out in the Schedule to the Regulations which is often the procedure which the parties agree to use. In any event, if the parties fail to agree an alternative procedure, the default procedure will apply.

The default procedure applies:

(a)   if the parties agree it should apply, or

(b)   if central management refuse to commence negotiations within 6 months of a valid request, or

(c)   if, 3 years after a valid request, the parties are still unable to achieve an agreement.

TICER Schedule para 6(1), defines the scope of the default procedure and provides that there must be information and consultation on matters which concern the community scale undertaking as a whole, or at least two of its establishments or group undertakings situated in *different* Member States. Therefore, in its default format, the EWC cannot be used for information and consultation on purely domestic matters (such as redundancies at one UK factory), unless these can be shown to impact in another Member State.

Under the default procedure, there is a right to meet with central management once a year to be informed and consulted. In particular the meeting will relate to 'the structure, economic and financial situation and of production and sales, the situation and probable trend of employment, investments and substantial changes concerning organisation, production, mergers, cut-backs or closures of undertakings, establishments or important parts thereof, and collective redundancies'.[48]

The default procedure also includes a right to be informed and meet whenever there are exceptional circumstances affecting the employees'

---

48   Schedule para 7 Art 12.

interests to a considerable extent, particularly in the event of relocations, closure of establishments or undertakings or collective redundancies.

Enforcement

15.21 Many employers are reluctant to comply with these Regulations as they feel that it involves the release of sensitive information which may adversely affect their share price. The Directive left the enforcement measures up to the Member States. In the UK, if an employer fails to adhere to their obligations, the remedy is to apply to the Central Arbitration Committee (CAC) for a declaration. They have no other sanction, however. Once a declaration has been granted then an application can be made to the Employment Appeal Tribunal (EAT) which has the power to fine the employer up to a maximum of £75,000. Other European countries have more effective remedies; for example, in France the courts can order that a transaction should be suspended until the appropriate consultation has taken place.

Disputes about whether or not the employer is a community scale undertaking, or community scale group of undertakings, can also be made to the CAC, as can disputes about whether a valid request has been made, failure of the employer to take steps to set up a SNB, and complaints about irregularities in the ballot within 21 days of publication of the result.

Domestic information and consultation procedures

15.22 Whereas TICER deals with transnational organisations, the Information and Consultation of Employees Regulations 2004 (ICER) deal with domestic undertakings. In terms of these Regulations, employees in larger undertakings have the right to request certain information from their employer. These Regulations implement the National Information and Consultation Directive.[49] An undertaking is defined, under Regulation 2, as 'a public or private undertaking which carries out an economic activity, whether or not for gain'.

The ICER Regulations apply to all private and public undertakings in the UK with more than 50 employees. The number of employees is

---

49 2002/14/EC.

calculated in accordance with Regulation 4 and is based on the average number of employees during the previous 12 months.

Under Regulation 5, an employer is obliged to provide on request to an employee, or employee representative, the necessary information to enable a calculation to be done to establish the number of employees within the UK and to calculate what constitutes 10% of the workforce. If the employer fails to provide this data, Regulation 6 provides for a complaint to be made to the CAC after a period of 1 month has elapsed from the date of the request. The CAC can order the employer to disclose specified data and an adverse inference can be drawn from a failure to comply with the order.[50]

The statutory procedure

15.23 The statutory procedure can be triggered in two ways:

(a)　a valid request by the employees or their representative

or

(b)　by the employer instigating negotiations.

A valid request is made for information and consultation where request is made on behalf of 10% of the workforce.

The request must:

(i)　be in writing and dated;

(ii)　be made on behalf of at least 10% of the workforce (subject to a minimum of 15 employees and maximum of 2,500). These numbers can be made up of more than one request from different sections of the workforce;

(iii)　specify the names of the employees making the request; and

(iv)　be sent to either the employer at its registered office, head office or principal place of business or to the CAC. If sent to the CAC, the CAC will notify the employer as soon as is reasonably practicable.

50　Regulation 35(3).

Once a valid request has been made the employer must start negotiations to establish a procedural framework for the information and consultation to take place. The employer and employees' representative must work together in a spirit of cooperation.[51]

The employees, or their representatives, and the employers are free to negotiate whatever procedures they wish covering whatever subject matter they feel should be the subject of information and consultation. In the event that the employer fails to negotiate, or negotiations have failed to achieve an agreement, within 6 months of a valid request then the default provisions under Regulation 18 will apply. These provisions provide that the subject matter of consultation and information will be:

(a) the recent and probable development of the undertakings' activities and economic situation;

(b) the situation, structure and probable development of employment within the undertaking and any anticipatory measures envisaged, in particular where there is a threat to employment within the undertaking;

(c) decisions which are likely to lead to substantial changes in work organisation or in contractual relations, including business transfers and collective redundancies.

The default provisions provide that information regarding these subjects should be provided at such time, in such fashion and with such content that the representatives will be able to conduct an adequate study and to prepare for consultation.

It should be noted that the right under these Regulations is only a right to be informed and consulted and not a right to make decisions.

One of the matters which concerns employers about mandatory information and consultation provisions is the fear that confidential and share price sensitive information will end up in the public domain. Regulations 25–26 attempt to alleviate this problem by providing that information received in confidence should be treated as confidential, unless the recipient believes that disclosure would be protected under the Employment Rights Act 1996 s 43A.

---

51   Regulation 21.

An employer may withhold information altogether if disclosing it to representatives would seriously harm the functioning of the business or be prejudicial to it.

If the employer has a pre-existing agreement for information and consultation which is:

(i)   in writing;

(ii)   covers all the employees and has been approved by them; and

(iii) specifies how the employer has to give information, and if the request was made by less than 40% of the employees employed in the undertaking when the request was made, there is no need to enter into a new agreement. The employer may instead conduct a ballot. If the majority of at least 40% of the employees employed in the undertaking endorse the request the employer is obliged to commence negotiations. If not the employer need not commence negotiations.

Complaints regarding the conduct of the ballot can be made by an employee or employee representative to the CAC.

Enforcement

15.24 Enforcement of the provisions of these Regulations is by complaint to the CAC.[52] The complaint must be made within 3 months of the act complained of and can only be brought by the information and consultation representatives, unless there are no such representatives, in which case complaints can be brought by individual employees or employee representatives or trade union representatives. If a complaint is upheld by the CAC then the complainant can apply to the EAT who can impose a financial penalty of up to £75,000. An example of this happening is *Amicus v Macmillan Publishers Ltd.*[53] Enforcement of purely voluntary arrangements, such as pre-existing agreements, is not by this method but is by court action.

---

52   Regulation 22.
53   [2007] IRLR 88.

Balloting requirements

15.25 Specific areas where ballots are now required are: (i) amalgamations, (ii) the adoption or retention by the union of political objectives, (iii) elections of trade union officials, (iv) recognition and de-recognition, and (v) official industrial action.

As the balloting requirements relating to (iv) and (v) are dealt with elsewhere in this chapter and in chapter 14, it is not necessary to give them detailed consideration here. The trade unions were not required by law to hold secret ballots until relatively recently (1984) unless it was a requirement in the union rule book. The exception was the requirement, under the Trade Union Act 1909, that if the union wanted to have a political fund they had to hold a ballot of their membership. What this meant was that ballots were not held and decisions were made without them or where they did proceed it would be carried out openly possibly, by a show of hands, which meant there was the possibility of ballot rigging.

Amalgamations of trade unions

15.26 The rules regarding balloting originally provided by the Trade Union (Amalgamations) Act 1964 and now are contained in ss 97-106 TULR(C)A 1992.

In 1900 there were 1323 trade unions and in 1991 there were only 309. At the end of 1990 there were 23 unions with over 100,000 members accounting for 82% of total membership of 9.8 million. Until recently[54] the total number of unions stood at 67 unions, with TUC membership, representing nearly 7 million people.

An amalgamation is where two or more unions come together to form an entirely new union, eg UNISON was NALGO and CPSA etc. A transfer occurs where one union transfers their membership and assets to another union and in the process cease to exist legally. The union only requires a simple majority of the membership in favour of ballot.

---

54   (2005 – 6.78 million) see http://www.tuc.org.uk/

Political funds of trade unions

15.27 It has long been possible for trade unions to support political parties financially by having political objectives and a political fund. It was traditionally left to the unions to decide how to make this decision. Union members would pay part of their subscription towards a political fund which the union would hold and this money needed to be paid from the general funds of the union. The law changed with the case of *Amalgamated Society of Railway Servants v Osborne*,[55] where a member of the ASRS sought a declaration from the court that a rule of the union under which it levied contributions on members to finance Labour Party candidates was ultra vires the union. The House of Lords decided that any expenditure not specifically authorised in the 1871 Trade Union Act was unlawful. This included political contributions. As this meant that unions could not legitimately support political parties, legislation was quickly introduced to overrule this decision in the form of the Trade Union Act 1913. This provided that the unions were allowed to have such levies provided they balloted their membership and they were in agreement (ie supported by a simple majority). Also until 1984, once a ballot had been held to determine if the union membership wanted to pursue or support political objectives, and agreement had been reached, there was no need for further ballots. The rules on political ballots were changed by Trade Union Act 1984 which provided that a ballot must be held every 10 years to reaffirm union membership support. However, no ballot was required if a union want to cease pursuing political objectives. Under the Employment Act 1988 unions were required to undertake postal ballots.

The rules regarding political funds can now be found in ss 71-91 of TULR(C)A 1992.[56] Trade Unions must appoint a qualified independent person known as a 'scrutineer' to: (a) Supervise production and distribution of voting papers in political fund ballots, (b) Act as a returning officer (c) Compile a report on conduct of ballot proceedings. Union members have the right to complain to the certification officer where political fund ballot is not held in accordance with rules submitted to Certification Officers

---

55 (1910) AC 87.
56 For detailed rules re political funds www.dius.gov.uk/assets/.../10-817-trade-union-political-funds-guide.pdf

(ss 79-81 TULR(C)A 1992). Also where unions have misapplied funds, in breach of s 71 TULR(C)A, then a union member can complain to the Certification Officer. Most ballots held by unions to reaffirm political objectives and funds were in favour of continuing. An exception was the Civil and Public Services Association (now part of UNISON) in 1997. In 1996 nearly 4.9 million union members contributed to a political fund which reached a combined total of £15.2 million donated to political parties etc. The Labour party threatened to axe its links with one of the unions which helped found the party, after five branches of the railway workers union decided to affiliate to the Scottish Socialist Party in protest at Tony Blair's policies on the railways and support for privatisation. Then, on 7 February 2004, the Labour leadership expelled the RMT because they had made a special conference decision to uphold the right of branches and regions to support parties other than the Labour Party. The trade-union percentage of the Labour Party's income went down from 66% in 1992 to 33% in 2001. From 2001 to 2006, the unions gave the Labour Party £45 million in cash.

The political fund must be separate from general funds of the union although the last Government introduced the main purpose test which allowed campaigns to protect jobs and other members interests to be funded from general fund.[57]

Expenditure for political objects is covered by s 72 TULR(C)A and can include any contributions to funds of political parties for various purposes including: services; property; holding ballots; maintenance of any holder of a political office; holding of a conference or meeting by political party and producing advertising or publicity material of any kind with respect to political candidature.[58]

Trade union elections

15.28 Prior to 1984, it was at the discretion of trade union rules what arrangements may apply to appointment of trade union officials. The rules might not necessarily require an election, and even where they did, the method of voting was not always fair and impartial. The Trade Union

---

57   *Paul v NALGO* (1987) IRLR 413.
58   *ASTMS v Parkin* (1983) IRLR 448.

Act 1984 stated unions must hold an election for all officials and the Employment Act 1988 confirmed that elections must be carried out every five years for all voting members of the principal executive committee. The General Secretary of the union is often excluded from the balloting requirement where he is a career trade unionist.

A failure to hold a ballot entitles union members to make a complaint to the Certification Officer or the Court of Session.[59] The Certification Officer can make an enforcement order requiring union to hold a new election or to remedy the fault or impose a requirement that they abstain for certain acts in the future. The court has a similar power to the Certification Officer in that it can make a declaration highlighting the breach of rules taken place and make an order requiring the union to remedy the defects. In *AB v CD*,[60] two candidates gained an identical number of votes in an election using the single transferable vote system. The rules did not have any provision for such an eventuality. The court implied a term into the standing orders that the candidate with the most votes in the initial voting should be declared the winner. An independent scrutineer must be appointed and they have responsibility to conduct the ballot as per s 51(A) of TULR(C)A 1992 and s 52 provides detailed rules regarding the content of the scrutineer's report.

Future developments

15.29 The pioneering use of e-balloting has significantly increased turnouts in union votes where it is allowed (ie pay ballots, minor elections) but the Employment Relations Act 1999 prevents its use for major ballots including those governing industrial action, union elections and political funds.

The TUC have claimed that the current balloting rules are so complex that they are almost impossible to follow and all too often end in unions being brought before the courts on minor technical challenges,[61] eg the

---

59   Section 108 of TULR(C)A 1992.
60   (2001) IRLR 808.
61   In *RMT v London Underground Ltd* [2001] IRLR 228 the union balloted in total 7,000 workers for industrial action at four different companies and secured large majorities overall. However, the action was held by the High Court and the Court of Appeal to be unprotected because the union gave insufficient information to the employer.

Unite case (see chapter 16). According to the International Labour Office, the complexity of the UK balloting laws is inconsistent with the right to strike guaranteed in ILO Convention 87.

COLLECTIVE AGREEMENTS

15.30 Under s 179 of TULR(C)A 1992, 'any collective agreement shall be conclusively presumed not to have been intended by the parties to be legally enforceable unless the agreement (a) is in writing and (b) contains a provision which (however expressed) states that the parties intended that the agreement shall be a legally enforceable contract.'

The parties to the agreement are the trade union and the employer or employer's association. In order for an employee to enforce a term of a collective agreement it must be incorporated into the employee's contract of employment. A term may be incorporated into a contract of employment from a collective bargain expressly which may arise from the parties agreeing verbally or in writing that all or part of a particular collective agreement shall be binding upon them.[62] It may also become incorporated by implication provided the term is apt for incorporation.[63] As we mentioned in Chapter 3, in order for an individual employee to rely on a term in a collective agreement, or an employer to rely on such a term against the employee, the provision must be validly incorporated into the individual employee's contract of employment. Incorporation does not happen automatically, but rather the normal rules of contract apply to the situation. Terms can become incorporated into a contract in two ways, either expressly or by implication.

Express incorporation occurs when the contract of employment specifically states that the collective agreement (or particular provision of the collective agreement) will become part of the contract. This can be in writing or it can be verbal. The usual method is to insert an express clause into the written contract of employment, stating that the employee's contract will be subject to the terms and conditions contained in relevant collective agreement(s) between the employer and the trade union. Often the clause is found in the written statement of terms and conditions, issued

---

62 *NCB v Galley* (1958) 1 WLR 16 CA.
63 *Alexander v Standard Telephones and Cables (No2)* [1990] ICR 291.

under s 1 of the Employment Rights Act 1996, but it must be remembered that this statement is merely evidence of the terms and conditions of the contract of employment and not the contract itself.

Implied incorporation of a provision in a collective agreement will occur by custom and practice of the industry, reasons of business efficacy or by inference that it was the intention of the parties to the contract of employment (ie the employer and employee) that the agreement be incorporated into the contract of employment.

An example of implied incorporation by custom and practice can be seen in *Arthur H Wilton Ltd & ors v Peebles*,[64] where the EAT held that where it had been the practice of the employers and employees over a period of more than 20 years that the employer paid, and the employees accepted, the rates negotiated between the employer's association and the trade union, it was open to the tribunal to hold that it was an implied term of the contract that this would continue to happen.

Another example of custom and practice resulting in implied incorporation can be seen in *McLea v Essex Line Ltd*,[65] where the court held that the custom and practice of the shipping industry that (unless there was an agreement to the contrary) seamen would be engaged on the terms and conditions of the National Maritime Board resulted in those terms and conditions being incorporated into an individual seaman's contract. In order for a term to be incorporated by custom and practice that term must be 'certain and notorious'.[66] Terms will be implied into the contract for reasons of business efficacy when they are 'Imposed by law as a necessary incident of the contract, without which that contract would be inefficacious, absurd or futile'.[67] An example of incorporation of provisions of a collective agreement on the ground of business efficacy is *Scally v Southern Health and Social Services Board*.[68] The approach the court will take in deciding whether the provision has been incorporated into the contract of employment by the actions of the parties, and the

---

64   EAT Case 835/93.
65   (1933) 45 LlL Rep 254.
66   *Henry v London General Transport Services Ltd* 2002 IRLR 472.
67   *Tadd v Eastwood and the Daily Telegraph Limited* [1983] IRLR 320 at 327.
68   [1991] IRLR 522 HL.

factors which will influence the decision, were set out by Hobhouse J in *Alexander v Standard Telephones and Cables Ltd* (No 2).[69]

'The relevant contract is that between the individual employee and his employer; it is the contractual intention of those two parties which must be ascertained. In so far as that intention is to be found in a written document, that document must be construed on ordinary contractual principles. In so far as there is no such document or that document is not complete or conclusive, their contractual intention has to be ascertained by inference from the other available material including collective agreements. The fact that another document is not itself contractual does not prevent it from being incorporated into the contract if that intention is shown as between the employer and the individual employee.

Where a document is expressly incorporated by general words it is still necessary to consider, in conjunction with the words of incorporation, whether any particular part of that is apt to be a term of the contract; if it is inapt, the correct construction of the contract may be that it is not a term of the contract. Where it is not a case of express incorporation, but a matter of inferring the contractual intent, the character of the document and the relevant part of it and whether it is apt to form part of the individual contract is central to the decision whether or not the inference should be drawn.'

It is up to the court to ascertain the contractual intention of the parties. From Hobhouse J's statement, and from examining other case law, it is possible to identify several basic principles which the courts will apply when ascertaining this intention:

(a)   The normal rules of contractual construction will be applied to the situation. In order to ascertain whether it was the intention of the parties that the provision should be incorporated into the contract of employment the wording of the contract of employment will be examined closely.

(b)   If there is no written contract, or the written contract is incomplete or inconclusive, the whole circumstances of the case

---

69   [1991] IRLR 286.

will be examined to see whether it can be inferred that it was the intention of the employer and employee that the provision of the collective agreement should be incorporated. In *National Coal Board v National Union of Mineworkers*,[70] Scott J stated that the intention of the parties was to be inferred from the language of the contract and the industrial relations background between the parties. An important part of the process of ascertaining the intention of the employer and employee involves the court examining the provision to see whether or not the **particular** provision is *apt* for inclusion as a contractual provision. The main consideration is whether the term is part of the 'normative' provisions of the collective agreement rather than 'procedural'.

A normative term is one which is intended to benefit the individual employee, for example rates of pay, hours of work. A procedural provision is one which is intended to regulate dealings between the employer and the trade union, for example timescale for negotiations, composition of negotiating committees, etc. In order to be incorporated into the contract of employment the term must have been intended to confer rights/impose duties on the parties to the employment contract. Therefore, only normative provisions can be incorporated into the employment contract. In *National Coal Board v National Union of Mineworkers* (above), it was held that the procedural requirements of a dispute resolution procedure were held to be intended for resolving industrial disputes between the parties (ie employer and trade union) and not intended to be enforceable by individual employees. Rules and procedures tend, therefore, to be considered unilateral and not suitable for incorporation. In *Cadoux v Central Regional Council*,[71] the Outer House of the Court of Session held that the rules of a life insurance scheme were unilateral and, therefore, were not suitable for incorporation, despite having been formulated in consultation with the union.

---

70   [1986] ICR 736.
71   1986 SLT 117.

In *Wandsworth LBC v D'Silva*, the Court of Appeal held that a sick pay code was not apt for incorporation because, when its content and character were examined, it was clear that it was merely providing guidance for supervisors and employees as to the procedure to be followed in relation to long term absence. A particular type of provision which courts and tribunals have in the past considered inapt for incorporation, are provisions regarding procedures to be followed in the event of redundancy. This type of provision in a collective agreement was regarded as something which was not part of the day-to-day activities between employers and employees, and not intended to confer rights on individual employees and, therefore, inapt for incorporation. In more recent cases, however, it seems that such provisions can be incorporated if they can be seen to be intended to create legal obligations between the employer and the employee. One example of this can be seen in the case of *Kaur v MG Rover Group.*[72] Mrs Kaur was a member of staff at Rover's Longbridge plant. Her written terms and conditions of employment contained a provision that her employment would be 'in accordance with collective agreements made from time to time with the recognised trade unions representing employees within the company'. Rover had two agreements with recognised trade unions. The first of these agreements was known as the 'New Deal' and included a clause to the effect that employees who work with Rover would be able to stay with the company. The second agreement was known as 'The Way Ahead' and applied only to the Longbridge plant, at which Mrs Kaur worked, and contained a provision that stated 'It will be our objective to ensure that the application of the 'Partnership Principles' will enable employees who want to work with Rover to stay with Rover. As with the successful introduction of 'Rover Tomorrow – The New Deal' THERE WILL BE NO COMPULSORY REDUNDANCY' Mrs Kaur argued that both of these agreements had the effect of incorporating a clause into her contract which prevented Rover

---

72   [2004] IRLR 279.

from making her compulsorily redundant. The Court of Appeal followed the approach recommended by Hobson J, in *Alexander v Standard Telephones and Cables* (No 2) (see above), and held that the provisions were purely aspirational, any commitment was purely on a collective basis, not intended to confer individual rights and not apt for inclusion and, therefore, not legally binding. The Court of Appeal has made it clear that there is a distinction between provisions which state a policy and those which confer rights. This is not to say that procedural matters can never be intended to confer rights on individual employees. In *Keeley v Fosroc International Ltd*,[73] the Court of Appeal considered whether enhanced redundancy payments contained in a staff handbook were apt for incorporation into Keeley's contract of employment. Auld LJ, at para 34, was of the view that 'Provision for redundancy, notwithstanding statutory entitlement, is now a widely accepted feature of an employee's remuneration package and as such is particularly apt for incorporation by reference'. Also, in *Edinburgh City Council v Brown*,[74] the EAT distinguished the *Cadoux* case (above) when it found that a policy that employee re-gradings would be retrospective to the date the application for re-grading was made had been incorporated and, therefore, could not be unilaterally varied by the employer. Similarly, in *Barber v Manchester Regional Hospital Board*,[75] the contract of a consultant employed at a hospital stated that it incorporated terms contained in a document issued by the Minister of Health including procedures to be followed in the event of a dismissal. It was held that these procedures were validly incorporated and a failure to follow them was a breach of contract.

(c)   In the case of *Corus UK Ltd v Anderson and Ors*,[76] there could be no incorporated term because the union and employer had not actually reached an agreement on the provision; however, provided the parties have reached an agreement, the legal

---

73   [2006] EWCA Civ 1277.
74   [1999] IRLR 208.
75   [1958] 1 WLR 181.
76   EAT 18 May 2007.

enforceability of the collective agreement itself is largely irrelevant in deciding whether or not a provision has been incorporated into the employment contract.

A collective agreement which is itself not legally binding can still be incorporated into a contract of employment and will, therefore, be enforceable by the employee (or employer) in a situation where it could not be enforced by the trade union. One example of this situation is the case of *Anderson v Pringle of Scotland Ltd.*[77] In 1986, Pringle entered into a collective agreement with the GMB trade union. Part of the agreement stated that redundancy selection procedures would be on a 'last-in-first-out' (LIFO) basis. The collective agreement expressly stated that it was not to be legally enforceable. Anderson's terms and conditions of employment contained a clause which stated that his terms were 'in accordance with, and subject to, the provisions of the agreement made by GMB'. In 1987, when making employees redundant, Pringle used a different selection procedure. The new procedure would have resulted in Anderson being selected, while the agreed LIFO system would have resulted in him keeping his job. The Court of Session held that the clause in his terms and conditions had the effect of incorporating the whole collective agreement, including the redundancy procedures, into his contract and, therefore, he could insist on the LIFO procedure being used. An order of suspension and interdict was granted against Pringle to prevent them using the new selection procedure. *Alexander v Standard Telephones & Cables Ltd* (No 1) and *Wall v Standard Telephones & Cables Ltd* (No 2) (see above), is another example of how a collective agreement which is unenforceable between the parties can give rise to legally enforceable obligations.

Alexander and Wall were both employed by Standard Telephones & Cables. They were members of different unions but their terms of employment stated that their basic terms were in accordance with the collective agreement negotiated with the union. Both collective agreements provided that selection for redundancy would be on the basis of service within the group, which the unions argued meant a last-in-first-out basis. Although it refused to grant an injunction in the particular circumstances of this case, the court stated that it was arguable that the term had been

---

77   [1998] IRLR 64.

incorporated into the employee's contract of employment. If so, then the remedy in this case would be an action for damages for breach of contract. In *Marley v Forward Trust Group Ltd*,[78] the terms of a collective agreement which contained an express provision that it was binding in honour only was incorporated into the employee's contract.

Practical implications of incorporation

15.31

1. Once incorporated the clause is like any other contractual term. It binds both the employer and the employee. An example of the employee being bound by a provision can be found in *National Coal Board v Galley*,[79] where there was an express provision in the employee's contract which referred to the national agreements for the time being in force. The employee was found to be in breach of the contract when he refused to work a Saturday shift, even though this had been agreed in a collective agreement.

2. Furthermore, the provision will be binding even if the employee was not aware of the terms of the agreement. In the case of *Gray Dunn & Co Ltd v Edwards*,[80] the employee was bound by a term in a recently concluded collective agreement of which he had no knowledge, and which stated that being under the influence of alcohol at work could result in summary dismissal.

3. Even if the provision is incorporated, it is essential to determine whether the provision is to be regarded as a term (which cannot be unilaterally varied) or a condition which can be unilaterally varied by the employer. In order to ascertain which it is, it is necessary to look closely at the wording of the provision itself. In *Airlie v Edinburgh District Council*,[81] a provision regarding a bonus scheme was incorporated into the contract of employment; however, since there were provisions in the collective agreement which allowed the Council to control the scheme and make

---

78   [1986] ICR 891.
79   [1958] 1 WLR 16 CA.
80   [1980] IRLR 23.
81   [1996] IRLR 516.

adjustments to it, the EAT held that the employers could unilaterally vary the scheme provided proper consultations had taken place.

4. Once incorporated, a term, on the other hand, may be altered *only* by the agreement of both parties. This variation will often happen when a new collective agreement is reached or by an agreement between the employer and the individual employee. It is not possible for either party to unilaterally alter a term.

5. Once incorporated into the individual contract the terms of the collective agreement remain binding even though the agreement itself no longer exists (see *Morris v CH Bailey Ltd*).[82] Even if the collective agreement is terminated there may still be a term in the employee's contract of employment.[83]

6. It is possible to incorporate the terms of a collective agreement into the contract of an employee who is not a union member.

7. If the employee is transferred to a new employer, under TUPE, any subsequent changes to the collective agreement will not apply if the new employer is not a party to that agreement.[84]

Remedies for breach of an incorporated term

15.32 The remedies available for a breach of a properly incorporated provision of the collective agreement are the same as those available for any other breach of the employment contract. The party who has suffered as a result of the other's breach may raise a court action for damages and various orders including declarator, interdict, and specific implement. A breach of the term by an employer may be sufficiently serious to allow the employee to resign and make an unfair dismissal application to an employment tribunal claiming constructive dismissal. The usual rules regarding statutory procedures apply, as does the 3 month time limit for

---

82   [1969] 2 Lloyds Rep 215 CA.

83   *Robertson v British Gas Corporation* [1983] IRLR 302 CA, *Gibbons v Associated British Ports* [1985] IRLR 376 QBD and *Lee v GEC Plessey Communications* [1993] IRLR 383 QBD).

84   *Werhof v Freeway Traffic Services GmbH & Co KG* (C-499/04), [2006] IRLR 400.

lodging a claim. The employment tribunal also has jurisdiction to hear claims for compensation arising from a breach of contract which arises or is outstanding on the termination of the employee's employment where the sum claimed is £25,000 or less.

If the breach of contract amounts to an unlawful deduction from wages, the employee will also have the right to make a claim to an employment tribunal under s 23 of the Employment Rights Act 1996. The claim must be made within 3 months of the date of the payment from which the deduction was made (or the last payment in a series of payments from which deductions were made). In this case there is no cash limit to the amount which the tribunal can order to be paid.[85]

ARTICLE 11 ECHR (FREEDOM OF ASSOCIATION)

15.33 Article 11 of the European Convention of Human Rights states that

(1)   Everyone has the right to freedom of peaceful assembly and to freedom of association with others, including the right to form and to join trade unions for the protection of his interests.

(2)   No restrictions shall be placed on the exercise of these rights other than such as are prescribed by law and are necessary in a democratic society in the interests of national security or public safety, for the prevention of disorder or crime, for the protection of health or morals or for the protection of the rights and freedoms of others. this article shall not prevent the imposition of lawful restrictions on the exercise of these rights by members of the armed forces, of the police or of the administration of the State.

The rights under Article 11 include the right to join a trade union and the right to refuse to join it,[86] the right to collectively bargain[87] and the right to take industrial action including strikes[88] and picketing.[89]

---

85   *Arthur H Wilton Ltd v Peebles* EAT Case 835/93.
86   *Sørensen v Denmark and Rasmussen v Denmark* (2008) 46 E.H.R.R. 29; 20 BHRC 258.
87   *Demir v Turkey* [2009] IRLR 766; (2009) 48 EHRR 54.
88   *Enerji Yapi-Yol Sen v Turkey.*
89   *Gate Gourmet London Ltd v Transport and General Workers Union* [2005] EWHC 1889 (QB), [2005] IRLR 881.

EMPLOYEE'S INDIVIDUAL RIGHTS UNDER TULR(C)A 1992

15.34 Under the domestic law the rights of trade union members are contained in the Trade Union and Labour Relations (Consolidation) Act 1992 which must be construed in a way which is consistent with Article 11 (see chapter 3 for more information on human rights)

Employees and the trade union

15.35 The relationship between the trade union and its members is essentially one of contract, however the law provides many statutory minimum rights which affect this relationship. These rights ensure freedom of choice as to whether or not to join a union and protection of the employee from an abuse of power by the union and must be construed in so far as possible to give effect to the parties Article 11 rights.

Protection from unjustified exclusion or expulsion from the trade union

15.36 Prior to this legislation trade unions were free to choose their members provided they did not act arbitrarily and trade unions would enter into agreements dividing up groups of potential members between themselves. This is no longer possible.

Trade unions may only exclude or expel members in accordance with the rules set out in the membership agreement. In addition to this trade union's freedom to exclude or expel workers from membership is restricted by statute. They are only permitted to exclude or expel for the reasons set out in s 174 TULR(C)A 1992.

Section 174 states that the only permissible grounds for excluding or expelling an individual from a trade union are:

(a)   he does not satisfy, or no longer satisfies, an enforceable membership requirement contained in the rules of the union,

(b)   he does not qualify, or no longer qualifies, for membership of the union by reason of the union operating only in a particular part or particular parts of Great Britain,

(c)   in the case of a union whose purpose is the regulation of relations between its members and one particular employer or a number of particular employers who are associated, he is not, or is no longer, employed by that employer or one of those employers, or

(d)   the exclusion or expulsion is entirely attributable to conduct of his (other than excluded conduct) and the conduct to which it is wholly or mainly attributable is not protected conduct .

The enforceable membership requirements are listed in s 174(3) and are:

•   employment in a specified trade, industry or profession;

•   occupational description (including grade, level or category of appointment);

•   possession of specified trade, industrial or professional qualifications or work.

An employee therefore has the right to join any union he pleases provided he meets the enforceable membership requirements set out by the union, any geographical restrictions and works for an employer with whom the union negotiates and does not commit any misconduct.

Expulsion or exclusion for conduct

15.37 Under s 174, an employee can only be expelled or excluded for conduct which is not excluded or protected. A failure to grant his application within a reasonable time will amount to exclusion under s 177.

Conduct which is 'excluded' and which *cannot* be used as a reason for excluding or expelling the employee is defined as:

(a)   conduct which consists in his being or ceasing to be, or having been or ceased to be, a member of another trade union,

(b)   conduct which consists in his being or ceasing to be, or having been or ceased to be, employed by a particular employer or at a particular place, or

(c)   conduct for which an individual may not be disciplined by a union under s 65 (see below).

'Protected conduct' is conduct which consists in the individual's being or ceasing to be, or having been or ceased to be, a member of a political party. In *ASLEF v UK*,[90] the trade union had expelled a member because of his membership of the British National Party. They had been forced to readmit him because s 174 TULR(C)A 1992 stated that they were not permitted to exclude or expel a member because of his membership of a political party.

The European Court of Human Rights held that under Article 11, just as an employee or worker should be free to join or not join a trade union, so should the trade union be equally free to choose its members. There was a conflict between the Article 11 rights of the trade union and the union member and accordingly the State had to find a fair and proper balance between these rights, The employee's expulsion from the union did not significantly impinge on the exercise of his Article 10 right to freedom of expression or his lawful political activities; nor had he suffered any particular detriment apart from the loss of his membership because he did not require to be a union member to find employment. Therefore there had been a breach of the union's rights under Article 11.

As a consequence of the *ASLEF* case, TULR(C)A 1992 was amended by s 19 of the Employment Act 2008 to make it clear that conduct which consists in an individual's being or having been a member of a political party is not protected conduct if membership of that political party is contrary to a rule of the trade union, or an objective of the trade union, if it is reasonably practicable for the objective to be ascertained by a person working in the same trade, industry or profession as the individual. Political activities are not included in protected conduct. Additionally the exclusion or expulsion is not permitted if:

(a) the decision to exclude or expel is taken otherwise than in accordance with the union's rules;

(b) the decision to exclude or expel is taken unfairly; ie if he is not given notice of the proposal to exclude or expel him, a fair opportunity to make representations and fair consideration of his representations.

(c) the individual would lose his livelihood or suffer other exceptional hardship by reason of not being, or ceasing to be, a member of the union.

---

90   [2007] IRLR 361; (2007) 45 EHRR 34.

It is arguable that this amendment went further than was necessary to comply with the *ASLEF* decision.[91]

Under s 176 the remedy for unlawful expulsion or exclusion is to apply to the employment tribunal within six months (or if that was not practicable within such time as the tribunal decides is reasonable) of the date of expulsion or exclusion. If the complaint is well founded the tribunal will make a declaration. It will also make a declaration if the reason is protected conduct or if the exclusion or expulsion was wholly or mainly because of conduct of the claimant which was in contravention of the union rules or reasonably ascertainable objectives of the union. Once the declaration is made there is a four week period after which the claimant may apply for compensation. The claim must be made within 6 months of the date of the declaration. This gives the union a chance to act on the declaration and admit or readmit the claimant. The tribunal will award such compensation as is just and equitable taking into account any contributory conduct and the duty to mitigate loss. If the claimant is not re admitted by the time he makes a claim for compensation then a minimum award applies of £8,100. This minimum award does not apply if the tribunal made a declaration that the exclusion or expulsion was wholly attributable to the complainants conduct in contravention of the rules or objectives of the union. In any event the maximum award is £85,200 being the aggregate of:

(a)   an amount equal to thirty times maximum amount of a week's pay for basic award in unfair dismissal cases currently £430), and

(b)   the maximum compensatory award in unfair dismissal cases (currently £72,300)

The right not to be unjustifiably disciplined by the trade union

15.38 In order to prevent oppressive conduct by a trade union against its members the situations in which the trade union is entitled to discipline a member are very limited.

---

91   Employment Act 2008: implementing the ASLEF decision – a victory for the BNP? Ewing KD, ILJ 2009, 38(1), 50–57.

Under s 64 the trade union will have disciplined a member if they have made a determination that:

(a)   he should be expelled from the union or a branch or section of the union;

(b)   he should pay a sum to the union, to a branch or section of the union or to any other person;

(c)   sums tendered by him in respect of an obligation to pay subscriptions or other sums to the union, or to a branch or section of the union, should be treated as unpaid or paid for a different purpose;

(d)   he should be deprived to any extent of, or of access to, any benefits, services or facilities which would otherwise be provided or made available to him by virtue of his membership of the union, or a branch or section of the union;

(e)   another trade union, or a branch or section of it, should be encouraged or advised not to accept him as a member, or

(f)   he should be subjected to some other detriment.

In *National and Local Government Officers Association v Killorn* the identification in the union newsletter of a member who had broken a strike was held to be a detriment.

A recommendation that one of these things should be done does not amount to a determination.

Discipline will be unjustified if the actual or supposed conduct or reason for disciplining him is that he:

(a)   failed to participate in or support a strike or other industrial action or indicated opposition to or a lack of support for such action;

(b)   failed to breach his contract of employment, for a purpose connected with such a strike or other industrial action or he encouraged or assisted someone else to perform a contract of employment.

(c)   asserted that the union, an official, trustee or representative of the union has contravened, or is proposing to contravene, a rule of the union, an agreement or legal requirement (whether by bringing proceedings or otherwise) or encouraged anyone else to do so (unless the accusation was false and made in bad faith);

(e) contravened a requirement imposed by or in consequence of a determination which infringes the individual's or another individual's right not to be unjustifiably disciplined;

(f) failed to agree, or withdrew agreement, to the deduction of payments to the union from his wages;

(g) resigned or proposed to resign from the union or from another union, became or proposed to become a member of another union, refused to become a member of another union, or was a member of another union;

(h) worked with, or proposed to work with, individuals who are not members of the union or who are or are not members of another union;

(i) worked for, or proposed to work for, an employer who employs or who has employed individuals who are not members of the union or who are or are not members of another union, or

(j) required the union to do an act which the union is required to do on the requisition of a member (section 65).

The remedy for a member who has been unjustifiably disciplined is to apply to the employment tribunal within 3 months of the act or omission complained of. This time limit may be extended by such time as the tribunal considers reasonable if it was not reasonably practicable for the complaint to be presented before the end of that period, or that any delay in making the complaint was wholly or partly attributable to a reasonable attempt to appeal against the determination or to have it reconsidered or reviewed. If a complaint of unjustifiable discipline is held to be well founded there should be no complaint of unjustifiable exclusion or expulsion on the same ground.

The tribunal may make a declaration that the discipline was unjustified. After 4 weeks of the declaration and within 6 months of the declaration the claimant can apply for compensation. The tribunal can award the repayment of any sum the claimant paid to the union in respect of the discipline and shall award such compensation as it feels is just and equitable having regard to any contributory conduct and the duty to mitigate loss. The maximum award is £85,200 being the aggregate of:

(a)   an amount equal to thirty times the maximum amount of a week's pay for basic award in unfair dismissal cases (currently £430), and

(b)   the maximum compensatory award in unfair dismissal cases (currently £72,300). If the trade union has not revoked the discipline then a minimum award applies of £8,100

OTHER RIGHTS AGAINST THE TRADE UNION

15.39 Another right which the members enjoy against their trade union is the right to a ballot before industrial action under s 62 TULR(C)A 1992. This right can be enforced by application to a court for an interdict or other order as the court sees fit.

Under s 63, although the provisions of the union rules may provide for disputes to be settled by mediation or conciliation, if after 6 months there has been no resolution the member cannot be prevented from having access to the courts.

Section 68 provides the right not to suffer unauthorised deduction or excessive deduction of union subscriptions. If this occurs his remedy is to apply to a tribunal within 3 months of the deduction (unless it was not reasonably practicable to do so). The tribunal may order the sum to be repaid.

Under s 69 the member has as an implied term of his membership agreement the right to resign his trade union membership at any time on the giving of reasonable notice and complying with any reasonable requirements of the membership agreement.

The union member has the right to certain information from his union including the right to inspect the accounts and the register of members.

He has the right to prevent the union from taking unprotected industrial action (see chapter 16) and, under s 15, indemnifying unlawful acts or under s 16 from making unlawful use of trade union property.

EMPLOYEES AND THE EMPLOYER

15.40 The rights enjoyed by the employee against his employer in relation to his trade union membership/non membership can be found in Chapter IX Part III of TULR(C)A 1992 and consist of:

(1)   The right not to be refused employment on grounds related to union membership (s 137);

(2)   the right not to be subjected to detriment on grounds related to his trade union membership or non membership (s 146);

(3)   the right not to be offered inducements not to participate in trade union membership, activities or collective bargaining;

(4)   the right not to be dismissed or selected for redundancy on grounds because of his trade union membership or non membership (s 152).

Following the decision of the European Court of Human Rights in *Young, James and Webster v UK*[92] that closed shops were a breach of a worker's Article 11 rights, the 1992 Act has provided that it is unlawful to refuse a worker employment because of his union membership or non membership. This provision is contained in s 137 of the 1992 Act and applies to employment agencies as well as employers. A third party who puts pressure on the employer or the agency can be joined to the proceedings. Unfortunately the courts have made a distinction between the term trade union membership and trade union activities leaving a wide margin for an employer to refuse employment because the worker had been regarded as a militant trade unionist. See for example *Birmingham District Council v Beyer*[93] and *Harrison v Kent County Council*[94] but see *Fitzpatrick v British Railways Board.*[95]

Section 146 provides that a worker has the right not to be subjected as an individual,[96] to any detriment (other than dismissal) by any act, or any deliberate failure to act, by his employer for the sole or main purpose of preventing or deterring him from (or penalising him for):

---

92   *TGWU v Webber* [1990] ICR 711.
93   *Young, James and Palmer v UK* [1981] 44 ECHR.
94   [1977] IRLR 211.
95   [1995] ICR 434.
96   [1992] ICR 221.

(A)

(a) joining an independent trade union, or penalising him for doing so;

(b) taking part in the activities of an independent trade union at an appropriate time, or penalising him for doing so;

(c) from making use of trade union services at an appropriate time, or penalising him for doing so, or

(B) compelling him to be or become a member of any trade union or of a particular trade union or of one of a number of particular trade unions.

An appropriate time for participating in activities or making use of services is a time outside working hours, or agreed with the employer and an employee will lose the protection of s 146 for participating at an inappropriate time.[97]

The original wording of s 146 (right not to be subjected to a detriment) left a gap which allowed employers to offer inducements to workers to opt out of collective bargaining and the 1992 Act had to be amended as a consequence of the judgement of the European Court of Human Rights in *Wilson and Palmer v UK*[98]. The legislation was amended and the gap filled by ss 145A and 145B which make it unlawful for the employer to offer inducements to the worker

(a) not to be or seek to become a member of an independent trade union,

(b) not to take part, at an appropriate time, in the activities of an independent trade union,

(c) not to make use, at an appropriate time, of trade union services, or

(d) to be or become a member of any trade union or of a particular trade union or of one of a number of particular trade unions.

Section 145B makes similar provision in relation to inducements to opt out of collective bargaining. Under s 146 a worker also has the right not to be subjected to any detriment as an individual by any act, or any

97 *FW Farnsworth v McCoid* [1999] ICR 1047; *Gallagher v Department of Transport* [1994] ICR 967.
98 *Robb v Leon Motor Services Ltd* [1978] ICR 506; *Brennan and Ging v Ellward (Lancs) Ltd* [1976] IRLR 378.

deliberate failure to act, by his employer if the act or failure takes place because of the worker's failure to accept an inducement.

The remedy for breach of s 145A and 146 is for the claimant to apply to the employment tribunal within 3 months of the act or omission complained of (or such other time as the tribunal thinks is reasonable if it is not reasonably practicable to meet the time limit). The remedy may include compensation including compensation for hurt feelings (subject to the limit in force for compensation for unfair dismissal). The tribunal may make a declaration and award compensation. It may also make a recommendation that the employer take action to reduce the adverse effect on the complainant. The amount of the compensation awarded shall be such as the tribunal considers just and equitable in all the circumstances including any expenses reasonably incurred or benefits lost by the complainant in consequence of the act or failure complained of. It may include compensation for hurt feelings. The tribunal shall have regard to the duty to mitigate loss and contributory conduct (except the conduct of refusing or accepting an inducement). No account will be taken of pressure put on the employer by threats of industrial action. In accordance with s 150, an award can be made against a third party who has been sisted to the proceedings.

In respect of the offer by the employer of an inducement the tribunal shall under s 15E make an award to be paid by the employer to the complainant of £3,500. Where an offer made in contravention of s 145A or 145B is accepted the employer cannot enforce the agreement to vary, or recover any sum paid or other asset transferred by him under the agreement to vary but if as a result of the acceptance the worker's terms of employment are varied, this does not make the variation unenforceable by either party.

Section 152 prohibits the dismissal of an employee on grounds related to union membership or activities.

Dismissal will be unfair if the reason for it was that the employee:

(a)   was, or proposed to become, a member of an independent trade union,

(b)   had taken part, or proposed to take part, in the activities of an independent trade union or had used or proposed to use the services of a trade union at an appropriate time, (see above for discussion of 'appropriate time'

(c)   had failed to accept an offer made in contravention of s 145A or 145B, or

(d)   was not a member of any trade union, or of a particular trade union, or of one of a number of particular trade unions, or had refused, or proposed to refuse, to become or remain a member. This includes membership or non membership of a particular branch of the union.

An application can be made to sist a third part to the proceedings if they have put pressure on the employer to dismiss the employee or select him for redundancy on one of these grounds.

Under s 153 selection for redundancy on grounds related to union membership or activities where the reason or principal reason for the dismissal of an employee was that he was redundant, but it is shown that the circumstances constituting the redundancy applied equally to one or more other employees in the same undertaking who held positions similar to that held by him and who have not been dismissed by the employer, **and** that the reason or principal reason why he was selected for dismissal was one of those specified in s 152(1) (see above) the dismissal shall be regarded as unfair. The requirement for a year's (or 2 years) qualifying service in order to make a claim of unfair dismissal will be disapplied, the amount of the basic award of compensation, before any reduction is made shall be not less than £5,300 (although this can be reduced on grounds of contributory fault)

The employee may also apply to the tribunal for interim relief on or before 7 days of the effective date of dismissal by presenting a certificate in writing signed by an authorised official of the independent trade union of which the employee was or proposed to become a member stating:

(a)   that on the date of the dismissal the employee was or proposed to become a member of the union, and

(b)   that there appear to be reasonable grounds for supposing that the reason for his dismissal (or, if more than one, the principal reason) was one alleged in the complaint.

DISMISSAL FOR OTHER TRADE UNION RELATED REASONS

15.41 Dismissal in connection with Industrial Action is considered in Chapter 16.

Protection from detriment and dismissal for reasons relating to the statutory recognition procedure are discussed earlier in this chapter.

RIGHTS TO TIME OFF

15.42 There are several situations in which a trade union official or member is entitled to reasonable time off :

– Right for reasonable paid time off for trade union duties if the employee is an official of the trade union (s 168 TULR(C)A 1992);

– Right to reasonable time off for trade union activities without pay if a trade union member (s 170 TULR(C)A);

– Right to reasonable time off with pay to carry out duties as a trade union learning representative (S 168A TULR(C)A);

– Time off without pay for a member to consult the trade union learning representative (S 168A TULR(C)A).

In each case the remedy for refusal is to apply to the tribunal within three months for a declaration and compensation.

FUTURE OF TRADE UNION LAW

15.43 There have been important changes in the economy of most countries, including the UK, that have influenced developments in the aims and the role of trade union law. Globalization for example has emphasised the need for cooperation between trade unions on a global scale to counteract the unscrupulous employment practices which have been introduced by certain global organisations. There is also a need for international labour standards to be introduced which are realistic and enforceable.

The fact that, in Europe at least, the structure of the trade union movement has remained based territorially on the national State this has not helped it in meeting these European or global challenges.

The protection of fundamental human rights in the development of trade union law, both within the UK and internationally, is also an important development and has been considered in the context of chapter 3 and chapter 16. The following quote signifies the importance of this: 'Labour rights are at the heart of the fight for human rights. The freedom to associate, to organise, and to have equal opportunities in the workplace – every year we see these rights under attack around the world.'[99]

The most obvious source of human rights for individuals in the UK in respect of trade union law is the European Convention of Human Rights (ECHR) which, since the passing of the Scotland Act 1998, is now part of Scottish law and the European Union Fundamental Charter of Social Rights. Human rights will undoubtedly play a major role in the development in labour law through implementation by the UK courts of the rights in the European Convention primarily against public authorities.

FURTHER READING

Books

Hanson, *Taming the trade unions: A Guide to the Thatcher Government's Employment Reforms 1980–90* (Macmillan, 1991).

Pelling, *A History of British Trade Unionism* (Penguin Books 1987 also Macmillan Press 1987). Standard but easily readable history of British Trade Unionism from its origins in 1825.

Reid, *United We Stand: A History of Britain's Trade Unions* (Penguin, 2004).

Webb and Webb, *The History of Trade Unionism* (Reprint). The classic, detailed but readable study of trade unionism from its origins until 1920, with comprehensive footnotes Longmans Green & Co; 1950 (was also available in Kelley Reprints series from Merlin Press.)

Wrigley, *British Trade Unions Since 1933*. (Cambridge University Press, 2002).

---

99   Kate Allen, Director, Amnesty International UK.

Journal article

Lorber 'Reviewing the European Works Council Directive: European progress and the United Kingdom perspective'. ILJ 2004, 33(2), 191–199

Websites

http://www.bis.gov.uk/policies/employment-matters/rights/trade-unions 2010 membership statistics http://stats.bis.gov.uk/UKSA/tu/TUM2010. pdfFurther Reading

http://www.berr.gov.uk/employment/employmentlegislation/ employment-directives/eu-workscouncil/page20049.htmlhttp://www.berr. gov.uk/files/file26086.pdf

Chapter 16

Trade Union Law and Industrial Action

OVERVIEW OF INDUSTRIAL ACTION

16.1 In this chapter we will look at the types of industrial action that individual employees, trade unions, and their officials, instigate, and/or pursue, and the impact that they have on employers. The legal treatment of industrial action, including liability for actions associated with industrial action, and the protection afforded to trade unions and their members from such liability, will be detailed.

TYPES OF INDUSTRIAL ACTION

16.2 A simple definition of industrial action, is a withdrawal of cooperation, or a refusal, by employees, to do something that is used as a bargaining weapon against the employer.

There are various types of action that they can be pursued: strikes; working to rule; go slow; overtime ban and other actions short of strike which are particular to the circumstances. The use of strikes as a means of pressuring employers to concede to demands in collective bargaining, or outside any bargaining process, has a very long history.

Strike action, often simply called a strike, is a work stoppage caused by the mass refusal by employees to perform work. A strike usually takes place in response to employee grievances. It is a withdrawal of labour often in response to the actions of the employer. A strike is defined in Employment Rights Act 1996 s 235 (5), as:

> '(a) the cessation of work by a body of employed persons acting in combination, or (b) a concerted refusal, or a refusal under a common understanding, of any number of employed persons to continue to work for an employer in consequence of a dispute, done as a means of compelling their employer or any employed person or body of employed persons, or to aid other employees in compelling their employer or any

employed person or body of employed persons, to accept or not to
accept terms or conditions of or affecting employment'.[1]

Occasionally, workers decide to strike without the authorisation of a
trade union, either because the union refuses to endorse such a tactic, or
because the workers concerned act quickly without seeking the support
of the union. Strikes without formal union authorisations are known as
unofficial, and where taken on the spot, without any notice, are known as
wildcat strikes. As will be seen, the trade unions must seek the support for
official industrial action through a ballot and give notice to an employer
before pursuing it, or they and their members will lose any statutory
protection.

Work-to-rule is a type of industrial action in which employees do no
more than the minimum required by the rules of a workplace, and follow
safety or other regulations to the letter, in order to cause a slowdown. This
is considered less disruptive than a strike, and just obeying the rules is
less susceptible to disciplinary action. Examples could include nurses
refusing to answer telephones, and teachers refusing to work after the end
of the school day or cover the work of sick colleagues. This could involve
applying, to the letter, rules that are normally set aside, or interpreted less
literally, to increase efficiency, or refraining from activities which are
customary but not required by rule or the job description (see *Secretary of
State for Employment v ASLEF* below).

Go-slow is a form of protest by workers, in which they deliberately
slow down in order to cause problems for their employers. This is more
clearly a breach of someone's contract of employment, because the work
is often being carried out at a lesser rate than that expected by the contract.

Overtime ban is where workers refuse to work hours over and above
those specified in their contract. This is particularly effective where the
employer relies on workers undertaking overtime to achieve production
targets etc.

Other action specific to a job or occupation can be taken by employees
in protest about a management decision, or to make demands. Examples of
other action could be action taken by teachers in educational institutions,

---

1   There is a much shorter definition in s 246 of TULR(C)A 1992, where a 'strike' is
    defined simply as 'any concerted stoppage of work'.

which could include refusing to: prepare classes and mark work; provide cover for absent colleagues; follow the directions of a head teacher or principal; go to out-of-hours meetings; do extra or unreasonable workload or duties, and teach or supervise a particular pupil or student. (In practice this is a common issue leading to industrial action.)

LEGAL CONSEQUENCES OF INDUSTRIAL ACTION

16.3 Lord Denning stated in *Express Newspapers v McShane*[2] that 'Parliament granted immunities to the leaders of Trade Unions. It did not give them the right to break the law or to do wrong by inducing people to break contracts. It only gave them immunity if they did'.

At common law, employees who withdraw labour will not be entitled to remuneration or other contractual benefits. They will be regarded as being in breach of their employment contract and this will entitle the employer to repudiate it, and discipline, or dismiss, the employee. The Trade Union and Labour Relations (Consolidation) Act 1992 (TULR(C)A 1992), provides protection to such employees in limited circumstances, which are discussed below.

An employee need not totally withdraw his labour to be regarded as being in breach of contract. In *Secretary of State for Employment v ASLEF (No 2)*,[3] workers who worked to rule, although not in breach of the express terms of the contract, were held by the Court of Appeal to be in breach of implied terms in the contract covering the 'lack of good faith with which performance was carried out' (a term used by Lord Denning in the case) which relates to the implied duties of obedience to, and cooperation with, the employer.[4]

An employee who is dismissed by his employer while taking industrial action, may lose his right to claim unfair dismissal. With certain exceptions, the law prevents an employment tribunal from considering a claim of unfair dismissal on its merits, if the employee was dismissed while taking part in industrial action. This means that the employment tribunal cannot find the dismissal of the employee to be unfair.

---

2 [1989] ICR 210.
3 (1972) 2 QB 455.
4 See also *British Telecom v Ticehurst* 1992 ICR 382

Legal liability of trade unions for industrial action

16.4 There are a range of possible actions which could be pursued against unions in the context of industrial action, eg defamation and trespass, but there are certain delicts which are well established in this context as the appropriate remedy, known as industrial delicts, and what follows is consideration of them. The employee, trade union, or trade union official, may all be liable and that liability will be owed, not only to the employer, but to third parties who it is reasonably forseeable will be affected by the act or omission.

The industrial delicts include: (i) Conspiracy, (ii) Intimidation, (iii) Inducing a breach of contract (indirect interference with the performance of a contract), and (iv) Interference with trade or business by unlawful means.

Civil conspiracy

16.5 There are two types of actions in delict for civil conspiracy. (1) Conspiracy to Injure, and (2) Conspiracy to Commit an Unlawful Act.

(1) **A Conspiracy to Injure** is a combination of two, or more, persons whose predominant motive is to cause economic loss to another, rather than pursue their own legitimate interests. The other affected by the conspiracy must suffer damage.

Almost any strike, or other industrial action, will require collective action which will adversely affect an employer. Through judicial rulings, the trade unions have been provided with a valuable defence. If it can be proven that the predominant purpose of industrial action is to defend union members' legitimate interests, then there is no liability for the union. This was decided in *Crofter Harris Hand-Woven Tweed Co Ltd v Veitch*,[5] when a group of mill owners on the island of Harris made tweed cloth from locally spun yarn and sold it. One of their number decided to import cheap yarn from the mainland. The mill owners contacted the union, the Transport and General Workers Union (TGWU), and persuaded them to refuse to handle the goods, with the consequence that they could not be transported or unloaded onto the island. An action was taken against the

---

5   (1942) AC (HL).

union for conspiracy to injure, but the union successfully argued that the action was taken to protect the interests and job security of their members. For the first time this was accepted as a legitimate defence by the House of Lords.

(2) **A Conspiracy to Commit an Unlawful Act**. To establish that this delict applies, it is necessary to show that the defendants acted with the intent to injure the claimant, see *Lohnro v Fayed*.[6] Also they have to prove a person committed another unlawful act (eg a separate delict such as inducing a breach of contract or, as in *Rookes v Barnard*,[7] conspiracy to intimidate).

The claimant for both actions in delict must show actual pecuniary or financial loss, rather than injury to reputation.

Intimidation

16.6 As intimated above, the delict of intimidation was an example of judicial creativity, where the courts took an existing delict used in other areas of law, and applied it to industrial action. Put simply, because there was no immunity for intimidation in 1964, when first applied in the case of *Rookes v Barnard*,[8] trade union officials could be successfully sued by the employer facing industrial action for damages or an interdict. In this case, an informal closed shop operated in the workplace (no one could be employed who was not a union member). Mr Rookes decided to leave the trade union. The union went to the employer and said that, unless they sacked Rookes, they would go out on strike. Rookes was dismissed by the employer. He sued the trade union for civil intimidation. This was the first time this type of action in delict had been successfully pursued in the context of industrial relations. It was held that the threat to go on strike, was as much a threat to commit an unlawful act, as threat to commit a crime. It constituted the delict of intimidation, and there was no statutory immunity against this delict for trade union officials at the time.

---

6   (1992) 1 AC 448.
7   (1964) AC 1129.
8   (1964) AC 1129.

The second case, that is also an example of a case brought on the basis of the delict of intimidation, is *Messenger Group Ltd v NGA*.[9] Following a dispute about closed shop arrangements, the company sought damages for losses caused by the delictual acts of the union that were not covered by the immunities, and involved secondary picketing, and other forms of secondary action. It was held that the company were entitled to recover exemplary and aggravated damages.

Inducing a Breach of Contract

16.7 When trade unions, or trade union officials, or others, call for, or otherwise organise, industrial action they are in practice calling for breach, or interference with the performance, of contracts. They may also be interfering with the ability of the employer of those taking the industrial action, and of other employers, to fulfil commercial contracts.

Under the common law, it is unlawful to induce people to break a contract, or to interfere with the performance of a contract, or to threaten to do either of these things. Accordingly trade unions or trade union officials face the possibility of legal action being taken against them for inducing breaches of contract every time they call a strike. The first case to decide that inducing a breach of contract was a heading of delict, was *Lumley v Gye*,[10] where an opera singer was persuaded to leave the theatre with which she had a contract, and join another theatre. The persuader was liable. 'A person who knowingly interrupts the performance of a subsisting contract by inducing its breach will be liable for any damage caused to the innocent party.'

In a commercial contract where a trade union, or trade union official, persuades a customer, or supplier of the employer in dispute, not to continue his contractual relations with them, and in an employment contract where a trade union, or trade union official, persuades employees of the employer in dispute to go out on strike, or take other industrial action this can amount to inducement to breach a contract. It can also apply where a trade union, or trade union official, persuades employees of a secondary employer (not in dispute) to breach their contract in support

---

9   (1984) IRLR 397 (QBD).
10 (1853) 2 E & B 216.

of the primary action.[11] Another example of judicial creativity, arose in the case of *Torquay Hotel v Cousins*,[12] where Lord Denning was unable to establish a breach of contract and argued that interference with the performance of a contract, by unlawful means, was a separate heading of delict. In the *Torquay Hotel v Cousins* case, a trade union official was involved in a dispute with the owner of a hotel and went on strike. The union, as a result of picketing, persuaded suppliers of oil not to deliver the goods as per their contract with the hotel. There was a force majeure clause in the supply contract between the hotel and the supplier, the effect of which was, when industrial action disrupted performance of the contract, there was no breach. Lord Denning was determined to find union officials liable (by inventing a new delict with no immunity), and he came up with new tort (delict) of interference with the performance of a contract by unlawful means. Here no breach of contract was required.

Interference with the performance of a contract by unlawful means

16.8 In *Merkur Island Shipping Corporation v Laughton*,[13] a cargo vessel had a foreign crew on low wages, well below the UK standard. Because of this, the ITF (UK), a trade union, decided to black the vessel (refused to deal with it in any way), after the ship had unloaded their cargo at Liverpool, and persuaded tug men not to tow the ship out of harbour, thereby inducing a breach of their employment contracts. There was a clause in the contract between the Shipping Corporation and tugboat owners, anticipating industrial action, and providing that where it occurs, there is no breach of their commercial contract. The House of Lords confirmed that the ITF was liable for the economic tort (delict) of interference, with an employer's (commercial) contract by the indirect and unlawful means of inducing breach of employment contracts. Other examples of this would be where pickets persuade a supplier or customer of the employer in dispute, not to enter his workplace and deliver goods or provide services.

---

11 See *Merkur Island Shipping Corporation v Laughton* below.
12 [1969] 2 Ch 106 CA.
13 [1983] ICR 490 HL.

Interference with trade or business by unlawful means

16.9 The last industrial delict/tort is interference with trade, or business, by unlawful means. This was first discussed as a possible heading of delict in the case of *Torquay Hotel v Cousins*,[14] and, clearly, this was not covered by the immunities. To establish that this delict applies, the pursuer needed to show that the interference with trade or business must be by unlawful means, and that its predominant purpose was to cause harm to the employer in dispute. In *Barretts & Baird (Wholesale) v Institution of Professional Civil Servants*[15] inspectors were employed by the Meat and Livestock Commission, to certify suitability of animals or carcasses in abattoirs. Their union, the Institution of Professional Civil Servants, called a series of one-day strikes. The plaintiffs were meat companies whose business was disrupted because of the interruption to the certification process. They claimed that there was interference with their trade by unlawful means. The court didn't agree as the striker's predominant purpose was not injury to the plaintiff as required here, but improved pay and conditions of their members through a re-grading claim. This is a similar defence to that employed in *Crofter Hand Woven Harris Tweed Co Ltd v Veitch*.[16]

These actions in delict can easily be pursued against trade unions, and their officials, for taking industrial action, and where they are liable for breach of them they could be liable for substantial damages and/or an interdict (usually interim in nature) to bring about cessation of the action. It is vital that unions have immunities against legal action, because they could, over time, be bankrupted through paying out damages, or their ability to take industrial action would be severely circumscribed.

Immunities from actions in delict for trade unions

16.10 When a trade union organises industrial action, it faces the prospect of legal action taken against it and its officers, by the employer for committing an industrial delict (for example, by causing someone to

---

14 (1969) 2 CH 106 CA.
15 (1987) IRLR 3 QB.
16 1942 SC(HL) 1.

break the terms of their contract), and by third parties. If the law did not offer trade unions some protection against actions for compensation, the economic consequences of being sued by an employer for organising industrial action would easily bankrupt them, and the threat of legal proceedings for an interdict would prevent unions from taking industrial action, thereby interfering with rights under Article 11 ECHR.

Vicarious liability for action of officials

16.11 Vicarious liability of trade union for the actions of their officials is dealt with under s 20 of TULR(C)A 1992. When actions in delict are brought against a trade union on a ground specified in s 219, then for the purposes of determining if the union is liable, the act shall be taken to have been done by the union, when it is done (or authorised or endorsed) by its: Principal Executive Committee; General Secretary or President; any person given power under the union's own rules to do so; or any other committee, of the union or any official of the union, including those who are employed by the union and those, like shop stewards, who are not.

Given the wide definition of vicarious liability for the actions of trade union officials, under s 20 of TULR(C)A 1992, basing liability on the authority or support of any official, including shop stewards, it will be difficult for a trade union to distance themselves from industrial action taken by their members.

In order to avoid liability, the Principal Executive Committee, President or General Secretary of the union must repudiate the act, as soon as reasonably practicable after it has come to the knowledge of any of them, and the union must, without delay, give written notice of the repudiation to the committee or official in question; and do its best to give individual written notice of the fact, and date of the repudiation, to (i) every member of the union who it has reason to believe is taking part – or might otherwise take part – in industrial action as a result of the act; and (ii) the employer of every such member.

Immunities from civil action

16.12 Trade union immunities were originally brought in to provide protection for trade unions following on from the decision in *Taff Vale*

Railway Co v Amalgamated Society of Railway Servants,[17] when it was decided that unions had sufficient legal status to be sued in their own name. The Trade Disputes Act 1906, then provided a blanket immunity against all actions in delict for unions and immunities against specific delicts, for example inducing a breach of contract for trade union officials. What followed, particularly in the 1960's, was a period of judicial creativity to make union officials liable for specific delicts (for example the *Rookes v Barnard* case, discussed above). All the immunities were removed by Industrial Relations Act 1971, but were reinstated by Trade Union and Labour Relations Act 1974, and the TULR(C)A (Amendment) Act 1976. The blanket immunity was removed again by the Employment Act 1982. As a consequence of losing their blanket immunity, trade unions only have the same immunities as their officials against specific industrial delicts.

Immunities – current law

16.13 Section 219 of the Trade Union and Labour Relations (Consolidation) Act 1992 (TULR(C)A), provides independent recognised unions and their officials with immunity against civil actions against them for wrongs committed in relation to industrial action. It is important to note that the immunities only apply in limited circumstances, and provided the trade union has taken the appropriate steps in relation to balloting and notice.

It should be noted that the immunities protect principally those who call for, threaten to call for, or otherwise organise, industrial action. They do not protect individual workers who take industrial action from legal action by their employer for breaking their contracts. In certain circumstances, there is protection from dismissal for them, provided by TULR(C)A 1992, and this is discussed below. The immunities are very specific and cover certain of the industrial delicts mentioned above, namely inducing a breach of contract, interference with performance of contract by unlawful means, intimidation, and civil conspiracy. Any delicts not specifically mentioned in s 219 will not be covered, for example, interference with trade or business by unlawful means, or breach of a statutory duty.

The circumstances in which industrial action is appropriate and will be protected by the statutory immunity under s 219 are:

---

17 (1901) AC 426.

1.   There is a trade dispute, and the action is called in contemplation or furtherance of that dispute (explained below);

2.   A trade union that calls for (or otherwise organises) the action has first held a properly conducted secret ballot;

3.   A trade union that calls for (or otherwise organises) the action, has provided the required notice of official industrial action to employers likely to be affected, following the ballot;

4.   The action is not 'secondary action', namely action that is not taken in respect of the primary dispute (often supportive action of trade unions);

5.   The action is not intended to promote union closed shop practices, or to prevent employers using non-union firms as suppliers;

6.   The action is not in support of any employee dismissed while taking unofficial industrial action;

7.   The action does not involve unlawful picketing (see below).

Contemplation of, or furtherance of, a trade dispute

16.14 In order to be protected, the delict must have been in contemplation of, or furtherance of, a trade dispute. Section 244 of TULR(C)A 1992 states that a trade dispute means a dispute between workers and *their* employers,[18] that relates *wholly or mainly* to one or more of the following:

(1)   terms and conditions of employment, or to the physical conditions in which any workers are required to work;

(2)   the engagement or non-engagement or termination or suspension of employment or the duties of employment of one or more of the workers;

(3)   allocation of work or duties of employment between workers or groups of workers;

(4)   membership or non membership of a trade union, on the part of a worker;

---

18 Immunity will be lost if the dispute is not with *their own* employer see *Dimbleby& Sons Ltd v NUJ* [1984] ICR 386.

(5)   matters of discipline, membership or non-membership of a trade union;

(6)   facilities for officials of trade unions;

(7)   machinery for negotiation and consultation in representing workers (including the recognition by employers of the right of unions to representation), for the purpose of negotiation, in respect of any of the above matters.

In deciding whether the dispute is a trade dispute, the court must look at the predominant purpose of the dispute.[19] The definition is wide enough to cover any genuine dispute between employer and employee. Therefore, a dispute which was predominantly about change in identity of an employer was a trade dispute,[20] as was industrial action relating to refusal to obey instructions to teach a disruptive pupil,[21] but the situation where a trade union calls action to support political or other wider aims, does not fall within this definition, and will be unprotected. In *BBC v Hearn*,[22] technicians refused to allow transmission of television programmes from South Africa, because they were opposed to the South African Government's policy of apartheid. Their action was not a trade dispute covered by the immunities. A similar result applied in *Express Newspapers Ltd v Keys*,[23] when the union went on strike because of the anti-working class policies of the Government.

Even where a trade dispute exists, the delict must have been committed in contemplation or furtherance of that dispute. The dispute must have been more than a mere possibility and action taken in preparation for future disputes will not be protected.[24] Actions taken in connection with the dispute will be examined by the court to ascertain the motive behind them, and if the motive is not furtherance of the dispute they will be unprotected. In *Conway v Wade*,[25] the trade union took action to persuade the employer to dismiss an employee, but the motive was to persuade

---

19 *Mercury Communications v Scott-Garner* [1983] IRLR 485.
20 *Westminster City Council v Unison* [2000] ICR 1046.
21 *P v National Association of School Masters* [2003] UKHL 9, [2003] IRLR 307.
22 [1977] IRLR 273.
23 [1980] IRLR 247 (QBD).
24 *Bents Brewery Co Ltd v Hogan* [1945] 2 All ER 570.
25 [1908–10] All ER Rep 344.

the employee to pay his union dues, and therefore the action was not in furtherance of a trade dispute.

Balloting and notice to employer

16.15 It is a condition for the immunity to apply that, before calling a strike or other industrial action, a trade union must first obtain the support of its members through a properly conducted ballot, and that it must provide at least seven days' notice to an employer of official industrial action to be taken against him. Sections 226–234A of the Trade Unions and Labour Relation (Consolidation) Act 1992,[26] as amended by TURERA 1993, set out the requirements of the ballot and notice. The Code of Practice on Industrial Action Ballots and Notice to Employers should also be consulted. The stringent requirements relating to balloting have come under the scrutiny of the courts in recent years. It is not a requirement to hold ballot where taking unofficial industrial action, but unofficial action is always unlawful and is unprotected by the immunities. Unofficial strikers have no protection under unfair dismissal legislation.

The ballot itself should include all members who at the time of balloting, it is reasonable for the union to believe, will be called upon to take part in the industrial action.[27] It must be a secret postal ballot[28] and, if more than 50 members are involved, a scrutineer should be appointed to report on the proceedings.[29] A simple majority of those voting is required in support of the action.[30] In order for immunity to apply the action must take place within 4 weeks of the ballot, or within such other period as may be agreed between the union and the employer, but not exceeding eight weeks.[31]

The union must take such steps, as are reasonably necessary to ensure that any employer that the union reasonably believes will be the employer of any of its members entitled to vote, receives certain information

---

26 Originally in the Trade Union Act 1984.
27 *London Underground Ltd v National Union of Rail Maritime and Transport Workers* [1996] ICR 170.
28 Section 239.
29 Section 226B.
30 Section 226(2).
31 Section 234.

in advance of the intended opening day of the ballot. No later than the seventh day before the intended start of the ballot the employer must get written notice: stating that the union intends to hold the ballot; specifying the date which the union reasonably believes will be the opening day of the ballot; providing a list of the categories of employee to which the affected employees belong, figures on the number of employees in each category, figures on the numbers of employees at each workplace and the total number of affected employees, together with an explanation of how these figures were arrived at. No later than 3 days before the ballot the employer must receive a sample voting paper.

Consequences of loss of immunity

16.16 The situations where the immunities will be lost, or removed, are set out in s 219, ss (3) and (4), TULR(C)A 1992. The immunities are lost where union is involved in: (a) Secondary picketing (eg picketing falling outside immunities defined in s 220 of TULR(C)A 1992; see below); (b) Secondary action as defined by s 224, ss (2), of TULR(C)A 1992; (c) Pressure imposed on an employer to impose a union membership requirement in a contract, s 222 of TULR(C)A (eg against recruitment of non-union employees); (d) Taking official industrial action without a ballot as per s 226 of TULR(C)A 1992; and (e) An act is not protected if the reason for it is in connection with the dismissal of one or more employees who are not entitled to protection from unfair dismissal by reason of their taking unofficial industrial action.

If the action does not fall within the statutory protection afforded by s 219, or immunity has been lost, or balloting and notice requirements are not carried out correctly, the consequences are that the proposed industrial action may be subject to an interdict, and the employer, and affected third parties, may sue for damages for losses suffered as a consequence of any unprotected action which has taken place. Any damage recovered will be subject to the limitations detailed below.

Where employer wants to stop the action taking place or prevent it from continuing, the normal remedy is interdict in Scotland. An interdict may be granted on an interim basis pending a full hearing of the case, but the union, or individual against whom the order is sought, will have the legal right to put forward their case. This is the primary remedy in industrial conflict cases. Under s 221(1) of TULR(C)A 1992, when the union has not got a chance to respond, or is likely to claim that the immunities apply, then the court must make sure the union has got notice of the application and an opportunity of being heard.

The standard of proof necessary to convince a judge to grant an interim interdict is the balance of convenience. This test is explained in an English case[32] where the terminology is different, but the principle is the same, as: 'This is an interlocutory application and it is usual on such application to pay particular attention to the balance of convenience ... until trial and to require of a plaintiff no more than an arguable case be shown.' Most disputes are resolved soon after the interim interdict is granted, and it is rare for a dispute to go all the way to a full hearing of the case to obtain a permanent injunction. If the matter does go all the way, then the appropriate remedy by then is likely to be damages, rather than an interdict. A failure to comply with an order of court is contempt of court. The person who sought the interdict will apply to the court to have the person failing to comply found in contempt of court. This is a breach of the criminal law and may face heavy fines or other penalties, which the court may consider appropriate, for example, a union may be deprived of its assets through sequestration (where the funds are frozen and placed in the control of a person appointed by the court).

The employer is most likely to seek a court order to prohibit industrial action from taking place, however, all members entitled to vote in the ballot, and those wrongly excluded, can apply for an interdict to stop the industrial action under s 62 of TULR(C)A 1992.

A third party (eg a member of the public) also has a right to get action 'called off' whenever it is unlawful. This will include any action that represents a delict unprotected by immunities, or actions not approved by ballot. In *Falconer v ASLEF and NUR*,[33] a commuter who was delayed from attending an important meeting sued the trade union successfully, and was awarded damages. It was not necessary for the union to have intended to harm the commuter.

---

32 *Thomas v NUM* (1985) IRLR 136 CD.
33 (1986) IRLR 331.

In *Network Rail Infrastructure Ltd v National of Rail, Maritime & Transport Workers*,[34] the applicant rail company applied for an interim injunction to prevent a strike by the respondent who had called a four-day national strike of its signallers. The applicant maintained that the union had not complied with the statutory requirements for a ballot under TULR(C)A, s 226a, s 231, s 234A and s 227, as it had conducted the ballot on the basis of inaccurate information, included irrelevant workplaces in the ballot for the purposes of the ballot notice, and had failed to provide complete information for a number of workplaces listed in the ballot notice. So the union had not taken all reasonably practicable steps to ensure that the information contained in the ballot notice was accurate in accordance with the law. The application was granted.

Procedural failures and Article 11

16.17 Article 11 of the European Convention of Human Rights, states that 'Everyone has the right to freedom of peaceful assembly and to freedom of association with others, including the right to form and join trade unions for the protection of his interests.' Any restrictions on the right must of course be proportionate.[35]

The right to collectively bargain,[36] and the right to take industrial action[37], are considered to be part of the right of freedom of association under Article 11 and therefore any restriction by interdict or procedural requirements will have to be proportionate.

In *University College London Hospital NHS Trust v Unison*[38] the ECtHR held that on principle an injunction preventing a strike was a breach of Article 11 rights since it prevents the trade union taking action to protect the rights of its members, but on the facts of the particular case it was proportionate and necessary in a democratic society for the protection of the rights of others and in *Enerji Yapi-Yol Sen v Turkey*[39] a

---

34 [2010] EWHC 1084, [2010] All ER (D) 191 (Jan).
35 Article11(2).
36 *Demir v Turkey* [2009] IRLR 766.
37 *Enerji Yapi –Yol Sen v Turkey* ECtHR 68959/01; *Unison v UK* [2002] IRLR 128.
38 [2002] IRLR 497.
39 ECtHR 68959/01.

ban preventing public sector employees from participating in a one day strike in support of the right to a collective bargaining arrangement, was a violation of their Article 11 rights.

In recent years the procedural requirements which must be fulfilled in order to achieve the immunity have been subject of litigation on this point. In *Metrobus v Unite the Union*,[40] the union held that the requirements of balloting and notice to employers under s 226A, 20(c), 231A and 234(3)(a), were held to be proportionate. The effect of this case on the union was that, the outlook for the unions improved. However, in *British Airways v Unite*,[41] when a less stringent approach was taken by the Court of Appeal, it was held that the requirement of s 231, that unions 'take such steps as were reasonably necessary' to inform members and employer of the results of the ballot as soon as reasonably practicable, were fulfilled by posting it on the website and including it in a newsletter. LJ Smith held that a minor infringement of the procedures relating to which had no adverse effect on anyone's rights or interests did not invalidate the ballot, stating that '[the policy behind the procedural requirements] is not to create a series of traps or hurdles for the union to negotiate. It is to ensure fair dealing between employer and Union and to ensure a fair, open and democratic ballot'

The trade unions were also successful in opposing injunctions in two other recent cases[42] In *National Union of Rail, Maritime & Transport Workers v Serco Docklands*,[43] the trade union had mistakenly allowed 2 members to vote (out of a total of 600). An injunction prohibiting the industrial action had been granted on the ground that the union had breached s 2A (2D) TULR(C)A 1992, in that the explanation given to the employers of how the numbers of employees involved was calculated, was not as accurate as reasonably practicable, and a breach of s 230(2) in that the union had sent voting papers to 2 persons not entitled to vote and this could not be disregarded as accidental. The Court of Appeal overturned the injunction, on the basis that entitlement to vote was not the

---

40 [2009] IRLR 114.
41 [2010] EWCA Civ 669, [2010] ICR 1316.
42 *National Union of Rail, Maritime & Transport Workers v Serco Docklands*; *Associated Society of Locomotive Engineers and Firemen v London and Birmingham Railway Limited t/a London Midland* [2011] EWCA Civ 226, [2011] IRLR 399.
43 [2011] EWCA Civ 226, [2011] IRLR 399.

same as opportunity to vote, and the union was not in breach of s 230(2) but s 226A (2) which could be disregarded if accidental which they held it was in this case. In any event the *de minimus* rule would have applied. The duty imposed on the union by s 226A (2) was limited by reference to the information possessed by the union, and was not an onerous one. The defence available under s 232B was not available where the union conferred the opportunity to vote on those who it must have known were not entitled to vote, but did apply on cases where the union had not done what was reasonably practicable and this section should have been applied. It is clear, therefore, that small errors will not affect the validity of the procedures in such a way as to deprive the union of immunity. The RMT has lodged a challenge with the European Court of Human Rights to the balloting and notice requirements, and to the prohibition against secondary industrial action. At the time of writing, the outcome of that challenge is awaited with interest.

LIMITATION ON DAMAGES

16.18 It is possible to claim damages for losses suffered as a result of action which is not protected under s 219, however under see s 25 of TULR(C)A 1992, there are upper limits on the amounts which can be awarded by way of damages in any proceedings in delict against a trade union. These limits depend on the size of the membership of trade unions and are currently as follows:

Number of Members	Limit (£)
Fewer than 5,000	10,000
5,000 or more but fewer than 25,000	50,000
25,000 or more but fewer than 100,000	125,000
100,000 or more	250,000

It is important to note that this limit applies **per action**. The limit does not apply to proceedings for personal injury as a result of negligence, or breach of duty, proceedings for breach of duty in connection with the ownership, occupation, possession, control or use of property, and proceedings brought under Part 1 of the Consumer Safety Act 1998.

PICKETING

16.19 An aspect of trade union liability that deserves separate consideration is the law of picketing. What follows is a breakdown of this topic. Although the emphasis will be on the position in Scotland, the law in England and Wales, which is quite different, will also be analysed.

Definition of picketing

16.20 There is no legal definition of picketing, but the following definition is commonly used: 'a congregation of persons outside a particular place, whose purpose it to prevent entry to that place.' This is probably too simplistic, given the reasons for picketing, because picketing is also used to: highlight or publicise industrial action, give an opportunity to distribute information to people, and persuade other secondary employers or workers to join the industrial action, etc. A better definition is: 'a form of industrial action in which employees gather outside a workplace, in which there is a trade dispute, usually a strike. The pickets, so gathered, often form a picket line, past which they attempt to discourage other workers, delivery lorries, and customers' collection lorries, from passing. The purpose is to reinforce the effects of the strike and to encourage the maximum number of employees to join it.'[44] So picketing can have a number of aims, but it is generally done to put pressure on the party targeted to meet particular demands, usually an employer in dispute but not always. This pressure is achieved by harming the business through loss of customers and negative publicity, or by discouraging, or preventing, workers from entering the site, and thereby preventing the business from operating normally. Picketing is a common tactic used by trade unions during strikes to try to prevent dissident members of the union, members of other unions, and non-unionised workers, from working.

---

44 *Dictionary of Business*, Oxford University Press, http://www.encyclopedia.com/
doc/1O18-picketing.html

Immunity for Picketing

16.21 What follows is a description of the immunity to civil actions, under the law of delict, for trade unions in the context of picketing, which is provided by s 220 of Trade Union and Labour Relations (Consolidation) Act 1992) (TULR(C)A 1992). 'It is unlawful for a person in contemplation or furtherance of a trade dispute to attend: (a) at or near their place of work,[45] or (b) if he/she is an official of a trade union, at or near the place of work of a member of the union whom he is accompanying, and whom he represents, for the purposes only of peacefully obtaining or communicating information or peacefully persuading any person to work or abstain from working'.

This only provides immunity when the picketing is *peaceful*, and is *primary*, which means it is only carried out by a worker at their own employer's premises. Peaceful picketing means that the picketers (also known as pickets) are not obstructive to persons or vehicles entering or leaving the premises, destructive to property, or harassing or threatening in their words or actions. Unfortunately, when there is mass picketing involving large numbers of primary pickets, and possibly secondary pickets, then picketing can be anything but peaceful. Primary picketing is defined by s 220, and will require the picketing to be at or near their place of work. In *Rayware Ltd v TGWU*,[46] the pickets positioned themselves at the entrance to an industrial estate within which their employer's premises were situated. Although they were some distance away from their workplace, it was held to be sufficiently near to qualify for immunities. What about the situation when it is difficult or impossible to picket an employer's premises? This is also dealt with by s 220. Sub-section (2) states: If a person works or normally works: (1) otherwise than at any one place; or (2) at a place, the location of which is such that attendance there for a purpose mentioned in sub-section (1) is impracticable, (eg oil platforms in the sea), the place of work shall be any premises of the employer from which he/she works, or from which his/her work is

---

45 See *Rayware Ltd v TGWU* (1989) ICR 457 CA.
46 Ibid.

administered, in other words the headquarters or regional offices of the employer.

Secondary Picketing

16.22 This is a form of secondary action that is defined by s 224(2) of TULR(C)A 1992. Unlawful action of secondary picketers falls outside the immunities, and their involvement could make the primary union in dispute liable for civil conspiracy. It commonly arises when a secondary union is indirectly affected by the issues behind the industrial action, or they simply want to support the action of the trade union in dispute with employer (sympathetic action).

Permissible Number of Pickets

16.23 An issue that often arises in legal cases concerns the permissible number of pickets outside each entrance of the employers. Although this is not dealt with directly by statute, a Code of Practice on Picketing was issued in 1980, and revised in 1992, which recommends that the permissible number at each entrance to the workplace is six. Although this is not legally binding, the courts they have followed this in their decisions.[47]

Mass Picketing

16.24 This is not defined, but usually involves a large numbers of pickets which is far in excess of the permissible number. In *Thomas v NUM (South Wales)*,[48] the courts indicated their poor view of mass picketing by holding that, irrespective of what heading of tort (delict) was applied to the mass picketers' actions, their behaviour was unlawful. The Miners Strike, that took place from 1983 to 1984, involved the worst example of conflict with police arising from mass picketing. During the dispute

---

47 *Messenger Newspapers Group v NGA* (1984) ICR 345).
48 (1985) IRLR 136.

there were several instances of physical confrontation between the police and the miners, and over this period 1,483 people in Scotland, and 9,808 people in England and Wales were arrested. The chance of civil and criminal offences is higher when there is mass picketing. If there are 20 or more people on a picket line, the police in England and Wales, under the Public Order Act 1986, can use special powers if the picketing is likely to cause serious public disorder, or serious damage to property. If the police are concerned that there's a threat to the safety of others, they can order those picketing to stop, and may arrest those not complying.

SCOTTISH POSITION

16.25 The vast majority of the statutes that apply to picketing south of the border do not apply in Scotland, but s 241 of TULR(C)A 1992 is regarded as one generic offence in Scotland. There are various offences provided by s 241 of TULR(C)A 1992 which could apply to picketing and these are set out as follows: Every person with a view to compelling any person to abstain from doing an act which he has a legal right to do, for example:

(a)   Using violence to intimidate such a person or his wife or children or injures his property;

(b)   Watching and besetting. Here a picket commits an offence when, with a view to compelling some person from abstaining from that which he will has a legal right to do, he watches and besets any place where that other happens to be;[49]

(c)   Following such a person with two or more other persons in a disorderly manner along any street or road;

(d)   Hiding any tools, clothes or property, or hinder in their use;

(e)   Persistently following such a person from place to place.

---

49 *Galt v Philip* [1984] IRLR 146.

Section 243 of TULR(C)A 1992 offers the limited possibility of prosecution for criminal conspiracy.[50] What is more likely is that common law crimes, such as breach of the peace, malicious mischief, vandalism or assault, will apply, as well as the obstruction of a police officer in the execution of his duty.[51] There is also the possibility of a civil action for nuisance, when the action of the union interferes with the property rights of neighbours of the employer, etc, and trespass in Scotland, particularly when the union occupies the premises of the employer, or they stray on to someone else's land.

BREACH OF THE PEACE

16.26 The Police have a duty to preserve the peace and can prevent conduct which in itself is lawful, if there is a real danger that the conduct is likely to lead to a breach of the peace, and this applies in both jurisdictions[52] but is widely utilised in Scotland. However, the conduct necessary to constitute a breach of the peace must now be severe enough to cause alarm to ordinary people, and threaten serious disturbance to the community. The case of *Smith v Donnelly*,[53] highlights the importance

---

50 Under 243 of TULR(C)A: (1) An agreement or combination by two or more persons to do or procure to be done an act in contemplation or furtherance of a trade dispute is not indictable as a conspiracy if that act committed by one person would not be punishable as a crime. (2) A crime for this purpose means an offence punishable on indictment, or an offence punishable on summary conviction, and for the commission of which the offender is liable under the statute making the offence punishable to be imprisoned either absolutely or at the discretion of the court as an alternative for some other punishment. (3) Where a person is convicted of any such agreement or combination as is mentioned above to do or procure to be done an act which is punishable only on summary conviction, and is sentenced to imprisonment, the imprisonment shall not exceed three months or such longer time as may be prescribed by the statute for the punishment of the act when committed by one person. (4) Nothing in this section (a) exempts from punishment a person guilty of a conspiracy for which a punishment is awarded by an Act of Parliament, or (b) affects the law relating to riot, unlawful assembly, breach of the peace, or sedition or any offence against the State or the Sovereign.(5) This section extends to Scotland only.

51 Section 41 of the Police (Scotland) Act 1967.

52 *Piddington v Bates* (1961) 1 WLR 162.

53 (2001) SLT 1007.

of this in determining the essence of the offence.[54] So less serious behaviour (eg verbal not threatening comments), occurring in the context of picketing will no longer be covered by the offence.

RELATED CRIMES AND OFFENCES IN ENGLAND AND WALES

16.27 One of the most common crimes committed in the context of picketing is Public Nuisance, which occurs when someone causes substantial inconvenience to the public at large. To establish this crime has been committed, it would probably be necessary to show that there is some element of violence, obstruction, annoyance or molestation.

Obstruction of the Highway is an offence that is defined in s 137 of the Highways Act 1980 as: to wilfully obstruct the free passage of public traffic along a highway without lawful authority or excuse,[55] for example it is a criminal offence when a picket tries to force a driver to stop against his will by lying down, or standing in front of, his vehicle.

As seen already, there are various separate offences provided by s 241 of TULR(C)A 1992 which could apply to picketing.

A person with a view to compelling any person to abstain from doing an act which he has a legal right to do, for example: (a) uses violence to intimidate such a person or his wife or children or injures his property; (b) watches and besets them; (c) following such a person with two or more other persons in a disorderly manner along any street or road; (d) hiding any of their tools, clothes or property, or hinder in their use; (e) persistently follow such a person from place to place, commits an offence under this section.

There are further offences provided by the Public Order Act 1986 namely:

> *Riot*, where 12 or more people use, or threaten to use, violence for a common purpose.

> *Violent Disorder*, where three or more persons use, or threaten to use, violence.

---

54 Supra 11, pp 654–655.
55 *Broome v DPP* [1974] ICR 84 HL.

Affray, where at least one person commits a violent act.

Fear or Provocation of Violence, where someone use threatening, abusive, or insulting, words etc, with the intent to make a person fear immediate violence, or to provoke it.

Harassment alarm or distress, the same as fear of provocation of violence. There is the defence that there is no reason to believe that a person who was alarmed was within his/her hearing or sight, or that his/her conduct was unreasonable

Also, as already mentioned, under the Public Order Act 1986, the police are given the power to disperse or limit the number of a crowd of 20 or more persons when actions are likely to lead to a serious breach of the peace, damage to property, or disruption to the public.

OTHER RELEVANT STATUTES

16.28 Section 154 of the Criminal Justice and Public Order Act 1994, creates the offence of intentional harassment. The picket must do something threatening, abusive, or insulting, which causes another person harassment alarm or distress.

Under the Protection from Harassment Act 1997 there are two offences which might apply to harassment or physical intimidation in the context of picketing. The two offences are harassment (under s 1 of the Act), and putting in fear of violence (under s 4). There is also a civil action for harassment under the Act.[56]

REMEDIES

16.29 Where the union, in the context of picketing, breaches the civil law then they may be covered by the immunities for industrial delicts when the picketing complies with the legal parameters (eg peaceful and primary picketing) but, other torts, such as nuisance and trespass, will never be covered, nor will the criminal offences cited above. When immunities do not apply or they have been removed (eg because of secondary picketing),

---

56 *Majrowski v Guy's and St Thomas NHS Trust* (2006) UKHL 34.

then the employer can sue the trade unions for damages and/or for an interim interdict, usually with the effect of stopping the picketing.

With respect to criminal penalties, these vary depending on sentencing practice for common law offences and the penalties set out under the relevant statutes in England and Wales. But usually it will involve actions being brought under summary procedure (with set fines and small periods of imprisonment), unless it is a serious crime involving intimidation or violence. The individual perpetrator of the crime will be liable, but the trade union itself could be liable for certain statutory offences (eg under the Public Order Act 1986), but not for common law crimes.

HUMAN RIGHTS ACT 1998 AND PICKETING

16.30 Article 10 of the European Convention of Human Rights covers right of freedom of speech or expression, and Article 11 covers right to freedom of assembly. Both could be relevant here; for example, when the picketers in the process of picketing give information to other workers, customers, etc, about the dispute, then courts should be reluctant to grant an interdict as this may be subject to challenge under Articles 10 and 11. Courts may have to review their policy of granting interim interdicts to employers to restrain picketing by trade unions in light of human rights, but see *Gate Gourmet London Ltd v TGWU*,[57] where the employer obtained an interim injunction for Gate Gourmet against the TGWU, whereby 17 named individuals and persons unknown were prevented from assaulting, threatening, intimidating, harassing, molesting or otherwise abusing employees who were continuing to work.

UNFAIR DISMISSAL AND INDUSTRIAL ACTION

16.31 Participating in industrial action is regarded as a breach of contract but, because of the protection conferred by TULR(C)A 1992, it is only in very limited circumstances that the employee participating in such action can be dismissed without notice. If that is the case such an employee will

---

57 [2005] EWHC 1889 (QB), [2005] IRLR 881.

not be entitled to a redundancy payment as redundancy is not the reason for dismissal.[58]

Section 237 TULR(C)A 1992 states that an employee who is dismissed *whilst* taking part in unofficial industrial action, may not claim unfair dismissal unless the dismissal was for a protected reason (see below). If the dismissal is before, or after, the industrial action then the tribunal will be able to hear a claim of unfair dismissal. Also ss 237-239 of TULR(C)A 1992 afford a degree of protection to the employee. The amount of protection varies, and depends on whether those involved in the action are all members of a recognised independent trade union or not, whether the action was official or unofficial. It is possible for a strike to be official for members of one union, yet unofficial for members of another.[59] If there is an unfair dismissal then the mere fact that the employee took the industrial action cannot be regarded as contributory conduct, which would justify a reduction in the award of compensation under ERA 1996.[60]

There are five possible situations which may occur.

(1) The employees who are on strike are all union members, and the strike is official, and protected (ie subject to s 219 immunity).

In this case, the employees taking part in industrial action are protected from dismissal under s 238A TULR(C)A. If s 238A applies, then it will be automatically unfair to dismiss such an employee for participating in the action, even if the dismissal takes place after the action has ceased. The employee will have six months after the effective date of dismissal to claim, will not need qualifying service to make a claim, and there will be no upper limit on compensation.[61] The protection from dismissal applies to dismissals which become effective during the *'protected period.'* The basic protected period is 12 weeks, beginning with the first day of industrial action, plus any period during which the employer operated a lock out. If the employee

---

58 *Baxter v Limb Group of Companies* [1994] IRLR 572; *Sanders v Ernest A Neale Ltd* [1974] IRLR 236.
59 *Balfour Kilpatrick Ltd v Acheson and ors* [2003] IRLR 683.
60 *Tracy and others v Crossville Wales Ltd* [1997] ICR 862.
61 Section 239(1).

ceases to take part in industrial action during the protected period, then the protection of s 238A continues after the end of the protected period. If the employer unreasonably fails to take such procedural steps as would have been reasonable to end the dispute, the employee will continue to enjoy the protection of s 238A after the end of the protected period. In deciding whether or not the employer has failed to take such steps no regard will be had to the merits of the dispute but regard will be had, in particular, to:

(a)   Whether the employer, or a union, had complied with procedures established by any applicable collective or other agreement;

(b)   Whether the employer, or a union, offered or agreed to commence or resume negotiations after the start of the protected industrial action;

(c)   Whether the employer, or a union, unreasonably refused, after the start of the protected industrial action, a request that conciliation or mediation services be used;

If the union repudiates the industrial action, it will become unofficial at the end of the next working day.

(2)   The employees who are on strike are all union members and the strike is endorsed by the union, ie official, but unprotected by s 219. If the action is official, but unprotected, the employee will not be able to claim unfair dismissal for a dismissal whilst taking part in such action, unless he can show that:

(a)   the dismissal was for a protected reason such as jury service, family, health and safety, working time, employee representative, protected disclosure and flexible working cases;[62] or

(b)   the employer has been picking and choosing those who he has dismissed (see the no 'picking or choosing' rule below).

The protection of s 219 can be lost for the following reasons:

---

62 Section 237(10(A)).

- the industrial action was in order to enforce trade union membership,

- the industrial action was a reaction to the dismissal of unofficial strikers,

- the action involved secondary action,

- the action was an attempt to impose a trade union recognition requirement,

- notice and/or balloting requirements were not complied with.

The employer is therefore entitled to dismiss, provided he dismisses all the employees involved in the action, and provided the real reason for dismissal is not a protected one.

Again if the union repudiates the industrial action, it will become unofficial at the end of the next working day.

(3)   The employees who are participating in the strike are union members, or a mixture of union members and non union members, and the strike is not authorised by the trade union unofficial.

This is regarded as unofficial action. Section 237 states, that an employee (union member or not) has no right to claim unfair dismissal if, at the time of dismissal, he was taking part in unofficial strike or other industrial action, unless he can show that the dismissal was for a protected reason, such as pregnancy maternity, statutory rights, such as emergency leave or working time or health and safety.[63] The employer can pick and choose who he dismisses in such a situation.

(4)   The employees are on strike are all non union members.

In this case then the strike is not unofficial. Section 237(2), s 238(1)(b), and 2(b) apply and the employee may not claim unfair dismissal unless they can show that the employer has been picking and choosing who he has dismissed.

(5)   There is a lock out.

A lock out is where the employer refuses to continue to employ his employees, closes the place of work or suspends the work

---

63 Section 237(1A).

being done. This is in order to compel the employees to accept a new contract of employment. The employee cannot claim unfair dismissal, unless the no picking and choosing rule applies.

THE NO PICKING AND CHOOSING RULE

16.32 The rule applies to s 23(8) (1) (a) dismissal in connection with a lockout, s 237 (dismissal in the case of an unofficial strike), s 238(1) (b), 2(b) (dismissal in the case where none of the participating employees are union members) and s 238(2) where the action is official but not protected.

Where this rule applies, the employee will be prohibited from claiming unfair dismissal if the employer dismisses all the employees involved in the action, and either reengages them all within 3 months, or does not reengage any of them within 3 months. If the claimant employee can show that one or more of the employees taking part in the industrial action was not dismissed or, if dismissed, was offered reengagement within three months of the claimant's dismissal, but that the claimant was not offered re engagement then the claimant will be allowed to bring an unfair dismissal claim. (There is nothing to prevent the employer from re-engaging employees after the 3 months limit is up).

This rule applies even if the employer reengaged the employee in error.[64] In that situation the employee must show the decision to dismiss fell within the range of reasonable responses test and, in particular, the decision to reengage some employees and not others, satisfied the usual requirements of reasonableness.[65] It may not be difficult for the employer to satisfy the reasonableness test. In *Sandhu and others v Gate Gourmet*,[66] the EAT decided that 'where large numbers of employees deliberately absent themselves from work in a manner which is plainly liable to do serious damage to the employer's business, it seems to us plain beyond argument that dismissal of those taking part in the action will be within the range of reasonable responses open to an employer.'

---

64 *Bingham v GKN Kwikform Ltd* [1992] IRLR 4.
65 *Edwards v Cardiff City Council* [1979] IRLR 303.
66 [2009] IRLR 907.

Chapter 17

Immigration and Employment Law

17.1 The rules relating to immigration and employment law have undergone substantial amendment over the last few years in response to changes introduced by Parliament. This change has been prompted by new political, sociological and economic approaches and attitudes to this issue (outlined below).

EMPLOYMENT LAW AND IMMIGRATION LAWS

17.2 Once an immigrant is legally employed in an organisation in the UK as an employee or a worker, they need to be treated the same as employees or workers born (or naturalised) in the UK. So they would be entitled to protect their rights in terms of unfair dismissal (see below) and redundancy (provided they have the requisite period of continuous employment with the respondent employer). They can also make claims in respect of: the national minimum wage; rights under Working Time Regulations; maternity and parental rights; and discrimination of various kinds (see below) etc.

UNFAIR DISMISSAL

17.3 It is a criminal offence, under the Immigration, Asylum and Nationality Act 2006, for an employer to employ a person knowing that he or she is not legally entitled to work in the UK. It is understandable that employers will be tempted to take immediate action in relation to a particular employee on discovering such circumstances apply in their organisation. The case law underlines the fact that, even in these circumstances, a legitimate disciplinary procedure should be followed which involves employers giving careful consideration to their own decision-making process.[1] The case of *Klusova v London Borough*

---

1   ACAS Code of Practice on Discipline and Grievance 2009.

of Hounslow[2] heard by the Court of Appeal is a good illustration of the difficulties that employers may encounter when trying to avoid contravention of the immigration legislation. Ms Klusova was a Russian national, who had leave to remain and work in the UK until May 2004. In November 2000, she began working for Hounslow Council and in March and May 2004 she applied to the Home Office twice for further leave to remain, but both applications were refused. However, the May application was not actually dealt with until a formal refusal letter was sent to Ms Klusova at the end of 2005. When a worker applies before the expiry of their permit for an extension to their right to remain, permission to do so continues until the request has been dealt with.[3] Hounslow Council received contradictory advice from the Home Office but was told that Ms Klusova was an 'overstayer'. She maintained that she had applied for an extension, but did not provide satisfactory evidence to this effect. Believing that continuing to employ her would contravene the Asylum and Immigration Act 1996, the Council dismissed her in August 2005. It did not follow the normal statutory dismissal procedures as it believed these did not apply when the dismissal was for breach of a statutory restriction. As it turned out, the Council was mistaken in its belief that continuing to employ Ms Klusova was an offence under the immigration legislation. Ms Klusova brought a claim for unfair dismissal.

The Court of Appeal found that the Council's mistaken belief that Ms Klusova's employment was unlawful was not sufficient for it to justify her summary dismissal.[4] The employment must actually be unlawful for such justification to be relied on. However, given that the Council had received conflicting advice and had genuinely believed it could not lawfully continue to employ Ms Klusova, her dismissal was potentially fair for 'some other substantial reason.'[5]

Unfortunately, for the Council, however, the statutory dismissal procedures[6] did apply in these circumstances. As the Council had failed to

---

2 [2007] EWCA Civ 1127, [2008] ICR 396.
3 www.uk-visa-appeal.co.uk. If an adverse decision is reached and should the applicant appeal, leave is again effectively extended on identical conditions until the appeal is heard.
4 Instant dismissal without notice being given.
5 Section 98(1)(b).
6 Set up under the Employment Act 2002 and repealed in 2008.

follow the procedures, Ms Klusova's dismissal was automatically unfair (eg presumed to be unfair from the outset unless the employer can show otherwise and employee not requiring any continuity of employment before qualifying for the right to bring a claim).

The case was remitted back to the employment tribunal to determine the appropriate compensation. Since the repeal of the statutory procedures, the same difficulty is unlikely to arise again, however, the case illustrates the difficulties encountered by employers in this area. Part One of the Employment Act 2008 repealed the Statutory Dispute Resolution Procedures (SDDP), which had been introduced six years earlier under the Employment Act 2002. With the repeal of the SDDP, the law has returned, in part, to the law prior to the 2002 Act. So where the employer in dismissing his employee has acted in breach of the ACAS Code they will be found to have unlawfully dismissed their employee. But there are significant changes, notably the new provision that allows an employment tribunal to increase or decrease an employee's award by up to 25% if either the employer or employee has 'unreasonably' failed to comply with the 2009 ACAS Code on Disciplinary and Grievance Procedures. The Code does not apply to dismissals for illegality or some other substantial reason so employers are now unlikely to be caught in the *Klusova* trap provided they act reasonably.

DISCRIMINATION

17.4 Employers who consider and take action in response to immigration issues too early face the added risk of a discrimination claim being successfully pursued against them. In the leading case of *Osborne Clarke* (considered below), the matter was dealt with under the old work permit scheme. Under this scheme the Home Office had to make the decision as to whether or not the criteria for employing a migrant worker were met or not.[7] In *Osborne Clarke Services v Mr A Purohit*,[8] the firm had a policy of not considering any applications for training contracts from

---

7 Rather than consider them under the points based system that now applies.
8 [2009] IRLR 341.

individuals who required permission to work in the UK. They believed that such positions could be filled by workers who were already resident in the UK. The Employment Appeal Tribunal (EAT) found that the policy was indirectly discriminatory on the grounds of nationality,[9] because the proportion of non-EEA nationals who could comply with it was considerably smaller than the proportion of EEA nationals who could comply, and the policy was not justifiable.[10]

It is worth noting that, whilst the work permit regime has since been replaced by a five tier permission system (see below), the Tier 2 skilled worker category is particularly relevant and similar considerations apply. Namely, employers should consider carefully and record any decision against applying for a sponsor licence (the rules relating to this are considered below) because employers have to sponsor a worker before he will be allowed entry into the country under the Tier 2 rules. They must ensure that they can justify such a decision against legal and commercial criteria in the event that it is ever challenged by a potential employee who considers that he or she should be sponsored by the employer. Claims could be brought where someone who is an immigrant is refused employment on the basis of their race or nationality, or on the ground of their religion or belief, under the EA 2010. Any question of their entitlement to stay in the country should be left aside from consideration in the recruitment and selection process until the other aspects of the decision making process have been complete.

IMMIGRATION RULES

17.5 Immigration under the new Coalition Government is determined by a Points Based System. This system was originally introduced by the Labour Government in 2009, but has gone through considerable

---

9 Under the Race Relations Act 1976 now the Equality Act 2010.

10 The employer sought to rely on the guidance of the UK Border and Immigration Agency (now simply the UK Border Agency) to justify its policy. The guidance required employers, when completing a work permit application form, to set out reasons why the post could not be filled by resident EEA workers. In rejecting this argument, the EAT referred to the Code of Practice of Racial Equality and Employment which makes it clear that, as far as possible, selection should be based purely on merit and work permit considerations should only come into play at the last stages of selection.

amendment since then.[11] The system was intended to be more objective, consistent, straightforward and transparent than the previous one.[12]

Points based system

17.6 Under the new Points Based System, the application for permission to stay in the UK is always made by the individual seeking entry or leave to remain under one of 5 'Tiers.' In each situation applications will be points-based[13] with applicants requiring sufficient points to be given the right to enter or remain in the UK.[14]

The Points Based System is made up of the following 5 tiers, or levels:

–   Tier 1 is aimed at highly skilled individuals who will contribute to the growth and productivity of the UK economy. Applicants under this category do not require a job offer or sponsorship from a UK organisation.

–   Tier 2 is aimed at skilled workers with a job offer, required to fill gaps in the UK labour force. Applications made under this Tier require sponsorship from an employing organisation.

–   Tier 3 is aimed at low skilled workers in order to fill specific temporary labour shortages. Applications under this tier also need be sponsored by employers. This tier may only be activated when relevant temporary labour shortages are identified.

–   Tier 4 is aimed at students and applications made under this tier must be supported by the educational institution.

---

11 Eg if someone had previously requested a review of decision of the UK Border Agency and the Agency had refused it solely because the person did not have valid permission to stay in the UK when he requested the review, they will now automatically review the decision.

12 Revised guidance of Borders Agency 22 November 2010.

13 The PBS replaces more than 80 existing routes into the UK for the purposes of work and study.

14 There will also be an English language requirement.

–   Tier 5 is designed to allow entry to youth mobility[15] and temporary workers who are coming to the UK to satisfy primarily non-economic objectives.

Most applicants (except Applicants under Tier 1)[16] seeking entry to the UK under the Point Based System will require a Certificate of Sponsorship.

Sponsorship requirement

17.7 A Certificate of Sponsorship must be issued to workers or students by their potential employer, or the educational institution they attend in the UK. Before they are able to issue these certificates of sponsorship, employers and educational institutions must obtain and maintain their place on the UK's National Sponsor's Register. This involves making a fairly detailed application, supported by business-related documents, and agreeing to what is effectively a code of practice, including a number of responsibilities and obligations such as reporting, record keeping and compliance-related activities. There are also specific additional duties associated with each tier under which the organisation wishes to sponsor migrant workers. In order to maintain their position on the register, they will need to comply with all of these responsibilities. Employers are required to take responsibility for assisting the UK Border Agency in ensuring that workers comply with the immigration laws by verifying that applications are legitimate. Employers must demonstrate that they are established in the UK, are in a position to employ people, and establish that they have advertised the position and have checked that the immigrant employed has suitable skills and qualifications. They are also responsible for informing the Border Agency if the person fails to start work or leaves their employment. If employers do not comply with their responsibilities one potential outcome may be suspension from the sponsors register. The applications for entry to work or study in the UK will be handled by the Border Agency and individuals can submit their application on line.

---

15 Set up in 2008 the youth mobility scheme is for young people from participating countries who would like to come and experience life in the UK. The countries in the scheme are: Australia, Canada, Japan, New Zealand and Monaco. The country from where a person originates will sponsor their visit.

16 Applicants under Tier 1 are able to apply based purely on their own attributes and achievements.

IMMIGRATION, ASYLUM AND NATIONALITY ACT 2006

17.8 Under the Immigration, Asylum and Nationality Act 2006[17] it is a criminal offence for an employer to employ a person in the knowledge that he or she is not legally entitled to work in the UK.[18] On conviction the maximum penalty is two years imprisonment and/or a fine.[19]

Civil penalties

17.9 The Act also imposes civil penalties on employers of illegal workers.[20] A notice of liability (NOL) to pay a civil penalty of a specific amount can be served by the UK Border Agency on behalf of the Secretary of State.

These apply even when an employer was unaware that the worker had no right to work in the UK, subject to an exemption where the employer can show a statutory excuse. In all cases, the excuse must be established before the employment begins. To establish a statutory excuse against liability for a civil penalty a prospective worker must provide the employer with an original version of one of the specified documents from List A,[21] or a specified combination of two documents from List B. These are documents which provide an excuse for the worker to stay in the UK for up to 12 months.[22] The statutory excuse requires that the employer: takes all reasonable steps to check the validity of specified documents; keeps copies of those documents and retains them for not less than two years

---

17 As amended by the Borders, Citizenship and Immigration Act 2009.

18 Section 21.

19 Section 50 (3) of the 2006 Act repealed and replaced the Asylum and Immigration Act 1996 s 8.

20 Summary conviction previously led to a fine not exceeding level 5 on the standard scale. However, under the rules that have applied since 29 February 2008 the penalties are substantially increased and can be: an unlimited fine and/or a prison sentence of up to two years for employers who employ an adult who they know is not legally entitled to work in the UK; or a civil penalty of up to £10,000 per employee if the employer did not made specified checks and did not know that the worker was not legally entitled to work in the UK.

21 Passports, birth certificates etc.

22 Eg a passport or travel document endorsed to show that the holder is allowed to stay in the United Kingdom and is allowed to do the type of work in question, work permit.

after the employment has come to an end.[23] The Home Office has said that 'the new civil penalties for employers who unknowingly hire illegal workers ... allow it to save criminal prosecution for more serious cases'.[24]

It is contrary to section 15 of the Immigration, Asylum and Nationality Act to employ an adult subject to immigration controls if (a) he has not been granted leave to enter or remain in the United Kingdom, or (b) his leave to enter or remain in the United Kingdom (i) is invalid, (ii) has ceased to have effect (whether by reason of curtailment, revocation, cancellation, passage of time or otherwise), or (iii) is subject to a condition preventing him from accepting the employment. This is a measure which comprehensively covers the situations where someone is employed or will be employed illegally. Section 15 (2) provides that the Secretary of State may give an employer who acts contrary to this section a notice requiring him to pay a penalty of a specified amount. However, under 15(3) an employer is excused from paying a penalty if he can show that he complied with any prescribed requirements in relation to the employment.[25] Employers are required to make ongoing checks when, for example, employees need to extend their permission to remain and they must be vigilant and put in place proper systems to ensure that an employee does escape their notice and expose them to liability. Under s 15(6), a penalty notice must (a) state why the Secretary of State thinks the employer is liable to the penalty, (b) specify the amount of the penalty (c) specify a date, at least 28 days after the date specified in the notice as the date on which it is given, before which the penalty must be paid, (d) explain: how the penalty must be paid; how the employer may object to the penalty and explain how the Secretary of State may enforce the penalty.

Under s 16, there are rules governing the possibility of objection by an employer to the penalty notice where (a) he is not liable to the imposition of a penalty (b) he is excused payment by virtue of s 15(3) or (c) the

---

23 The civil consequences for an employer where an individual is found to be employed illegally by them can be up to a penalty of up to £10,000. In 2008, the UK Border Agency served civil penalties against companies for infringing these regulations to the value of over £1 million.
24 BBC News, 29 February 2008 'Fines for hiring illegal workers' http://news.bbc.co.uk/1/hi/business/7268807.stm
25 15 (4) But the excuse in subsection (3) shall not apply to an employer who knew, at any time during the period of the employment, that it was contrary to this section.

amount of the penalty is too high. Under s 16 (4), where the Secretary of State receives a notice of objection to a penalty he shall consider it and undertake the following: (a) cancel the penalty (b) reduce the penalty (c) increase the penalty or (d) determine to take no action.

Where the employer is dissatisfied with the outcome of his notice of objection to the penalty notice he can appeal to the court, under s 17, on the ground that (a) he is not liable to the imposition of a penalty (b) he is excused payment by virtue of s 15(3) or (c) the amount of the penalty is too high.[26] Section 17 (5) provides that an appeal may be brought by an employer irrespective of whether he has objected to the Secretary of State under s 16 and the outcome of any objection.

Criminal penalties

17.10 Under s 21 of the 2006 Act, an employer may commit a criminal offence if he or she knowingly employs an illegal migrant. On summary conviction, the maximum penalty an employer may be given will be a fine of no more than the statutory maximum for each person employed illegally and/or imprisonment for up to 6 months. Following conviction on indictment, there is no upper limit to the level of fine and the employer may also be subject to imprisonment for up to two years. It also introduces corporate liability whereby: the employer will be treated as knowing that an employee cannot lawfully work, if a person who has responsibility within the organisation for 'an aspect of the employment' knows that the employee does not have the right to work in the UK. If found guilty the responsible individuals can face the same term of imprisonment and/or a fine as an employer.

As discovered recently by Primark, the stigma attached to employing illegal workers or foreign workers on poor terms and conditions can sometimes be significant, even if those workers are not actually the company's own employees. In this case the workers in question were employed by a sub-contractor called TNS Knitwear. An article featured in the newspaper the News of the World, alleged that TNS Knitwear had breached UK employment, tax, and immigration laws, although the company itself strenuously denied that this was the case. It was discovered

---

26 Under s 16 (2) the court may (a) allow the appeal and cancel the penalty (b) allow the appeal and reduce the penalty or (c) dismiss the appeal.

through an undercover BBC investigation[27] that TNS Knitwear was employing illegal workers in poor conditions at its Manchester factory and the factory workers making clothes destined for the fashion chain Primark worked up to 12 hours a day and for £3.50 an hour.[28]

BUSINESS VISITORS

17.11 Prior to 2008 a business visitor did not require special permission to visit the UK on condition that these visitors did not charge members of the public for services provided or goods received. Accordingly, business visitors were generally able to attend trade fairs and meetings; negotiate and conclude contracts; conduct site visits and promotional activities, and attend conferences without any restriction. However, under the new rules, all visa nationals who want to come to the UK on business for up to six months must apply for a dedicated new business visa and prove that they will be carrying out specific activities, such as these mentioned above, before the visa is granted.

ENFORCEMENT

17.12 Police officers and immigration officers had wide powers given to them allowing them to enter premises and conduct searches for evidence under the Immigration Act 1971 and the Immigration and Asylum Act 1999. These powers were extended by the Nationality, Immigration and Asylum Act 2002[29] and further extended by the UK Borders Act 2007. The Borders Act 2007 set up the UK Border Agency as a law enforcement agency with a single force at the border working collaboratively with police officers and other law enforcement agencies.[30] The UK Border

---

27 A previous BBC investigation had found that Primark contractors were employing children in slum workshops in India. The findings were the result of an investigation carried out by the BBC Panorama programme and the Observer newspaper which were broadcast on a Panorama special titled 'Primark: On the Rack' 23 June 2008.

28 Primark linked to UK sweatshops Monday 12 January 2009, http://news.bbc.co.uk/1/hi/7824291.stm

29 Sections 153 to 155.

30 In these acts immigration officers are given the power: to detain; to set reporting conditions; to arrest a person liable to detention; to enter and search premises or search a detained person, fingerprinting etc.

Agency claim that by supporting the police and responding to communities they are using the immigration laws to protect communities and prosecute and remove people from the UK. The Border Agency has to work closely with the Migration Advisory Committee which advises the Government on migration issues. The Committee is a non-statutory, non-time-limited, non-departmental public body, sponsored by the UK Border Agency of the Home Office. It is made up of a chair and four others all of whom are independent economists. Additionally, the Commission for Employment and Skills and the UK Border Agency are represented on the committee.

CURRENT DEVELOPMENTS

17.13 To control the numbers coming to the UK the Government, in July 2010,[31] announced they were committed to: introducing an annual limit of 21,700 for those coming into the UK under the skilled and highly skilled routes (20,700) under Tier 2 (General) and 1,000 under the new 'exceptional talent' route; raising to £40,000 the minimum salary for those coming under the Tier 2 (Intra company transfer) route[32] for more than 12 months and working up to five years,[33] and requiring occupations in Tier 2 (General) to be at graduate level.[34] These were interim arrangements which applied until April 2011 after which a permanent cap operated.[35] The number of foreign staff entering Britain on intra-company transfers has increased dramatically since the Government announced in July 2010 that such work permits would be exempt from the immigration cap but

---

31 www.ukba.homeoffice.gov.uk
32 This category is for employees of multi-national companies who are being transferred by their overseas employer to a UK branch of the organisation.
33 Those earning between £24,000–£40,000 in their job in the UK will be able to work in the UK for up to 12 months.
34 www.ukba.homeoffice.gov.uk
35 All foreign nationals seeking to work in a Tier 2 (General) category that is subject to the cap will need a Restricted Certificate of Sponsorship. These Certificates of Sponsorship will be capped at 20,700 for April 2011 to April 2012. This annual cap will be divided into 12 monthly allocations, 4,200 Certificates for April 2011 and 1,500 for each month thereafter.

subject to the limitations outlined above.[36] The UK Government was required to legislate to implement a European Union Directive which gave the right of citizens of the European Union to move and reside freely within its Member States,[37] The measures were designed, among other things: to encourage European Union citizens to exercise their right to move and reside freely within Member States;[38] to reduce administrative formalities; to provide a better definition of the status of family members; to limit the scope for refusing entry or terminating the right of residence and to introduce a new right of permanent residence.[39] In the UK, the directive has been introduced into UK law by the Immigration (European Economic Area) Regulations 2006[40] and amended by The Immigration (European Economic Area) (Amendment) Regulations 2009.[41] The UK law introduces all the rights mentioned above. It includes within its coverage same-sex relationships and unmarried/unregistered partners. It also allows free movement when a UK citizen is moving back to the UK after living abroad.

---

36 Official figures of the Home Office show that between July and September 2010 more than 8,000 non-EU workers arrived in the UK on ICTs up by 30 per cent on the same period in 2009.

37 European Parliament and Council Directive 2004/38/EC of 29 April 2004 on the right of citizens of the Union and their family members to move and reside freely within the territory of the Member States.

38 Defines the right of free movement for citizens of the European Economic Area (EEA), which includes the European Union (EU) and the three European Free Trade Association (EFTA) members Iceland, Norway and Liechtenstein.

39 This applies automatically after a period of 5 years.

40 SI 2006/1003.

41 SI 2009/1117.

Chapter 18

Alternative Dispute Resolution

18.1 The aim of the last Government was to try and avoid employment tribunal claims where possible. There are many alternative ways of sorting out complaints and legal problems. Together they are often called 'alternative dispute resolution' (ADR) and include things like mediation, arbitration and conciliation.

(1) MEDIATION

18.2 Most employers up to now have avoided using mediation in employment, opting instead for the legal route before an employment tribunal. This is surprising given that mediation can provide a structured, effective means of resolving a workplace dispute, which avoids the expense and inconvenience of claims being brought before employment tribunals.

Process

18.3 Mediation involves using an independent, third party to facilitate the negotiations between the parties. The mediator may be someone from within the organisation or an external consultant. It can often help to defuse difficult situations in the workplace and can be cost effective, discrete and provide certainty for the parties. It can also deliver to the parties benefits unavailable in an employment tribunal. Where the relationship looks as if it might be salvaged, the parties can plot both steps for change to achieve harmony, as well as strategies for dealing with future conflict, including potentially, an exit strategy. That way, if the old personality clashes rear their ugly heads again, the parties will already have agreed how they will deal with this conflict, or ultimately part ways. If the relationship is beyond repair, benefits can be obtained which cannot be ordered by tribunals: agreed references, effective restrictive covenants and secrecy.

Employers need to develop effective strategies for introducing mediation into the workplace, not only when relationships have already broken down, but also as a means of avoiding a breakdown. Mediation services are offered by a range of providers, ranging from specialist employment lawyers to mediation specialists such as the Centre for Effective Dispute Resolution (CEDR) and independent mediation consultants. In addition, ACAS provides a variety of dispute resolution services including conciliation, mediation in certain cases, and arbitration.

According to CIPD, employers whose HR specialists are trained in mediation, techniques have 50% fewer employment tribunal claims than those who do not offer such training. This may be more an indication that well trained staff will inevitably get better results than those who act in a rather more haphazard way in terms of dispute resolution. However, it does underline the benefits of having a developed mediation strategy.

Given the economics, one must ask why it is employers have been so shy of using mediation in the past. Creating a mediation forum can be used as an opportunity to resolve disputes before someone is forced to go down either the disciplinary or grievance route.

One of the greatest costs for employers is losing good staff and many good staff leave because they consider that their grievance has not been satisfactorily resolved, because they do not want to be seen as a trouble-maker by starting a formal grievance procedure or because they believe their employer will not do anything to resolve the dispute. The grievance procedure necessarily involves a win-lose situation and, therefore, often results in a complete breakdown of relationships and trust.

Bringing in somebody entirely neutral to act as an intelligent guide to the negotiation process can be an effective means of resolving disputes in a way that addresses the needs of all parties to the dispute. An employer who uses mediation as one of their tools puts themself in a stronger position with regard to its employees both to identify unreasonable practices and to provide a non-contentious means of resolving disputes.

Employers who fail to make use of the full range of dispute resolution techniques can often pay a high price for their lack of investment.

The Gibbons Report

18.4 The Gibbons Report[1] on reviewing employment dispute resolution practice represented a compelling call for a change in the way employment tribunals conduct their affairs, and raises the prospect of a much greater role for mediation in resolving workplace disputes. The strength of the report lay in its plain-speaking critique of the existing employment tribunal system and its 17 practical and achievable positive recommendations.

In March 2007, Michael Gibbons wrote his report Better Dispute Resolution: A Review of Employment Dispute Resolution in Great Britain. In his foreword letter to the Secretary of State for the DTI, he stated that 'the headline recommendation is the complete repeal of the statutory dispute resolution procedures set out in the 2004 Dispute Resolution Regulations'. He also presented a suite of complementary recommendations which, in aggregate, are 'genuinely deregulatory, and simplifying'. Importantly, he also stated: 'I would like to comment on how employment disputes not solved in the workplace should be resolved in the future. My vision is of a greatly increased role for mediation; my attitude is based, as you know, on my knowledge of the use of mediation in resolving difficult family disputes, and also with some involvement in alternative dispute resolution through the civil courts. Encouraged by signs of success in the context of employment disputes elsewhere in the world, I commend increased use of mediation to employers, employees and practitioners in Great Britain'.

This vision was further expounded on in his Executive Summary, and mediation and other ADR techniques were seen as effective means of achieving early resolution with positive experience from New Zealand, the US and in the civil courts. Although the Gibbons Report did not recommend a 'near mandatory' approach to ADR, it did recommend that the Government should offer a free early dispute resolution procedure and there should be incentives to use early resolution techniques. It envisaged giving employment tribunals discretion to take into account the parties' efforts to settle the dispute when making awards and costs offers. It also

---

1   Gibbons M, A Review of Employment Dispute Resolution in Great Britain (2007) DTI.

recommended that the fixed periods for ACAS to conciliate should be abolished.

Less predictability

18.5 So how is the move made from the current prescriptive and complex dispute resolution process to one that, while being simpler, gives tribunals more discretion to decide cases and so has less predictability in results? Litigation by its very nature is uncertain. To ensure the success of a new regime, it will be crucial to see the stance that employment tribunal chairs take in conducting directions and final hearings, and to have consistency applied.

It may turn out to be idealistic to fulfil Gibbons' hope that claimants be encouraged to present succinct cases, as a significant portion of parties (including well-paid advisers) cannot resist writing chapter and verse on their cases when a few words will do the job more effectively, but any movement in this area is welcome.

The right emphasis

18.6 Gibbons rightly places a strong emphasis on mediation as a way to resolve employment disputes. Mediation will be the way forward in this new workplace environment as it works in at least 80% of cases, with the right mediator, and represents the most effective way of helping business to resolve disputes and avoid red tape.

Mediation is informal, generally less expensive than taking the matter to court, and encourages personal responsibility by requiring a solution crafted by those involved rather than one imposed by a third party. Overall, there is still a lack of understanding about the subject, and the use of mediation is considered to be a sign of weakness. The nature of employment law, which is based on an adversarial legal system where there can often be points scoring between parties, can lead to parties being afraid to mediate. By embracing mediation, legal representatives and HR professionals will offer another way of enabling organisations to avoid potentially costly disputes and to divert management time away from dealing with litigation. Employers can include mediation clauses within their firm's contracts of employment. Such a step will allow reference to a third party to be triggered when notice of a dispute is given.

Some would say that the Gibbons Report echoed Judges' views in the civil courts for a number of years. In *Frank Cowl & Ors v Plymouth City Council*,[2] Lord Woolf stated that there is a:

> 'paramount importance of avoiding litigation whenever this is possible'. This means that litigants 'must by now be acutely conscious of the contribution alternative dispute resolution can make to resolving disputes in a manner which both meets the needs of the parties and the public and saves time, expense and stress… The courts should…make appropriate use of their ample powers under the CPR to ensure that the parties try to resolve the dispute with the minimum involvement of the courts. The legal aid authorities should co-operate in support of this approach'

and that

> 'Today sufficient should be known about ADR to make the failure to adopt it, in particular when public money is involved, indefensible'.

Brooke LJ stated in *Dunnett v Railtrack plc*[3] that 'Skilled mediators are now able to achieve results satisfactory to both parties in many cases which are quite beyond the power of lawyers and courts to achieve'. In *Halsey v Milton Keynes NHS Trust*,[4] the Court of Appeal decided that all lawyers conducting litigation should now routinely consider with their clients whether their disputes are suitable for ADR. Parties could not be ordered against their wishes to mediate, but successful parties at trial or appeal could be the subject of adverse costs orders if they had unreasonably refused to agree to mediation.

In many employment tribunal cases, the costs may be out of proportion to the claim, but, in general terms, costs orders will not be made. Costs orders may however be made in circumstances where the paying party has, in bringing or conducting the proceedings, acted vexatiously, abusively, disruptively or otherwise unreasonably, or where the bringing or conducting of the proceedings by the paying party has been misconceived.

---

2   [2001] EWCA Civ 1935, [2002] 1 WLR 803.
3   [2002] EWCA Civ 303, [2002] 2 ALL ER 850.
4   [2004] EWCA Civ 576, [2004] 1 WLR 3002.

There is, of course, no reason why refusal to consider mediation could not have been brought within the parameters of the costs rules.

Judicial Mediation Schemes

18.7 In July 2006, it was announced that a trial Judicial Mediation Scheme was to be run in Birmingham, London Central and Newcastle Employment Tribunals. These pilot schemes have been encouraging. However, as in the civil courts, mediation must be voluntary so judicial mediation will only be contemplated with the consent of both sides and, even then, the Tribunal Regional Judge has to be satisfied that mediation is appropriate to the case. Moreover, there are not, as yet, sufficient statistics to gauge the schemes' success. The evidence is perhaps anecdotal but certainly, in the authors' experiences, tribunal hearings of many days have been obviated by settlements at judicial mediations. The fact that the parties did not have to pay for these mediations was a considerable attraction, but nevertheless the mediations did not appear to be as effective as private mediations.

Employment Act 2008

18.8 The Employment Act 2008 (EA 2008) received the Royal Assent on 6 December 2008. It was originally introduced into Parliament as the Employment Simplification Bill on 11 July 2008. As that name implied, it was intended to remove the horrendous complications of the technicalities surrounding the Dispute Resolution Procedures introduced by the Employment Act 2002 and the 2004 Disciplinary, Dismissal and Grievance Procedures. The EA 2008 repeals the legislation which introduced these procedures. The indications were that mediation would play a significant part in the new legislation and Codes of Practice. Those indications were: the Gibbons Report which recommended reform; the many pronouncements in favour of mediation at the highest judicial level; and the apparent successes of pilot schemes at several Tribunal centres.

The EA 2008 and the ACAS Code have not adopted any form of compulsion for mediation in the Tribunals and the references to mediation were not as positive as some had expected.

As to the EA 2008, s 3 inserts a new s 207A to the Trade Union and Labour Relations (Consolidation) Act 1992 which provided that an employment tribunal may increase or decrease any award it makes by no more than 25%, if the employer or employee has unreasonably failed to comply with any Code of Practice issued under the Act. Also, ss 5 and 6 of the 2008 Act removed the fixed time limits for conciliation and ACAS has been given access to free resources for pre-claim conciliation.

As to Codes, the new ACAS Code of Practice on Disciplinary and Grievance Procedures (CoP 1) introduced a new 9-page Code which came into force on 6 April 2009, when the 2008 Act came into force. The brevity of the Code compared with the 81-page ACAS Guidance, Discipline and Grievances at Work, which will not have statutory effect. The only reference to mediation in the Code is in the non-binding foreword which states that, if the employer and employee cannot resolve their differences… employers and employees should consider using an independent third party to help resolve the problem. The third party need not come from outside the organisation but could be an internal mediator, so long as they are not involved in the disciplinary or grievance issue. In some cases, an external mediator might be appropriate.' The Guidance (also non-binding) refers in two short pages to mediation (pages 7 and 8).

ACAS continues to champion mediation, for example through its recent publication ACAS/CIPD – Mediation: An Employer's Guide as of 17 September 2008. That identified the significant advantages of mediating employment disputes:

'It is a cheaper alternative to employment tribunal claims, which carry immediate financial costs to the organisation and the individual claimant as well as non-financial burdens. Mediation is also a speedier option and can nip potentially damaging disputes in the bud… Moreover employment tribunals do not resolve systemic problems at work that may underlie an individual dispute. Mediation is more likely to enable the employer to get beneath the problem and make changes to working practices that can benefit employees and the organisation more generally in the long term.'

We hope these significant advantages will lead to a greater increase in mediating employment disputes and greater encouragement of mediation by the tribunals. We hope, too, that the provision for increasing or decreasing awards for failure to comply with Codes of Practice will be interpreted by the tribunals so that a failure to mediate will produce such a result. However, it is regrettable that the legislation was not explicit that an unreasonable failure to agree to mediation would have such a result. It is also regrettable that the legislation contains no formal costs compunction against parties who unreasonably refuse to agree to mediate employment disputes. It seems that the recent reforms have been a missed opportunity.

What did the Act means for employers?

18.9 Existing statutory procedures for dealing with dismissal, disciplinary and grievance procedures issues were repealed by a non-binding ACAS Code.

Employment tribunals were given the discretionary power to adjust awards, up or down, by up to 25%, if employers or employees have unreasonably failed to comply with the Code. If cases reached the tribunal stages decisions of the ET would be based on what was 'fair and reasonable' rather than a nit-picking analysis of the procedure. Informal action was encouraged wherever possible. At each stage employers and employees should consider mediation and all issues should be dealt with promptly and consistently

Dismissal and Disciplinary

18.10 The Code states that formal action involves: investigation; meeting; decision; appeal and, even where gross misconduct was suspected an employer, should follow a fair disciplinary process before dismissing for that reason.

The Code represents 'best practice': it recognises that it may sometimes be impracticable for all employers to take all of the steps set out in the Code.

The size and administrative resources of the employer will be taken into account

The Code does not apply to redundancies or to the non-renewal of fixed-term contracts on their expiry.

Grievance

18.11 Informal action is again encouraged wherever possible: 'often a quiet word is all that is needed.' Employees are encouraged, but not required, to set out the grievance in writing. Because a written grievance is no longer a condition of bringing a claim, employers should expect more surprise claims

Where an employee raises a grievance during a disciplinary process, the disciplinary process may be temporarily suspended in order to deal with the grievance.

Where the grievance and disciplinary cases are related, it may be appropriate to deal with both issues concurrently.

EHRC Mediation Service

18.12 The Equalities Mediation Service is a body which is funded by the Equality and Human Rights Commission. It offers free conciliation for employment disputes which involve claims for any kind of discrimination. If an employee believes they have been treated unfairly in the workplace because of their; gender, race, religion or belief, sexual orientation or disability then this is another option for them. Referrals to this service will be made through the Equality and Human Rights Commission.

Future for Mediation

18.13 For mediation to take hold as a mechanism for resolving workplace disputes in the United Kingdom, employers need to be convinced of the desirability of their developing effective strategies for mediation into the workplace, not only to be utilised when relationships break down, but also for avoiding future breakdowns. Employment tribunals in England and Wales now offer a Judicial Mediation Scheme which, since 2009, is available throughout both countries. There were plans to extend this to Scotland as well but to date this hasn't happened. Judicial mediation is entirely voluntary and provides parties to an employment tribunal claim with a confidential, alternative settlement option that tries to avoid the need for a full merits hearing. The judicial mediation takes place in the employment tribunal but is held in private.

A number of mediation providers are registered members of the Scottish Mediation Register managed by the Scottish Mediation Network (for Scotland).[5] These providers declare that they meet certain standards covering: training, practice development, codes of conduct, complaints handling and indemnity insurance.

The Scottish Mediation Network[6] was established in 1990 to raise the profile of mediation in Scotland, act as a professional body for mediators in Scotland and provide access to quality assured mediation services. As well as establishing a register of mediators in Scotland they have issued standards for membership and for accreditation of providers of training in mediation.

(2) ARBITRATION

18.14 In arbitration both parties allow an independent and impartial outsider called an arbitrator to determine the outcome of a workplace problem. Arbitration differs from conciliation (considered below) and mediation because the arbitrator, after reviewing the evidence presented by the parties, acts like a judge and makes a firm decision in the case. This decision is binding on the parties and can be enforced through the civil courts if it is not complied with.

Process of arbitration

18.15 Like mediation, arbitration is voluntary, so if both parties agree for a matter to go to an arbitrator it can be a quick, informal and efficient way of resolving a workplace problem without the stress and expense of taking a case before an employment tribunal. Unless the parties agree in advance that an arbitrator's decision will not be legally binding it will normally be binding and accordingly if the parties are unhappy with the arbitrator's decision they are unable to take the case to an employment tribunal or court except on very limited grounds. However, certain decisions reached

---

5   Civil Mediation Council (CMC) (for England and Wales). A list of registered workplace
     mediation providers for England and Wales can be found at www.cmcregistered.org.
6   http://www.scottishmediation.org.uk/

by an ACAS (Advisory, Conciliation and Arbitration Service) arbitrator can be legally binding.

Arbitration is as an alternative to a court of law, and is not subject to its formality and strict procedural and evidential rules. Unlike the court procedure, which is normally conducted in public, arbitration hearings are undertaken in private. In an arbitration hearing the arbitrator will ask the questions and there is no formal examination or cross-examination of witnesses or swearing of oaths. Arbitration can be used for resolving individual or collective problems at work.

In England, Wales and Northern Ireland arbitration is defined, and the rules set out, in the Arbitration Act 1996. Under the 1996 Act there is very limited scope for appeal against an arbitrator's award. Usually, appeals can only be based on a claim that the arbitrator behaved unfairly. In Scotland arbitration was based mainly on the common law until the introduction of the Arbitration (Scotland) Act 2010. This Act put the Scottish law of arbitration on a statutory footing and borrowed many of the principles from the English legislation and the UNCITRAL model of international arbitration. The Act introduced the English term arbitrator into Scots law replacing the old term arbiter. The principles of arbitration are contained in s 1 of the Act namely:

(a)   That the object of arbitration is to resolve disputes fairly, impartially and without unnecessary delay or expense.

(b)   That parties should be free to agree how to resolve disputes, subject only to such safeguards as are necessary in the public interest.

(c)   That the court should not intervene in an arbitration except as provided by the 2010 Act.

Schedule 1 of the Act contains the Scottish Arbitration Rules. These are rules of procedure which will apply to any Scottish arbitration. Some of these rules are mandatory and cannot be altered by the parties and some are discretionary and can be disapplied by the agreement of the parties. The mandatory rules relate to eligibility of the arbitrator and duties of the arbitrator and parties, to duties of impartiality, confidentiality and resolution of the arbitration speedily and without incurring unnecessary expense.

Part 8 of the Scottish Arbitration Rules set out the grounds of challenge of an award. The parties can challenge an award in the Outer House of the Court of Session on the grounds that:

–   the arbitrator has no jurisdiction,

–   serious irregularity, or

–   legal error.

Serious irregularity includes the tribunal failing to conduct the arbitration in accordance with the arbitration agreement, the Scottish Arbitration Rules and any other agreement of the parties, acting out with its powers, failing to deal with all the issues put to it, uncertainty or ambiguity as to the award's effect, the award being contrary to public policy, or obtained by fraud or in a way which is contrary to public policy, an arbitrator having not been impartial and independent, an arbitrator having not treated the parties fairly, an arbitrator having been incapable of acting as an arbitrator, an arbitrator not having a qualification which the parties agreed (before the arbitrator's appointment) that the arbitrator must have, or any other irregularity in the conduct of the arbitration, or in the award which is admitted by the tribunal,

Arbitration Clauses

18.16 Although the parties can enter into an agreement to arbitrate at any stage, contracts of employment can include a clause stating that arbitration will be used to resolve any dispute between the parties. This will be agreed at the time the contract is signed and the clause is intended to prevent disputes ending up in employment tribunals or court. A contract with an arbitration clause included is usually binding on the parties, which means they must allow disputes to go to arbitration. The arbitrator's decision is also binding and there is no appeal from the decision. Under the Arbitration (Scotland) Act 2010 the parties may nominate Scotland as the seat of arbitration, in which case the 2010 Act will apply even though there is no connection with Scotland. If Scotland is selected as the seat of arbitration then Scots law will apply unless another law is specified by the parties.

Role of ACAS

18.17 ACAS offer arbitration in collective disputes between employers and trade unions. This is often used in collective employment related disputes, particularly where a stalemate in negotiations is reached between the parties. The union and the employer would need to agree to ask ACAS to appoint an independent arbitrator from a panel to hear the case of either side and then make an independent and impartial decision.

ACAS can also be used to settle individual disputes. For example, an individual and an employer might decide to go to arbitration to avoid the stress and expense of an employment tribunal. However, as with any workplace dispute, it is important to make use of all internal procedures to resolve the issue in question, before proceeding, via ACAS conciliation, to arbitration.

The ACAS Arbitration Scheme

18.18 ACAS runs a free Arbitration Scheme that can decide cases of unfair dismissal and disputes about flexible working,[7] where there are no complex legal issues involved. Entry to the Scheme is via an Arbitration Agreement reached with the assistance of an ACAS conciliator or in the format of a Compromise Agreement (see below) drawn up by appropriate representatives. The arbitrator will use an inquisitorial rather than adversarial approach. The parties will be invited to submit a written statement of their case in advance of the hearing and they must comply with any instruction given by the arbitrator, and will be expected to co-operate in the production of relevant documents, and the attendance of appropriate witnesses. Hearings will be held at a convenient and

---

7   ACAS was given the power to draw up the Scheme in the Employment Rights (Dispute Resolution) Act 1998 and was implemented in England and Wales by the ACAS Arbitration Scheme (England and Wales) Order Statutory Instrument 2001 No 1185. As from 6 April 2004 the original unfair dismissal scheme was replaced by a version which applied to Scotland as well as to England and Wales, ACAS Arbitration Scheme (Great Britain) Order 2004, SI 2004/753. As from 1 October 2004 the flexible working scheme was also replaced by a version which applied to Scotland as well as England and Wales (see the ACAS (Flexible Working) Arbitration Scheme (Great Britain) Order 2004, SI 2004/2333).

accessible location to the parties and will not normally last for more than half a day.

Once the parties have reached an agreement to undertake an ACAS arbitration they are free, at any time, to pull out of the process and try and reach agreement between themselves, however, they can't make a claim to an employment tribunal.

This is because decisions reached by an ACAS arbitrator, under the Arbitration Scheme, on certain unfair dismissal claims or requests to work flexibly are legally binding. If a claim is upheld, an arbitrator can order the same remedies as an employment tribunal.

There are very limited grounds for challenging an arbitrator's award.

(3) CONCILIATION

18.19 Conciliation is similar to mediation but is normally used when there is a particular legal dispute rather than more general problems. A conciliator will normally be there to encourage the two sides to come to an agreement between themselves, whereas a mediator will often suggest their own solution. The decision of an employment tribunal is not affected by a decision to try conciliation.

Process of conciliation

18.20 A trained conciliator who is appointed by the parties, or through ACAS, will: talk through the issues with each side; look at opportunities for settling the case; explain any legal issues involved and assist both parties to agree on a legally binding agreement. The conciliator is impartial and independent and the discussions are confidential. The benefits are that: the parties get a better understanding of the issues; they might sort the problem without a tribunal hearing; the parties can arrive at a solution in the form of an agreed settlement that can include things that can't be covered in a tribunal judgement (like making sure an employee gets a good reference or consideration for promotion).

Role of ACAS

ACAS pre-claim conciliation (PCC) service

18.21 The pre-claim conciliation service is available for any type of workplace issue that could turn into an employment tribunal claim and employees, workers, employers and representatives on both sides can utilise it. When this service is asked for through ACAS the parties will be put in touch with a specially trained pre-claim conciliator who will talk through the problem with them, answer any questions and make sure they fully understand the situation and the different courses of action available. The dialogue will be as flexible as necessary and the conciliator will try to explore all alternatives to find a mutually acceptable way forward. If the parties can find a basis for settlement, the conciliator will also offer to help them draw up a binding written agreement to record the terms. The benefits of pre-claim conciliation are:

- it is quick with most cases being resolved within two weeks;
- it takes place early in the dispute process which means there is a better chance of avoiding a permanent breakdown of the employment relationship;
- it is voluntary so both parties must agree to take part before the process starts and they can change their mind at any time;
- there is little formality involved as the process simply involves talking the problem through and looking for a solution;
- it is confidential and
- it is impartial as conciliators don't make judgements on the rights and wrongs of the matter in dispute or impose outcomes the parties don't want.

To be eligible to use this services the parties must have already tried to resolve the problem in question internally without external help, for example by making use of their discipline or grievance procedures, and the dispute must be likely to end with a tribunal claim if the parties don't get help to resolve it. ACAS conducted a trial of the service in 2008. This involved reviewing 900 cases, where they found that most of the companies involved were small businesses with 15 or fewer staff. Of those that took part, 60% were satisfied with the outcome of the PCC service while the remainder proceeded to tribunal. The service was offered nationwide in April 2009.

ACAS Conciliation

18.22 ACAS offers information, advice and conciliation to employees and employers involved in workplace disputes.[8] If both parties choose to use conciliation, the ACAS conciliation officer works with both of them to try to reach a mutually acceptable settlement. This is usually done on the phone. The officer can explain tribunal proceedings and the tribunal's approach, but will not advise parties on their legal position. ACAS is required by law to conciliate as a precursor to all employment disputes presented to employment tribunals. Where a settlements is reached through ACAS conciliation it is legally binding. The parties will sign an agreement called a COT3. However it is important that the terms of the COT3 are clear as illustrated in the case of *McLean v TLC Marketing Plc*[9] where the claimant entered into a COT3 in order to settle her claims for equal pay, sex discrimination and victimisation. Under the agreement, Ms McLean accepted the sum of £28,000: 'In full and final settlement of her employment tribunal claims against the Respondents and of any other claim whatsoever arising out of or connected with her employment with the Respondent and its termination.' The company failed to pay the full amount due under the COT3, or to provide her with a reference as agreed, so Ms McLean brought a further claim of victimisation. The tribunal refused to accept her claim on the grounds that the COT3 agreement precluded any such claim. On appeal, the EAT disagreed and the claim was remitted to a tribunal to be considered on its merits. The EAT held that the language used in the COT3 was not sufficiently clear to support a finding that the parties intended to exclude future claims.

---

8   In Northern Ireland, the Labour Relations Agency (LRA) performs essentially the same functions as ACAS does in England, Wales and Scotland.
9   Case No. 0429/08/0512.

Collective Conciliation

18.23 Collective conciliation is a process whereby a neutral third party meets with the opposing sides of a collective dispute and tries to help them reconcile their differences and reach an agreement.[10] This service is undertaken by the ACAS Collective Conciliation Service. The emphasis is on the parties reaching an agreement themselves with the conciliator using reason and persuasion to get the parties to reconsider their positions. ACAS conciliators have been helping the parties to resolve their collective employment disputes for over 30 years. The service is known within ACAS as 'collective conciliation'.

Compromise Agreements

18.24 Another form of legally binding settlement in an employment context is a 'Compromise Agreement'. These agreements are used in the United Kingdom where ACAS isn't involved. A compromise agreement is a specific type of contract between an employer and his employee (or ex-employee) which is regulated by statute.[11] Under this agreement an employee will receive a negotiated financial settlement in exchange for agreeing that he or she will have no further legal claim against the employer resulting from their breach of a statutory obligation. Except when ACAS has been involved in an employment dispute, and arranged a COT3 settlement, the Compromise Agreements are the only means whereby an employee can waive their statutory claims for unfair dismissal, discrimination, redundancy etc.

The Agreement will only be valid where (i) it is in writing, and (ii) where the employee has received independent advice from a solicitor who has professional indemnity insurance.[12] An employee cannot compromise

---

10 Under the terms of the Trade Union and Labour Relations Consolidation Act 1992 in situations where 'a trade dispute exists or is apprehended ACAS may, at the request of one or more parties offer its assistance with a view to bringing about a settlement'.

11 For employees to validly sign away their rights to sue their employer for breach of their statutory employment rights the requirements for Compromise Agreements in s 203 of the Employment Rights Act 1996 must be fully complied with. The requirements are strict and detailed.

12 The agreement must name the adviser but doesn't have to be signed by them.

potential future claims but, claims that have already arisen but are unknown to the employee can be waived under the Agreement. Conciliation Agreements (COT3) and Compromise Agreements are legally binding and once agreement has been reached the employee will no longer be able to pursue their employment tribunal claims.

Employment tribunals do have the jurisdiction to decide if Compromise Agreements are valid. They may be invalid, for example because the requirements of s 203 of ERA 1996 have not been complied with or because the employee has been induced to enter the Agreement following a misrepresentation on the part of his employer.

The facility to compromise claims through a Compromise Agreement is contained in each piece of legislation giving employees particular rights, for example, under s 147 Equality Act 2010. Employers are now increasingly using Compromise Agreements at an early stage as a mechanism for preventing possible future complaints to a tribunal especially in redundancy situations. Often the Compromise Agreement will also deal with references, the notice element in a contract of employment and may provide for a payment in lieu of working notice to be made as part of the settlement.

What terms does a Compromise Agreement need to contain?

18.25 The Compromise Agreement will give the full breakdown of the payments the employee is receiving, including the extent to which the sums will be paid free of tax. The Compromise Agreement will also provide for confidentiality both in terms of an employer's trade secrets and business affairs, but also in respect of the Terms of the Agreement itself. Employees can be paid a small additional sum for agreeing to this privacy restriction. The Compromise Agreement may also confirm any existing post-termination restrictive covenants that are in place under an employee's contract of employment. In some cases the restrictive covenants will be new having only appeared in the compromise agreement for the first time. There will often be a long list of statutes mentioned in the compromise agreement such as the Equality Act 2010, the Employment Rights Act 1996 and many more, under which the employee will agree not to bring a claim. Because the Compromise Agreement is intended to be in full and final settlement of all claims by the employee, the employer needs to list these independently from each other to be able to enforce the Agreement.

McWilliam & Others v Glasgow City Council,[13] was the first case to consider the requirements of s 77 of the SDA 1975. Section 77 (similar provisions are now contained in the Equality Act 2010 s 147) set out the criteria for a valid Compromise Agreement and in particular the need for the complainant to receive independent advice as to the terms and effect of the proposed contract. Most importantly, the vice-president of the Scottish employment tribunals, Employment Judge Walker, held that it is not necessary that the advice is such as would allow the complainant to make an informed decision. All that is required is that the complainant is advised what the terms of the Compromise Agreement are and what they mean. This would include the scope of the claims, what claims are being compromised, how any payment would be treated for tax purposes etc. This is to be distinguished from an assessment of whether or not the agreement is a 'good deal'.

Compromise Agreements are becoming increasingly common, especially in the financial services sector. The Agreements are predominantly used in cases of redundancy, unfair dismissal or unlawful discrimination. As the economic crisis deepens it seems certain that there will be a major increase in demand for compromise deals both from employers and employees.

The case of *Collidge v Freeport plc*[14] shows what can go wrong if a Compromise Agreement is breached by an employee. The facts were that Mr Collidge was the chief executive and a director of Freeport, a leading developer and operator of retailer outlet centres in Europe. In early 2006, allegations of financial impropriety were made against him and in March 2006, the board proposed he be suspended while these allegations were investigated. He said he would rather resign, which the board agreed to, but the company told him its investigation would still go ahead.

The terms of a Compromise Agreement were reached, stating that Freeport would pay Collidge £445,680 subject to terms in the Agreement being met. However, Clause 7 stated: 'you warrant as a strict condition of this agreement that... there are no circumstances of which you are aware

---

13   S132316/07.
14   [2007] EWHC 1216 (QB), [2007] All ER (D) 457 (May).

or of which you ought to be aware which would constitute a repudiatory breach on your part of your contract of employment which would entitle the company to terminate your employment without notice'.

Before payment was made to him Freeport's investigation had revealed that Mr Collidge was in breach of Clause 7 of the Agreement. Therefore, the board did not authorise payment to him. He brought a claim in the High Court, arguing that Clause 7 was not a pre-condition to the enforceability of the Agreement and therefore the payment should be made. The High Court, however, held that the clause was a pre-condition to Freeport's liability to perform its own obligations under the agreement. Therefore, Freeport was under no obligation to pay Mr Collidge. The Court of Appeal[15] rejected an appeal against the High Court decision that an employer did not have to make a payment due under a Compromise Agreement, if the employee was in breach of a warranty he had given as part of the Compromise Agreement. They held that the parties clearly intended the warranty to be a condition precedent of making the payment.

In *Byrnell v British Telecommunications plc*[16], the EAT held that the employment tribunal was correct to conclude that it had no jurisdiction to entertain claims in relation to a Compromise Agreement, except to satisfy itself that the Compromise Agreement met the conditions set out in s 203 of the ERA 1996.

In 2005 the IRS Employment Review carried out a survey of 94 UK organisations into the use of Compromise Agreements and found that more than three-quarters of them had used Compromise Agreements to avoid potential employment tribunals claims.[17] The most common reason was the belief that the cost of contesting a tribunal hearing would outweigh the cost of reaching a settlement. However, just under half had used them to avoid potential damage to their reputation with customers and employees, or because they knew they were in the wrong.

Section 401 of the Income Tax (Earnings and Pensions) Act provides that payments and other benefits which are received 'directly or indirectly in consideration or in consequence of, or otherwise in connection with the

---

15   [2008] EWCA Civ 485, [2008] IRLR 697.
16   [2004] All ER (D) 78 (Nov) EAT.
17   Compromise agreements used to keep organisations clear of the courtroom Personnel Today 29, November 2005, www.personneltoday.com.

termination of a person's employment, a change in the duties of a person's employment, or a change in the earnings from a person's employment...' are subject to deduction of tax and national insurance by the employer before payment to the employee. This provision is subject to an exemption for sums up to £30,000. Contractual payments in lieu of notice are liable to tax under s 62 of the Act and therefore the exemption does not apply to them. Damages for personal injury and hurt feelings are not liable to tax and national insurance. The taxation of sums received under compromise agreements is therefore a complex matter and it is very important to apportion the elements of a payment correctly. This is particularly true in light of the recent cases of *Norman v Yellow Pages Sales*[18] and *Oti-Obihara v HMRC Tax*.[19] In the former case the Court of Appeal held that where the parties did not apportion a damages award between taxable and non-taxable elements it was for the employee (not the employer) to sort out the position with HMRC and the employer should deduct tax from the whole amount over £30,000 in the meantime. In the latter case the tribunal judge felt that a large amount of the compensation arising from discrimination represented financial loss resulting from the termination of the contract and was liable to tax and national insurance (apart from the exempt amount of £30,000).

To avoid complications later the compromise agreement should identify the separate elements of the payment at the outset.[20]

---

18 [2010] EWCA Civ 1395, [2010] All ER (D) 272 (Dec).
19 [2010] UKFTT 568.
20 See Ingle M, '*Norman v Yellow Pages Sales* and *Obi Hara v HMRC*: tax and compensation for discrimination – pose a challenge for employers and employees alike', [2011] BTR 150 for guidance on how best to do this.

Index

[references are to paragraph]

639

Apprentice
equality clause applies, 11.29
national minimum wage, 11.3, 11.6
Arbitration, 2.34, 18.14–18.18
ACAS role, 2.34, 18.17, 18.18
appeal or challenge to award, 18.15,
18.18
CAC, 2.36, 15.4, 15.21
clause, 18.16, 18.24, 18.25
compromise agreement, 18.18
nature of, 18.14
procedural rules, 18.15
process of, 18.15
Scotland, principles in, 18.15
Armed forces member
national minimum wage exemption,
11.6
working time protection exclusion,
12.18, 12.19
Assistance by way of representation, 2.6
Atypical employment, 5.1 *et seq*
see also Agency worker etc
legal protection afforded to, 5.6
meaning, 5.2
national minimum wage applies to, 11.4
Award, *see* Compensation; Damages

B
Ballot, *see* Industrial action; Trade union
Basic award, 7.40
Behaviour, *see* Conduct
Bonus, entitlement to, 8.36, 8.57, 10.9
Border Agency
immigrant worker controls, 17.7, 17.9,
17.12
Breach of contract
see also Express terms; Implied terms
incorporated term, 15.32
industrial action, 16.2, 16.13
calling as inducement to breach, 16.7,
16.8
participation as breach, 16.3, 16.30,
16.31
remedies in civil court, 4.52–4.57, 11.45
court for claim, 4.51
damages, 4.55, 7.12
declarator, 4.57
interdict, 4.53, 7.13
lien and retention, 4.56
specific implement, order of, 4.53

Breach of contract – *contd*
remedies in employment tribunal, 4.50,
4.51, 7.14, 11.45
breach of collective agreement
incorporated term, 15.32
maximum award, 7.14, 11.45
repudiatory, 7.32
serious, effect of, 4.54
unilateral variation as, 4.47

C
**Capability, dismissal reason, 7.21,
7.26–7.30**
changed nature of job and employee
cannot adapt, 7.30
Code of Practice, 7.26
illness causing mental or physical
inability, 7.28
incapability examples, 7.26
incompetence, deliberate or neglectful,
7.29
inherent inability to do job, 7.27
qualification prerequisite, failure in, 7.31
reasonableness of employer, 7.26
Capacity
contract, to enter, 4.3–4.6
dismissal for lack of mental capacity,
7.28
Career break, 6.3
Case management discussion, 2.14
Casual worker, 5.16
casual or umbrella contracts, and
continuity, 6.5
national minimum wage applies, 11.3
**Central Arbitration Committee, 2.36,
15.4, 15.21**
Certification Officer, 2.34, 15.5
complaint on trade union ballot to,
15.27, 15.28
Child, employee with
child benefit, 10.19
rights to leave etc, *see* Adoption leave;
Flexible working; Maternity/
pregnancy; Parental leave;
Paternity rights
time off work in case of accident, illness
etc, 10.22
Civil courts, 2.20, *see also* Court of
Session
breach of contract claim, 4.52–4.57

6